THE
100
BEST
STOCKS
YOU CAN BUY
2009

JOHN SLATTER, CFA

ADAMS MEDIA
AVON, MASSACHUSETTS

Dedication

To my wife Beverly, my daughter Carol, and my son Steve

Acknowledgments

Writing a book is far easier than finding a publisher. My first book, *Safe Investing*, didn't find a home until I latched on to my dutiful agent, Edythea Ginis Selman. Edy knows how to find a publisher, and she knows how to convince the editor that I am worth paying a living wage.

My publisher, Adams Media, has treated me like a king. That could be because my editor is Peter Archer, easy to do business with.

Also, a vote of thanks to George G. Morris, CFA, my broker with Wachovia Securities, who helped me gather research. If you need a full-service broker, George is your man in Cleveland at (800) 222-4633.

Published by Adams Business,
An imprint of Adams Media, an F+W Publications Company
57 Littlefield Street
Avon, MA 02322
www.adamsmedia.com

ISBN-10: 1-59869-846-X
ISBN-13: 978-1-59869-846-6

Printed in Canada.

J I H G F E D C B A

Library of Congress Cataloging-in-Publication Data
is available from publisher.

This book is available at quantity discounts for bulk purchases.
For information, please call 1-800-289-0963.

Contents

PART I

THE ART AND SCIENCE OF INVESTING IN STOCKS

Is This the Right Investment Book for You?

The last time I stopped by the investment section of my local bookstore, there was no shortage of books about investing in the stock market. Fortunately, several copies of the latest edition of *The 100 Best Stocks You Can Buy* were prominently displayed.

However, I saw only one lonely soul trying to find a book to his liking. I was tempted to suggest that mine was the best one on the shelf. But I refrained. I recalled that on my previous trip to the bookstore I made a similar suggestion and had been totally ignored. He didn't even look up to see who was offering him this sage advice. (I was tempted to report that recalcitrant cad to the manager but thought better of it.)

Since you have the book in your hands and are wondering whether this is the one for you, let me give you a song and dance that will convince you that your search has ended; you don't need to look any further.

To begin, let me congratulate you on making the decision to educate yourself on the intricacies of the stock market. Many people totally ignore the importance of saving money for the future. It could be that they believe their company 401(k), along with Social Security, will do the job. The odds are that you will need more, particularly if you work for a firm that insists your 401(k) should be stuffed with your employer's company stock.

If you want to build a solid portfolio, it makes better sense to buy stocks on a regular basis—at least once a year. I suggest setting aside at least 10 percent of your gross income every year for stock purchases. And don't skip a year because you don't like the antics of the stock market at that particular time. Forecasting the market is a no-no. You can't do it—nor can anyone else.

Why People Don't Read about Investing

One reason that people don't read about investing is that they are overwhelmed by the complexity of the financial scene. I heartily concur—it *is* overwhelming. That's because there are thousands of mutual funds, common stocks, preferred stocks, certificates of deposit, options, bonds, annuities, and assorted investment products.

Even if you simply confined your search to the stocks listed on the New York Stock Exchange, the task would be daunting, since some 3,000 stocks are traded there. Or you might decide to "Let George do it," by investing in mutual funds. There, too, you will encounter infinite decisions, since there are over 14,000 mutual funds—most of which underperform such market indexes as the Dow Jones Industrial Average (called the Dow, Dow Jones, or DJIA) or the Standard & Poor's 500 (S&P 500).

If you are like many buyers of my books, you are not a sophisticated investor. You have a good job, have an income that is well above average, and you are serious about your career. That means that you spend time improving yourself by reading trade journals and taking courses at a local college.

Why Not Burn the Midnight Oil?

In other words, your day is already taken up with reading. How can you possibly start poring over annual reports, Standard & Poor's reports, *Fortune, Value Line Investment Survey*, the *Wall Street Journal, Forbes,*

BusinessWeek, *Barron's*, and a half-dozen books on the stock market? Easy. Drink lots of coffee and stay up until two in the morning.

If you object to this routine, you will be better off with my book, since I try to make investing a lot simpler than you thought it would be. For one thing, my style of writing is easy to understand. At least that's what people tell me.

Incidentally, I am one of the few authors who take calls from readers. My phone number is on the last page of this book. I assume you will confine your calls to regular business hours, based on Eastern Standard Time, since I live in Vermont.

Whenever I buy a book, I always check to see if the writer has good credentials. For my part, I have been on the investment scene for a good forty years. I started as a plain vanilla stockbroker, and then became editor of a publication devoted to mutual funds, followed by several years as a securities analyst for a brokerage firm. I spent a few years as a portfolio manager and started operating my own firm, managing portfolios on a fee basis for investors with assets of $250,000 or more.

During these years, I did a lot of writing, first for *Barron's Financial Weekly*, and later for such publications as *Physician's Management* and *Better Investing*. During the same period, I wrote tons of reports on stocks for the brokerage firms that paid my salary. In recent years, I have written a slew of books: *Safe Investing*, *Straight Talk About Stock Investing*, and eleven previous editions of *The 100 Best Stocks You Can Buy*.

I also wrote two great novels, but no publisher seems to agree that they are great, so I am not currently getting royalties on those.

As I mentioned previously, the number of stocks and mutual funds out there is infinite. Besides the 3,000 stocks on the New York Stock Exchange, plus the thousands of mutual funds, there are also thousands of stocks listed on the Nasdaq and thousands more traded on markets in Europe, Asia, Latin America, and Canada.

The beauty of my book is that I whittle the number of stocks you need to know about down to 100. Among those 100 are four types of stocks, depending on your particular temperament: Income, Growth and Income, Conservative Growth, and Aggressive Growth.

Diversification, the First Rule of Investing

Of course, there is no need to confine your investing exclusively to one category. A well-diversified portfolio could have half a dozen from each sector. Incidentally, diversity is the key to investing. Whenever you concentrate on one type of stock, such as technology, energy, banks, utilities, or pharmaceuticals, you expose yourself to extra risk. Don't do it. Let me emphasize that again—don't do it.

When I was a portfolio strategist in Cleveland a few years ago, I examined portfolios submitted to our firm for analysis. About 100 percent of them were not diversified. They were typically concentrated in only three industries: public utilities, banks, and oil.

Before you make up your mind about which stocks to buy, you will want to collect some information. If you have access to a brokerage house, you can easily get a copy of a report called *Value Line Investment Survey*. You can also subscribe yourself, but be prepared to spend $600 a year for this service, which covers about 1,700 well-known stocks. A less expensive alternative is the same service limited to 600 stocks. Still another good source is Standard & Poor's tear sheets, which can be obtained from a broker or library. Finally, most brokerage houses have a staff of analysts that turn out reports on a multitude of stocks.

My Sources of Information

A final source of information is this book, which is updated every year. I believe that my write-ups are valuable in ways that the other sources are not. When I first began writing this series of books, I obtained my information from each company's annual report, as well as from the two services mentioned. Now, I go much further afield. On a daily basis, I collect information on these companies from such sources as *Barron's, Forbes, Better Investing, BusinessWeek,* and other monthly investment publications. In addition, I consult well-known newspapers across the country, including the *Boston Globe* and *New York Times,* as well as papers in Chicago, Philadelphia, Atlanta, Denver, St. Louis, Houston, Milwaukee, Los Angeles, Detroit, San Francisco, Miami, and Dallas.

Whenever I see an article on one of my companies, I clip it out and file it for future reference and examine it again when I sit at my computer to prepare a report. Using this vast collection, I sift through the facts to find the reasons that this stock is attractive. I also look for factors that have a negative tone. In other words, I don't want to give you a purely one-sided view of this stock. By contrast, if you read the company's annual report, you will only hear about the attributes of the company and not about its problems and deficiencies.

Similarly, if you read a report from a brokerage house, it is rarely negative. The analyst normally tells you to buy—rarely to sell. One reason for this is the tie brokerage houses have to these companies that can lead to extremely lucrative underwriting and corporate finance deals. If the analyst tells investors to avoid the stock, the company may decide to avoid the brokerage house and give its business to someone else.

Obviously, I have no reason to be anything but unbiased.

Forty Years of Experience Is the Key

Finally, the 100 stocks have to be selected. The publisher is not the one who picks the stocks. I do. My forty years of varied experience on the investment scene give me an edge in this regard. And, of course, I am intimately involved in stock selection from a personal perspective. I have a large portfolio of stocks, more than fifty at present, which have made my wife and me millionaires.

If you would like to reach the same comfortable plateau, why not invest $14.95 and start reading?

Oh, and here's one more thing. If you read the rest of these introductory chapters, you will see that I have provided a helpful glossary that explains all the terms you need to know to understand the fundamentals of investing.

I also have a chapter on asset allocation that will tell you what percentage of your holdings should be in stocks and how much in such fixed-income vehicles as bonds and money-market funds. Finally, there also are chapters on how I select my stocks, an intriguing way to reduce risk, and still another on how to analyze stocks. There is also a short chapter that focuses on the four essentials of successful investing. You'll be surprised at how simple investing can be if you read this chapter.

Before You Invest in a Mutual Fund

I always look forward to Sunday, partly because it gives me the opportunity to read the Sunday *New York Times Book Review*. One page I pay particular attention to is the one listing the current bestsellers. As you might expect, I check the nonfiction list to see if it includes *The 100 Best Stocks You Can Buy*.

Alas, my book never seems to make it. One reason is that I am not a great promoter. It's one thing to write a great book, but in order to get on the list, you must make a concerted effort to tell your story on radio, television, or on a book tour. For my part, I confine my promoting to talking to investment clubs. This gives me an opportunity to address fifteen or twenty eager listeners. For some reason, most of the clubs I have met with are made up mainly of women. Men are singularly lacking.

Of course, in order to make my talk interesting, I have to pick a topic that will get the ladies' attention. One evening in April, I met with seventeen women—and three men. My topic stressed diversification, with particular emphasis on the ten sectors that are discussed elsewhere in this book. For the most part, the sector concept met with good reception, since they had not heard of this strategy from any previous speaker.

Of course, one reason I make these talks is to sign my autograph to the most recent edition of my book. Amazingly, the club members usually line up with their checkbooks in hand, eagerly awaiting me to write carefully something like "To my good friend Allisa Sheng." It's not sufficient, of course, merely to sign my name. Some want to discuss their own situation.

When all the eager buyers had drifted away, one club member came forward and said, "Mr. Slatter, that was one of the best talks we've had—and I really enjoyed your humorous approach. Most of the speakers are far too serious."

After she had made those flattering comments, I racked my brain to remember how I had signed her book. What was her name? Then, it came to me. It was Linda Brunswick. The reason I remembered was because when I autographed her book, it occurred to me that Johnson & Johnson's home office is in Brunswick, New Jersey. For some reason, several pharmaceutical manufacturers are situated in New Jersey.

Unlike the other ladies, Linda Brunswick didn't scurry away to chomp on the cookies and sandwiches at a table on the other side of the room. "I know you have written over a dozen books on the stock market, Mr. Slatter, and you seem to have an engaging style," she said. "Have you ever tried writing a novel or a book on another topic?"

"Yes," I replied. "As a matter of fact, I tried a couple of novels about twenty years ago and really enjoyed the challenge. However, my agent says that novels are tough to market. Too many would-be writers are also trying to impress publishers with their pitiful attempts at literature."

"Why don't you try something on another topic?" she asked. "Don't you have interests outside of the stock market? A man with your talents shouldn't give up so easily."

"As a matter of fact, Mrs. Brunswick, I do have interests in such things as the Supreme Court, baseball, philosophy, ancient history, geography, medicine, economics, evolution, the Civil War, and U.S. Presidents."

"Those are all interesting topics. What's holding you back?"

"Even though I have many interests," I told her, "Roman history tops them all. Ever since high school I have been reading about ancient Rome. My library has far more books on Rome than on the stock market—or any other subject, for that matter. For that reason, I am giving serious thought to a book on famous Romans, which I intend to call *Roman Lives*, with a subtitle, *Biographies of fifty-seven famous Romans, such as Julius Caesar, Horace, Caligula, Trajan, Virgil, Epictetus, Pliny the Younger, and Marcus Aurelius.*"

"Wow, that sounds intriguing!" she said. "But how in the world could you dig up enough information to write interesting sketches about so many famous Romans? I would think you would have to do a tremendous amount of research. When would you have the time?"

"You are right, Mrs. Brunswick, the task would be a bit daunting. Fortunately, I don't have to spend twelve months a year writing *The 100 Best Stocks*. Normally, after I send in my manuscript in early May, I can goof off until the corrected proofs arrive back from the publisher for my approval. Once that task is completed, I can bask in the sun until after Labor Day."

"Are you convinced you could write a 400-page book on ancient Rome when you should be out enjoying Vermont's great summer weather?" she asked.

"Not necessarily," I answered. "My first hurdle is to convince my agent and a publisher to accept my idea. Sitting beside my desk are seventy-seven books on Roman history and culture—including biographies on quite a number, such as Caesar, Constantine the Great, Cicero, Pompey the Great, and Marc Antony. I plan to select ten Romans and write a five- or ten-page biography of each. The list would include two or three emperors, a couple generals, one or two historians, a poet,

a philosopher, among others. Next, I would go through my books and record notes on three-by-five cards on each of the ten. When I have 200 cards on a particular Roman, I will be ready to get to work on my computer and create a scintillating sketch of his life. By the end of the summer, I expect to have ten lives created to my satisfaction, ready to submit them to an editor for his decision."

"That sounds like you have your work cut out for you, Mr. Slatter," she said. "No more basking in the sun. Oh, I almost forgot. One reason I wanted to chat with you is to ask you for more information on mutual funds. I get the impression that maybe you don't like them."

"Exactly. There are all sorts of reasons why you should invest in individual stocks. One major problem with mutual funds is deciding how to make a selection. Can you believe that there are now 4,800 mutual funds trying to get you as a customer? Frankly, I haven't discovered a good way to pick the best ones."

"That does sound like a daunting task. It seems to me that I have seen lists of the best ones in various magazines. Maybe that would work," said Mrs. Brunswick.

"Perhaps," I agreed. "However, I have seen studies on that idea, and it turns out they base their recommendations on recent performance. While that may sound logical, it doesn't seem to work out in practice.

"The thing that really disturbs me is the fact that mutual funds don't deliver what investors want—performance. For instance, they rarely do as well as the market, as measured by the Dow Jones Industrial Average or the S&P 500. In the period from 1984 through 2002, the Standard & Poor's 500 climbed an average of 12.2 percent per year, compared with only 9.3 percent for equity mutual funds—those that invest in common stocks."

"I'm beginning to see why you prefer common stocks," she said. "By the way, how did your 100 stocks perform in 2007?"

"I had a few losers and a few big winners, but on average my 100 stocks climbed 8.2 percent last year—that was considerably better than the general market. The Dow Jones average was up 6.4 percent, and the S&P 500 less than 4 percent."

"So far, I am wondering why people buy mutual funds," she observed. "Do you have any theories?"

"I suppose there are many reasons," I answered. "Some people don't do their homework. They leave it up to stockbrokers. Incidentally, stock brokers sell lots of mutual funds. Mutual fund companies don't sell many of their funds directly to investors. About 90 percent are sold through brokerage houses. It's no secret that the funds with the lowest costs are not sold through brokers. In fact the fees received by mutual fund companies amounted to $37 billion in 2004—and are probably even higher now. That's money that investors are not getting."

"I assume that about wraps up the reasons why I shouldn't be investing in mutual funds. Many thanks for your enlightening help, Mr. Slatter."

"Don't leave just yet, Mrs. Brunswick," I cautioned. "There's one more important point. Don't forget taxes. As you are aware, every time you sell one of your profitable stocks, you have to let Uncle Sam know about it, so that he can get his pound of flesh, currently about 15 percent. But when you own a mutual fund that is not in a tax shelter, such as an IRA, the bite is even

more severe. For whatever reason, mutual fund managers are nervous critters who like to churn their portfolios. On average, the turnover in a mutual fund portfolio is close to 100 percent each year. If the profitable trades exceed the unprofitable ones, that profit is taxable to you, whether or not you have reinvested your dividends."

"How does that compare to owning your own stocks?"

"As I pointed out, you can't avoid taxes entirely when you invest in common stocks. On the other hand, you can control the time and frequency of your trades. If you buy a stock for $30 a share and it runs up to $50 a year or two later, there is no tax to pay if you simply hold on to your holdings. If you are a long-term investor, for instance, you might hold on to a stock for ten or fifteen years and not have to worry about taxes. And if you want to reduce your taxes, you can simply wait until one of your stocks proves a loser and sell it the same year you sell one that has been profitable. Subtract the loss from the gain and pay a tax on the difference. By contrast, when you own a mutual fund, you don't have that privilege."

"I'm amazed at what you have told me," she said. "Are there any books on what I should know about mutual funds?"

"A recent one might give you some insight into the subject: *The Investor's Dilemma: How Mutual Funds Are Betraying Your Trust And What To Do About It*, published by Wiley, $29.95."

Investment Mistakes You Shouldn't Make

Although I am in robust health—thanks to two hours of exercise each day—I still have to sit in waiting rooms to see a physician now and then. If there is the slightest hint that I might need some kind of nostrum to cure my suspected ailment, the first step is to schedule a diagnostic test. This past week, for instance, my doctor was concerned that I might have faulty circulation in my lower limbs. As it turned out—after a half hour of multiple blood pressure tests taken on arms, thighs, calves, ankles, and big toes—the doctor determined that the circulation in my legs and feet was not a problem that would prompt him to scribble a hasty prescription.

Next, he suspected that my heart was not running on all eight cylinders. The answer: have the hospital perform an echocardiogram—which is far different from the popular electrocardiogram. Although I am not a fan of diagnostic schemes, this one is not one to fret about.

All I had to do was to perch on my left side on a comfortable examination table and let the nurse, Giles Drumlin, hold a gel-tipped wand (called a sound-wave transducer) on various parts of my chest and watch a screen on an electrocardiograph monitor and periodically manipulate a huge bank of computer keys.

After about forty-five minutes of very minimum torture, I was through. As you might expect, Giles gave me no hint as to whether I was hale and hearty or whether death would intervene before my next birthday.

Just out of curiosity, I asked Giles (a trained cardiac sonographer) how much the instrument in front of him cost the hospital. A cool $258,000. No wonder health care costs are out of sight.

When we had finished my little ordeal, I asked the still-youthful operator how much training I would need to switch careers and begin to rake in cash examining people's hearts. In his case, he had been a cardiac nurse for seven years before taking an additional period of training in manipulating his fancy echo equipment. On the other hand, if someone with no medical training entered the picture, it would require enduring two years of training followed by six months working in the hospital of your first employer. It didn't take much urging for me to decide that writing books was an easier way to buy food and the other necessities of life.

However, I felt much more comfortable in knowing that my vital organ was being scrutinized by Giles Drumlin, an experienced and able cardiac sonographer.

Becoming Wealthy Through Investing

Since I was the last patient of the day, and we were getting well acquainted, I finished dressing and pulled out my business card and mentioned that he could become a wealthy sonographer merely by reading the latest edition of *The 100 Best Stocks You Can Buy*. To my surprise, Giles expressed an immediate interest. "I have been buying stocks for eight or ten years and have not always made the right moves. Maybe I need your book."

"Unfortunately, I don't have one handy," I said, "but I would be happy to chat with you and give you some off-the-cuff advice, if you have an extra half hour available."

"Well, it's only 4 P.M., and there are no more patients lurking in the waiting room. Why don't we sit down and chew the fat," said Giles Drumlin.

"That's fine with me. You said you had made a few blunders. My first question is: how many stocks do you own?'

"Not that many. I think it might be seven or eight."

"That's a good start, but you have a long way to go before you achieve adequate diversification. A good portfolio should have a minimum of twenty stocks, but thirty would be even better. For my part, my wife and I probably have too many—close to fifty, I think.

"However, the actual number of stocks is not the whole story. I have examined scores of portfolios of investors with $100,000 or $200,000 invested in stocks, and yet they are not diversified. Owning thirty or forty stocks may be deceptive."

"I thought you said that would be a good number to own," said Giles. "Could you elaborate a bit?"

"Glad to. As I said, many investors have dozens of stocks, but they are concentrated in a handful of industries, typically banks, oil companies, and public utilities. As you know, this strategy has been a disaster in 2008. Even the largest banks and financial institutions have been badly bruised in recent weeks."

"I know what you mean," said Giles Drumlin. "I own two banks myself. I assume you will tell me where I went wrong."

Owning in Different Sectors

"In a properly diversified list of stocks," I told him, "I suggest owning stocks in as many as ten different sectors. One sector is financial, such as banks, insurance companies, mutual fund companies like T. Rowe Price, and credit card companies such as American Express. Still another sector would be Energy, companies such as Exxon, Devon Energy, and Nabors."

"I'm beginning to get the picture," he said. "What are some of the other sectors?"

"If you are concerned about the antics of the market of late, you should not neglect the Consumer Staples sector, which includes Procter & Gamble, Walgreen, and Kellogg. Of course, public utilities can also provide some stability to your holdings. A few that are included in my latest book are MDU Resources, Dominion Resources, and FPL Group."

"I can appreciate that these stocks are safe and sane, but suppose I were a little more aggressive. What kind of fare would you suggest?" asked the cardiac sonographer.

"The first sector that comes to mind is Information Technology, which includes IBM, Microsoft, and Hewlett-Packard. There is a very broad group called Industrials, which includes such stocks as United Parcel, Norfolk Southern, United Technologies, and Ingersoll-Rand."

"Have you left out anything?"

"There are several more that a good list should contain. One sector that I have neglected in previous books is Telephone. I will feature AT&T in my 2009 book. Then, there is one group that I use extensively, Health Care. The woods are full of stocks in this group, such as Johnson & Johnson, Becton, Dickinson, Dentsply, and Abbott Laboratories. That group should do well in the years ahead, as the population ages."

"You're right there, Mr. Slatter. That's what keeps my paychecks rolling in. What's next?"

"I don't think I mentioned Consumer Discretion stocks. These are a bit more risky than Consumer Staples and include such companies as Target, Omnicom Group (a large advertising firm), Johnson

Controls, and McGraw-Hill. Still another interesting group is referred to as Materials, and includes Praxair (industrial gases), Lubrizol, and Ecolab, which is not very well known to most investors."

"I assume that about covers all the sectors idea. Right?"

Don't Neglect Sectors

"I think I have hit the high points of the sector idea. The next thing to bear in mind is not to go whole hog on just a few sectors, such as three or four. You may recall that I mentioned earlier that too many people neglect all the sectors except Energy, Financials, and Utilities. That is a blunder of the first order. Of course, there are some people who get all excited with tech stocks—many of which are traded on Nasdaq—neglecting entirely the other nine sectors. Those people risk a really bumpy ride, sometimes up dramatically and other times down in the dumps."

"I think I get the picture," said Giles Drumlin. "Now I am wondering how much emphasis I should put on each sector."

"As I pointed out, Giles, most investors not only neglect all ten sectors, but they often over-emphasize a few sectors and typically neglect the others. My strategy is to invest at least 5 percent of your portfolio in each sector—even those that turn you off. On the other hand, keep a lid on your favorites, not investing more than 15 percent in each."

"I think you have made me a better investor, Mr. Slatter. I can't wait to tell my wife that we are now on the road to riches, thanks to your sage advice."

"Hold on a minute, Giles, you can't get away just yet," I said. "That's just the beginning of avoiding the pitfalls that await the unwary investor. Your wife can hold supper until we finish my words of wisdom."

"Well, it's only 4:15, so I guess there's no hurry. What's next?"

"The next pitfall that might hurt your royal road to riches is sloth. Investing wisely requires a reasonable amount of effort. Not all stocks are born equal. In order to stay away from losers, it helps to do some reading. For my part, I read the *Wall Street Journal, Barron's, BusinessWeek. Forbes*, and *Value Line Investment Survey*. To be sure, I do more reading than most individual investors, but it would pay you to invest a reasonable amount of time studying a stock before you invest $5,000 in it. Of course, my book can be part of your required reading. Since there are 3,000 stocks on the New York Stock exchange and scads that trade on Nasdaq and elsewhere, I make your chore simpler by giving you 100 stocks to examine, instead of tens of thousands."

"You sound a bit like my high school teachers who used to assign homework every night," Giles said, laughing. "I guess I have to tell my kids that there will be no more shooting baskets in the backyard. I'll assign my wife to take care of grooming them to become champions of the court."

"If you want to be rich, you have to pay a price, Giles. Now, let's move on to the next important piece of advice. Most people think that becoming rich means you have to be able to pick winning stocks. To be sure, that's important, but the real key to riches is very simple—start early in life. It would appear that you have already started your portfolio before becoming gray and bald. I assume you're in your mid-thirties.

"How did you guess? Yes, I'm just shy of thirty-seven. Why is it so important to start early?"

"The earlier the better. Let's say you had begun when you were twenty-five and invested $5,000 each year until age sixty-five and made 12 percent a year on average. By the time you reach sixty-five, your holdings would be worth $3,835,457. However, if you delayed getting into equities until age thirty-five and invested $5,000 each year, you would get the company's gold watch with far less, only $1,206,663. Now, let's move to age forty-five before buying your first stock, once again investing $5,000. This time, you hit the sixty-five mark with only $360,262. Of course, the story gets even more depressing for those who frittered their money away until age fifty-five. In this instance, you would end up with $87,744. Does that convince you that beginning early makes sense?"

"Of course, getting 12 percent on your stocks may not be that easy, but I see your point."

"If you don't spend too much time teaching your kids to shoot baskets, you should be able to do it, Giles. Going back to 1926, that has been the history of the stock market. Let's hope the future is more of the same. Next, still another factor to bear in mind is developing a habit of thrift. If you are going to invest a substantial amount of money on a regular basis—let's say 10 percent or 15 percent of your income—you may have to tighten your belt a bit. One way to save money is to buy used cars, not new ones. I drive a 1998 Cadillac, which I bought when it was three years old. I haven't bought a new car in forty years. I also buy books and DVDs from Amazon, usually used. One other interesting way to obtain bargains when you buy things is to go to yard sales; some people call them garage sales. I have seven exercise machines in my workout room, and four of them I picked up in mint condition at garage sales for $25 or less each. In other words, I live a sensible, but frugal life. It has helped me to become a millionaire—and then some!"

"I never considered buying used cars, but maybe I should give it some thought. What else do you have up your sleeve?"

Avoid Debt

"Next, let's look at credit cards. Some people have a wallet stuffed with them. What's even worse, each is piled high with debt, with interest rates as high as 18 percent. I have one credit card and no outstanding obligations. I send out a check the day after I receive the statement. My wife does the same thing with hers."

"I'm with you there, Mr. Slatter. So far, I haven't found fault with your ideas," said Giles Drumlin.

"Glad to see you have avoided credit card mania. Next, let's find out how to forecast the stock market. Perhaps you have figured out how to do this, Giles."

"I'm afraid that gift has eluded me, Mr. Slatter," he said. "I assume you will clue me in on how to do it. I think it would really help."

"As far as I know, Giles, no one has been able to predict which direction the market is headed—and that includes stockbrokers, financial advisers, mutual fund managers, bankers and armchair investors like you. Remember this: whenever you sell your stocks because you are convinced the market is headed south, you have to be right twice, not once. If you correctly predict it is going to take a dive, you then have to predict when to get back into the market before it starts heading back up. In all likelihood, you will be wrong at least once. You will probably sell too late and then buy back too soon or too late. Meanwhile, buying and selling costs brokerage commissions and capital gains taxes. Capital gains taxes, of course, are the worst part."

"I'm sorry to hear that. With all your experience in writing books, I would assume you could figure out how to beat the market and its antics of rising and falling. With that comment, I suppose it's time to head out of here to enjoy some home cooking."

"Hold on, Giles, there is more to come. One mistake that aggressive investors make is paying to much for an attractive stock—often one that is popular. It may have a price/earnings ratio, or P/E, that is thirty, forty or fifty times earnings. History shows that such expensive stocks do not perform well in the long run. I suggest you avoid paying more than thirty times earnings.

"I'm getting close to the end. As you know, you can't be an investor without having a brokerage firm to handle your transactions. Too often, investors stumble on to a broker who calls them on the telephone out of the blue. Such brokers are often new to the business, and they are given a list of names of people who might be willing to open an account with a total stranger. If you receive an unsolicited call, don't listen. Just hang up. The way to find a good broker is to talk with people you know who have established a good relationship with a broker who knows what's going on and is not trying to sell you something that includes a hefty commission."

"I know what you mean," said Giles Drumlin. "I have two brokerage accounts. One is a full-service broker and one is a discount broker. I see no reason to listen to anyone else."

"One last piece of advice is to buy the latest edition of my book, *The 100 Best Stocks You Can Buy.* I don't happen to have a copy with me, but if you send me a check, I will mail you an autographed copy, postage-free. How does that sound."

"That's the least I can do for your taking time for a busy schedule to get me on the straight and narrow."

The good news is that the cardiac sonographer actually sent me a check. What's more, my doctor didn't send me a report indicating that my heart was scheduled to stop beating anytime soon.

The Essentials of Successful Investing

You don't have to be a brilliant stock-picker to become a successful investor. Here are a few factors that matter more.

Start Early

Starting your program at an early age wins hands down. Let's say you want to reach age sixty-five with investments worth a million dollars. If you buy your first stock at age thirty-five and pick stocks that appreciate at a rate of 10 percent (dividends included), you will have to set aside $6,079 each year. But if you delay until age forty-five, the amount needed leaps to $17,460. Waiting until you're fifty-five boosts your annual contribution to a real back-breaker—$62,746.

Don't Be a Spendthrift

Also important is your ability to set aside money out of your current income. You will have a lot of trouble if you buy a new car every two or three years. In fact, if you buy new cars at all, you will have trouble. I buy used cars, usually Buicks that are three years old but are in top condition. And don't buy the best house in town and saddle yourself with a huge mortgage. Buy an older home that has been well taken care of. And never fail to pay off your credit card balance before it includes interest charges. In short, don't be a spendthrift. If you need help, read *The Millionaire Mind*, by Thomas J. Stanley.

Stocks Are the Answer

Next, make sure you invest mostly in common stocks. Over the years, stocks have provided 11 or 12 percent a year in total return. If you buy bonds, CDs, preferred stocks, or leave your cash in a money-market fund, you may not be able to pay your bills during retirement. On the other hand, you may want to have a portion of your investment money—let's say 30 percent—in short-term bonds, particularly if you are retired.

Still another alternative to be avoided are mutual funds. Why? Because the people who manage mutual funds scoop off about 1.5 percent of your holdings each year. They call it the "expense ratio." In addition, picking a good fund is made difficult because there are many thousands to choose from—and no effective way to separate the wheat from the chaff. In fact, there are not very many good ones. The average fund underperforms the market. Finally, mutual funds trade stocks as if they were going out of style, which means they distribute capital gains to you that are subject to income tax.

The Keys to Picking Stocks

And now we come to the final factor: picking a good list of stocks.

The most important factor is diversification. I suggest owning at least twenty to thirty stocks. However, that doesn't mean you have to accomplish this objective on day one. Let's say you have $5,000 and will be able to save $5,000 each year. In the first year, you buy one or two stocks. That certainly is not a diversified portfolio—but don't let that worry you. If you start investing at age forty and buy one stock a year, you will have twenty-five stocks at age sixty-five.

The one thing you want to avoid is buying too many stocks that are similar. In 1998 and 1999, many investors were convinced that tech stocks were the wave of the future, so they loaded up on them, often to the exclusion of everything else—no oil stocks, no bank stocks, no drug stocks, no utilities, no REITs, no food stocks, and so forth—just tech stocks. Well, as you know, they crashed big time. Many were down 90 percent, and some didn't even survive the bear market of 2000–2002.

As far as picking stocks is concerned, don't fret over picking all winners. You can't do it. Don't worry about it. Just keep picking stocks from my book, *The 100 Best Stocks You Can Buy*, that appeal to you, and time will take care of the rest.

A Few Guidelines

But whichever route you care to traverse, you still have to make up your mind which stock or stocks you will purchase. Ideally, a stock should have these characteristics:

- A rising trend of earnings, dividends, and book value
- A balance sheet with less debt than other companies in its particular industry
- A Standard & Poor's rating of B+ or better
- A price/earnings ratio no higher than average
- A dividend yield that suits your particular needs
- A below-average dividend payout ratio (For instance, if a company has annual earnings per share of $4, I would prefer that it pays out $2 or less in the form of dividends.)
- Company's return on shareholders' equity is 15 percent or higher

Sources of Information

You can obtain this information from *Value Line Investment Survey*, which is available at most brokerage offices and some libraries. *Value Line* covers about 1,700 stocks with one page devoted to each stock; these are revised every three months. What's more, all the stocks in a given industry are presented together.

An equally helpful source of information is Standard & Poor's, which publishes a two-page report on nearly any stock you can think of. You can also find these sheets online. For instance, I have an account at Charles Schwab, so I merely bring up my portfolio and click on News/Chart, then scroll down Select a Report until I see *S&P Stock Report*. I click Go, and the report appears on the screen, which I can print out.

Finally, there's no law against calling the company and ordering the latest annual report. Or, if you are computer literate, you can find a wealth of information on the company's Web site. The easiest way to get to the Web site is to bring up the financial section of the *New York Times* and enter the ticker symbol where it offers to give you a quote. When that comes on your screen, you will see a place to click on the company's Web site. Then click Investor Relations, and the rest is easy.

Once you sink your hard-earned cash into a stock, you will immediately start wondering when to sell. This is not an easy decision, but I think you should use the list of characteristics that I discussed above, such as the trend of earnings, the P/E ratio, and the return on equity. If your stock no longer measures up, it may be time to sell. Even so, the more you tinker with your holdings, the worse your performance will be. Buy and hold is the best strategy.

Twenty Ways to Reduce Investment Risk

No matter where you invest your money, there is always risk. Even bonds are not safe from inflation and rising interest rates. CDs also suffer from inflation. Stocks, as everyone knows, are regarded as the riskiest investments. However, they are also the most profitable—at least in the long run. In the short run, who knows what they will do.

Based on my long experience in the stock market, I have figured out twenty ways you can reduce this risk. Since I use most of them myself and for my clients, I have emerged from the recent bear market relatively intact. Since more bear markets are not out of the question, here are my thoughts on ways to mitigate your discomfort.

You will find some of these same ideas discussed in greater detail in other chapters of this book. This may seem repetitive, but sometimes repetition is one of the best ways to cram new knowledge into your gray matter. Here are the twenty ways to reduce your risk:

1. The first rule of investing is *diversification*. Although most investors are aware of this concept, most do not know how to implement it. Of course, the most grievous blunder is to invest your whole portfolio in one stock. I have seen what this can do.

A few years ago, I met an architect after delivering a lecture. He had more than a million dollars invested in an obscure stock called Comdisco, which was selling around $30 a share. I convinced him to sell $300,000 worth and have me manage that portfolio, which is now worth about $500,000. Meanwhile, Comdisco climbed to $57 a share, which made the architect happy. However, by the end of 2001 it was worth only fifty-two cents a share, and my client had failed to sell it.

Still another investor came to me with all his money invested in WorldCom. He had bought the shares much lower and was well ahead of the game. He agreed to sell it all and have me manage his portfolio by buying twenty-five stocks. It's no secret what has happened to WorldCom.

When I was in Cleveland, I had the task of evaluating portfolios for a firm's clients. Almost without exception, these customers had some diversification. They often had twenty, thirty, or forty stocks, which is considered adequate. But most of these stocks were in three industries: oil, utilities, and banks. That's certainly a far cry from prudent diversification.

2. Not to be forgotten is asset allocation. This concept is similar to diversification, but it goes one step further. Instead of investing all your money in stocks, you should spread it around in such assets as bonds, foreign stocks, and money-market funds. No one knows what the market is going to do, so it makes sense to hedge your bets with prudent asset allocation. In the past three years, bonds have far outperformed stocks. That doesn't mean you should sell all your stocks and concentrate in bonds. Who knows? Now may be the time to be in stocks. Still, it pays to have some money in fixed-income assets, even if you think a new bull market is just ahead.

3. One way to measure whether a stock is overpriced is to calculate its price-earnings ratio (known as the P/E ratio). Simply divide the stock price by the company's most recent twelve-month earnings per share. P/E ratios can vary all the way

from 10 to 100 or more. In most instances, a high ratio indicates a company with good prospects for the future. A low P/E ratio often means the company has a lackluster future. Although I am not suggesting that you stuff your portfolio with low P/E stocks, I am suggesting that you avoid stocks that are selling at very high P/E ratios. I would avoid any stock with a ratio of 30 or higher. In the long run, they don't do well. Many studies prove this point.

4. Many investors ignore real estate investment trusts, usually known as REITs. They look stodgy and dull and typically have a dividend yield of 5 percent or higher. In the past two years, REITs have not only avoided the debacle that has engulfed most other stocks, but they have also actually risen in value. That's because REITs act counter to the market. In a rising market, for instance, they would not do as well as growth stocks.

For my own part, I own several of them. REITs are not all alike. Some invest in apartment buildings, some in office buildings, and some in shopping malls. And there are others, as well. Most REITs are well diversified geographically.

5. In recent years, dividends have largely been ignored. Historically, however, dividends have played a prominent role in investing. About half of the 11 or 12 percent annual return that investors enjoy can be attributed to dividends. Lately this has not been the case, as companies have tended to buy back their own shares, rather than pay out profits to shareholders. Even so, when I pick stocks, I look for a dividend and a history of regular increases. Stocks that pay a dividend are less likely to plunge in value than those that prefer to reinvest their profits in growth.

6. A strong balance sheet is an essential for a company that you want to consider. It's simply a relationship between the amount of debt as a percentage of capitalization. My preference is for 75 percent in equity (the book value of the common stock). A strong balance sheet makes it easier for the company to finance an acquisition. If you have access to *Value Line Investment Survey*, it's easy to find out this percentage.

7. If you elect to buy bonds, don't look for the highest yield. For one thing, a high yield is often characteristic of a weak company. When the yield gets too large, the bonds are referred to as "junk bonds." The safest bonds are those issued by the federal government. In today's market, you can't get much more of a return than 5 percent, and that's for bonds that mature in twenty or thirty years. Shorter maturities are typically lower. It's best to stick to maturities of five years or less. The reason is that the bond will sink like a stone if interest rates start climbing. This does not happen for bonds due in less than five years, since all you have to do is wait and you'll get the face value of the bond. A bond due in thirty years, by contrast, will drop, and you may not live long enough to get the face value.

8. In an effort to avoid the risk of owning stocks, some people think it pays to buy preferred stocks, convertible bonds, annuities, or commodities, or to sell short. None of these vehicles are recommended— at least not by me. Here's why:

• **Preferred stocks sound safe and sound? Not necessarily.** A preferred stock is somewhat like a bond, in that the dividend is paid regularly and never changes. But a preferred stock—unlike a bond—never matures. In other words, you can't get your money back by waiting for the maturity date. Unlike a common stock, the dividend will never be increased. But if the company has problems, the dividend can be cut. If interest rates go up, the value of a preferred stock will decline.

• **Convertible bonds** appeal to some investors because they have a higher yield than the same company's common stock. They can also be converted into the company's common stock. On the other hand, unless you really know what you are doing, you may find that the company calls in the convertible when it suits their purposes. If you are bound and determined to buy convertibles, I advise you to do it by investing in a mutual fund that is managed by professionals. Even so, I'm not so sure you will be a happy camper.

• **Annuities** are issued by insurance companies. There are two main types. The more conservative is invested in such things as bonds and mortgages. When you are ready to retire, the insurance company will set up a monthly payment plan that will assure you of the same amount each month until you die. Assuming you leave behind a husband or wife, the income will not continue to that survivor. However, if you are willing to take a smaller monthly payment, the company will continue paying that amount to your survivor until his or her death, too. Finally, insurance companies charge a pretty penny for their products, since they have to pay the agent for talking you into it.

• **Variable annuities** are another version of annuity, called "variable" since it is invested in common stocks and other assets of your choosing. Here again, the cost of these products is high. You would be better off buying a conventional mutual fund. The costs are usually about 1.5 percent a year.

• **If you are a speculator, you may find an interest in options, such as puts and calls, and many variations.** A call enables you to buy a particular common stock some weeks or months in the future at today's price. If the stock goes up substantially, this works out fine. But if it drops or advances only modestly, you lose the price of the option. "Puts" work for stocks that are expected to decline. But if they don't decline, you lose. In short, options are best avoided.

• **Commodities** have to do with speculating in such agricultural items as corn, wheat, soybeans, and pork bellies. It is possible to make a lot of money quickly in commodities. But very few people actually do because Mother Nature has a hand in your results. If you think a drought will help the price of your commodity, you might get rich—unless it starts raining, which can lead to a surplus and too much of that commodity, thus reducing prices drastically. This is no game for amateurs.

• **Selling short** is similar to calls and puts. If you think a stock is likely to decline in price, you can make money by selling short. You simply instruct your broker to borrow the shares from one of the firm's accounts. You then sell those shares at today's price. Let's say the stock is selling for $50 a share. Then, when the price drops to $30, you buy shares in the market and give them back to the investor who loaned them to you. Thus, you make a tidy profit of $20 a share. The catch is that the price may very well shoot up to $75, and what do you do then? If you buy back at this level, you lose $25 a share. There is no limit to the amount you can lose when you sell short. If you wait until the price goes to $150, you lose $100 a share. This is not my idea of having fun.

9.   Some investors can't stand inaction. Instead of buying and holding, they insist on selling winners and holding losers. All you do that way is end up with a portfolio of losers. It's better to let your winners

run. The more you buy and sell, the more taxes you will have to pay.

10. Be careful in selecting a stockbroker. Most people start with a traditional full-service firm, since their salespeople are aggressively seeking new clients. Brokerage firms can supply you with research material, but these firms rely heavily for their profits on investment banking and their analysts may not be impartial. For their part, the salespeople make their money from commissions, which are much higher than such discount firms as Schwab or Scottrade. Even worse, they tend to recommend products that have a high commission and limited prospects.

11. If you invest in stocks, avoid companies that are losing money. Instead, look for companies with a long history of profitable operation, with a rising trend in earnings per share. If you buy stocks that are losing money, you are a speculator, not an investor.

12. Stocks are traded on the New York Stock Exchange, the American Stock Exchange, and Nasdaq. The leading companies are usually listed on the New York Stock Exchange. Those traded elsewhere are less mature and often of lower quality.

13. If you buy mutual funds, make sure you examine the "expense ratio." Even no-load funds are not free. To pay the salary of analysts and other employees, along with expenses like advertising, rent, and travel, mutual funds subtract these costs from your profits. The average expense ratio is about 1.5 percent per year. Studies show that funds with the highest expense ratios perform worst, while those with the lowest perform the best.

14. Although I am not a fan of mutual funds, if advising on how to invest in them,

I would say avoid those with new management. Before you invest, call the company and ask the age of the manager and how long he has been in charge. I would prefer a manager at least forty years of age and a tenure of at least five years.

15. Avoid stocks with excessively high yields, at least in relation to other companies in that industry. Those with high yields are often in trouble and are likely to cut their dividend.

16. Seek companies that are financially strong. This can be determined in two ways. Standard & Poor's rates stocks by letter. The highest rating is A+. An average rating is B+. Avoid those with a rating below B+. *Value Line* uses a similar rating, but its highest rating is A++, and an average one is B++. Again, don't go below B++.

17. Examine the dividend payout ratio. It's calculated by dividing the annual dividend by the annual earnings per share for the past twelve months. If the dividend is $1, and the earnings per share are $4, the payout ratio would be 25 percent. That signifies a company that is plowing back earnings into research, new products, stock repurchase, debt reduction, or acquisitions. If the payout ratio is high, let's say 75 percent, this is an indication that the company has limited growth potential.

18. The economy has an impact on most companies, but there are some industries that are considered cyclical, such as chemicals, autos, appliances, machinery, metals and mining, paper, and railroads. Most of these have limited long-term growth. The only way to make money is by buying them when they are in trouble and selling them when money is rolling in. It's not that easy to be able to jump in and out with any consistency. Instead of cyclical stocks,

concentrate on industries that are more stable, such as food processors, banks, REITs, utilities, food supermarkets, life insurance, medical supplies, and household products.

19. When a major company buys another major company, avoid the buyer. A good case in point is the purchase of Compaq by Hewlett-Packard. Rarely is there an exception to this rule.

20. Most investors are busy people such as doctors, accountants, executives, and business owners. That means their time is limited. Even so, some time must be allotted for reading annual reports, the *Wall Street Journal*, *Business Week*, and *Value Line*. To be a successful investor, you have to know how the game is played. This should also include reading at least one book on investing every year.

Basic Terminology

If you are new to the investment arena, you may have difficulty understanding parts of this book. To get you over the rough spots, I have listed some common expressions that appear frequently in books on investing. You will also encounter them in the *Wall Street Journal*, *Forbes*, *BusinessWeek*, *Barron's*, and other periodicals devoted to investing.

This is not a glossary but merely a brief list of terms essential to understanding this book.

Analyst

In nearly every one of the 100 articles, you will note that I refer to "analysts" and what they think about the prospects for a particular stock. Analysts are individuals who have special training in analyzing stocks. Typically, they have such advanced degrees as M.B.A. or C.F.A. Many of them work for brokerage houses, but they may work for banks, insurance companies, mutual funds, pension plans, or other institutions. Most analysts specialize in one or two industries. A good analyst can tell you nearly everything there is to know about a particular stock or the industry it's a part of.

However, analysts can be dead wrong about the future action of a stock. The reason: surprises. Companies are constantly changing, which means they are acquiring, divesting, developing new products, restructuring, buying back their shares, and so forth. When they make a change and announce this change to Wall Street, the surprise can change the course of the stock. In short, analysts can be helpful, but don't bet the store on what they tell you.

As you can see, analysts are usually intelligent, hardworking, and conscientious. Even so, they don't always succeed in guiding you to riches. Perhaps the biggest beef most people have is the tie that analysts have to the companies they follow. They know these people well and may be reluctant to say anything negative.

One reason for this is economic. Most brokerage firms make a ton of money from their investment banking division. If the analyst antagonizes the company, that company may give its investment banking business to a firm that says nice things rather than pointing out its warts and all.

This reluctance to see no evil and speak no evil can be seen when you examine the number of times that analysts advise investors to sell. According to the research firm First Call, more than 70 percent of the 27,000 recommendations outstanding in November 2000 were strong buys or buys. Fewer than 1 percent were sells or strong sells. To recap: Of the 27,000 recommendations, 26.6 percent were holds, 36.8 percent were buys, 35.7 percent were strong buys, and a mere 0.9 percent were sells or strong sells. I rest my case.

Annual Report

If you own a common stock, you can be certain that you will receive a fancy annual report a couple of months after the close of the year. If the year ends December 31, look for your annual report in March or April. If the fiscal year ends some other time of the year, such as September 30, the annual report will appear in your mailbox two or three months later.

Not all investors read annual reports, but they might be better off if they did. Although most companies will not list their problems, you can usually get a pretty good idea how things are going. In particular, read the report by the president or CEO. It's usually one, two, or three pages long and is written in language you can understand.

If you want detailed information on the company's various businesses, the annual report will often overwhelm you with details that may be difficult to fathom. If you are really curious about what they are trying to say, feel free to call the investor contact. I have provided the phone number of this person for all 100 stocks listed. Have a list of questions ready, and call during the person's lunch hour, leaving your name and phone number. This sneaky little strategy means the cost of the call back will be paid by the company, not you. By the way, don't assume you will be intimidated by the investor contact. Investor contacts are usually quite personable and helpful.

Argus Research Company

Argus is an independent research organization that provides information on stocks to institutions, such as brokerage houses, banks, and mutual funds. It is normally not available to individual investors. However, you may be able to obtain Argus reports through your broker. You will note that I have quoted liberally from Argus in the analysis of my 100 stocks. You should be able to obtain this information from a brokerage house, such as Charles Schwab & Company. Analysts with Argus typically revise their reports quite often, depending on changes in earnings and important developments.

Asset Allocation

This is not the same as diversification. Rather, it refers to the strategy of allocating your investment funds among different types of investments, such as stocks, bonds, or money-market funds. In the long run, you will be better off with all of your assets concentrated in common stocks. In the short run, this may not be true, since the market occasionally has a sinking spell. A severe one, such as that of 2000–2002, can cause your holdings to decline in value by 20 percent or more. To protect against this, most investors spread their money around. They may, for instance, allocate 50 percent to stocks, 40 percent to bonds, and 10 percent to a money-market fund. A more realistic breakdown might be 70 percent in stocks, 25 percent in bonds, and 5 percent in a money-market fund.

Balance Sheet

All corporations issue at least two financial statements: the balance sheet and the income statement. Both are important. The balance sheet is a financial picture of the company on a specific date, such as December 31 or at the end of a quarter.

On the left side of the balance sheet are the company's assets, such as cash, current assets, inventories, accounts receivable, and buildings. On the right side are its liabilities, including accounts payable and long-term debt. Also on the right side is shareholders' equity. The right side of the balance sheet adds up to the same value as the left side, which is why it is called a balance sheet.

In most instances, corporations give you figures for the current year and the prior year. By examining the changes, you can get an idea of whether the company's finances are improving or deteriorating.

Bonds

Entire books have been written on the various kinds of bonds. A bond, unlike a stock, is not a form of ownership. A bond is a contractual agreement that means you have loaned money to some entity and that entity has agreed to pay you a certain sum of money (interest) every six months until that bond matures. At that time, you will also get back the money you originally invested—no more, no less. Most bonds are issued in $1,000 denominations. The safest bonds are those issued by the U.S. government. The two advantages of bonds are safety and income. If you wait until the maturity date, you will be assured of getting the face value of the bond. In the meantime, however, the bond will fluctuate, because of changes in interest rates or the creditworthiness of the corporation. Long-term bonds, moreover, fluctuate far more than short-term bonds. But enough about bonds. This book is about stocks.

Capital Gains

When you buy common stocks, you expect to make money in two ways: capital gains and dividends. Over an extended period of time, about half of your total return will come from each sector. If the stock rises in value and you sell it above your cost, you are enjoying a capital gain. The tax on long-term capital gains is a maximum of 15 percent if the stock is held for twelve months.

Chief Executive Officer (CEO)

This is the executive of a company who reports to the board of directors. That corporate body can terminate the CEO if he or she fails to do an effective job of managing the company. In some instances, the CEO may also have the title of either president or chairman of the board, or both.

Closed-End Investment Company

A managed investment portfolio, similar to a mutual fund, a closed-end investment company is generally traded on a stock exchange. The price fluctuates with supply and demand, not because of changes in the assets within the trust. An open-end investment trust, or mutual fund, changes in size as investors buy new shares or surrender

their shares for cash. A closed-end trust, by contrast, does not permit new money to be invested, nor can shares be redeemed by the company. Thus, the number of shares remains the same once the trust begins trading. One feature of the closed-end trust is worth mentioning: They often sell at a discount to their asset value. An open-end trust always sells at precisely its asset value.

Common Stocks

We might as well define what a common stock is, since this whole book is devoted to them. All publicly owned companies—those that trade their shares outside of a small group of executives or the founding family—are based on common stocks. A common stock is evidence of partial ownership in a corporation. Most of the stocks described in this book have millions of shares of their stock outstanding, and the really large ones may have in excess of 100 million shares. When you own common stock, there are no guarantees. If the company is successful, it will probably pay a dividend four times a year. These dividends may be raised periodically, perhaps once a year. If, however, the company has problems, it may cut or eliminate its dividend. This can happen even to a major company, such as IBM, Goodyear, or General Motors. As I said, there are no guarantees.

Investors who own common stock can sell their shares at any time. All you do is call your broker, and the trade is executed a few minutes later at the prevailing price—which fluctuates nearly every day, sometimes by a few cents or sometimes two or three points.

Current Ratio

The current ratio is calculated by dividing current assets by current liabilities. Current assets include any assets that will become cash within one year, including cash itself. Current liabilities are those that will be paid off within a year. A current ratio of 2 is considered ideal. Most companies these days have a current ratio of less than 2.

Diversification

Since investments are inherently risky, it pays to spread the risk by diversifying. If you don't, you may be too heavily invested in a stock or bond that turns sour. Even well-known stocks such as Alcoa, International Paper, Eastman Kodak, and American Express can experience occasional sinking spells.

To be on the safe side, don't invest more than 5 percent of your portfolio in any one stock. In addition, don't invest too heavily in any one sector of the economy. A good strategy is to divide stocks among ten sectors: drugs and health care, industrials, materials, energy, telecommunications, utilities, consumer staples, consumer discretionary, financials, and information technology.

Here's a rule of thumb that will keep you out of trouble: Invest at least 5 percent in each sector but not more than 15 percent. That means that you should own at least ten stocks so that you have representation in all ten sectors.

Dividends

Unlike bonds, which pay interest, common stocks may pay a dividend. Most dividends are paid quarterly, but there is no set date that all corporations use. Some, for instance, may pay on January 1, March 1, July 1, and September 1. Another company may pay on February 10, May 10, August 10, and November 10. If you want to receive checks every month, you will have to make sure you buy stocks that pay dividends at different times of the year. The Standard & Poor's *Stock Guide* is a source for this information, as is the *Value Line Investment Survey*. Most companies like to pay the same dividend every quarter until they can afford to increase

it. Above all, they don't like to cut their dividends, since investors who depend on this income will sell their shares, and the stock will decline in price. If you use good judgment in selecting your stocks, you can expect that your companies will increase their dividends nearly every year.

Dividend Payout

If a company earns $4 a share in a twelve-month period and pays out $3 to shareholders in the form of dividends, it has a payout ratio of 75 percent. However, if it pays only $1, the payout ratio is 25 percent. In the past, many investors looked favorably on a low payout ratio. The thinking was that such a company was plowing back its earnings into such projects as research, new facilities, acquisitions, and new equipment. It sounds logical.

Now, there is evidence that you are better off buying a company with a higher payout ratio. Mark Hulbert, who writes frequently for the Sunday *New York Times*, has come up with some studies that focus on this concept. According to work done by Michael C. Jensen, currently an emeritus professor of business administration at the Harvard Business School, "The more cash that companies have now (beyond what is needed for current projects), the less efficient they will be in the future."

Two other scholars concur that a higher payout ratio serves investors better than a low one. They are Robert D. Arnott of First Quadrant and Clifford S. Asness of AQR Capital Management. For one thing, they found that, "For the overall stock market between 1871 and 2001, corporate profits grew fastest in the ten years following the calendar year in which companies had the highest average dividend payout ratio." What's more, their study showed that in the period from 1946 to 1991, there was a strong correlation that demonstrates conclusively that companies with a high payout ratio performed far better than the ones who were stingy with their dividend distributions.

Mr. Hulbert concludes that, "The common theme that emerges from these various studies is a very unflattering portrait of corporate management: give executives lots of rope and they too often end up hanging themselves. It would appear that a high dividend payout ratio is an effective way to reduce the length of that rope."

Dividend Reinvestment Plans

Unless you are retired, you might like to reinvest your dividends in more shares. Many companies have a dividend reinvestment plan (also known as a DRIP) that will allow you to do this, and the charge for this service is often minimal. Most of these companies also allow you to mail in additional cash, which will be used to purchase new shares, again at minimal cost.

In recent years, a few companies have created "direct" dividend reinvestment plans. Unlike most plans, direct plans enable you to buy your initial shares directly from the company. To alert you to which companies have direct plans, I have inserted the word *direct*. Companies with such plans include ExxonMobil, McDonald's, Procter & Gamble, Merck, and Lilly. Incidentally, you can rarely buy just one share. Many companies have a minimum purchase amount, such as $500.

This may sound like a good way to avoid paying brokerage commissions, but there are some drawbacks to bear in mind. For one thing, you can't time your purchases, since it may be a week or more before your purchase is made.

Even worse is calculating your cost basis for tax purposes. By the time you sell, you may have made scores of small investments in the same stock, each with a different cost basis. Make sure you keep a file for each company so that you can make these calculations when the time comes. Or, better still, don't sell.

Dollar-Cost Averaging

Dollar-cost averaging is a systematic way to invest money over a long period, such as ten, fifteen, or twenty years. It entails investing the same amount of money regularly, such as each month or each quarter. If you do this faithfully, you will be buying more stock when the price is lower and less stock when the price is higher. This tends to smooth out the gyrations of the market. Dollar-cost averaging is often used with a mutual fund, but it can just as easily be done with a company that has a dividend reinvestment plan (DRIP).

Hedge Fund

Most investors are familiar with mutual funds, but hedge funds may not ring a bell. For the most part, they are marketed to wealthy investors. Let's start out with a definition that I obtained from Google, my favorite Internet site for answering any question that pops into my head. The following definition was provided by investorwords.com:

"A fund, usually used by wealthy individuals and institutions, which is allowed to use aggressive strategies that are unavailable to mutual funds, including selling short, leverage, program trading, swaps, arbitrage, and derivatives. Hedge funds are exempt from many of the rules and regulations governing other mutual funds, which allows them to accomplish aggressive investing goals. They are restricted by law to no more than 100 investors per fund, and as a result most hedge funds set extremely high minimum investment amounts, ranging anywhere from $250,000 to over $1 million. As with traditional mutual funds, investors in hedge funds pay a management fee; however, hedge funds also collect a percentage of the profits (usually 20%)."

One of my favorite columnists is Jonathan Clements who writes a weekly column for the *Wall Street Journal*—it appears nearly every Wednesday. On September 20, 2006, Mr. Clements said: "Consider a study by Roger Ibbotson, founder of Ibbotson Associates—now a unit of Chicago researchers Morningstar, Inc.—and Peng Chen, the firm's president.

"The authors note that, based on the TASS database, hedge funds appear to have clocked an eye-popping 16.5 percent a year between year-end 1994 and April 2006, easily outpacing the 11.6 percent average for the Standard & Poor's 500-stock index. Yet this 16.5 percent average is mighty misleading, for two reasons.

"First, when hedge funds are added to performance databases, they sometimes include earlier results. This 'backfill bias' skews the average upward, because only funds with stellar returns typically report their prior performance. Second, when poorly performing hedge funds go out of business, their dismal results are often ignored, leading to so-called survivorship bias.

"What happens if you eliminate survivorship bias and backfill bias? Messrs. Ibbotson and Chen calculate that hedge funds returned just 9 percent a year, less than the S&P 500's 11.6%."

Let me close this definition with a cogent observation by the erudite Alan Abelson, who writes a thoughtful weekly column for *Barron's*. Here is what he said on July 31, 2006: "As we've said before (we quote ourselves, a la George Bernard Shaw, to spice our conversation), we've nothing against hedge funds or the filthy rich losing their money in them; the benefit of being filthy rich, after all, is that there's always plenty more where that came from. But the notion that Jane and Joe Doaks should entrust their retirement pittance to untutored pups or grasping geezers who live (and die) by leverage and operate in the shadows is positively indecent."

Income Statement

Most investors are more interested in the income statement than they are in the balance sheet. They are particularly interested in the progress (or lack of it) in earnings per share (EPS). The income statement lists such items as net sales, cost of sales, interest expense, and gross profit. As with the balance sheet, it makes sense to compare this year's numbers with those of the prior year.

Inflation-Indexed Treasury Bonds

Conventional bonds—those that pay a fixed rate of return, such as 5 percent—have one big drawback: They are vulnerable to rising interest rates. For example, if you buy a bond that promises to pay you 5 percent for the next fifteen or twenty years, you will lose principal if interest rates climb to 7 percent. The reason is that new bonds being issued give investors a much better return. Thus, those that pay only 5 percent will sag in price until they hit a level that equates them to the new bonds that pay 7 percent. The loss of principal, moreover, is much greater with long-term bonds, such as those due in fifteen, twenty, or thirty years.

By contrast, short-term bonds, those coming due in three or four years, are much less volatile because you can often hold the bonds until the maturity date. Thus, you are certain to receive the full face value. Of course, you can do the same thing with a twenty-year bond, but twenty years is a long time.

The way to beat this disadvantage is to buy the relatively new bonds being issued by the U.S. government, since they are indexed to inflation. For this reason, you are unlikely to lose principal. To be sure, they pay less initially, currently 3.8 percent. But the ultimate return may be much better if inflation continues to impact the economy.

Suppose you invested $1,000 in inflation bonds at the current yield of 3.8 percent. If consumer prices rose 2.5 percent over the next year, your principal would climb to $1,025, and you would earn interest equal to 3.8 percent on this growing sum. Thus, if you spent the interest but didn't cash in any bonds, you would enjoy a rising stream of income while keeping your principal's spending power intact.

One thing to bear in mind is that with inflation-indexed treasury bonds, you have to pay federal income taxes each year on both the interest you earn and also the increase in the bonds' principal value. One way to take the sting out of this tax is to use these bonds in a tax-deferred account, such as an IRA.

Despite the tax implications, inflation bonds may be useful outside an IRA. Because these bonds don't perform as erratically as conventional bonds, they can be a good place to park money you may need if something unexpected comes along, such as a medical bill not fully covered by insurance. If inflation-indexed bonds ring a bell, ask the teller at your bank to get you started. She won't charge you a fee, and there is no red tape.

Investment Advisor

Investors who do not have the time or inclination to manage their own portfolios may elect to employ an investment advisor. Most advisors charge 1 percent a year. Thus, if you own stocks worth $300,000, your annual fee would be $3,000. Advisors differ from brokers, since they do not profit from changes. Brokers, by contrast, charge a commission on each transaction, which means they profit from changes in your portfolio. Advisors profit only when the value of your holdings increases. For instance, if the value of your portfolio increases to $500,000, the annual fee will be $5,000. You, of course, will be $200,000 richer.

Moving Average

Some investors use the moving average to time the market. The strategy is to buy a stock when it is selling above its moving average and sell when it falls below. A popular moving average is the 200-day version. A dotted line is drawn, taking the average price of the stock over the previous 200 days. The actual price of the stock is plotted on the same graph. Studies show that this method of timing the market does not work on a consistent basis.

PEG Ratio

The PEG ratio is supposed to be helpful in determining if a stock is too expensive. It is calculated by dividing the price-earnings ratio by the expected earnings growth rate. Let's say the P/E ratio of American International Group is 34.39, which is calculated by dividing the price ($98) by the expected EPS in 2001 of $2.85. Meanwhile, the earnings per share in the 1989–1999 period expanded from $0.67 to $2.18, a compound annual growth rate of 12.52 percent. When you divide 34.39 by 12.52, the PEG ratio is 2.75. According to Michael Sivy, a writer for *Money* magazine, "Stocks with a PEG ratio of 1.5 or less are often the best buys."

By that rule, you would avoid American International Group. Curiously, Mr. Sivy includes AIG on his list of "100 Stocks for Long-Term Investors," published in January 2001. By his calculation, AIG had a PEG ratio at that time of 2.5.

Once again, I am a doubting Thomas. Who is to say what a company's future growth rate will be? You can easily determine what it has been in the past. And that may give you some indication of the future, but it is far from reliable. The P/E ratio is also a slippery number, since you are expected to base it on the EPS for the year ahead. I prefer to base it on the most recent twelve months, since that is a figure that does not depend on a crystal ball.

Preferred Stock

The name sounds impressive. In actual practice, owning preferred stocks is about as exciting as watching your cat take a bath. A preferred stock is much like a bond. It pays the same dividend year in and year out. The yield is usually higher than a common stock. If the company issuing the preferred stock does well, you do not benefit. If it does poorly, however, you may suffer, since the dividend could be cut or eliminated.

Price-Earnings Ratio (P/E)

This is a term that is extremely important. Don't make the mistake of overlooking it. Whole books have been written on the importance of the P/E ratio, which is sometimes referred to as "the P/E" or "the multiple."

The P/E ratio tells you whether a stock is cheap or expensive. It is calculated by dividing the price of the stock by the company's earnings per share over the most recent twelve months. For instance, if you refer to the *Stock Guide*, you will see that Leggett and Platt had earnings of $2.23. At the time, the stock was selling for $52. Divide that figure by $2.23, and you get a P/E of 23.32.

A high P/E ratio tends to indicate a stock with good prospects for the future. However, this evaluation tends to be overdone. In an article written by Mark Hulbert for the *New York Times* on January 25, 2004, Mr. Hulbert said, "Although the stock market is not as expensive as it was in 2000, it has many 'pockets of craziness,' in the view of Josef Lakonishok, a finance professor at the University of Illinois at Urbana-Champaign.

Professor Lakonishok bases his assessment on a historical study that found that companies trading at high price-to-earnings ratios almost never grow as quickly as they need to justify their valuations."

The study was conducted by the above professor and two other academics.

Mr. Hulbert went on to say, "The professors concluded that very high P/E ratios were hardly ever justified."

Profit Margins

Profit margins fall into two categories: Net Profit Margin and Operating Profit Margin.

Net Profit Margin is simply net income divided by sales. It measures profitability after all expenses and taxes have been paid—and after all accounting adjustments have been made.

Operating Profit Margin is operating income divided by sales. It measures profitability after only those expenses related to current operations have been paid.

Reverse Stock Split

Stock splits are normally a happy occasion. If you have 100 shares of a stock selling for $80 a share, the company may announce a two-for-one stock split. In due course, you will have 200 shares, each worth $40. You are no richer, but you may be happier.

A reverse stock split, however, is not good news. If you have 200 shares of a stock selling for $1.25, the company may be contemplating upgrading your shares by announcing a reverse stock split. They will issue new shares worth, say, ten times as much. Now you have only twenty shares, each one worth $12.50. Again, you are no richer. But you may be unhappy. You should be. Studies show that a reverse stock split is a bad omen.

In July 1997, the *Journal of Business* measured all reverse stock splits from 1926 to 1991. The authors were two professors of accounting, Hemang A. Desai of Southern Methodist University and Prem C. Jain of Georgetown. According to an article in the *New York Times* by Mark Hulbert (dated November 3, 2002), "They found that, over the year after the announcement, the average stock undergoing a reverse stock split performed 8.5 percent worse than the stock market."

Mr. Hulbert explained why some companies resort to this device. "David L. Ikenberry, a finance professor at the University of Illinois at Urbana-Champaign, and Sundaresh Ramnath, an accounting professor at Georgetown, have developed a theory that does explain it. They believe that when management lacks confidence in its company's stock, it is more likely to use a reverse split. By contrast, they say, if management believes that the low price is just temporary, it will be more likely to leave the stock alone."

Standard & Poor's *Stock Reports*

S&P is a major provider of financial information, primarily to institutions, such as stockbrokers, mutual funds, and banks. However, individuals can tap into this information by requesting a "tear sheet" on almost any stock. You will note that I have quoted liberally from Standard & Poor's in the analysis of my 100 stocks. S&P stock tear sheets are revised quite frequently, depending on earnings changes and important developments.

Stock Split

Corporations know that investors like to invest in lower-priced stocks. Thus, when the price of the stock gets to a certain level, which varies with the company, they will split the stock. For instance, if the stock is $75, they might split it three-for-one. Your original 100 shares now become 300 shares. Unfortunately, your 300 shares are worth exactly the same as your original 100 shares. What it amounts to is this: Splits please small investors, but they don't make them any richer. One company, Berkshire Hathaway, has never been split. It is now worth a huge amount per share: over $100,000. It also pays no dividend. The company is run by the legendary Warren Buffett, and has made a lot of people very wealthy without a stock split or dividend.

Technician

There are two basic ways to analyze stocks. One is *fundamental*; the other is *technical*.

Fundamental analysts examine a stock's management, sales and earnings potential, research capabilities, new products, competitive strength, balance sheet strength, dividend growth, political developments, and industry conditions.

Technicians, by contrast, rarely consider any of these fundamental factors. They rely on charts and graphs and a host of other arcane statistical factors, such as point-and-figure charts, breadth indicators, head-and-shoulders formations, relative strength ratings, and the 200-day-moving average. This technical jargon is often difficult for the average investor to fathom. The fundamental approach predominates among professional portfolio managers, although some institutions may also employ a technician.

The question is, do technicians have the key to stock picking or predicting the trend of the market? Frankly, I am a skeptic, as are most academic analysts. Among the nonbelievers is Kenneth L. Fisher, the long-time columnist for *Forbes* magazine whom I mentioned earlier. His columns are among my favorites. Here is what Mr. Fisher says about technicians: "One of the questions I hear most often is, 'Can charts really predict stock prices?' Naturally, there is only one answer: a flat 'No.'"

Mr. Fisher goes on to say, "There is virtually nothing in theory or empiricism to indicate anyone can predict stock prices based solely on prior stock price action. Nevertheless, a big world of chartists continues to exist, amplified by recent Internet day trading. Yet the world of investors with long-lasting success is devoid of them."

Such eminently successful portfolio managers as Peter Lynch and Warren Buffett, for instance, don't resort to charts and other technical mumbo jumbo.

Value Line Investment Survey

Value Line provides one-page reports on about 1,700 stocks. It is normally available in brokerage houses and libraries. You will note that I have quoted liberally from *Value Line* in the analysis of my 100 stocks. Although *Value Line* is too expensive for most individual investors, the company does have a much less expensive version that covers 600 major corporations. Stocks are revised by *Value Line* every three months.

Yield

If your company pays a dividend, you can relate this dividend to the price of the stock in order to calculate the yield. A $50 stock that pays a $2 annual dividend (which amounts to fifty cents per quarter) will have a yield of 4 percent. You arrive at this figure by dividing $2 by $50. Actually, you don't have to make this calculation, since the yield is given to you in the stock tables of the *Wall Street Journal*. Here are some typical yields: Coca-Cola, 1.5 percent; ExxonMobil, 2.0 percent; General Electric, 1.3 percent; Illinois Tool Works, 1.2 percent; Kimberly-Clark, 1.8 percent; and 3M Company, 2.0 percent. Although the yield is of some importance, you should not judge a stock by its yield without looking at many other factors.

Yield Curve

The yield curve is a graphic representation of yields on U.S. Treasury securities. Most of the time, the yield is less on short-term debt and higher on bonds that mature ten or fifteen years from now. If this difference is represented by a graph, you will see a curve going to the right of the graph, gradually rising as it proceeds toward the future.

Ordinarily, short-term bonds carry lower yields to reflect the fact that an investor's money is under lower risk. The longer you tie up money, the theory goes, the more you should be rewarded for the extra risk you are taking. After all, who knows what's going to happen over the next two or three decades? In that period, there may be such developments as high inflation, a recession, or devastation from war.

If this curve does not act in this way, it is referred to as an "Inverted Yield Curve." Such a curve means that short-term rates are higher than long-term rates. Analysts tend to think an inverted yield curve is a sign of a pending recession. In May 2005, the curve was approaching an inverted status. The difference between short-term rates (overnight federal funds rates) and long-term rates on ten-year Treasury notes was only 112 basis points (or just over 1 percent). By contrast, in June 2004, the spread was more normal, at 387 basis points, or close to 4 percent.

Although analysts are cautious when they see a flat or inverted yield curve, at least one observer did not agree. "Be careful how you interpret a very narrow yield curve in the context of structural forces that may have flattened it," said former Fed Governor Laurence Meyer in early June 2005. "It doesn't mean the same thing that it used to mean."

How to Choose a Broker

According to my wife and family, I'm a compulsive book buyer. Even though I already own several hundred books, (including three encyclopedia sets) on such topics as baseball, tennis, philosophy, economics, politics, biography, geography, the Supreme Court, medicine, Greek, Roman, and American history, and U.S. presidents, I still buy more. It all started in high school when I bought a used edition of The Harvard Classics for $25. They are still unread.

However, I rarely buy a book without considerable study and investigation (unless it's at a library sale or garage sale). Usually, I cruise around Barnes & Noble and pick up books that appear interesting and then settle down in one of their incredibly comfortable over-stuffed chairs to read a few pages here and there. And I also read the biography inside the back cover to see if the author has good credentials. If I go through a half dozen books while I am making these assessments, I rarely buy more than one book, and sometimes none.

Of course, I am not the only bookworm in Barnes & Noble who is hunkered down with a book or two under consideration. I rarely notice what they are reading, but one day I was caught by surprise when I noticed an auburn-haired lady in her mid-thirties who was studiously absorbed in a copy of *The 100 Best Stocks You Can Buy*. She seemed intent on giving the book a thorough going-over. I was hesitant to interrupt her perusal, for fear she might not buy the book. And so I went back to studying the books piled in front of me.

Finally, I could not restrain myself any longer. I said, "I see you are reading a book on investing. Would you like me to introduce you to the author?"

She looked up in amazement. "You mean the author lives in Vermont? And you know him personally?"

"Well, not exactly," I said. "I happen to be John Slatter. But don't let me disturb you from examining my book. I need all the customers I can get so that the publisher will keep sending me royalty checks. So far, the book has been selling well for the past ten years, and I am currently working on the next edition."

"I can't believe you are the author. Do you have a business card? I'm a tough person to convince."

When she had examined my card, she said, "I like your introductory chapters, but there is one that seems to be missing. I haven't come across one on how to pick a broker. I am new to the investment game, and I haven't the faintest idea how to find someone that I could have confidence in."

"After ten years of writing my book, I seem to have neglected to provide that information. Is now a good time to give you a few ideas on that subject?" I asked her.

"Are you trying to tell me that a busy author like you is willing to spend his time to indoctrinate a total novice and do it free of charge?"

"Before I begin, it might be helpful if I knew your name, since you already know mine."

"Oh, I'm sorry; my name is Valletta Hamamett. I'm a nurse, and this is my day off."

"Let me tell you how I picked a company to put a new roof on my house," I told her. "That will give you a hint on how my mind works. Whenever I need someone to fix a problem in our house, I call a pal down the street who is also a client of mine. I'll call him Fred. In this instance, Fred called a roofer who does work for him. Fred happens to own a lot of rental real estate, so he has a stable of plumbers, electricians, carpenters and the like. When I call these people and tell them Fred recommended them, they usually come to my rescue. On this occasion, the man never called. Of course, it was early August, and he probably was already swamped with work, so he never got around to me.

Next, I checked with some of my neighbors, mostly those I have met when I jog along Beech Street getting some exercise. Mostly, they are out walking their dogs, and they notice me and strike up a conversation. One lady said she had had her roof replaced a couple years earlier and was satisfied with the results. I called the roofing contractor she recommended and got a quote for $12,800. That seemed too high, so I next talked to my next-door neighbor who was in the midst of having his roof replaced. I accosted the person in charge and told him my roof was in dire straits, and that I would like to get an idea of what he could do to alleviate my predicament. He said he would come over to my house later that afternoon. Over the next three weeks, he failed to make an appearance. I was beginning to get desperate.

"I checked with my friend Fred again, and he gave me another name. I called him and left my name on his answering device, but got no response. A week or so later I called him again and finally got to talk to him. He said he was too busy but gave me the name of his cousin, and he promised he would make an appraisal and give me a quote. I am still waiting.

"I was about ready to burn down my house and collect on the insurance when

I had a lucky break. One of my neighbors had recently sold their house and moved to New Mexico. One Saturday morning, I decided I had better introduce myself and welcome the new family into the community. During the conversation, I happened to mention that I was about to burn down my house, and he gasped in disbelief—apparently he was unaware that I was joking. When I told him my problem, he immediately said, 'Heavens, I am sure I can solve your problem. My good friend and former partner, Clint Sandhaven, is an experienced, capable roofer. I'll have him give you a call.'"

At that point, Valletta interrupted. She said, "That's quite a tale of frustration, Mr. Slatter. I hope getting a broker is not that difficult."

"I haven't quite finished my story, Valletta. Let me continue. A few days later, Clint called and made an appointment with my wife and me. We were both convinced beyond the shadow of a doubt that Clint Sandhaven was our man. His price was a couple thousand lower than the other guy, and his whole manner impressed us to the extent that we now have a new roof—and my insurance company is unaware of my plans to resort to the torch on our dandy five-bedroom abode."

"I'm beginning to get the idea that I should not pick a broker by leafing through the yellow pages," said Valletta Hamamett.

"Exactly. And another thing. Don't deal with a rookie who calls you on the telephone. Such brokers have a purchased list of prospects in front of them and are 'cold calling' one after another, looking for clients. You don't need someone who is just getting started in the business. I assume you have friends or associates who are investors. Talk with them and find out if they have enjoyed good results with brokers who are not trying to sell you a mutual fund or some product their company has dreamed up that has a fat sales commission tied into it. What you want is a broker who deals in stocks and not one who tries to sell you something else or who tries to convince you that you should have your portfolio managed on a fee basis, which is often 2 percent or so."

"You are right, Mr. Slatter. I do know a number of people who are investing in the stock market. I'm an RN, so I know nurses and doctors who might give me some ideas. Anything else?"

"Yes, there is one more decision you have to make, Valletta. There are two types of brokers. The better known are full-service brokers, such as Edward Jones, Smith Barney, UBS Financial, A. G. Edwards, and Wachovia Securities. Most people start with a full-service broker since they have a staff of brokers who are well trained and are willing to answer your questions and offer suggestions on how to build a portfolio.

"The advantages of dealing with a full-service broker are several. For one thing, the brokerage firm usually has a staff of research analysts who can provide reports on stocks you may have an interest in. Secondly, their account executives may be quite knowledgeable and experienced. On the negative side, the cost of doing business with them is quite high, often $200 or $300 per trade, with a minimum of at least $50.

"The other type of broker is quite different. They are called discount brokers and include Scottrade, Charles Schwab, E*Trade, Ameritrade, and Fidelity. And there are scores of others.

"The chief advantage of a discount broker is the low cost of buying or selling a stock, often $25 or less. Scotttrade is at the low end, only $7, regardless of the number of shares involved in the trade. The disadvantages are primarily an absence of a research department. In addition, you won't get much sophisticated help from your account executive. They will execute your trade and answer questions concerning how

to make trades on the Internet, which is typically less costly than on the phone or in person.

"If you are in doubt as to which route to take, there's no reason why you can't have a full-service broker as well as a discount broker. In my own case, I have an account with Wachovia Securities and two discount brokers: Schwab and Fidelity."

"I am beginning to get an understanding of what's out there, Mr. Slatter. But before you head downstairs to pay for your books, can you outline again what I should look for when I select a full-service broker? I forgot to take notes."

"Glad to. Here are the types of broker to avoid:

- Those who sell mostly mutual funds, rather than stocks.
- Those who are new in the business. Make sure the broker you select has at least five years of experience.
- Those who call you once or twice a month with the hot stock of the week. You are better off making your own selections.
- Those who tell you that you need a professional advisor on a fee basis. The annual fee for such advisory firms is often 2 percent per year, and your portfolio is rarely managed with you in mind. It is typically invested in the same stocks that everyone else is getting. Even worse, such portfolios are not likely to outperform the market—at least not on a consistent basis—particularly when you take the 2 percent fee into account."

"On a more positive note, what you want is a broker who will alert you to poor diversification in your list of holdings. There are ten sectors in the economy—at least according to Standard & Poor's—and you should invest in a minimum of six or seven sectors, or better still, all ten. The sectors include:

1. Industrials, such as United Technologies, Caterpillar, and General Electric.

2. Utilities, such as Piedmont Natural Gas, FPL Group, and MDU Resources.

3. Telephone, such as Alltel, Verizon, and AT&T.

4. Financials, such as Kimco Realty, T. Rowe Price, and Washington REIT.

5. Consumer Staples, such as PepsiCo, McCormick, and Procter & Gamble.

6. Consumer Discretionary, such as Black & Decker, Coach, and Walt Disney.

7. Materials, such Bemis, Praxair, and Ecolab.

8. Drugs and Health, such as Eli Lilly, Pfizer, and Medtronic.

9. Information Technology, such as Intel, IBM, and Microsoft.

10. Energy, such as ExxonMobil, Chevron, and Devon Energy."

After listening to my lengthy and erudite lecture on investing and sector diversification, Valletta Hamamett said, "I can't thank you enough, Mr. Slatter, for such a professional and interesting lesson in common stock investing. If I follow your advice, I should be able to be one of the few nurses in Vermont who can retire with a million-dollar portfolio. Now, I am wondering whether I really need to buy a copy of your book. For the time being at least, I think I'll return it to the shelf."

A Novel Approach to Asset Allocation

I'm not sure whether my neighborhood is characteristic of Vermont as a whole, but Beech Street in Essex Junction seems to teem with dog-walkers. One dog-walker, in particular, is a real puzzle. The lady who leads this little canine is an attractive widow who looks younger than her fifty-eight years.

But Brutus Kutch III, her little overwrought monster, is about as big as an Alley Cat *Felis domestica*. I am convinced this diminutive wretch is bent on having me for lunch. As soon as he sees me—even from a block away—he starts to yap with ferocity and petulance. Apparently, he is convinced that I am guilty of some heinous crime. Fortunately, the other dogs in the area are unaware of my crimes against the family Canidae, since rarely do any of them bare their fangs or utter a word of discontent when I encounter them on my daily walk through the streets of Essex Junction.

I have not tried petting Brutus (I value my hands), but I have offered him some delicious morsels of fancy dog food. But to no avail—I am still his mortal enemy. It's too bad, because I enjoy chatting with Alice Hardleigh, the lady at the other end of the leash who lives nearby on Taffeta Trail. She tells me that Brutus is the only Mongolian toy mastiff in Chittenden County. That's certainly good news!

One day, when Brutus had finally calmed down after Ms. Hardleigh held the little cuss in her arms, she said, "Mr. Slatter, I have been reading your book, but I'm not sure how I should set up my portfolio. I wonder whether you could have lunch with me at the Lincoln Inn sometime and get me headed in the right direction."

"I assume you'll bring Brutus with you," I said.

"Only if you insist. He's never liked the Lincoln Inn."

Once the waiter had taken our orders for Diet Cokes, Alice opened the conversation about her situation. (She doesn't like me to call her Ms. Hardleigh, but persists in addressing me as Mr. Slatter. It must be my gray hair. Hers is blonde, with no trace of old age.)

"I know you have a chapter in your book on asset allocation, but somehow I thought I would feel more comfortable getting your thoughts on my particular situation. Does that make sense?"

"Everyone is different, Alice. I assume that your late husband left you with adequate finances. Can you give me an idea of what your holdings are?"

"Yes, you're right, Mr. Slatter, I'm not exactly a pauper. Besides a pension, Fillmore left me an insurance policy worth $300,000. Right now, I don't have to touch the principal, since I manage to keep the bills paid from my piano lessons. I have a waiting list, so I guess it has paid to keep my fingers limber over the years. Fillmore and I used to entertain our friends with my playing and his singing."

"I get the feeling that your $300,000 is still in cash," I said.

"In a money market, which is yielding only 4 percent. I know I should put this money to work, but I think I need a little nudge."

"Unfortunately, there is no secret formula for asset allocation," I said. "A few people invest entirely in stocks or mutual funds, with no bonds and very little cash. If you start investing young enough, let's say in your twenties or thirties, stocks are the best way to go. Over the years, stocks (including dividends) have returned about 11 percent a year, compounded. By contrast, bonds, CDs, and other fixed-income vehicles have rarely done much better than 6 percent. That's quite a difference. Let's say you were thirty-five years of age and had $300,000 to invest, and you put it all in stocks. By age sixty-five, your nest egg would be worth more than $8.8 million. On the other hand, if you invested the same $300,000 at 6 percent, you would have only $2.5 million when you reached retirement age."

"Are you suggesting that I invest all my money in common stocks, Mr. Slatter? That sounds a little scary to me. I think Fillmore would turn over in his grave."

"I'm not surprised. Most people know that stocks involve risk—sometimes a lot of risk—and they simply can't stand the worry that it may involve. Of course, diversification can help some. If you own twenty or thirty stocks, you are spreading the risk of owning only a half dozen. However, the risk of stock ownership is still there.

"There are a number of formulas that have been devised. A simple rule of thumb is to invest 70 percent in stocks and the rest in fixed income, such as bonds. This percentage might be suitable for an average investor. But for someone who tends to be conservative, a more suitable breakdown might be 60 percent stocks, with the rest in bonds and money-market funds. Finally, for those who are ultraconservative, the best formula would be to balance stocks and fixed income fifty-fifty."

"I'm not sure which camp I might fall into. Do you have any other magic formulas?" asked Alice, as she munched on her Caesar salad.

"Another one that I devised is based on age. My thinking is that younger people should be more aggressive than older people. At fifty-eight, you're kind of in the middle."

"How does it work?"

"It's quite simple and revolves around the investor who is sixty-five years old. At that age, I suggest having 65 percent in stocks and the rest in bonds and other fixed-income vehicles. But if you are older than sixty-five, you should edge toward the fixed-income sector. My formula says to deduct 1 percent each year from the common stock sector, so that when you reach seventy, you will have 60 percent invested in stocks. Going a step further, when you reach eighty, you'll be fifty-fifty."

"I can't see how that works for me. I'm only fifty-eight." said Alice, as she broke her club sandwich into small portions.

"I was just getting to that. For those younger than sixty-five, the strategy is to add to the percentage invested in common stocks. For each year younger, add 1 percent. That means that for you we would add 7 percent, bringing the total to 72 percent. How does that sound?"

"I can see the logic of your formula, but somehow I don't think I would sleep at night knowing I had more than $200,000 in stocks. How could I afford food for Brutus if the stock market went into a tailspin? I think we had better go to plan C. Do you have any more strategies?"

"Just one more. If you don't like this one, I'm afraid there is no plan D."

"I see you have finished off your prime rib," she said. "Why don't we get another cup of coffee before you start?"

When the coffee arrived, I began my explanation of plan C. "Incidentally, this strategy is not in any of my other books. So, pay close attention."

"I guess I had better takes notes. Okay, my pen is ready to record your words of wisdom. If I like this one, I will give specific orders to Brutus Kutch III to stop barking at you."

"Thanks. Now I won't have to carry a gun when I walk by 36 Taffeta Trail. I think you'll like this one—it's got a little bit of everything. Let's take your $300,000. We divide it into three equal segments, with $100,000 in each. The first $100,000 is invested in twenty blue-chip stocks, with $5,000 in each. These are all huge companies, most of them in the Dow Jones Industrial Average—stocks like General Electric, United Technologies, Coca-Cola, Citigroup, ExxonMobil, Home Depot, IBM, Johnson & Johnson, Merck, 3M Company, Procter & Gamble, Wal-Mart, Anheuser-Busch, Colgate-Palmolive, Costco, FedEx, United Parcel, Lowe's, and Walgreen. How does that sound so far?"

"Great. I think we're onto something. I will alert Brutus that you are not all bad."

"On to the second part. There are those who think that index funds are the best way to invest. They contend that actively managed mutual funds can't compete against them because of the high cost of management, usually about 1.5 percent a year. I agree. A good index fund is the Standard & Poor's 500. You can buy it on the American Stock Exchange. It trades there as an exchange-traded fund with a ticker symbol of IVV. In effect, you are buying all 500 stocks, so diversification is outstanding. One big advantage of an index fund is the low cost. Those managed by Vanguard have an expense ratio of less than 0.25 percent, compared with 1.5 percent for a typical managed mutual fund. I suggest putting $33,000 in IVV.

"The next $33,000 should go into another index fund. This one is called DIA-MONDS, or DIA. It invests in the thirty stocks that make up the Dow Jones Industrial Average.

"The third $33,000 goes into a very broad group of stocks that are not in the S&P 500. In other words, they are stocks that are smaller. Many smaller companies may not be familiar, but they are nonetheless worth owning for their future growth. If past history is any indication of the future,

small stocks are somewhat more volatile (or more risky), but they tend to perform better than industry giants over the long haul. This index fund is called the Vanguard Extended Market Index, and has a symbol of VXF.

"According to my friend Don Dempsey, an investment advisor in Burlington, Vermont, the Extended Market Index is designed to track the performance of the Wilshire 4500 Completion Index, a broadly diversified index of small and medium-size U.S. companies. The Wilshire 4500 Index contains all of the U.S. common stocks regularly traded on the New York and American Exchanges and the Nasdaq over-the-counter market, except those stocks included in the S&P 500.

"By investing in these three market indexes, Alice, you should do well—assuming the stock market does well."

"I'm beginning to like your idea," said Alice Hardleigh. "That still leaves $100,000. So far, we have lots of stocks."

"Right. The rest is left in a money-market fund or in U.S. treasury bonds that mature in less than five years. Bonds that mature within a few years, as opposed to those that mature twenty or thirty years from now, are much less volatile, and are far better to hold when interest rates start back up.

"Thus, if stocks have a temporary sinking spell, you will still have an anchor to the windward to preserve a good part of your holdings. To be sure, this is a conservative strategy, but I think it fits the bill for you and Brutus. But before we go ahead with it, you will want to consult with him. After all, he's the one that wants to have me for lunch."

"I still can't understand why he has such a loathing for you, Mr. Slatter. He's normally such a mild-mannered pooch—like all the other Mongolian toy mastiffs. They're a wonderful breed."

The next day I walked by her house on Taffeta Trail and heard the familiar yapping of Brutus Kutch III. It was coming from inside the house, so I knew I was safe from attack.

For Busy Investors, a Strategy that Rarely Fails

One way to simplify the investment enigma is to concentrate your investing in the thirty stocks that make up the Dow Jones Industrial Average. The venerable Dow—which is what investors mean by "the market," dates back more than 100 years. It currently includes such giant blue chips as Alcoa, Boeing, Caterpillar, DuPont, ExxonMobil, General Electric, Hewlett Packard, IBM, Johnson & Johnson, 3M Company, Procter & Gamble, and Wal-Mart Stores.

If you are a busy investor, the complexities you face in managing your holdings may seen daunting and time-consuming. You have your choice of more than 10,000 mutual funds, thousands of hedge funds, investment advisors, and individual stocks (there are some 3,000 on the New York Stock Exchange alone), plus tens of thousands of foreign stocks.

None of these choices are free of short-comings:

Mutual funds, for instance, charge too much (normally 1.5 percent per year) and they churn their holdings at a fierce pace—100 percent annual turnover is typical. At the end of each year, all the capital gains are credited to your account for the IRS to take its bite. What's even worse, there are precious few mutual funds that do as well as the Dow or the S&P 500. Quite often, the ones that were spectacular performers one year are among the biggest losers the next year.

The Truth about Hedge Funds

Hedge funds charge even more than mutual funds—and they are not regulated.

Every year, about a thousand hedge funds go out of business. One of my favorite columnists is Jonathan Clements who writes a weekly column for the *Wall Street Journal*—it appears nearly every Wednesday. On September 20, 2006, Mr. Clements said: "Consider a study by Roger Ibbotson, founder of Ibbotson Associates—now a unit of Chicago researchers Morningstar, Inc.—and Peng Chen, the firm's president.

"The authors note that, based on the TASS database, hedge funds appear to have clocked an eye-popping 16.5 percent a year between year-end 1994 and April 2006, easily outpacing the 11.6 percent average for the Standard & Poor's 500-stock index. Yet this 16.5 percent average is mighty misleading, for two reasons.

"First, when hedge funds are added to performance databases, they sometimes include earlier results. This 'backfill bias' skews the average upward, because only funds with stellar returns typically report their prior performance. Second, when poorly performing hedge funds go out of business, their dismal results are often ignored, leading to so-called survivorship bias.

"What happens if you eliminate survivorship bias and backfill bias? Messrs. Ibbotson and Chen calculate that hedge funds returned just 9 percent a year, less than the S&P 500's 11.6%."

In another realm, investment advisors come and go, and they charge fees for managing your account—whether successful or not. Finally, some people subscribe to advisory letters. According to Mark Hulbert, who writes frequently for the *New York Times* and also publishes a service that tracks market letters, only a tiny fraction of them do as well as the general market.

Save Time and Minimize Taxes

Enough of the negatives. Since you have your hands full earning a living, it stands to reason you might profit from a simple method of investing to save time and aggravation. You might also prefer one that has no fees that will detract from performance. Most important, you look kindly on a strategy that minimizes taxes. Mutual funds, hedge funds, and advisors make multiple switches, and you pay for their activity in payments to your uncle in Washington, DC. If you invest in the thirty Dow stocks, there is no reason to churn your own account. If you don't sell anything, you have no capital gains taxes to pay.

If you decide to switch some of your assets to the Dow thirty strategy, you will have some choices to make. If you get rid of all your mutual funds, hedge funds, and advisors, you will be saddled with buying the thirty Dow stocks yourself. Since you are a busy person, doesn't it make sense to keep track of thirty blue chip stocks instead of the tens of thousands of stocks, mutual funds and hedge funds, that dot the landscape? Because the Dow stocks are huge and important companies, they are frequently in the news. Articles on these companies appear almost daily in such publications as the *Wall Street Journal, Barron's, Forbes* and *BusinessWeek*.

One last comment. There is no reliable evidence that professional investors can beat or even equal the performance of the market—at least not on a consistent basis. Why should you pay for their services and keep the IRS happy, when owning the Dow thirty will probably perform better than any of the alternatives?

In brief, here are some reasons to adopt this strategy:

If you have a large portfolio and buy stocks in large chunks, you are not likely to disturb the market when you buy a Dow thirty stock. By contrast, if you invest in a Nasdaq stock or some other outfit with fewer shares outstanding, your purchase of 25,000 or 100,000 shares could cost you an extra two or three points when you buy or sell.

If you own most of the thirty Dow stocks, you are not likely to be left at post when the market makes a major move. In effect, you are the market. And remember, precious few investors of any stripe are successful in outperforming the S&P 500 or the Dow thirty.

When you concentrate on the Dow thirty, your research is simplified. You don't have to examine the performance of 10,000 mutual funds or 5,000 hedge funds, or 3,000 stocks listed on the Big Board. Your thirty candidates are there in plain sight, with instant information readily available in the *Wall Street Journal* and *New York Times*, as well as other leading journals. Of course, you can also read the company's annual report or check in at its Web site.

There are no fees to pay to advisors, hedge fund managers, or investment advisors.

There are no capital gains taxes to pay unless you sell one or two of your stocks. Incidentally, the best ones to sell are the ones that are up the least or the ones that have been big disappointments. Once again, the IRS is kept out of your wallet.

Investors often fret at how to determine when to sell. With the Dow thirty, the decision is made by Dow Jones & Company, which publishes the *Wall Street Journal* and *Barron's*. Every so often, the staff decides to do a little surgery on the index by deleting two or three components and replacing them with stocks it likes better. On average, about one stock per year is shunted aside and replaced with a new candidate. That's when you sell the discarded stock and invest the proceeds in the new kid on the block. Normally, the stock dumped is deleted because it was a dog. That means you may not have to pay Uncle Sam a nickle when the *Wall Street Journal* wields the ax.

Fees paid to stockbrokers can be kept at a minimum by dealing with a discount broker, such as Charles Schwab, Fidelity, or Scottrade.

If you want to beat the market, you can do it by buying all thrity stocks, but giving greater weight to those you like best. Here is a simple strategy: Invest 4 percent in each of the ten stocks you like best. Invest 3 percent in the next ten and only 2 percent in the ten with the least appeal.

Save 10 percent for a money-market fund or a short-term bond to give you a bit of protection if the Dow heads south. Or, better still, why not consider am ETF that invests in foreign stocks. A good way to do this is through PowerShares International Dividend Achievers.

That way, you are investing in sixty stocks that have each raised its dividend for five consecutive years. PID, which has outperformed the Dow in recent years, is traded on the American Stock Exchange. It includes stocks from such countries as China, Britain, Australia, Spain, Canada, Norway, and Sweden. Many are bank stocks.

Beware of Small Stocks— They May Be Overpriced

In the past few years, this strategy of investing in large companies has not done as well as those which favor small-capitalization stocks. But the tide could turn, as it has in the past. Over time, small stocks do not beat the market. They tend to do about as well as large-cap stocks. At present, moreover, small stocks appear to be overpriced,

at least when you examine the price/earnings ratio. In the spring of 2007, the fifty largest companies in the S&P average had a P/E of about 19, compared with 60.7 in March of 2000. By contrast, the smaller companies in the Index had a price/earnings ratio of 30.7, versus 20.3 seven years ago. Now may be an ideal time to switch to the Dow thirty.

If concentrating on the Dow Jones Industrial Average makes sense, you can find the list frequently in the *Wall Street Journal* (notably on Monday in the Money & Investing section) or in *Barron's*. As of March 2007, these were the thirty stocks in the Index, broken down according to sectors. Although not perfect, this makes an excellent portfolio, in terms of quality and diversification:

Industrials: 3M Company (MMM), Boeing (BA), Caterpillar (CAT), General Electric (GE), Honeywell (HON), United Technologies (UTX)

Materials: Alcoa (AA), DuPont (DD)

Consumer Staples: Altria (MO), Coca-Cola (KO), Procter & Gamble (PG), Wal-Mart (WMT)

Dow Financials: American Express (AXP), American International Group (AIG), Citigroup (C), JP Morgan (JPM)

Telecommunication Services: AT&T (T), Verizon (VZ)

Energy: Exxon (XOM)

Consumer Discretionary: General Motors (GM), McDonald's (MCD), Walt Disney (DIS)

Information Technology: Hewlett-Packard (HPQ), Intel (INTC), IBM (IBM), Microsoft (MSFT)

Health Care: Johnson & Johnson (JNJ), Merck (MRK), Pfizer (PFE)

When to Sell

Deciding when to sell is often a wrenching experience. Not long ago, I was fretting over whether to sell Eli Lilly. For one thing, it was not acting well, often sagging when the rest of the market was moving ahead. For another, I was concerned that Lilly was hurting my overall performance, since it was my largest holding. Those are two good reasons to sell a stock—or at least part of it. I ended up selling 300 shares.

Over the years, I have read a number of articles on when to sell, such as one written by Manuel Schiffres for *Kiplinger's Personal Finance* magazine in February 1994. He said, "There are some general rules for when to sell a stock—such as when it reaches preposterous valuation levels or when the reason you bought it no longer applies. For example, if you bought a stock because you had high hopes for a new product, you should sell if the product is a lemon. Or, if you owned a stock for its high dividends—as many IBM investors did—and the company slashes the payout, that is also a strong signal to sell.

"Consider selling if your goals change, you desire a more defensive investment posture or you want to establish a gain or loss for tax reasons. Also consider selling if a more attractive opportunity comes along. Always ask yourself, 'What's my potential for this stock over the next twelve months?'" says Michael DiCarlo, who runs the John Hancock Special Equities fund. "If it's 15 percent, and you have something you think can make 50 percent, that's an easy swap to make."

Advice from Better Investing

To be sure, there are any number of reasons to sell one of your holdings. Here are seven that are enumerated by the National Association of Investors Corporation (NAIC), which gives assistance and advice to the nation's investment clubs. NAIC also publishes an outstanding monthly magazine, *Better Investing*—I am a faithful subscriber. Here are the sell signals featured by NAIC:

- Sell because an issue of equal or better quality offers the potential for higher returns.
- Sell because of an adverse management change.
- Sell because of declining profit margins or a deteriorating financial structure.
- Sell because direct or indirect competition is affecting the prosperity of the company.
- Sell because a company has great dependence on a single product whose cycle is running out.
- Sell to increase quality or decrease quality as circumstances dictate.
- Sell companies that have become cyclical and have low-growth-rate issues because prosperity is about to succumb to recession.

Helpful Criteria to Use when Judging a Stock

If those reasons for selling don't cover all the bases, perhaps you should consider some of my own ideas on the subject. In an earlier chapter, I discussed what to look for when you are buying a stock. If you examine that list of factors—a version of which is given below—and find that the stock in question does not measure up, that could be a signal to sell:

- A rising trend in earnings, dividends, and book value per share. This information can be obtained from such publications as *Value Line Investment Survey* or Standard & Poor's tear sheets. You'll find them at most brokerage offices and some libraries.
- A balance sheet with less debt—compared with equity—than other companies in its particular industry. In most instances, I look for 75 percent or more in shareholders' equity and the rest in long-term debt.
- An S&P quality rating of B+ (which is average) or better. If you refer to *Value Line*, their average financial strength rating is B++.
- A P/E ratio no higher than average for that industry.
- A dividend yield—such as 2 percent or 3 percent—that suits your particular needs. If a $30 stock has an annual dividend of seventy-five cents, that's a yield of 2.5 percent (seventy-five cents divided by $30).
- A stock that insiders—such as officers and board members—are not selling in significant quantities.
- A below-average dividend payout ratio. For instance, if a company earns $4 a share and pays out $3 in dividends, it doesn't have much left to invest in new facilities, acquisitions, research, or marketing. A payout ratio of 25 percent would be far better.
- A history of earnings and dividends not pockmarked by erratic ups and downs.
- Companies whose return on equity is fifteen or better.
- A ratio of price to cash flow that is

not too high when compared to other stocks in the same industry. Here again, you can obtain this information from *Value Line* or Standard & Poor's.

To be sure, you are not likely to find a company that fits all of those criteria precisely. But if the stock you are worried about misses the mark on the majority of those benchmarks, perhaps the time has come to make a switch. What's more, if you already have a stock in mind that does fit the above criteria, you have a good reason to sell the one that doesn't.

Is the Stock Priced Too High?

One good reason to sell a stock is price. Even though the company has most of the other features, if it has climbed to a level that doesn't make sense, it may be prudent to unload it. One of the best gauges to determine price level is the price/earnings ratio. If you bought the stock when it had a P/E of 22, for example, and it is now in the high 30s, it may be a good time to find something that's more reasonably priced, assuming it also fits the pattern described above. The P/E is calculated by dividing the price by the annual earnings per share. If a stock sells for $40 and earned $1.32 in the past twelve months, that works out to a P/E of 30.3—which is much higher than stocks in general. But if the earnings were $2.75, that would be a multiple of 14.6, which is below the market, and might be a bargain if it has the features described above.

Don't Fall in Love with a Stock

You may recall that one reason I sold 300 shares of Eli Lilly was because I owned too much of the stock. A good rule of thumb is to invest no more than 5 percent of your portfolio in any single stock. That means that you should own at least twenty stocks. I own more than fifty stocks.

I can appreciate that you may be reluctant to pare back one of your large holdings, since the price has risen appreciably, and you would have to cough up a chunk of cash for the tax collector. That used to make sense, but no more. The maximum capital gains tax is now a mere 15 percent.

One thing to bear in mind when you are giving thought to selling a stock is portfolio turnover. Most conservative investors should avoid too much trading. Buy and hold is a good strategy. Most mutual funds, however, don't adhere to this dictum. They often hold their stocks for no more than twelve months. According to an article in *Fortune* magazine on August 23, 2004: "As it turns out, most of that activity is not paying off for investors. Quite the opposite, in fact," says the author Janice Revell. "A recent Morningstar study shows that managers who adhere to a buy-and-hold strategy—and stifle the impulse to react to short-term market gyrations—tend to outperform their faster-fingered rivals.

"Morningstar analyst Kerry O'Boyle first screened the universe of actively managed equity funds for 1992–1998 to find those that fell into the lowest quartile for both portfolio turnover and the number of stocks held. He then went back and tracked the five-year performance for each fund, year by year, from 1992 through 2003. The result: Among all style categories, the concentrated low-turnover funds overwhelmingly beat their peers."

My thought is to make occasional changes, but don't get carried away with change. If your annual turnover is 10 or 20 percent, that should be sufficient. On the other hand, if you never bother to update your portfolio, you will end up with too many dogs that should have been sold long ago.

A New Retirement Strategy

Although I have previously addressed a strategy for arranging your portfolio for retirement, here is another idea that might appeal to you—particularly if you have a substantial portfolio—let's say $400,000 or more. It's simple and logical.

First, you should examine carefully your asset allocation. My favorite breakdown of assets is based on your age. For instance, if you are age sixty-five, you should have 65 percent of your assets in common stocks. The other 35 percent can be in a money-market fund or short-term bonds.

The Laddered Bond Portfolio

I tend to prefer short-term bonds, since they are unlikely to fluctuate in an adverse market. One alternative is a "laddered" approach to bonds. Long-term bonds typically pay better than short-term bonds. With a "ladder," you can own a batch of bonds, from one-year maturities to those that mature five or ten years from now. The strategy is to sell the short-term bond when it matures at face value and invest the proceeds in the one with a maturity five or ten years from now. That way, you are always selling a bond when it matures, which assures you the full face value. A longer-term bond, by contrast, is more volatile and could decline substantially when interest rates are climbing.

As you get older, the percentage in equities should decrease 1 percent each year. Thus, if you are seventy, you should have only 60 percent in stocks. And at age eighty, you should have a fifty-fifty breakdown.

On the other hand, if you are *younger* than sixty-five, you should *increase* the amount in equities by 1 percent each year.

Thus, at age fifty-five, you would have 75 percent in stocks. The rest would be in the fixed-income sector, usually money-market funds or short-term bonds.

Don't Forget Diversification— It's Vital

Next, you should make sure you have at least fifteen or twenty stocks, preferably more. (Of course, if you are a younger investor, it would not make sense to own a large number of stocks if you have a modest portfolio of $10,000, $25,000, or $50,000.) In this exercise, I have shown you a portfolio with twenty-five stocks. And most important, you should make sure you don't concentrate too heavily in any two or three sectors. In the breakdown below, I use a total of nine different sectors. The only sector left out is telephone, since there are no telephone stocks in this edition. Here are the twenty-five stocks, along with their sectors and symbols:

SECTOR	STOCK	SYMBOL
Industrials	Boeing	BA
Industrials	FedEx	FDX
Industrials	Illinois Tool Works	ITW
Energy	ExxonMobil	XOM
Energy	EnCana	ECA
Energy	ConocoPhillips	COP
Consumer Discretionary	Costco	COST
Consumer Discretionary	Lowe's	LOW
Consumer Discretionary	McGraw-Hill	MHP
Utilities	Piedmont Natural Gas	PNY
Utilities	MDU Resources	MDU
Utilities	Dominion Resources	D
Materials	Ecolab	ECL
Materials	Praxair	PX
Financials	Kimco Realty	KIM
Financials	Wells Fargo	WFC
Information Technologies	Microsoft	MSFT
Information Technologies	IBM	IBM

SECTOR	STOCK	SYMBOL
Information Technologies	Intel	INTC
Consumer Staples	Procter & Gamble	PG
Consumer Staples	Walgreen	WAG
Consumer Staples	PepsiCo	PEP
Health Care	Medtronic	MDT
Health Care	Johnson & Johnson	JNJ
Health Care	Teva Pharmaceuticals	TEVA

The Big Problem— and How to Solve It

Let's say that your portfolio is worth $400,000. What do you do next? Unless you are filthy rich, you will need some income to supplement Social Security and perhaps an IRA or a 401(k), an annuity, or a company pension (a rare benefit these days).

The problem is that most stocks don't provide much dividend yield, perhaps 2 percent or so—and many companies pay no dividend at all. Nor will you get rich with bonds or money-market funds. The only solution is to dip into capital. Many investors refuse to do this, fearing that they will exhaust their holdings and end up broke before they die. After all, people are living to older ages these days, frequently passing from the scene in their mid-eighties. What's more, if you have good genes and do lots of exercising, reaching age ninety is a good possibility.

The question is: what percentage to take out each year. If you get a bit greedy and take out 7 or 8 percent, you may end up in trouble, particularly if the market sags during an extended period. Studies show that 7 or 8 percent might eventually eat up all your assets, particular if you live into your late eighties or early nineties.

My solution is not to take out too much. I suggest liquidating 5 percent each year. You may assume that this means you will have a steady income of $20,000 each year, regardless of what the market does. My strategy is based on 5 percent of the *current* value at the beginning of each year, not 5 percent of the beginning value of $400,000.

As an example, if you take out 5 percent the first year, and the market dips a little after that, you may end the year with only $385,000. That means you should take out 5 percent of that figure for the ensuing year, or $19,250. On a more positive note, let's say the market enjoys itself during the next twelve months, and now you have assets worth $420,000. Taking 5 percent of that is $21,000.

A Twenty-five-Year Look at the Dow Jones Average

Taking out 5 percent of your portfolio is not likely to deplete it anytime soon. For evidence, I checked how the DJI has performed over the past twenty-five years— excluding dividends. The average is an 11 percent gain per year (plus dividends). In that span, the Dow was higher at the end of the year eighteen times, and lower only seven times. In other words, the market advanced 72 percent of the time. To be sure, projecting this performance into the future may not be a good idea, since the future is not exactly something you can predict. Here is the year-by-year breakdown of the Dow Jones Industrial Average:

2005:-0.61%	2004:+3.15%	2003:+25.32%
2002:-16.76	2001:-7.10	2000:-6.18
1999:+25.22	1998:+16.10	1997:+22.64
1996:+26.01	1995:+33.45	1994:+2.14
1993:+13.72	1992:+4.17	1991:+20.32
1990:-4.34	1989:+26.96	1988:+11.85
1987:+2.26	1986:+22.58	1985:+27.66
1984:-3.74	1983:+20.27	1982:+19.60
1981:-9.23		

Picking the Best Stock to Sell or Reduce

It stands to reason that you can't take the whole 5 percent entirely out of your money-market fund. That would upset the percent breakdown of stocks and cash. There are a number of approaches that you might like to consider when making this decision as to which stock to sell or reduce.

A New Retirement Strategy

One way to evaluate the future prospects of a stock is to see what leading analysts are saying. You can do this by going on the Internet and checking the business section of the *New York Times*. Click on Company Research at the top of the page and then the ticker symbol, and it will show what analysts are saying. For instance, I checked Lowe's, and here are the results of sixteen analysts:

Buy 8

Overweight 2

Hold 6

Underweight none

Sell none

On this particular day, most analysts liked Lowe's. By contrast, if you looked at General Motors on the same day, this is what you would have seen:

Buy 2

Overweight 1

Hold 4

Underweight 1

Sell 4

In my last two books, I have used this device throughout.

If you have an account at Fidelity, you can consult Research, followed by Stocks and Browse Research. Next, type in the ticker symbol of the stock in question. Detailed comments are made by such brokerage houses as Lehman Brothers and Prudential Equity. There is also information from Argus Research (an independent research firm) and Standard & Poor's. S&P is one of my favorites.

One more source of advice can be the research department of a full-service brokerage firm, such as Wachovia, Smith Barney, A.G. Edwards or UBS Financial. These firms typically have dozens of well-qualified analysts covering a broad array of industries. Your broker may have access to recent reports on some of the companies you have an interest in.

Finally, you can go to a brokerage house or a public library and read what *Value Line Investment Survey* thinks of the stock. If you do all of these things, you should be able to make up your mind whether this stock should be whittled back. Of course, if you go through this ritual on all twenty-five stocks, you may have to give up your Saturday golf outing, or your day on the ski slopes.

If you are too busy or not inclined to do this extensive research, there are four simple alternatives:

- Sell a stock from your IRA, since there will be no taxes to pay—unless you have reached the age when the IRS makes it mandatory for you to begin withdrawing part of your IRA, all of which is taxable.
- Simply cut back on your largest holding, which will enhance your diversification.
- Sell the stock that shows the worst profit—assuming you don't have any stocks in your IRA. If you don't like to pay capital gains taxes, this is a good strategy.
- A fourth alternative is to sell a really dinky holding, one that makes up only 1 percent of your list. Such small stocks are rarely large enough to make you rich, even if they double.

Pros and Cons of My Strategy

The disadvantage of my strategy is that you will have a varying income, not a steady one. On the other hand, the advantage is that it is unlikely that you will ever use up your principal. To be sure, you may have an up-and-down income, but you won't end up a pauper late in life.

In actual practice, it is difficult to see how you would be unhappy with this method of dipping into capital, since the market historically has gone up more often than it has sagged. Then, too, the common stocks in your portfolio are not your only assets, assuming you use my formula for allocating some of your holdings to a money-market fund, short-term bonds, or a laddered portfolio of bonds. Thus, if the stock portfolio declines 10 percent in a given year, your entire holdings will decline much less. On a more positive note, if the market goes up 15 or 20 percent, your spendable income will go up substantially.

One other factor to bear in mind: your income will not depend entirely on your stocks and bonds. Your Social Security will actually increase every year, based on an adjustment for the cost of living. Then, too, you may have a 401(k), an IRA, an annuity, or a pension that will be steadying factors.

Of course, if you have been enjoying a substantial income prior to retirement— let's say $125,000—there is no way a portfolio of $400,000 will enable you to live high on the hog during retirement. The answer is, of course, that you set aside enough during your working years so that you can still buy a new car once in a while and take an occasional trip to Finland, India, Egypt, or Patagonia, if the spirit moves you. I suggest setting aside a minimum of 10 percent of your income every year, putting most of it in common stocks. Finally, don't skip a year merely because you think stocks are headed for the woodshed.

Index Funds vs. Exchange-Traded Funds (ETFs)

I barely recognized the voice of Hans Gelderland when he called me out of the blue in early 2007. You may recall that Hans is the author of the acclaimed book, *How to Make $37,000 a Year as a Full Time Free-lance Writer*. Some time ago, I had helped him write a magazine article on the major mistakes that investors make.

"It's been a long time, Hans," I said. "What are you working on these days?"

"I'm busy writing another book. So far, I don't have a publisher, but I have some sample chapters that I intend to send out soon. It should be a big bestseller, since it's a biography of Sancho III of Navarre. He's usually referred to as Sancho the Great. He was king of Navarre from 1000 A.D. until his death in 1035. During his lifetime, Sancho III was the most important Christian monarch of the Iberian Peninsula."

"I do quite a bit of reading, Hans, and I'm afraid that Sancho III of Navarre doesn't ring a bell. Why not try a more famous person such as Peter the Great, Mithradates of Pontus, Cleopatra, Cicero, Cardinal Richelieu or Martin Luther."

"That's all well and good, Slats, but I . . ."

I broke in with more names, "and don't forget Erasmus, Leibniz, Gustave Flaubert, Queen Elizabeth I, Millard Fillmore, Hannibal and Charlemagne?"

"They're all good names, Slats, but my mind is made up. The reason is simple: Sancho was Spanish, and with the tens of thousands of Mexicans streaming across the Rio Grande, there will be a stampede to Barnes & Noble to buy a copy of *Sancho the Great*. It can't miss."

"You might have a point, Hans, since you've done a lot of research on your famous Spaniard. I suppose you're calling to invite me to have lunch at my favorite restaurant, the Windjammer on Williston Road in South Burlington. I love their Reuben sandwiches."

"I hadn't thought of that, but perhaps we could get together to talk about a financial article I want to write on exchange-traded funds. It will tide me over till I get an advance on my book on Sancho III. I notice that you have never written anything on ETFs."

"Not so far, Hans, but my good buddy George Morris, a broker with Wachovia Securities in Cleveland, has been after me to tackle ETFs. I have a raft of material on the subject, but so far I haven't put pencil to paper. However, I do have the makings of an article in my brain that I could share with you."

A few days later, we met at the Windjammer to put some flesh on the article on exchange-traded funds for Hans Gelderland. I awaited eagerly for my tasty Reuben sandwich. Hans ordered a grilled chicken teriyaki salad wrap. I led off the discussion. "Not everyone knows the difference between index funds and ETFs," I said. "To begin with, index funds got into the act when Vanguard's Jack Bogle dreamed up the concept a few decades ago. He reasoned that most mutual funds, despite being managed by sophisticated analysts, typically fail to do as well as the market, as represented by the S&P 500 or the Dow Jones Average.

"As it turned out, skeptics on Wall Street abounded when they heard about Jack Bogle's novel concept. But his idea began to gather momentum when his funds outpaced most managed funds. One reason they did well was because the cost of managing an index fund was close to zip. Whereas open-end mutual funds (as opposed to closed-end funds) had fees and costs of about 1.5 percent per year, index funds could boast fees that were only a fraction of that, often .20 percent."

"I think that covers the essence of the subject. When did ETFs come on the scene?" asked Hans, after he swallowed a bite of his teriyaki wrap.

"The first ETF was introduced on the Toronto Stock Exchange in 1990. In the United States, the first exchange-traded fund, an S&P 500 index fund, began trading on the American Stock Exchange in January 1993. A second ETF—which tracked the S&P MidCap 400 index—was added in 1995, and seventeen ETFs linked to international stock exchanges began trading in 1996. As of January 2007, there were 387 ETFs, with assets of $422 billion, mostly traded on the American Stock Exchange. What's more, twenty-eight new ones were added in January 2007.

"Index mutual funds, of course, are not traded on any stock exchange—unless they are the closed-end variety. You have to invest in them directly through the mutual fund company that creates them, such as Fidelity or Vanguard. And the price you pay is directly determined by the value of the assets at the closing bell on the stock exchange. When you sell, the same price applies. And there is no commission to pay.

"By contrast, exchange-traded funds are traded just like a stock such as IBM, Procter & Gamble, FedEx or Bed Bath & Beyond. Thus, you don't have to wait until 4 p.m. to find out what you paid. The price of an ETF fluctuates throughout the day and is not necessarily the same as the assets held by the fund, although, of course, they are very close to that amount."

"If you have to pay a commission for an ETF, what motivates an investor to select that investment rather than a traditional index fund?" asked Hans Gelderland.

"That's a good question. Frankly, I wouldn't. On the other hand, I am a conservative investor who prefers to buy and hold. I am not a trader. But the investment scene is well populated with people who aren't content to sit around and wait to become rich. They want action, and the ETF gives them action. For instance, if they think Portugal or France—or some other country—is poised to take off, they can buy an ETF that invests exclusively in that sector of the world economy and not be bothered finding the best stock or two in that particular market."

"Is it true that you can buy an ETF on margin or sell short?"

"Exactly. What's more, you can use limit orders or stop-loss order with an ETF. In short, an ETF is just another stock."

"I've heard that ETFs are getting very popular, and new ones are being added to the mix at a breath-taking pace. What's going on?"

"Open-end index funds are typically based on large segments of the market. When you buy an S&P 500 index fund, your results will be essentially the same as the index. But when you look at the ETF realm, you have a much wider choice. Many ETFs are based on single industries or countries, for instance. This appeals to aggressive investors who are not content to simply mirror the general market. They think they can outwit the conservative investor by picking their shots on hot segments of the market. Of course, they are not always right."

Advantages and Disadvantages

"I think I'm getting a bit confused," said Hans Gelderland. "Maybe it would make sense to outline when it makes sense to go the index fund route and when it would be better to use an ETF."

"Good thinking. There are pros and cons in each realm," I said. "If you are a small investor and want to invest $2,000 in a fund and then add to it by investing $200 a month, you should not consider the ETF route. You would have to pay a commission every time you mailed in a payment. In fact, ETFs are not even set up for such programs. The traditional open-end mutual fund is the only way to go. On the other hand, if you have very limited capital, such as $300, most mutual funds would not do business with you, since they often have a minimum entry fee of $500, $1,000, or more. By contrast, you can buy any number of shares on the American Stock Exchange. There is no minimum. Naturally, your commission would be quite large as a percentage of your small purchase."

"How about taxes? I have heard that ETFs are a better bet tax-wise. Is that correct? If so, why?" said Hans.

"Both are a good bet when income taxes are considered. That's because index funds and ETFs are not managed. They consist essentially of a group of stocks that represent a fixed group of stocks, such as the stocks in an industry, such as utilities, food stocks, banks, or technology. Those groups occasionally change, but those changes are infrequent. That means that capital gains are also minimal. By contrast, if you buy a managed mutual fund, there is often a great deal of trading. On average, the portfolio switches are about 100 percent per year. Whenever a stock is sold for a profit, that profit is passed on to the investor, even if you reinvest such capital gains. That's one reason I am death on managed mutual funds."

"Are you telling me that index funds and ETF funds are both equal when it comes to paying the IRS?" said Hans Gelderland.

"Not exactly. The ETF holds a modest edge. That's because the fund itself is not involved when you sell your shares on the American Stock Exchange. However,

if you own an open-end index fund, you are getting your money from the fund itself, which may have to sell some of its holdings to pay you. When that happens, it may involve selling a stock that was purchased at a lower price, thus creating a tax liability for all investors who own that particular index fund. Of course, this tax problem is a drop in the bucket when compared with a managed portfolio."

"I think I am getting the hang of how index funds differ from ETFs," Hans said. "One more question. I know that index funds have low costs, since there is no management. I assume that ETFs are about the same."

"Not exactly," I said. "Most ETFs have a lower expense ratio than comparable mutual funds. Mutual funds may charge between 1 percent and 3 percent, since most of them are managed. ETFs, by contrast, are rarely managed, and they usually charge as little as 0.1 percent to 1 percent. It would seem that exchange-traded funds have the advantage. On the other hand, if you deal with a low-cost provider, such as Vanguard, you won't have to worry about a high expense ratio. In most instances, it is less than 0.2 percent per year. It's only when you get into managed mutual funds that the expense ratio is a real burden, typically 1.5 percent, and sometimes more than 2 percent. Over the long term, the expense ratio can impact your results big time. It's a major reason to avoid them."

"Once again, you have given me some good ammunition for my magazine article. I get the impression that you have an aversion to exchange-traded funds, Slats."

"Well, for one thing, I have never given any thought to buying one. However, I have recommended a few for my clients. As long as you don't get involved in those that invest in small segments of the market, I see no reason to avoid them. My preference is to invest in index funds or ETFs that buy a broad selection of stocks, such as the S&P 500, the Dow Jones Industrial Average, or the Russell 2000. I would avoid those that zero in on individual countries or a narrow sector such as health care, utilities, banks, or tech stocks."

"Enough said, Slats. I guess it's my turn to foot the bill for a great repast at the Windjammer."

I didn't fumble for my wallet. I figured Hans Gelderland would soon get a huge advance on his new book on Sancho III of Navarre. On the other hand, my choice would have been to stick with someone famous such as Millard Fillmore or Cardinal Richelieu.

After I had my meeting with Hans Gelderland, I came across an article in the *Wall Street Journal*, dated February 8, 2007.

Here's what Justin Lahart had to say, "The next time you hear advice from an investment expert about a hot sector, the best strategy might be to ignore it.

"Analysts and fund companies like to advise investors to 'overweight tech' or 'underweight energy.' In plain English, that means they are saying to put extra cash into technology shares or less of it into energy stocks. And over the years, they have come up with a well-worn set of terms and guidelines. If the economy is heading for a rough patch, for instance, it is time to buy 'defensive' stocks; if it is pulling itself out of the doldrums, it is time to buy 'early cyclicals.'

"The problem with well-worn ideas in financial markets is they tend to stop working, and that might be happening with sector pickers now."

PART II

100 BEST STOCKS
YOU CAN BUY

100 Best Stocks

In the following table are listed the 100 stocks discussed in this book. A brief description of the stock appears here. The ticker symbol is given so that you can use the quote machine in your broker's office. Or, if you call your broker on the phone, it makes it easier if you know the ticker symbol, since your broker may not.

In the table, "Industry" refers to one of the company's main businesses. This is not always easy to express in one or two words.

For instance, United Technologies is involved in such industries as aircraft engines, elevators, and air conditioning equipment. To describe the company succinctly, I arbitrarily picked the designation, "aircraft engines."

Similarly, General Electric presents an even more daunting problem since it owns NBC, makes appliances, aircraft engines, medical devices and a host of other things.

The designation "Sector" indicates the broad economic industry group that the company operates in, such as Energy, Financial, Drug & Health Care, Consumer Staples, Consumer Discretionary, Information Technology, Industrials, Materials, Telecommunications, and Utilities. A properly diversified portfolio should include at least one stock in each of the ten sectors.

"Category" refers to one of the following: 1) Income (Income) 2) Growth & Income (Gro Inc) 3) Conservative Growth (Con Grow) or 4) Aggressive Growth (Aggr Gro). As above, it might make sense to have some representation in each category, even though you have a strong preference for only one.

I have not included the page numbers because of space limitations. In any event, it is easy enough to find a particular stock, since they appear alphabetically in the book.

Company	Symbol	Industry	Sector	Category
—A—				
Abbott Laboratories	ABT	Med Supplies	Health Care	Gro Inc
Air Products	APD	Gases	Materials	Con Grow
Alcoa	AA	Aluminum	Materials	Aggr Gro
Apache Corporation	APA	Exploration	Energy	Aggr Gro
AT&T*	T	Telephone	Telecomm	Gro Inc
—B—				
Bard, C. R.	BCR	Hosp Products	Health Care	Con Grow
Becton, Dickinson	BDX	Med Supplies	Health Care	Con Grow
Boeing Company	BA	Aerospace	Industrials	Aggr Gro
—C—				
Campbell Soup	CPB	Packaged Foods	Cons Staples	Con Grow
Canadian National	CNI	Railroad	Industrials	Con Grow
Carnival Corporation	CCL	Cruise Lines	Cons Discret	Aggr Gro
Cash America Int'l	CSH	Financial Services	Financials	Aggr Gro
Caterpillar, Inc.	CAT	Machinery	Industrials	Aggr Gro
Chevron Texaco	CVX	Gas & Oil	Energy	Gro Inc
Cintas	CTAS	Uniforms	Industrials	Aggr Gro

Company	Symbol	Industry	Sector	Category
Clorox	CLX	Household Pd.	Cons Staples	Con Grow
Coach	COH	Leather Goods	Cons Discret	Aggr Gro
Coca-Cola*	KO	Beverages	Cons Staples	Gro Inc
Colgate-Palmolive	CL	Household Products	Cons Staples	Con Grow
ConocoPhillips	COP	Oil & Gas	Energy	Gro Inc
CONSOL Energy*	CNX	Coal & Gas	Energy	Aggr Gro
Costco Wholesale	COST	Wholesale	Cons Staples	Aggr Gro
CVS Corporation	CVS	Pharmacy	Cons Staples	Con Gro
—D—				
Deere & Company	DE	Farm Equipment	Industrials	Aggr Gro
Dentsply Int'l	XRAY	Dental Products	Health Care	Con Gro
Devon Energy	DVN	Oil & Gas Explor	Energy	Aggr Gro
Dominion Resources	D	Gas & Electric	Utilities	Gro Inc
Donaldson	DCI	Filtration	Industrials	Con Grow
Dover	DOV	Ind Machinery	Industrials	Aggr Gro
DuPont	DD	Chemicals	Materials	Gro Inc
—E—				
Eaton Corporation	ETN	Machinery	Industrials	Gro Inc
Ecolab	ECL	Specialty Chem.	Materials	Con Gro
Emerson Electric	EMR	Elect. Equip.	Industrials	Gro Inc
EnCana Corporation	ECA	Oil & Gas	Energy	Aggr Gro
Energen	EGN	Oil & Gas	Utilities	Cons Gro
Entergy*	ETR	Energy	Utilities	Gro Inc
ExxonMobil	XOM	Petroleum	Energy	Gro Inc
—F—				
Fastenal Company*	FAST	Fastener Distrib	Industrials	Aggr Gro
FedEx Corporation	FDX	Air Freight	Industrials	Aggr Gro
FMC Corporation*	FMC	Feeding World	Materials	Aggr Gro
FPL Group	FPL	Elect Power	Utilities	Gro Inc
—G—				
General Dynamics	GD	Aerospace	Industrials	Con Grow
General Electric	GE	Elect. Equip.	Industrials	Gro Inc
General Mills	GIS	Packaged Foods	Cons Staples	Gro Inc
Goodrich*	GR	Aerospace	Industrials	Aggr Gro
Gentex*	GNTX	Electro-optical	Cons Disc	Gro Inc
Grainger, W. W.	GWW	Supplies	Industrials	Con Gro
— H—				
Harris Corp.*	HRS	Communications	Inform Tech	Aggr Gro
Hewlett Packard	HPQ	Printers	Inform Tech	Aggr Gro

Company	Symbol	Industry	Sector	Category
Honeywell	HON	Aerospace	Industrials	Aggr Gro
Hormel Foods	HRL	Packaged Foods	Cons Staples	Con Gro
—I—				
Idex	IEX	Fluid, Meter	Industrials	Con Grow
Illinois Tool Works	ITW	Machinery	Industrials	Con Grow
Ingersoll-Rand	IR	Equipment	Industrials	Aggr Gro
Intel	INTC	Computers	Inform Tech	Aggr Gro
Int'l Business Mach	IBM	Computers	Inform Tech	Con Gro
International Paper*	IP	Packaging	Materials	Aggr Gro
—J—				
Johnson Controls	JCI	Elect. Equip.	Cons Discret	Con Grow
Johnson & Johnson	JNJ	Med Supplies	Health Care	Con Grow
—K—				
Kellogg	K	Packaged Foods	Cons Staples	Con Grow
Kimco Realty	KIM	REIT	Financial	Gro Inc
—L—				
Lowe's Companies	LOW	Retail	Cons Discret	Con Grow
Lubrizol	LZ	Specialty Chem	Materials	Gro Inc
—M—				
McCormick & Co.	MKC	Spices	Cons Staples	Con Gro
McGraw-Hill	MHP	Publishing	Cons Discret	Con Gro
MDU Resources	MDU	Oil & Gas	Utilities	Gro Inc
Medtronic	MDT	Med Devices	Health Care	Aggr Gro
Meredith	MDP	Publishing	Cons Discret	Con Gro
—N—				
Nabors Industries	NBR	Oil & Gas	Energy	Aggr Gro
Nordson*	NDSN	Coatings	Industrials	Aggr Gro
Norfolk Southern	NSC	Railroads	Industrials	Con Gro
Northern Trust*	NTRS	Bank	Financials	Con Gro
—O—				
Omnicom Group	OMC	Advertising	Cons Discret	Cons Gro
Oshkosh Corporation	OSK	Trucks	Industrials	Aggr Gro
—P—				
Parker Hannifin	PH	Industrial Mach	Industrials	Aggr Gro
Patterson Companies	PDCO	Dental	Health Care	Aggr Gro

Company	Symbol	Industry	Sector	Category
Paychex	PAYX	Payroll Services	Inform Tech	Aggr Gro
PepsiCo	PEP	Beverages	Cons Staples	Con Grow
Piedmont Nat'l Gas	PNY	Nat'l Gas	Utilities	Income
Praxair	PX	Indust Gases	Materials	Con Grow
Procter & Gamble	PG	Household Products	Cons Staples	Con Grow
—R—				
Raytheon*	RTN	Defense	Industrials	Con Grow
Rohm & Haas*	ROH	Spec Chem	Materials	Gro Inc
—S—				
Schlumberger*	SLB	Oilfield Services	Energy	Aggr Gro
Sigma–Aldrich*	SIAL	Life Science	Inform Tech	Con Grow
St. Jude Medical	STJ	Medical Devices	Health Care	Aggr Gro
Staples*	SPLS	Office Products	Cons Discret	Aggr Gro
Stryker	SYK	Medical Sup.	Health care	Aggr Gro
Sysco Corporation	SYY	Food Distrib.	Cons Staples	Con Grow
—T—				
Target Corporation	TGT	Gen. Merchandise	Cons Discret	Aggr Gro
Teva Pharmaceutical	TEVA	Pharmaceuticals	Health Care	Aggr Gro
3M Company	MMM	Diversified	Industrials	Con Grow
TJX	TJX	Retailer	Cons Discret	Aggr Gro
T. Rowe Price	TROW	Asset Management	Financials	Aggr Gro
—U—				
United Parcel	UPS	Expr Carrier	Industrials	Con Gro
United Technologies	UTX	Aircraft Eng	Industrials	Con Grow
—V—				
Varian Medical	VAR	Med Devices	Health Care	Aggr Gro
Vulcan Materials Co.	VMC	Construction	Materials	Aggr Gro
—W—				
Walgreen	WAG	Drugstores	Cons Staples	Con Grow
Wells Fargo	WFC	Divers Bank	Financial	Gro Inc

*New in this edition (16 stocks).

Abbott Laboratories

100 Abbott Park Road □ Abbott Park, IL 60064-6400 □ (847) 937-3923 □ Dividend reinvestment plan available □ Web site: *www.abbott.com* □ Ticker symbol: ABT □ Listed: NYSE □ S&P rating: A− □ Value Line financial strength rating: A++

On February 15, 2008, Abbott received U.S. Food and Drug Administration (FDA) approval for SIMCOR®, the first fixed-dose combination of two widely prescribed cholesterol therapies, Niaspan® (Abbott's proprietary niacin extended-release) and simvastatin. SIMCOR is approved for use along with diet to lower levels of elevated total cholesterol, LDL "bad" cholesterol and triglycerides, and to raise HDL "good" cholesterol in patients with complex lipid disease when treatment with simvastatin or Niaspan monotherapies are not considered adequate.

"Managing cholesterol encompasses many factors, not just lowering LDL. There is a clear need for medicines that both raise good and comprehensively lower the bad components of cholesterol," said Christie Ballantyne, M.D., the Methodist DeBakey Heart and VascularCenter, Houston, and lead SIMCOR investigator. "SIMCOR represents an important new option to help patients reach healthy lipid levels."

An estimated 80 million Americans have high levels of the bad LDL cholesterol, and more than 44 million have low levels of the good HDL cholesterol, which the body uses to remove bad cholesterol from the bloodstream. Studies have shown that along with diet, SIMCOR can help patients with lipid disorders reach their treatment goals by addressing more than just bad cholesterol, targeting multiple lipids with one pill.

The FDA's approval was based on SIMCOR safety and efficacy trial data from more than 640 patients with mixed dyslipidemia and type II hyperlipidemia. In the SEACOAST clinical trial, patients receiving SIMCOR 1000/20 mg achieved significant cholesterol improvements over and above what simvastatin 20 mg alone provided. Patients treated with SIMCOR 1000/20 mg had additional lipid improvements beyond simvastatin 20 mg treated baseline, with additional LDL reductions of 12 percent and an additional 21 percent HDL increase compared to a 7 percent decrease in LDL and an 8 percent increase in HDL with simvastatin 20 mg alone. Furthermore, SIMCOR reduced triglycerides by an additional 27 percent compared to 15 percent with simvastatin 20 mg alone.

"With SIMCOR, doctors now have a new option for helping patients reach their LDL and HDL cholesterol treatment goals with a combination of two proven therapies," said Eugene Sun, M.D., Vice President of Global Clinical Development for Abbott. "Abbott is committed to bringing forward new cholesterol therapies, and SIMCOR represents a new treatment option for patients in Abbott's rapidly expanding portfolio of cholesterol treatments for lipid disorders."

Company Profile

Abbott Laboratories is one of the largest diversified health care manufacturers in the world. The company's products are sold in more than 130 countries, with about 40 percent of sales derived from international operations. ABT has paid consecutive quarterly dividends since 1924.

Abbott's major business segments include Pharmaceuticals & Nutritionals (prescription drugs, medical nutritionals and infant formulas) and Hospital & Laboratory Products (intravenous solutions, administrative sets, drug-delivery devices, and diagnostic equipment and reagents).

The company's leading brands are:

- AxSym systems and reagents (immunodiagnostics)
- Biaxin/Biaxin XL/Klalcid/Klaricid (macrolide antibiotic)
- Depakote (bipolar disorder; epilepsy; migraine prevention)
- Depakote ER (migraine prevention)
- Ensure (adult nutritionals)
- Humira (rheumatoid arthritis)
- Isomil (soy-based infant formula)
- Kaletra (HIV infection)
- MediSense (glucose monitoring products)
- Mobic (to control pain)
- Similac (infant formula)
- Synthroid (hypothyroidism)
- Tricor (a lipid-control agent)
- Ultane/Sevorane (anesthetic)

Although revenue growth in Abbott's infant formula and diagnostics businesses has slowed in recent years, new drugs (such as the antibiotic clarithromycin), new indications (including the BPH claim for Hytrin), the launch of disease-specific medical nutritionals and cost-cutting (diagnostics and hospital supplies) continue to boost the company's profits.

Shortcomings to Bear in Mind
- On September 1, 2007, Bruce Japsen, a reporter with the *Chicago Tribune*, said, "While Abbott Laboratories awaits word from the Food and Drug Administration on when or whether the agency will review its experimental drug-coated stent, a rival has jumped ahead in what could be a critical review process for the troubled market for devices that unclog heart arteries.

"Because the only two drug-coated stents on the U.S. market have raised concerns among doctors and consumer groups over the potentially harmful and even deadly risk of blood clots, the FDA is expected to take a closer look at stents made by North Chicago-based

Abbott and Medtronic Inc., which are seeking approval for marketing in the U.S.

"What's more, the safety issues have caused the worldwide market to become smaller, putting more pressure on Abbott and Medtronic as they try to make inroads in a $5 billion worldwide market for drug-coated stents—tiny metal, scaffold-like devices that are snaked into coronary arteries via a balloon-tipped catheter."

Reasons to Buy
- "We believe Abbott will outpace its pharmaceutical peers in 2008 revenue growth, with help from strong sales of pharmaceuticals and medical devices," said the Standard & Poor's weekly publication, *The Outlook*, on March 12, 2008. "In the pharmaceutical unit, Humira, a treatment for rheumatoid arthritis and Abbott's flagship drug, should continue to be the top performer in the business. It accounted for 50 percent of sales growth in 2007, and we expect a more than 30 percent increase in 2008."
- On February 4, 2008, Argus Research Company rated Abbott a BUY. Martha Freitag, CFA, said, "We expect Abbott's continued investment in pharmaceuticals and higher-growth medical product lines to translate into more robust growth. In our view the acquisition of Guidant's vascular business and Kos Pharmaceuticals have the potential to accelerate Abbott's long-term growth beyond its stated goal of 10 percent.
- "A Food and Drug Administration panel yesterday backed an Abbott Laboratories drug-coated stent despite concerns about the long-term risk of developing blood clots," said Jennifer Corbett Dooren, writing for the *Wall Street Journal* on November 30, 2007.

"Members of the panel of outside medical experts overwhelmingly said they believed the device was effective at keeping previously blocked cardiac arteries open and said the device appeared to be safe for at least one year."

- On August 9, 2007, Abbott received a supplemental Premarket Approval from the U.S. Food and Drug Administration for its recently introduced RealTime HIV-1 viral load test. The approval allows Abbott to market a number of enhancements to the test, including a new design feature that will give laboratories the flexibility to perform HIV-1 viral load tests with smaller amounts (0.6 ml) of blood plasma. Abbott markets the m2000™ system and a menu of tests throughout the world as part of a strategic alliance with Celera.

"It can be challenging to obtain blood samples from some people, particularly critically ill patients," said Timothy Stenzel, M.D., Ph.D., medical director, Abbott Molecular. "This improvement will give labs the ability to use a smaller sample size while still maintaining the highest sensitivity and precision of any HIV-1 viral load test. It's easier on the patient and at the same time better for the lab."

Initially approved in the United States on May 11, 2007, the RealTime test, based on real-time polymerase chain reaction (PCR) technology, is the most sensitive HIV-1 viral load test available and the only test of its kind validated to detect and quantitate (precisely measure) the common strains of HIV-1 as well as all known genetic variations of the virus, including group O, group N, and non-B subtypes.

- "After a chilly spring and summer for Abbott Laboratories, Wall Street seems to have started warming up again to the medical-products giant," said Johanna Bennett, writing for *Barron's* on November 7, 2007. "It has, however, been a gradual thaw.

"Up 13 percent over the last twelve months due to expectations surrounding Abbott's experimental Xience V heart stent, Abbott has been hit by recent concerns that the Food and Drug Administration could delay approving the device next year, curtailing profit growth.

"Yet Abbott's earnings could climb substantially in 2008, even if Xience gets held up by regulators, thanks to rising sales of Abbott's blockbuster rheumatoid arthritis drug, Humira and new drug launches."

- On April 15, 2008, Abbott introduced the ARCHITECT® i1000SR® immunochemistry analyzer, expanding its ARCHITECT family of diagnostics instrument systems for clinical laboratories. Designed for labs that typically perform fewer than 200 immunoassay tests per day, the instrument addresses many of the workflow challenges common in today's laboratories.

With the increased demand for diagnostic testing, laboratories, both large and small, need to process tests as quickly and efficiently as possible. By providing continuous access to reagents and samples while the instrument is running, the ARCHITECT i1000SR enhances laboratory productivity. Additionally, a wide test menu, user-friendly software and low maintenance make it easy to train new laboratory personnel on the instrument's operation.

"Because time and ease of use are so critical in the testing environment, Abbott worked extensively with customers very early in the development phase and designed an instrument that could help smaller labs overcome the same productivity obstacles faced by larger labs," said Cass Grandone, Divisional Vice President, Systems Development, Abbott Diagnostics. "The ARCHITECT i1000SR analyzer is ideal for facilities running fewer than 200 tests per day and offers productivity benefits, such as highly efficient sample processing, usually reserved for larger testing facilities. Since ARCHITECT utilizes common reagents, consumables and software user interfaces, larger laboratories may be interested in using the instrument as a backup system to the i2000SR."

The ARCHITECT i1000SR analyzer can process up to 100 tests per hour. The instrument accommodates sixty-five patient samples and has the capability to priori-tize emergency test results and turn them around in less than sixteen minutes.

SECTOR: **Health Ccare**
BETA COEFFICIENT: **.75**
10-YEAR COMPOUND EARNINGS PER SHARE GROWTH: **7.8%**
10-YEAR COMPOUND DIVIDENDS PER SHARE GROWTH: **9.2%**

	2007*	2006*	2005	2004	2003	2002	2001	2000
Revenues (Mil)	25,914	22,476	22,338	19,680	19,681	17,685	16,285	13,746
Net Income (Mil)	3,606	3,881	3,351	3,566	3,479	3,243	1,550	2,786
Earnings per share	2.84	2.52	2.50	2.27	2.21	2.0	6.99	1.78
Dividends per share	1.30	1.18	1.10	1.0	3.9	7.9	2.8	2.76
Price high	59.5	49.9	50.0	47.6	47.2	58.0	57.2	56.2
low	48.5	39.2	37.5	38.3	33.8	29.8	42.0	29.4

*Extraordinary items have been excluded.

CONSERVATIVE GROWTH

Air Products and Chemicals, Inc.

❑ 7201 Hamilton Boulevard ❑ Allentown, PA 18195-1501 ❑ (610) 481-5775 ❑ Direct dividend reinvestment plan available ❑ Web site: *www.airproducts.com* ❑ Listed: NYSE ❑ Fiscal years end September 30 ❑ Ticker symbol: APD ❑ S&P rating: A ❑ Value Line financial strength rating: B++

On February 13, 2008, Air Products and Applied Process Technology, Inc. announced the signing of a license agreement for Applied's patented HiPOx™ technology. The license agreement provides Air Products exclusive rights to market the technology in the United States and Canada for municipal wastewater and drinking water applications at greater than 1 million gallons per day water flow rate. The agreement also provides Air Products nonexclusive access to other geographic regions, as well as industrial wastewater and groundwater remediation applications of the technology.

HiPOx technology uses an advanced oxidation process, which combines ozone and hydrogen peroxide to form hydroxyl radicals. The hydroxyl radicals oxidize organic contaminants in water without creating additional waste streams. Unlike other ozone-based advanced oxidation systems, HiPOx technology minimizes the formation of by-products,

such as bromate, making it ideal for drinking water applications in addition to remediation, wastewater and process water clean up. The applications for the technology include taste, odor, and color reduction, destruction of volatile organic compounds (VOCs), water disinfection for reuse, and removal of microcontaminants such as endocrine disruptors.

"This technology is a significant building block for our water treatment business. Water treatment is an important growth area for Air Products, building on our gases experience and expanding into new equipment-based solutions. Our existing water treatment business has focused primarily on industrial wastewater applications. HiPOx technology combined with other internally developed offerings provides an entry for Air Products into the drinking water and water reuse segments," said Deborah Anderson, business development manager for North America Merchant Gases at Air Products.

Company Profile

Here is a solid view of the company, which I extracted from the company's Web site on the Internet. To be sure, it's a bit self-serving.

"Air Products touches the lives of consumers around the globe in positive ways every day. We serve customers in healthcare, technology, energy, and industrial markets worldwide with a unique portfolio of products, services and solutions, providing atmospheric gases, process and specialty gases, performance materials and chemical intermediates. The company has built leading positions in key growth markets, such as semiconductor materials, refinery hydrogen, home healthcare services, natural gas liquefaction, and advanced coatings and adhesives.

"Founded more than 60 years ago, Air Products is recognized for its innovative culture, operational excellence and commitment to safety and the environment. In fact, we are the safest company of our kind in the nation. With annual revenues of $8.1 billion and operations in more than thirty countries, Air Products' more than 20,000 employees build lasting relationships with their customers and communities based on understanding, integrity and passion.

Over 60 Years of Growth

"Air Products was established in 1940 in Detroit, Michigan, on the strength of a simple, but then revolutionary, idea: the 'on-site' concept of producing and selling industrial gases, primarily oxygen. At the time, most oxygen was sold as a highly compressed gas product in cylinders that weighed five times more than the gas itself. Air Products proposed building oxygen gas generating facilities adjacent to large-volume users, thereby reducing distribution costs. The concept of piping the gas directly from the generator to the point of use proved sound and technically solvable.

"Today, Air Products ranks 281st in sales and 276th in total assets among *Fortune* magazine's April 2005 list of the 500 largest corpo-

rations in the U.S. Corporate headquarters are at the company's 600-acre campus in eastern Pennsylvania's Lehigh Valley, near Allentown; European headquarters are at Hersham, near London; and Asian headquarters are in Singapore, with offices in Tokyo and Hong Kong.

Serving a Diversity of Markets

"Air Products is one of the world's largest industrial gas producers, supplying a broad range of industrial gases—chiefly oxygen, nitrogen, argon, hydrogen and helium and related equipment for their production, distribution and use—to hundreds of thousands of customers throughout the world. These gases are used in most industries, including food and metal processing, semiconductor manufacturing, healthcare, aerospace and chemical production.

"Air Products' $1.9 billion chemicals business includes polymers, polyurethane intermediates and additives, amines, and specialty and epoxy additives used in applications such as adhesives, coatings, polyurethane foams, textiles, herbicides, pesticides, water treatment chemicals, reinforced composites and inks.

Positioned for Growth

"As international competition continues to intensify, Air Products is well positioned to compete with the best anywhere in the world. In addition to a broad product line and invested presence in more than thirty countries, the company has world-class production and applications technology and a long-standing commitment to safety, efficiency and cost-effectiveness in every facet of its operations. The corporation also has firmly established continuous improvement processes which will yield further productivity gains and even higher levels of customer satisfaction, ensuring a future for Air Products as bright as its past."

Shortcomings to Bear in Mind

■ On January 20, 2008, Standard & Poor's weekly publication, *Outlook,* gave Air Products a HOLD rating, with this comment,

"APD holds strong positions in several growth products and markets for industrial gases and specialty chemicals. However, we expect the equipment business to have sharply lower profits in fiscal 2008, and believe APD will soon sell its polymer emulsion business."

Reasons to Buy

- "This was a milestone year," said CEO John E. McGlade in fiscal 2008. "For the first time, we reached $1 billion in net income on sales of $10 billion, up 43 and 15 percent, respectively, from the prior year. This marked our fourth consecutive year of double-digit sales and earnings per share growth. Operating income from continuing operations of $1,390 million increased 23 percent, and diluted EPS of $4.37 was up 25 percent."

He also said, "We further strengthened our balance sheet, continuing to improve our solid financial position. Cash flow from continuing operations was $1.5 billion, including pension contributions of $290 million. Our debt-to-debt plus equity ratio ended the year at 39.3 percent, placing us squarely within an 'A' credit rating range."

- "As a global gases, specialty chemicals, equipment and services provider, Air Products is unique," according to a company official. "We serve many of today's highest-growth markets, including technology, performance materials, energy, healthcare, and other industries."

Leading supply positions

- "We supply atmospheric gases, process and specialty gases, performance materials and chemical intermediates to customers throughout the world. With our culture based on innovation, operational excellence, and a commitment to safety and the environment, we have built leading supply positions in key growth markets, including semiconductor and flat panel display materials, refinery hydrogen, home healthcare services, natural gas liquefaction, and advanced coatings and adhesives."

Global scope

- "We are geographically diversified, with operations in over thirty countries and half our revenues outside of the U.S. Our 20,700 employees differentiate Air Products by building lasting relationships with customers and communities based on understanding, integrity and passion."

Earnings stability

- "There is a high degree of stability in our earnings. We have a strong balance sheet with "A" bond ratings, and we generate strong cash flow. We also have attractive business models in how we go to market. For example, the majority of our business is supplied under long-term contracts. We have energy and raw material pass-through capability for the vast majority of the company's sales."

Growing with discipline

- "And most importantly, we're growing. We have substantial operating leverage as we load our existing assets with good business. We are driving increased productivity across our businesses at all levels. We are focused on growth businesses: Electronics, Performance Materials, Refinery Hydrogen, Healthcare and Asia. And we remain disciplined in our capital spending, pursuing leadership positions and choosing only the best opportunities. Each and every day, we work hard to improve our business portfolio, shifting it toward a higher growth, higher return mix for our shareholders."

- On October 29, 2007, Air Products, through its subsidiary Air Products San Fu Co. Ltd. in Taiwan, signed a long-term contract with Rexchip Semiconductor Corporation, a joint venture company between Powerchip Semiconductor Corporation and Elpida Memory Inc., for the supply of nitrogen and bulk gases. The gases will be supplied to Rexchip's two new twelve-inch fabrication facilities (Fab R1 and R2), which are under construction in Central Taiwan

Science Park (CTSP) in Houli, Taichung. Under this contract, Air Products will build, own, and operate two new nitrogen air separation plants in the CTSP.

Rexchip is a new joint venture company between Powerchip Semiconductor Corporation and Elpida Memory Inc. to operate DRAM fabrication facilities in Central Taiwan Science Park with a total planned capacity of 240,000 twelve-inch wafers per month, making the Rexchip Houli site the largest concentration of twelve-inch DRAM fabrication facilities in the world.

SECTOR: **Materials**
BETA COEFFICIENT: **1.00**
10-YEAR COMPOUND EARNINGS PER SHARE GROWTH: **9.1%**
10-YEAR COMPOUND DIVIDENDS PER SHARE GROWTH: **10.1%**

		2007	2006	2005	2004	2003	2002	2001	2000
Revenues (Mil)		10,038	8,850	7,768	7,411	6,297	5,401	5,858	5,467
Net Income (Mil)		1,036	723	712	604	397	525	466	533
Earnings per share		4.67	3.18	3.08	2.64	1.78	2.42	2.12	2.46
Dividends per share		1.52	1.34	1.25	1.04	0.88	0.82	0.78	0.74
Price	high	105.0	72.4	65.8	59.2	53.1	53.5	49.0	42.2
	low	68.6	58.0	53.0	46.7	37.0	40.0	32.2	23.0

AGGRESSIVE GROWTH

Alcoa, Inc.

201 Isabella Street at 7th Street Bridge □ Pittsburgh, PA 15212-5858 □ (212) 836-2674 □ Dividend reinvestment plan available □ Web Site: *www.alcoa.com* □ Listed: NYSE □ Ticker symbol: AA □ S&P rating: B+ □ Value Line financial strength rating: A

On December 21, 2007, Alcoa announced it had agreed to sell its packaging and consumer businesses to New Zealand's Rank Group Limited for $2.7 billion in cash. Alcoa's packaging and consumer businesses generated $3.2 billion in revenues and $95 million in after-tax operating income in 2006, representing 10 percent of Alcoa 2006 revenues and 3 percent of after-tax operating income. Alcoa announced in April 2007 its plan to explore strategic alternatives for this segment. Businesses included in the sale are:

■ Closure Systems International, a global leader in the manufacture of plastic and aluminum packaging closures and capping equipment for beverage, food, and personal care customers;

■ Consumer Products, a leading manufacturer of Reynolds Wrap branded and private label foil, wraps, and bags;

■ Flexible Packaging, manufacturers of laminated, printed, and extruded nonrigid packaging materials such as pouch, blister packaging, unitizing films, high quality shrink labels, and foil lidding for the pharmaceutical, food and beverage, tobacco, and industrial markets; and

■ Reynolds Food Packaging, makers of stock and custom products for the foodservice, supermarket, food processor, and agricultural markets including foil, film, and both plastic and foil food containers.

In total, these packaging businesses have 10,000 employees in twenty-two countries around the world. Alcoa will continue to operate its flat-rolled can sheet products serving the packaging market. Lehman Brothers acted as financial advisor to Alcoa on this transaction.

Company Profile

Alcoa (formerly Aluminum Company of America), founded in 1888, is the world's leading integrated producer of aluminum products. The company is active in all major aspects of the industry—technology, mining, refining, smelting, fabricating, and recycling.

Alcoa's aluminum products and components are used worldwide in aircraft, automobiles, beverage cans, buildings, chemicals, sports and recreation, and a wide variety of industrial and consumer applications, including such Alcoa consumer brands as Alcoa wheels, Reynolds Wrap aluminum foil, and Baco household wraps.

Related businesses include packaging machinery, precision castings, vinyl siding, plastic bottles and closures, fiber optic cables, and electrical distribution systems for cars and trucks.

Since aluminum is expensive and has difficulty competing against steel—even though it has some admirable qualities—it might appear to be a rare element. Not so.

Aluminum is an abundant metal and, in fact, is the most abundant metal in the earth's crust. Of all the elements, only oxygen and silicon are more plentiful. Aluminum makes up 8 percent of the crust. It is found in the minerals of bauxite, mica, and cryolite, as well as in clay.

Until about 100 years ago, aluminum was virtually a precious metal. Despite its abundance, it was very rare as a pure metal. The reason: it was so difficult to extract from its ore.

This is because aluminum is a reactive metal, and it cannot be extracted by smelting with carbon.

To solve the enigma, displacement reactions were tried, but metals such as sodium or potassium had to be used, making the cost prohibitive.

Electrolysis of the molten ore was tried, but the most plentiful ore, bauxite, contains aluminum oxide, which does not melt until it reaches 2,050 degrees centigrade.

The solution to the problem of extracting aluminum from its ore was discovered by Charles Hall in the United States and by Paul Heroult in France—both working independently. The method now used to extract aluminum from its ore is called the Hall-Heroult process.

I won't bore you with the steps taken to effect this process. The important fact to remember is that it is far from cheap. Even so, it can be done economically enough to make aluminum the second most widely used metal. However, it is not likely to replace iron and steel any time soon. Iron makes up more than 90 percent of the metals used in the world.

The main cost in the Hall-Heroult process is electricity. So much energy is required that aluminum smelters have to be situated near a cheap source of power, normally hydroelectric.

The price of entry into the business is so high that it discourages most upstarts from taking the plunge.

On the other hand, this frustrating effort to produce commercial aluminum is worth the cost, since the white metal has a number of valuable attributes: It has a low density. It is highly resistant to corrosion. It is lightweight—one-third the weight of steel. It is an excellent reflector of heat and light.

It is nonmagnetic. It is easy to assemble. It is nontoxic.

It can be made strong with alloys. It can be easily rolled into thin sheets. It has good electrical conductivity. It has good thermal conductivity. Aluminum doesn't rust.

Shortcomings to Bear in Mind

■ Alcoa is labeled an Aggressive stock because it is in a cyclical industry. Earnings don't advance every year. In the past ten years, EPS have had three down years. What's more, the Beta coefficient is a very high 1.45. That means that it is likely to decline 45 percent more than the market in a bad year. On the other hand, it would be expected to climb 45 percent more than the market in a good year.

Reasons to Buy

■   On February 1, 2008, Alcoa announced that it would join forces with Aluminum Corporation of China ("Chinalco") to acquire 12 percent of the UK common stock of Rio Tinto plc. Alcoa will contribute up to $1.2 billion to the total investment.

Commenting on the investment, CEO Alain Belda said, "We have long believed that Rio Tinto has a world-class portfolio of assets and is very well positioned to prosper in the current mining cycle. This investment, made in partnership with Chinalco, allows us to mutually benefit from developments in the sector. We have known Chinalco for many years, dating back to our participation in the successful launch of Chalco's IPO, and are looking forward to this new venture."

Highlights of 2007

■   2007 revenues at an all-time record of $30.7 billion

■   On August 8, 2007, Alcoa announced that its Juruti bauxite mining project in Brazil was recognized during the IV Corporate Architecture Grand Prix, a corporate architectural awards program promoted by Brazilian publishing house Flex Eventos. Architect Márcio Mazza won the prestigious award in the Sustainability Category for extensive use of sustainable materials in the construction of the Juruti site.

There are more than thirty buildings, corresponding to some 15,000 square miles of construction area, using recycled materials.

"The architectural project includes not only works for the Alcoa facility, but also for those of the Positive Agenda, a set of voluntary initiatives developed in partnership with the community and municipal authorities, to improve the quality of life of the local population, with immediate action in the areas of education, health and infrastructure," said Mauricio Macedo, Alcoa's Sustainability and Corporate Affairs Manager in Juruti.

Construction of the airport, Municipal Court and the Senai Professional Education Center are also being carried out using sustainable materials, such as small concrete columns made with cardboard molds and certified wood from the region.

"Before starting this project, we researched local characteristics and discussed the feasibility of this work with the people in the community. From our learnings, we drew up the architectural plans. Today, the town is beginning to receive modern buildings that preserve natural resources," says architect Márcio Mazza.

For masonry construction, unfired clay bricks dried in the shade and made from raw materials from the region were selected. The unfired bricks were produced by local town people following training. "This is a major contribution by Alcoa to the region, because IBAMA (the federal government's environment department) had already closed two brickworks in the town for the illegal burning of wood," says Mazza.

■   Through the years, Alcoa aluminum has been used in everything from airplanes to food packaging to Ferraris, but recently, the sustainable metal was cast again into one of the first items it had originally been used for over 100 years ago—a teapot.

New York-based industrial designer Joey Roth's unique Sorapot evolved from an unlikely combination of the artist's love of tea and an engineering class on the topic of bridges. The design of the pot, Roth said, emphasizes tea making as a ritual while showcasing the brewing of either green or white tea leaves. Roth chose to use Alcoa aluminum for the Sorapot because of its advantages over other materials. The majority of the aluminum plate used to make the teapot is sourced from Alcoa Bohai, located in Qinhuangdao, China.

"I was originally going to cast it from stainless steel, but aluminum's light weight and better flow rate gave me the freedom to design exactly the shapes I had in mind," Roth said on August 2, 2007. In addition, he said that aluminum is ideal for its ability to transfer heat without allowing the water to get too hot for delicate tea leaves. Roth said there is no other metal he could cast in the shape he needs for the pot.

It was for some of the same shape- and weight-related benefits that a teakettle was one of the first products made with Alcoa aluminum in 1895, when Arthur Vining Davis created the piece of cookware to display a new use for aluminum. The owner of the company he showed the teapot to—the

Griswold Company of Erie, Pennsylvania— was so impressed that an order was placed for 2,000 kettles. Despite Davis's attempts to explain that he only wanted to sell Griswold the aluminum, Alcoa was forced to enter the fabricating business to prove there was a market for the metal.

While Alcoa's original aluminum teapots can now only be found in museums and antique collections, Roth's new design is available through his Web site, *www.joeyroth.com.*

■ Alcoa makes a very sustainable product: almost 70 percent of the aluminum ever produced is still in use, equaling 480 million metric tons (529 million tons) of a total 690 million metric tons (761 million tons) manufactured since 1886.

SECTOR: **Materials**

BETA COEFFICIENT: **1.45**

10-YEAR COMPOUND EARNINGS PER SHARE GROWTH: **10.5%**

10-YEAR COMPOUND DIVIDENDS PER SHARE GROWTH: **10.5%**

		2007	2006	2005	2004	2003	2002	2001	2000
Revenues (Mil)		30,748	30,379	26,159	23,478	21,504	20,351	22,859	22,936
Net Income (Mil)		2,564	2,248	1,233	1,310	938	420	908	1,484
Earnings per share		2.95	2.57	1.40	1.49	1.08	.49	1.05	1.80
Dividends per share		0.68	0.60	0.60	0.60	0.60	0.60	0.60	0.50
Price	high	48.8	37.0	32.3	39.4	38.9	39.8	45.7	43.6
	low	28.1	26.4	22.3	28.5	18.4	17.6	27.4	23.1

AGGRESSIVE GROWTH

Apache Corporation

One Post Oak Central ❑ 2000 Post Oak Boulevard ❑ Suite 100 ❑ Houston, TX 77056-4400 ❑ (713)296-6662 ❑ Dividend reinvestment plan available ❑ Web site: *www.apachecorp.com* ❑ Listed: NYSE ❑ Ticker symbol: APA ❑ S&P rating: A ❑ Value Line financial strength rating: A

On January 24, 2008, Apache Corporation reported the first two discoveries from its 2008 exploration program.

■ The Hydra-1X exploration well in Egypt's Western Desert test-flowed 41.6 million cubic feet (MMcf) of natural gas and 1,313 barrels of condensate per day from the Jurassic Lower Safa formation. The discovery,

which is located in a sparsely drilled area in Apache's 100 percent interest Shushan "C" Concession, logged 178 feet of net pay in the Lower Safa—one of the thickest Lower Safa pay zones identified since Apache's 2003 discovery at Qasr—as well as forty-five feet of probable gas-condensate pay in the Jurassic Alam El Bueib (AEB) Unit 6 sand

and thirty feet of probable oil pay in the Lower Cretaceous AEB Unit 3.

■ The Brulimar-1 discovery on Australia's Northwest Shelf encountered 113 feet of net pay in the Upper Triassic Mungaroo sandstone. Brulimar-1 is the fourth consecutive exploration success in the Apache-operated WA-356-P block; Apache owns a 65 percent interest in the block in a joint venture with Kufpec.

"Although the accumulation is not as large as Qasr, the Hydra-1X penetrated the same Lower Safa sandstone that we discovered twenty-five miles away at Qasr—the largest field we've ever discovered, with estimated proved reserves of 2.3 trillion cubic feet of gas and 80.4 million barrels of condensate," said CEO G. Steven Farris. "The latest discovery extends the known Lower Safa production trend across Apache acreage an additional nine miles north of the Kahraman B-22 Lower Safa discovery, which flowed 16 MMcf of natural gas and 480 barrels of condensate per day after a fracture stimulation when it was tested in October 2006.

"The Brulimar-1 is also a significant discovery because it continues to validate our use of advanced geophysical techniques to identify specific stratigraphic targets and accurately predict reservoir thickness before we drill a well.

"With the most extensive inventory of quality exploration prospects in our fifty-three-year history, each of our core growth areas of Australia, Canada, and Egypt has a significant exploration drilling program planned for 2008. It's nice to ride out of the chute with two meaningful discoveries in Egypt and Australia in the first month of the year."

Company Profile

Established in 1954 with $250,000 of investor capital, Apache Corporation has grown to become one of the world's top independent oil and gas exploration and production companies with $155 billion in assets.

Apache's domestic operations are focused in some of the nation's most important producing basins, including the Outer Continental Shelf of the Gulf of Mexico, the Anadarko Basin of Oklahoma, the Permian Basin of West Texas and New Mexico, the Texas-Louisiana Gulf Coast, and East Texas.

In Canada, Apache is active in British Columbia, Alberta, Saskatchewan, and the Northwest Territories. The company also has exploration and production operations in Australia's offshore Carnarvon, Perth, and Gippsland basins, Egypt's Western Desert, the United Kingdom sector of the North Sea, China, and Argentina.

The Company's Strategy

Apache's strategy is built on a portfolio of assets that provide opportunities to grow through both grassroots drilling and acquisition activities. The company has seven core areas—two in the United States, and in Canada, Egypt, the United Kingdom sector of the North Sea, Australia, and Argentina.

The company's portfolio also is balanced in terms of gas versus oil, geologic risk, reserve life, and political risk.

Natural gas now represents 53 percent of production, while oil is 47 percent—a balanced product mix that provides upside potential in either market. Each core area has significant producing assets and large undeveloped acreage to provide running room for the future, but no single region contributes more than 25 percent of production or reserves. In each core area, the company's goal is to build critical mass that supports sustainable, lower-risk, repeatable drilling opportunities, balanced by higher-risk, higher-reward exploration.

How APA allocates its capital resources is reviewed quarterly, as management assesses its portfolio of drilling opportunities, service costs and the market for producing assets.

When acquisition opportunities are identified, operational and technical teams participate in the evaluation process, enabling our personnel to move in quickly to execute exploitation activities (including workovers, re-completions and drilling) that will increase production and reserves, reduce costs per unit produced and enhance profitability. Over time, the company builds teams that have the technical knowledge and sense of urgency to maximize value. This knowledge of producing basins and the company's culture provides a platform for continued growth through strategic acquisitions and drilling.

Apache has increased reserves in each of the last twenty-one years and production in twenty-seven of the last twenty-eight years. Management believes the company's portfolio of assets provides a platform for profitable growth through drilling and acquisitions across the cycles of the industry.

Operations Overview

Apache's U.S. operations are focused in some of the nation's most important producing basins, including the Outer Continental Shelf of the Gulf of Mexico, the Anadarko Basin of Oklahoma, the Permian Basin of West Texas and New Mexico, the Texas-Louisiana Gulf Coast, and East Texas. In Canada, Apache is active in British Columbia, Alberta, Saskatchewan, and the Northwest Territories. The company also has exploration and production operations in the Carnarvon, Perth and Gippsland basins offshore Australia, Egypt's Western Desert, the United Kingdom sector of the North Sea, and Argentina.

Shortcomings to Bear in Mind

■ According to the company's latest 10-K report, "Our estimated proved reserves, revenues, profitability, operating cash flows and future rate of growth are highly dependent on the prices of crude oil, natural gas and natural gas liquids, which are affected by numerous factors beyond our control. Historically, these prices have been very volatile. A significant downward trend in commodity prices would have a material adverse effect on our revenues, profitability and cash flow, and could result in a reduction in the carrying value of our oil and gas properties and the amounts of our estimated proved oil and gas reserves."

(The 10-K report is issued annually by all publicly owned companies and is far more technical and detailed than its annual report. Most investors do not read it.)

Reasons to Buy

■ "Apache had a record year in 2007 by virtually all financial and operational yardsticks," said CEO G. Steven Farris on February 7, 2008. "In addition to record earnings, Apache achieved these record results:

■ Cash from operations before changes in operating assets and liabilities totaled $6.2 billion in 2007, up 22 percent from 2006. Fourth-quarter cash from operations totaled $1.9 billion, up 50 percent from the year-earlier period.

■ Production averaged 561,239 barrels of oil equivalent (boe) per day during 2007—a 12 percent increase and the twenty-eighth annual increase in the last twenty-nine years. Fourth-quarter production averaged 574,646 boe per day, up 8 percent from the prior-year period.

Proved reserves totaled 2.45 billion boe, up 6 percent from 2006 and the twenty-second consecutive annual increase. Apache replaced 167 percent of its 2007 production, including 140 percent from drilling activity.

"With exploration success at the Julimar complex in Australia, discoveries in Egypt, and encouraging results at the Ootla shale play in northern British Columbia, we built tremendous momentum that set the stage for 2008," Mr. Farris said.

"We have the largest portfolio of quality exploration prospects in the fifty-three-year history of the company, with significant exploration drilling programs planned in our 'ACE' core growth areas of Australia, Canada and Egypt. We also have six major development projects that are expected to add production of more than 100,000 boe per day by 2011."

■ On December 3, 2007, Apache Corporation reported that its Jade-4 well in Egypt's Western Desert test-flowed 23.8 million cubic feet (MMcf) of natural gas and 2,107 barrels of condensate per day from the Jurassic Alam El Bueib-3G (AEB) formation.

The Jade-4 is adjacent to the Jade-1x discovery, which logged 217 feet of AEB pay and 66 feet in the Jurassic Upper Safa formation in March 2007. The discovery was completed as a gas producer from the Upper Safa after a test of 25.6 MMcf of gas per day. The Jade-4 was drilled to test the potential of the AEB—one of the most prolific reservoirs in the greater Khalda Concession. The latest well logged 234 feet of net pay in the AEB.

"After drilling three wells in the Jade Field along the Matruh Ridge, Apache has successful tests in four discrete reservoir intervals," said Farris. "We are planning appraisal and development drilling, and we expect to drill additional exploration prospects along the Jade trend during 2008."

In addition to the discovery well, the Jade-2x well is producing gas and condensate after testing over 20 MMcf of gas per day from each of two AEB sands, and the

Jade-4 is being completed as a gas and condensate producer. In addition, oil pay was identified in another AEB sand behind casing in the Jade-1x and Jade-4.

The Jade Field is located in the quarter-million-acre Matruh Concession. Apache holds a 100 percent contractor interest in the block.

"The Jade discovery was one of several higher-risk, higher-reward exploration prospects we have developed across the 37 million acres we have assembled in our core growth regions of Australia, Canada and Egypt," Mr. Farris said. "This field and other recent discoveries will enable Apache to deliver strong growth through the end of the decade."

■ On February 26, 2008, Argus Research Company gave Apache a BUY rating, with this comment by Philip Weiss, CFA, CPA, "Robust and organically driven production growth, together with industry-leading operating efficiency, should fuel Apache's earnings for the foreseeable future, in our opinion."

SECTOR: **Energy**
BETA COEFFICIENT: **.95**
10-YEAR COMPOUND EARNINGS PER SHARE GROWTH: **28 %**
10-YEAR COMPOUND DIVIDENDS PER SHARE GROWTH: **17.5 %**

	2007	2006	2005	2004	2003	2002	2001	2000
Revenues (Mil)	9,978	8,289	7,584	5,333	4,190	2.560	2,791	2,291
Net Income (Mil)	2,812	2,552	2,618	1,670	1,246	566	764	721
Earnings per share	8.39	7.64	7.84	5.03	3.74	1.84	2.50	2.48
Dividends per share	0.60	0.50	0.36	0.26	0.22	0.19	0.17	0.09
Price high	109.3	76.2	78.2	52.2	41.7	28.9	31.5	32.1
low	63.0	56.5	47.4	36.8	26.3	21.1	16.6	13.9

GROWTH AND INCOME

AT&T Inc.

175 East Houston □ San Antonio, TX 78205 □ (210) 821-4105 □ Dividend reinvestment plan available □ Web site: *www.att.com* □ Ticker symbol: T □ Listed: NYSE □ S&P rating: B+ □ Value Line financial strength rating: A+

On February 25, 2008, AT&T announced that Deutsch, a multinational electronics corporation, had signed a new two-year agreement for AT&T's Multiprotocol Label Switching

(MPLS) Virtual Private Network (VPN) service. The service will link Deutsch's facilities in the U.S., Germany, Italy, India, Japan, Mexico, Israel, and the United Kingdom.

In order to achieve its goal of becoming a global company, Deutsch sought a common network platform for various applications, such as e-mail, data sharing, video conferencing, and phone systems. The AT&T VPN solution will be deployed across fifteen company sites and will allow them to be linked together regardless of location, application or time zone.

Once the AT&T VPN solution is fully deployed, Deutsch plans to introduce Voice over Internet Protocol (VoIP) services, such as local and international calling, mobile call routing, telecommuting, centralized Internet access, video streaming, virus control, content-filtering, and spam management.

"We are very pleased AT&T customized a solution that is reliable and consistent," said Sylvio Duguay, chief information officer at Deutsch. "It's this type of superior network services and support that solidified our relationship with AT&T."

Through the secure AT&T Business Direct® portal, Deutsch has around-the-clock access to real-time information about the performance of its network services and a direct connection to electronic billing and ordering systems. Additionally, AT&T currently provides local and long distance voice, Internet access, and private lines to Deutsch.

The expanded business agreement renews and extends a long-standing relationship between the two companies that spans more than ten years.

Company Profile

AT&T Inc. is the largest communications holding company in the United States and worldwide, by revenue. Operating globally under the AT&T brand, AT&T is recognized as the leading worldwide provider of IP-based communications services to busi-

nesses and the leading U.S. provider of wireless, high-speed Internet access, local and long distance voice, and directory publishing and advertising services. As part of its "three screen" integration strategy, AT&T is expanding video entertainment offerings to include such next-generation television services as AT&T U-verse℠ TV.

The merger of AT&T and BellSouth, along with the ownership consolidation of Cingular Wireless and Yellowpages.com, will speed convergence, competition and continued innovation in the communications and entertainment industry, creating new solutions for consumers and businesses.

AT&T continues to build on the heritage of its predecessor companies that have served customers for more than a century. The new AT&T will earn customer trust and loyalty with a continuing commitment to the deployment of innovative products and services, reliable, high-quality service and excellent customer care.

Shortcomings to Bear in Mind

■ Over the past ten years, earnings per share have not been particularly impressive. Nor have dividend increases.

Reasons to Buy

■ "We believe cost reductions and growth stemming from wireless and broadband will enable AT&T to generate strong free cash flow in 2008 and 2009," said Todd Rosenbluth on February 21, 2008, writing for the Standard & Poor's *Stock Reports*. "We think as competitors face challenges, AT&T will gain share in nonwireline voice markets." The *Stock Reports* gave AT&T five stars, or STRONG BUY.

■ On January 24, 2008, Argus Research Company regarded AT&T as a BUY. Joseph Bonner, CFA, said, "AT&T is moving forward with initiatives across a number of fronts in both it Wireless and Wireline businesses. Large merger synergies are set to be realized in 2008, large share repurchases are planned, and the substantial dividend remains intact."

■ Operates one of the world's most advanced and powerful global backbone networks, carrying more than 10.17 petabytes of data traffic on an average business day to nearly every continent and country, with up to 99.999 percent reliability.

■ The nation's premier wireless carrier based on subscribers, serving 63.7 million customers.

■ The largest provider of broadband—more than 13.3 million lines in service (as of 2Q07)—and a major Wi-Fi provider, with nearly 50,000 hot spots in eighty countries.

■ Ranks as one of the world's largest providers of IP-based communications services for businesses, with an extensive portfolio of Virtual Private Network (VPN), Voice over IP (VoIP) and other offerings, all backed by innovative security and customer support capabilities.

■ Offers one of the most extensive VoIP service portfolios for businesses, enabling enterprises to migrate seamlessly between traditional and next-generation services.

■ The only communications provider to deliver interoperability with the world's five leading IP PBX vendors

■ The leading U.S. provider of local and long distance voice services.

■ The nation's largest directory publisher, delivering 178 million directories a year and publishing more than 1,250 different directories in twenty-two states.

■ Through Yellowpages.com, operates a leading Internet Yellow Pages network that received more than 1 billion local searches in 2006.

■ The world leader in transport and termination of wholesale traffic and recognized by numerous industry experts for its industry-leading wholesale services portfolio.

■ AT&T provides communications services to customers in virtually every country and territory in the world. Remote access solutions,

for example, are provided from more than 60,000 points of presence in 164 countries.

AT&T delivers the widest international coverage of any U.S.-based wireless carrier, giving customers the ability to make calls using an internationally enabled phone on six continents and 190 countries, with wireless data roaming in 130 countries for laptops, hand-held devices and other data services.

■ AT&T provides an unsurpassed array of wireless, voice, entertainment and Internet communications products and services for consumers and small businesses. By offering comprehensive, innovative service bundles, AT&T enables millions of consumers and small businesses to take advantage of competitive pricing and a single bill for wireline and wireless voice and data, broadband Internet and messaging services. The AT&T portfolio of services is perhaps the most robust in today's market, featuring choice, value and convenience across a range of service options that includes:

• High-speed Internet access
• Wi-Fi connectivity at nearly 50,000 hot spots in the United States and around the world, offering broadband service for on-the-go customers in more than eighty countries globally (including company-owned and third-party roaming locations)
• Home and small business networking
• Wireless services
• Satellite television services through strategic alliances
• AT&T Homezone[SM], which combines AT&T | DISH Network with AT&T Yahoo!® High Speed Internet
• Limited availability of AT&T U-verse[SM] services, including AT&T U-verse TV and AT&T Yahoo! High Speed Internet U-verse Enabled
• Local and long distance voice services
• Messaging services and call-management features

- Print and online directory services, listings and advertising

■ AT&T Labs has a long history of innovation, with thousands of patents issued or pending worldwide, and is a successor to a heritage that produced seven Nobel Prizes.

BellSouth was the first major communications provider to commercially launch wireless broadband using pre-WiMAX technology and a leader in fiber deployment with fiber-to-the-curb facilities to more than 1.3 million homes.

AT&T is a leader in third-generation wireless technology, launching the first widely available service in the world to use HSDPA technology. It launched the world's first commercial deployment of wireless services using EDGE, a third-generation high-speed mobile data and Internet access technology.

Researchers and engineers at AT&T Labs have developed some of the world's major technological inventions, including the transistor, the solar cell, the cell phone, and the communications satellite. These groundbreaking technologies have enabled today's computers and electronic devices, wireless phones and VoIP.

AT&T Labs has been an industry leader in the development of DSL and other broadband Internet transport and delivery systems, wireless data networks, and new technologies and applications for networking and enterprise business needs. AT&T's predecessor companies pioneered new technologies and developed promising new products and services in a wide range of areas, including IP network management and VoIP.

■ On December 10, 2007, AT&T announced the completion of the acquisition of Ingenio, a leading provider of Pay Per Call® technology. The combination will allow AT&T to better serve business directory and local search customers across its entire advertising and publishing portfolio. AT&T plans to quickly begin integrating Ingenio within AT&T's Yellowpages.com and the organization will be overseen by Charles Stubbs, president and CEO of Yellowpages.com.

SECTOR: **Telecommunications Services**
BETA COEFFICIENT: **1.00**
10-YEAR COMPOUND EARNINGS PER SHARE GROWTH: **.5%**
10-YEAR COMPOUND DIVIDENDS PER SHARE GROWTH: **4.7%**

		2007	2006	2005	2004	2003	2002	2001	2000
Revenues (Mil)		118,928	63,055	43,862	40,787	40,843	51,755	54,301	53,313
Net Income (Mil)		16,950	9,014	5,803	4,884	5,051	7,219	7,972	7,746
Earnings per share		1.94	1.89	1.72	1.47	1.52	2.16	2.35	2.26
Dividends per share		1.42	1.33	1.29	1.25	1.3/	1.0/	1.02	1.01
Price	high	43.0	36.2	26.0	27.7	31.7	41.0	53.1	59.0
	low	32.7	24.2	21.8	23.0	18.8	19.6	36.5	34.8

CONSERVATIVE GROWTH

C.R. Bard, Inc.

730 Central Avene ◻ Murray Hill, NJ 07974 ◻ (908) 277-8413 ◻ Direct dividend reinvestment plan available
◻ Web site: *www.crbard.com* ◻ Listed: NYSE ◻ Ticker symbol: BCR ◻ S&P rating: A ◻ Value Line Financial Rating: A

On December 7, 2007, C.R. Bard announced that it had signed an agreement to acquire the assets of the LifeStent® product family from Edwards Lifesciences

Corporation, headquartered in Irvine, California. Bard's Peripheral Vascular division, located in Tempe, Arizona, will assume marketing responsibility for the product.

Edwards Lifesciences recently completed the one-year follow-up of 206 patients in a randomized trial named Resilient. In the study, the LifeStent device was compared to standard percutaneous transluminal angioplasty (PTA) in the treatment of superficial femoral artery (SFA) and proximal popliteal stenotic disease. In one year, the PTA plus stenting arm of the study demonstrated clear superiority with 80 percent primary patency compared to 38 percent patency in the PTA only arm. These results were highly statistically significant (p less than 0.0001). Additionally, in the SFA, the LifeStent device was found to have a low fracture rate of only 2.9 percent at one year. Edwards Lifesciences has submitted a Pre-Market Approval application to the United States Food and Drug Administration (FDA) and is currently responding to the agency's follow-up questions. The LifeStent product family is currently available in the United States for biliary indications only.

CEO Timothy M. Ring commented, "The acquisition of the LifeStent product family is a significant strategic addition to our portfolio of noncoronary stent and stent graft products. Pending FDA approval, the LifeStent SFA product, the Flair™ Arteriovenous Access Stent Graft and E-Luminexx™ Iliac Stent will together give Bard one of the broadest product offerings for peripheral vascular stenting."

Company Profile

Founded in 1907 by Charles Russell Bard, the company initially sold urethral catheters and other urinary products. One of its first medical products was the silk urethral catheter imported from France.

Today, C.R. Bard markets a wide range of medical, surgical, diagnostic and patient-care devices. It does business worldwide with hospitals, individual health care profession-als, extended care facilities, and alternate site facilities. In general, Bard's products are intended to be used once then discarded.

The company offers a complete line of urological diagnosis and intervention products (about one-third of annual sales), including the well-known Foley catheters, procedure kits and trays, and related urine monitoring and collection systems; urethral stents; and specialty devices for incontinence.

Urology

The Foley catheter, introduced by Bard in 1934, remains one of the most important products in the urological field. Foley catheters are marketed in individual sterile packages, but, more importantly, they are included in sterile procedural kits and trays, a concept pioneered by Bard. The company is the market leader in Foley catheters, which currently are Bard's largest-selling urological product.

Newer products include the Infection Control Foley catheter, which reduces the rate of urinary tract infections; an innovative collagen implant and sling materials used to treat urinary incontinence, and brachytherapy services, devices, and radioactive seeds to treat prostate cancer.

Oncology

In the realm of oncology, C.R. Bard's products are designed for the detection and treatment of various types of cancer. Products include specialty access catheters, and ports; gastroenterological products (endoscopic accessories, percutaneous feeding devices and stents); biopsy devices; and a suturing system for gastroesophageal reflux disease. The company's chemotherapy products serve a well-established market in which Bard holds a major market position.

Vascular Products

The company's line of vascular diagnosis and intervention products includes peripheral angioplasty stents, catheters, guide wires, introducers and accessories, vena cava filters and biopsy devices; electro physiology products such as cardiac mapping and laboratory systems, and diagnostic and temporary pacing electrode catheters; fabrics and meshes; and implantable blood vessel replacements.

Bard's memotherm nitinol stent technology from the company's Angiomed subsidiary established the company as a major player in this peripheral growth market. With the acquisition of Impra, Inc. in 1996, Bard has the broadest line available of vascular grafts.

Surgical Products

Surgical specialties products include meshes for vessel and hernia repair; irrigation devices for orthopedic and laparoscopic procedures; and topical hemostatic devices.

The innovation of Bard's PerFix plug and Composix sheet has significantly improved the way hernias are repaired and has reduced the time needed for repair from hours to minutes. Hernia operations can now be done in an outpatient setting in about twenty minutes. What's more, the patient generally can return to normal activity with little or no recovery time.

The balance of sales (about 4 percent) fall into the "other" category.

International

Bard markets its products through twenty-two subsidiaries and a joint venture in ninety-two countries outside the United States. Principal markets are Japan, Canada, the United Kingdom and continental Europe.

Shortcomings to Bear in Mind

■ In the past ten years, the company's record of growth is excellent. But dividend increases have lagged far behind. On the other hand, earnings are more important than dividends for a growth company.

Reasons to Buy

■ On January 31, 2008, the company said that in 2007, income from continuing operations was $406.4 million and diluted earnings per share from continuing operations were $3.84, an increase of 29 percent and 31 percent, respectively, as compared to full year 2006 results. Adjusting for items that affect comparability between periods, full year 2007 income from continuing operations and related diluted earnings per share increased 15 percent and 16 percent, respectively, as compared to full year 2006 results.

CEO Timothy M. Ring said, "We are pleased to conclude our centennial year with solid fourth quarter and full year results. Our 2007 performance marks the fifth consecutive year that Bard has delivered adjusted EPS growth above the company's target of 14 percent. This success demonstrates the effectiveness of our strategy, and the ability of our organization to execute. We look forward to making 2008 another successful year for Bard and its shareholders."

■ On November 8, 2007, the company announced that it had received clearance from the United States Food and Drug Administration to market its Agento™ IC silver-coated endotracheal tube. The clearance includes claims for the reduction of microbiologically confirmed ventilator associated pneumonia (VAP). Management is currently evaluating the benefits of launching the Agento IC product in conjunction with the potential publication of the clinical trial results in a major peer-review medical journal. The product will be marketed by Bard's Medical division located in Covington, Georgia.

VAP is one of the most costly hospital acquired infections and is associated with high patient mortality and morbidity. It is especially prevalent in hospital intensive care units in cases where a ventilated patient has an endotracheal tube in place for more than twenty-four hours. The Agento IC product incorporates Bard's proprietary silver colloid polymer technology, which allows the tube to elute microbicidal levels of silver ions.

■ "A rapidly aging population and an increasing focus by Ob/Gyn physicians on the gynecological side of their practices are driving the growing demand for continence and pelvic floor reconstruction products," said Mr. Ring. "Bard's broad array of continence products, including surgical slings, pelvic floor reconstruction devices and urethral bulking products, compete in a $350 million global market growing nearly 20 percent annually. As clinicians seek ever less-invasive methods for surgery, we believe products such as our new Avaulta biosynthetic support system are well positioned to claim a growing share of this attractive market."

■ "In the United States, Bard's Fluency stent graft helps return the breadth of life to patients whose airways have become narrowed due to malignant tissue growth," said Mr. Ring. "In Europe, the product is also indicated for opening arteries in the vascular system. Sales of our Conquest and

Atlas percutaneous transluminal angioplasty balloon catheters (used to relieve partial or complete blockage in blood vessels) have grown at a compounded 42 percent rate over the last three years, securing our leadership position in the arteriovenous access and large vessel segments of the vascular patency market. The success of these products in 2005 helped drive sales in our endovascular business at a double-digit pace."

■ C.R. Bard has an acquisition strategy that targets small research or developing companies as well as larger established companies with market leadership positions. In addition to acquiring companies, Bard has expanded its business in the medical field by acquiring product lines, entering into licensing agreements and joint ventures, and making equity investments in companies with emerging technologies.

SECTOR: **Consumer Health Ccare**
BETA COEFFICIENT: **.65**
10-YEAR COMPOUND EARNINGS PER SHARE GROWTH: **16.6%**
10-YEAR COMPOUND DIVIDENDS PER SHARE GROWTH: **5.5%**

		2007	2006	2005	2004	2003	2002	2001	2000
Revenues (Mil)		2,202	1,985	1,771	1,656	1,433	1,274	1,181	1,099
Net Income (Mil)		406	352	312	263	204	177	143	125
Earnings per share		3.84	3.29	3.12	2.45	1.94	1.68	1.38	1.23
Dividends per share		0.60	0.56	0.50	0.47	0.45	0.43	0.42	0.41
Price	high	95.3	85.7	72.8	65.1	40.8	32.0	32.5	27.5
	low	76.6	59.9	60.8	40.1	27.0	22.0	20.4	17.5

CONSERVATIVE GROWTH

Becton, Dickinson and Company

1 Becton Drive □ Franklin Lakes, NJ 07417-1880 □ (201) 847-5453 □ Direct dividend reinvestment plan available □ Web site: *www.bd.com* □ Fiscal years end September 30 □ Ticker symbol: BDX □ S&P rating: A □ Value Line financial strength rating: A+

On January 2, 2008, BD Diagnostics, a segment of Becton, Dickinson and Company announced that it had received clearance from the U.S. Food and Drug Administration (FDA) for the BD GeneOhm™ StaphSR assay. This new assay is the first

test available to rapidly and simultaneously identify two deadly health care-associated infections (HAIs)—Staphylococcus aureus (SA) and methicillin-resistant Staphylococcus aureus (MRSA)—from patients with positive blood cultures. It will help enable physicians to implement the right treatment at the right time for patients with bloodstream infections, thereby transforming patient care and significantly reducing health care costs.

"The BD GeneOhm StaphSR assay provides a rapid, definitive identification of SA and MRSA from blood cultures. This allows for more appropriate isolation procedures and agent-specific antimicrobial therapy, resulting in reduced patient morbidity and mortality as well as an overall reduction in health care costs," said Thomas Davis, M.D., PhD, director of Clinical Microbiology, Wishard Memorial Hospital, Indianapolis, Indiana.

"The launch of the BD GeneOhm StaphSR assay in the United States further demonstrates BD's commitment to helping health care providers rapidly identify, prevent, and control HAIs," said Vince Forlenza, executive vice president of Becton, Dickinson. "It also illustrates our desire to provide customers with a complete menu of assays and tools to combat these potentially deadly infections."

The BD GeneOhm StaphSR assay provides results within two hours, directly from positive blood cultures. It is easy to perform and requires less technologist time than traditional microbiology algorithms, which can take two days to generate results. Studies have shown that providing physicians with critical microbiology information earlier will result in decreased mortality, length of stay and variable costs.

Currently, the BD GeneOhm™ MRSA assay rapidly identifies patients who are colonized with MRSA and allows infection control professionals to break the chain of MRSA transmission. Becton, Dickinson has recently submitted subsequent applications to the FDA for the BD GeneOhm StaphSR assay to add nasal swab and wound claims. The company is also developing rapid tests for the detection of two other organisms that cause severe HAIs. These tests will identify the vanA and vanB genes associated with vancomycin-resistant enterococci and the toxin gene associated with Clostridium difficile. These rapid assays will further complement the company's portfolio of HAI-related products.

Company Profile

Becton, Dickinson is a medical technology company that serves health care institutions, life science researchers, clinical laboratories, industry and the general public. BD manufactures and sells a broad range of medical supplies, devices, laboratory equipment and diagnostic products.

Becton, Dickinson focuses strategically on achieving growth in three worldwide business segments—BD Medical (formerly BD Medical Systems), BD Biosciences, and BD Diagnostics (formerly BD Clinical Laboratory Solutions). BD products are marketed in the United States both through independent distribution channels and directly to end-users. Outside the United States, BD products are marketed through independent distribution channels and sales representatives and, in some markets, directly to end-users.

BDX generates close to 50 percent of its revenues outside the United States. Worldwide demand for health care products and services continues to be strong, despite the ongoing focus on cost containment. The health care environment favors continued growth in medical delivery systems due to the growing awareness of the need to protect health care workers from accidental needlesticks and legislative/regulatory activity favoring conversion to safety-engineered devices.

BD Biosciences, one of the world's largest businesses serving the life sciences, provides research tools and reagents to study life—from normal processes to disease states—and accelerate the pace of biomedical discovery. Throughout the world, clinicians and researchers use BD Biosciences' tools to study genes, proteins, and cells to better understand disease, improve technologies for diagnosis and disease management, and facilitate the discovery and development of novel therapeutics.

BD Diagnostics (formerly BD Clinical Laboratory Solutions) offers system solutions for collecting, identifying and transporting specimens, as well as advanced instrumentation for quickly and accurately analyzing specimens. The business also provides services that focus on customers' process flow, supply chain management, and training and education.

BD Medical holds leadership positions in hypodermic needles and syringes, infusion therapy devices, insulin injection systems and prefillable drug-delivery systems for pharmaceutical companies. It offers the industry's broadest, deepest line of safety-engineered sharps products, as well as surgical and regional anesthesia, Ophthalmology, critical care and sharps disposal products.

BDX is dedicated to producing solutions—and the best solution of all is helping all people live healthy lives. Its vision is to become a great company, defined by great performance, great contributions made to society, and being a great place to work.

Shortcomings to Bear in Mind

■ Nearly half of the company's sales come from abroad. This exposes Becton, Dickinson to the risks associated with foreign currency rates, which could create increased volatility in reported earnings. On the other hand, BDX has done a good job of managing foreign currency exposure, and the impact on earnings has typically been limited to only 1 or 2 percent.

Reasons to buy

■ "This timely, top-quality issue offers worthwhile three-to-five-year price appreciation potential," said Erik A. Antonson, writing for *Value Line Investment Survey* on February 29, 2008. "Solid revenue growth, steady margin expansion, and share buybacks should help drive earnings growth

over the pull to 2011-2013. BD also keeps a relatively clean balance sheet, and generates a sizable amount of cash, which should comfort conservative investors."

■ On March 19, 2008, Standard & Poor's *The Outlook* rated BDX a STRONG BUY. Its analyst said, "We think BDX will continue to benefit from recovering end user demand in the life sciences industry, momentum in the diagnostics and diabetes management areas, and exposure to cancer diagnostics following the December purchase of TriPath."

■ "The company's BioSciences and Diagnostics segments are seeing strong demand for their products," said David H. Toung, an analyst with Argus Research Company. "Moreover, management provided upbeat comments about the future contributions from GeneOhm and TriPath, two recent acquisitions." On January 28, 2008, Argus rated Becton, Dickinson a BUY.

■ On August 7, 2007 Becton, Dickinson, a leading global medical technology company, announced that it had named Scott P. Bruder, MD, PhD, as the company's senior vice president and chief technology officer.

In this new position, Dr. Bruder will provide R&D, strategy and development leadership to BD as it focuses on advancing innovation in medical devices, diagnostics and biosciences. He will oversee the integration and alignment of the company's business and product technology planning with its R&D and business development activities.

■ The company's use of computer-aided design and manufacturing technology enables Becton to bring quality products to market faster and at a lower cost. One such technology is stereo lithography, which uses a laser system to quickly create a three-dimensional physical object from a computer-aided design model. Engineers can use this extremely accurate model as a prototype, improving both the quality of the product design and the speed of the product development process.

Becton, Dickinson has the technology to help reduce the medical errors that have received attention of late. A U.S. government scientific panel found that about 75,000 hospital patients die each year from medical mistakes. Yet, only 9 percent of the facilities have invested in equipment to address the problem.

For its part, BDX is offering two hand-held devices, based on 3Com's Palm Computing technology. One tracks drugs from the initial order through their administration. The other serves a similar purpose for specimen collection, testing and patient file management.

■ Domestic sales of insulin needles and syringes are expected to increase in the high-single digits during the next few years, fueled by the estimated five percent annual growth in the number of Americans suffering from diabetes, plus the trend toward multiple insulin injections. Recent scientific studies have shown that the use of multiple daily injections of insulin reduces the severity of the disease's longer-term deleterious effects.

Becton, Dickinson, which accounts for about 90 percent of the domestic insulin syringe market, has entered into an arrangement with Eli Lilly, the largest domestic producer of insulin products, and Boehringer Mannheim, a major manufacturer of glucose monitoring devices, to provide information to diabetics regarding the best manner in which to control their disease. Over time, this program should accelerate the trend toward multiple daily insulin injections.

The company is also reviewing a number of noninvasive techniques to monitor glucose levels in diabetics. This device could reach the market before the end of the decade and further enhance the company's overall position in the diabetic sector.

SECTOR: **Health Care**
BETA COEFFICIENT: **.75**
10-YEAR COMPOUND EARNINGS PER SHARE GROWTH: **12.2%**
10-YEAR COMPOUND DIVIDENDS PER SHARE GROWTH: **14.2%**

	2007	2006	2005	2004	2003	2002	2001	2000
Revenues (Mil)	6,560	5,835	5,415	4,935	4,528	4,033	3,746	3,618
Net Income (Mil)	978	841	692	582	547	480	402	393
Earnings per share	3.84	3.28	2.66	2.21	2.07	1.79	1.63	1.49
Dividends per share	0.98	0.86	0.72	0.60	0.40	0.39	0.38	0.37
Price high	85.9	74.2	61.2	58.2	41.8	38.6	39.3	35.3
low	69.3	58.1	49.7	40.2	28.8	24.7	30.0	21.8

AGGRESSIVE GROWTH

The Boeing Company

100 North Riverside ❑ Chicago, IL 60606 ❑ (312) 544-2140 ❑ Dividend reinvestment plan available ❑ Web site: *www.boeing.com* ❑ Ticker symbol: BA ❑ Listed: NYSE ❑ S&P rating: B+ ❑ Value Line financial strength rating: A++

On November 7, 2007, Boeing said that Southeast Asia airlines will need 1,930 airplanes worth $290 billion over the next twenty years. Strong demand for new airplanes will lead to a world fleet with significantly improved environmental performance, according to The Boeing Company's updated annual forecast for the commercial airplane market.

Air travel within Southeast Asia will grow 6 percent during this period, above the world average growth of 5 percent—compared to China's 8.8 percent forecasted domestic growth rate.

Deliveries to airlines in Southeast Asia will represent about 10 percent of the deliveries measured by dollar value worldwide between 2006 and 2026.

During the next twenty years, deliveries of new airplanes in Southeast Asia will consist of:

- 6 percent regional jets—less than ninety seats
- 45 percent single-aisle airplanes—ninety seats and above
- 38 percent twin-aisle airplanes—200–400 seats, tri-class, and
- 11 percent airplanes 747-size or larger—more than 400 seats, tri-class

Combined with the retained fleet and used airplane acquisitions, these new deliveries will more than double and result in a Southeast Asia commercial airplane fleet of 2,310 airplanes by 2026.

The Boeing Southeast Asia Current Market Outlook projects that single-aisle and twin-aisle airplanes in the 100- to 400-seat categories will account for 83 percent of the regional growth in air travel during the next twenty years.

The Boeing product strategy centers on this growth market, offering a family of airplanes that allows customers to maximize their efficiency, increase profitability and provide the frequency choices passengers want.

"Boeing understands aviation better than anyone else and will continue to provide the right products and solutions for Southeast Asia to sustain growth," said Randy Tinseth, vice president, marketing, Boeing Commercial Airplanes. "Taiwan's carriers operate one of the youngest and most efficient fleets in the world."

Worldwide, Boeing forecasts a $2.8 trillion market for new commercial airplanes during the next twenty years and projects a need for approximately 28,600 new commercial airplanes (passenger and freighter),

doubling the world fleet by 2026. The vast majority of these new airplanes will be in the single-aisle (ninety seats and above) and twin-aisle (200–400 seats) categories. The Boeing market forecast is widely regarded as the most comprehensive and respected analysis of the commercial aviation market.

Company Profile

With a heritage that mirrors the first 100 years of flight, The Boeing Company provides products and services to customers in 145 countries. Boeing has been the premier manufacturer of commercial jetliners for more than forty years and is a global market leader in military aircraft, satellites, missile defense, human space flight, and launch systems and services.

Boeing continues to expand its product line and develop new technologies to meet customer needs. Creating new models for its family of commercial airplanes; developing, producing, supporting, and modifying aircraft for the U.S. military; building launch vehicles capable of lifting more than fourteen tons into orbit; and improving communications for people around the world through an advanced network of satellites, Boeing is carrying forward a long tradition of technical excellence and innovation.

Boeing is organized into four major business units: Boeing Capital Corporation, Boeing Commercial Airplanes, Connexion by Boeing℠, and Boeing Integrated Defense Systems. Supporting these units is the Boeing Shared Services Group, which contributes common services and efficient infrastructure services that enable the company's business units to concentrate on profitable growth. In addition, Phantom Works provides advanced research and development, including advanced concepts for air traffic management. Phantom Works partners with the company's business units to identify technology needs and address them with innovative and affordable solutions.

Boeing has been the premier manufacturer of commercial jetliners for more than forty years. With the McDonnell Douglas merger in 1997, Boeing's legacy of leadership in commercial jets now is joined with the lineage of Douglas airplanes, giving the combined company a seventy-year heritage of leadership in commercial aviation. Today, the main commercial products consist of the 717, 737, 747, 767, and 777 families of airplanes, and the Boeing Business Jet. New product development efforts are focused on the Boeing 7E7, a super-efficient airplane that is expected to be in service in 2008. The company has nearly 13,000 commercial jetliners in service worldwide, which is roughly 75 percent of the world fleet. And through Boeing Commercial Aviation Services, the company provides unsurpassed, round-the-clock technical support to help operators maintain their airplanes in peak operating condition; further, through Commercial Aviation Services, Boeing offers a full range of world-class engineering, modification, logistics and information services to its global customer base, which includes the world's passenger and cargo airlines as well as maintenance, repair and overhaul facilities. Boeing also trains maintenance and flight crews in the 100-seat-and-above airliner market through Alteon, the world's largest and most comprehensive provider of airline training.

Shortcomings to Bear in Mind

- On March 1, 2008, *Washington Post* writer Dana Hedgpeth said, "The Pentagon yesterday passed over Boeing's bid for a $40 billion contract to build a fleet of refueling tankers for the Air Force, instead choosing a team that includes Boeing's European rival Airbus.

"The team of Northrop Grumman and European Aeronautic Defence and Space (EADS), Airbus's parent company, will build an initial fleet of 179 tankers. The contract to supply the tankers had initially been awarded to Boeing, but was withdrawn in 2004 over a procurement scandal that resulted in officials from Boeing and the Air Force being sent to prison."

Reasons to Buy

- On December 28, 2007, "Boeing said that it finalized a deal with British Airways, notching 790 orders for its long-awaited 787 Dreamliner plane during the last three years," according to an article by the Associated Press.

"British Airways' order for 24 Dreamliners gives the plane one of the industry's most successful launches ever—even though the airliner has yet to take flight.

"The Chicago-based aerospace company expects to fly the first 787 around the end of the first quarter of 2008 and begin deliveries in late November or December. It expects to deliver 109 airplanes in 2009.

"The 787, Boeing's first newly designed jet since the 777 began service in 1995, will be the world's first large commercial airplane made mostly of light, durable and less-corrosive carbon-fiber composites. Boeing says its new plane will be cheaper to maintain and will offer better fuel efficiency and more passenger comforts than planes flying today."

- On September 24, 2007, Christopher Leonard, an Associated Press business writer, said, "Boeing Co. delivered the first Super Hornet EA-18G aircraft to the U.S. Navy on Monday as part of a $9.2 billion contract.

"Instead of carrying missiles or cannons, the so-called Super Hornet 'Growler' is equipped with radar-jamming equipment and other gear to knock out a wide array of electronic devices. The aircraft will fly with teams of conventional bombers and help disrupt enemy air defenses.

"'It's essential to keep them guessing where you're coming from,' said Navy Rear Adm. Kenneth Floyd.

"The Navy will buy three Growlers to test during 2008. The aircraft are scheduled to be deployed in 2010, and the Navy has agreed to buy a total of eighty-five by 2013—though the timing of the contract is flexible, according to Mike Gibbons, Boeing's program manager for the Growler project."

■ On February 22, 2008, Boeing received full acceptance of its SBInet Project 28 (P28) border security prototype from U.S. Customs and Border Protection (CBP).

A demonstration of the SBInet security solution, P28 network cameras, radars, sensors and communications took place along twenty-eight miles of the U.S.-Mexico border near Sasabe, Arizona. Developed as a proof-of-concept of Boeing's overall SBInet technology solution, P28 serves as a test and evaluation system in an operational environment.

Using P28 technology, Border Patrol agents apprehended more than 2,000 illegal immigrants during initial operations testing between September 2007 and February 2008. In the coming months, CBP will conduct operational and technical tests of P28.

"We're very happy the customer has accepted P28," said Jack Chenevey, Boeing SBInet program manager. "While we've learned a lot from the integration work we've completed, the information we'll capture from actual frontline field use of the system is invaluable to our systems engi-neering and design efforts for future SBInet technology deployments."

By the end of the year, Boeing will replace P28 mobile surveillance towers as part of the larger Tucson Sector deployment with permanent towers equipped with camera, radar and communications technology that incorporate feedback from operational tests.

■ On January 31, 2008, Boeing announced that it had been awarded a $73.7 million U.S. Navy contract to design and develop the Harpoon Block III missile, a next-generation weapon system that will enhance naval surface warfare capabilities.

The system design and development (SDD) contract will result in a kit upgrade program for existing Navy weapons that will return 800 enhanced surface- and air-launch Harpoon missiles and fifty ship-launch systems to the service's inventory.

"The start of SDD is a big milestone for the Harpoon program and is the first major development for the U.S. Navy on Harpoon for many years," said Jim Young Jr., Boeing Harpoon Block III program manager. "Harpoon Block III will provide the warfighter with a capable, near-term solution to over-the-horizon, surface warfare threats."

SECTOR: Industrials
BETA COEFFICIENT: 1.05
10-YEAR COMPOUND EARNINGS PER SHARE GROWTH: 23.7%
10-YEAR COMPOUND DIVIDENDS PER SHARE GROWTH: 9.6%

		2007	2006	2005	2004	2003	2002	2001	2000
Revenues (Mil)		66,387	61,530	53,621	52,457	50,485	54,069	58,198	51,321
Net Income (Mil)		4,074	3,014	2,572	1,872	809	2,275	2,316	2,511
Earnings per share		5.28	3.62	2.39	2.30	1.00	2.82	2.79	2.84
Dividends per share		1.40	1.20	1.05	0.77	0.68	0.68	0.68	0.59
Price	high	107.8	92.0	72.4	55.5	43.4	51.1	69.9	70.9
	low	84.6	65.9	49.5	38.0	24.7	28.5	27.6	32.0

Campbell Soup Company

1 Campbell Place ❑ Camden, NJ 08103-1799 ❑ (856) 342-6428 ❑ Dividend reinvestment plan available ❑ Fiscal years end July 31 ❑ Web site: *www.campbellsoupcompany.com* ❑ Ticker symbol: CPB ❑ Listed: NYSE ❑ S&P rating: B+ ❑ Value Line financial strength rating: B++

In 2007, Campbell Soup Company, the world's largest soup company, outlined its entry strategy and product plans for Russia and China, the world's two largest soup consumption markets.

Since 2001, Campbell has revitalized its core North American soup business and streamlined its international operations through the sale of its businesses in the United Kingdom and Ireland. Campbell is now expanding its global focus to include the two soup markets with the highest growth potential. Soup consumption in Russia and China far exceeds that of the United States, where there are approximately 14 billion soup servings consumed per year. In Russia, there are about 32 billion soup servings annually, some 225 servings per capita, and in China, annual soup servings are approximately 320 billion, more than 241 servings per capita, with nearly all of it in both countries being homemade.

Campbell's expansion into Russia and China supports two of the company's five key strategies: to expand the company's icon brands within the simple meals and baked snacks categories; and to make its products more broadly available in existing and new markets.

CEO Douglas R. Conant said, "The soup markets of China and Russia represent an extraordinary opportunity for Campbell. Soup is consumed in huge amounts in these countries, and Campbell is exceptionally qualified to lead the soup commercialization activity due to our unrivaled understanding of consumers' soup consumption behavior, innovative technology capabilities, supply chain excellence, and our superior marketing prowess within the simple meals category. We call this the Campbell advantage.

"We have invested the time and resources to understand each market, partnered with strong local companies, and developed delicious products that we believe will appeal to the unique tastes of the people in each country," Mr. Conant continued. "Our timing is right. Income levels are rising in both countries, and consumers are increasingly time pressed and seeking more convenient ways to prepare nourishing meals while maintaining their central role in family meal preparation. Campbell's new products can play a key role in minimizing the time it takes to prepare homemade soup, a staple of peoples' diets in both countries."

Campbell conducted extensive research and development in both markets and studied consumers' soup preparation practices and eating habits, including more than 10,000 consumer interviews and thousands of household tests. The company plans to introduce a variety of delicious broths designed to serve as a base for the soups and other meals Russian and Chinese consumers prepare at home. These broths are customized for the tastes, trends, and eating habits of consumers in each country.

"During our immersion in the Russian and Chinese markets, we recognized that in order to convert homemade behavior, we would have to offer products that enabled the preparer to use them as foundations for their favorite recipes," said Larry McWilliams, president, Campbell International.

Company Profile

"Soup lovers across America consume more than 10 billion bowls of soup each year—and by a wide margin, their favorite soups are Campbell's condensed soups in the familiar red and white can," said a company spokesman in fiscal 2007. "Our two most popular Campbell's soups are chicken noodle and tomato. These are among the top ten food items sold in grocery stores. Cooking with soup is also extremely popular in the U.S., where one out of every ten homemade dinners is made with a can of Campbell's condensed soup. In addition to our Campbell's condensed brand, Campbell is also known for many other soup brands, including our two popular ready-to-serve varieties Campbell's Chunky and Campbell's Select, which feature easy-open pop-top lids for greater convenience. These two varieties are also offered in microwavable bowls. For individuals with special dietary requirements, Campbell's Healthy Request is lower in sodium, fat, and cholesterol, and contains no MSG. Other U.S. Soup offerings include the Swanson broths and Campbell's Soup At Hand microwavable soups.

"Each year, nearly 90 percent of American households purchase Campbell's soups and on average, consumers stock eleven cans of Campbell's soup in their pantries at all times. With a 69 percent share of the U.S. wet soup market, Campbell sells almost 3 billion cans of soup every year. Away from home, soup consumption is on the rise, with half of U.S. food dollars spent on food consumed outside the home. Today, Campbell has several thousand self-service, branded kettles in high traffic venues such as college, healthcare, and business cafeterias across the country. In the restaurant marketplace, co-branding with Campbell's is growing.

Beyond Soup

"Campbell Soup Company owns some of the world's most powerful sauce, beverage, and indulgent snack brands, including Prego, Pace, V8, SpaghettiOs, Pepperidge Farm, and Godiva. Each of these brands is number one or two in its segment. Since its introduction over two decades ago, Prego pasta sauce has become a popular part of Italian meals prepared in American homes. Created more than fifty years ago, Pace Mexican sauces have built unwavering loyalty with consumers in western U.S. markets. V8 vegetable juice, introduced almost seventy years ago, remains on trend for today's health conscious consumers.

"Pepperidge Farm is consistently ranked by consumers among the top two percent of brands worldwide in brand equity. Pepperidge Farm has almost 5,000 employees and 3,000 independent distributors. Pepperidge Farm products are available nationwide and in forty countries around the world. There are eight Pepperidge Farm production sites throughout the United States, which produce indulgent cookies and treats, fresh breads, fun snacks, and meal solutions. Pepperidge Farm has been committed to quality in all of its products for nearly seventy years.

"Godiva is recognized around the world as the leader in fine chocolates. From its famous truffles to its European style biscuits, and gourmet coffees, Godiva Chocolatier has been dedicated to excellence and innovation in the Belgian tradition for nearly eighty years."

Shortcomings to Bear in Mind

■ Campbell Soup has a dismal record of growth for both earnings and dividends. However, new management is having a decided impact on reviving the company.

Reasons to Buy

■ On December 20, 2007, Campbell Soup announced it had entered into an agreement to sell its Godiva Chocolatier business for $850 million to Yildiz Holding A.S., which is the owner of the Ülker Group, a diversified food company based in Istanbul, Turkey. Godiva has annual sales of approximately $500 million.

CEO Douglas R. Conant said, "We are very pleased with the value we obtained for Godiva. The sale price reflects the strength of the Godiva business. Godiva is one of the world's leading premium chocolate businesses and is an excellent strategic fit within Ülker's portfolio. The agreement allows Ülker to expand and diversify its portfolio with an elite, global luxury brand and enables Campbell to sharpen our strategic focus on simple meals, anchored by soup, baked snacks, and vegetable-based beverages. I truly believe we have reached an agreement that benefits all parties—Campbell, Ülker, and Godiva and its employees."

■ "We took a major step in fiscal 2007 as part of our strategy to align with consumer wellness needs, introducing thirty-two new or reformulated Campbell's lower-sodium soups," said Mr. Conant in fiscal 2008. "We also added seventeen new or reformulated Campbell's lower-sodium products to be launched for the 2008 soup season. In Canada, we lowered the sodium in many of our Campbell's soups in fiscal 2007."

Mr. Conant also said, "In June 2007, we entered into an agreement with Coca-Cola North America and Coca-Cola Enterprises Inc. for distribution of our refrigerated single-serve beverages in the United States and Canada through the Coca-Cola bottler network. Beginning in fiscal 2008, this will enhance our presence in convenience stores, which account for the majority of single-serve beverage sales.

"In Baked Snacks, Pepperidge Farm continued its strong performance. Pepperidge Farm Goldfish snack crackers represented an estimated 25 percent of all category growth for crackers in fiscal 2007 on the strength of the brand's wholesome positioning, increased advertising investment, and new points of distribution. Pepperidge Farm breads continued to grow significantly, with additional offerings in the whole grain segments."

■ On February 18, 2008, Campbell Soup announced a major new step in its innovative sodium reduction efforts by adding thirty-six reformulated ready-to-serve varieties under the name "Campbell's Select Harvest" soups to its industry-leading portfolio of lower sodium products and reformulating its twelve condensed kids favorite soups to meet the government criteria for "healthy" foods.

Campbell will reduce the sodium in these forty-eight soups to the heart-healthy level of 480 milligrams of sodium per serving. This sodium reduction effort marks the next phase in the company's ongoing commitment to reduce sodium across its portfolio and builds upon previous new and reformulated lower sodium products introduced over the last two years.

With the introduction of these new soups in the fall of 2008, Campbell's portfolio of low and reduced sodium soups will include more than eighty-five varieties across the condensed, ready-to-serve and microwavable platforms. Currently, Campbell's low and reduced sodium soups and broth in total are now a $650 million business at retail, up from $100 million in 2003.

SECTOR: **Consumer Staples**
BETA COEFFICIENT: **.85**
10-YEAR COMPOUND EARNINGS PER SHARE GROWTH: **.53%**
10-YEAR COMPOUND DIVIDENDS PER SHARE GROWTH: **.90%**

		2007	2006	2005	2004	2003	2002	2001	2000
Revenues (Mil)		7,867	7,343	7,548	7,109	6,678	6,133	6,664	6,287
Net Income (Mil)		771	681	707	652	626	625	649	714
Earnings per share		1.95	1.66	1.71	1.58	1.52	1.28	1.55	1.65
Dividends per share		0.82	0.74	0.69	0.64	0.63	0.63	0.90	0.90
Price	high	42.7	40.0	31.6	30.5	27.9	30.0	35.4	37.5
	low	34.2	28.9	27.3	25.0	20.0	19.7	25.5	23.8

Canadian National Railway Company

935 de la Gauchetiere Street West ❑ Montreal, Quebec, Canada H3B 2M9 ❑ (514) 399-0052 ❑ Dividend reinvestment plan not available ❑ Web site: *www.cn.ca* ❑ Ticker symbol: CNI ❑ Listed: NYSE ❑ S&P rating: A ❑ Value Line financial strength rating: B++

"Ten years ago, CN set out with a goal that many thought grandiose: to become North America's best railroad," said CEO E. Hunter Harrison in 2007. "Today, many people would agree that we've achieved that goal: service reliability that consistently ranks in the top of independent surveys; an operating ratio that leads the industry by a wide margin; a strong culture of innovation developed over the years, from our precision railroading model to our unique hourly labor agreements; solid, consistent, profitable performance through a number of ups and downs in the economy.

"We've proven a lot, no question. But, as I say every year, there's much more to prove. We continue to get better at leveraging our business model to improve customer service, safety performance and shareholder value. But that's a given. That's always the goal.

"Now we're setting our sights on new directions for CN. Something we can strive for over the next decade. North America's best railroad, why stop there? Why not strive to become one of the world's best transportation companies?

"We're a company that differentiates itself from others by continuously defining new horizons for profitable growth. A good example is CN WorldWide, our international freight forwarding service subsidiary, launched in Europe two years ago to leverage CN's extensive North American route knowledge for trans-Atlantic shippers. In October 2006, CN WorldWide started operations in China with offices in Shanghai, Beijing and Shenzhen. While it's still early in the development process, CN WorldWide has begun to prove that it can deliver an excellent product by applying the CN precision approach beyond rail."

Company Profile

Canadian National Railway, which was controlled by the Canadian government until 1995, operates the largest Canadian railroad. The acquisition of Illinois Central in 1999 enables CNI to cross the continent both east-west and north-south, linking customers in Canada, the United States, and Mexico.

Since late 1998, the company has offered scheduled train service. Railroads typically hold trains until enough cars accumulate. With a time schedule, CNI runs shorter trains, but has realized greater operating efficiency and timeliness, with service peaks and valleys smoothed out. Its operating ratio is among the best in the industry.

Canadian National Railway is a leader in the North American rail industry. Following its acquisition of Illinois Central in 1999, WC in 2001 and GLT in 2004, as well as its partnership agreement with BC Rail in 2004, CNI provides shippers with more options and greater reach in the rapidly expanding market for north-south trade.

CNI has one of the best operating ratios in this industry and is committed to moving more freight, more quickly and with fewer assets.

Canadian National is the only railroad that crosses the continent east-west and north-south, serving ports on the Atlantic, Pacific and Gulf coasts while linking customers to all three NAFTA nations.

CNI is a more diverse railroad. The company's revenues derive from the movement of a diversified and balanced portfolio of goods, including petroleum and chemicals, grain and fertilizers, coal, metals and minerals, forest products, intermodal and automotive.

Quick Facts about Canadian National Railway

■ Operates the largest rail network in Canada and the only transcontinental network in North America. The company operates in eight Canadian provinces and sixteen U.S. states.

■ Spans Canada and mid-America from the Atlantic and Pacific oceans to the Gulf of Mexico, serving the ports of Vancouver, Prince Rupert, B.C., Montreal, Halifax, New Orleans, and Mobile, Alabama, and the key cities of Toronto, Buffalo, Chicago, Detroit, Duluth, Minnesots/Superior, Wisconsin, Green Bay, Wisconsin, Minneapolis/St. Paul, Memphis, St. Louis, Jackson, Mississippi, with connections to all points in North America.

■ Has the shortest route from the Atlantic coast to the U.S. Midwest through the St. Clair Tunnel between Sarnia, Ontario, and Port Huron, Michigan.

■ Originates approximately 85 percent of traffic, allowing the company to capitalize on service advantages, efficient asset utilization and negotiations with other carriers on revenue division arrangements.

Shortcomings to Bear in Mind

■ Although the company has had an impressive record of growth in recent years, it must be remembered that railroads—like chemical companies, car companies, home builders, and paper companies—are very cyclical and depend on the health of the economy.

Reasons to Buy

■ In 2008, Mr. Harrison had this comment on results of last year: "CN faced strong headwinds in 2007, but we turned in a solid performance for both the fourth quarter and the year. The major challenges were weak housing markets in the United States, the continuing strength of the Canadian dollar that affected our U.S. dollar-denominated revenues, a strike in the first quarter, and a number of weather-related issues, particularly in western Canada.

"During the final quarter of 2007, four of our commodity groups—intermodal, petroleum and chemicals, metals and minerals, and coal—generated increased revenues. However, tough market conditions reduced forest products revenues by 19 percent. Operating expenses declined three percent in the quarter, allowing the company to deliver an operating ratio of 62.1 percent."

■ "Intermodal business should be a bright spot for Canadian National this year," said Craig Sirois, an analyst with *Value Line Investment Survey*, on March 7, 2008. "The railway began operations last September out of the new Port of Prince Rupert container terminal, and service levels have been consistently on target."

■ "Transportation stocks have fared well in recent years as investors have gone long on global trade," said Matthew Craft, writing for *Forbes* magazine on May 5, 2008. "Warren Buffett also helped raise the profile of rail stocks by becoming the top investor in Burlington Northern Santa Fe. Even so, Canadian National stands out. It boasts the industry's highest net profit margin, at 27 percent. It also has shorter-term freight contracts than its peers, which gives it flexibility in times when prices are rising, like now, to hike rates, points out Keith Schoonmaker, an analyst at Morningstar in Chicago."

■ Canadian National has a strong stake in intermodal transportation, which involves a combination of shipping companies, typically utilizing a railroad, as well as a trucking company or a seagoing vessel. For instance, a shipment of goods that starts out from Asia on a ship could be loaded on to a railroad flatcar—still in its original container—for several hundred miles and then be transferred to a trucking company for its final destination.

Intermodal is by far the company's most complex business, with a high degree of randomness, uneven flow of traffic and numerous points in the chain for delays to occur. CNI launched Intermodal Excellence, called IMX, in 2003 to smooth traffic flows, increase speed and reliability, as well as to improve asset utilization and margins.

At the heart of IMX is the application of scheduled railroading's discipline and precision to intermodal transportation. IMX requires shippers to make reservations to get on trains, while pricing encourages the shift to traffic to off-peak days. This, along with required gate reservations at the company's largest terminals, enables Canadian National to align traffic with equipment and gate capacity and improve speed and asset utilization. Even though implementation throughout the entire CNI system was not complete until year end, the company had already seen improvements in profit margins. What's more, customers were aware of the benefits: better speed and reliability of service.

A Passion for Seeing Things Differently

"It's been a tradition throughout CN's history as a publicly held corporation to look beyond the conventions of traditional railroading to drive excellence. Those of you familiar with CN's track record know that is our central theme.

"Since that moment in the Memphis yard long ago, getting the absolute maximum out of rail assets has been a major focus of mine, and it's a passion here at CN. It's one of the five guiding principles of successful railroading.

- The first is providing good service—consistently doing what you say you'll do.
- The second is controlling your costs.
- The third is asset utilization.
- The fourth is to make sure to operate safely.
- The fifth is developing your people.

"I've always believed if I focus 90 percent of my time as a leader on the fifth principle, the other four will follow naturally."

On December 24, 2007, CN announced that it would acquire the Athabasca Northern Railway Ltd. (ANY) to preserve a critical rail link to the oil sands region of northern Alberta.

CN's purchase and rail-line rehabilitation plan are premised on long-term traffic volume guarantees that the company has negotiated with shippers Suncor Energy Inc., OPTI Canada Inc., and Nexen Inc.

Mr. Harrison said, "CN's investment and partnership agreements with key shippers will allow the parties to maintain important rail service to Lynton, Alberta, a point near Fort McMurray, home of existing and future oil sands development.

SECTOR: **Industrials**
BETA COEFFICIENT: **1.10**
10-YEAR COMPOUND EARNINGS PER SHARE GROWTH: **21%**
10-YEAR COMPOUND DIVIDENDS PER SHARE GROWTH: **23.7%**

		2007	2006	2005	2004	2003	2002	2001	2000
Revenues (Mil)		7,897	7,716	7,240	6,548	4,531	3,874	3,555	3,637
Net Income (Mil)		2,158	2,087	1,556	1,258	782	667	615	590
Earnings per share		4.25	3.91	2.77	2.17	1.35	1.11	1.03	0.98
Dividends per share		0.92	0.59	0.43	0.32	0.26	0.18	0.17	0.16
Price	high	58.5	51.2	41.4	31.0	21.3	17.9	16.5	11.0
	low	41.6	38.6	27.7	18.3	13.2	12.0	9.6	7.5

Carnival Corporation & PLC

3655 N.W. 87ᵗʰ Avenue □ Miami, FL 33178-2428 □ (305) 406-4832 □ Dividend reinvestment plan
available □ Fiscal years end November 30 □ Web site: *www.carnivalcorp.com*
□ Listed: NYSE □ Ticker symbol: CCL □ S&P rating: A+ □ Value Line financial strength rating: B+

On December 13, 2007, Carnival Corporation & plc ordered two 71,000-ton cruise ships for its AIDA Cruises brand, which caters exclusively to the German-speaking market. These two newbuilds mark six new ships that the German cruise operator has ordered in just the past three years.

The 2,174-passenger vessels, which will be built at Germany's Meyer Werft shipyard at an all-in cost of €380 million and €385 million, are scheduled to enter service in April 2011 and May 2012, respectively.

Additionally, the company announced that it has contracted with Meyer Werft to increase the size of the fourth vessel in the series, set to debut in April 2010, to 71,000 tons with a passenger capacity of 2,174, making it a sister to the two ships ordered today. The all-in cost for that vessel has been increased from €335 million to €350 million.

All of these vessels will operate under AIDA Cruises' informal "club resort" cruise concept which is marketed exclusively to German-speaking clientele and offers a product aimed at younger, more active guests who enjoy a host of on-board amenities and facilities.

"With the interest in cruise vacations among Europeans continuing to grow significantly, we are committed to investing in our European brands," said CEO Micky Arison. "The addition of these 71,000-ton 'club resort' newbuilds and the increase in capacity for the fourth in the series will help to ensure that we have adequate capacity to meet growing demand, while further reinforcing AIDA's position as the leader in the German cruise industry."

Company Profile

Carnival Corporation & plc is the largest cruise vacation group in the world, with a portfolio of cruise brands in North America, Europe and Australia, comprised of Carnival Cruise Lines, Holland America Line, Princess Cruises, Seabourn Cruise Line, Windstar Cruises, AIDA Cruises, Costa Cruises, Cunard Line, Ocean Village, P&O Cruises, Swan Hellenic, and P&O Cruises Australia.

Together, these brands operate eighty-one ships totaling approximately 144,000 lower berths with eighteen new ships scheduled to enter service between March 2007 and spring 2010. Carnival Corporation & plc also operates the leading tour companies in Alaska and the Canadian Yukon, Holland America Tours, and Princess Tours. Traded on both the New York and London stock exchanges, Carnival Corporation & plc is the only group in the world to be included in both the S&P 500 and the FTSE 100 indices.

Carnival Corporation and its British affiliate is a global cruise company with a portfolio of twelve distinct brands, comprised of the leading cruise operators in North America, Europe and Australia. Included in this group are: Carnival Cruise Lines (twenty ships), Holland America Line (thirteen), Princess Cruises (fourteen), AIDA (four), Costa Cruises (ten), Cunard Line (three), P&O Cruises (four), Windstar Cruises (three), Seabourn Cruise Line (three), Ocean Village (one), Swan Hellenic (one). All told, these seventy-nine vessels have more than 137,000 lower berths.

The company has sixteen new ships scheduled for delivery between February 2006 and the fall of 2009.

Carnival also operates two tour companies, which include seventeen hotels or lodges in Alaska and the Canadian Yukon, more than 500 motor coaches, and twenty domed rail cars, and two-day boats.

Some Background

Although the name Carnival Corporation didn't come into existence until 1993, the foundation for the company was laid when its flagship brand, Carnival Cruise Lines, was formed in 1972 by cruise industry pioneer, the late Ted Arison.

After achieving its position as the world's most popular cruise line, Carnival made an initial public offering of 20 percent of its common stock in 1987, which provided the influx of capital that enabled the company to begin expanding through acquisitions.

Over a fourteen-year span, Carnival acquired representation in virtually every market segment of the cruise industry, including premium operator Holland America Line in 1989 (the purchase also included niche cruise line Windstar Cruises and Alaskan/Canadian tour operator Holland America tours); luxury brand Seabourn Cruise Line in 1992; contemporary operator Costa Cruises, Europe's leading cruise company, in 1997; and premium/luxury Cunard Line in 1998, which built the world's largest ocean liner, the 150,000-ton *Queen Mary 2*.

On April 17, 2003, agreements were finalized to combine Carnival Corporation with P&O Princess Cruises, plc, creating a global vacation leader with twelve brands, making it one of the largest leisure travel companies in the world.

Shortcomings to Bear in Mind

■ "We are maintaining our HOLD rating on Carnival Corp.," said Paul Kleinschmidt, writing for Argus Research Company on March 19, 2008. "The improvement in the operating environment in the Caribbean is being offset by skyrocketing fuel prices. It now appears certain average bunker prices will be higher this year than last." The analyst also said, "We remain bullish on Carnival for the long term, given its leading position in an industry that should benefit from increased demand for cruise vacations among affluent baby boomers."

■ Standard & Poor's *Stock Reports* also had some reservations about the company on January 17, 2008. "Although we look for at least near-term results to show improved demand versus year-earlier periods, for the company's Caribbean cruises, we have become wary that a slower-growth United States economy may dampen overall future cruise demand."

Reasons to Buy

■ Commenting on results in 2007, Mr. Arison said, "Our European brands enjoyed another record year absorbing substantial new capacity and driving significant improvement in unit operating profit. Although operating performance for our North American brands was hampered by pricing pressure in the Caribbean early in the year, demand for Caribbean cruises strengthened considerably as the year progressed and we expect this trend to continue into 2008. Despite the continuing increases in fuel costs throughout the year, we still managed a six percent improvement in earnings over 2006."

■ With an array of brands, Carnival can offer something for every breed of cruise fanatic. There's the high-end yachts of Seabourn, which feature onboard lectures by Ivy League professors. At the other end of the spectrum are the Carnival "Fun Ships," which offer midnight buffets and dancing until 4 A.M.

■ "In general, all-inclusive cruise vacations can be 20 percent to 30 percent less expensive than vacations on land," said Sandra Ward, writing for *Barron's* on April 7,

2008. "That's why Carnival expects more cost-conscious consumers to consider cruises rather than foregoing a vacation altogether. Families clearly are finding cruises offer good value and choice: More than a million children now cruise every year, according to the Cruise Lines International Association."

- In the April 7, 2008, issue of *Forbes* magazine, columnist John W. Rogers Jr. said, "Carnival Chairman Micky M. Arison became president of the company in 1979, at thirty. He was experienced well beyond his years, as he had started working for his father, Ted Arison, in 1972, when Carnival's fleet consisted of one ship. Now it has eighty-five. Wall Street frets about Carnival's ability to withstand high fuel costs and a weakening economy. But Arison has shown before he knows how to sail in such headwinds. He expands into new markets, such as starting a line to serve Spanish and Italian passengers. Carnival shares trade at a 40 percent discount to my estimate of its private market value."

- Encouraged by the positive trend of its cruises in Asia, Costa Cruises (which is part of Carnival) will increase its presence by positioning a second cruise ship in the region, beginning in March 2009.

Costa Cruises, the leading cruise line in Italy and Europe, was the first international company to schedule regular cruises in China and Asia. Its operations began on July 2, 2006, with the *Costa Allegra*, which flies the Italian flag. A year and a half later, following the success of the product marketed both in China and internationally, Costa has decided to strengthen its presence in Asia from March 2009 onward with the deployment of a second ship—the 53,000 gross tonnage *Costa Classica*. With accommodations for 1,680 guests and 590 crewmembers, this refined and elegant vessel epitomizes Costa's signature Italian style and ambience for which it is known worldwide. With this second cruise ship in the Asian market, Costa will offer nearly 55,000 additional berths with a total of over sixty cruises, thus bringing its overall capacity in the region to 85,000 berths. Since Costa began operations in the Far East, more than 50,000 guests have sailed on the *Costa Allegra* on a total of approximately 100 cruises.

The *Costa Allegra* will offer thirty cruises from November 2008 through November 2009, some of which will be fourteen-day cruises, with departures from Hong Kong and Singapore on itineraries visiting some of the most exciting ports of call in the region. Meanwhile, the *Costa Classica* will be deployed from March 27 through November 7, 2009, on thirty-three cruises lasting between four and fourteen days, with departures out of Singapore, Shanghai, Tianjin and Hong Kong on itineraries offering the finest destinations in several Asian countries.

SECTOR: **Consumer Discretionary**
BETA COEFFICIENT: **1.15**
10-YEAR COMPOUND EARNINGS PER SHARE GROWTH: **10.2%**
10-YEAR COMPOUND DIVIDENDS PER SHARE GROWTH: **19.1%**

	2007	**2006**	**2005**	**2004**	**2003**	**2002**	**2001**	**2000**
Revenues (Mil)	13,033	11,839	11,087	9,727	6,717	4,368	4,536	3,778
Net Income (Mil)	2,408	2,279	2,257	1,854	1,194	1,016	926	965
Earnings per share	2.95	2.77	2.70	2.24	1.66	1.73	1.58	1.60
Dividends per share	1.38	1.02	0.80	0.52	0.44	0.42	0.42	0.42
Price high	52.7	56.1	59.0	58.3	39.8	34.6	34.9	51.3
low	41.7	36.4	45.8	39.0	20.3	22.1	17.0	18.3

Cash America International, Inc.

1600 West 7th Street □ Fort Worth, TX 76102-2599 □ (817) 335-1100 □ Direct dividend reinvestment plan available □ Listed: NYSE □ Web site: *www.cashamerica.com* □ Ticker symbol: CSH □ S&P rating: B □ Value Line financial strength rating: not

covered

In 2007, Cash America began offering online cash advances to short-term unsecured loans to consumers throughout the United Kingdom.

Commenting on the entrance into the new market for Cash America, CEO Daniel R. Feehan said, "The flexibility to reach new markets quickly is an important attribute of Cash America's online cash advance distribution platform. We see our entrance into the United Kingdom as a demonstration of our ability to touch new markets where we determine that the customer demand is sufficient to generate long-term opportunities for our company. The UK market for online cash advance services does not appear to be as well developed as the U.S. market, and we expect a more moderate level of initial growth, but with attractive long-term potential."

Company Profile

Cash America International, Inc. is a provider of specialty financial services to individuals in the United States with 896 total locations. Cash America is the largest provider of secured nonrecourse loans to individuals, commonly referred to as pawn loans, through 467 locations in twenty-one states under the brand names Cash America Pawn and SuperPawn. The company also offers short-term cash advances in many of its locations including 291 locations that offer this service under the brand names Cash America Payday Advance and Cashland. In addition, check-cashing services are provided through its 138 franchised and company-owned "Mr. Payroll" check-cashing centers.

Pawn Lending Activities

Pawnshops are convenient sources of consumer loans and are also retail sellers of merchandise, primarily of previously owned merchandise acquired from customers who do not redeem the pawned goods. When receiving a pawn loan from the company, a customer pledges personal property to the company as security for the loan; the company does not have recourse against the customer for the loan.

The customer who does not repay the loan or redeem the property forfeits the property to the company, which relies on the disposition of pawned property to recover the principal amount loaned plus a yield on the investment. As a result, customer credit-worthiness is not a factor in the loan decision, and a decision not to redeem pawned property does not affect the customer's personal credit status. Goods pledged to secure pawn loans are generally tangible property such as jewelry, tools, television sets, stereos, musical instruments, firearms, and other miscellaneous items.

Shortcomings to Bear in Mind

- The stock has a very high Beta of 2.02, which means it is twice as volatile as stocks in general. Cash America is not for the faint of heart and is definitely an Aggressive Growth stock.

Reasons to Buy

- On January 24, 2008, Cash America announced that its fourth quarter 2007 earnings per share rose 24 percent to 88 cents on $26,287,000 in net income, compared to 71 cents per share on net income of $21,699,000 for the fourth quarter of 2006. The successful fourth quarter 2007 period, which ended on December 31, is attributable to a 21 percent increase in total revenue for the period, which reached $261,129,000, up from $215,714,000 in the same period in 2006. The year-over-year revenue growth continued a trend that has existed throughout 2007, as revenue from the company's various loan products increased 23 percent to $138.3 million and revenue from the sale of merchandise increased 20 percent to $119.5 million in the fourth quarter of 2007 compared to the fourth quarter of 2006.

Commenting on the results of the quarter, Mr. Feehan said, "Our company emerged from one of the most challenging fourth quarter economic environments in recent history with strong and improving trends in our key business metrics. During the period, we experienced the second consecutive quarter with a sequential decrease in loan losses and the disposition of merchandise in our stores increased year over year while gross profit margins expanded. These factors led to a sequential improvement in our marginal profitability compared to the third quarter and positions us well as we move ahead into fiscal 2008."

Total revenue for the fiscal year ended December 31, 2007, was $929.4 million, up 34 percent from $694.5 million in 2006. Cash America finished fiscal year 2007 with a 30 percent increase in net income to $79,346,000 ($2.61 per share) for the twelve-month period compared to $60,940,000 ($2.00 per share) in fiscal 2006. Included in the 2007 total is an after-tax gain of 13 cents per share from a pretax gain of $6.3 million from the company's third quarter sale of its notes receivable related to the 2004 sale of its overseas pawn lending business, Svensk Pant-belåning. Included in the 2006 total is an after-tax gain of 5 cents per share from a $2,167,000 pretax gain on proceeds from a lease contract that was terminated during the second quarter of that year. Excluding these gains, income from continuing operations was up 26 percent to $75,290,000 ($2.48 per share) for the full year of 2007 compared to the full year of 2006.

- On March 5, 2008, Cash America reported that it had increased its existing line of credit with a ten-bank syndicate from $250 million to $300 million. All other terms of the line of credit, including pricing and maturity, remain the same.

Commenting on the completion of the financing, CEO Feehan said, "The expansion of our credit facility affords Cash America additional flexibility for capital investments in 2008 and beyond. We will continue our strategy of seeking investment opportunities that achieve growth and return on capital objectives, grow our business organically through expansion of earning assets and complete the terms of previously announced acquisitions." As of December 31, 2007, the company's last fiscal year end, the existing line of credit balance was $171.8 million.

- "In addition to being the country's first publicly owned chain of pawn lending locations, Cash America continues to be a leader in transforming the pawnshop experience," said a company officer in 2006. "Well-lit, inviting locations filled with well-trained, professional customer service representatives provides a pleasant experience for customers and co-workers alike. Most importantly, we've created a culture based on positive core values. We've created a family. To protect this culture, all of our operations-level management co-workers have graduated from our own in-house management-training program, and many members of our operations team participate in our multifaceted training as part of CA University. These efforts are designed to develop co-workers who are ready and willing to make a positive difference.

"Whether we're accepting merchandise as collateral for a pawn transaction or selling merchandise, the quality of our people changes everything. Because of them, Cash America locations have become bright spots on the American horizon."

■ The company spokesman went on to say, "In order to create a more rewarding experience for everyone involved, our customer service representatives are provided with the very latest in information technology, including a nationwide proprietary network that makes it possible to put a consistent estimate on the value of property pledged as collateral. It gives even the newest co-worker instant knowledge and puts our full resources at their fingertips. We also have a customer database linked to all our locations, as well electronic-based training programs with modern advancements like streaming video.

"We've made, and will continue to make, a large investment in our infrastructure, the look and feel of our brick-and-mortar stores, and the information systems that connect them. It has always been a focus of Cash America to change the industry, to help it not only grow, but grow up. Being able to employ the latest technology certainly calls for a significant investment. However, it allows Cash America to elevate the way our industry functions, and therefore the way it is perceived by all our audiences: customers, regulators, law enforcement, co-workers, and potential co-workers, the media and investors."

■ "The people we serve are the people who get up and go to work each day across America," said a company spokesman in 2006. "Some people call them the 'fabric of the American workforce,' the factory workers, bricklayers, bakers, and healthcare providers.

"Because these Americans are frequently disenfranchised from traditional banking institutions, they seek alternative financial services that work for them. One such service is the traditional pawn lending business that Cash America was created to provide. These are smaller dollar loans (typically under $100) secured by collateral. But as the needs of our customers change, Cash America responds. We add products and services to meet demand.

One such addition is our cash-advance product which offers larger loans, based on the customer's personal credit, without relying on collateral. Here's how it works: A customer brings in proper paperwork such as a current pay stub, bank statements, and utility bills and applies for a short-term loan. When approved, the customer signs a promissory note and related documents and, in many cases, leaves a personal check for the loan amount plus fees. The customer has the option of paying off the loan in cash or allowing the lender to deposit or electronically process the check at the end of the loan term, which is usually about two weeks. Over 23 percent of total revenue we generated this year was from cash advances. Investing in our customers and responding to their changing needs benefit everyone."

SECTOR: Financials
BETA COEFFICIENT: 2.02
10-YEAR COMPOUND EARNINGS PER SHARE GROWTH: 14.2%
10-YEAR COMPOUND DIVIDENDS PER SHARE GROWTH: 10.8%

	2007	2006	2005	2004	2003	2002	2001	2000
Revenues (Mil)	929	693	594	469	438	388	356	364
Net Income (Mil)	79.3	60.9	44.8	35.0	30.0	18.5	12.7	−1.73
Earnings per share	2.48	2.00	1.48	1.18	1.13	0.75	0.51	−0.07
Dividends per share	0.14	0.10	0.10	0.07	0.06	0.05	0.05	0.05
Price high	48.0	48.0	30.0	30.4	21.5	10.3	10.5	13.0
low	29.8	22.1	13.4	18.6	8.1	6.5	4.3	3.6

Caterpillar, Inc.

100 N. E. Adams Street □ Peoria, Illinois 61629-5310 □ (309) 675-4619 □ Direct dividend reinvestment plan is available
□ Web site: *www.cat.com* □ Listed: NYSE □ Ticker symbol: CAT □ S&P rating: A □ Value Line financial strength rating: A+

On November 5, 2007, Caterpillar and Blount International, Inc. announced that Caterpillar had acquired the assets of Blount's Forestry Division. Under the agreement, Caterpillar acquired two Blount manufacturing facilities—a sales office and a service parts warehouse and product support operation in North America as well as an assembly operation in Sweden. These operations joined Caterpillar's global facilities that produce and support forestry equipment. Since 2003, Caterpillar and Blount have had an agreement to jointly produce and market products globally under the Caterpillar and former Timberking brands.

"Caterpillar and Blount have worked closely together since our initial agreement, leveraging Caterpillar's unmatched worldwide distribution and long forestry heritage with Blount's legacy of product excellence," said John Heller, Caterpillar vice president with responsibility for forestry. "This acquisition will provide greater opportunities for integrating Caterpillar's state-of-the-art design and components into the forestry products that previously have been manufactured by Blount."

Blount International, Inc., headquartered in Portland, Oregon, is a diverse, high-performing industrial company consisting of two business segments: The Outdoor Products Group and the Industrial and Power Equipment Group, which includes its Forestry Division. For more than fifty years, Blount's Forestry Division has manufactured market-leading products such as timber harvesting and processing equipment, loaders and attachments.

Company Profile

Caterpillar's distinctive yellow machines are in service in nearly every country in the world. About 48 percent of the company's revenues is derived from outside North America. Europe/Africa/Middle East contributes 27 percent, Asia/Pacific, 13 percent and Latin America, 8 percent. What's more, about 71 percent of Cat's 220 independent dealers are based outside the United States.

Headquartered in Peoria, Illinois, Caterpillar is the world's largest manufacturer of construction and mining equipment, diesel and natural gas engines and industrial gas turbines. It is a *Fortune* 50 industrial company with more than $37 billion in assets.

Caterpillar's broad product line ranges from the company's new line of compact construction equipment to hydraulic excavators, backhoe loaders, track-type tractors, forest products, off-highway trucks, agricultural tractors, diesel and natural gas engines and industrial gas turbines. Cat products are used in the construction, road-building, mining, forestry, energy, transportation, and material-handling industries.

Caterpillar products are sold in more than 200 countries, and rental services are offered through more than 1,200 outlets worldwide. The company delivers superior service through its extensive worldwide network of 220 dealers. Many of these dealers have relationships with their customers that have spanned at least two generations. More than 80 percent of Cat's sales are to repeat customers.

Caterpillar products and components are manufactured in forty-one plants in the United States and forty-three plants in Australia, Brazil, Canada, England, France, Germany,

Hungary, India, Indonesia, Italy, Japan, Mexico, The Netherlands, Northern Ireland, China, Poland, Russia, South Africa, and Sweden.

The company conducts business through three operating segments: Machinery, Engines, and Financial Products.

Machinery

Caterpillar's largest segment, the Machinery unit (60 percent of revenues, and 74 percent of operating profits) makes the company's well-known earthmoving equipment. Machinery's end-markets include heavy construction, general construction, and mining quarry and aggregate, industrial, waste, forestry, and agriculture.

End markets are very cyclical and competitive. Demand for Caterpillar's earthmoving equipment is driven by many volatile factors, including the health of global economies, commodity prices, and interest rates.

Engines

For decades, the Engine segment (32 percent of sales and 11 percent of operating profits) made diesel engines solely for the company's own earthmoving equipment. Now, Engine derives about 90 percent of sales from third-party customers, such as Paccar, Inc., the maker of well-known Kenworth and Peterbilt brand tractor/trailer trucks. Engine's major end markets are electric power generation, on-highway truck, oil and gas, industrial/OEM, and marine.

Financial Products

The Financial Products segment (7.6 percent of revenues and 20 percent of operating profits) primarily provides financing to Caterpillar dealers and customers. Financing plans include operating and finance leases, installment sales contracts, working capital loans, and wholesale financing plans.

Shortcomings to Bear in Mind

■ Caterpillar has a very leveraged balance sheet—too much debt. About 67 percent of its capitalization is in long-term debt.

Reasons to Buy

■ On February 11, 2008, Caterpillar released its latest United States exports figures, showing a dramatic increase in the sale of U.S.-made Caterpillar machinery and engines shipped to customers around the world. For 2007, Caterpillar exported more than $12.676 billion of products from the United States, a 20 percent increase compared to 2006 exports of $10.539 billion.

"Due to the dedication and hard work of Team Caterpillar, our company has nearly doubled in size since 2003, growing from about $22 billion in sales to nearly $45 billion," said CEO Jim Owens. "This incredible growth is being fueled by strong demand for our products around the world and is being aided by trade agreements that allow Caterpillar to effectively compete from a U.S. manufacturing base."

Mr. Owens also said, "As a nation, we should be crafting policies that allow U.S. companies to compete successfully in the world market. Instead, some U.S. policy makers seem to want to turn inward by creating barriers to trade and investment. Such short-sighted actions would undoubtedly damage U.S. firms competing in the international marketplace."

■ On April 22, 2008, Standard & Poor's *Stock Reports* rated CAT a STRONG BUY, with this analysis by Michael W. Jaffe, "We expect demand for CAT's products in foreign markets, particularly emerging ones, to remain robust for an extended period."

■ "We still like CAT's story based on its exposure to the fast-growing nonresidential construction and infrastructure markets," said Rashid Dahod, writing for Argus Research Company on April 21, 2008. "And despite some headwinds from higher material costs, we are encouraged that the company is operating at or near full manufacturing capacity for many products, which may allow it to raise prices further." The rating was BUY.

- In the March 2008 issue of *SmartMoney*, Eric Marshall, Portfolio Manager, Hodges Capital Management, said, "For the first time in U.S. history, more people are living in urban areas than rural areas. That means cities need to build more roads, airports and power plants, all of which will benefit Caterpillar. The long-term outlook is good."

- Over the years, Caterpillar has earned a reputation for rugged machines that typically set industry standards for performance, durability, quality and value. The company's goal is to remain the technological leader in its product lines. Today, thanks to accelerated design and testing, computer-based diagnostics and operations and greatly improved materials, the company can deliver to customers new and better products sooner.

- Caterpillar is an innovator and spends heavily on research and development. Historically, the company invests about 3.1 percent of annual revenues on R&D.

- Caterpillar's commitment to customer service is demonstrated by the fastest parts delivery system in its industry. Caterpillar's customers can obtain replacement parts from their dealers usually upon request. If not, Caterpillar ships them anywhere in the world within twelve hours, often much sooner.

- "For over two decades, we've been helping customers use Cat generator sets to produce power from alternative fuels—including methane from landfills, livestock manure, sewage treatment facilities and underground coal seams that would otherwise contribute to climate change," said a company spokesman in 2007. "At mine sites in Australia, for example, our generator sets fueled by coal seam gas are powering roughly 30,000 homes while significantly reducing GHG emissions. In the United States, cow manure—an abundant, endlessly renewable resource—is increasingly being tapped as a source of clean power and a growing business opportunity. Farmers are using the animal waste to generate electricity that they then sell to local utilities."

- "Chile's vast Atacama Desert is one of the driest regions in the world, a desolate landscape rich in mineral deposits," said a company official in 2007. "Antofagasta PLC's El Tesoro copper mine exclusively uses Cat machines in this demanding environment—and benefits from equipment design that enables the rebuilding of components for maximum equipment performance and reliability.

"El Tesoro and other mine operations in the area also benefit from one of the world's largest and most advanced manufacturing facilities nearby. Caterpillar dealer Finning Chile S. A.'s new Component Rebuild Center (CRC) is equipped to rebuild and test all major components of even Caterpillar's largest equipment. Capable of completing 3,000 component rebuilds per year, Finning's world-class CRC minimizes downtime and maximizes productivity for all of the Chilean mines."

SECTOR: **Industrials**
BETA COEFFICIENT: **1.20**
10-YEAR COMPOUND EARNINGS PER SHARE GROWTH: **9.4%**
10-YEAR COMPOUND DIVIDENDS PER SHARE GROWTH: **10.6%**

	2007	**2006**	**2005**	**2004**	**2003**	**2002**	**2001**	**2000**
Rev (Mil)	44,958	41,517	36,339	30,251	22,763	20,152	20,450	20,175
Net Income (Mil)	3,541	3,537	2,854	2,035	1,099	798	805	1,051
Earnings per share	5.37	5.17	4.04	2.88	1.57	1.15	1.16	1.51
Dividends per share	1.32	1.20	0.96	0.78	0.72	0.70	0.70	0.67
Price high	87.0	82.0	59.9	49.4	42.5	30.0	28.4	27.6
low	58.0	57.0	41.3	34.3	20.6	16.9	19.9	14.8

Chevron Corporation

6001 Bollinger Canyon Road ▫ San Ramon, CA 94583-2324 ▫ (925) 842-5690 ▫ Direct
dividend reinvestment plan is available ▫ Web site: *www.chevrontexaco.com*
▫ Listed: NYSE ▫ Ticker symbol: CVX ▫ S&P rating: A− ▫ Value Line financial strength rating: A++

On January 31, 2008, Chevron Corporation announced the successful completion of an appraisal well at its Big Foot prospect in the deepwater Gulf of Mexico. Big Foot is located in over 5,000 feet of water on Walker Ridge 29, some 225 miles south of New Orleans, and 180 miles offshore. The appraisal well, Big Foot no. 3, Sidetrack no. 2, confirmed the same pay intervals of the previously announced discovery and sidetrack wells, and found the main pay sand full of oil to the base.

Operated by a Chevron subsidiary, the appraisal well reached a measured depth of 25,113 feet (including water) at a location to the northwest of, and deeper than, the previous wells. Chevron is evaluating a range of production development options for the Big Foot prospect.

Chevron owns a 60 percent working interest in Big Foot. Partners are Statoil-Hydro (27.5 percent) and Shell Gulf of Mexico Inc. (12.5 percent).

Chevron is the largest leaseholder in the U.S. Gulf of Mexico and is one of the world's leading integrated energy companies. The company has 59,000 employees, and operates across the entire energy spectrum—exploring for, producing and transporting crude oil and natural gas; refining, marketing and distributing fuels and other energy products and services; manufacturing and selling petrochemical products; generating power; and developing and commercializing the energy resources of the future, including biofuels and other renewables. Chevron is based in San Ramon, California.

Company Profile

Chevron is the world's fourth largest publicly traded, integrated energy company based on oil-equivalent reserves and production. It is engaged in every aspect of the oil and gas industry, including exploration and production; refining, marketing and transportation; chemicals manufacturing and sales; and power generation.

The corporation traces its roots to an 1879 oil discovery at Pico Canyon, north of Los Angeles. This find led to the formation, in the same year, of the Pacific Coast Oil Company. Active in more than 180 countries, ChevronTexaco has reserves of 11.9 billion barrels of oil and gas equivalent and daily production of 2.6 million barrels.

In addition, it has global refining capacity of more than 2.3 million barrels a day and operates more than 24,000 retail outlets (including affiliates) around the world. The company also has interests in thirty power projects now operating or being developed.

Chevron's upstream success includes:

■ The number one oil and gas producer in the U.S. Gulf of Mexico Shelf and number two in the Permian Basin.

■ The number one oil producer in the San Joaquin Valley in California.

■ The number one oil and natural gas producer in Kazakhstan.

■ The number one oil producer in Indonesia and Angola.

■ The number one natural gas resource holder in Australia.

■ The number one deepwater leaseholder and number three oil and gas producer in Nigeria.

- One of the top producers and lease-holders in the deepwater Gulf of Mexico.

Its downstream business includes:
- Four refining and marketing units, which operate in North America; Europe and West Africa; Latin America; and Asia, the Middle East and southern Africa. Downstream also has five global businesses: aviation, lubricants, trading, shipping, and fuel and marine marketing.
- The company's global refining network comprises twenty-three wholly owned and joint-venture facilities, which process more than 2 million barrels of oil per day.
- Chevron sells more than 2 million barrels of gasoline and diesel per day through more than 24,000 retail outlets under three well-known consumer brands: Chevron in North America; Texaco in Latin America, Europe and West Africa; and Caltex in Asia, the Middle East and southern Africa.
- CVX is the number one jet fuel marketer in the United States and third worldwide, marketing 550,000 barrels per day in eighty countries.
- The company's industrial and consumer lubricants business operates in more than 180 countries and sells more than 3,500 products, from specialized hydraulic fluids to leading branded products, such as Delo, Havoline, Revtex, and Ursa.
- Chevron's global trading business buys and sells more than 6 million barrels of hydrocarbons per day in some sixty-five countries.
- The company's fuel and marine marketing business is a leading global supplier and marketer of fuels, lubricants and coolants to the marine and power markets, with about 500,000 barrels of sales per day.
- CVX's shipping company manages a fleet of thirty-one vessels and annually transports more than a billion barrels of crude oil and petroleum products.

Shortcomings to Bear in Mind
- "Chevron is spending millions of dollars trying to reshape its image as an energy company that cares about climate change just as much as ordinary folk do," said Guy Chazan, writing for the *Wall Street Journal* on October 18, 2007.
  "'Imagine that—an oil company as part of the solution,' intones a TV spot in a new global advertising campaign, the biggest Chevron has ever run.
  "But some think it may take more than that to burnish Chevron's image. Big Oil has been taking a battering in the court of public opinion in the past couple of years, blamed for everything from global warming to high energy prices and human-rights abuses in oil-producing countries. Most recently, Chevron has come under fire for its investments in Myanmar, after the country's military regime brutally suppressed pro-democracy protests in Yangon last month."

Reasons to Buy
- On October 31, 2007, Chevron and the U.S. Department of Energy's National Renewable Energy Laboratory (NREL) announced that they had entered into a collaborative research and development agreement to study and advance technology to produce liquid transportation fuels using algae.
  Chevron and NREL scientists will collaborate to identify and develop algae strains that can be economically harvested and processed into finished transportation fuels such as jet fuel. Chevron Technology Ventures, a division of Chevron U.S.A. Inc., will fund the initiative.
  The research project is the second under a five-year strategic biofuels research alliance between Chevron and NREL announced in October 2006. The first involves bio-oil reforming, a process by which bio-oils derived from the decomposition of biological feedstocks are then converted into hydrogen and biofuels.

"We are extremely pleased to join Chevron in this path-breaking research," said NREL director Dan Arvizu. "NREL operated the Aquatic Species Program for the Department of Energy for nearly twenty years, giving us unique insights into the research required to produce cost-effective fuels from algal oils or lipids. Our scientists have the advanced tools and the experience to rapidly increase the yield and productivity of key species of algae. In Chevron we have found an ideal research partner with the skills and knowledge to transform these algal lipids to cost-competitive fuels and to distribute those fuels to consumers."

"Biofuels will play an increasingly important role in diversifying energy supplies to meet the world's growing energy needs. Chevron believes that nonfood feedstock sources such as algae and cellulose hold the greatest promise to grow the biofuels industry to large scale," said Chevron's Don Paul, vice president and chief technology officer. "Collaboration between industry, universities, research institutions and government is essential to overcoming the technological and commercial challenges of manufacturing high-quality transportation fuels from unconventional feedstocks. Chevron is pleased to partner with the nation's preeminent renewable energy laboratory in this important research."

Algae are considered a promising potential feedstock for next-generation bio-fuels because certain species contain high amounts of oil, which could be extracted, processed and refined into transportation fuels using currently available technology. Other benefits of algae as a potential feedstock are their abundance and fast growth rates. Key technical challenges include identifying the strains with the highest oil content and growth rates and developing cost-effective growing and harvesting methods.

■ Chevron's upstream business, encompassing exploration and production activities, is the company's primary source of value growth. Its upstream portfolio is rich and broadly based, with premier resource, reserves and production positions in many of the world's largest and most abundant oil and natural gas regions, including Angola, Australia, Indonesia, Kazakhstan, Nigeria, the United States, and Venezuela.

■ Chevron is one of the world's largest producers of heavy crude oil, which represents about one-third of the world's hydrocarbon reserves. Industry production of heavy oil is projected to grow by 30 percent by the end of this decade. Because the company is committed to extracting greater value from its extensive heavy-oil resource base, it is implementing improved technologies and processes for producing, transporting, refining, and marketing this challenging resource.

SECTOR: Energy
BETA COEFFICIENT: .95
10-YEAR COMPOUND EARNINGS PER SHARE GROWTH: 13.7%
10-YEAR COMPOUND DIVIDENDS PER SHARE GROWTH: 7.4%

	2007	2006	2005	2004	2003	2002	2001	2000
Rev (Mil)	220,904	210,118	198,200	150,865	121,761	98,913	106,245	52,129
Net Income (Mil)	18,688	17,138	14,099	13,034	7,230	1,132	3,288	5,185
Earnings per share	8.77	7.80	6.54	6.14	3.48	0.54	1.55	3.99
Dividends per share	2.32	2.01	1.75	1.53	1.43	1.40	1.33	1.30
Price high	95.5	76.2	66.0	56.1	43.5	45.8	49.2	47.4
low	65.0	53.8	49.8	41.6	30.7	32.7	39.2	35.0

Cintas Corporation

Post Office Box 625737 ❑ Cincinnati, Ohio 45262-5737 ❑ (513) 459-1200 ❑ Dividend reinvestment plan not available ❑ Web site: *www.cintas.com* ❑ Fiscal years end May 31 ❑ Listed: Nasdaq ❑ Ticker symbol: CTAS ❑ S&P rating: A+ ❑ Value Line financial strength rating: B++

"America's workforce is looking spiffier these days, along with the companies that outfit a growing number of waiters, doormen, drivers and other employees," said J.R. Brandstrader, writing for *Barron's* on October 8, 2007. "Twenty-six million civilians now wear uniforms at work, and their ranks are expected to grow by more than a million a year as companies seek to differentiate their workers from competitors and better identify them in an age of greater security risks."

The *Barron's* article also said, "Uniform companies profit chiefly from contracts for laundering and repairing rental uniforms, with five-year deals now the norm, up from two- or three-year pacts a decade ago. Some 90 percent of contracts are renewed, producing a solid, predictable cash stream."

Mr. Brandstrader goes on to say, "The industry's big players have used their cash wisely in recent years to buy smaller concerns, repurchase shares, boost dividends and find clients outside the manufacturing sector, which has contracted supply. The savviest uniform outfits also have developed their route-based businesses. For example, they provide fire extinguishers, document shredders and entrance and other mats, all with maintenance contracts. About half the industry's new growth has come from customers who previously weren't in uniform-rental programs."

Company Profile

Cintas is North America's leading provider of corporate identity uniforms through rental and sales programs, as well as related business services, including entrance mats, hygiene products, clean room services and first aid and safety supplies.

Cintas serves businesses of all sizes, from small shops to large national companies employing thousands of people. Today, more than 5 million people go to work wearing a Cintas uniform every day. That is well over 3 percent of the nonfarm, civilian work force in the United States and Canada.

Cintas provides its award-winning design capability and top quality craftsmanship to the high end of the market—hotels, airlines, cruise ships and the like. The company delivers the proper uniform to anyone in any job classification from the doorman to the cocktail waitress in a hotel; from the mechanic to the pilot at the airlines; and even people working in the retail sector.

According to a Cintas spokesman, "Companies use Cintas uniforms to identify their employees to their customers. An employee who wears a clean, crisp, and attractive uniform is always viewed as more professional than someone in ordinary work clothes. Uniforms also complement a company's esprit de corps by building camaraderie and loyalty. Bottom line—we don't just sell uniforms—we well image, identification, teamwork, morale, pride and professionalism." Put another way, Cintas believes that when people look good, they feel good. And when they feel good, they work better. What's more, their improved attitude results in a decline in absenteeism and turnover.

Shortcomings to Bear in Mind

■   Growth seems to be slowing down in recent years. For the past ten years, earnings climbed an impressive 12.6 percent compounded. However, in the most recent six years, that rate has dropped to 8.2 percent. Also disturbing is the action of the stock in the past several years. It sagged from $56.6 in 2002 to as low as $30.39 in 2008.

Reasons to Buy

■ On July 18, 2007, CEO Scott D. Farmer said, "I am pleased to announce that we have recently completed our thirty-eighth consecutive year of growth in both revenue and earnings. This achievement is due to the dedication and effort put forth by our 34,000 employee-partners. They are our driving force, enabling us to provide world-class service to some 800,000 business customers.

"Our efforts and success as a company continue to be recognized. This year we were again selected by *Fortune* magazine as one of 'America's Most Admired Companies' and were listed as the number one company in the 'Diversified Outsourcing Industry' category. We were presented the Matthew 25 Ministries 'Humanitarian Hall of Fame Award' for our assistance to this charitable organization. And, we were ranked as one of the top military-friendly businesses as chosen by *G.I Jobs* magazine."

Addressing current year results, Mr. Farmer stated, "We experienced economic pressure throughout the year from the continued off-shoring of manufacturing jobs as well as the ripple effect felt at other customers that serve these manufacturing businesses. In addition, the restructuring of our sales force has taken longer and been more costly in the current year than we anticipated. Despite these conditions, we achieved 8.9 percent revenue growth and experienced growth in all of our business units."

Mr. Farmer added, "We are a leader in business services, with a wide array of products and services for businesses of any size and any type. There is hardly a business or industry that you can think of that does not need one or more of our products and services. With approximately 14 million businesses in the United States and Canada and our vast field presence allowing us to reach over 90 percent of the population, we continue to be excited about our future growth opportunities, especially as our new sales organization gains strength."

■ On March 8, 2008, Standard & Poor's *Stock Reports* gave Cintas a BUY rating. Kevin Kirkeby said, "Valuations have steadily compressed during the past two years and are now at a discount to the S&P 500. We think this is partly due to a slowing in revenue growth as CTAS's traditional customer base in manufacturing has generally been reducing head count. At the same time, CTAS has been investing heavily to achieve sufficient scale in its nonuniform service offerings. As these businesses mature and the economy begins to improve, we see free cash flow growth accelerating. In the meantime, we see the company pursuing additional fill-in acquisitions."

■ According to an analytical report issued by Robert W. Baird & Co. (a brokerage firm, with offices in the United States, France, Spain, Germany, and the United Kingdom), "In addition to the current market served, there are another roughly 25 million employees (according to American Apparel Manufacturer) that currently purchase work apparel specific for their occupation through retail outlets, which we believe could potentially be served by the industry.

"Furthermore, we believe that there are another 20–25 million employees in occupations that could be conducive to a uniform program, but that do not currently utilize one. If the industry penetrated these two potential markets, we estimate that the direct sales market could potentially reach $11 billion."

■ Many large corporations are re-engineering all aspects of their business, and they are consolidating their source of supply of products and services. They prefer to deal with fewer suppliers to reduce purchasing and administrative costs. They often prefer to do business with Cintas because the company is a complete uniform service, whether the customer wants to rent, lease or buy their uniforms. In addition, Cintas also provides online ordering, inventory control and paperless systems.

■ According to the company, "When on-the-job injuries occur, businesses need to handle them. Cintas can help by delivering our Xpect line of first aid and safety products and services.

"Cintas regularly and reliably stocks first aid cabinets, provides safety and emergency products and conducts training to ensure that work places are safer and more prepared. Our products and services run the gamut—everything from pain relievers to defibrillators, from back injury prevention to emergency oxygen, from ergonomics to OSHA compliance."

■ On April 12, 2008, Standard & Poor's *Stock Reports* gave Cintas four stars, or BUY. Kevin Kirkeby said, "CTAS has been investing heavily to achieve sufficient scale in its nonuniform service offerings. As these businesses mature and the economy begins to improve, we see free cash flow growth accelerating. In the meantime, we see the company pursuing additional fill-in acquisitions."

■ Here is a comment by a company spokesman in 2008, "If you are considering an investment in Cintas, here are some facts you should know:

• We are the largest company in our industry.

• We have grown thirty-eight consecutive years, through all economic cycles.

• We are a market leader with an excellent reputation.

• We have an outstanding management team, most of whom have been with the Company for many years. We are experienced, knowledgeable, and committed.

• We are ownership-driven. Most of the executives have the majority of their net worth invested in Cintas stock. We are motivated more by the long-term value of Cintas than by salaries, bonuses, and perks.

• We do extensive benchmarking by comparing costs and productivity—line item by line item—or every Cintas operation throughout North America. This stimulates competition within our team and sets the scene for outstanding performance.

These are the reasons we have been successful in the past—and the reasons why we will continue to grow in the future."

SECTOR: **Industrials**
BETA COEFFICIENT: **1.05**
10-YEAR COMPOUND EARNINGS PER SHARE GROWTH: **12.6%**
10-YEAR COMPOUND DIVIDENDS PER SHARE GROWTH: **14.6%**

		2007	2006	2005	2004	2003	2002	2001	2000
Revenues (Mil)		3,707	3,404	3,067	2,814	2,687	2,271	2,161	1,902
Net Income (Mil)		334	327	301	272	249	234	222	193
Earnings per share		2.09	1.94	1.74	1.58	1.45	1.36	1.30	1.14
Dividends per share		0.39	0.35	0.32	0.29	0.27	0.25	0.22	0.19
Price	high	42.9	44.3	45.5	50.5	50.7	56.2	53.3	54.0
	low	31.13	4.63	9.53	0.63	9.23	3.82	3.22	6.0

The Clorox Company

1221 Broadway □ Oakland, CA 94612 □ (510) 271-2270 □ Dividend reinvestment plan available □ Web site: *www.clorox.com*
□ Listed: NYSE □ Fiscal years end June 30 □ Ticker symbol: CLX □ S&P rating: A □ Value Line financial strength rating: B++

On October 31, 2007, the Clorox Company, as part of its strategy to grow in and beyond its core in fast-growing, higher-margin consumer-product categories, announced it would acquire Burt's Bees, a leader in the natural personal care category.

The highly fragmented U.S. natural personal care market represents about $6.4 billion in sales and is currently growing at about 9 percent annually. Founded in 1984, the Burt's Bees® brand today is regarded among many consumers who purchase natural personal care products as the "most natural" personal care brand and as the leading natural brand in the U.S. The acquisition of Burt's Bees is strongly aligned with Clorox's Centennial Strategy to pursue growth in areas aligned with consumer "megatrends" in health and wellness, sustainability, convenience and a more multicultural marketplace.

"This acquisition allows us to enter a growing market that's consistent with consumer megatrends," said CEO Donald R. Knauss. "With this transaction, we're entering into a new strategic phase for our company, enabling us to expand further into the natural/sustainable business platform. The Burt's Bees® brand is well anchored in sustainability and health and wellness, and we believe it will benefit from natural and "green" tailwinds. It's in an economically attractive category with a margin structure that will be highly accretive to Clorox. Combined with our new Green Works™ line of natural cleaning products, and Brita® water-filtration products, we can leverage Burt's Bees' extensive capabilities and credibility to build a robust, higher-growth platform for Clorox."

"Burt's Bees' mission, 'We make people's lives better every day—naturally,' is a terrific complement to Clorox's mission: 'We make everyday life better, every day,'" Mr. Springer said. "Burt's Bees' values align strongly with Clorox's and provide a solid foundation for working together and creating synergies between our management teams."

Company Profile

Clorox has a solid stake in the manufacture and marketing of cleaning products. It offers laundry products, which include liquid bleaches, laundry stain removers, and dry and liquid color-safe bleaches; and water filtration systems and filters. Some of its better-known brands include Formula 409, Handi-Wipes, Clorox Bleach, Lestoil, Liquid-Plumr, Pine-Sol, Tilex, Kingsford and Match Light charcoal, Kitchen Bouquet, Fresh Step, Armor All, Glad, Hidden Valley, Brita, and S.O.S.

The company's home care cleaning products primarily comprise disinfecting sprays and wipes, toilet bowl cleaners, carpet cleaners, drain openers, floor mopping systems, toilet and bath cleaning tools, and premoistened towelettes.

Clorox also provides professional products for institutional, janitorial, and food service markets, which include bleaches, toilet bowl cleaners, disinfectants, food-storage bags, trash bags, barbecue sauces, mildew removers, soap scum removers, and bathroom cleaners.

Its auto care products consist of protectants, cleaners and wipes, tire- and wheel-care products, washes, gel washes and waxes, and automotive fuel and oil additives.

The cat litter products include clumping cat litter and scoopable and silica-gel crystals cat litter.

In addition, the company offers food products, which include salad dressings and dip mixes, seasoned mini-croutons, seasonings, sauces, and marinades. Clorox sells its products to grocery stores and grocery wholesalers primarily through a network of brokers; and through a direct sales force to mass merchandisers, warehouse clubs, and military and other retail stores in the United States. It also sells its products outside the United States through subsidiaries, licensees, distributors, and joint-venture arrangements with local partners.

The company was founded in 1913 as Electro-Alkaline Company and changed its name to Clorox Chemical Corporation in 1922. It changed its name to Clorox Chemical Co. in 1928 and then to The Clorox Company in 1957.

Shortcomings to Bear in Mind

■ Some analysts worry that the cost of the Burt's Bees acquisition will delay international deals, the area where they see the most need for growth. International markets are "where their competitors are growing fastest," said Wachovia Capital Markets analyst Jason Gere.

Reasons to Buy

■ "The Burt's Bee's acquisition suggests that 'Clorox could be a very different company at its centennial in 2013 than it is today,' wrote Lehman Brothers analyst Lauren Lieberman in a research brief to investors this week," said Anjali Cordeiro, writing for the *Wall Street Journal* on November 14, 2007. 'We believe Burt's Bees is only the first move in a longer-term and further-reaching portfolio strategy than we'd previously expected.'"

■ On April 4, 2008, Jerome H. Kaplan, writing for *Value Line Investment Survey*, said, "These neutrally ranked shares offer worthwhile appreciation potential out to 2011–2013. Moderate growth from existing businesses, lower interest expenses and margin expansion should propel profits higher. Moreover, we expect more emphasis on higher-margined health and wellness products."

■ On August 2, 2007, The Clorox Company announced earnings results for the fiscal fourth quarter, which ended June 30, 2007. For the quarter, the company reported mixed top-line results but earnings within its previously communicated outlook range. Clorox also announced that solid sales growth, gross margin expansion and cost savings contributed to favorable operating results for fiscal year 2007.

"I'm pleased that we delivered on our earnings outlook for the quarter," said Mr. Knauss. "Although we are disappointed that sales and volume growth were lower than anticipated, we delivered overall strong results when you look at the back half of the fiscal year. As I've said before, results will vary by quarter, and we continue to manage our business for the long term."

Commenting on the company's fiscal year 2007 results, Mr. Knauss said, "I'm happy with our overall performance for the year. Despite challenging commodity and competitive environments, we expanded gross margin, achieved our sixth consecutive year of strong sales growth and cost savings greater than $100 million, and delivered earnings results in line with our outlook. Importantly, we also introduced our Centennial Strategy to drive long-term growth. I'm extremely proud of the hard work and dedication of Clorox employees worldwide, and excited about the future of our company as we look ahead to our centennial anniversary in 2013."

For fiscal year 2007, Clorox reported net earnings from continuing operations of $496 million, or $3.23 per diluted share. This compares with fiscal year 2006 net earnings from continuing operations of $443 million, or $2.89 diluted EPS, which included the aforementioned $23 million of charges, for an increase of 34 cents per diluted share, or 12 percent.

■   Amid growing concern about the rise in hospital-acquired infections, McKesson Provider Technologies and Clorox announced on March 26, 2008, a strategic relationship focused on helping customers enhance patient safety. Clorox and McKesson together will develop and promote disinfection protocols for mobile equipment and handheld electronic devices. These devices—which include computers on wheels, tablet PCs, mobile medication cabinets, and handheld bar-code scanners for medication administration, specimen tracking and blood verification—are commonly used by clinicians in and between patient rooms.

McKesson will team with Clorox to offer jointly developed disinfection protocols in conjunction with McKesson's Patient Care Advantage™ solution. The solution, which drives a "one patient, one care team, one plan" approach to care delivery, is designed to enable hospitals to provide safer, more efficient care. More than 2 million clinicians nationwide rely on McKesson solutions, and each year more than 100 million medications are scanned at the bedside using McKesson solutions. Clorox manufactures a complete line of hospital-grade surface-disinfecting products and alcohol-based hand sanitizers.

"McKesson is the only single-source provider of integrated software, automation, packaging, distribution and consulting solutions that help organizations improve efficiency and prevent medication errors at each stage where they can occur," said Mary Beth Navarra, R.N., M.B.A., chief patient safety officer for McKesson Provider Technologies. "Our solutions also address broader patient safety issues by helping to improve communication among caregivers, reduce variability in care, and develop a metric-driven culture focused on performance improvement," said Navarra. "Infection control is a key element of patient safety. By collaborating with Clorox, we can help customers lower the risk of inadvertently transporting harmful microorganisms among patient rooms."

For example, surfaces that are touched frequently such as door knobs, bed rails, mobile devices, and lavatories may accumulate microbes, according to the Centers for Disease Control, which recommends adhering to a regular schedule of cleaning and disinfection as an important adjunct measure to hand hygiene.

"Surface disinfection and proper hand hygiene both provide necessary lines of defense for helping to reduce the spread of pathogens that can lead to hospital-acquired infections," said Craig Stevenson, general manager, Clorox Professional Products. "In working closely with hospitals, we've found that explicit protocols for disinfection are very important to ensuring compliance and reducing the risk of infection."

SECTOR: **Consumer Staples**
BETA COEFFICIENT: **.65**
10-YEAR COMPOUND EARNINGS PER SHARE GROWTH: **10.3%**
10-YEAR COMPOUND DIVIDENDS PER SHARE GROWTH: **11.7%**

		2007	2006	2005	2004	2003	2002	2001	2000
Revenues (Mil)		4,847	4,644	4,388	4,324	4,144	4,061	3,903	4,083
Net Income (Mil)		496	443	517	546	514	322	325	394
Earnings per share		3.23	2.89	2.88	2.43	2.33	1.37	1.63	1.75
Dividends per share		1.60	1.14	1.10	1.08	0.88	0.84	0.80	0.72
Price	high	69.4	66.0	66.0	59.4	49.2	47.9	40.8	56.4
	low	56.2	56.2	52.5	46.5	37.4	31.9	30.0	28.4

Coach, Incorporated

516 West 34ᵗʰ Street ▫ New York, NY 10001 ▫ (212) 594-1850 ▫ Web site: *www.coach.com* ▫ Dividend reinvestment plan available not available ▫ Fiscal years end June 30 ▫ Listed: NYSE ▫ Ticker symbol: COH ▫ Standard & Poor's rating: Not rated ▫ Value Line financial strength rating: A

Coach Inc., a leading marketer of modern classic American accessories, announced on January 31, 2008, plans to enter the Russian market through an arrangement with Jamilco, a domestic distributor with significant luxury brand experience. The company expects to open at least fifteen locations in Russia over a five-year period, initially concentrating development in Moscow and St. Petersburg. The first free-standing Coach store is expected to open in April 2008 and will be located at the Seasons Kutuzovsky shopping center in central Moscow. The company also expects to open in the GUM development on Red Square in the fall of this year.

"Russians are fast becoming important consumers of luxury accessories, both domestically and in key travel retail markets such as the Middle East, where Coach has established a retail presence with ten locations. Opening in Russia is part of our strategy to capitalize on the increasing popularity of the brand with emerging luxury consumers globally," said Ian Bickley, president, Coach International.

The Seasons Kutuzovsky location is being designed by Reed Krakoff, executive creative director, with the Coach Architecture Group. The material palette used reflects Coach's signature style, with a stainless steel storefront, Venetian plaster walls, polished stainless details, white maple fixtures, and Calacatta white marble flooring. The store will occupy 1,500 square feet (approximately 140 square meters) and will feature an assortment of Coach's products, including handbags, small leather goods, outerwear, sunwear, and travel accessories.

Company Profile

"Coach was founded in 1941 as a family-run workshop. In a Manhattan loft, six artisans handcrafted a collection of leather goods using skills handed down from generation to generation. Discerning consumers soon began to seek out the quality and unique nature of Coach craftsmanship.

"Now greatly expanded, Coach continues to maintain the highest standards for materials and workmanship. Coach's exceptional work force remains committed to carefully upholding the principles of quality and integrity that define the company. We attribute the prominence of the Coach brand to the unique combination of our original American attitude and design, our heritage of fine leather goods and custom fabrics, our superior product quality and durability and our commitment to customer service.

"During the last decade, Coach has emerged as America's preeminent designer, producer, and marketer of fine accessories and gifts for women and men including handbags, business cases, luggage and travel accessories, wallets, outerwear, eyewear, gloves, scarves, and fine jewelry. Continued development of new categories has further established the signature style and distinctive identity of the Coach brand. Together with our licensing partners, we also offer watches, footwear, and office furniture bearing the Coach brand name."

Coach's distribution strategy is multichannel. There are currently over 300 Coach stores in the United States, with more expected to open this calendar year. In addition, Coach has built a strong presence in the U.S. through Coach boutiques located within select department stores and specialty retailer locations. The catalogue is an important advertising and sales vehicle for Coach, both domestically and abroad. In 1999, Coach launched its online store at *www.coach.com.*

While Coach continues to be one of the best-recognized accessories brands in the United States, its long-term strategic plan is to increase international distribution and target international consumers, with an emphasis on the Japanese consumer. Through Coach Japan, Inc., now wholly owned by Coach, the company is leveraging a significant growth opportunity in this important market. Intent on maintaining a consistent brand strategy domestically and abroad, this ownership structure provides Coach with complete control of its distribution in Japan. With a global vision in place, Coach now operates stores and shops in nearly 200 locations in nineteen countries outside the United States.

Shortcomings to Bear in Mind

■ This not exactly a cheap stock. You may find the price/earnings ratio above 30. On the other hand, its growth record is most impressive.

■ "A difficult macroeconomic landscape is pressuring Coach's domestic franchise," said Andre J. Costanza, an analyst with *Value Line Investment Survey*, on February 8, 2008. "A falling housing market and lofty oil prices have shaken consumer confidence and prompted many would-be shoppers to tighten purse strings in recent months."

Reasons to buy

■ In fiscal 2007, direct-to-consumer sales rose 30 percent to $2.10 billion from $1.61 billion generated in fiscal 2006. Overall, North American comparable store sales for the fiscal year increased 22.3 percent, with retail stores up 16.4 percent and factory stores up 30.0 percent, while comparable location sales in Japan rose mid-single-digit. For the year, sales in Japan rose 19 percent on a constant-currency basis, while dollar sales rose 16 percent, impacted by the exchange rate.

Indirect sales on a continuing operations basis increased 34 percent to $111 million in the fourth quarter from the $83 million reported for the prior year. For the year, indirect sales on a continuing operations basis rose 20 percent to $511 million, up from $424 million recorded for fiscal 2006. Results for the quarter and fiscal year reflected strong gains in U.S. department stores where sales at POS rose about 30 percent in both periods. In addition, sales at retail increased at a double-digit pace at International Wholesale locations.

Lew Frankfort, CEO of Coach, Inc. added, "The strength of our fourth quarter results was reflected in all of our businesses. Our successful spring and summer collections drove our performance, as we continued to improve productivity through our well-received product offerings. In April, Ergo, the third new lifestyle platform of 2007, was introduced in North America with considerable success. For May, we launched a new summer program, featuring a Legacy Cotton Signature assortment, which was built on the success of last year's small capsule group. In June, Patchwork, a perennial favorite, returned across a variety of Ergo silhouettes along with new styles and fabrications in Signature Stripe.

"For July, we successfully introduced an expanded collection of Chelsea handbags, including novelty and limited edition styles. Last week we installed our August floorset, featuring Hamptons and Legacy. Hamptons, appealing to the more classic consumer, is anchored by our bestselling carryall updated with improved function and new detailing in lightweight leathers and Signature. The Legacy line debuted last October; this fall's version features unique new shapes and a fresh color palette. In September, we will introduce a belted version of Ergo with hardware in a range of fabrications, including several sophisticated patchwork styles inspired by early twentieth century art. Importantly, we will also be launching an expanded jewelry offering across all geographies, inspired by the success of the capsule collection introduced last holiday to select North American Coach Stores.

"In Japan, we were particularly pleased with our outstanding sales and market share growth in both the fourth quarter and for the year, which we achieved despite continued softness in the imported accessories market. Our rapidly expanding sales in Japan reflect the success of our distribution strategy, and demonstrate how well the Coach proposition resonates with the stylish Japanese consumer. This was clearly evidenced by the success of Ergo, reflecting the appeal of these lightweight leather handbags with minimal hardware."

▪ Mr. Frankfort also said: "During the fourth quarter of fiscal 2007, the company opened fifteen North American Coach retail stores—including two in new markets for Coach—and three factory stores, bringing the total to 259 retail stores and ninety-three factory stores at June 30, 2007. This was a net increase of forty-one Coach retail stores from the 218 in operation a year ago. In Japan, six new locations were opened in the fourth quarter, bringing the total to 142 at fiscal year end. This was a net increase of twenty locations from the 122 at year-end 2006.

"As usual, our overall sales growth in 2008 will be driven by both distribution—through new and expanded stores—and higher productivity—fueled by product innovation and excellent service. During fiscal 2008, we will open about forty new North American retail stores, at least six U.S. factory outlets, and fifteen to twenty new locations in Japan,

along with expanding key locations in both geographies. In addition, we expect to open about thirty international wholesale locations, working with our distributors, including at least five in Mainland China."

▪ On July 31, 2007, Coach announced a 43 percent increase in earnings per diluted share on a continuing operations basis for its fourth fiscal quarter ended June 30, 2007. For the full fiscal year, earnings per share increased to $1.69, up 41 percent versus the prior fiscal year on the same continuing operations basis.

During the fourth quarter, net sales were $652 million, 30 percent higher than the $502 million generated in the prior year's fourth quarter. Net income rose 41 percent to $159 million, or $0.42 per diluted share, compared with $113 million, or $0.29 per share, in the prior year. For the fiscal year 2007, net sales were $2.61 billion, up 28 percent from the $2.04 billion recorded in fiscal year 2006. Net income rose to $637 million, up 37 percent from the $464 million earned in the prior year. Diluted earnings per share rose 41 percent to $1.69, versus $1.19 a year ago.

Mr. Frankfort said, "We're extremely pleased with our fiscal fourth quarter and full year results. This quarter's performance demonstrated a continuation of the strength we have seen throughout the year as our market share continued to grow across all channels and geographies. Our performance also reflects the vibrancy of the premium handbag and accessory category in North America, where we continue to see significant growth."

SECTOR: Consumer Discretionary
BETA COEFFICIENT: 1.10
7-YEAR COMPOUND EARNINGS PER SHARE GROWTH: 42.7%
7-YEAR COMPOUND DIVIDENDS PER SHARE GROWTH: none paid

		2007	2006	2005	2004	2003	2002	2001	2000
Revenues (Mil)		2,612	2,111	1,710	1,321	953	719	616	548
Net Income (Mil)		637	494	389	262	147	866	439	
Earnings per share		1.69	1.27	1.00	0.68	0.40	0.24	0.19	0.14
Dividends per share		—	—	—	—	—	—	—	—
Price	high	54.0	45.0	36.8	28.8	20.4	8.9	5.3	3.7
	low	29.2	25.2	24.5	16.9	7.3	4.3	2.5	2.0

Colgate-Palmolive Company

300 Park Avenue □ New York, New York 10022-7499 □ (212) 310-2291 □ Dividend reinvestment plan available □ Web site: *www.colgate.com* □ Listed: NYSE □ Ticker symbol: CL □ S&P rating: A+ □ Value Line financial strength rating: A++

"We are delighted to have ended the year so strongly on both the top and bottom lines," said CEO Ian Cook on January 31, 2008. "The excellent results were truly across the board with every operating division increasing both sales and operating profit in the quarter.

"Pleasingly, the 90 basis point (there are 100 basis points in each percentage point) improvement in gross profit margin worldwide and other savings programs allowed for strong levels of advertising investment behind our global brands while still generating higher than expected operating profit, net profit and earnings per share for the quarter.

"Consistent with our strategy to present higher value offerings to the consumer, new premium priced products are driving market share gains across categories in key countries around the world. Colgate's global market shares in toothpaste, manual toothbrushes, mouth rinse, bar soaps, shower gels and fabric conditioners all finished the year at record highs."

Mr. Cook further commented, "Sales have started off well in 2008 across all divisions, and we are confident that the strong top-line growth momentum will continue, driven by our very full new product pipeline with an array of impactful, integrated marketing campaigns to support them. We expect gross profit margin, excluding restructuring charges, to be up within our targeted range of 75 to 125 basis points for the year, as a result of our ongoing cost-savings initiatives, the benefits from restructuring, efficiencies in promotional programs and a continued shift toward higher-margin products.

"All this adds to our confidence that we will again deliver our planned double-digit earnings per share growth in 2008."

For the full year 2007, worldwide sales increased 12.5 percent to $13,789.7 million, an all-time high, including 6.5 percent unit volume growth, 1.0 percent higher pricing and 5.0 percent positive foreign exchange. Global sales and global unit volume grew 13.0 percent and 7.0 percent, respectively, excluding divestitures.

Net income and diluted earnings per share for the full year 2007 were $1,737.4 million and $3.20, respectively. Full year 2007 results include $183.7 million of after-tax charges related to the 2004 Restructuring Program, and other items totaling to a net after-tax gain of $85.4 million.

Net income and diluted earnings per share for the full year 2006 were $1,353.4 million and $2.46, respectively. Full year 2006 results include restructuring charges of $286.3 million and a gain on the sale of the company's household bleach business in Canada of $38.2 million. Excluding restructuring charges and other items in both periods, net income and diluted earnings per share for full year 2007 increased 15 percent and 16 percent, respectively.

Company Profile

Colgate-Palmolive is a leading global consumer products company, marketing its products in over 200 countries and territories under such internationally recognized brand names as Colgate toothpaste and brushes, Palmolive, Mennen Speed Stick deodorants, Ajax, Murphy Oil Soap, Fab, and Soupline/Suavitel, as well as Hill's Science Diet and Hill's Prescription Diet.

With two-thirds of its sales and earnings coming from abroad, Colgate is making its greatest gains in overseas markets. Travelers, for instance, can find Colgate brands in a host of countries:

- They'll find Total toothpaste, with its proprietary antibacterial formula that fights plaque, tarter and cavities, in more than seventy countries.
- The Care brand of baby products is popular in Asia.
- Colgate Plax makes Colgate No. 1 in mouth rinse outside the U.S.
- The Colgate Zig Zag toothbrush, popular in all major world regions outside the United States, helps make Colgate the number one toothbrush company in the world.
- Axion is an economical dishwashing paste popular in Asia, Africa, and Latin America.

Shortcomings to Bear in Mind

- The company has far too much debt. It is nearly twice the value of shareholder's equity. I prefer 75 percent in shareholder's equity.

Reasons to Buy

- "Colgate is apt to continue reporting good results in 2008 and 2009," said Jerome H. Kaplan, an analyst with *Value Line Investment Survey*, on April 4, 2008. "We expect that Latin America, the company's largest market with 25 percent of sales and 31 percent of operating profits, will lead the way. Colgate has numerous premium-priced value-added products slated for introduction this year."
- "BUY-rated Colgate-Palmolive reported 2007's fourth quarter earnings slightly above our estimate, benefiting from strong international operations as well as solid domestic growth," said Erin Ashley Smith, writing for Argus Research Company on February 8, 2008. "Margins expanded for the quarter and full year despite significant cost inflation and a double-digit increase in marketing spending. The majority of Colgate's sales and profits are generated abroad, which should insulate the company from the expected economic slowdown in the United States this year."
- Standard & Poor's *Stock Reports* joined the BUY bandwagon on April 5, 2008, with this comment by Loran Braverman, CFA, "Our STRONG BUY opinion reflects our view that CL's restructuring plans are likely to drive EPS (earnings per share) growth in the low double-digits from 2006 onward for at least several years."
- Technology-based new products and veterinary endorsements are driving growth at Hill's, the world's leader in specialty pet food. Hill's markets pet foods mainly under two trademarks: Science Diet, which is sold through pet supply retailers, breeders and veterinarians; and Prescription Diet for dogs and cats with disease conditions. Hill's sells its products in eighty-five countries.

Recent introductions gaining wide acceptance are Science Diet Canine and Feline Oral Care, Science Diet Canine Light Small Bites and new Prescription Diet Canine b/d, a clinically proven product that reduces the effect of canine aging.

- Colgate concentrates research expenditures on priority segments that have been identified for maximum growth and profitability. For example, the fast-growing liquid body-cleansing category has benefited from continuous innovation. The result: European sales of Palmolive shower gel have nearly tripled during the past four years. The latest innovation, Palmolive Vitamins, uses unique technology to deliver two types of Vitamin E to the skin, thus providing both immediate and long-lasting protection.

In another sector, focused R&D at Colgate's Hills subsidiary has resulted in a superior antioxidant formula that helps protect pets from oxidative damage, including to the immune system. This discovery led to a significant nutritional advance of Hill's Science Diet dry pet foods, introduced in the U.S. in 2000. The product has gained excellent reception from vets, retailers and their customers, aided by national media advertising. Hill's scientists have also developed a new Prescription Diet brand formulation that nutritionally helps avoid food-related allergies.

■ Adding to region-specific initiatives is the company's vast consumer intelligence. Colgate interviews over 500,000 consumers in more than thirty countries annually to learn more about their habits and usage of the company's product.

■ To best serve its geographic markets, Colgate has set up regional new product innovation centers. From these centers, in-market insight from thousands of consumer contacts is married with R&D, technology and marketing expertise to capitalize on the best opportunities. Early on, the consumer appeal, size and profitability of each opportunity are assessed. Once a new product concept is identified, it is simultaneously tested in different countries to assure acceptance across areas. Then, commercialization on a global scale takes place rapidly.

A prime example is Colgate Fresh Confidence, a translucent gel toothpaste aimed at young people seeking the social benefits of fresh breath and oral health reassurance. The process from product concept to product introduction in Venezuela took only one year.

Within another six months, Colgate Fresh Confidence had been expanded throughout Latin America and began entering Asia and Europe. Today, less than a year after its first sale, Colgate Fresh Confidence is available in thirty-nine countries and is gaining new Colgate users among the targeted age group. Colgate Fresh Confidence, moreover, has expanded even faster than Colgate Total, the most successful toothpaste introduction ever.

The U.S. Surgeon General recently cited oral disease as a "silent epidemic," of which the primary victims are inner city children. Initially designed to improve the oral health of urban youngsters in the United States, Colgate's Bright Smiles, Bright Futures program has expanded to address oral care needs in eighty countries.

In the midst of expanding the company's reach, Colgate dental vans are stopping in cities across the country. New York, Houston, Atlanta, Chicago, and Los Angeles are examples of the many cities where children benefit from the expertise of volunteer dental professionals. Colgate's partnership with retail giants such as Wal-Mart and Kmart reaches children and their families outside stores across the U.S. Each year, this campaign reaches 5 million children in the United States as well as another 49 million around the world.

SECTOR: **Consumer Staples**
Beta Coefficient: **.65**
10-YEAR COMPOUND EARNINGS PER SHARE GROWTH: **10.1%**
10-YEAR COMPOUND DIVIDENDS PER SHARE GROWTH: **10.5%**

		2007	2006	2005	2004	2003	2002	2001	2000
Revenues (Mil)		13,790	12,238	11,397	10,584	9,903	9,294	9,084	9,358
Net Income (Mil)		1,737	1,353	1,351	1,327	1,421	1,288	1,147	1,064
Earnings per share		3.20	2.46	2.43	2.33	2.46	2.19	1.89	1.70
Dividends per share		1.44	1.28	1.11	0.96	0.90	0.72	0.68	0.63
Price	high	81.3	67.1	57.2	59.0	61.0	58.9	64.8	66.8
	low	63.8	53.4	48.2	42.9	48.6	44.1	48.5	40.5

ConocoPhillips

600 North Dairy Ashford ❑ Houston, TX 77079-1175 ❑ (212) 207-1996 ❑ Direct dividend reinvestment plan available ❑ Web site: *www.conocophillips.com* ❑ Listed: NYSE ❑ Ticker symbol: COP ❑ S&P rating: B+ ❑ Value Line financial strength rating: A+

On February 19, 2008, ConocoPhillips announced 2007 preliminary net proved reserve additions of 1.338 billion barrels of oil equivalent (BOE), including equity affiliates. The company's reserve replacement ratio was 159 percent, based on 842 million BOE of production. The amounts above exclude 16 million BOE of 2007 Venezuelan production and 1.089 billion BOE of reserves associated with the expropriation of the company's Venezuelan oil projects. The reserve replacement ratio including the impact of the expropriation was 29 percent. ConocoPhillips' total proved reserves at year-end 2007 were 10.6 billion BOE.

ConocoPhillips' organic reserve replacement ratio, which excludes sales, acquisitions, and the Venezuela impacts noted above, was 122 percent. Sales of reserves during the year were related to producing assets sold as part of the company's asset rationalization program. Acquisitions were mainly Canadian oil sands reserves associated with the upstream EnCana business venture.

Year-end proved reserves exclude 0.2 billion barrels associated with the company's Canadian Syncrude operations. U.S. Securities and Exchange Commission (SEC) regulations define the company's Syncrude operations as mining related; therefore, these operations are not reported as part of the company's oil and gas proved reserves.

Total reserve additions, including revisions, improved recovery, purchases, and extensions, and discoveries, were 1.433 billion BOE. Costs incurred, as defined by Statement of Financial Accounting Standards No. 69 (SFAS No. 69), are expected to be $16.292 billion. The company's five-

year average reserve replacement was 176 percent and its estimated five-year average finding and development cost per BOE was $10.11.

"In 2007, we advanced several key projects that positively impacted the company's reserves, including projects in the U.S. Lower 48, Alaska, Qatar and the Asia Pacific region," said John Lowe, executive vice president of Exploration and Production. "In addition, reserves improved as a result of our business venture with EnCana and our equity ownership in LUKOIL. We remain committed to sustaining our production and proved reserve base over the long-term, and we will strive to do so at a competitive finding and development cost."

Company Profile

ConocoPhillips is an international, integrated energy company. It is the third-largest integrated energy company in the United States, based on market capitalization, oil and gas proved reserves and production; and the largest refiner in the United States. Worldwide, of nongovernment controlled companies, ConocoPhillips has the eighth-largest total of proved reserves and is the fourth-largest refiner in the world.

ConocoPhillips is known worldwide for its technological expertise in deepwater exploration and production, reservoir management and exploitation, 3-D seismic technology, high-grade petroleum coke upgrading, and sulfur removal.

Headquartered in Houston, Texas, ConocoPhillips operates in more than forty countries. The company has about 35,800 employees worldwide and assets of $86 billion. ConocoPhillips stock is listed on the New York Stock Exchange under the symbol COP.

The company has four core activities worldwide:

- Petroleum exploration and production.
- Petroleum refining, marketing, supply and transportation.
- Natural gas gathering, processing and marketing, including a 30.3 percent interest in Duke Energy Field Services, LLC.
- Chemicals and plastics production and distribution through a 50 percent interest in Chevron Phillips Chemical Company LLC.

In addition, the company is investing in several emerging businesses—fuels technology, gas-to-liquids, power generation and emerging technologies—that provide current and potential future growth opportunities.

Shortcomings to Bear in Mind

- "ConocoPhillips has grand plans," said Moira Herbst, writing for *BusinessWeek* on December 24, 2007. "With demand for oil soaring, the company announced on December 7 that it will boost its exploration and production budget by 8 percent, to $11 billion, a war chest intended to fund massive projects from Canada to China to the Caspian Sea.

"But there's a potential obstacle to the company's vision: not enough people to get the work done. Half of Conoco's employees are for retirement within five years. Unless older employees can be replaced, Conoco's expansion could be costlier and slower than planned. In an interview with *BusinessWeek*, CEO James J. Mulva said the lack of talent is one of the most dangerous threats to his company's long-term health."

Reasons to Buy

- On January 22, 2008, Mr. Mulva said, "We were pleased to recently advance two important initiatives. Before year-end, ConocoPhillips acquired a 50 percent equity interest in the Keystone crude oil pipeline. This pipeline will play a critical role in supplying North American crude oil to refineries in the U.S. mid-continent region. In addition, we signed a Memorandum of Understanding with Qatar Petroleum International to pursue and develop international energy projects outside of Qatar, which represents an exciting opportunity for both companies.

"ConocoPhillips also recently announced its decision to join and support the World Bank's Global Gas Flaring Reduction partnership. We are committed to minimizing the environmental impact and improving the energy and material efficiency of our operations, and are confident this partnership will lead to major progress in reducing gas flaring around the world.

"As planned, we repurchased $7 billion of ConocoPhillips common stock during the year, and the number of weighted-average diluted shares outstanding during the fourth quarter was 1,612 million. For the first quarter of 2008, we anticipate share repurchases will be between $2 billion and $3 billion.

"Our asset rationalization program remains on target, with proceeds of approximately $3.8 billion since inception. We expect to continue our rationalization efforts in 2008, including the completion of the disposition of our U.S. retail assets. We will evaluate additional opportunities to optimize and strengthen our asset portfolio as the year progresses.

"We anticipate the company's first-quarter E&P segment production will be approximately 1.8 million BOE per day, and we expect exploration expenses to be in the range of $250 million to $300 million for the quarter. Downstream, we anticipate the worldwide refining crude oil capacity utilization rate in the first quarter to be in the mid-90-percent range. Turnaround costs are expected to be approximately $125 million before-tax for the quarter.

"Our previously announced capital program of $15.3 billion for 2008 supports our value-generating growth strategies, as well as a complementary financial strategy designed to strengthen distributions to shareholders through increased dividends and continued share repurchases."

- On November 12, 2007, ConocoPhillips announced that its refinery in Billings, Montana, had earned the Environmental Protection Agency's (EPA) 2007 Energy Star® for superior energy performance. In 2006, the facility became the nation's first refinery to earn the Energy Star® designation.

"We are proud to earn our second Energy Star,®" said Mike Wirkowski, refinery manager, ConocoPhillips Billings refinery. "Receiving this designation two years in a row is a testament to the dedication of our employees and reflects the company's commitment to reducing energy consumption."

The Billings refinery earned this award by emphasizing energy-efficient equipment design and operational excellence, placing the facility among the top 25 percent of refineries nationwide for energy efficiency. The plant is particularly efficient in capturing and recycling thermal energy, an important factor in helping to reduce greenhouse gas emissions.

Energy Star® is a program of the EPA that encourages businesses and consumers to protect the environment through superior energy efficiency. EPA awards the Energy Star® to refineries achieving top-quartile energy efficiency based on an energy intensity index. The EPA works closely with the petroleum refining industry as well as eight other industries to promote strategic energy management at all levels.

- On July 23, 2007, Peabody Energy and ConocoPhillips announced they had entered into an agreement to explore development of a commercial scale coal-to-substitute natural gas (SNG) facility using proprietary ConocoPhillips E-GAS™ technology.

The project will be developed as a mine-mouth facility at a location where Peabody has access to large reserves and existing infrastructure. It will be designed to annually produce 50 billion to 70 billion cubic feet of pipeline quality SNG from more than 3.5 million tons of Midwest sourced coal. In addition, presuming there is a supportive regulatory framework in place, the project scope will provide for carbon capture and storage.

"Our agreement with ConocoPhillips combines the strength of global industry leaders and proven technology that further demonstrates coal's ability to build energy reliability, security and price stability," said Gregory H. Boyce, CEO of Peabody. "The energy value in Peabody's vast coal reserve base exceeds the energy in the oil or gas reserves in the continental United States, offering strategic advantages for coal-to-gas projects and other Btu conversion projects."

Peabody and ConocoPhillips will participate in project ownership along with other potential equity partners. The preliminary design and economic assessment is expected to be complete in early 2008.

"ConocoPhillips believes the key to a secure energy future is the development and efficient use of diverse energy sources," said Mr. Mulva, "This project, as currently envisioned, will be designed to deliver over 1.5 trillion cubic feet of SNG in its first thirty years of operation from proven, domestic coal reserves. It also offers an excellent opportunity to use our company's project management capabilities, manufacturing expertise, and advanced technology to help increase the supply of alternative fuels."

Gasification has been used for the refining, chemical and power industries for more than fifty years. E-GAS™ technology converts coal or petroleum coke into a clean synthesis gas, allowing virtually all impurities to be removed.

SECTOR: Energy
BETA COEFFICIENT: 1.00
10-YEAR COMPOUND EARNINGS PER SHARE GROWTH: 15.4%
10-YEAR COMPOUND DIVIDENDS PER SHARE GROWTH: 9.4%

	2007	2006	2005	2004	2003	2002	2001	2000
Revenues (Mil)	187,400	183,700	179,400	135,076	104,196	56,748	26,729	20,835
Net Income (Mi)	11,891	15,550	13,640	8,107	4,591	1,511	1,709	1,916
Earnings per share	7.22	9.66	9.55	5.79	3.35	1.56	2.90	3.74
Dividends per share	1.64	1.44	1.18	0.90	0.82	0.74	0.70	0.68
Price　　high	90.8	74.9	71.5	45.6	33.0	32.1	34.0	35.0
low	61.6	54.9	41.4	32.2	22.6	22.0	25.0	18.0

AGGRESSIVE GROWTH

CONSOL Energy Inc.

1800 Washington Road □ Pittsburgh, PA 15241 □ (412) 831-4000 □ Dividend reinvestment plan not available □ Web site: *www.consolenergy.com* □ Ticker symbol: CNX □ Listed: NYSE □ S&P rating: Not rated □ Value Line financial strength rating: B++

On September 7, 2007, CONSOL Energy entered into multiyear, multimillion dollar coal supply agreements with scrubbed utilities in the Midwest and the Southeast. The transactions consist of an aggregate of 9.3 million tons of Northern Appalachia coal to be supplied to new electricity generating units owned by We Energies and Santee Cooper.

"These two contracts are significant," said CEO J. Brett Harvey, "because they show that the market-reach of our high-Btu Northern Appalachian coal will expand as power generators install scrubbers. We believe that both of these customers recognized the value of our product and designed new coal-fired generating units that are capable of accommodating Pittsburgh 8 seam coal." Since the beginning of 2006, CONSOL Energy has signed six separate multiyear, multimillion ton supply agreements for high-Btu coal. Three of these six contracts are with customers that are located in the Midwest and the Southeast.

Harvey added that CONSOL Energy also has the opportunity to expand the company's geographic footprint by doubling the amount of thermal coal that is exported to Europe, primarily by increasing the utiliza-

tion of its export facility at the Baltimore Terminal. The company expects to export at least 4 million tons of thermal coal to scrubbed power generating units in Europe in 2007.

The agreement with Santee Cooper requires CONSOL Energy to supply 6.5 million tons for the 2007–2011 timeframe. The coal is expected to be shipped from CONSOL Energy's Bailey Mine to Santee Cooper's new Cross *3 and Cross *4 units that are based in South Carolina. The Cross *3 unit came online in 2007 and the Cross *4 unit is scheduled to come online in 2009.

Under the agreement with We Energies, CONSOL Energy will supply 2.8 million tons for a period of 2.5 years starting in July 2008. The coal is expected to be shipped from CONSOL Energy's Bailey, Enlow, and Blacksville mines for consumption at We Energies' two new units at the Oak Creek Power Plant site. The units were designed to burn Pittsburgh 8 seam coal and will be at full capacity in 2011.

Mr. Harvey said that over the next five years there will be more than seventy additional gigawatts of scrubbed capacity, which equates to about 170 million tons of high-Btu coal, scheduled to come online east of the Mississippi River. "Because of the broader market appeal for Northern Appalachian coal as a result of the scrubbers, we have tremendous opportunities to capture market share in regions of the country that just a few years ago were unable to purchase our product."

Company Profile

Through expansion and acquisitions, CONSOL Energy has evolved from a single-fuel mining company into a multi-energy producer of coal, gas and electricity. CONSOL produces both high-Btu coal and gas, which collectively fuels two-thirds of all U.S. power generation, from reserves located mainly east of the Mississippi River.

CONSOL Energy is a major fuel supplier to the electric power industry in the northeast quadrant of the United States. In addition, CONSOL Energy has expanded the use of its vast property holdings by brokering various industrial and retail development projects and overseeing timber sale and forestry management activities both in the U.S. and abroad. The company also maintains the largest private research and development facilities devoted exclusively to coal and energy utilization and production.

Quick Facts about CONSOL Energy:

■ Began operations in 1864.
■ Mines more high-Btu bituminous coal than any other U.S. coal producer.
■ In terms of tons produced, is the largest U.S. coal producer east of the Mississippi River.
■ Is the largest U.S. producer of coal from underground mines.
■ Has 4.3 billion tons of proven and recoverable coal reserves, the most among U.S. coal producers.
■ Is the second largest natural gas producer from the Appalachian Basin.
■ Controls 1.3 trillion cubic feet of net, proved reserves of gas.
■ Operates more than 2,600 wells connected by approximately 1,030 miles of gathering lines and infrastructure.

■ Produces a daily net of 158.9 million cubic feet per day of pipeline-quality coalbed methane for commercial use.
■ Through its subsidiary, CNX Land Resources Inc., has timber and farming operations, as well as commercial development ventures.
■ Maintains a fleet of twenty-two vessels and 600 barges. In 2006, river operations transported 24.5 million tons of coal, including 11.1 million tons of coal produced by CONSOL Energy operations.
■ Has a private R&D facility currently working with the U.S. Department of Energy and others on advanced technology for coal and coalbed methane production and utilization.
■ During 2006, contributed nearly $1 million in charitable donations and awarded $400,000 through scholarships and grants to colleges and universities.
■ Has a safety record of almost two times better than the industry average for underground bituminous coal mines.

Shortcomings to Bear in Mind

■ This is no stock for widows and orphans. The Beta coefficient tells the story. With a Beta of 1.45, the stock can rise or fall 45 percent more than the market. Look at the history of earnings and dividends if you are tempted to invest in this stock. In 2002 and 2003, the dividend was cut substantially. The reason: earnings per share slumped in both years. On the plus side, earnings have mushroomed in recent years.

Reasons to Buy

■ On October 5, 2007, CONSOL Energy acquired Tri-River Fleeting Harbor Services, Inc., and Tri-River Marine, Inc. With the arrangement, CONSOL Energy acquired control of eight towboats that operate along the Monongahela and Ohio rivers.

"The addition of eight additional vessels through this acquisition will increase our efficiency and expand our fleeting services for our traditional customers along the Upper Ohio River System," said James C. Grech, senior vice president, CONSOL Energy Sales Company. "It will also enable CONSOL to take advantage of Tri-River's current market of transporting aggregates and materials other than coal to a new customer base.

"CONSOL Energy's more than 125 years of experience along the inland rivers dovetails nicely with the successful operations of Tri-River's assets, especially when you include our purchase of Mon River and J.A.R. assets from the Guttman Group in 2006."

With the Tri-River acquisition, CONSOL Energy adds sixty new employees and increases its fleet of towboats to twenty-seven vessels. With the purchase, no additional barges were added to CONSOL's current fleet of 650 barges.

■   On September 6, 2007, CONSOL Energy entered into an agreement to investigate the development of coal-based gasification facilities to produce feedstock for various industrial chemical manufacturers. CONSOL Energy and SES will also investigate the feasibility of producing substitute natural gas (SNG) to meet the demand for clean, affordable energy.

"If this agreement develops as we hope," said Mr. Harvey, "it will expand significantly our total energy production profile and will meet our continuing objective of capturing the full value of all our assets. In this case, the achievement of the goal is amplified because the process creates an asset of a waste stream that would otherwise be on the balance sheet as a liability."

■   "CONSOL should really hit its stride in 2009," said Sigourney B. Romaine, writing for *Value Line* on March 14, 2008. "Coal production should rise a few million tons from this year, and average coal prices will probably be up substantially. Demand for CONSOL's coal should rise as power plants in its area bring scrubbers on line and foreign demand increases, due to economic growth in China and India. China became a coal importer last year, and its needs should only grow."

■   On March 14, 2008, CONSOL Energy was honored by the National Wild Turkey Federation (NWTF) with its Energy for Wildlife Corporate Achievement Award. The award recognizes corporations that demonstrate outstanding efforts to improve wildlife habitat and promote conservation and the country's hunting heritage.

Energy for Wildlife is a membership-based certification program for all energy companies with the primary goal of enhancing wildlife habitat on company-managed, -owned or -influenced lands. These lands include power line and gas rights of way, plant sites, woodlands, and other properties.

CONSOL is also a Centurion Corporate Life Sponsor of the NWTF, and is currently working with the Federation to write and implement management plans on select properties. During the last ten years, the company has allocated 50,000 acres of wildlife habitat to states for public access, and donated more than $50,000 for the purchase of conservation equipment.

Dennis Fredericks, manager of conservation properties accepted the award on behalf of CONSOL Energy. "Together, CONSOL and the NWTF are doing a lot of good things, not only for wild turkeys, but other species as well," Mr. Fredericks said.

"CONSOL Energy has always supported the NWTF's conservation programs," said Jay Jordan, NWTF's Energy for Wildlife Program Coordinator. "The folks at CONSOL have made great partners as we work together for wildlife. We're proud to have them on our team, and we look forward to continued success together in the future."

SECTOR: **Energy**
BETA COEFFICIENT: **1.45**
8-YEAR COMPOUND EARNINGS PER SHARE GROWTH: **9.7%**
8-YEAR COMPOUND DIVIDENDS PER SHARE GROWTH: **9.1%**

	2007	2006	2005	2004	2003	2002	2001	2000
Revenues (Mil)	3,762	3,544	3,377	2,777	2,222	2,184	2,137	2,095
Net Income (Mil)	267.8	380.1	253.5	115.2	12.6	11.7	129.3	107.0
Earnings per share	1.45	2.04	1.37	0.63	0.08	0.08	0.82	0.68
Dividends per share	0.40	0.28	0.28	0.28	0.28	0.42	0.56	0.56
Price high	74.2	49.1	39.9	22.0	13.4	14.2	21.2	14.0
low	29.2	28.1	18.6	10.1	7.3	4.9	9.1	5.0

AGGRESSIVE GROWTH

Costco Wholesale Corporation

999 Lake Drive ▫ Issaquah, WA 98027 ▫ (425) 313-8203 ▫ Direct dividend reinvestment plan is available ▫ Web site: *www.costco.com* ▫ Listed: Nasdaq ▫ Fiscal years end Sunday nearest August 31 ▫ Ticker symbol: COST ▫ S&P rating: A— ▫ Value Line financial strength rating: A

"Costco's membership trends continue to be in great shape," said Kevin Downing, writing for *Value Line Investment Survey* on February 8, 2008. "Currently, COST has the most members in the industry at 27.8 million, which includes the 400,000 who joined in the first quarter. Membership fees were up 13 percent for the first quarter, including executive membership, which rose an impressive 5 percent. Executive members enjoy additional cost savings and account for more than half of the company's revenue.

"Lastly, the membership renewal rate remains the best in the industry at 87 percent."

Company Profile

Costco Wholesale Corporation operates an international chain of membership warehouses, mainly under the "Costco Wholesale" name, that carry quality, brand name merchandise at substantially lower prices than are typically found at conventional wholesale or retail sources. The warehouses are designed to help small-to-medium-sized businesses reduce costs in purchasing for resale and for everyday business use. Individuals may also purchase for their personal needs.

Costco's warehouses present one of the largest and most exclusive product category selections to be found under a single roof. Categories include groceries, candy, appliances, television and media, automotive supplies, tires, toys, hardware, sporting goods, jewelry, watches, cameras, books, housewares, apparel, health and beauty aids, tobacco, furniture, office supplies, and office equipment. Costco is known for carrying top quality national and regional brands, with 100 percent satisfaction guaranteed, at prices consistently below traditional wholesale or retail outlets.

Members can also shop for private label Kirkland Signature products, designed to be of equal or better quality than national brands, including juice, cookies, coffee, tires, housewares, luggage, appliances, clothing and detergent. The company also operates self-service gasoline stations at a number of its U.S. and Canadian locations.

Additionally, Costco Wholesale Industries, a division of the company, operates manufacturing businesses, including special food packaging, optical laboratories, meat processing, and jewelry distribution. These businesses have a common goal of providing members with high quality products at substantially lower prices.

According to CEO Jim Sinegal, "Costco is able to offer lower prices and better values by eliminating virtually all the frills and costs historically associated with conventional wholesalers and retailers, including salespeople, fancy buildings, delivery, billing and accounts receivable. We run a tight operation with extremely low overhead which enables us to pass on dramatic savings to our members."

Costco is open only to members and offers three types of membership: Business, Gold Star (individual), and the Executive membership. Business members qualify by owning or operating a business, and pay an annual fee ($50 in the U.S.) to shop for resale, business and personal use. This fee includes a spouse card. Business members may purchase up to six additional membership cards ($40 each) for partners or associates in the business.

Gold Star members pay a $50 annual fee (in the U.S.), and is available to those individuals who do not own a business. This fee includes a free spouse membership.

The company also has a third membership level, called the Executive membership. In addition to offering all of the usual benefits, it allows members to purchase a variety of discounted consumer services (auto and homeowner insurance, real estate and mortgage services, long-distance telephone services, auto buying, personal check printing, financial planning) and/or discounted business services (merchant credit card processing, health insurance, business lending, payroll processing, communication solutions, check and forms printing) at substantially reduced rates. Executive members also receive a 2 percent annual reward

(up to $500) on most of their warehouse purchases. Executive members pay an annual fee of $100.

Costco warehouses generally are open seven days per week for all members.

Costco is a Washington corporation, publicly traded under the Nasdaq ticker symbol "COST," with its home office in Issaquah, Washington.

Key Information

Number of warehouses: 520
Areas of operation: 385 locations in thirty-eight U.S. states and Puerto Rico;
Seventy-one locations in nine Canadian provinces;
Nineteen locations in the United Kingdom;
Four locations in Taiwan;
Five locations in Korea;
Six locations in Japan;
Thirty locations in eighteen Mexican states
Membership Data:
49.0 million cardholders
26.7 million households
18.0 million Gold Star
5.3 million Business
3.4 million Business add ons
Warehouse sizes: 70,000 to 205,000 square feet
(average 140,000 square feet)

Shortcomings to Bear in Mind

■ "Costco Wholesale Corp.'s eclectic product mix and customer-friendly policies have created fiercely loyal shoppers," said Kris Hudson, writing for the *Wall Street Journal* on August 27, 2007. "But some on Wall Street think Costco should focus more on profit and have been pressuring Chief Executive Jim Sinegal to squeeze customers a little harder."

The article goes on to say, "The retailer's stock trades at 21.2 times its projected per-share earnings for the next four quarters, far ahead of most other retailers. But some have begun to worry Costco could slip if it doesn't show more profit growth."

■ On April 11, 2008, Ned Davis Research Inc. rated Costco a SELL, with this comment, "The Fundamental Risk Model remains in the high risk zone, while the Technical Model continues to show a neutral stance. Stocks that have a combined model reading that is negative will have a SELL rating until a neutral or positive combined model reading is produced."

Reasons to Buy

■ Net sales for fiscal 2007, the fifty-two weeks ended September 2, 2007, were $63.09 billion, an increase of 7 percent from $58.96 billion during the prior 53-week fiscal year ended September 3, 2006. Comparable warehouse sales increased 6 percent over the comparable fifty-two-week period of the prior year.

According to Costco's chief financial officer, Richard Galanti, "Historically, membership fee revenue was recognized using a 'monthly' convention starting from the month the membership payment was received. We are now recognizing membership fees using a 'daily' convention, based on the specific membership terms and timing of payments. The net cash flow effect to the company is slightly positive, due to a reduction of current income taxes payable of approximately $20 million."

Net income for fiscal 2007 was $1.08 billion, or $2.37 per diluted share, compared to $1.10 billion, or $2.30 per diluted share, during fiscal year 2006. Excluding the adjustment to membership fee revenue, outlined above, as well as the following items recorded in the second and third quarters of fiscal 2007: a $95.3 million noncash pretax charge ($48.1 million taken in the second quarter and $47.2 million taken in the third quarter) related

to revisions to the reserve for estimated sales returns; a pretax charge of $47.3 million associated with reducing adverse income tax consequences to employees arising from the review of stock options by a special committee of the board of directors; and a $10.1 million pretax benefit primarily to merchandise costs for an excise tax refund on prior merchandise sales of phone cards, net income for the 2007 fiscal year would have been $1.20 billion, or $2.63 per diluted share, representing a 14 percent increase in earnings per share over the prior fiscal year.

■ Costco's policy generally is to limit advertising and promotional expenses to new warehouse openings and occasional direct mail marketing to prospective new members. These practices result in lower marketing expenses as compared to typical discount retailers and supermarkets.

In connection with new warehouse openings, Costco's marketing teams personally contact businesses in the region that are potential wholesale members. These contacts are supported by direct mailings during the period immediately prior to opening.

■ On March 5, 2008, Standard & Poor's *Stock Reports* rated Costco as a BUY. Joseph Agnese said, "We expect COST to maintain or increase its market share, reflecting what we view as a strong value proposition and a relatively upscale product mix that appeals to a more affluent customer base. We see category strength in fresh foods and electronics, with additional growth provided by expansion of ancillary businesses. We think the company is well positioned to generate future earnings growth due to improved labor cost controls and an acceleration of new store expansion."

SECTOR: **Consumer Staples**
BETA COEFFICIENT: **.90**
10-YEAR COMPOUND EARNINGS PER SHARE GROWTH: **11.2%**
4-YEAR COMPOUND DIVIDENDS PER SHARE GROWTH: **not meaningful**

		2007	2006	2005	2004	2003	2002	2001	2000
Revenues (Mil)		64,400	60,151	52,935	48,107	41,693	37,993	34,797	32,164
Net Income (Mil)		1,083	1,103	989	882	721	700	602	631
Earnings per share		2.37	2.30	2.03	1.85	1.53	1.48	1.29	1.35
Dividends per share		0.55	0.49	0.45	0.20	—	—	—	—
Price	high	72.7	57.9	51.2	50.5	39.0	46.9	46.4	60.5
	low	51.5	46.0	39.5	35.0	27.0	27.1	29.8	25.9

CONSERVATIVE GROWTH

CVS/Caremark Corporation

One CVS Drive □ Woonsocket, RI 02895 □ (914) 722-4704 □ Direct dividend reinvestment plan is available □ Web site:
www.cvs.com □ Listed: NYSE □ Ticker symbol: CVS □ S&P rating: A □ Value Line financial strength rating: A

Continuing on a path of national growth, MinuteClinic, a subsidiary of CVS and the pioneer and largest provider of retail health care in the United States, has surpassed the 200 clinic mark with a new center opening last week in Hartford, Connecticut. MinuteClinic's goal of placing high-quality treatment of common family illnesses in the pathway of consumers is helping to meet the public demand for a more patient-centric approach to healthcare.

"We're delighted with the continued expansion of MinuteClinic and with the enthusiastic response of healthcare consumers to this expansion in access to quality healthcare for common ailments," said Michael Howe, MinuteClinic CEO. "We're bringing innovation and change to the marketplace and consumers who are looking for more accessible and convenient options are responding to our approach to quality care."

MinuteClinic has plans to enter all markets where CVS/pharmacy stores are located. "By the end of 2007," said Howe, "we expect to have more than 400 MinuteClinic locations and longer term, based on consumer demand, we expect to have MinuteClinics in over 2,500 CVS/pharmacy locations."

MinuteClinic has also distinguished itself as the first and only retail clinic provider to achieve accreditation from The Joint Commission, the national evaluation and certifying agency for nearly 15,000 health care organizations and programs in the United States.

MinuteClinic health care centers are staffed by masters-prepared, board-certified nurse practitioners and physician assistants who specialize in family health care and are trained to diagnose, treat and write prescriptions (when clinically appropriate) for common family illnesses such as strep throat and ear, eye, sinus, bladder, and bronchial infections. MinuteClinic also offers common vaccinations such as influenza, tetanus, MMR and hepatitis A and B. The clinics are also supported by physicians who collaborate with the practitioners to assure the highest quality of care.

Every MinuteClinic patient assessment and treatment follows nationally established clinical practice guidelines from the American Academy of Family Physicians and the American Academy of Pediatrics that are embedded in MinuteClinic's electronic medical records system.

MinuteClinic nurse practitioners make it a point to stress the importance of a regular medical exam with every patient they see. If a patient doesn't have a primary care physician, MinuteClinic will provide a list of physicians in the area who are accepting new patients. MinuteClinic will also provide a record of the visit to a patient's primary care provider (so long as the patient consents) to facilitate continuity of care.

MinuteClinic health care centers are located in twenty states in the following metropolitan areas: Atlanta, Austin, Baltimore, Charlotte, Chicago, Cleveland, Columbus, Detroit, Hartford, Indianapolis, Jacksonville, Kansas City, Knoxville, Las Vegas, Minneapolis-St. Paul, Nashville, New York City, northern New Jersey, Orlando, Phoenix, Providence, Raleigh-Durham, Seattle, southern Connecticut, south Florida, Winston-Salem, and the Maryland suburbs of the nation's capital.

Company Profile

Stanley and Sid Goldstein were distributing health and beauty products in the early 1960s when they decided to branch out into retailing. The brothers then opened their first Consumer Value Store in Lowell, Massachusetts in 1963. The CVS chain had grown to forty outlets by 1969, the year they sold the business to Melville Shoes. Melville underwent a restructuring in the mid-1990s, spinning off CVS and other retail units.

CVS Corporation is now the largest domestic drugstore chain, based on store count. CVS operate 5,474 retail and specialty pharmacy stores in thirty-eight states and the District of Columbia. The company holds the leading market share in thirty-two of the 100 largest U.S. drugstore markets, or more than any other retail drugstore chain.

Stores are situated primarily in strip shopping centers or free-standing locations, with a typical store ranging in size from 8,000 square feet to 12,000. Most new units being built are based on either a 10,000 square foot or 12,000 square foot prototype building that typically includes a drive-thru pharmacy. The company says that about one-half of its stores were opened or remodeled over the past five years.

Celebrating more than forty years of dynamic growth in the pharmacy retail industry, CVS is committed to being the easiest pharmacy retailer for customers to use. CVS has created innovative approaches to serve the health care needs of all customers through nearly 4,200 CVS/pharmacy® stores; its online pharmacy, CVS.com®; and its pharmacy benefit management and speciality pharmacy subsidiary, PharmaCare Management Services. The pharmacy industry has some of the best long-term growth dynamics in all of retail, and CVS is extremely well positioned to seize further growth opportunities

Shortcomings to Bear in Mind

■ Drugstores face growing competition from major retailers. Wal-Mart, Target and Costco, for instance, are among the big chains that have added pharmacies.

■ Mail-order prescriptions are still a small segment of all drug sales. On the other hand, consumers who need maintenance drugs to treat chronic health ailments, such as hypertension, diabetes and arthritis, may find that their health plans now require that they use mail-order suppliers.

Reasons to Buy

■ On January 31, 2008, CEO Thomas Ryan had these comments on the financial results in 2007, "2007 was a milestone year for CVS Caremark, and we accomplished a great deal across our business units. At the same time, we remained focused on service, execution, and expense control, which yielded exceptional financial performance. Solid revenue growth and improved gross margins in both the Retail and PBM segments drove expanded operating margins and healthy earnings growth. We attained our goal of generating $2 billion in free cash flow, and launched a $5 billion share repurchase program, slated to be fully complete by the end of the first quarter of this year."

Mr. Ryan continued, "We also set the stage for significant future growth with the completion of our transformational merger. From this platform, we are creating a unique and differentiated position in the marketplace, which will enable us to reduce the costs and complexities of healthcare for payors and consumers, while improving health outcomes."

■ "Even though CVS has rallied 27 percent in the past twelve months, to $39.62, it changes hands for seventeen times 2008 estimates of $2.32 a share, about the same as Walgreen's 17.4 times," said Tom Sullivan, writing for *Barron's* on October 15, 2007.

"This reflects outmoded thinking, suggests Lisa Gill, an analyst at JPMorgan, who raised her CVS rating last month to OVERWEIGHT, from NEUTRAL. As a healthcare company, she says, CVS ought to be compared with fellow PBMs Medco Health (MHS), which fetches twenty-one times future earnings, and Express Scripts, which also sports at P/E of 21."

■ "Earnings growth ought to remain strong for the foreseeable future," said Andre J. Costanza, writing for *Value Line* on March 28, 2008.

■ Standard & Poor's *Stock Reports* gave CVS five stars, or STRONG BUY, on April 5, 2008. Analyst Joseph Agnese said, "We believe the March 2007 acquisition of Caremark will provide an opportunity for accelerated earnings growth not only through overhead savings, but also from new customer wins as the company leverages retail offerings to gain new clients. Additionally, we anticipate earnings benefits from ongoing improvement from 700 drugstores acquired from Albertson's in June 2006."

■ On November 1, 2006, Caremark Rx, Inc. and CVS Corporation announced that they had entered into a definitive merger agreement to create the nation's premier integrated pharmacy services provider, combining one of the nation's leading pharmaceutical services companies with the largest pharmacy chain.

The merger is expected to create significant benefits for employers and health plans through more effective cost management and innovative new programs, and for consumers through expanded choice, unparalleled access, and more personalized services. It is also expected to drive substantial value for shareholders through a number of benefits anticipated from the combination. These anticipated benefits include increased competitive strength, the ability to achieve significant synergies from the combination, accretion to earnings in the first full year, powerful cash flow generation opportunity, and a platform from which to accelerate growth. The combined business is expected to fill or manage over 1 billion prescriptions per year. The new company will be called CVS/Caremark Corporation and be headquartered in Woonsocket, Rhode Island. The new pharmacy services business, including the combined pharmacy benefits management (PBM), specialty pharmacy, and disease management businesses, will be headquartered in Nashville, Tennessee. Combined projected revenues for CVS and Caremark for 2006 are estimated to be approximately $75 billion, after adjusting for inter-company transactions.

"Combining Caremark's expertise in serving employers and health plans with CVS's expertise in serving consumers will create a powerful force for change in pharmacy services," said Mac Crawford, chairman, CEO, and president of Caremark. "Caremark has been focusing on moving our services closer to the consumer as the consumer is being asked to become more involved in their own healthcare decisions through changes in plan designs, the adoption of consumer

directed plans and, of course, the introduction of Medicare Part D. This merger
creates a significant platform to address
the needs of both payors and consumers
by providing high-quality, cost-effective
services in a manner that is convenient,
flexible and easy for the consumer to navigate and understand."

SECTOR: **Consumer Staples**
BETA COEFFICIENT: **.75**
10-YEAR COMPOUND EARNINGS PER SHARE GROWTH: **13.5%**
10-YEAR COMPOUND DIVIDENDS PER SHARE GROWTH: **8.1%**

	2007	2006	2005	2004	2003	2002	2001	2000
Rev (Mil)	76,330	43,814	37,006	30,594	26,588	24,182	22,241	20,088
Net Income (Mil)	2,637	1,369	1,225	959	847	719	638	734
Earnings per share	1.92	1.60	1.45	1.15	1.03	0.88	0.78	0.90
Dividends per share	0.24	0.16	0.14	0.13	0.12	0.12	0.12	0.12
Price high	42.6	36.1	31.6	23.7	18.8	17.9	31.9	30.2
low	30.5	26.1	22.0	16.9	10.9	11.5	11.5	13.9

AGGRESSIVE GROWTH

Deere & Company

One John Deere Place ▫ Moline, IL 61265 ▫ (309) 765-4491 ▫ Direct dividend reinvestment plan available ▫ Web site:
www.deere.com ▫ Listed: NYSE ▫ Fiscal years end October 31 ▫ Ticker symbol: DE ▫ S&P rating: A– ▫ Value Line financial
strength rating: A++

"Ask people in Waterloo, Iowa. There, at
a factory, thousands of workers are building high-tech John Deere tractors that are
equipped with satellite-tracking technology
and are intended for export to China, India,
Central Europe, and the former Soviet
republics in Central Asia, among other
destinations," said William J. Holstein,
writing for the *New York Times* on March
11, 2007.

"Foreign sales of these tractors have
doubled in the last five years. 'There are
more lines of computer code in these
tractors than there is in the space shuttle,'
says Dave Everitt, president of the North
America, Australian and Asian regions
of the agricultural division of Deere &
Company.

"Although the cheaper dollar has
helped, particularly in sales to Western
Europe, the tractors are selling because
they can be guided precisely by satellite and
because of an 'intelligent power' system that
can provide extra horsepower when needed
while still meeting emission requirements.
'We are not competing on cost. We are not
competing on volume,' Mr. Everitt says.
'We are competing on providing value to
the customer.'

Company Profile

Deere & Company, founded in 1837, grew
from a one-man blacksmith shop into a worldwide corporation that today does business in
more than 160 countries and employs more
than 40,000 people around the globe. Deere
consists of three equipment operations, credit
operations and four support operations:

Equipment Operations

Agricultural Equipment: John Deere
has been the world's premier producer of
agricultural equipment since 1963. Products
include tractors; combines, cotton and sugar

cane harvesters; tillage, seeding and soil-preparation machinery; hay and forage equipment; materials-handling equipment; and integrated agricultural management systems technology for the global farming industry.

Construction and Forestry Equipment: The world's leading manufacturer of forestry equipment, and a major manufacturer of construction equipment, whose key products are backhoes, four-wheel-drive loaders, graders, excavators, crawler dozers, log skidders, skid steer loaders, wheeled and tracked harvesters, forwarders, and log loaders.

Commercial and Consumer Equipment: Deere is the world leader in premium turf-care equipment and world vehicles. The company produces a broad range of outdoor power products for both homeowners and commercial users, including tractors, mowers, utility vehicles, golf and turf equipment, and hand-held products.

Credit Operations

John Deere Credit is one of the largest equipment finance companies in the United States, with more than 1.8 million accounts and a managed asset portfolio of nearly $16 billion. It provides retail, wholesale and lease financing for agricultural, construction and forestry, commercial and consumer equipment, including lawn and ground care—and revolving credit for agricultural inputs and services. John Deere Credit also provides financing in Argentina, Australia, Brazil, Canada, Finland, France, Germany, Italy, Luxembourg, Spain, and the United Kingdom.

Support Operations

Parts: John Deere is a major supplier of service parts for its own products as well as those of other manufacturers.

Power Systems: A world leader in the production of off-highway diesel engines in the 50- to 600-horsepower range, supplying heavy-duty engines and drive train systems for OEM (original equipment) markets in addition to John Deere Equipment Operations.

Technology Services: Offers a wide range of electronic, wireless-communication, information system, and Internet-related products and services to Deere and outside customers.

Health Care: John Deere Healthcare subsidiaries provide health care management services to about 4,400 employer groups and cover about 4,400 employer groups and cover more than 515,000 members.

Shortcomings to Bear in Mind

▪ Deere does not have a consistent record of earnings and dividend increases. In fact, its earnings have sometimes been quite volatile. In 1999, EPS dropped from $2.08 per share to $.51.

In 2001, earnings fell from $1.03 to $0.32. Dividends have not been as volatile. However, from 1998 to 2003, the company paid the same $.44 annual dividend. More recently, the payout has been advancing a good clip.

Reasons to Buy

▪ On February 29, 2008, Deere announced it would expand its presence in the world's largest and fastest growing market for construction equipment by entering into a joint venture in China.

Deere said it has signed a definitive agreement to own 50 percent of Xuzhou Xuwa Excavator Machinery Co., Ltd. (XCG)—a subsidiary of Xuzhou Bohui Science and Technology Development Co. Ltd. (Bohui). The companies are seeking review of the transaction by government approval authorities in China.

"Today's action provides Deere with a foundation in this important and rapidly expanding marketplace with an opportunity to leverage the expertise of XCG in China," said Samuel R. Allen, president, Worldwide Construction and Forestry Division. "XCG is a leader in providing quality machines that perform to high standards for customers, which is a key to enhancing our construction equipment business in this growing market."

XCG was viewed as a viable partner for the Chinese market because of its strong domestic position as a leading Chinese manufacturer of construction equipment with a broad excavator product line of fourteen models. Currently XCG is the third largest domestic excavator manufacturer in China with dealers covering all but two provinces of the Chinese market.

"Excavators are a vital segment of the construction equipment market," Mr. Allen said. "XCG is well positioned to provide Deere recognition as a key provider of construction equipment in China."

While Deere has a long-term presence in the manufacturing of agricultural equipment in China, this is the company's first manufacturing operation in construction equipment in the country. Deere's construction and forestry division is the world's leading producer of equipment for forestry and a leading provider of a broad range of construction equipment in North America.

■ "Profit-taking was in the forefront as traders settled up bets for a year that saw abundant turmoil, along with investment gains of 7 percent to 9 percent," said William Sluis, writing for the *Chicago Tribune* on December 30, 2007.

"Among winners, the stock of Deere & Co. continued its surge, as a renewed emphasis on biofuels prompted investors to decide that farmers will need additional equipment. The world's largest maker of tractors and agricultural gear has seen its stock blossom as Congress tries to encourage additional production of ethanol. Lawmakers have called for a fivefold increase in the use of biofuels."

■ While many companies are having tough sledding this year, Deere had a banner year in fiscal 2007. For the full year, net income was $1.822 billion, or $4.01 per share, compared with $1.694 billion, or $3.59 per share, last year. Full-year income from continuing operations was $1.822 billion, or $4.01 per share, in comparison with $1.453 billion, or $3.08 per share, a year ago.

"Deere's continuing strong performance reflects improving execution of our plans to create a fundamentally more profitable, resilient business," said CEO Robert W. Lane. "As a result, the company has delivered four successive years of record results, and done so in the face of mixed market conditions." In 2007, Deere benefited from an improving global farm economy yet saw weakening in the construction, forestry, commercial and consumer sectors, chiefly as a result of the U.S. housing downturn. Said Mr. Lane, "In addition to our ongoing focus on cost and asset management, Deere has successfully entered new markets, made important acquisitions, and expanded its global customer base with advanced lines of innovative products and services."

■ Argus Research Company called Deere a BUY on February 22, 2008, with this comment by Rashid Dahod: "Deere is reaping the benefits of stronger conditions for agricultural producers, driven by economic growth and the increasing demand for renewable fuels. In addition, Deere has increased its investments in Brazil, China and India, and has benefited from the introduction of new equipment and services."

■ On April 25, 2008, *Value Line Investment Survey* awarded Deere its highest Timeliness rating, a 1, with this analysis by Morton L. Siegel, "Deere's farmer customers are benefiting from the high cost of grains, which is permitting them to spend heavily on new equipment. Of course, farmers have to deal with increased energy and supplies costs, but the balance is quite favorable for the potential buyers of agricultural equipment, and this company as the leading maker of farm equipment in the world, is a prime beneficiary of the very strong demand."

■　Michael Santoli, writing for *Barron's* on September 17, 2007, had this to say: "Since our bullish feature on the green-and-yellow tractor maker was published nearly 12 months ago, nearly everything has gone Deere's way. Corn prices are almost as high as an elephant's eye, having risen by a third to a recent $3.30 a bushel on the September contract, thanks in part to ramped-up ethanol production. Wheat and poultry prices have also surged, as a hungry world boosts its food-purchasing power. This means that farmers—Deere's prime customers—are flush."

■　On June 19, 2006, Deere & Company announced that it had acquired Roberts Irrigation Products, a manufacturer of high-performance plastic micro and drip irrigation products for the agricultural, nursery, and greenhouse markets.

Roberts Irrigation will continue to be headquartered in San Marcos, California. The acquisition of Roberts Irrigation provides Deere a foundation to grow its new business initiative in precision water systems.

"Among Deere & Company's strategic growth opportunities, the water industry is one that makes very good sense," said Mike McGrady, president of John Deere's Precision Water Systems. "Water is an important natural resource for customers of John Deere equipment. Management of this limited resource will become even more critical in the future."

SECTOR: **Industrials**
BETA COEFFICIENT: **1.25**
10-YEAR COMPOUND EARNINGS PER SHARE GROWTH: **7.8%**
10-YEAR COMPOUND DIVIDENDS PER SHARE GROWTH: **9.6%**

		2007	2006	2005	2004	2003	2002	2001	2000
Revenues (Mil)		24,082	22,148	21,931	19,635	13,349	11,703	11,077	11,169
Net Income (Mil)		1,822	1,694	1,447	1,406	643	319	153	486
Earnings per share		4.01	3.59	2.89	2.78	1.32	0.67	0.32	1.03
Dividends per share		1.00	0.88	0.61	0.53	0.44	0.44	0.44	0.44
Price	high	93.0	50.7	37.4	37.5	33.7	25.8	23.1	24.8
	low	45.1	33.5	28.5	28.4	18.8	18.8	16.8	15.2

CONSERVATIVE GROWTH

Dentsply International, Inc.

P.O. Box 872 ❑ 221 West Philadelphia Street ❑ York, PA 17405-0872 ❑ (717) 849-4243 ❑ Dividend reinvestment plan not available ❑ Web site: *www.dentsply.com* ❑ Listed: Nasdaq ❑ Ticker symbol: XRAY ❑ S&P rating: A− ❑ Value Line financial strength rating: B++

More than 50 percent of all dental restorations today are repairs of previously placed fillings, indicating a strong market need for a dental filling material that performs more satisfactorily. The major reason for the failure of existing dental materials is secondary caries that develop due to the access of bacteria at the interface of the restoration and the tooth.

Dentsply recently completed a comprehensive licensing agreement with Doxa AB to develop and commercialize products within the dental field, based on Doxa's bioactive ceramic technology. The novel technology was originally developed in Sweden in cooperation with the Department of Engineering Sciences at the University of Uppsala's world-renowned Angstrom Laboratory. Doxa, a Swedish biomaterial technology company, also located in Uppsala, is an ideal business partner for Dentsply. They have since undertaken significant work to advance the unique calcium aluminate hydrate and bioactive ceramic technology to the point where physical properties and product handling and delivery are supportive of its use in dentistry.

The Doxa technology is designed to induce chemical integration between the bioactive ceramic material and dentition or bone structure. The bioactive calcium aluminate induces the formation of a substance similar to hydroxyapatite, the main mineral component of teeth. This leads over time to micro structural integration with dentin, enamel and bone, providing a long-lasting material seal.

With virtually no micro-leakage at the interface with the tooth structure, it will provide a breakthrough platform for the introduction of new and advanced restorative dental materials and cements and may also have application for improved dental implant surface coatings and endodontic root canal filling materials. In the words of a company spokesman, "Our market leadership, global strength and strategic focus uniquely position the company to successfully bring this new technology to market."

Company Profile

Dentsply designs, develops, manufactures and markets a broad range of products for the dental market. The company believes that it is the world's leading manufacturer and distributor of dental prosthetics, precious metal dental alloys, dental ceramics, endodontic instruments and materials, prophylaxis paste, dental sealants, ultrasonic scalers, and crown and bridge materials; the leading United States manufacturer and distributor of dental X-ray equipment, dental handpieces, intraoral cameras, dental

x-ray film holders, film mounts, and bone substitute/grafting materials; and a leading worldwide manufacturer or distributor of dental injectable anesthetics, impression materials, orthodontic appliances, dental cutting instruments, and dental implants.

Dentsply International Inc. is among the largest manufacturers of dental products in the world. The company has a presence in more than 120 countries, though its main operations take place in Canada, Germany, Switzerland, Italy, the UK, Japan, and Italy. The company markets its products under the following brand names: Caulk, Cavitron, Ceramco, Dentsply, Detrey, Gende.

Dentsply International is a major company involved in the manufacture of dental products. Many of the company's products are bestsellers in the domestic dental market. The company's operations encompass the design, manufacture and marketing of a variety of dental products.

The company has an extensive sales network of around 1,800 sales representatives, distributors, and importers. Its products are manufactured both domestically and internationally and have some of the most well-established brand names in the industry, such as Caulk, Cavitron, Ceramco, Dentsply, Detrey, Midwest, R&R Rinn, and Trubyte.

The company's operates under the following segments: U.S. dental consumables, UK dental consumables, endodontics/professional division dental consumables, Africa/European dental laboratory business; Australia/Canada/Latin America/U.S. pharmaceutical; U.S. dental laboratory business/implants/orthodontics, and all others.

The dental consumables

The U.S. and Europe/Japan/nondental segment produces small equipment, chairside consumable products, and laboratory products. The segment is also engaged in design in its nondental business of the company. The operations of this segment are concentrated in Germany, Scandinavia, the United States, Iberia, Eastern Europe, and Japan.

The endodontics/professional division

The dental consumables/Asia segment designs and manufactures endodontic products for Switzerland, Germany and U.S. markets. The segment also produces small equipment and chair-side consumable products for the domestic market. For the Chinese market, the segment produces laboratory products. The segment's operations also encompass sale and distribution of all products of the company to the Asian market and sale of endodontic products to regions that include Canada, Switzerland, Scandinavia, Benelux, and the United States.

The Australia/Canada/Latin America/U.S. pharmaceutical segment focuses largely on the design, production, sale, and distribution of the company's dental anesthetics.

This segment caters to the dental anesthetics demand of U.S. and Brazil markets. Furthermore, the segment also handles the selling and distribution of all the company's products to Canada, Australia, Mexico and Latin America.

The U.S. dental laboratory business/implants/orthodontics segment caters to the U.S. market's demand for laboratory products. The segment is primarily focused on the design, manufacture, sale and distribution of laboratory products. It also handles the global sale and distribution of the dental implant, bone generation, and orthodontic products of the company.

Shortcomings to Bear in Mind

■ To be sure, Dentsply has an enviable record of earnings and dividend growth. However, Wall Street is well aware of this and has awarded the stock a generous multiple that is well above the market.

Reasons to Buy

■ On February 5, 2008, CEO Bret Wise said, "We are pleased with the acceleration of our sales growth and earnings performance in 2007, as many strategic initiatives implemented in 2006 and 2007 began to contribute to results. During the year, we achieved an important milestone with sales exceeding $2 billion for the first time, just six years after reaching $1 billion in sales. Our broad product portfolio, focus on consumables, and global footprint position us well for future success. Despite the volatility in the broader global markets, we remain confident in our ability to grow and experience another year of solid performance in 2008."

■ "More sustainable low double-digit percentage gains are likely in 2008 and 2009," said George Rho, an analyst with *Value Line Investment Survey*, on February 29, 2008. "The economic headwinds in the United States, notwithstanding, we expect organic revenue growth to approximate 6 percent this year. Dentsply's broad geographic presence is certainly a positive, as the company derives two thirds of its sales abroad, where business is more buoyant."

■ On June 21, 2007, Dentsply International Inc. announced that it had entered into an agreement to acquire the assets of Sultan Healthcare, Inc. Sultan Healthcare, based in New Jersey, is a well-known U.S. dental consumable manufacturer recognized primarily for infection control products, dental materials and preventive products. It is expected that this acquisition will add about $45 to $50 million on an annualized basis to Dentsply's sales. The transaction is also expected to be neutral to earnings per share in 2007 and slightly accretive to earnings per share in 2008.

The Sultan tradition began in 1872, when Edward Sultan founded the original Sultan Pharmacy on 23rd Street in New York City. Paul Seid, president of Sultan

Healthcare, commented, "Partnering with the industry leader was a natural choice. DENTSPLY offers a rich history of dental traditions and product innovation that aligned well with the Sultan management team's growth strategies and our commitment to quality and service."

Over the course of its 135-year history, Sultan Healthcare's portfolio of products has significantly broadened and includes products for both domestic and international markets sold under the following leading brands: Purevac®, Comfit®, Prosonic™, Assure®, Genie®, Sensitemp®, Versatemp®, Hydrocast®, Topex®, and Upgrade®.

Mr. Wise said, "Sultan Healthcare provides Dentsply with important entries into new consumable categories such as infection control, while complementing Dentsply's offerings in dental materials and preventive products. We look forward to welcoming the associates of Sultan Healthcare to Dentsply International."

■ Dentsply has joined forces with the Georgia Institute of Technology's Dental Technology Center (DenTeC) to partner on several innovative research projects. DenTeC is a nonprofit, multidisciplined research center focused on advancing dental science and technology.

The Institute brings engineering expertise to dentistry by integrating engineering and dental science to introduce new products and technology for dentists, via research, testing, and education. What's more, DenTeC will pursue dentistry-related research in nanotechnology, photonics and optics, imaging, rapid prototyping, material development and testing, tissue-material interface evaluation, and software and hardware development.

SECTOR: **Health Care**
BETA COEFFICIENT: **.75**
10-YEAR COMPOUND EARNINGS PER SHARE GROWTH: **13.8%**
10-YEAR COMPOUND DIVIDENDS PER SHARE GROWTH: **8.6%**

		2007	2006	2005	2004	2003	2002	2001	2000
Revenues (Mil)		2,010	1,810	1,715	1,694	1,571	1,514	1,129	890
Net Income (Mil)		259.7	223.7	215.5	195.8	172.6	146.1	109.9	101.0
Earnings per share		1.68	1.41	1.34	1.20	1.07	0.92	0.70	0.65
Dividends per share		0.16	0.14	0.12	0.11	0.10	0.09	0.09	0.09
Price	high	47.8	33.8	29.2	28.4	23.7	21.8	17.4	14.5
	low	29.4	26.1	25.4	20.9	16.1	15.7	10.9	7.7

AGGRESSIVE GROWTH

Devon Energy Corporation

20 North Broadway, Suite 1500 ❑ Oklahoma City, OK 73102-8260 ❑ (405) 552-4526 ❑ Dividend reinvestment plan not available ❑ Web site: *www.devonenergy.com* ❑ Ticker symbol: DVN ❑ Listed: NYSE ❑ S&P rating: A– ❑ Value Line financial strength rating: B++

The Barnett Shale in north Texas has been called the hottest natural gas play in the United States, and Devon is its largest producer. "Since acquiring our original ownership in the field in 2002, we have drilled about 1,600 wells and increased our net daily production from 350 million cubic feet of natural gas equivalent to more than 710 million today," said a company official in 2007.

"In 2006, we leapt ahead in the play by acquiring the assets of another Barnett operator, Chief Holdings. Devon acquired more than 600 billion cubic feet of proven reserves through the $2.2 billion transaction. Importantly, the deal also grew our land position to 736,000 net acres, representing thousands of potential drilling locations.

"Devon's dominance in the low-risk Barnett Shale is reaping huge rewards for the company and our shareholders. We now have more than 2,700 producing wells in the Barnett, representing one-third of Devon's total gas production in the United States. Devon produces nearly half of the field's overall daily production and more than twice that our of nearest competitor.

"Application of technology is an important element of Devon's leadership position in the Barnett. We first introduced horizontal drilling in the play in 2002 and drilled our 600th horizontal Barnett Shale well in 2006. We have also partnered with a leading university to develop proprietary, cutting-edge underground imaging to identify optimal drilling locations.

"We are accelerating production in the Barnett by increasing drilling density. The twenty-acre infill program we started in 2005 is delivering impressive results, and we have now begun drilling twenty-acre wells outside the borders of the original core pilot area. The successful infill program, the addition of Chief's assets and expansion of our operations in Johnson and Parker counties are currently keeping thirty drilling rigs running."

Company Profile

Devon Energy Corporation is the largest U.S.-based independent oil and gas producer and one of the largest independent processors of natural gas and natural gas liquids in North America.

The company's portfolio of oil and gas properties provides stable, environmentally responsible production and a platform for future growth. About 86 percent of Devon's production is from North America. The company also operates in selected international areas, including Brazil, West Africa, the Middle East, and China. The company's production mix is about 60 percent natural gas and 40 percent oil and natural gas liquids, such as propane, butane, and ethane.

Headquartered in Oklahoma City, Devon has about 4,000 employees worldwide. Devon is a *Fortune* 500 company and is included in the S&P 500 index.

The company's primary goal is to build value per share by:

- Exploring for undiscovered oil and gas reserves.
- Purchasing and exploiting producing oil and gas properties.
- Enhancing the value of its production through marketing and midstream activities.
- Optimizing production operations to control costs.
- Maintaining a strong balance sheet.

On January 20, 2005, Devon Energy Corporation announced that it had completed a multiyear program to divest noncore midstream assets. The midstream divestiture program was launched in 2002 and has involved nine separate transactions. The final transaction took place in mid-2005. Aggregate proceeds from these transactions are about $330 million.

"Devon's midstream operations continue to perform exceptionally well," said Darryl G. Smette, senior vice president of marketing and midstream. "These divestitures, which are in addition to the divestitures of producing oil and gas properties we announced in September, have allowed us to bring increased focus to our core midstream assets."

·The divested assets include six gas processing plants and about 7,000 miles of gas gathering pipelines. The assets are situated in Oklahoma, Texas, Louisiana, Kansas, and Wyoming. The midstream asset sold in 2004 and expected to be sold in 2005 contributed about $48 million to Devon's marketing and midstream operating margin in 2004.

Following the divestitures, Devon is still one of the largest independent gas processors in North America. The company retains ownership in sixty-four gas processing plants in the United States and Canada, with aggregate net processing capacity of nearly 2.1 trillion cubic feet of natural gas per day. The company also owns an interest in 11,320 miles of gas gathering pipelines.

Shortcomings to Bear in Mind

- Although earnings share have fared well over the past ten years, they seem to have stalled of late. EPS reached a high of $6.70 in 2005, but have failed to equal those results since. Nor is it likely 2008 will be any better.

Reasons to Buy

- On February 6, 2008, Devon Energy reported record net earnings of $3.6 billion for the year ended December 31, 2007, a 27 percent increase compared with full-year 2006 earnings. Earnings per share in 2007 increased 26 percent to a record $8.08 per common share ($8.00 per diluted common share). In the year ended December 31, 2006, Devon earned $2.8 billion, or $6.42 per common share ($6.34 per diluted common share).

For the quarter ended December 31, 2007, Devon earned a record $1.3 billion, or $2.96 per common share ($2.92 per diluted common share). This was 126 percent greater than reported net earnings of $582 million or, $1.31 per common share ($1.29 per diluted common share) in the fourth quarter of 2006.

"Devon's 2007 results were exceptional, both financially and operationally," said CEO J. Larry Nichols. "We set earnings and cash flow records, increased production by 12 percent and drilled 2,440 wells with a 98 percent success rate. Our 2007 drilling program added 390 million barrels of proved reserves at very competitive finding

and development costs setting the stage for continued production growth in the future. In 2008 we expect to deliver similar organic growth of reserves and production."

- On July 30, 2007, Devon Energy Corporation announced the commencement of production from its Polvo oil field in Brazil. Polvo was discovered in 2004. It is situated on block BM-C-8 in the Campos Basin offshore Rio de Janeiro in about 300 feet of water. Gross production is expected to peak by the end of 2008 at 50,000 barrels of oil per day.

Production facilities include a fixed production and drilling platform connected to a floating production, storage and offloading vessel. First sales are expected to begin in October when the initial shipment of oil will be offloaded from the FPSO and transported to market.

"Development of the Polvo discovery was a significant engineering project carried out efficiently within a rapid three-year discovery-to-production cycle time," said Stephen J. Hadden, senior vice president of exploration and production. "The project is expected to contribute about 26,000 barrels per day in 2008 to Devon's continuing production growth forecast. With Polvo and nine additional offshore leases, we have a solid future in Brazil with potential for additional discoveries."

Polvo has estimated resource potential in excess of 50 million barrels. Devon is the operator of the BM-C-8 development with a 60 percent interest. SK Corporation of Korea holds the remaining 40 percent interest.

- On July 18, 2007, Devon Energy Corporation announced that its board of directors had approved a plan to form a new, publicly traded master limited partnership (MLP). The MLP will own a minority interest in Devon's U.S. onshore marketing and midstream business. This business includes natural gas gathering and processing assets located in Texas, Oklahoma, Wyoming and Montana.

A Devon subsidiary will serve as the general partner of the MLP, and Devon expects to own a majority of the partnership units following completion of the initial public offering. Following the offering, Devon will continue to own a majority interest in its domestic onshore marketing and midstream business.

■   Devon's production is weighted toward natural gas, and most of its operations are in North America.

■   60 percent of production is natural gas.

■   40 percent is oil and natural gas liquids, such as propane, butane, and ethane.

■   More than 80 percent of both production and proved reserves are in North America, including the United States, Canada, and the Gulf of Mexico.

■   The majority of Devon's international production and proved reserves are found in West Africa, Egypt, Azerbaijan, and China.

■   Devon produces 2.4 billion cubic feet of natural gas each day, or nearly 4 percent of all gas consumed in North America.

■   On January 22, 2008, *Fortune* magazine ranked Devon Energy Corporation among

its "100 Best Companies to Work For," distinguishing the Oklahoma City-based independent oil and gas producer as one of the nation's most desirable employers.

Devon is ranked forty-eight on the 2008 list of 100, the highest among energy producers. The company is fourth among companies with the lowest turnover and eighth in work-life balance. Fortune also distinguished Devon for maintaining a healthy corporate culture despite rapid growth. The company underwent five multibillion dollar acquisitions from 1999 through 2003 and grew from 764 employees to more than 5,000 worldwide.

"Being ranked among the best companies to work for is a great honor for us," said Mr. Nichols. "Among all the resources that comprise Devon, we consider our people to be at the foundation of our strength. Because of that, we strive to be an employer of choice, and we are gratified to be included on *Fortune's* prestigious list."

SECTOR: **Energy**
BETA COEFFICIENT: **1.00**
10-YEAR COMPOUND EARNINGS PER SHARE GROWTH: **22.1%**
10-YEAR COMPOUND DIVIDENDS PER SHARE GROWTH: **18.8%**

	2007	2006	2005	2004	2003	2002	2001	2000
Revenues (Mil)	11,362	10,578	10,622	9,189	7,352	4,316	3,075	2,784
Net Income (Mil)	3,606	2,846	2,930	2,176	1,731	549	674	715
Earnings per share	8.00	6.35	6.70	4.38	4.04	1.71	2.52	2.73
Dividends per share	0.56	0.45	0.30	0.20	0.10	0.10	0.10	0.10
Price high	94.8	74.8	70.4	41.6	29.4	26.5	33.4	32.4
low	62.8	48.9	36.5	25.9	21.2	16.9	15.3	15.7

GROWTH AND INCOME

Dominion Resources, Inc.

P.O. Box 26532 ❑ Richmond, VA 23261-6532 ❑ (804) 819-2156 ❑ Direct dividend reinvestment plan available ❑ Web site: *www.dom.com* ❑ Listed: NYSE ❑ Ticker symbol: D ❑ S&P rating: B+ ❑ Value Line financial strength rating: B++

On January 24, 2008, Dominion Resources announced that it had acquired a 50 percent interest in the Fowler Ridge Wind

Farm from BP Alternative Energy Inc. The facility is in Benton County, Indiana, about ninety miles northwest of Indianapolis.

"This project is a perfect fit for Dominion's plans to increase our renewable energy portfolio substantially in light of the nation's growing demand for clean energy," said CEO Thomas F. Farrell II. "The site is located in an area with an excellent wind resource in PJM, and we are pleased to be partnering with BP, a company that is well known as a premier renewable energy developer."

The Fowler Ridge facility is expected to be built in two phases and generate a total of 750 megawatts. Dominion and BP are partners for 650 megawatts, with BP retaining sole ownership of 100 megawatts. The first phase of approximately 222 turbines producing up to 400 megawatts is expected to be operating by the end of this year. Dominion has entered into a long-term power purchase agreement for 200 megawatts. Construction of the second phase of 350 megawatts could begin as early as 2009. Terms were not disclosed.

The entire facility will be in PJM Interconnection, the independent operator of the electric transmission system and the wholesale energy market in thirteen states and the District of Columbia. PJM's regional grid stretches from Chicago to the Mid-Atlantic.

The Fowler Ridge Wind Farm is Dominion's second wind-to-electricity project. The company is a 50 percent partner in a 264-megawatt facility in Grant County, West Virginia. Dominion has another 413 megawatts of renewable generation already in place, providing enough electricity to power more than 100,000 homes during times of peak demand.

Company Profile

Dominion is one of the nation's largest producers of energy, with a portfolio of more than 26,500 megawatts of generation and 7,800 miles of natural gas transmission pipeline. Dominion also owns and operates the nation's largest underground natural gas

storage system with about 960 billion cubic feet of storage capacity and serves retail energy customers in eleven states.

Dominion's strategy is to be a leading provider of electricity, natural gas and related services to customers in the energy-intensive Midwest, Mid-Atlantic and Northeast regions of the United States, a potential market of 50 million homes and businesses where 40 percent of the nation's energy is consumed.

On August 13, 2007, Dominion announced that it would realign its business units and services company to reflect the company's refocused strategic positioning and the sale of most of its natural gas and oil exploration and production assets, effective Oct. 1.

The new operating business units and service company leadership changes are:

- Dominion Virginia Power is responsible for all regulated electric distribution and electric transmission operations in Virginia and North Carolina. It is also responsible for Dominion Retail and all customer service.

- Dominion Generation is responsible for Dominion's 26,500 megawatts of regulated and merchant power generation.

- Dominion Energy is now responsible for all natural gas distribution, transmission and storage operations. It also will be responsible for the Appalachian-based natural gas and oil exploration and production operations and producer services.

- Dominion Resources Services is now the company's shared services division.

"This new structure is designed to help Dominion take advantage of its strengths and maximize opportunities to serve our customers and shareholders to the best of our ability," said Mr. Farrell

Mr. Farrell noted that the vast majority of Dominion's income and revenues will now come from regulated and energy infrastructure businesses. The planned sale of most of the company's E&P operations is nearly complete, electric re-regulation legislation was adopted in Virginia earlier this year, and other planned asset sales are expected to be completed by the end of the year.

In addition, the company announced the creation of a new Climate Change Initiative to determine if there are business opportunities for Dominion in light of increasing demand for ways to reduce greenhouse emissions from fossil-fueled power stations and other sources.

"Dominion has a long history of operational excellence at its power stations and of getting ahead of the curve in reducing other emissions," Mr. Farrell said. "We want to see if this expertise can be transferred to help ourselves and others reduce greenhouse gas emissions."

Also new is a Governance Department, which provides oversight of corporate governance matters for the board of directors. This group includes the corporate secretary's department.

Shortcomings to Bear in Mind

▪ Although this stock is classified for growth and income, the company's record of dividend increases is suspect. From 1995 through 2003, the annual dividend per share was locked in place at $1.29 and only modestly increased to $1.58 in 2008.

Reasons to Buy

▪ On January 30, 2008, Dominion announced unaudited net income determined in accordance with generally accepted accounting principles (GAAP) for the 12 months ended Dec. 31, 2007 of $2.54 billion ($3.88 per share) compared to net income of $1.38 billion ($1.96 per share) for the same period in 2006.

Mr. Farrell said: "We completed the divestiture of our non-Appalachian natural gas and oil exploration and production businesses in 2007, while continuing to

deliver exceptional results across the rest of our businesses. We posted impressive results in all business areas, from merchant generation and unregulated retail sales to our regulated electric and gas operations.

"Our newly aligned operating segments, combined with expanded disclosure of earnings drivers detailed in the 2008 Earnings Guidance Kit that will be posted this morning on Dominion's Web site, will better highlight Dominion's earnings power and growth prospects. We are providing 2008 operating earnings guidance of $3.05 to $3.15 per share and are confident that we can deliver long-term annual operating earnings per share growth of at least 6 percent after 2008."

▪ "We look for higher earnings in 2008 and 2009," said an analyst Paul E. Debbas, CFA, with *Value Line Investment Survey*, on February 29, 2008. "The full recovery of power costs will help this year, and higher profits from the nonregulated generating assets should help each year."

▪ On January 30, 2008, Argus Research Company called Dominion a BUY, with this analysis by Gary F. Hovis, "Dominion has a solid base of high-return, nonregulated operations and a core regulated utility operation, and we believe that the D shares are quite attractive at current prices. We believe that Dominion's strong fundamentals and diverse range of businesses (which include regulated electric utilities, natural gas pipeline and storage operations, and exploration and production activities in Appalachia) will continue to drive EPS (earnings per share) growth."

▪ Standard & Poor's *Stock Reports* said Dominion was a BUY on April 12, 2008. Christopher B. Muir explained why, "We view the company's recently completed sale of its E&P (exploration and production) assets as positive, allowing it to focus on its core businesses."

■ XTO Energy Inc. (NYSE: XTO) purchased Dominion's operations in the Rocky Mountains, San Juan Basin, and the Gulf Coast region for $2.5 billion. These operations include proved reserves of 1 Tcfe on Dec. 31, 2006.

Proceeds from the sales will be used to repurchase stock under the company's outstanding tender offer that expires on August 7, 2007, unless extended.

With these sales, Dominion has closed on more than 85 percent of the natural gas and oil reserves the company plans to sell. In June, Dominion reached an agreement to sell the other 15 percent, about 780 billion cubic feet equivalent (Bcfe), to Linn Energy, LLC for $2.05 billion.

■ On August 16, 2007, Dominion announced that it had secured firm, long-term commitments to receive natural gas supplies from a new pipeline, Rockies Express (REX), and deliver it to major natural gas markets in the Northeast and Mid-Atlantic regions.

Dominion's project, named Dominion Hub I, is the first transportation project to provide firm access from the REX pipeline to the Northeast and Mid-Atlantic regions.

"We are proud to offer Rocky Mountain basin producers market access for this new gas supply," said Gary Sypolt, president of Dominion Transmission. "The robust Dominion natural gas pipeline and storage grid ensures that REX shippers will have year-round access to local distributors, industrial consumers and power generation markets throughout the eastern seaboard."

SECTOR: **Utilities**
BETA COEFFICIENT: **.75**
10-YEAR COMPOUND EARNINGS PER SHARE GROWTH: **10%**
10-YEAR COMPOUND DIVIDENDS PER SHARE GROWTH: **2%**

	2007	2006	2005	2004	2003	2002	2001	2000
Revenues (Mil)	15,674	16,482	17,971	13,972	12,078	10,218	10,558	9,260
Net Income (Mil)	2,539	1,380	1,033	1,425	1,261	1,378	775	624
Earnings per share	3.88	2.40	1.50	2.13	1.96	2.41	1.49	1.25
Dividends per share	1.58	1.38	1.34	1.30	2.58	1.29	1.29	1.29
Price high	49.4	42.2	43.5	34.5	33.0	33.6	35.0	34.0
low	39.8	34.4	33.3	30.4	25.9	17.7	27.6	17.4

CONSERVATIVE GROWTH

Donaldson Company, Inc.

P.O. Box 1299 ▫ Minneapolis, MN 55440 ▫ (952) 887-3753 ▫ Dividend reinvestment plan available ▫ Web site: *www.donaldson.com* ▫ Fiscal years end July 31 ▫ Listed: NYSE ▫ Ticker symbol: DCI ▫ S&P rating: A+ ▫ Value Line financial strength rating: B++

You expect to see Donaldson Company's filtration products on the heavy-duty truck traveling the interstate highway, or on the construction equipment on the side of the road. "After all, that's where our company began," said a company senior official.

"But you aren't as likely to expect our filters in the camera that captures memories of your daughter's birthday party. Or in the backup generator providing electricity to your computer center or office.

"Donaldson filters and related products are in many unexpected places—in products you see, touch and use every day. Our long-term, focused investment in filtration technology has created the leverage to carry us into new product lines, new markets and new geography. This diversification in end markets, linked by a common technology base, has enabled us to smooth out the ups and downs of the various market segments and to achieve our twelfth consecutive year of double-digit earnings growth—no small feat in these turbulent economic times.

"Donaldson holds more than 450 U.S. patents and related patents filed around the world, and our employees are constantly developing new ways to utilize superior filtration and acoustic technology for products that are still years away from market."

Company Profile

Donaldson Company is a leading worldwide provider of filtration systems and replacement parts. Founded in 1915, Donaldson is a technology-driven company committed to satisfying customers needs for filtration solutions through innovative research and development.

The company's product mix includes air and liquid filters, as well as exhaust and emission-control products for mobile equipment; in-plant air-cleaning systems; air intake systems for industrial gas turbines; and specialized filters for such diverse applications as computer disk drives, aircraft passenger cabins, and semiconductor processing.

Donaldson operates plants throughout the world. Of these, fourteen facilities are in the United States, three in the United Kingdom, two each in Germany, Japan, China, South Africa, and Mexico. Finally, the company has one plant in each of the following countries: Australia, France, Hong Kong, Italy, Belgium, and India.

The company has two reporting segments engaged in the design, manufacture and sale of systems to filter air and liquid and other complementary products:

The Engine Products segment makes air intake systems, exhaust systems, and liquid filtration systems. The company sells to original-equipment manufacturers (OEMs) in the construction, industrial, mining, agriculture, and transportation markets, independent distributors, OEM dealer networks, private-label accounts, and large private fleets. This segment is further subdivided as follows:

Off-Road Equipment includes products sold to industrial equipment and defense contractor OEMs (original equipment manufacturers) for agriculture, construction, mining, and military applications.

The company's Truck operation produces products sold to manufacturers of light-, medium-, and heavy-duty trucks.

In the Aftermarket sector, Donaldson sells a broad line of replacement filters and hard parts for all of the equipment applications noted above.

Industrial Products consist of dust, fume, and mist collectors, static and pulse-clean air filter systems of industrial gas turbines, computer disk drive filter products and other specialized air-filtration systems. DCI sells to various industrial end-users, OEMs of gas-fired turbines, and OEMs and users requiring highly purified air. This segment is further broken down, as follows:

Under Industrial Air Filtration, the company sells under such trade names as Donaldson Torit and Donaldson Torit DCE. It provides equipment to control and capture process dust, fumes and mist in manufacturing and industrial processing plants.

Under Gas Turbine Systems, Donaldson provides complete systems to deliver clean air to gas-fired turbines. Products include self-cleaning filter units, static air filter units, inlet ducting and silencing, evaporative coolers, chiller coils, inlet heating, and anti-icing systems.

Under Ultrafilter, the company provides a complete line of compressed air filters and a wide assortment of replacement filters, a complete offering of refrigeration and desiccant dryers, condensate management devices, and after-sale services.

Under Special Applications, the company provides a wide range of high-efficiency media, filters, and filtration systems for various commercial, industrial and product applications.

Shortcomings to Bear in Mind

■ Some analysts point out the risk factors for Donaldson because of greater shortages of steel and an inability of the company to recover these higher costs, along with unrest in parts of the world, most notably Iraq.

Reasons to Buy

■ In fiscal 2008, CEO Bill Cook said, "This past year, we continued to grow and diversify our business. A strong business climate, particularly in Europe and Asia, contributed to overall revenue growth of 13 percent, leading to another record revenue year and our eighteenth consecutive year of record earnings. In short, we once again delivered excellent results. The highlights include:

- Full-year operating margins of 11 percent.
- Record earnings per share, which were up 18 percent, from last year.
- Return on shareholders equity of 25.7 percent.

"We achieved these results in spite of a significant downturn in our North American truck business. The NAFTA heavy-duty truck business is still a very important part of our company. However, as a result of our diversification efforts over the past two decades, it is now about 6 percent of our total sales."

■ Mr. Cook also said, "Historically, we have grown through a combination of internal growth and small, strategic acquisitions to our targeted markets. I

am pleased to report that we completed two acquisitions during the past year. In March, we announced the acquisition of Aerospace Filtration Systems (AFS). AFS, located in St. Charles, Missouri, is the U.S. leader in the design, development, and manufacture of high-performance air filters for military and commercial helicopters. The acquisition of AFS nicely complements our existing aerospace and defense business. In June, we completed the acquisition of Rawsen Equipment in South Africa. Rawsen is a specialist in the purification of compressed air."

■ In fiscal 2007, a Donaldson spokesman said, "Our PowerCore filtration technology—the recipient of the 2006 Frost & Sullivan Automotive Air Filters Aftermarket Product Innovation of the Year Award—is poised to become the industry standard for air filtration over the next few years. Introduced in 2000, PowerCore air filtration systems have been approved on sixty of our customers new equipment platforms. In addition, we had proposals at our customers for an additional sixty-seven platforms.

"PowerCore employs a proprietary combination of high-density filtration construction and nano-fiber technology which together results in improved particle collection efficiency and higher air flow—all in a package half the size of competing technologies. These advantages make PowerCore systems ideally suited to meet size, weight and efficiency demands of our customers's new equipment designs. And, PowerCore's proprietary media and design means we will capture most of the replacement filter sales for equipment installed with our PowerCore air filtration systems."

■ "Our Ultra-Web nano-fiber media is a technology that remains unequaled in usefulness, functionality—and potential," said a company spokesman in fiscal 2007. "This technology application extends all the way from large and demanding industrial applications to high-tech bio-chemical frontiers.

"Our award-winning Downflo Oval technology is a great filtration solution for those large and demanding industrial applications. By employing Ultra-Web filtration media, our Downflo Oval collector provides a 25 percent increase in airflow capacity; improved airflow path; and a 29 percent increase in pulse cleaning pressure, giving our customers improved filtration efficiency without increasing the size of the collector."

■ On February 4, 2008, Donaldson announced that it had acquired the assets of LMC West, a manufacturer of industrial dust collection and filtration systems.

LMC West, based in Riverbank, California, designs and manufactures dust collectors and industrial filtration systems for woodworking, agricultural and industrial applications. LMC West had annual sales of $10 million in 2007.

"The acquisition of LMC West complements our existing Donaldson Torit® dust collection products well," said Tod Carpenter, vice president, Global Industrial Filtration Solutions. "Through the leadership of President Mike Clark and his team, LMC West has built a great reputation for quality products and successful installations. Their continued leadership from the California location will allow us to be more responsive to our West Coast Customers."

SECTOR: **Industrials**
BETA COEFFICIENT: **1.05**
10-YEAR COMPOUND EARNINGS PER SHARE GROWTH: **13.8%**
10-YEAR COMPOUND DIVIDENDS PER SHARE GROWTH: **14.9%**

	2007	2006	2005	2004	2003	2002	2001	2000
Revenues (Mil)	1,919	1,694	1,596	1,415	1,218	1,126	1,137	1,092
Net Income (Mil)	150.7	132.3	110.6	106.3	95.3	86.9	75.5	70.2
Earnings per share	1.83	1.55	1.27	1.18	1.05	0.95	0.83	0.76
Dividends per share	0.36	0.32	0.24	0.22	0.18	0.16	0.15	0.14
Price high	48.4	39.0	33.9	34.4	30.8	22.5	20.2	14.4
low	33.6	30.2	28.6	25.0	16.1	15.0	12.2	9.4

AGGRESSIVE GROWTH

Dover Corporation

280 Park Avenue ❑ New York, NY 10017-1292 ❑ (212) 922-1640 ❑ Direct Dividend reinvestment plan available ❑ Web site: *www.dovercorporation.com* ❑ Listed: NYSE ❑ Ticker symbol: DOV ❑ S&P rating: A− ❑ Value Line financial strength rating: A

On December 18, 2007, DE-STA-CO, an operating company within the Material Handling platform of Dover Corporation's Industrial Products segment, and worldwide leader in robotic tooling, work-holding and flexible industrial automation solutions, announced the acquisition of Industrial Motion Control, LLC.

Serving a global customer base, IMC is one of the world's leading industrial automation manufacturers of mechanical motion control products, including high precision cam-actuated index drives, parts handlers, and precision link conveyors, which are integrated into advanced factory automation systems used in a wide variety of industries, including paper conversion, consumer products, packaging, semiconductor, automotive, medical and pharmaceuticals. IMC's industry leading brand names of CAMCO and Ferguson have a proven reputation in the market for high load, high speed and high accuracy industrial automation applications. IMC is headquartered in Wheeling, Illinois, with additional facilities in Belgium and China.

"IMC's products serve a variety of attractive end markets and are a key upfront consideration in the design of new industrial automation systems," said Pat Carroll, president of DE-STA-CO. "Their products' strong brand names and channels combined with early visibility into industrial automation project requirements will pull through additional DE-STA-CO automation products."

Jeff Peterson, president of IMC added "We are very excited about this new partnership, knowing that DE-STA-CO products are very complementary to IMC's product portfolio. It gives us the opportunity to offer a more comprehensive solution to our customers as they concept and design their industrial automation systems."

DE-STA-CO, a Dover Company, is a worldwide leader in the innovation, design, manufacture and support of clamping, gripping, transfer and robotic tooling solutions for workplace and industrial automation needs. The company is committed to the Team DE-STA-CO philosophy, a progressive approach to doing business that focuses on providing consistent, standard-setting service and products to every customer, regardless of geographic location.

Company Profile

Dover Corporation is a diversified industrial manufacturer with over $6 billion in annual revenues and is comprised of about fifty operating companies that manufacture specialized industrial products and manufacturing equipment.

Dover's overall strategy is to acquire and develop platform businesses, marked by growth, innovation, and higher-than-average profits margins. Traditionally, the company has focused on purchasing entities that could operate independently (stand-alones). However, over the past ten years, Dover has put increased emphasis on also acquiring businesses that can be added to existing operations (add-ons).

On October 1, 2003, Dover completed its largest-ever acquisition with the $326 million purchase of WARN Industries, the world's most recognized brand in winches and wheel hubs for off-road vehicles. WARN makes equipment and accessories to enhance the performance of four-wheel-drive and all-terrain vehicles. The Oregon-based company, founded in 1948 to manufacture locking hubs to convert World War II Jeeps into on-road vehicles, developed the first recreational winch in 1959. In addition to specialized wheel hubs, WARN makes self-recovery, towing and utility winches.

A New Breakdown of Operations

In the fall of 2004, Dover announced that it would expand its existing subsidiary structure from four to six reporting market segments and concurrently realigned its forty-nine operating businesses in thirteen more focused business groupings. Management believes that this realignment will better-position Dover for "enhanced growth by providing increased management oversight of its operating businesses by expanding the company's acquisition capacity and by supporting the development of future executive management talent."

Effective January 1, 2005, the four subsidiaries and their respective operating company groups were:

Dover Diversified

- Industrial Equipment: Crenlo, Performance Motorsports, and Sargent
- Process Equipment: Graphics Microsystems, Hydratight Sweeney, SWEP, Tranter PHE, and Waukesha Bearings.

Dover Electronics

- Components: Dielectric, Dow-Key, K&L Microwave, Kurz-Kasch, Novacap, and Vectron.
- Commercial Equipment: Hydro Systems, and Triton.

Dover Industries

- Mobile Equipment: Heil Environmental, Heil Trailer, Marathon, and Somero.
- Service Equipment: Chief Automotive, Koolant Koolers, PDQ, and Rotary Lift.

Dover Resources

- Petroleum Equipment: C. Lee Cook, Energy Products Group.
- Fluid Solutions: Blackmer, OPW Fluid Transfer Group, OPW Fueling Components, RPA Technologies, and Wilden.
- Materials Handling: De-Sta-Co Industries, Texas Hydraulics, Tulsa Winch, and WARN Industries.

Shortcomings to Bear in Mind

■ I have labeled Dover as an Aggressive Growth stock because it has a Beta coefficient of 1.25, which means it can fluctuate as much as 25 percent more than the market. Which means it is not for widows and orphans. On the other hand, *Value Line* likes the stock and gives it a 2 rating for Timeliness, as of April 26, 2008.

Reasons to Buy

■ On January 30, 2008, commenting on results in 2007, CEO Ronald L. Hoffman, said, "We are pleased to report Dover's fourth quarter and full-year

results. Our diluted EPS for the full year surpassed our previous high by 12 percent. This performance was even more impressive given that it was accomplished in the face of headwinds in portions of our Electronic Technologies and Industrial Products segments. Company-wide organic growth (thus not including acquisitions) for the fourth quarter was 2.8 percent and 2.3 percent for the full year. Organic growth for our core industrial businesses (excluding Electronic Technologies) was 4.6 percent for the fourth quarter and 5.2 percent for the full-year indicating solid performance across our broad industrial business base.

"In addition to our strong financial results, Dover undertook several major initiatives in 2007 to enhance the long-term success of our company. First, we optimized Dover's operating structure by re-aligning into four defined industry segments with six business platforms. This new simplified structure gives us sharper focus on our major end markets and related acquisition program, accelerates the sharing of best practices and realization of business synergies, and facilitates management development. Second, we adjusted our capital allocation to reflect the value we felt was inherent in our company versus the available external opportunities, by announcing two successive share repurchase programs during the year which will reduce the outstanding share count by roughly 10 percent. In 2007, we repurchased 12.4 million shares for $591 million and have added another million shares to that total in early 2008. Additionally, we spent $274 million on strategic add-on acquisitions, including Pole/Zero and Camco, which considerably strengthened both our Microwave Products Group and Material Handling Platform. Lastly, we launched a new initiative to capture synergies throughout our organization. Although we are early in the process, we are highly encouraged by the scope of the potential synergy opportunities and are confident they can bring meaningful improvement to our bottom line.

"Looking forward to 2008, assuming a reasonably stable global economy, we are encouraged that our recent strategic initiatives will enable Dover to improve full year earnings per share in the 10 percent-plus range, despite headwinds in a few of our end-markets. We strongly believe in the positive direction Dover is headed and are confident our new structure, capital allocation model and synergy initiatives have laid solid groundwork for future growth. We also anticipate increased opportunities to expand our identified platforms through value-creating add-on acquisitions. Lastly, I'd once again like to thank the 34,000 employees of Dover around the globe for their tireless efforts, professionalism and dedication to improving Dover every day. Without their vital daily contributions, none of our current or future successes would be possible."

■ Dover has built its group of companies largely through acquisitions. However, management is extremely careful when considering which companies to bring into the fold. Management has these strict rules to guide its decisions:

- We seek manufacturers of high value-added, engineered products.
- Our focus is on equipment and machinery sold to a broad customer base of industrial and/or commercial users.

- We prefer companies that are niche-oriented market leaders with either a number one or a strong number two market position.
- Candidates should have strong national distribution (if not international, which is preferred).
- Dover is decentralized—we will only buy businesses that have strong management teams in place. We expect management of each operating company to behave as the emotional owners of that business and we have longer-term financial incentives designed to encourage continued growth of the business.
- Our judgment on the skill, energy, ethics and compatibility of the top executives at each acquisition candidate is one of the most critical factors in our decision making.
- We expect that operating companies will continue to be run by the management team in place upon acquisition. This reflects our decentralized structure and the fact that Dover buys companies for the long term; we do not have a "portfolio" mentality.
- Since we seek market leaders, we expect outstanding operating financial performance that can be built upon. EBIT's above 15 percent are the norm in Dover operating companies. We also expect that any business we own will generate significant real growth over time.

SECTOR: **Industrials**
BETA COEFFICIENT: **1.25**
10-YEAR COMPOUND EARNINGS PER SHARE GROWTH: **6.5%**
10-YEAR COMPOUND DIVIDENDS PER SHARE GROWTH: **8.3%**

	2007	2006	2005	2004	2003	2002	2001	2000
Revenues (Mil)	7,226	6,512	6,078	5,488	4,413	4,184	4,460	5,401
Net Income (Mil)	661	562	510	413	285	211	167	525
Earnings per share	3.26	2.73	2.50	2.00	1.40	1.04	0.82	2.57
Dividends per share	0.80	0.71	0.65	0.62	0.57	0.54	0.52	0.48
Price high	54.6	51.9	42.2	44.1	40.4	43.6	43.6	54.4
low	44.3	40.3	34.1	35.1	22.8	23.5	26.45	34.1

GROWTH AND INCOME

E. I. DuPont De Nemours

1007 Market Street ❑ Wilmington, DE 19898 ❑ (800) 441-7515 ❑ Dividend reinvestment plan available ❑ Web site: *www.dupont.com* ❑ Ticker symbol: DD ❑ Listed: NYSE ❑ S&P rating: B ❑ Value Line financial strength rating: A++

"DuPont is a science company. The core of our capability and competitive advantage is market-driven scientific discovery and new product innovation," said CEO Chad Holliday on March 1, 2008. "Our strengthened science capability has been the driving force behind the transformation of DuPont over the past decade, and has reshaped our businesses. In particular, DuPont is leading the rapid convergence of biology and chemistry to create additional competitive advantage and open new global markets for superior-performing products.

"Today, over 5,000 DuPont scientists worldwide are delivering high-margin, high-value-added products that are aimed directly at unmet market needs. Sales of these products have been instrumental in helping us overcome higher energy and ingredient costs, including record high oil prices.

"Based on important measures such as new product introductions, U.S. patent applications filed and U.S. patents granted, DuPont has demonstrated superior R&D performance, which helped boost average selling prices about 3 to 5 percent annually for the past three years. In 2007, 36 percent of our revenues—or about $10.5 billion—

were generated by products introduced in the last five years—up from 24 percent in 2001. In the face of a near tripling of oil prices, this has been critical.

"DuPont has a rich pipeline of new products, particularly in Agriculture, Safety & Protection, Electronics, and applied biosciences, with more projects underway than ever before. Our applied biosciences businesses promise significant future growth, particularly in biofuels and biomaterials where we have a clear technology leadership position and strong partnerships that will facilitate market access. These strengths are backed by a world-class intellectual property portfolio in biotechnology."

Company Profile

DuPont was founded in 1802 and was incorporated in Delaware in 1915. DuPont is a world leader in science and technology in a range of disciplines, including:

- Biotechnology
- Electronics
- Materials and Science
- Safety and Security
- Synthetic Fibers

Recently, the company strategically realigned its businesses into five market- and technology-focused growth platforms.

The growth platforms are:

- Agriculture and Nutrition
- Coatings and Color Technologies
- Electronic and Communication Technologies
- Performance Materials
- Safety and Protection

These growth platforms are designed to address large, attractive market spaces that allow the company to leverage its science and technology, products and brands, market access and global reach to bring innovative solutions to meet specific customer needs. A sixth platform was also formed to prepare it for separation from the company.

The growth platforms, together with Textiles and Interiors and Pharmaceuticals, comprise the company's seven reportable segments.

The company has operations in about seventy-five countries worldwide and about 55 percent of consolidated net sales are made to customers outside the United States. Subsidiaries and affiliates of DuPont conduct manufacturing, seed production, or selling activities, and some are distributors of products manufactured by the company.

The company utilizes numerous firms as well as internal sources to supply a wide range of raw materials, energy, supplies, services and equipment. To ensure availability, the company maintains multiple sources for fuels and most raw materials, including hydrocarbon feedstocks. Large volume purchases are generally procured under competitively priced supply contracts.

The major commodities, raw materials and supplies for the company's reportable segments include the following:

Agriculture and Nutrition: carbamic acid related intermediates; polyethylene; soybeans; soy flake; 5-choroindanone; soy lecithin; sulfonamides.

Coatings and Color Technologies: butyl acetate; chlorine; HDI based poly alaphatic isocyanates; industrial gases; ore; petroleum coke; pigments.

Electronic and Communications Technologies: chloroform; fluorspar; hydrofluoric acid; kraton; oxydianiline; perchloroethylene; polyester; polyethylene; precious metals; pyromellitic dianhydride.

Performance Materials: adipic acid; butanediol; ethane; ethylene glycol; fiberglass; hexamethylenediamine; methacrylic acid; methanol; natural gas; paraxylene.

Safety and Protection: ammonia; aniline; benzene; high-density polyethylene; isophthaloyl chloride; metaphenylenediamine; methyl methacrylate; natural gas; paraphenylenediamine; polyester fiber; polypropylene; propylene; terephthaloyl chloride; wood pulp.

Textiles and Interiors: acetylene; adipic acid; ammonia; butadiene; cyclohexane; natural gas; paraxylene; terephthalic acid.

Shortcomings to Bear in Mind

▪ According to the company's form 10-K (similar to an annual report, but much more detailed, sophisticated and technical), "The company's businesses compete on a variety of factors, such as price, product quality, and performance or specifications, continuity of supply, customer service and breadth of product line, depending on the characteristics of the particular market involved and the product or service provided.

"Major competitors include diversified industrial companies principally based in the United States, Western Europe, Japan, China and Korea. In the aggregate, these competitors offer a wide range of products from agricultural, commodity and specialty chemicals to plastics, fibers and advanced materials. The company also competes in certain markets with smaller, more specialized firms who offer a narrow range of products or converted products that functionally compete with the company's offerings."

Reasons to Buy

- DuPont has introduced more than 1,000 new products each year for the past several years.
- On April 18, 2008, *Value Line Investment Survey* gave DuPont a 1 rating, tantamount to a STRONG BUY, with this analysis by Michael Napoli, CPA, "DuPont's Pioneer Hi-Bred business has recently introduced Optimum AcreMax. This new insect-protection system aims to improve corn growers' productivity. Pioneer expects to launch the first phase of this system in 2009, pending regulatory approval. In addition, DuPont has formed a collaboration agreement with Arcadia Biosciences, whereby Pioneer Hi-Bred will utilize Arcadia's technology to improve nitrogen use efficiency in corn."

According to DuPont's form 10-K, "The company believes that its patent and trademark estate provides it with an important competitive advantage. It has established a global network of attorneys, as well as branding, advertising, and licensing professionals, to procure, maintain, protect, enhance, and gain value from this estate."

What's more, "The company owns approximately 19,600 worldwide patents and approximately 13,600 worldwide patent applications. In 2004, the company was granted almost 490 U.S. patents and about 1,740 international patents."

On November 3, 2006, DuPont introduced DuPont Tyvek ThermaWrap, a breathable, metallized product for the home-building industry. Designed to enhance the thermal performance of walls, DuPont Tyvek ThermaWrap provides all the additional benefits of a water-resistive barrier. The product helps thermal management by managing radiant heat, while helping to protect structures from air and water intrusion and ultraviolet rays.

DuPont Tyvek ThermaWrap is a specially engineered housewrap with a breathable aluminum layer. Its combination of high vapor permeability and thermal protection forms a quality wall defense against moisture condensation, which can lead to mold and mildew growth. Previously, non-DuPont generations of radiant barriers were commonly made solely of aluminum foils, which act as barriers, do not permit water to pass through, and can lead to moisture accumulation and possible damage.

"This is a truly revolutionary product that delivers sustainable solutions through science and innovation," said Tom Powell, vice president and general manager, DuPont Surfaces and Building Innovations. "DuPont Tyvek ThermaWrap has been engineered to provide the best possible balance of breathable barrier properties, so it's light and flexible, highly vapor permeable, but still air-tight, water-resistant, wind-tight and will last the entire lifetime of any building. We're focused on ensuring homes are sealed, protected from harsh weather, while at the same time create aesthetically pleasing, comfortable living environments."

As part of its new Clean Technologies solutions, DuPont announced on March 13, 2008, that it has started up a plant in El Paso, Texas, and is in the process of starting up a facility in Linden, New Jersey, that will help refineries reduce their environmental footprints with on-site spent sulfuric acid regeneration and sulfur gas recovery services with significant reductions in sulfur dioxide emissions. The custom-designed DuPont facilities that are built on refiners' facilities will provide for efficient and environmentally superior management of the sulfur gas processing while providing a cost effective and reliable sulfuric acid regeneration service for the refineries.

SECTOR: Materials
BETA COEFFICIENT: 1.05
10-YEAR COMPOUND EARNINGS PER SHARE GROWTH: −1.1%
10-YEAR COMPOUND DIVIDENDS PER SHARE GROWTH: 2.1%

	2007	2006	2005	2004	2003	2002	2001	2000
Revenues (Mil)	30,653	28,982	26,639	27,340	26,996	24,006	24,726	28,268
Net Income (Mil)	2,988	3,148	2,100	2,390	1,607	2,012	1,236	2,884
Earnings per share	3.22	2.88	2.32	2.38	1.65	2.01	1.19	2.73
Dividends per share	1.52	1.48	1.46	1.40	1.40	1.40	1.40	1.40
Price high	53.9	49.7	54.9	49.4	46.0	49.8	49.9	74.0
low	42.3	38.5	37.6	39.9	34.7	35.0	32.6	38.2

CONSERVATIVE GROWTH

Ecolab, Inc.

370 Wabasha Street North ❑ St. Paul, MN 55102-1390 ❑ (651) 293-2809 ❑ Dividend reinvestment program available ❑ Web site: *www.ecolab.com* ❑ Listed: NYSE ❑ Ticker symbol: ECL ❑ S&P rating: A ❑ Value Line financial strength rating: A

On November 12, 2007, Ecolab Inc. announced that it had expanded its infection prevention expertise in the health care industry with the purchase of Microtek Medical Holdings Inc. (Nasdaq: MTMD). The Alpharetta, Georgia-based manufacturer and marketer of infection control products for health care and acute care facilities specializes in infection barrier equipment drapes, patient drapes, fluid control products, and operating room cleanup systems. Microtek's 2006 sales were $142 million.

Commenting on the transaction, CEO Douglas M. Baker Jr. said, "Microtek represents a terrific addition to the Ecolab family, and furthers our efforts to become a leader in providing comprehensive solutions to significantly reduce infections and contamination in the healthcare environment. By combining Microtek's excellent barrier product lines with our complementary strength in skin care, disinfectants and central sterile, Ecolab is now the only company that can offer system-wide solutions for healthcare facilities that help improve operational efficiencies, reduce infections,

and most importantly, improve patient safety."

According to the U.S. Centers for Disease Control and Prevention, more than 2 million health care patients contract hospital-acquired infections (HAIs) annually in North America alone. The cost to treat these individuals is estimated to be $30 billion to $50 billion annually, and even with treatment, approximately 100,000 are believed to die each year. With the Centers for Medicare and Medicaid Services recently announcing they are considering excluding funding for "preventable" HAIs, health care leaders are looking for help in solving this complex problem more than ever before.

"Ecolab can provide the layers of protection healthcare facilities are looking for," Mr. Baker said. "Our clinically trained healthcare experts can offer healthcare facilities the latest in innovative products and technologies; integrated clinical and support services; data utilization and process improvement; training and continuing education; quality assurance testing; thought leadership; and best practices. We can help our customers clean the patient, break the vectors that could contaminate the patient, and clean the healthcare facility environment."

Company Profile

According to a company officer, "When it comes to delivering premium commercial cleaning and sanitizing solutions on a truly global basis, Ecolab is the one. No other company comes close to rivaling our worldwide reach or the extraordinary breadth of products, systems and services we offer.

"We meet the varied and specialized needs of thousands of diverse businesses and institutions in North America, Europe, Asia, Latin America, Africa, the Middle East—the list of countries in which we do business reads like an atlas. In 2001, we took decisive actions to ensure that Ecolab remains number one in the world for many years to come."

Founded in 1923, Ecolab is the leading global developer and marketer of premium cleaning, sanitizing, pest elimination, maintenance and repair products and services for the world's hospitality, institutional and industrial markets.

In the early years, Ecolab served the restaurant and lodging industries and has since broadened its scope to include hospitals, laundries, schools, retail and commercial property, among others.

The company conducts its domestic business under these segments:

The Institutional Division is the leading provider of cleaners and sanitizers for warewashing, laundry, kitchen cleaning and general housecleaning, product-dispensing equipment and dishwashing racks and related kitchen sundries to the foodservice, lodging, and health care industries. It also provides products and services for pool and spa treatment.

Food & Beverage offers cleaning and sanitizing products and services to farms, dairy plants, food and beverage processors, and pharmaceutical plants.

The Kay Division is the largest supplier of cleaning and sanitizing products for the quick-service restaurant, convenience store, and flood retail markets.

Ecolab also sells janitorial and healthcare products (detergents, floor care, disinfectants, odor control, and hand care under the Airkem and Huntington brand names; textile care products for large institutional and commercial laundries; vehicle care products for rental, fleet, and retail car washes; and water-treatment products for commercial, institutional, and industrial markets.

Other domestic services include institutional and commercial pest elimination and prevention; and the GCS commercial kitchen equipment repair services.

Around the world, the company operates directly in nearly seventy countries. International sales account for 22 percent of sales. In addition, the company reaches customers in more then 100 countries through distributors, licensees and export operations. To meet the global demands for its products, Ecolab operates more than fifty state-of-the-art manufacturing and distribution facilities worldwide.

Shortcomings to Bear in Mind

■   Wall Street seems well aware that Ecolab has a bright future, since it has tagged it with an above-average multiple, typically twenty-five times earnings or higher.

Reasons to Buy

■   On February 11, 2008, Mr. Baker said, "We are very pleased with our fourth quarter results. We enjoyed strong growth in our U.S. and Latin America regions, improving sales trends in Asia Pacific and we are well underway with our plans to enhance our European business performance. Our U.S. Cleaning and Sanitizing segment realized very good margin development that drove the quarter's profit improvement and more than offset our business investments elsewhere.

"In total, 2007 was an excellent year. We introduced exciting new products and services that enhance customer results and reduce their costs, improved our operating efficiency, undertook critical investments to strengthen our business for the future, and did all that while delivering excellent earnings growth and improved shareholder value. We are proud of our accomplishments for the year and the people that made them happen.

"We expect another good year in 2008 and look to once again outperform our markets through aggressive sales, outstanding service, innovative solutions, and close attention to customer needs. We will use our strength to continue to make significant investments to strengthen and reinvigorate our European business and integrate and build upon our exciting new acquisitions in healthcare and water management. These investments should lead to stronger earnings momentum as the year progresses while strengthening our growth opportunities for years to come. We have an outstanding future and an outstanding team to realize it. We look forward to making terrific progress on these goals in 2008 and delivering another year of superior shareholder returns."

■ Standard & Poor's *Stock Reports* said Ecolab was a BUY on April 12, 2008, with this analysis by Richard O'Reilly, CFA, "We expect ECL to post ongoing solid sales and EPS (earnings per share) gains in coming periods, based on our belief that conditions will remain healthy in the global industries that it serves."

■ On March 14, 2008, *Value Line Investment Survey* awarded a 2 rating to Ecolab, tantamount to a BUY. Frederick L. Harris III said, "We are optimistic about Ecolab's prospects in 2008 and 2009. Sales ought to be boosted nicely by aggressive efforts to attract and retain accounts and product introductions, with businesses in the United States, Asia Pacific, and Latin America leading the way."

■ Ecolab has a highly skilled research and development team, which continues to turn out innovative new products. According to a company spokesman, "Never content

with the status quo, we strive for constant improvement, so far earning nearly 2,600 patents worldwide. And we boast the industry's most sophisticated R&D facilities—where breakthroughs happen every day."

■ On August 7, 2007, Ecolab Inc. announced it had agreed to purchase Microtek Medical Holdings Inc., an Alpharetta, Georgia-based manufacturer and marketer of infection control products for healthcare and acute care facilities. Microtek's specialized product lines include infection barrier equipment drapes, patient drapes, fluid control products, and operating room cleanup systems. Microtek's 2006 sales were $142 million.

Mr. Baker said, "This represents another strong step to significantly expand Ecolab's growing presence in healthcare cleaning and infection prevention. As the global leader in premium cleaning and sanitation, we have a long-standing record of bringing new, innovative and effective solutions to the foodservice, lodging, food and beverage processing and healthcare industries, helping them to deliver cleaner, safer, and healthier products, experiences and outcomes. We are continuing to build on our capabilities, particularly in the healthcare market, as we focus on improving cleaning and sanitizing solutions for patients and staff, and simultaneously reduce healthcare associated infections (HAIs).

"Microtek will combine with our existing hand hygiene, medical instrument, and surface and environmental cleaning and disinfection offerings to comprise a critical part of our strategy to offer broad and complete product solutions for the healthcare market, and especially HAIs," Baker continued. "Further, Microtek's strong team and excellent customer relationships will provide us new avenues to pursue future growth with our existing products.

"We expect dilution from the transaction to be $0.01 per share in the fourth quarter 2007, but we believe our current business momentum will enable us to offset that; as a result, we continue to look for 2007 earnings per share to be in the $1.64 to $1.66 range. We expect dilution from Microtek to represent $0.02 per share in 2008, and show accretion building thereafter."

SECTOR: **Materials**
BETA COEFFICIENT: **.95**
10-YEAR COMPOUND EARNINGS PER SHARE GROWTH: **13%**
10-YEAR COMPOUND DIVIDENDS PER SHARE GROWTH: **12.5%**

		2007	2006	2005	2004	2003	2002	2001	2000
Revenues (Mil)		5,470	4,896	4,535	4,185	3,762	3,404	2,321	2,264
Net Income (Mil)		427	369	320	310	277	210	188	209
Earnings per share		1.70	1.43	1.23	1.19	1.06	0.80	0.73	0.79
Dividends per share		0.52	0.40	0.35	0.33	0.29	0.27	0.26	0.24
Price	high	52.8	46.4	37.2	35.6	27.9	25.2	22.1	22.8
	low	37.0	33.6	30.7	26.1	23.1	18.3	14.3	14.0

GROWTH AND INCOME

Emerson Electric Company

8000 W. Florissant Avenue ❑ P. O. Box 4100 ❑ St. Louis, MO 63136-8506 ❑ (314) 553-2197 ❑ Dividend reinvestment plan available ❑ Web site: *www.gotoemerson.com* ❑ Listed: NYSE ❑ Ticker symbol: EMR ❑ Fiscal years end September 30 ❑ S&P rating: A ❑ Value Line financial strength rating: A++

"David Farr isn't the only chief executive officer who gets giddy when he talks about his company's venture into new wireless products," said Christopher Leonard, writing for the Associated Press on December 30, 2007.

"But Emerson Electric Co. is not selling the kind of wireless technology that lets you download songs while sipping a latte. It is selling the kind of wireless products that keep oil refineries from exploding and killing hundreds of people.

"'In this industry, you make a mistake and things do go boom,' Farr said in a recent interview.

"Emerson's foray—wireless sensors that monitor liquid levels and pressure in the vast maze of pipes that run through oil refineries—symbolizes the company's business strategy. It is profitable, it is growing, and virtually no one outside a specific niche industry has ever heard of it.

"With $22.6 billion in annual revenue and a rank of 115th on the *Fortune* 500 list last year, St. Louis-based Emerson has a global footprint of manufacturing and design facilities in more than 150 countries. But the company operates largely behind the scenes, making almost nothing that is sold directly to consumers.

"While it may not have a flashy public image, Emerson's low-key strategy is getting a lot of notice on Wall Street. The company's stock is trading at an all-time high after Emerson reported a strong profit this fall and forecast profit growth for next year."

Company Profile

Emerson is a leading manufacturer of a broad list of intermediate products such as electrical motors and drives, appliance components and process-control devices. The company also produces hand and power tools, as well as accessories.

Founded 110 years ago, Emerson is not a typical high-tech capital goods producer.

Rather, the company makes such prosaic things as refrigerator compressors, pressure gauges, and In-Sink Erator garbage disposals—basic products that are essential to industry.

Here are the company's five segments:

Industrial Automation

This segment of the company provides integral horsepower motors, alternators, electronic and mechanical drives, industrial valves, electrical equipment, specialty heating, lighting, testing, and ultrasonic welding and cleaning products for industrial applications. Key growth drivers for the segment include the embedding of electronics into motors and other equipment to enable self-diagnosis and preventative maintenance functionality, as well as alternators for diesel and natural gas generator sets to create reliable distributed power solutions.

Appliance and Tools

This operation includes the Emerson Storage Solutions, Emerson Tools, Emerson Appliance Solutions, and Emerson Motors brand platforms. Customer offerings feature an extensive range of consumer, commercial and industrial storage products; market-leading tools; electrical components and systems for appliances; and the world's largest offering of fractional horsepower motors. Key growth drivers include professional-grade tools serving the fast-growing home center market, as well as advanced electrical motors, which create entirely new market opportunities for Emerson.

Climate Technologies

This segment is known for leading technologies and solutions for heating, air conditioning, and refrigeration applications that provide homeowners with a whole new level of comfort and efficiency, while lowering their energy bills. Climate Technologies's remote monitoring capabilities help assure food safety and quality for grocery stores.

Process Management

Award-winning technologies help oil and gas, refining, power generation, chemical, pharmaceutical, and other process businesses increase plant uptime, improve productivity, and identify and eliminate problems before they occur. Emerson offers intelligent control systems and software, measurement instruments, valves, and expertise in engineering, project management, and consulting.

Network Power

Businesses depend on the company's Network Power for reliable power to run data centers, telecommunications networks, and other mission-critical applications. Emerson leads the industry in the design, manufacture, installation, and service of power solutions such as AC and DC backup systems and precision cooling equipment.

Shortcomings to Bear in Mind

■ Emerson Electric is an excellent company with a consistent growth rate. However, the compound growth rate of earnings per share and dividends is just over 7 percent, hardly a spectacular showing. That's why I have classified it as a Growth and Income stock.

Reasons to Buy

■ On November 6, 2007, Emerson Electric announced record net sales for fiscal 2007 of $22.6 billion, an increase of 12 percent from the prior year. Sales for the fourth quarter ended September 30, 2007 were $6.1 billion, an increase of 11 percent over the $5.5 billion reported in the same period last year. The company achieved underlying sales growth in the quarter of 7 percent, which excludes increases of 3 percent due to favorable currency exchange rates and 1 percent from acquisitions, net of divestitures.

Earnings per share for the fourth quarter of $.78 represented an increase of 20 percent over the $.65 achieved in the fourth quarter of 2006. The company translated strong sales performance during the quarter into expanded operating profit margin, which was a key component of the 20 percent increase in earnings per share. Operating profit margin during the quarter was 16.6 percent, an improvement of 70 basis points from the prior year period. This improvement was driven by a continued focus on cost reduction programs and leverage on sales increases. Pretax earnings margin was 14.8 percent compared to 14.1 percent in the prior year period.

"Emerson had a great finish to 2007 and enters 2008 with solid momentum," said Farr. "End market conditions tracked expectations and the company's ability to execute in this environment led to performance in sales, earnings and cash generation that exceeded our expectations.

"Emerson's performance has been outstanding over the last five years. We have focused on the correct strategies to grow across the business platforms while also enhancing shareholder returns. This is a proven formula that Emerson will continue to follow as it pursues future opportunities."

■ On February 5, 2008, Standard & Poor's *Stock Reports* named Emerson Electric a BUY. Its analyst, Christopher Lippincott, said, "We believe EMR's business prospects over the next two years remain strong, as the company gains continued organic revenue from international sales, globally valued brand platforms, and new product introductions in key business segments, as well as opportunistic bolt-on acquisitions and favorable currency translation."

■ On April 11, 2008, *Value Line* gave the stock a 2 rating, essentially a BUY. Kevin Downing had this to say, "Double-digit sales growth from four of the company's five segments drove the top line (sales) advance in 2007. The Process Management division's sales grew 18 percent over the year-ago period, thanks to strong results in Asia, and continued

expansion of the world's energy markets. Network Power was also a standout, posting sales growth of 17 percent, most of which came from internal gains in the United States and Asia. The Climate Technologies and Industrial Automation units rounded out the company's top-line growth with respective gains of 11 percent and 13 percent."

■ Argus Research Company had good things to say about Emerson on February 6, 2008, giving the company a BUY rating. Rashid Dahod said, "Propelled by continued sales growth in the Process Management, Industrial Automation, Network Power and Climate Technologies segments, and with help from its restructuring efforts, Emerson continues to demonstrate earnings momentum. We believe that EMR's broad global footprint and its combination of strong end markets, acquisitions and margin expansion should keep earnings on a growth path."

In the magazine's January issue, *Institutional Investor* credited Farr with "positioning his company to withstand more difficult times ahead," noting that while leading the company through difficult restructuring earlier in the decade, Farr maintained important investments in technology and innovation. He was also credited with helping position Emerson for strong global growth that, in fiscal year 2007, resulted in 52 percent of the company's sales occurring outside the U.S., compared with 40 percent when Farr took over in 2000. Farr has served as CEO of Emerson since October 2000 and was named chairman in September 2004. He is only the third chief executive of Emerson in the past fifty-plus years. He assumed the title of company president in November 2005.

Under Farr's leadership, Emerson has grown its position in global markets, increased its focus on customer-oriented services and solutions, and invested in industry-leading technologies to enhance its long-term growth and market position. With his management team, Farr has kept the company focused on creating long-term value and maintaining Emerson's solid financial performance relative to growth in sales, earnings, cash flow, and return on capital.

■ Technology is fundamental to Emerson's sales growth. As a consequence, the company has been increasing its investment in Engineering & Development, notably in such sectors as communications, software, and electronics. E&D investment, moreover, has risen every year since 1973.

■ Emerson is now supplying the world's leading windmill manufacturer with more than 3,000 wind turbine generators, helping deliver electricity to the national grid for twenty-eight different countries.

SECTOR: **Industrials**
BETA COEFFICIENT: **1.00**
10-YEAR COMPOUND EARNINGS PER SHARE GROWTH: **7.8%**
10-YEAR COMPOUND DIVIDENDS PER SHARE GROWTH: **7.4%**

		2007	2006	2005	2004	2003	2002	2001	2000
Revenues (Mil)		22,572	20,133	17,305	15,615	13,958	13,748	15,480	15,545
Net Income (Mil)		2,136	1,845	1,487	1,257	1,013	1,060	1,032	1,422
Earnings per share		2.66	2.24	1.78	1.49	1.21	1.26	1.25	1.65
Dividends per share		1.10	0.89	0.85	0.80	0.79	0.78	0.77	0.72
Price	high	59.1	45.2	38.9	35.5	32.5	33.1	39.8	39.9
	low	41.3	36.8	30.4	28.1	21.9	20.9	22.0	20.3

AGGRESSIVE GROWTH

EnCana Corporation

P. O Box 2850 □ Calgary, Alberta □ Canada T2P 2S5 □ (403) 645-4737 □ Dividend reinvestment plan not available □ Web site: *www.encana.com* □ Ticker symbol: ECA □ Listed: NYSE □ S&P rating: B+ □ Value Line financial strength rating: B++

On November 5, 2007, a subsidiary of EnCana Corporation entered into an agreement to acquire all of the Deep Bossier natural gas and land interests of privately owned Leor Energy in Texas for US$2.55 billion.

"We are acquiring our partner's 50 percent interest in the prolific Amoruso Field, centered in one of the fastest-growing natural gas trends in North America—the Deep Bossier formation. These assets are a seamless fit with our existing production and operations, and they hold tremendous growth potential in the near and longer term. Strengthening our Deep Bossier position exemplifies EnCana's core strategy—being a leading North American unconventional gas producer," said CEO Randy Eresman.

"We began to work on acquiring Leor's remaining interest this spring and becoming the 100 percent owner of the Amoruso Field is the culmination of more than two years of development work along the Deep Bossier geological trend in East Texas. As operator of the Amoruso Field, we have led the exploration, definition and systematic development of this exciting new geological resource since our entry in 2005 until today. In just over twenty-four months, production from the Amoruso Field has grown from zero to more than 215 million gross cubic feet per day. This is an exciting long-life asset that is at the earliest days of development. It has the potential to be the leading resource play in our North American portfolio."

The Amoruso Field is home to some of the largest producing onshore gas wells in the United States during the past five years. Two of the country's five largest wells since 2002—Bonnie Ann 1 and South McLean B1—are in the Amoruso Field. Initial gross production rates in these wells have exceeded 50 million cubic feet per day. The most recent Amoruso well, Laxson, is producing about 65 million gross cubic feet of gas per day. EnCana has seven rigs working in the field now and expects to increase that to about ten next year.

"This is a resource acquisition. We are investing today for tomorrow's reserves and production growth. This acquisition follows our successful practice of entering a play early, locking up a large land position, applying the right technology and generating value that was previously unrecognized. It is similar to what we have done in plays such as Jonah in Wyoming and Cutbank Ridge in British Columbia," Mr. Eresman said.

EnCana estimates the Deep Bossier lands acquired from Leor have about 200 net well locations. Each well costs about $10 million to drill, complete and tie in and is expected to recover between 8 billion and 13 billion cubic feet of gas. This results in estimated ultimate recovery of between 1.3 trillion to 1.8 trillion cubic feet of gas net after royalties. At the midpoint of this range, EnCana estimates that would result in a full-cycle finding, development and acquisition cost of about $3.00 per thousand cubic feet.

When combined with EnCana's existing Deep Bossier interests, the company estimates that it would have a total of about 370 potential drilling locations with a similar range of estimated gas recovery per well. This would put estimated ultimate recovery, on a net after-royalty basis, at between 2.4 trillion and 3.3 trillion cubic feet, resulting, at the midpoint, in a full-cycle finding, development and acquisition cost of about

$2.50 per thousand cubic feet. In addition to the Deep Bossier formations, the acquired lands have significant potential in shallower formations that is expected to enhance the ultimate gas recovered and the play's economics.

Company Profile

EnCana is one of North America's leading independent crude oil and natural gas exploration and production companies. EnCana pursues growth from its portfolio of unconventional long-life resource plays situated in Canada and the United States. The company defines resource plays as large contiguous accumulations of hydrocarbons, located in thick and extensive deposits, which typically have low geological and commercial development risk and low average decline rates.

EnCana's disciplined pursuit of these unconventional assets enabled it to become North America's largest natural gas producer and a leading developer of oil sands through in-situ recovery. The term in-situ means that the thick bitumen from subsurface oil sands is mobilized through injecting steam into specialized wells.

According to an article in *Barron's* October 12, 2005, Andrew Bary said, "It costs about $20 a barrel to transform bitumen, the heavy tar-like oil found in abundance in northern Alberta, into conventional crude oil that can be pumped to refineries in Canada and the U.S. When oil prices stood at the $20-to-$30-a-barrel range, the oil sands had limited appeal. But with crude trading above $60 a barrel, the economics of the oil sands becomes compelling."

The Barron's writer also said, "Producing crude from oil sands is dirty: The bitumen typically is strip-mined, then separated from the surrounding sands in a process that produces waste water that sits in giant pools. Once separated, bitumen needs to be heated, usually with natural gas, to produce crude oil. Environmental critics decry the strip-mining, its ugly aftereffects and the energy-intensive upgrading process, which produces greenhouse gases and other emissions."

The company is also engaged in exploration and production activities internationally and has interests in midstream operations and assets, including natural gas storage facilities, natural gas processing facilities, power plants and pipelines.

EnCana operates under two main divisions: Upstream and Midstream and Marketing.

Upstream

The Upstream division manages EnCana's exploration for, and development of, natural gas, crude oil and natural gas liquids and other related activities. Following the merger in 2002, the majority of EnCana's Upstream operations are situated in Canada, the United States, Ecuador, and the United Kingdom's central North Sea. From the time of the merger through early 2004, EnCana focused on the development and expansion of its highest growth, highest return assets in those key areas. In 2004, the company sharpened its strategic focus to concentrate on its inventory of North American resource play assets. In focusing its portfolio of assets, EnCana completed a number of significant acquisitions during the past three years.

Midstream and Marketing

EnCana's Midstream and Marketing division encompasses the corporations's midstream operations and market optimization activities. EnCana's midstream activities are comprised of natural gas storage operations, natural gas liquids processing and storage, power generation operations and pipelines. The company's marketing groups are focused on enhancing the sale of Upstream proprietary production. Correspondingly, the marketing groups undertake market optimization activities, including third-party purchases and sales of product, which provides operational flexibility for transportation commitments, product type, delivery points, and customer diversification.

Shortcomings to Bear in Mind

- On March 14, 2008, Adam Rosner, an analyst with *Value Line Investment Survey*, said "Our projections indicate that EnCana's stock holds below average appreciation potential for the next three to five years. Despite a sharp rise in profits in 2007, advances will likely become less robust, reflecting a higher operating cost environment."

Reasons to Buy

- On February 14, 2008, EnCana said that it had achieved strong increases in 2007 cash flow and operating earnings during a year of solid growth in natural gas and oil production. Financial results were enhanced by EnCana's favorable gas price hedges, which offset weaker gas prices, and excellent performance from the company's downstream segment of the integrated oil business. EnCana also achieved very strong proved reserves additions at competitive costs.

"EnCana delivered tremendous operational and financial performance in 2007, a direct result of our sharpened focus on North American unconventional natural gas and integrated oil resource plays," said Eresman. "The sustainable value creation capacity of our resource play strategy is becoming increasingly evident. With strong production growth of 11 percent per share and successful price hedges that delivered a $1 billion benefit to 2007 cash flow, our company's cash flow, operating earnings and free cash flow all increased substantially in a year when our industry faced many challenges. In 2007, production from our key natural gas resource plays grew 14 percent, while production from our integrated oil projects increased 25 percent. Our newly established refining business also delivered great results, achieving twice the cash flow we expected during its inaugural year. Completing the year's success story, proved reserves additions were also substantial, replacing more than two times the amount of oil and gas we produced. Most importantly, these reserves additions were achieved at a highly competitive finding and development cost of $1.65 per thousand cubic feet equivalent. EnCana's energy resources lie beneath its more than 25 million net acres of land in North America, largely in the heart of the unconventional fairway. Our low-risk, long-life resource play assets hold the potential to deliver strong shareholder value creation for many years ahead. As a reflection of the company's confidence in the sustainability of its business model, EnCana's board of directors has approved a doubling of our quarterly dividend to 40 cents per share," Mr. Eresman said.

■ "EnCana's geographic focus is North America, which has among the highest known concentration of unconventional natural gas and oil sands resources in the world," said a company official. "Compared to conventional plays, these long-life reservoirs typically have lower-than-average long-term decline rates and lower geographical and commercial development risk.

"EnCana's people have the skills, expertise, and technology to maximize the value from its 26 million net acres of North American onshore lands, 17 million of which are undeveloped. EnCana has currently identified 37,000 future drilling locations and more than 24 trillion cubic feet of gas equivalent of unbooked resource potential.

"EnCana defines unbooked resource potential (URP) as quantities of oil and natural gas on existing land holdings that are not yet classified as proved reserves, but which EnCana believes may be moved into the proved reserves category and produced in the future."

SECTOR: **Energy**
BETA COEFFICIENT: **.90**
10-YEAR COMPOUND EARNINGS PER SHARE GROWTH: **27.4%**
10-YEAR COMPOUND DIVIDENDS PER SHARE GROWTH: **19%**

	2007	2006	2005	2004	2003	2002	2001	2000
Revenues (Mil)	21,446	16,399	14,573	11,810	10,216	7,064	6,333	4,835
Net Income (Mil)	3,959	3,270	3,241	1,976	1,375	794	822	696
Earnings per share	5.18	3.91	3.64	2.11	1.44	0.82	1.58	1.37
Dividends per share	.80	.38	0.28	0.20	0.16	0.13	0.13	0.13
Price high	75.9	55.9	59.8	28.7	20.0	16.2	14.8*	
low	42.4	39.5	26.4	19.0	15.0	11.4	11.3*	

*EnCana was formed from a merger between PanCanadian Energy Corporation and Alberta Energy Company on April 5, 2002.

CONSERVATIVE GROWTH

Energen Corporation

605 Richard Arrington Jr. Boulevard North □ Birmingham, AL 35203-2707 □ (205) 326-8421 □ Direct dividend reinvestment plan available □ Web site: *www.energen.com* □ Listed: NYSE □ Ticker symbol: EGN □ S&P rating: A □ Value Line financial strength rating: A

The San Juan Basin in New Mexico and Colorado has long been an important source of domestic natural gas. This mountainous region is home to abundant conventional natural gas, natural gas liquids and coalbed methane reserves. The San Juan Basin is Energen Resources's largest area of operation and represents 53 percent of the company's proved reserves and some 314,000 net acres.

Energen Resources first established a presence in the San Juan Basin in 1997 with the acquisition of 319 Bcfe (billion cubic feet equivalent) of proved reserves from Burlington Resources; the company has substantially expanded its operations there through subsequent acquisitions and successful development.

Energen Resources cumulative production in the San Juan Basin totals more than 270 Bcfe, and the company today is the seventh-largest gas producer in the basin. Underscoring the company's preference for long-lived reserves, Energen Resources's reserves-to-production ratio in the San Juan Basin exceeds twenty-one; this means that, at current rates of production, it would take twenty-one years to exhaust the company's existing proved reserves.

Energen Resources focuses on four key reservoirs in the San Juan Basin. These range from coalbed methane in the over-pressured Fruitland Coal to conventional gas and natural gas liquids in the Pictured Cliffs, Mesa Verde and Dakota formations; these targets are all at depths of about 3,000 feet to 8,500 feet.

The company invested about $100 million of capital in the region in 2007 to drill sixty-one net wells and perform other devel-opment-related activities. Over the last few years, Energen Resources has experienced excellent results from drilling some thirty-five horizontal wells in the over-pressured Fruit-land Coal; Energen Resources has drilled more horizontal wells in the basin than any other operator. Included in its drilling plans for 2007 are thirty more horizontal wells and sixteen horizontal sidetracks from existing vertical wells.

Company Profile

Energen is a diversified holding company engaged primarily in the acquisition, development, exploration, and production of oil, natural gas, and natural gas liquids in the continental United States. It also has a stake in the purchase, distribution, and sale of natural gas, principally in central and north Alabama. Its two subsidiaries are Energen Resources Corporation and Alabama Gas Corporation (Alagasco).

Energen was incorporated in Alabama in 1978 in connection with the reorganization of its oldest subsidiary, Alagasco. Alagasco was formed in 1948 by the merger of Alabama Gas Company into Birmingham Gas Company, the predecessors of which had been in existence since the mid-1800s. Alagasco became a public company in 1953. Energen Resources was formed in 1971 as a subsidiary of Alagasco and became a subsidiary of Energen in the 1978 reorganization.

Oil and Gas Operations

Energen's oil and gas operations focus on increasing production and adding proved reserves through the acquisition and development of oil and gas properties. To a lesser extent, Energen Resources explores for and develops new reservoirs, primarily in areas in which it has an operating presence. Substantially all gas, oil and natural gas liquids production is sold to third parties. Energen Resources also provides operating services in the Black Warrior Basin in Alabama for its partners and third parties. These services include overall project management and day-to-day decision-making, relative to project operations.

At the end of the latest fiscal year, Energen Resources inventory of proved oil and gas reserves totaled 1,364.9 billion cubic feet equivalent (Bcfe). Substantially all of the company's 1.4 trillion cubic feet equivalent of reserves are situated in the San Juan Basin in New Mexico, the Permian Basin in west Texas, the Black Warrior Basin in Alabama, and the north Louisiana/east Texas region. About 81 percent of Energen Resources's year-end reserves are proved developed reserves. Energen Resources reserves are long-lived, with a year-end reserves-to-production ratio of sixteen. Natural gas represents about 65 percent of Energen Resources's proved reserves, with oil representing about 23 percent, and natural gas liquids making up the rest.

Natural Gas Distribution

Alagasco is the largest natural gas distribution utility in the state of Alabama. Alagasco purchases natural gas through interstate and intrastate marketers and suppliers. It then distributes the purchased gas through its distribution facilities for sale to residential, commercial, and industrial customers and other end-users of natural gas. Alagasco also provides transportation services to industrial and commercial customers located on its distribution system. Those transportation customers, using Alagasco as their agent or acting on their own, purchase gas directly from producers, marketers or suppliers and arrange for the delivery of the gas into the Alagasco distribution system. Alagasco charges a fee to transport such customer-owned gas through its distribution system to the customers's facilities.

Alagasco's service territory is situated in central and parts of north Alabama and includes some 185 cities and communities in twenty-eight counties. The aggregate population of the counties served by Alagasco is estimated to be 2.4 million. Among the cities served by Alagasco are Birmingham, the center of the largest metropolitan area in Alabama, and Montgomery, the state capital. During the most recent year, Alagasco served an average of 427,413 residential customers and 35,463 commercial, industrial and transportation customers. The Alagasco distribution system includes about 9,810 miles of main and more than 11,494 miles of service lines, odorization and regulation facilities, and customer meters.

Alagasco's distribution system is connected to two major interstate natural gas pipeline systems: Southern Natural Gas Company (Southern) and Transcontinental Gas Pipe Line Company (Transco). It is also connected to several intrastate natural gas pipeline systems and to Alagasco's two liquified natural gas (LNG) facilities.

Shortcomings to Bear in Mind

■ Unlike most public utilities, Energen has an extremely low dividend yield of barely 1 percent. Typically, utilities have yields of 3 percent to 5 percent. Thus, this is not a stock you would buy for income.

Energen has not been particularly generous to investors seeking a rising trend of dividends. In the past ten years (1997 to 2007), the dividend per share advanced from $.30 to $0.48, for a compound annual growth rate of only 4.8 percent. On a more positive note, the earnings per share growth has been impressive. EPS climbed from $.58 to $4.28 in the same span, for a growth rate of 22.1 percent.

Reasons to Buy

▪ On January 23, 2008, Energen reported that its 2007 earnings per diluted share (EPS) increased 15 percent to $4.28, marking the diversified energy company's sixth straight year of record earnings. Energen also affirmed its 2008 earnings guidance and initiated earnings guidance for 2009 with a range of $4.45—$4.85 per diluted share.

"Our natural gas hedging, strong prices applicable to our unhedged oil and natural gas liquids (NGL) volumes, and accelerated development of our undeveloped reserves combined to generate record earnings at Energen for the sixth straight year," said CEO James T. McManus. "I think it is important to emphasize that we achieved record earnings in 2007 even though prior-year earnings included some 56 cents per diluted share of one-time gains associated with the sale of half of our October 2006 acreage position in Alabama shales to Chesapeake Energy Corporation and a settlement of our Enron bankruptcy claim."

"The expectation that Energen would deliver in 2007 helped generate for shareholders a total return of 38 percent. Over the last five years, Energen's annualized total return to shareholders is 36 percent a year.

"The just-completed 2007 year also was marked by record production of 98.6 billion cubic feet equivalent (Bcfe) for Energen Resources Corporation, our oil and gas exploration and production company," Mr. McManus said. "Not only did we increase our capital spending to accelerate the production of our undeveloped reserves, but our horizontal drilling activities in the San Juan Basin performed even better than expected. With year-end proved reserves of 1.75 trillion cubic feet equivalent (Tcfe), Energen demonstrated its ability to replace reserves organically by bringing into production its extensive undeveloped reserves."

▪ Energen Resources attempts to lower the risks associated with its oil and natural gas business. A key component of the company's efforts to manage risk is its acquisition versus exploration orientation and its preference for long-lived reserves. In pursuing an acquisition, Energen Resources primarily uses the then-current oil and gas futures prices in its evaluation models, the prevailing swap curve and, for the longer term, its own pricing assumptions.

After a purchase, Energen Resources may use futures, swaps and/or fixed-price contracts to hedge commodity prices on flowing production for up to thirty-six months to help protect targeted returns from price volatility. On an on-going basis, the company may hedge up to 80 percent of its estimated annual production in any given year, depending on its pricing outlook.

SECTOR: **Utilities**
BETA COEFFICIENT: **95**
10-YEAR COMPOUND EARNINGS PER SHARE GROWTH: **22.1%**
10-YEAR COMPOUND DIVIDENDS PER SHARE GROWTH: **4.8%**

		2007	**2006**	**2005**	**2004**	**2003**	**2002**	**2001**	**2000**
Revenues (Mil)		1,435	1,394	1,128	93784	2677	785	556	
Net Income (Mil)		309	274	173	127	110	70.6	67.9	53.0
Earnings per share		4.28	3.73	2.37	1.74	1.55	1.05	1.09	0.88
Dividends per share		0.48	0.44	0.40	0.38	0.37	0.36	0.35	0.34
Price	high	70.4	47.6	44.3	30.1	21.0	16.0	20.1	16.8
	low	43.8	32.2	27.0	20.0	14.1	10.8	10.8	7.4

Entergy Corporation

639 Loyola Avenue ◻ New Orleans, LA 70113 ◻ (504) 529-5262 ◻ Dividend reinvestment plan available ◻ Web site: *www.entergy.com* ◻ Ticker symbol: ETR ◻ Listed: NYSE ◻ S&P rating: A— ◻ Value Line financial strength rating: A

"Given our strong point of view on the environment, there are two broad strategies we are pursuing at Entergy," said CEO J. Wayne Leonard in 2007. "First, we are taking action to reduce our impact on global climate change. We already have one of the lowest CO_2 (carbon dioxide) emission rates among our peers.

"As of 2005, we were the fifth-lowest among the largest 100 power generators in the United States. In 2006, we made our second five-year commitment to voluntarily stabilizing our CO_2 emission at 20 percent below 2000 levels, from 2006 to 2010, after successfully completing our first commitment with emission levels that were 23 percent lower than our target.

"These results were achieved at a time when business as usual would have meant a steady four percent per year increase in absolute emissions as we grew our business. We are also exploring a number of other actions to combat global climate change, including:
- "Expanding our use of safe, emission-free nuclear generation through high-capacity factors, upgrades and the construction of new nuclear facilities.
- Using newer, more efficient generation technologies such as combined-cycle gas turbine plants.
- Investing in equipment upgrades, carbon sequestration projects and carbon credits to lower CO_2 emissions.
- Considering the future cost of carbon when making investment decisions.
- Encouraging energy efficiency.
- Seeking opportunities to expand utilization of renewable resources.

"Second, we are aggressively advocating positive actions on global climate changes at all levels of government and within our communities. We participate in ten organizations advocating equitable regulation of greenhouse gases in all industries."

Company Profile

Entergy Corporation is an integrated energy utility engaged primarily in electric power production and retail electric distribution operations. Entergy owns and operates power plants with about 30,000 megawatts (MW) of electric generating capacity. Entergy delivers electricity to 2.6 million utility customers in Arkansas, Louisiana, Mississippi, and Texas.

The company operates primarily through two business segments: U.S. Utility and Non-Utility Nuclear. U.S. Utility generates, transmits, distributes, and sells electric power in a four-state service territory that includes portions of Arkansas, Mississippi, Texas, and Louisiana, including the city of New Orleans; and operates a small natural gas distribution business. Non-Utility Nuclear owns and operates five nuclear power plants located in the northeastern United States and sells the electric power produced by those plants primarily to wholesale customers. This business also provides services to other nuclear power plant owners. Entergy also operates the Energy Commodity Services segment and the Competitive Retail Services business. The company's Commodity Services includes Entergy-Koch, LP and Entergy's non-nuclear wholesale power marketing business. Entergy Koch is a nonoperating entity, which prior to the fourth quarter of 2004, owned and operated an energy marketing/trading and gas transportation/storage business. The Competitive Retail Services business markets and sells electricity, thermal energy, and related services in competitive markets, primarily in the ERCOT region in Texas. Entergy decided to divest the retail electric portion of the Competitive Retail Services business operating in the ERCOT region of Texas, and now reports this portion of the business as a discontinued operation. Management of Entergy Corporation and its subsidiaries has prepared and is responsible for the financial statements. To meet this responsibility, management establishes and maintains a system of internal control designed to provide reasonable assurance regarding the preparation and fair presentation of financial statements in accordance with generally accepted accounting principles. This system includes communication through written policies and procedures, an employee Code of Integrity, and an organizational structure that provides for appropriate division of responsibility and the training of personnel. This system is also tested by a comprehensive internal audit program. Entergy management assesses the effectiveness of its internal control over financial reporting on an annual basis. In making this assessment, management uses the criteria set forth by the Committee of Sponsoring Organizations of the Treadway in Internal Control, Integrated Framework. As a supplement to management's assessment, Entergy's independent auditors conduct an objective assessment of the degree to which management meets its responsibility for fairness of financial reporting and issue an attestation report on the adequacy of management's assessment. They evaluate Entergy's internal control over financial reporting and perform such tests and other procedures as they deem necessary to reach and express an opinion on the fairness of the financial statements.

Shortcomings to Bear in Mind

■ On January 24, 2008, the company issued this statement:

"Entergy regrets the problems that repeatedly have arisen with the new, state-of-the-art alert system it has been designing, installing and testing for communities around the Indian Point Energy Center. We apologize to our neighbors in those communities for the delays that have occurred in making this new system operable.

"The missed deadlines have been taken most seriously and the $650,000 fine the Nuclear Regulatory Commission levied is ten times larger than the base-level fine the NRC could issue in a case such as this. We are working with the four counties surrounding Indian Point, the Federal Emergency Management Agency and the NRC to ensure that the remaining issues will be resolved and the system approved by FEMA as quickly as possible."

Reasons to Buy

■ On July 31, 2007, Entergy announced that its subsidiary, Entergy Arkansas, Inc. (EAI), had signed an Asset Purchase Agreement to acquire the Ouachita Power Facility, a nominally rated 789 megawatt power plant, from Quachita Power, LLC, an indirect subsidiary of Cogentrix Energy, Inc. EAI expects to sell approximately one third of the output of the plant to Entergy Gulf States, Inc. on a long-term basis under a separate agreement.

"The acquisition of a modern, highly efficient load-following generation resource such as Ouachita will help meet our objective of providing, safe, reliable service to customers at a reasonable cost," said Mr. Leonard. "This transaction is well aligned with our disciplined, market point of view for capital deployment. This dispatchable resource will provide fuel savings to customers, but also both the Facility's location and technology are well suited to meet the time-varying demands of customers and the System."

The facility, which entered commercial service in 2002, is a nominal 789-megawatt General Electric 7FA combined-cycle gas-fired generating facility located near Monroe, Louisiana. The plant will be 100 percent owned by EAI and closing is expected to be completed in 2008.

■ On April 5, 2008, the Standard & Poor's *Stock Reports* rated Entergy a STRONG

BUY. Justin McCann, its analyst, said, "In our view, the electric utility's plan to spin off its nonutility nuclear operations would enable the yet-to-be-named company to realize higher growth and P/E multiples than it would when combined with the parent."

■ Writing for Argus Research Company on January 29, 2008, Gary F. Hovis said, "With Entergy's solid base of high-return, nonregulated operations and its core regulated utility operation, we believe that the ETR shares are attractive at current prices. Entergy's strategy is to become a key regional energy provider. We expect the company to invest its expanding cash flow in energy-related assets that have potential for higher long-term returns."

■ "Fuel prices and dividends are usually big drivers of share prices of utilities," said Abby Schultz, writing in the *New York Times* on April 13, 2008. "Now there is a new variable to consider: how much carbon their power plants emit. Companies like Exelon Corporation, the Constellation Energy Group and Entergy Corporation, which operate nuclear power plants, would benefit from cap-and-trade plans under consideration."

She also said, "If carbon caps—limits on carbon emissions—eventually become law, the winners may include operators of nuclear power plants (which don't emit carbon)."

■ On February 27, 2008, Entergy and NuStart Energy Development announced the submittal of a combined construction and operating license application to the Nuclear Regulatory Commission for a potential new nuclear unit in Port Gibson, Mississippi.

The application seeks regulatory approvals to potentially build a new unit adjacent to Entergy's existing Grand Gulf Nuclear Station, a reactor that ranks third among the nation's 104 nuclear plants for total electricity output over its lifetime of commercial operations.

With energy demands rising across the nation, many energy companies are pursuing clean, safe nuclear options through the NuStart consortium and other avenues. The U.S. Department of Energy states 250 to 500 new baseload power plants—those designed to help meet basic electrical needs—will be needed across the country by 2030.

Although Entergy has made no decision to build a nuclear reactor at this time, seeking NRC approval and a license now will preserve the nuclear option for the future.

"The licensing and construction process for a nuclear reactor will take several years to complete, so strategically securing a license now will better position Entergy to build, should conditions prove favorable," said Paul Hinnenkamp, Entergy's vice president of nuclear business development. "Although Entergy may elect not to immediately exercise the option to build once a license is received, the license itself is a tangible resource that could be employed at a later time."

SECTOR: **Utilities**
BETA COEFFICIENT: **.85**
10-YEAR COMPOUND EARNINGS PER SHARE GROWTH: **9.5%**
10-YEAR COMPOUND DIVIDENDS PER SHARE GROWTH: **5.2%**

	2007	2006	2005	2004	2003	2002	2001	2000
Revenues (Mil)	11,484	10,932	10,106	10,124	9,195	8,305	9,621	10,016
Net Income (Mil)	1,135	1,133	943	933	874	878	717	711
Earnings per share	5.60	5.36	4.40	3.93	3.69	3.68	3.08	2.97
Dividends per share	3.00	2.16	2.16	1.89	1.60	1.34	1.28	1.22
Price high	125.0	94.0	79.2	68.7	57.2	46.8	44.7	43.9
low	89.6	66.8	64.5	50.6	42.3	32.1	15.9	23.7

ExxonMobil Corporation

5959 Las Colinas Boulevard □ Irving, TX 75039-2298 □ (972) 444-1538 □ Direct dividend reinvestment plan is available □ Web site: *www.exxonmobil.com* □ Listed: NYSE □ Ticker symbol: XOM □ S&P rating: A+ □ Value Line financial strength rating: A++

On August 14, 2007, ExxonMobil Chemical Company announced that it had introduced Vistalon™ EPM*rubber 722 which can cost effectively improve processability and cable flexibility in medium- and low-voltage wire and cable applications.

In comparison with conventional EPDM, the metallocene-based product can provide processing improvements while exhibiting similar performance. Compared with cross-linked polyethylene (PE), it offers improved performance and excellent flexibility at low temperatures. What's more, it has improved electrical properties compared with metallocene EPDMs.

"We have developed Vistalon EPM 722 for customers looking for improved productivity during cable manufacture and increased flexibility and durability in final cable construction. Exhibiting good electrical properties, it is highly successful in several commercial applications. Vistalon EPM 722 is just one of many examples of the exceptional opportunities and value that ExxonMobil's metallocene technology brings to our customers and we have more in development," said Ulf Nilsson, global EPDM product manager, ExxonMobil Chemical. The new product is supplied in pellet form, making it clean and easy to use.

Company Profile

ExxonMobil is engaged in the exploration, production, manufacture, transportation, and sale of crude oil, natural gas, and petroleum products. It also has a stake in the manufacture of petrochemicals, packaging films, and specialty chemicals.

Divisions and affiliated companies of ExxonMobil operate or market products in the United States and some 200 other countries and territories. Their principal business is energy, involving exploration for, and production of crude oil and natural gas, manufacture of petroleum products and transportation and sale of crude oil, natural gas and petroleum products.

The company is a major manufacturer and marketer of basic petrochemicals, including olefins, aromatics, polyethylene, and polypropylene plastics and a wide variety of specialty products. It also has interests in electric power generation facilities.

In a nutshell, here is ExxonMobil:

- The company conducts oil and gas exploration, development and production in every major accessible producing region in the world.
- ExxonMobil has the largest energy resource base of any nongovernment company, and it is the world's largest nongovernment natural gas marketer and reserves holder.
- Consumers know the company best by its brand names: Exxon, Mobil and Esso.
- ExxonMobil is the world's largest fuels refiner and manufacture of lube base stocks used for making motor oils.
- The company has refining operations in twenty-six countries, 42,000 retail service stations in more than 100 countries and lubricants marketing in almost 200 countries and territories.
- ExxonMobil markets petrochemical products in more than 150 countries. Ninety percent of the company's petrochemical assets are in businesses that are ranked number one or number two in market position.

Shortcomings to Bear in Mind

- Rob Cox and Cyrus Sanati, writing for the *Wall Street Journal* on September 24, 2007, had this comment: "Big Oil has a big problem. It may not be apparent from the huge profits that oil and gas companies are gushing. But the industry's future depends on its ability to rove the earth in search of new reservoirs of oil and gas. Yet as energy resources grow scarce, governments are restricting Western drillers access to their fields. They're fostering their own champions, many of which are flush with capital, have learned from the majors and can easily contract drilling expertise from firms like Schlumberger, a Franco-American oil-service company."

Reasons to Buy

- On February 1, 2008, CEO Rex W. Tillerson had this comment on financial results in 2007. "ExxonMobil's full year 2007 net income and earnings excluding special items were a record $40,610 million ($7.28 per share), reflecting strong results in all business segments.

"We continued to supply crude oil and natural gas volumes to meet the world's energy needs through disciplined development and operation of our globally diverse resource base. Capital and exploration project spending increased to $20,853 million in 2007, up 5 percent from 2006. Our long-term investment program, in projects often far from major consuming nations, continued to provide resources essential to the increasingly interdependent global energy supply network. Operations reliability in our global Downstream and Chemical businesses continued to supply the important products consumers require around the world.

"The Corporation distributed a total of $35.6 billion to shareholders in 2007 through dividends and share purchases to reduce shares outstanding, up $3.0 billion from 2006.

"ExxonMobil's fourth quarter earnings excluding special items were a record $11,660 million, up 18 percent from the fourth quar-

ter of 2006. Higher crude oil and natural gas realizations and gains on asset sales were partly offset by lower chemical margins."

- On November 20, 2007, ExxonMobil said that its subsidiary, ExxonMobil Libya Limited, signed an agreement to execute an Exploration and Production Sharing Agreement (EPSA) with Libya's National Oil Corporation to initiate exploration activity offshore Libya in the Sirte Basin.

The agreement includes four blocks located in Contract Area 21, approximately 110 miles off the Libyan coast. The contract area comprises 2.5 million acres and is situated in water depths ranging from approximately 5,400 feet to ultradeep areas of more than 8,700 feet.

ExxonMobil Libya Limited committed to a five-year work program consisting of at least 4,000 kilometers of 2D seismic acquisition, 2,000 square-kilometers of 3D seismic, and one deep water exploration well. The agreement also stipulates the payment of a signing fee, a training program to help upgrade the skills of nationals and other support for education in Libya.

"We are pleased that we have reached an agreement with National Oil Corporation of Libya in Contract Area 21 as we believe this to be one of the most prospective unlicensed areas in the Libyan offshore," said Phil Goss, president and general manager of ExxonMobil Libya Limited. "We expect to realize substantial technical, operational and cost reduction synergies with Exxon-Mobil deepwater exploration efforts in the adjacent Contract Area 20."

- ExxonMobil's world-class, geographically diverse upstream portfolio consists of 72 billion oil-equivalent barrels of oil and gas resources and activities in nearly forty countries. Large, highly profitable oil and gas operations in established areas, including North America, Europe, Asia, and West Africa, are the foundations of this portfolio. These areas include long-life fields and have significant near-term potential as new opportunities are developed using existing infrastructure. ExxonMobil also holds a strong position in the Caspian, Eastern Canada, the Middle East, and Russia, as well as in the deep waters of West Africa and the Gulf of Mexico. According to a company official, "Our financial strength allows us to pursue all profitable opportunities. We continually invest in our existing assets to extend their economic life and have an industry-leading portfolio of more than 100 major new projects."

■ ExxonMobil is the world's largest refiner, with an ownership interest in forty-six refineries in twenty-six countries and a total capacity of 6.3 million barrels per day. It has an extensive transportation network of oil tankers, pipelines and product terminals. Lube-refining capacity is 150,000 barrels per day.

■ Worldwide, ExxonMobil markets gasoline and other fuels at more than 40,000 service stations, serves more than 1 million industrial and wholesale customers, provides aviation services and products at more than 700 airports, and services ocean-going vessels in more than 300 ports.

■ On February 5, 2008, Standard & Poor's *Stock Reports*'s analyst rated Exxon-Mobil a STRONG BUY, its highest rating. Tina J. Vital said, "We believe XOM will benefit from 'big-pocket' upstream growth opportunities in deepwater, liquefied natural gas (LNG), and ventures with state-owned oil companies. We expect its upstream to benefit from strong crude oil prices, and its complex refineries from sig-

nificant cost discounts due to its ability to refine lower quality crude feedstocks."

■ "ExxonMobil Corp. plans to increase its spending by more than $1 billion a year to find and tap new oil and natural-gas resources, aggressively increasing exploration in politically stable countries not usually thought to be energy-rich, including Germany, New Zealand, and Greenland," said Russell Gold writing for the *Wall Street Journal* on March 6, 2008. "Exxon, the world's largest publically traded oil company, announced yesterday a 25 percent increase in annual capital spending for the next few years, to between $25 billion and $30 billion, to adjust for higher costs and to pay for wider exploration. Just a few years ago, it projected it would spend $20 billion a year.

"In recent years, the oil industry has developed the ability to drill wells in two-mile-deep water. That technology feat has encouraged Exxon, among others, to look for new opportunities in deep waters around the globe, including nations that haven't been big oil producers in the past."

■ Argus Research Company also gave Exxon its stamp of approval with a BUY rating on February 8, 2008. Philip Weiss, CFA, CPA said, "The company has delivered record earnings in each of the past two years, generating solid returns for shareholders. Based on the combination of our forecast for higher energy prices and the positive impact of the company's ongoing share repurchase program, we believe that ExxonMobil should continue to deliver robust profitability and cash flow."

SECTOR: **Energy**
BETA COEFFICIENT: **.95**
10-YEAR COMPOUND EARNINGS PER SHARE GROWTH: **16.1%**
10-YEAR COMPOUND DIVIDENDS PER SHARE GROWTH: **5.6%**

		2007	2006	2005	2004	2003	2002	2001	2000
Rev (Mil)		404,552	377,640	370,998	291,252	246,738	204,506	187,510	206,083
Net Income (Mil)		40,610	39,090	36,100	25,330	17,030	11,011	15,105	16,910
Earnings per share		7.28	6.62	5.71	3.89	2.56	1.69	2.18	2.41
Dividends per share		1.40	1.28	1.14	1.06	0.98	0.92	0.91	0.88
Price	high	95.3	79.0	66.0	52.0	41.1	44.6	45.8	47.7
	low	69.0	56.4	49.2	39.9	31.6	29.8	35.0	34.9

Fastenal Company

2001 Theurer Boulevard ❑ Winona, MN 55987-0978 ❑ (507) 454-5374 ❑ Dividend reinvestment plan not available ❑ Web site: *www.fastenal.com* ❑ Ticker symbol: FAST ❑ Listed: Nasdaq ❑ S&P rating: A ❑ Value Line financial strength rating: A

"Almost every day some one asks me, how is business at Fastenal?" said CEO Willard D. Oberton in 2008. "In 2007, it was a good year in most areas of our business, but there is a lot of work to do. The year started out very slowly with our daily sales growth at 12.6 percent in January. Our team worked hard, and we ended 2007 on a stronger note by reporting daily sales growth of 15.3 percent for the fourth quarter and 16.8 percent daily sales for the month of December. This was also a year of great change at Fastenal with the introduction of our new growth strategy called 'Pathway to Profit.'

"Our 2007 sales growth was 14 percent, and our total revenue for the year was about $2.1 billion. Two billion in revenue is a new milestone for Fastenal, and for me it represents a bit more. When I started with Fastenal in January 1980, we had annual revenue of two million dollars, which means our revenue is now one thousand times greater than it was when I started with Fastenal."

Company Profile

Fastenal was founded in 1967 in Winona, Minnesota, by CEO Bob Kierlin. From this beginning, Fastenal has expanded to become the fastest growing full-line industrial distributor, and is now the largest fastener distributor in the nation. Fastenal's service-oriented business network includes an in-house Manufacturing Division, a product Quality Assurance and Engineering Department, a strategic system of twelve distribution centers in the United States, and a fleet of over 275 company-owned semi-trucks and trailers.

Fastenal owns and operates more than 2,160 stores with locations in all fifty states,

Canada, Mexico, the Dominican Republic, Puerto Rico, Singapore, Europe, and China. Each store utilizes local inventory, outside sales staff, and on-site delivery vehicles to help save customers time and money.

The company employs 8,617 people at its stores. In addition, there are 3,396 people employed in various support positions.

Fastenal provides extensive employee training to ensure exceptional customer support for each product line. Management believes that, as new product categories are added, trained personnel must be available to support changing customer needs. "With this in mind, we pledge to remain specialists—not generalists—in each of the products we bring to the market."

Fastenal is the premiere fastener distributor in North America. "We couple our extensive product offering with a complete selection of Vendor-Managed Inventory programs. Our unique approach sets the benchmark for distributors serving MRO, OEM and Construction markets. Within the fastener category, we specialize in threaded fasteners and accessories for use in both industrial and commercial applications."

Fastenal's Cutting Tools Division specializes in metal removal tooling, custom design, and re-sharpening services using Computer Numeric Control (CNC) equipment.

The company's Hydraulics & Pneumatics product group is a one-stop shop for brand name fittings, hoses, pneumatic valves, and power transmission products. FAST also provides custom hydraulic and air hose assembly, as well as crimping, to meet any and all of your hydraulics, pneumatics, and fluid transfer needs.

A wide range of pipes, fittings, and filters can be found in Fastenal's Plumbing Division. Their stores offer copper, PVC/CPVC and black pipe tubing and fittings, pumps, and air filters.

Within the Material Handling, Storage, and Packaging category, Fastenal offers everything its customers need to move, store, lift, and package goods.

The company's Janitorial Supplies products include of a wide selection of brand name and private label items, all designed to deliver high quality at a low price.

Fastenal's Electrical Supplies Division specializes in a complete line of electrical products and supplies for MRO and OEM customers. The company offers a diverse selection of the most recognized electrical supplies and accessories in the industry, ranging from wire, switches, and fuses to fittings, conduits, and receptacles.

The company's complete line of Welding Supplies serves customers both in maintenance and repair departments as well as those in production manufacturing operations. In addition to an extensive product offering, Fastenal also offers access to local inventory: lowering customer inventory costs.

Shortcomings to Bear in Mind

■ Fastenal, because of its explosive growth in recent years is not on the bargain table. Its PE ratio can be well above average.

Reasons to Buy

■ The company has been completely free of long-term debt for the past decade.

■ On March 8, 2008, Standard & Poor's *Stock Reports* rated FAST a STRONG BUY. Michael W. Jaffe said, "We have a positive outlook on Fastenal's upcoming business trend, and an especially positive view of its recent change in growth strategy. We think its plan to attain sales and margin growth through larger sales staffs and a lower rate of new store openings will likely prove successful."

■ "The nut and bolt retailer's new strategy appears to be paying off," said Erik A. Antonson, an analyst with *Value Line*, on April 4, 2008. "In April 2007, management decided to alter the company's business model. For most of the last decade, Fastenal used store openings as the primary source of growth, adding more than 200 locations a year in some instances. Now, management is bolstering the staff in existing stores at a faster-than-historical clip. The company is funding this salesforce expansion with the occupancy savings generated by opening stores at a slower rate." *Value Line* gave Fastenal a BUY rating.

■ In 2008, Mr. Oberton said, "As I stated earlier, we introduced a new long-term growth strategy in 2007, which we call the 'Pathway to Profit.' We developed this strategy by analyzing the profitability of our stores based on age, sales volume, geographic location, staffing, and sales growth. We also factored in many of the things we learned from our CSP projects over the last several years.

"During this analysis, we confirmed some things and we learned some things. First off, we discovered the real 'sweet spot' for store profitability. This sweet spot is annual per store sales of about $1.5 million, or $125,000 per month. When our stores reach this sales level, they currently produce an average pretax operating margin of about 23 percent. By comparison, our pretax earnings margin was 17.7 percent in 2006, and our average annual per share sales were $955,000, or $79,500 per month.

"The 'Pathway to Profit' strategy is very straightforward—to grow our average store sales to $125,000 per month and to drive our pretax operating margin to 23 percent. To drive our average store volume to this level, we have transitioned from a growth strategy primarily focused on store openings to a strategy that blends store openings with a heightened investment in additional outside sale personnel in existing stores.

"We believe this new growth strategy will allow us to produce annual sales growth at or above 20 percent in a normal economic cycle. In addition, we believe it can produce an even greater profit growth and return on invested capital."

Mr. Oberton also said, "Our research shows for every store we don't open, we can hire four sales people. Based on results we had in our CSP2 stores, we believe we will achieve greater sales growth by adding these sales people to an existing store. If we are able to execute on the 'Pathway to Profit,' an 8 percent rate of new store opening, combined with 20 percent sales growth companywide, could raise our average store to $125,000 per month in five years. Our stated plan is to grow our pretax earnings margin from the current 18.3 percent to 23 percent over this five-year period. A simple way to think about this strategy—greater investment in people and lower investment in brick and mortar."

On another subject, Mr. Oberton said, "The inventory expansion project in our Indianapolis Distribution Center was a big focus in 2007. In 2006, we began to expand our inventory selection in that facility from 28,000 to about 120,000 items during 2005. We chose to do this project in Indianapolis due to its central location and because we can reach more than 70 percent of our customers in less than 48 hours using Fastenal's ground transportation. Because of the benefits we have seen from this program, we have continued to expand the number of stocked items at this location, and at year-end there were some 140,000 different items available. In 2008, we

plan to continue expanding the selection of inventory at this location by adding 25,000 to 50,000 more items throughout the year."

In still another sector, the company CEO said, "Our marketing department continues to work hard promoting the Fastenal name. In 2007, we decided to increase our presence in the NASCAR racing program by agreeing to sponsor the No. 40 Dodge in the Nationwide Series (formerly the Busch Series). The team is owned by Chip Ganassi Racing with Felix Sabates, and our lead driver will be Dario Franchitti, the 2007 Indianapolis 500 and IndyCar points champion. Both our research and our experience have told us that racing is a very popular sport with a high percentage of our customer base."

Finally, Mr. Oberton had these comments on another topic, "Product development and purchasing continue to search for the best suppliers. This group is tasked with putting our sales people in a position of having high-quality product at a competitive price. We continue to expand our foreign sourcing efforts and have greatly increased the number of field inspectors traveling to factories to check for both quality and social compliance. In 2007, we opened two quality-control laboratories, one in Kan Shan, Taiwan and the other in Shanghai, China. These investments were made to help with quality assurance and to speed up the product-development process. Both of these labs have received their A2LA quality certification."

SECTOR: **Industrials**
BETA COEFFICIENT: **1.25**
10-YEAR COMPOUND EARNINGS PER SHARE GROWTH: **19.1%**
10-YEAR COMPOUND DIVIDENDS PER SHARE GROWTH: **46%**

		2007	2006	2005	2004	2003	2002	2001	2000
Revenues (Mil)		2,062	1,809	1,523	1,239	995	905	818	746
Net Income (Mil)		232.6	199.0	166.8	131.0	84.1	74.8	70.1	80.7
Earnings per share		1.55	1.32	1.10	0.87	0.56	0.50	0.46	0.53
Dividends per share		0.44	0.40	0.31	0.20	0.11	0.03	0.02	0.02
Price	high	52.9	49.3	42.0	32.3	25.5	21.7	18.3	18.3
	low	33.1	33.2	25.5	21.9	13.8	13.3	11.7	8.9

FedEx Corporation

942 South Shady Grove Road □ Memphis, TN 38120 (901) 818-7200 □ Web site: *www.fedex.com*
□ Direct dividend reinvestment plan is available □ Fiscal years end May 31 □ Listed: NYSE
□ Ticker symbol: FDX □ Standard & Poor's rating: B+ □ Value Line financial strength rating: B++

"FedEx delivered solid financial results in fiscal 2007 even though we were restrained by a slowing U.S. economy," said CEO Frederick W. Smith. "The weakened industrial sector is currently limiting demand for transportation services, but we expect the U.S. economy to begin to show modest year-over-year improvement in the late summer to early fall timeframe. We remain optimistic about prospects for global economic growth, and will continue to invest in projects critical to achieving strong long-term financial performance."

FedEx reported the following consolidated results for the full year:

- Revenue of $35.2 billion, up 9 percent from $32.3 billion the previous year
- Operating income of $3.28 billion, up 9 percent from $3.01 billion a year ago
- Operating margin of 9.3 percent, unchanged from 9.3 percent the previous year
- Net income of $2.02 billion, up 12 percent from last year's $1.81 billion
- Earnings per share of $6.48, up 11 percent from $5.83 per share a year ago

Revenue grew due to strong FedEx Ground volume growth, as well as continued FedEx Express International Priority revenue growth. Revenue growth also reflected the acquisition of Watkins Motor Lines in September 2006. Fiscal 2007 results included costs associated with upfront compensation and benefits under the new pilot labor contract at FedEx Express, which reduced second quarter earnings by approximately $0.25 per diluted share. Fiscal 2006 results included a charge of $0.15

per diluted share to adjust the accounting for certain facility leases, primarily at FedEx Express. Capital spending for fiscal 2007 was $2.9 billion.

Company Profile

FedEx Corporation is the world's leading provider of guaranteed express delivery services. Using a $4 million inheritance as seed money, Frederick W. Smith founded FedEx in 1971 when he was only twenty-seven.

The company offers a wide range of express delivery services for the time-definite transportation of documents, packages and freight. Commercial and military charter services are also offered by FedEx. The company's operations are as follows:

- *FedEx Express* is the world's largest express transportation company, providing fast, reliable delivery to 214 countries, including every address in the United States.
- *FedEx Ground* is North America's second-largest ground carrier for small-package business shipments, including business-to-residential service through FedEx Home Delivery.
- *FedEx Freight* is the largest U.S. regional less-than-truckload freight company, providing next-day and second-day delivery of heavyweight freight within the United States and from key international markets.
- *FedEx Custom Critical* is the "24/7" option for urgent shipments, proving nonstop, door-to-door delivery in the contiguous United States, Canada, and Europe.
- *FedEx Trade Networks* facilitates international trade as the largest-volume customs filer in the United States, and a

one-stop source for freight forwarding, advisory services, and trade technology.

Shortcomings to Bear in Mind

■ On November 16, 2007, Alan B. Graf Jr., FedEx executive vice president and chief financial officer, said. "Since we provided earnings guidance for the second quarter in September, our fuel costs have increased more than eight percent, or $85 million. While we have dynamic fuel surcharges in place, they cannot keep pace in the short-term with rapidly rising fuel prices. In addition, less-than-truckload freight trends in the FedEx Freight segment remain weak, despite economic signs that the decline in U.S. industrial production has hit bottom. We are taking prudent steps to reduce expenses, and are reviewing our capital investment plans for further reduction."

Reasons to Buy

■ The company has had a reputation as a great place to work, with employees claiming they "bleed purple and orange"—the company's colors—and living by Smith's mantra: "people, service, profit." FedEx has repeatedly been on *Fortune* magazine's list of the "100 Best Companies to Work For" and its lists of best places for minorities and women to work.

■ On March 3, 2008, *Fortune* magazine released its annual report card on corporate reputation, listing FedEx in the top ten of both its U.S. and global rankings. Overall, FedEx was number six on *Fortune*'s list of the World's Most Admired Companies and number seven on *Fortune*'s list of America's Most Admired Companies.

"This honor is a testament to our 290,000 team members who daily go the extra mile to make every FedEx experience outstanding," said Mr. Smith. "At FedEx, our people and our culture distinguish us from the competition—and we are particularly proud of our unique focus on service and innovation."

FedEx has consistently ranked in *Fortune*'s list of the World's Most Admired Companies and *Fortune*'s list of America's Most Admired Companies since 2002 and 2001, respectively. FedEx has also been honored as one of *Fortune*'s Best Companies to Work For in ten of the past eleven years and was named to the Best Companies to Work For Hall of Fame in 2005.

■ Standard & Poor's *Stock Reports* classified FedEx as a STRONG BUY March 25, 2008, with this analysis by Jim Corridore, "While we think FDX's results are likely to be hurt by the slowing U.S. economy, we believe the shares have over-corrected, and think that any signs of renewed strength in the U.S. economy over the next twelve months could push this cyclical stock higher."

■ "FedEx transportation services provide the single most important element that every shipper needs—certainty," said Mr. Smith. "We deliver both shipments and the related information about them exactly as customers need, virtually anywhere in the world. We provide a broad portfolio of service options. And all of this is becoming crucial to businesses striving to transform complex supply chains into more efficient engines of growth and profitability."

■ According to Mr. Smith, "The new strategy we have put in place of the past several years has made us a full-service transportation company, offering the broadest array of services. With FedEx Express, FedEx Ground, FedEx Freight, FedEx Custom Critical, and FedEx Trade Networks, we can offer our customers an unprecedented array of shipping and supply chain services quickly and conveniently across the globe."

■ FedEx has been a part of the China free-trade success story for twenty years, helping build the air transportation infrastructure needed to support China's growing economic demands. Over that time, FedEx Express has grown to become the largest international express carrier in the country, with service to more than 220 cities and plans to expand to 100 more during the next five years.

With eleven flights every week through three major gateways—Beijing, Shanghai, and Shenzhen—FedEx serves its customers with more flights into and out of China than any other U.S.-based cargo carrier. "FedEx is benefiting enormously from the surge in China trade," said Michael L. Ducker, executive vice president of FedEx Express. "But we're also helping drive it. For the economic revolution to continue, China will need greater access to the global marketplace. That's what FedEx provides."

■ On May 26, 2006, FedEx announced an agreement to acquire the less-than-truckload (LTL) operations of Watkins Motor Lines and certain affiliates for $780 million, payable in cash. LTL freight customers will benefit from the additional choice that this new, reliable and cost-effective solution will add to the FedEx Freight portfolio of services.

Watkins Motor Lines, a privately held company headquartered in Lakeland, Florida, is a leading provider of long-haul LTL services. With over $1 billion in annual revenue, Watkins will be rebranded FedEx National LTL and operate as a separate network within the FedEx Freight segment.

With the acquisition, FedEx Freight will gain more than a leading provider of long-haul LTL; the two companies also share a strong commitment to employee culture and growth. Both companies have been recognized for their dedication to the workforce. FedEx Freight has the lowest driver turnover in the industry.

After the transaction closed, Watkins Motor Lines was renamed FedEx National LTL and functions as a separate operating network within FedEx Freight, one of four core operating companies at FedEx including FedEx Express, FedEx Ground, and FedEx Kinko's.

Founded in 1932, Watkins Motor Lines was a privately owned, nationwide LTL long-haul carrier and a subsidiary of Watkins Associated Industries. Known for its premium on-time service, the company has a workforce of approximately 10,000 and is one of a handful of trucking companies that has been consistently profitable since obtaining its transcontinental LTL operating authority in 1972. Today, with revenues in excess of $1 billion, it has 139 locations in forty-two states and Puerto Rico and operates more than 3,400 late-model city and line-haul tractors and 10,200-plus trailers.

SECTOR: **Industrials**
BETA COEFFICIENT: **1.00**
10-YEAR COMPOUND EARNINGS PER SHARE GROWTH: **16.0%**
10-YEAR COMPOUND DIVIDENDS PER SHARE GROWTH: **No dividend prior to 2002.**

		2007	2006	2005	2004	2003	2002	2001	2000
Revenues (Mil)		35,214	32,294	29,363	24,710	22,487	20,607	19,629	18,257
Net Income (Mil)		2,073	1,855	1,449	838	830	710	663	688
Earnings per share		6.67	5.98	4.82	2.76	2.74	2.39	2.26	2.32
Dividends per share		0.37	0.33	0.29	0.24	0.20	—	—	—
Price	high	121.4	120.0	105.8	100.9	78.0	61.4	53.5	49.8
	low	89.5	96.5	76.8	64.8	47.7	42.8	33.2	30.6

FMC Corporation

1735 Market Street □ Philadelphia, PA 19103 □ (215) 299-6000 □ Dividend reinvestment plan not available □ Web site: *www.fmc.com* □ Ticker symbol: FMC □ Listed: NYSE □ S&P rating: B− □ Value Line financial strength rating: B++

"Here's a Halloween nightmare: Suppose you had to bet all of your investment capital on just one stock and hold it for half a decade," said Jim McTague, writing for *Barron's* on October 29, 2007. "Where would you look for a treat in a market that lately has pulled more nasty tricks than a holiday haunted house?

"One good bet would be FMC, a mid-size and fast-growing chemical company that, despite an enviable track record, is as invisible as a ghost to most of Wall Street.

Mr. McTague goes on to say, "FMC, with a market value of about $4 billion, produces indispensable industrial chemicals like soda ash, high-demand specialty chemicals like soda ash, high-demand specialty chemicals like those processed from plant sources such as seaweed to enhance food products, and a palette of agricultural pesticides that sell particularly well in South America, which is becoming a winter cornucopia for North Americans. Just check out the labels on those off-season fresh tomatoes next time you visit the supermarket."

Company Profile

Feeding the world, protecting health, and providing the conveniences of life. That is the mission of FMC.

With FMC's superior technology and strong partnerships with customers, FMC's people are finding solutions that are helping to change people's lives for the better.

Ever since our beginning in California in 1883 when John Bean invented the first piston sprayer for agriculture, FMC has continued a proud heritage of pioneering solutions for its customers. Today, FMC uses an array of advanced technologies in research and development, mining and manufacturing to produce customized products and solutions for the many markets the company serves. As a global leader utilizing advanced technologies and customer-focused research and development, FMC provides innovative and cost-effective solutions to food and agriculture, pharmaceutical, health care, pulp and paper, textiles, glass and ceramics, rubber and plastics, lubricants, structural pest control, turf and ornamental markets, and specialty and related industries.

FMC Corporation is a diversified chemical company serving agricultural, industrial and consumer markets globally for more than a century with innovative solutions, applications and quality products. The company employs some 5,000 people throughout the world. FMC operates its businesses in three segments: Agricultural Products, Specialty Chemicals and Industrial Chemicals.

FMC Agricultural Products provides crop protection and pest control products for worldwide markets. The global business offers a strong portfolio of insecticides and herbicides. FMC is also a leader in innovative packaging for the industry.

In the Specialty Chemicals Group, FMC BioPolymer is the world's leading producer of alginate, carrageenan and microcrystalline cellulose. For more than half a century, manufacturers around the world have turned to FMC BioPolymer for the uncompromising performance and quality of these products. Also in the Specialty Chemicals Group, FMC Lithium is one of the world's leading producers of lithium-based products and is recognized as the technology leader in specialty organo-lithium chemicals and related technologies.

In the Industrial Chemicals Group, FMC Alkali Chemicals is the world's largest producer of natural soda ash and the market leader in North America. Downstream products include sodium bicarbonate, sodium cyanide, sodium sesquicarbonate and caustic soda. FMC Hydrogen Peroxide is the market leader in North America with manufacturing sites in the United States, Canada and Mexico. FMC Active Oxidants is the world's leading supplier of persulfate products and a major producer of peracetic acid and other specialty oxidants. Based in Barcelona, Spain, FMC Foret is a major chemical producer supplying customers throughout Europe, the Middle East, and Africa with a diverse range of products including hydrogen peroxide, peroxygens, phosphates, silicates, zeolites and sulfur derivatives.

Shortcomings to Bear in Mind

- FMC is not a conservative, dividend-paying stock. For many years, the company did not pay a dividend. Even now, its dividend yield is less than 1 percent.
- Earnings per share don't always advance. In 2000, for instance, EPS were $3.36. The next year, earnings per share slumped to $1.60. What's more, they sagged even further in 2002, to $1.28 and only $.95 the following year. Since then, however, the trend has been sharply up.

Reasons to Buy

- In 2007, revenue was $2,632.9 million, an increase of 12 percent, versus $2,345.9 million in the prior year. Net income was $132.4 million, or $1.71 per diluted share, as compared to $131.3 million, or $1.66 per diluted share, in the prior year. Net income in 2007 included restructuring and other income and charges of $107.3 million, or charges of $1.38 per diluted share versus restructuring and other income and charges of $84.4 million, or charges of $1.07 per diluted share in 2006. Excluding these items, the company earned $239.7 million, or $3.09 per diluted share for the full year 2007, versus

$215.7 million, or $2.73 per diluted share, for the full year 2006.

- On February 6, 2008, CEO William G. Walter said, "We expect another record year in 2008 with earnings before restructuring and other income and charges of $3.80 to $4.00 per diluted share. Industrial Chemicals carries strong operating momentum into the new year and should benefit from continued volume growth, higher pricing levels and improved power market conditions in Spain. We look for further growth in Agricultural Products through the successful application of its focused strategy, new product introductions and additional global supply chain productivity improvements. In Specialty Chemicals, earnings growth will be driven by strong commercial performance in BioPolymer and continued productivity improvements across the segment. We expect to achieve these results despite the headwinds of higher raw material costs across our businesses. We will derive significant benefit in 2008 from our global footprint, the noncyclical nature of our end-use markets and our limited exposure to rising petrochemical costs.
- "Innovation is essential to our creating long-term shareholder value," said Mr. Walter in 2007. "We are focused on pursuing innovation in all of our businesses through investing in both internal and external opportunities. Our innovation initiatives are tailored to build on the strengths and strategies of each business. Agricultural Products has shifted to its innovation paradigm from a longer-term internally focused discovery cycle to shorter-term multifaceted, external strategy aimed at bringing new products and technologies to market in a more targeted and rapid fashion. Through Innova Solutions, we have already seen benefits from this shift in strategy."
- Mr. Walter goes on to say, "Specialty Chemicals is investing in a number of internal development opportunities. In BioPolymer,

through our Healthcare Ventures, we are funding and nurturing the development of promising technology platforms targeted at drug dosage formulation as well as biomaterials for the medical device industry. In lithium, we are investing in high-growth energy storage markets and in alkali silica reactivity chemistries to extend the life of concrete.

"We are also expanding in China and India. Both BioPolymer and lithium are investing in manufacturing plants, research facilities and organizations in order to better serve our customers, lower costs and participate in the rapidly growing regional opportunities in Asia.

■ On December 14, 2007, FMC and Pronova BioPharma ASA announced the companies have entered into a worldwide license and development agreement to develop products using a novel capsule technology developed by FMC. The alginate-based capsule technology is expected to significantly strengthen the product life-cycle management of Pronova BioPharma's products and has the potential for use both with Pronova BioPharma's current active pharmaceutical ingredient, marketed as Omacor in Europe and Lovaza in the United States, as well as in future products under development.

Under the terms of the agreement, FMC will apply its technology to Pronova BioPharma's products while Pronova BioPharma will be responsible for the clinical development and for securing regulatory approval. Pronova BioPharma plans to initiate clinical trials in early 2009 and launch of the new capsule is expected in 2010–2011.

FMC's novel proprietary capsule technology uses alginate, a marine plant-derived biopolymer, as the main component in the capsule shell. Alginate is gastro-resistant, providing an enteric release profile that delays release of the drug until passage from the stomach into the intestine. The technology also has the benefit of producing a seamless capsule with a significantly thinner shell wall, reducing the size of the capsule by approximately 25 percent. The enteric release profile and smaller capsule size are expected to result in increased patient compliance.

Commenting on the announcement, Tomas Settevik, CEO of Pronova BioPharma, said: "The new alginate capsule technology has the potential to deliver significant benefits for patients, as well as creating important patent life-extensions for Omacor/Lovaza and other products under development in our pipeline. We look forward to working with FMC in bringing the new capsule technology to market, which we anticipate taking place by 2010–2011."

Ted Butz, vice president and general manager, FMC Specialty Chemicals Group said: "We are delighted to partner with Pronova BioPharma to combine our leading edge oral dose technology with such an important pharmaceutical product franchise."

SECTOR: **Materials**
BETA COEFFICIENT: **1.20**
10-YEAR COMPOUND EARNINGS PER SHARE GROWTH: **-1.9%**
10-YEAR COMPOUND DIVIDENDS PER SHARE GROWTH: **NM**

	2007	2006	2005	2004	2003	2002	2001	2000
Revenues (Mil)	2,633	2,347	2,150	2,051	1,921	1,853	1,943	3,926
Net Income (Mil)	132.4	216.4	171.9	135.2	67.5	87.5	99.6	212.3
Earnings per share	1.71	2.74	2.20	1.60	.95	1.28	1.60	3.36
Dividends per share	0.42	0.36	—	—	—	—	—	—
Price high	59.0	39.0	31.9	25.3	17.4	21.2	42.0	38.6
low	35.6	25.9	21.6	16.5	7.1	11.5	22.8	23.0

FPL Group, Inc.

700 Universe Boulevard □ Juno Beach, FL 33408 □ (561) 694-4697 □ Web site: *www.investor.fplgroup.com* □ Dividend reinvestment plan is available □ Listed: NYSE □ Ticker symbol: FPL □ S & P rating: A— □ Value Line financial strength rating: A+

On March 18, 2008, the Florida Public Service Commission (PSC) took a positive step toward securing the state's clean energy future with its approval of plans to build two nuclear power units at Florida Power & Light Company's Turkey Point generating complex in Miami-Dade County, according to FPL president Armando Olivera.

The PSC approved the additional nuclear plants and specifically agreed that FPL should proceed with making reservation payments on a key piece of equipment with long advance ordering requirements.

"This is a critical first step toward securing Florida's future with additional energy that is safe, reliable, cost-efficient and clean. Additional nuclear generation will help us achieve Governor Crist's goal of reducing the carbon emissions that scientists have determined contribute to climate change, and will protect customers from supply disruptions and unpredictable prices that can result from being too dependent on a single fuel source," Mr. Olivera said.

FPL is pursuing the option of constructing two advanced-design nuclear plants at Turkey Point that would add between 2,200 and 3,000 megawatts. If built, the units are expected to go into service in the years 2018 and 2020. FPL has safely operated two existing nuclear plants at Turkey Point for thirty-five years.

FPL, which serves 4.5 million customers in thirty-five counties, must increase its electrical generation capacity by nearly 33 percent to meet projected growth in electricity demand between 2011 and 2020. The two advanced-design nuclear plants would generate enough power to supply the needs of more than 1 million residential customers.

If constructed, Turkey Point Units 6 and 7, as the new units will be known, will also diversify FPL's fuel mix, which currently consists of 50 percent natural gas. Fuel diversity helps protect customers from price spikes that can result from being overly dependent on a single fuel source.

Over the long term, operating expenses for nuclear plants are projected to be much lower than expenses for fossil-fuel plants, despite higher initial investment costs. For example, between January 2000 and July 2007, FPL's existing nuclear units saved customers $8.7 billion in fuel costs compared to natural gas and oil.

Additional nuclear generation will also help Florida address global climate change. For example, the two proposed units will reduce carbon dioxide emissions by more than 7 million tons per year relative to fossil fuel plants. Reducing carbon emissions by 7 million tons is the equivalent of removing nearly 1.2 million cars from the road, according to the Environmental Protection Agency.

Company Profile

FPL Group, Inc. is one of the nation's largest providers of electricity-related services and is nationally known as a high-quality, efficient and customer-driven organization. Its principal subsidiary, Florida Power & Light Company, serves more than 8 million people along the eastern seaboard and southern portion of Florida.

FPL Energy, LLC, FPL Group's competitive energy subsidiary, is a leader in producing electricity from clean and renewable fuels. Together, FPL's and FPL Energy's generating assets represent nearly 33,000 megawatts of capacity. FLP FiberNet, LLC, provides fiber-optic services to FPL and other customers, primarily telecommunications companies in Florida.

Shortcomings to Bear in Mind

- If you are looking for a fat dividend yield, you had better look elsewhere. FPL's yield is a full percentage point below its peers. On the plus side, the stock's growth prospects are better than most other electric utilities.

Reasons to Buy

- "FPL Group performed exceptionally well in 2007, driven again by the outstanding performance of FPL Energy," said CEO Lew Hay on January 28, 2008. "Despite some weakness in revenues at Florida Power & Light, particularly late in the year, full-year results for FPL Group exceeded the expectations we set out in the fall of 2006.

"FPL Energy's strong results benefited from contributions from new investments as well as the roll-out of below-market hedges in the existing fleet. The merchant portfolio and our wholesale marketing operations also took advantage of market opportunities and delivered results at the high end of our expectations.

"Florida Power & Light delivered good results overall, although the latter part of the year was disappointing in terms of revenue growth. We expected 2007 to be a challenging year for Florida Power & Light on the cost front, and we had indicated some uncertainty about revenue growth. During the year, we were able to find offsetting productivity improvements in some of the cost pressures, but the revenue performance fell well short of our expectations."

Mr. Hay goes on to say, "Throughout 2007, FPL Energy and Florida Power &

Light continued laying the groundwork for future growth, and we are pleased with our progress. At FPL Energy, we expanded and accelerated our growth plans and outlined a program to add an additional 8,000 to 10,000 megawatts of wind to our portfolio by 2012. FPL Energy also invested significant effort in other growth areas, including adding new solar capacity and transmission facilities designed to leverage the overall growth of the renewable business."

The company's CEO also said, "Florida Power & Light also took steps to add incremental fossil, nuclear and renewable generation as it continues to meet the needs of the growing Florida market. At the same time, we continued to invest in strengthening our transmission and distribution infrastructure, and our advanced metering initiative yielded good early results. As a result of our success in 2007, FPL Group is well positioned for earnings growth in future years and we remain comfortable with our previously announced earnings expectations for 2008 and 2009. For 2008, we expect full year adjusted earnings per share to be in the range of $3.83 and $3.93. For 2009, we continue to see a reasonable adjusted earnings per share range of $4.15 to $4.35."

- For the fourth consecutive year, Florida Power & Light Company has received the ServiceOne™ Award for excellent customer service among utilities in the United States and Canada. PA Consulting Group, which presented the award to FPL on October 17, 2007, uses a broad range of measures to certify that specific "best practices" are in place to sustain long-term performance.

"I'm exceptionally proud of how hard our 2,400 customer service employees have worked to meet our customers' needs," said FPL vice president for customer service, Marlene Santos. "This is a reflection of their commitment to excellence that they bring to work every day."

The ServiceOne awards are presented annually by PA Consulting Group, a management, systems and technology consultancy, whose certification process defines, evaluates, and quantifies the performance of utilities worldwide. A group of industry experts assembled by PA Consulting Group evaluated five key areas of FPL's customer service organization—the call center, billing, meter reading, credit and collections, and field service. As a result of this benchmarking process, FPL received the 2007 ServiceOne award.

"What is particularly exciting about this award is how well we fared across the full spectrum of benchmarking categories," Mr. Santos said. "Every single area in customer service was rated at exemplary levels, which shows that we are good at every aspect of what we do."

Florida Power & Light Company is nationally known as a high quality, efficient and customer-driven organization focused on energy-related products and services. FPL Group is widely recognized as one of the country's premier power companies.

■ On January 28, 2008, Argus Research Company regarded FPL as a BUY. Gary F. Hovis said, "The company has a solid base of high-return, nonregulated operations and a core regulated utility operation, and we believe that the shares are quite attractive at current levels. While economic activity in Florida has eased, it is still strong, as businesses continue to relocate to the state."

■ In 2006, FPL Energy, LLC, a subsidiary of FPL Group, hosted about 200 guests near Abilene to dedicate the world's largest wind farm—the 735 MW Horse Hollow Wind Energy Center located in Taylor and Nolan County, Texas.

Texas State Representative Phil King and Dyess Air Force Base Commander Timothy Ray joined FPL Energy's senior vice president of development Mike O'Sullivan and more than 200 local and regional guests to celebrate the commercial operation of the Horse Hollow Wind Energy Center and all those that helped bring the facility to Texas.

"The Horse Hollow Wind Energy Center is a great example of a project put together by a terrific team that will benefit the state of Texas for many years to come," said Mr. O'Sullivan. "Wind is a clean, renewable source of energy that is emission-free and has a minimal impact on the local infrastructure, while contributing to the economic well-being of local communities."

State representative Phil King said, "The state legislature worked very hard last year to pass legislation to encourage the development of wind energy in our state. The Horse Hollow Wind project is an excellent example of the type of project we all envisioned. I look forward to working with FPL Energy and other wind developers to expand renewable energy across the state."

"The Air Force is the largest purchaser of renewable energy in the nation, and Dyess Air Force Base is leading the way as the first federal installation to use 100 percent wind-generated electricity," said Col. Timothy Ray, 7th Bomb Wing commander. "Dyess is a true success story, and we're proud to be part of this community that's so dedicated to making our nation a little cleaner for our children and grandchildren."

SECTOR: **Utilities**
BETA COEFFICIENT: **.75**
10-YEAR COMPOUND EARNINGS PER SHARE GROWTH: **6.2%**
10-YEAR COMPOUND DIVIDENDS PER SHARE GROWTH: **5.5%**

	2007	2006	2005	2004	2003	2002	2001	2000
Revenues (Mil)	15,263	15,710	11,846	10,522	9,630	8,311	8,475	7,082
Net Income (Mil)	1,312	1,261	885	887	883	710	796	719
Earnings per share	3.27	3.23	2.32	2.46	2.45	2.01	2.31	2.07
Dividends per share	1.64	1.50	1.42	1.30	1.20	1.16	1.12	1.08
Price high	72.8	55.6	48.1	38.1	34.0	32.7	35.8	36.5
low	53.7	37.8	35.9	30.1	26.8	22.5	25.6	18.2

CONSERVATIVE GROWTH

General Dynamics Corporation

2941 Fairview Park Drive □ Suite 100 □ Falls Church, VA 22042-4513 □ (703) 876-3195 □ Dividend reinvestment plan not available □ Web site: *www.generaldynamics.com* □ Ticker symbol: GD □ S&P rating: A+ □ Value Line financial strength rating: A++

On August 23, 2007, General Dynamics NASSCO, (a wholly owned subsidiary of General Dynamics), announced that it had reached an agreement with the U.S. Navy for options to build up to five additional T-AKE dry cargo ammunition ships. Contracts for the ships, valued at $2.5 billion if all options are exercised, are expected to be awarded over the next four years. Including the nine ships previously under contract, this agreement means the San Diego shipyard would build a total of 14 T-AKE ships for the Navy.

"This agreement clearly provides the best value to the government and NASSCO," said Frederick J. Harris, president of General Dynamics NASSCO. "The Navy-NASSCO team can now focus on building and delivering T-AKE ships as efficiently as possible."

Since October 2001, NASSCO has received contracts to build nine T-AKE ships and delivered the first three ships of the class. The fourth T-AKE ship was scheduled to be delivered in November 2007. Under the new agreement, NASSCO

would deliver the fourteenth ship in the fourth quarter of 2014.

NASSCO has incorporated international marine technologies and commercial ship-design features into the T-AKE class, including an integrated electric-drive propulsion system. The ships can deliver more than 10,000 tons of food, ammunition, fuel and other provisions to combat ships at sea. T-AKE ships are replacing single-mission ships that are reaching the end of their service lives.

General Dynamics NASSCO employs more than 4,600 people and is the only major ship construction and repair yard on the West Coast of the United States. In addition to the four T-AKE ships currently under construction, NASSCO will soon begin construction on the first of nine product carriers for U.S. Shipping Partners L.P.

Company Profile

General Dynamics was officially established February 21, 1952, although it has organizational roots dating back to the late 1800s. The company was formed after its predecessor and current operating division, Electric Boat, acquired the aircraft company Canadair Ltd. and began building the first nuclear-powered submarine, the *USS Nautilus*.

Through the years, General Dynamics has applied the wisdom of its experience and insight to recognize and act on change to build its position in the defense and technology business sectors. Building upon its marine business, the company added its first Combat Systems business unit, Land Systems, in 1982; its first Information Systems and Technology business unit, Advanced Technology Systems, in 1997; and returned to the aerospace business with Gulfstream in 1999.

Today, General Dynamics has leading market positions in business aviation and aircraft services, land and amphibious combat systems, mission-critical information systems and technologies, and shipbuilding and marine systems. The company is a leading supplier of sophisticated defense systems to the United States and its allies, and sets the world standard in business jets.

General Dynamics has four main business segments. Aerospace designs, manufactures and provides services for mid-size, large cabin and ultralong range business aircraft. Combat Systems supplies land and amphibious combat machines and systems, including armored vehicles, power trains, turrets, munitions and gun systems. Information Systems and Technology's expertise lies in specialized data acquisition and processing, in advanced electronics, and in battlespace information networks and management systems. Marine Systems designs and builds submarines, surface combatants, auxiliary ships and large commercial vessels.

Information Systems and Technology

General Dynamics Information Systems and Technology is a leading integrator of transformational, network-centric command-and-control, communications, computing, intelligence, surveillance, and reconnaissance (C4ISR) systems using digital information-sharing technologies. These systems provide today's war-fighters with secure, on-demand access to more mission-critical information than ever before, enabling U.S. forces and allies to prevail on the battlefield.

Combat Systems

General Dynamics Combat Systems is a market-leading provider of tracked and wheeled armored combat vehicles, armament systems, and munitions for customers in North America, Europe, the Middle East and the South Pacific—and the only producer of America's main battle tanks.

Marine Systems

General Dynamics Marine Systems designs, develops, manufactures, and integrates the complex naval platforms that are central to the U.S. Navy's transformation to a more lethal, flexible, network-centric sea force of the future. Its three advanced shipyards apply decades of development innovation, experience, and expertise to produce the world's most sophisticated maritime surface, sub-surface and support systems.

Aerospace

General Dynamics Aerospace is one of the world's leading designers and manufacturers of business-jet aircraft, and is a leading provider of services for private aircraft in select markets globally. Gulfstream business jets are among the most technologically advanced aircraft available, and the company provides a broad selection of planes to meet the demanding requirements of business and government customers alike.

Shortcomings to Bear in Mind

▪ On March 21, 2008, *Value Line Investment Survey* was less than enthusiastic about General Dynamics. Morton L. Siegel said, "These shares, now selling at over three times the low set in 2003, have below-average three-to-five-year gain potential."

Reasons to Buy

▪ Earnings from continuing operations for 2007 were $2.1 billion, or $5.10 per share on a fully diluted basis, compared with $1.7 billion, or $4.20 fully diluted, in 2006. This is an increase of 21.6 percent. Revenue for the full year 2007 was $27.2 billion, compared with $24.1 billion for 2006, an increase of 13.2 percent.

Net cash provided by operating activities from continuing operations totaled $1.07 billion in the quarter and $2.95 billion for the year. Free cash flow from operations, defined as net cash provided by operating activities from continuing operations less capital expenditures, was $891 million in the quarter and $2.48 billion for the year.

The company's funded backlog grew by $292 million in the fourth quarter of 2007, to $37.2 billion. Compared to year-end 2006, funded backlog increased $3.2 billion. Total backlog at year-end 2007 was $46.8 billion.

Operating margins for the fourth quarter 2007 increased to 11.6 percent from 10.8 percent for fourth quarter 2006. For the full year, company-wide operating margins increased by 50 basis points over 2006, to 11.4 percent.

▪ "The U.S. Senate recently approved a defense spending bill that includes $23 billion of funding for mine-resistant, ambush-protected (MRAP) vehicles," said the Standard & Poor's weekly publication, *The Outlook*, on October 24, 2007. "We believe that General Dynamics has a competitive MRAP offering. In addition, the company has a joint venture to manufacture MRAP models designed by Force Protection.

"At Gulfstream, we expect the business jet market will remain strong for some time, driven by an increase in global corporate wealth. We also see good growth at General Dynamic's information systems and technology segment and potential for future growth in the marine segment, where the company is one of only two U.S.

makers of nuclear-powered submarines and the second-largest military shipbuilder."

▪ On March 8, 2008, Standard & Poor's *Stock Reports* rated General Dynamics a BUY. Richard Tortoriello said, "Longer term, we see GD continuing to increase sales and EPS (earnings per share) via acquisitions, growth in business jet deliveries, and strength in land vehicles and munitions needed for current operations in Iraq and the replacement of lost and damaged equipment afterward. We see strong supplemental spending by Congress for the ongoing wars funding increased defense spending at GD. We see a significant amount of this funding being used for land vehicles for the Army."

▪ Argus Research Company rated General Dynamics a BUY on January 23, 2008. Its analyst, Suzanne Betts, said "While the IS&T segment continues to face downward pressure from contract runoffs and recent acquisitions, the segment is expected to post modest top-line gains in 2008. Management cited the Marine Systems group as having the strongest outlook for compound annual growth over the next few years, despite modest operations for 2008."

▪ "General Dynamics's chief, Nicholas Chabraja, is a deal maker," said Thomas G. Donlan, writing for *Barron's* on July 10, 2006. "He's made more than forty acquisitions, not to mention an occasional sale, in the past twelve years. To avoid expensive bidding contests or telegraphing his next move to rivals or targets, he plays his cards close to the vest. As he says, 'I don't tell people my strategies; maybe that's why they work.'

"There's no arguing with the results. Chabraja's roughly $8.5 billion of purchases have revived an outdated $3 billion tank and submarine builder that itself was on the sales block as the Cold War ended in the early 1990s, and turned it into a $21 billion high-technology colossus that serves the military, aerospace and business-jet markets."

Mr. Donlan goes on to say, "The company's erratic past has made some investors understandably wary of the shares. Until the early 1990s, it was a defense conglomerate making warplanes, rockets, ships and tanks. But the end of the Cold War threw defense companies into a tailspin, and by the end of 1993, GD had sold off several units and was set to unload its last two major businesses—submarine and tank manufacturing. However, taxes, binding labor contracts and potential environmental liabilities make a sales uneconomical for shareholders, Chabraja said in a recent interview.

"When he was named chief executive officer in 1997, he saw no choice but to grow."

SECTOR: **Industrials**
BETA COEFFICIENT: **1.00**
10-YEAR COMPOUND EARNINGS PER SHARE GROWTH: **15.1%**
10-YEAR COMPOUND DIVIDENDS PER SHARE GROWTH: **11%**

	2007	2006	2005	2004	2003	2002	2001	2000
Revenues (Mil)	27,240	24,063	20,975	19,178	16,617	13,829	12,163	10,356
Net Income (Mil)	2,072	1,856	1,448	1,203	998	1,051	943	901
Earnings per share	5.10	4.20	3.58	2.99	2.50	2.54	2.33	2.24
Dividends per share	1.16	0.89	0.78	0.70	0.63	0.60	0.55	0.51
Price high	94.6	78.0	61.2	55.0	45.4	55.6	48.0	39.5
low	70.6	56.7	48.8	42.5	25.0	36.7	30.3	18.2

GROWTH AND INCOME

General Electric Company

3135 Easton Turnpike ❏ Fairfield, CT 06828 ❏ (203) 373-2468 ❏ Direct dividend reinvestment plan available ❏ Web site: *www.ge.com* ❏ Ticker symbol: GE ❏ S&P rating: A+ ❏ Value Line financial strength rating: A++

"GE has six strong businesses: Infrastructure, Healthcare, Commercial Finance, GE Money, Industrial and NBCU," said CEO Jeffrey Immelt in 2007. "We expect these businesses to achieve 10 percent-plus earnings growth most years, with long-term returns of 20 percent. We expect them to be industry leaders in market share, value and profitability. We want businesses where we can bring the totality of the company—products, services, information, and financing—to capitalize on the growth trends I mentioned earlier.

"We run these businesses with common finance and human resource processes. We have one leadership development foundation and one global research infrastructure to achieve excellent results with a common culture. We have a few company-wide councils, like services, so we can share ideas with minimum bureaucracy.

"We compete hard and are tough-minded about winning. We invest to lead in our core businesses in good times and bad. Sometimes good businesses go through bad cycles and we must have the patience to fix them. However, when we find that a business cannot meet our financial goals or could be run better outside GE, we will exit that business rather than erode shareholder value."

Company Profile

General Electric, a superbly managed company, provides a broad range of industrial products and services. Under the stewardship of CEO Jack Welch (now retired), GE transformed itself from operating as a maker of diverse industrial equipment, to being a provider of a broad range of commercial and consumer services.

In 1980, manufacturing operations generated about 85 percent of operating profits; currently, services operations generate 70 percent of total operating profits. GE Capital (the company's enormous financing arm, and the world's largest nonbank financial operation) alone generates nearly 30 percent of operating profits.

General Electric is one of the world's largest corporations. Although GE can trace its origins back to Thomas Edison, who invented the light bulb in 1879, the company was actually founded in 1892.

The company's broad diversification is clearly evident if you examine its components: Operations are divided into two groups: product, service and media businesses and GE Capital Services (GECS).

Product, service and media includes eleven businesses: aircraft engines, appliances, lighting, medical systems, NBC, plastics, power systems, electrical distribution and control, information services, motors and industrial systems, and transportation systems.

In 2002, the company—often criticized for the complexity of its structure and the resulting opacity of its numbers—said it would break up GE Capital, by far its largest business, into four businesses. The new businesses are GE Commercial Finance, GE Insurance, GE Consumer Finance, and GE Equipment Management.

Shortcomings to Bear in Mind

■ General Electric has many attributes and is considered one of the bluest blue chips. However, its balance sheet is suspect, since 70 percent of capitalization is in long-term debt.

Reasons to Buy

■ In 2007, earnings from continuing operation were $22.5 billion, or $22.0 per share, up 16 percent and 18 percent, respectively. Full-year revenues from continuing operations were $173 billion, up 14 percent.

"We have built the company to outperform in this environment," said Mr. Immelt. "We have strengthened the portfolio for growth, restructuring to lower our cost, maintain our Triple A credit rating and stayed true to our risk management principles. We are also more global, with more than 50 percent of our revenues now coming from outside the United States. At the same time, we have been disciplined with capital allocation, returning $58 billion over the last three years to our shareholders in the form of dividends and buyback."

■ GE Healthcare, a unit of General Electric Company, announced on August 22, 2007, that it had received U.S. Food and Drug Administration (FDA) approval for its new mobile mammography product that will improve access to breast cancer screening for millions of women around the world. The mobile Senographe® Essential is built on the company's Senographe Essential platform, the next-generation of GE's proven Senographe Full Field Digital Mammography systems.

As medical organizations continue to offer full-field digital mammography in a mobile setting, GE Healthcare's newest mobile unit will feature the largest digital detector in the mammography market, advanced ergonomic design for the technologist, optimized patient comfort and seamless workflow connectivity. The foundation of the Senographe Essential imaging excellence is GE's advanced digital detector, which delivers the industry's highest Detective Quantum Efficiency (DQE)—the standard for quantifying digital X-ray image quality—at low doses.

"GE's goal is to enhance breast care for women worldwide and bring this technology to those who otherwise would not have access to it," said David Caumartin, general manager of Global Mammography for GE Healthcare. "GE offers customers the broadest portfolio when it comes to breast imaging and the new mobile Essential will be the top of the line mobile product in the market featuring all the proven advantages of our Senographe platform."

A study published in May 2007 by the National Cancer Institute found that use of mammography screening had dropped four percent from 2000 to 2005. In 2005, only 70 percent of women surveyed for the study reported getting an annual mammogram. During the same timeframe, among women fifty to sixty-four, the group most at risk for breast cancer, screening was down 7 percent, from 79 percent to 72 percent.

■ "General Electric's $8.13 billion deal with Abbott Laboratories in the latest step in GE Chairman Jeffrey Immelt's strategy to redouble investment in the conglomerate's market-leading businesses, from aviation to healthcare," said Kathryn Kranhold and Avery Johnson, writing for the *Wall Street Journal* on January 19, 2007.

"The companies confirmed that GE had agreed to acquire Abbott's laboratory-testing unit and a smaller blood-analysis division." The article goes on to say, "The acquisition would mark GE's entry into what is known as 'in vitro' diagnostics, or laboratory testing, while Abbott sheds a unit growing more slowly than other parts of its business."

The writers also said, "Mr. Immelt said the Abbott deal would give GE a 'pretty complete' healthcare business, which also includes information-technology systems."

■ The key to GE's business plan is the requirement that businesses be first or second in market share in their industries. Those that fail to achieve this status are divested.

■ "The company continues to benefit from its presence in global infrastructure markets, as well as from the solid base in its financial service businesses," said analyst Suzanne Betts, writing for Argus Research Company on January 18, 2008. "This year, GE plans to further realign its consumer finance portfolio and to take advantage of selective commercial finance opportunities that yield higher margins. The company has also indicated a willingness to pursue

industrial acquisitions that complement its existing portfolio."

■ Here are ten growth facts about General Electric in 2007:

• Third straight year of organic revenue growth of two to three time GDP growth.

• Earnings per share (EPS) of $2.20, an increase of 18 percent.

• Global revenue growth of 22 percent, more than half of revenues outside the United States.

• Orders growth of 18 percent.

• Equipment backlog of $49 billion, an increase of 54 percent; service backlog of $109 billion, an increase of 16 percent.

• Financial services assets growth of 16 percent.

• Free cash flow of $19 billion; industrial cash flow from operating activities growth of 15 percent.

• Dividend increase of 11 percent, thirty-second straight annual increase.

• $25.4 billion returned to investors through dividend and stock buyback.

• One of five "Triple-A"-rated U.S. industrial companies.

■ On March 8, 2008, Standard & Poor's *Stock Reports* gave GE a BUY rating. Analyst Richard Tortoriello had this to say, "Given what we see as an environment of increased investment risk, we view GE's S&P Quality Ranking of A+ as providing a measure of safety for shareholders. We also favor the repositioning of GE's portfolio of businesses that has taken place over the past few years, including recent acquisitions. We think various factors, including a strong aerospace market, increasing demand for energy infrastructure, and increased global wealth, will help GE's businesses continue to show moderately strong growth going forward."

■ *Value Line Investment Survey* concurred by rating the stock a BUY on April 11, 2008.

Richard Gallagher said,"Management has positioned General Electric for long-term growth. The company's global operations should help GE weather a downturn in any specific market. In fact, over 50 percent of GE's revenues come from outside the United States. What's more, General Electric's flexible business model and substantia resources allow it to quickly react to opportunities for growth."

■ "A reliable growth company must have the courage to invest and the discipline to deliver," said Mr. Immelt in 2007. "It took courage to invest over $1 billion in a new jet engine, such as the GE90, with minimal returns for more than ten years. Today, because of these investments, GE enjoys exceptional success in commercial aviation. The GE90 engine should generate $40 billion of revenues over the next thirty years."

SECTOR: **Industrials**
BETA COEFFICIENT: **.90**
10-YEAR COMPOUND EARNINGS PER SHARE GROWTH: **10.2%**
10-YEAR COMPOUND DIVIDENDS PER SHARE GROWTH: **12.0%**

	2007	2006	2005	2004	2003	2002	2001	2000
Revenues (Mil)	172,738	163,391	147,956	151,299	134,187	131,698	125,913	129,853
Net Income (Mil)	22,650	20,829	16,711	16,593	15,589	14,118	13,684	12,735
Earnings per share	2.20	2.01	1.58	1.59	1.55	1.51	1.41	1.27
Dividends/share	1.12	1.03	0.88	0.82	0.77	0.73	0.64	0.57
Price high	42.2	38.5	37.3	37.8	32.4	41.8	53.6	60.5
low	33.9	32.1	32.7	28.9	21.3	21.4	28.5	41.6

GROWTH AND INCOME

General Mills, Inc.

P.O. Box 1113 ◻ Minneapolis, MN 55440-1113 ◻ (763) 764-3202 ◻ Dividend reinvestment plan available ◻ Web site: *www.generalmills.com* ◻ Listed: NYSE ◻ Fiscal years end last Sunday in May ◻ Ticker symbol: GIS ◻ S&P rating: A-◻ Value Line financial strength rating: A

On September 24, 2007, General Mills said that its board of directors had elected Kendall J. Powell CEO. Mr. Powell, age fifty-three, joined the company in 1979 and was most recently president and chief operating officer. He succeeded Steve Sanger, age sixty-one, who served as General Mills's CEO since May 1995. Mr. Sanger will continue as chairman through the end of the current fiscal year in May 2008.

"The board and I have great confidence that Ken will be an outstanding chief executive officer of General Mills," said Mr. Sanger. "He has extensive knowledge of our global food categories, our customers, and our worldwide operations. This deep-seated understanding of our business, coupled with Ken's commitment to our culture and the development of our people, make him uniquely qualified to lead General Mills in the next phase of our long-term growth."

Mr. Powell has held a variety of general management assignments over his twenty-eight-year career with General Mills, including president of the Yoplait Division from 1996 to 1997; president of Big G Cereals from 1997 to 1999; and chief executive officer of the company's Cereal Partners Worldwide (CPW) joint venture with Nestle based in Switzerland from 1999 to 2004. Today, CPW generates $1.6 billion in annual net sales and sells ready-to-eat breakfast cereal in more than 130 international markets. Powell was named an executive vice president of General Mills in 2004 and was appointed CEO—U.S. Retail in 2005. He was named president and chief operating officer of General Mills in June 2006. Mr. Powell holds a bachelor's degree in biology from Harvard and an MBA from Stanford.

Company Profile

General Mills is the second-largest domestic producer of ready-to-eat breakfast cereals. It is also a leading producer of other well-known packaged consumer foods.

Major cereal brands, most of which bear the Big G label, include Cheerios, Wheaties, Lucky Charms, Total, and Chex. Other consumer packaged food products include baking mixes (Betty Crocker and Bisquick); meals (Betty Crocker dry packaged dinner mixes), Progresso soups, Green Giant canned and frozen vegetables); snacks (Pop Secret microwave popcorn, Bugles snacks, grain and fruit snack products); Pillsbury refrigerated and frozen dough products, frozen breakfast products and frozen pizza and snack products; organic foods and other products, including Yoplait and Colombo yogurt. The company's holdings include many other brand names, such as Haagen-Dazs frozen ice cream and a host of joint ventures.

The company's international businesses consist of operations and sales in Canada, Europe, Latin America, and the Asia/Pacific region. In those regions, General Foods sells numerous local brands, in addition to internationally recognized brands, such as Haagen-Dazs ice cream, Old El Paso Mexican foods, and Green Giant vegetables. Those international businesses have sales and marketing organizations in thirty-three countries.

Shortcomings to Bear in Mind

■ Dividends have grown at a snail's pace. In the 1997–2007 period, dividends per share advanced from $1.02 to $1.44, a compound growth rate of only 3.5 per-

cent. On a more positive note, earnings per share have outpaced dividends by a wide margin, climbing at a compound rate of 7.8 percent.

Reasons to Buy

■ For the fiscal year ended May 27, 2007, General Mills net sales grew 6 percent to $12.4 billion, outpacing 4 percent growth in unit volume. Segment operating profits increased 7 percent to $2.3 billion. Diluted earnings per share (EPS) totaled $3.18, up 10 percent from $2.90 in 2006.

Mr. Sanger said, "For the second year in a row, all three of our business segments achieved solid gains in net sales and operating profit. We increased our level of consumer marketing investment, which will help sustain our brands' growth momentum going forward. And we returned $1.8 billion in cash to shareholders through increased dividends and share repurchases." Total return to General Mills shareholders in fiscal 2007 through stock price appreciation and dividends exceeded 19 percent.

■ On February 19, 2008, Argus Research Report rated General Mills a BUY, with this comment by Erin Ashley Smith, "We are pleased with the company's optimistic outlook for fiscal 2008 and beyond, despite the challenging cost environment. GIS expects to increase margins and profits in the International segment and to deliver solid EPS growth in fiscal 2008."

■ "The stock has a number of attributes that will likely appeal to conservative investors in a turbulent market," said *Value Line Investment Survey* on February 1, 2008. Robert M. Greene, CFA, went on to say, "With its portfolio of well-established food brands, General Mills should be more recession-resistant than most companies."

■ In 2007, net sales for the Snacks division increased 10 percent to exceed $1 billion for the first time, led by grain snacks such as Nature Valley granola bars and new Fiber One bars. Yoplait sales grew 6 percent, led by

Yoplait light varieties, Go-gurt and Yoplait Kids yogurt fortified with DHA Omega 3. Net sales for the Meals division grew 5 percent, reflecting strong growth of Progresso ready-to-serve soups and Hamburger Helper mixes. Net sales for Pillsbury USA and the Baking Products division each grew 3 percent. Big G cereals posted a 2 percent sales increase, with strong performance from the market-leading Cheerios franchise and new cereals introduced during the year.

■ In 2007, net sales for the Bakeries & Foodservice division grew 5 percent to exceed $1.8 billion. Unit volume grew 1 percent, and pricing, favorable sales mix and productivity boosted operating profits 28 percent to $148 million.

■ After-tax earnings from joint ventures totaled $73 million in 2007, up 6 percent on strong earnings growth for Cereal Partners Worldwide (CPW). These results include a restructuring expense of $8 million after-tax in both years related to the CPW plant restructuring under way in the United Kingdom.

■ International net sales grew 16 percent in 2007 to exceed $2.1 billion. Unit volume grew 8 percent and favorable currency exchange contributed 4 points of sales growth. Operating profits rose 11 percent to $216 million despite double-digit growth in consumer marketing expense.

■ Cash flow from operations totaled nearly $1.8 billion in 2007. Capital expenditures totaled $460 million for the year. Dividends paid in 2007 grew 7.5 percent to $1.44 per share. On June 25, 2007, the company announced a two-cent increase in the quarterly dividend rate to 39 cents per share, effective with the August 1, 2007, payment.

■ Fiscal 2008 Outlook: "We expect fiscal 2008 to be another year of strong operating performance, consistent with our long-term goals," said Mr. Sanger. "Our growth model calls for low single-digit growth in net sales, mid single-digit growth in segment operating profits, and high single-digit growth

in earnings per share. We expect to meet these targets in 2008 despite the estimated 5 percent input-cost inflation and increased consumer marketing investment that is included in our plans."

■ On December 19, 2007, General Mills reported results for the second quarter of fiscal 2008. Net sales for the thirteen weeks ending November 25, 2007, rose 7 percent to $3.70 billion. Segment operating profits essentially matched last year's second quarter at $716 million, including higher input costs, a 10 percent increase in consumer marketing investment and $20 million pretax expense associated with a product recall of frozen pepperoni pizza. Net earnings totaled $391 million including restructuring and associated costs of $20 million pretax, $13 million after tax. Diluted earnings per share (EPS) totaled $1.14, up 6 percent from $1.08 a year ago. Product recall expenses reduced 2008 second-quarter EPS by 4 cents.

Mr. Powell said, "Our worldwide operations are continuing to generate good growth in fiscal 2008. Each of our three business segments reported net sales gains for the second quarter and first half. And segment operating profits were up 4 percent through the first six months despite significant input cost inflation, recall expenses and double-digit growth in our consumer marketing investment. This performance has us on track to achieve our full-year growth targets."

■ General Mills has a solid market share in most of its product lines, generally number one or number two: ready-to-eat cereals (number two), refrigerated yogurt (one), frozen vegetables (one), Mexican products (two), ready-to-serve soup (two), refrigerated dough (one), dessert mixes (one), frozen baked goods (one), microwave popcorn (two), frozen hot snacks (two), dry dinners (one), and fruit snacks (one).

■ Although some analysts are skeptical of the 2002 acquisition of Pillsbury, it now appears that the price paid was not excessive. According to a *Barron's* article, "In buying Pillsbury, its Minneapolis neighbor, General Mills doubled its annual sales. It picked up the leading maker of refrigerated dough; the Progresso, Old El Paso and Green Giant brands; a large domestic food-service business; international food operations; and one of the best-known corporate mascots, the Pillsbury Doughboy.

"One unfortunate legacy, however, was the addition of debt, issued to fund the cash portion of the deal. In all, General Mills paid $6 billion in stock and $4 billion cash to Pillsbury's former owner, Diageo. The company's debt load is one of the food industry's highest."

SECTOR: Consumer Staples
BETA COEFFICIENT: .65
10-YEAR COMPOUND EARNINGS PER SHARE GROWTH: 7.8%
10-YEAR COMPOUND DIVIDENDS PER SHARE GROWTH: 3.5%

		2007	2006	2005	2004	2003	2002	2001	2000
Revenues (Mil)		12,442	11,640	11,244	11,070	10,506	7,949	7,078	6,700
Net Income (Mil)		1,244	1,090	1,100	1,055	917	581	643	614
Earnings per share		3.18	2.90	2.74	2.85	2.43	1.70	2.20	2.00
Dividends per share		1.44	1.34	1.24	1.10	1.10	1.10	1.10	1.10
Price	high	61.5	59.2	53.9	50.0	49.7	51.7	52.9	45.3
	low	54.2	47.0	44.7	43.0	41.4	37.4	37.3	29.4

AGGRESSIVE GROWTH

Goodrich Corporation

Four Coliseum Center ▫ 2730 West Tyvola Road ▫ Charlotte, NC 28217 ▫ (704) 423-5517 ▫ Dividend reinvestment plan not available ▫ Web site: *www.goodrich.com* ▫ Ticker symbol: GR ▫ Listed: NYSE ▫ S&P rating: B ▫ Value Line financial strength rating: B+

On April 2, 2008, Goodrich was selected by Lockheed Martin to supply the air data system (ADS) for the F-35 Lightning II program. Initial work includes the System Development and Demonstration (SDD) and Low Rate Initial Production 1 and 2 phases of the program. SDD is expected to be completed in the first quarter of 2009, with ADS production deliveries also commencing in the first quarter of 2009. The ADS program has the potential of generating $300 million in revenue over the life of the program.

The ADS is designed, developed and produced by Goodrich's Sensors and Integrated Systems team in Burnsville, Minnesota, and provides all critical air data parameters to the vehicle management computers for the aircraft's flight control and pilot display systems. Its SmartProbe™ and SmartPort® air data sensing technology allows integration of multifunction sensing ports, pressure sensors and processing capability through the elimination of pneumatic lines. The total number of discrete product installations is reduced, overall weight is decreased, and reliability and maintainability are significantly improved. Commonality of the ADS for all F-35 variants will simplify logistics support and reduce overall life cycle costs.

"This award solidifies Goodrich's 'Smart' air data technology as the preferred architecture for next generation aircraft and modernization programs," said Jan Mathiesen, vice president, Goodrich Sensors and Integrated Systems. "We are proud to have the F-35 Lightning II join leading military and commercial aircraft using this technology, including the Lockheed Martin F-22 Raptor, Boeing C-130 AMP, Airbus A380, Dassault Falcon 7X, and Embraer 170/190 and Phenom programs."

Goodrich's content on the F-35, expected to be valued at more than $3 million per aircraft, includes landing gear, weapons bay door systems, engine and fuel quantity sensors, actuation systems and unique short takeoff/vertical landing (STOVL) engine and airframe components. Production takes place at company facilities in Australia, Canada, the UK, and the U.S.

Company Profile

Goodrich Corporation, a *Fortune* 500 company, is a global supplier of systems and services to the aerospace, defense and homeland security markets. With annual revenues of $5.9 billion, Goodrich is headquartered in Charlotte, North Carolina, and employs more than 23,000 people worldwide in over ninety facilities across sixteen countries.

Goodrich offers an extensive range of products, systems and services for aircraft and engine manufacturers, airlines and defense forces around the world. The company's transformation into one of the globe's largest aerospace companies has been driven by strategic acquisitions and internal growth fueled by innovation and quality. From aerostructures and actuation systems to landing gear, engine control systems, sensors and safety systems, Goodrich products are on almost every aircraft in the world.

Shortcomings to Bear in Mind

- I labeled Goodrich "Aggressive Growth" for several reasons. For one thing, its Beta is on the high side, at 1.25, which might scare away conservative investors who don't like stocks that tend to be volatile.

Also, I wasn't impressed with the company's dividend record. I prefer one that increases its dividend year after year. By contrast, Goodrich has paid the same eighty-cent annual dividend since 2003. And before that it paid $1.10 for a decade or more.

Finally, Goodrich is not exactly a blue chip and is rated only B+ by Value Line for Financial Strength. Similarly, Standard & Poor's awarded the stock only a B, which is below average. On a more positive note, earnings per share are bounding ahead at a good clip.

Reasons to Buy

- On January 31, 2008, CEO Marshall Larsen said, "Overall, 2007 was an excellent year for Goodrich, reflecting strong growth in all of our major market channels and improving margins and cash flow. Our strong fourth quarter results provide us with significant momentum as we look forward to 2008."

Mr. Larsen also said, "We anticipate strong sales growth in 2008, led by expected double-digit growth in sales to the large commercial airplane original equipment manufacturers. Our commercial aftermarket sales are expected to continue their strong growth, with the majority of our sales coming from non-U.S. customers. We do not believe that right-sizing of U.S. airlines' domestic fleets will affect our aftermarket sales since we have far less content on the airplanes that are likely to be retired over the next several years than we have on the airplanes that will remain in service, such as the Airbus A320 and Boeing 737NG aircraft. We believe steady growth in defense and space sales will continue to support our broad and balanced portfolio. In 2008, these sales are expected to drive strong, double-digit growth in earnings per diluted share and continued improvement in cash flow as we near completion of key development programs and focus on improving working capital performance."

■ On September 3, 2007, Neil A. Martin, writing for *Barron's*, had this comment from an analyst: "Goodrich has the best operating momentum and strongest growth profile of any of the aerospace suppliers," says Michael D. Rocco, a Philadelphia-based analyst for asset manager PNC Financial Services. "Earnings, margins and cash flow are all strong and expanding and should continue to improve," he says. "And the current up cycle in aircraft orders and deliveries is nowhere near its peak."

■ On April 1, 2008, Goodrich entered into an agreement with Airbus North America Customer Services Inc. to perform repair work on a variety of proprietary components at its Foley, Alabama maintenance, repair, and overhaul (MRO) facility known as the Alabama Service Center. Under the agreement, the facility becomes one of two Airbus-endorsed repair stations for structural components in the Americas; in addition, it is now one of three repair stations in the Americas that Airbus has chosen to work on its proprietary parts. The main product lines the facility expects to service include flight control surfaces, pneumatic ducting and access doors, such as landing gear doors.

Under the agreement, Goodrich and Airbus will jointly market these repair services to operators. Airlines will now have the option of routing damaged Airbus proprietary components, including those under new aircraft warranty, directly to the Goodrich facility for refurbishment. With the agreement, the facility will become a member of the extended Airbus "family," with direct access to Airbus support and resources including technical data, engineering and supply chain.

"This agreement creates a partnership between Goodrich and Airbus that benefits all Airbus operators in the Americas," said Stuart Kay, general manager of the Alabama Service Center. "It also elevates the level of MRO services that we provide and furthers our goal of being a total solutions provider."

The Foley, Alabama, facility is part of Goodrich's Aerostructures business headquartered in Chula Vista, California. Aerostructures also operates MRO facilities in Scotland, France, Singapore and Dubai, and plans to open an additional MRO facility in Brazil later this year.

■ On August 14, 2007, the U.S. Navy and U.S. Army contracted Goodrich to provide helicopter Vehicle Health Management Systems. The Naval Air Systems Command, Patuxent River, MD, ordered systems for installation on new MH-60R and MH-60S aircraft currently being produced as well as aircraft already in the fleet. Retrofit systems for the Marine Corporation Super Stallion (CH-53E) fleet have also been contracted. Furthermore, the Army Aviation and Missile Command, Redstone Arsenal, Huntsville, Alabama, also ordered additional systems to retrofit into UH-60L aircraft prior to deployment in Iraq.

"These operators are realizing tremendous dispatch reliability and maintainability improvements in aircraft equipped with our Vehicle Health Management Systems," said Kip Freeman, Government Systems Business Director for Goodrich's Sensors and Integrated Systems division. "It is very rewarding for our employees to supply equipment that is helping soldiers, sailors and Marines accomplish their missions," he added.

U.S. Sen. Patrick Leahy (D-VT), a key supporter of the Navy and Army programs, noted, "This equipment has already increased the safety of our men and women in combat, improving the readiness of helicopters to fly crucial medical evacuation and troop transport missions. As Goodrich continues to deliver system after system to the Army and Navy, it is helping to transform the difficult and time-consuming task of maintaining aircraft. I am pleased to see that more helicopters that we deploy will be equipped with this vital system, and I am proud that Vermonters are providing such an important contribution to our fliers."

Goodrich's fully integrated health management systems apply full-time diagnostic health monitoring of the entire helicopter mechanical drive train, from the engines to the rotor system, as well as monitoring of flight manual exceedances and hundreds of aircraft signals. The Navy and Army are using the system as the cornerstone of an initiative to move from flight-hour based maintenance of helicopters to actual health- or condition-based, maintenance practices.

Goodrich Sensors and Integrated Systems provides a broad range of systems to the aerospace industry worldwide including SmartProbe™ air data systems, Electronic Flight Bag systems, security and surveillance systems, fuel measurement and management systems, health and usage management systems, ice detection and protection systems, and rescue hoists and cargo winches. The Vergennes, Vermont facility produces aircraft health management systems for a wide variety of military and commercial helicopters including the: V-22; UH- 60A/L/M; MH-60R/S; AH-1Z; UH-1Y; CH-53E; and S-92/H-92.

SECTOR: Industrials
BETA COEFFICIENT: 1.20
10-YEAR COMPOUND EARNINGS PER SHARE GROWTH: 4.6%
10-YEAR COMPOUND DIVIDENDS PER SHARE GROWTH: - 2%

		2007	2006	2005	2004	2003	2002	2001	2000
Revenues (Mil)		6,392	5,878	5,396	4,724	4,383	3,910	4,184	4,364
Net Income (Mil)		484	336	244	172	38	244	306	318
Earnings per share		3.79	2.66	1.97	1.43	0.33	2.31	2.87	2.97
Dividends per share		0.90	0.80	0.80	0.80	0.80	0.88	1.10	1.10
Price	high	75.7	47.4	45.8	33.9	30.3	34.4	44.5	43.1
	low	45.0	37.2	30.1	26.6	12.2	14.2	15.9	21.6

GROWTH AND INCOME

Gentex Corporation

600 North Centennial Street □ Zeeland, MI 49464 □ (616) 772-1800 □ Dividend reinvestment plan available □ Web site: □ www.gentex.com □ Ticker symbol: GNTX □ Listed: Nasdaq □ S&P rating: B+ □ Value Line financial strength rating: A

On March 19, 2008, Gentex Corporation, the leading supplier of automatic-dimming rearview mirrors to the worldwide automotive industry, announced that it is supplying auto-dimming interior and exterior rearview mirrors for the 2008/2009 Jaguar XF. The XF was launched in Europe and will be introduced later in 2008 to the North American market.

The new Jaguar will feature a three-mirror auto-dimming system. Interior and exterior auto-dimming mirrors will be standard equipment on the Luxury, Premium Luxury and 4.2 trim levels in North America and standard on the two higher trim levels in other global markets. The North American model will also offer a HomeLink®-compatible garage door/entry gate opener feature on all three trim levels. All global exterior autodiming mirrors will be available with puddle lamps and side blind zone indicators. Gentex mirrors darken automatically in response to the headlamp glare of rearward-approaching vehicles. HomeLink® is Johnson Control's fully integrated wireless control system.

"Working closely with Jaguar Cars, Gentex has been able to produce auto-dimming and other visual safety products that can be used throughout the automaker's global market," said Gentex senior vice president Enoch Jen. "We are very pleased that Jaguar recognizes our value-added products and have made them available around the world."

Company Profile

Gentex Corporation develops, manufactures and markets proprietary electro-optical products—products combining photoelectric sensing devices with related electronic circuitry. Specifically, they make smoke detectors that "see" smoke and signal an alarm; rearview mirrors that sense glare and correspondingly dim.

Automotive Products Group
(96 percent of total company sales)

Gentex is the recognized world leader in the manufacture of electrochromic, automatic-dimming mirrors for the auto industry, selling to nearly every automotive manufacturer worldwide.

Gentex automatic-dimming mirrors are based on the science of electrochromics, which is the process of reversibly darkening materials by applying electricity. During nighttime driving, the mirrors use a combination of sophisticated sensors and electronic circuitry to detect glare from rearward approaching vehicles and darken accordingly to eliminate the glare and protect driver vision.

Although Gentex has earned the dominant market share, the industry still has incredible room for growth. Gentex mirrors are found on the majority of the vehicles offering auto-dimming mirrors, yet this represents only 18 percent of the light vehicles produced in the world.

Today, Gentex is making auto-dimming mirrors even smarter, helping them eliminate blind spots, display the compass heading and outside temperature, turn on your headlights and unlock your doors. They're rapidly becoming the preferred location as the driver interface for advanced electronic features and displays.

Gentex mirrors are offered as standard or optional equipment on over 250 2007 model year vehicles around the world. The company is producing mirrors at a rate of over 14 million units a year, with the current estimated capacity to produce 25 million units annually. Over 100 million mirror units have been shipped since 1987.

Gentex was the first company in the world to successfully develop and produce a commercial automatic-dimming rearview mirror. After more than twenty years of supplying these products in the highly competitive global automotive industry, the company remains the leading supplier of these mirrors.

Fire Protection Products Group
(4 percent of total company sales)

Gentex also maintains an extensive line of commercial fire protection products for the North American market, including smoke detectors and audible/visual signaling devices. Gentex's photoelectric method of smoke detection is preferred by hotels, hospitals, office buildings, and the like because they're less prone to false alarms yet are quick to detect slow, smoldering fires.

Founded in 1974, Gentex operates out of five manufacturing plants (four automotive and one fire protection) all located in Zeeland, Michigan; automotive sales/engineering offices in Livonia, Michigan; Munich and Sindelfingen, Germany; Nagoya and Yokohama, Japan; Seoul, South Korea; Coventry, England; Paris, France; and Gothenburg, Sweden. There are automotive sales, engineering, light assembly and warehouse facilities in Erlenbach, Germany, and Shanghai, China. There are four regional U.S. sales offices for the Fire Protection Products Group. The company is recognized for its quality products, its application of world class manufacturing principles, for its commitment to developing and maintaining a highly skilled workforce, and for encouraging employee ownership of the company's stock.

As of September 1, 2007, Gentex had approximately 2,600 employees worldwide.

Shortcomings to Bear in Mind

■ In 2008, a company spokesman said, "During the fourth quarter of 2007, the company's quarterly financial results were negatively impacted by approximately $358,000 (pretax, reported in Engineering, Research and Development Expense) in legal expenses related to litigation between the Company and K.W. Muth and Muth Mirror Systems LLC (collectively 'Muth'). The litigation, as previously announced, relates to exterior mirrors with turn signal indicators. A trial took place in Wisconsin in July 2007, and in December 2007, the court found that Muth's patents were invalid and unenforceable, and that Gentex's Razor Mirror product does not infringe the patents in suit. However, the Court did find that Gentex had breached the agreement between the two companies and, on January 24, 2008, entered a judgment against Gentex of $2.9 million. In accordance with generally accepted accounting principles, the company recorded a pretax charge of $2.9 million in the fourth quarter of 2007. It is uncertain at this time whether either party will appeal. (The $2.9 million judgment was recorded above the operating income line on the company's income statement as 'Litigation Judgment')."

Reasons to Buy

■ On January 29, 2008, CEO Fred Bauer said, "We are pleased to report that the company's sales continue to grow at a significant pace, despite the issues related to reduced vehicle production levels at the traditional 'Big Three' automakers in North America. Our business strategy many years ago was to work to diversify our business so that eventually our percentage of business with each automaker would reflect that automaker's percentage of global market share, and we believe that we are on our way to doing that.

"We also have an excellent portfolio of very popular, high value-added products to offer our customers, and a number of those products are just starting to get some traction, such as SmartBeam® and the new Rear Camera Display (RCD) Mirror. Each of those products have incremental average selling prices that are at least three times higher than the price of one base feature auto-dimming rearview mirror, and there appears to be significant market demand for each."

■ Even though most drivers consider backing up a "dangerous activity" and over half have experienced either a backup accident or "close call," few drivers actually take the time to walk behind their vehicle to check for potential obstacles. In fact, a study conducted by The Planning Edge, Inc., an independent research and analysis firm based in Birmingham, Michigan, determined that nearly 60 percent of drivers "rarely" or "never" look behind their vehicle before backing up.

This apparent lack of driver attentiveness, combined with the large rear blind spots associated with many of today's vehicles, are the primary contributors to millions of dollars in property damage accidents, thousands of injuries and nearly 200 backover fatalities annually. In response, automakers are increasingly offering "backup assist" features in the form of sensor-based audio and/or visual alerts and rear camera display (RCD) systems.

Rear camera systems enable drivers to see real-time video images of the area behind the vehicle while backing up. A typical system has a video camera located at the rear of the vehicle and a display located in the center console or instrument panel (usually as part of a navigation system) or in the rearview mirror.

The Planning Edge research, commissioned by Gentex Corporation, was conducted nationwide with current owners of 2005–2007 model vehicles. Survey participants included individuals who own vehicles with RCD in the navigation display, other vehicle owners who have a navigation system without RCD, and vehicle owners who did not have either system.

The study found that most drivers would want the rear camera feature on their next vehicle. Drivers also said they prefer that the display be located in the rearview mirror because the mirror is in the natural line of sight and allows the driver to view the display and reflected scene simultaneously. Gentex recently introduced technology that integrates the rear camera display in its auto-dimming rearview mirrors, and is currently shipping the product for five different vehicles. It is currently port- or dealer-installed equipment on the Mazda CX-9, and is factory-installed equipment as a stand-alone option on the Ford F-150 and Expedition, and the Lincoln Navigator and Mark LT.

"There is significant interest from our customers to offer mirror-based rear camera displays on their vehicles because they're easy to integrate, quick-to-market and are not tied to expensive navigation systems," said Mr. Bauer.

SECTOR: **Consumer Discretionary**
BETA COEFFICIENT: **1.20**
10-YEAR COMPOUND EARNINGS PER SHARE GROWTH: **13%**
10-YEAR COMPOUND DIVIDENDS PER SHARE GROWTH: **NM***

	2007	2006	2005	2004	2003	2002	2001	2000
Revenues (Mil)	653.9	572.3	536.5	505.7	469	395.3	310.3	297.4
Net Income (Mil)	122.1	108.8	109.5	112.7	106.8	85.8	65.2	70.5
Earnings per share	0.85	0.73	0.70	0.72	0.69	0.56	0.43	0.47
Dividends per share	0.40	0.37	0.35	0.31	0.08	—	—	—
Price high	22.6	21.0	20.3	23.5	22.5	16.8	17.1	19.9
low	14.9	12.7	15.4	15.1	12.0	11.8	9.2	8.1

*Not meaningful

CONSERVATIVE GROWTH

W. W. Grainger, Inc.

100 Grainger Parkway □ Lake Forest, IL 60045 □ (847) 535-0881 □ Dividend reinvestment plan not available □ Web site: *www.grainger.com* □ Ticker symbol: GWW □ Listed: NYSE □ S&P rating: A □ Value Line financial strength rating: A++

On February 4, 2008, Grainger, North America's leading distributor of facilities maintenance supplies, announced the release of its 2008 catalog featuring more than 183,000 facilities maintenance products. The new catalog includes an increase of 44,000 items over last year's offering.

"Our customers count on us to be the one-stop shop for all their facilities maintenance supplies and we bolstered our offering this year in several key categories including power transmission, raw material, and fleet maintenance products to help ensure that when they have a need, we are ready to offer solutions," said Y.C. Chen, president, Grainger Industrial Supply. "By providing easy access to a broad array of maintenance, repair and operating (MRO) products, Grainger helps customers be more productive in maintaining facilities."

Customer feedback drove the addition of more than:
■ 4,000 power transmission products such as bearings, couplings, linear motion products and belts;
■ 9,000 raw materials products such as metal, plastic, rubber and felt;

■ 4,200 fleet maintenance products such as lift equipment, battery chargers and accessories; as well as

■ 30,000 gap fill products across all major product categories including plumbing, electrical, tools and material handling.

In addition, the company launched Tough Guy™, a private label professional cleaning supplies brand designed to offer customers a quality, single-source facilities cleaning solution. The product category includes products such as degreasers, disinfectants, foam and lotion soaps and dispensers and polyethylene trash containers.

In order to drive down the high costs associated with procuring unplanned MRO items, customers including facilities managers, contractors and purchasing professionals need quick access to a wide array of facilities maintenance supplies across multiple product categories. Easy access to product helps provide businesses and institutions the opportunity to consolidate their MRO spending and drive efficiency in their businesses.

Company Profile

Grainger is North America's leading broadline supplier of facilities maintenance products, providing quick and easy access to products through a network of 582 branches, sixteen distribution centers, and award-winning Web sites.

Grainger operates in the United States through a network of more than 400 branches, ten distribution centers and its Web site, *www.grainger.com.* Grainger offers repair parts, specialized product sourcing and inventory management. Grainger sells principally to industrial and commercial maintenance departments, contractors and government customers. Sales are made to about 1.3 million customers.

Acklands-Grainger, Inc. is Canada's leading broad-line distributor of industrial, fleet and safety products. It serves a wide variety of customers through 166 branches and five distribution centers across Canada. It also offers bilingual Web sites and catalogs.

Grainger, S.A. de C.V. is Mexico's leading facilities maintenance supplier, offering customers more than 40,000 products. Local businesses have access through a Spanish-language catalog, online at grainger.com.mx or over the counter at one of six branches.

Lab Safety Supply (LSS) is a leading business-to-business direct marketer of safety and other industrial products in the United States and Canada. LSS primarily reaches its customers through the distribution of multiple branded catalogs and other marketing materials distributed to targeted markets. It is a primary supplier for many small and medium-size companies in diverse industries, including manufacturing, government and agriculture.

Grainger serves customers in eight categories that contain diverse businesses. Here's a snapshot of each:

■ Government customers include government offices, schools, and correctional institutions on the state and local levels and office buildings, many military installations, and the U.S. Postal Service on the federal level.

■ Heavy manufacturing customers are usually involved in textile, lumber, metals, and rubber industries.

■ Light manufacturing includes food, pharmaceutical and electronic customers.

■ Transportation customers are involved in the shipbuilding, aerospace, and automotive industries.

■ Retail customers include grocery stores, restaurants, and local gas stations.

■ Contractor includes contracting firms involved in maintaining and repairing existing facilities.

■ Reseller customers offer Grainger products to customers in different markets.

■ Commercial customers include hospitals, hotels, and theaters.

Many of Grainger's customers are corporate account customers, primarily *Fortune*

1,000 companies, that spend more than $5 million annually on facilities maintenance products. Corporate account customers represent about 25 percent of Grainger's total U.S. sales. Both government and corporate account customer groups typically sign multiyear contracts with facilities maintenance products or a specific category of products, such as lighting or safety equipment.

Shortcomings to Bear in Mind

- Although the company has a solid long-term record of earnings, there have been a few years when EPS declined. In 1999, earnings per share dipped to $1.92 from $2.44 the prior year. What's more, the next year was equally lackluster, as EPS slipped to $1.88. Finally, in 2003, per-share earnings failed to equal the $2.50 earned in 2002, declining a bit, to $2.46.

Reasons to Buy

- Grainger's 1.6 million customers comprise about 8 percent of the businesses and institutions in the United States. While each customer has unique facilities to run and different problems to solve, they share the same needs when maintaining those facilities: Does Grainger carry the products? If Grainger has it, can I get it from them faster and easier than from anyone else?

Customer purchases typically aren't planned. When something breaks and needs repair, customers may not know where to find the right product. Most facilities maintenance products aren't expensive. What's expensive is the time spent finding and buying them.

Customers work with Grainger in a number of ways that save them time and money. First, they can refer to one of Grainger's many catalogs, the largest of which is 3,818 pages containing 82,431 different products grouped in eleven categories. Grainger also has the industry's leading Web site with more than 200,000 products that customers can access. Once the item is iden-

tified, customers can place an order. Trained customer service professionals can help customers determine which product is right for their needs, connecting them with technical service people or specialists in repair parts. Finally, customers can stop by a branch where experienced employees can help diagnose the problem and find a solution.

No matter how they access the company, customers can choose the way their order gets fulfilled: they can have it shipped to them or they can buy it at a branch, either over the counter or as a will-call. About half of all transactions are picked up at a branch and half are shipped, mainly from the distributions centers. Because the size of the order is typically larger when a customer requests a shipped order, the ratio of sales dollars is roughly two-thirds shipped and one-third picked up.

- Through its expanded presence, Web site enhancements and improved telesales efforts, Grainger aims to gain market share in the $10 billion facilities maintenance market in Mexico.

- Customers buy facilities maintenance supplies in four basic ways. First, they buy the things they use every day, like janitorial supplies and light bulbs, looking to purchase these items in bulk for the lowest price. Second, they buy key products that keep their business running, such as a highly specialized motor for a production line. This type of product is often purchased at a premium and requires technical assistance from the manufacturer. Third, they buy simple products that they use frequently in their businesses, like belts for an auto mechanic or air filters for an HVAC (heating, ventilation and air conditioning) contractor. They're looking for product specialists who can offer uninterrupted availability.

While Grainger provides products in all of these instances, its value to the customer is in helping in the fourth instance:

unplanned, infrequently purchased items. A recent study of Grainger customers revealed that 40 percent of their facilities maintenance spend is on such items.

Over the period of a year, these customers purchased on average about 13,000 unique items from Grainger. Of these, 7,000 were purchased only twice. That's almost 75 percent of their purchases. Sourcing these products from many suppliers is very costly. By consolidating with Grainger, customers are able to get a great level of service from one source and save time and money.

■ "W.W. Grainger Inc. said Monday that 65-year-old Richard Keyser will step down as chief executive of the Lake Forest-based company on June 1, and President James Ryan will add the CEO title," said James P. Miller, writing for the *Chicago Tribune* on April 1, 2008.

"Keyser, who is concluding a 13-year tenure in the top job, will remain Grainger's chairman. Ryan, a 27-year veteran at the company and a director since last year, will become the fourth CEO in the 80-year history of the distributor of maintenance products.

"Ryan, who joined the company in 1980, has a master's degree in business administration from Chicago's DePaul University. He was named president in 2006 and added the title of chief operating officer in February 2007."

■ On March 15, 2008, Standard & Poor's *Stock Reports* gave Grainger a BUY rating. Stewart Scharf said, "Our BUY recommendation is based on favorable market trends in the commercial and government markets, and our valuation metrics. We expect strategic initiatives to enhance the branch-based distribution network. We see strong free cash flow, targeted for internal investments and additional share buybacks, while ROIC continues to expand."

SECTOR: **Industrials**
BETA COEFFICIENT: **1.10**
10-YEAR COMPOUND EARNINGS PER SHARE GROWTH: **8.1%**
10-YEAR COMPOUND DIVIDENDS PER SHARE GROWTH: **10.2%**

	2007	2006	2005	2004	2003	2002	2001	2000
Revenues (Mil)	6,418	5,884	5,527	5,050	4,667	4,644	4,754	4,977
Net Income (Mil)	420	383	346	277	227	236	211	175
Earnings per share	4.94	4.25	3.78	3.02	2.46	2.50	2.23	1.86
Dividends per share	1.40	1.16	0.92	0.79	0.74	0.72	0.70	0.67
Price high	98.6	80.0	72.4	67.0	53.3	59.4	49.0	56.9
low	68.8	60.6	51.6	45.0	41.4	39.2	29.5	24.3

AGGRESSIVE GROWTH

Harris Corporation

1025 West NASA Boulevard □ Melbourne, FL 32919 □ (321) 727-9383 □ Dividend reinvestment plan available □ Web site: *www.harris.com* □ Ticker symbol: HRS □ Fiscal years ends Friday closest to June 30 □ Listed: NYSE □ S&P rating: B+ □ Value Line financial strength rating: A

On February 20, 2008, Harris Corporation, an international communications and information technology company, delivered its 100th NEXIO AMP™ advanced media platform server during the first six weeks of the product's availability. Recent new customers include broadcasters in Germany, Japan and Canada, as well as two major television networks in the United States.

"NEXIO AMP™ builds on the success of the Harris® NEXIO™ server line, which has increasingly become the server of choice for customers around the world—including five of the eight major U.S. networks," said Tim Thorsteinson, president of Harris Broadcast Communications.

The Harris® NEXIO AMP™ advanced media platform pairs a high-performance, high-definition/standard-definition (HD/SD) server architecture with best-in-class content protection. The new system combines the highest levels of I/O, data pathway and storage redundancy with all the features broadcasters have come to expect in NEXIO servers—including integrated software codec support and automatic up/down/cross conversion. Recent new orders came from Germany's Astra APS through Teracue AG; the American Forces Network through Snader & Associates; Toyama Cable TV in Japan; FOX Sports Houston in the United States; Canal 9 in Argentina; and ExpressVu in Canada.

"The NEXIO AMP™ platform leverages the power of software in a number of innovative ways that provide immediate and future benefits for our operation," said Stefan Hennecke, vice president, Playout, APS Munich. "Today, we have a server that provides true format transparency with integrated software codec support and automatic up/down/cross conversion. In the near future, the platform will also have the ability to host software-enabled media applications, which will allow us to reduce our hardware expenditures, take the guesswork out of point-product compatibility and improve our overall workflow efficiency."

Company Profile

Harris is an international communications and information technology company serving government and commercial markets in more than 150 countries. Headquartered in Melbourne, Florida, the company has annual revenue of about $4 billion and more than 14,000 employees, including more than 6,000 engineers and scientists. Harris is

dedicated to developing best-in-class assured communications™ products, systems, and services for global markets, including government communications, RF communications, broadcast communications, and wireless transmission network solutions.

Major Product Areas

Government Communications

Harris conducts advanced research studies, develops prototypes, and produces and supports state-of-the-art, highly reliable communications and information systems that solve the mission-critical communications challenges of its military and government customers, and provides the technology base for the company's diverse commercial businesses.

RF Communications

Harris is a leading worldwide supplier of tactical radio communication products, systems and networks to military and government organizations, and a provider of high-grade encryption solutions. These solutions address the demanding requirements of U.S., NATO, and Partnership for Peace Forces, as well as government agencies and embassies around the world.

Broadcast Communications

Digital technology dominates today's world of television and radio broadcasting. Harris has solidified its leadership position in this industry with total content delivery solutions, including advanced digital transmission, automation, asset management, digital media, network management and video infrastructure solutions. Solutions from Harris Broadcast Communications transform rich media content into a usable asset and provide it to the right person, on the right device, at the right time.

Harris Stratex Networks, Inc.

Harris Stratex Networks, Inc., a majority-owned subsidiary of Harris Corporation, is the world's leading independent supplier of turnkey wireless network solutions. The company offers reliable, flexible and scalable wireless network solutions, backed by comprehensive professional services and support. Harris Stratex Networks serves all global markets, including mobile network operators, public safety agencies, private network operators, utility and transportation companies, government agencies, and broadcasters. Customers in more than 135 countries depend on Harris Stratex Networks to build, expand and upgrade their voice, data and video solutions. Harris Stratex Networks is recognized around the world for innovative, best-in-class wireless networking solutions and services.

Shortcomings to Bear in Mind

■ In recent years, earnings per share have been somewhat erratic, falling in 1999 from $1.42 to $0.42 the following year. Although EPS climbed in subsequent years, it was not until 2005 that earnings per share reached $1.46. Similarly, dividends have been up and down, as well. In 2000, for instance, dividends per share fell to $0.20, from $0.48 the previous year. What's more, not until 2007 did the payout reach the $0.44 level.

Reasons to Buy

■ On December 20, 2007, Harris entered into a patent licensing agreement with VT Miltope, a company of VT Systems, covering several Harris U.S. and international patents for aviation applications.

The Harris Ground Data Link patents cover core inventions in wireless communications that support flight operations, maintenance operations, quality assurance, electronic flight bags and in-flight entertainment data that is exchanged between an aircraft and ground-based systems. The Harris Wireless Engine Monitoring Systems patents cover core inventions in the wireless communication of engine performance and engine monitoring data between aircraft engines and ground-based systems.

"This agreement represents yet another step in the development and deployment of our industry-leading wireless technologies for aviation and expands Harris Corporation's role of providing the aviation industry with new capabilities," said Bob Henry, executive vice president and chief operating officer of Harris. "VT Miltope is an acknowledged industry leader in the design, development, and manufacture of innovative computers, computer peripherals and networking products for the global aviation industry."

■ On April 11, 2008, *Value Line Investment Survey* had a favorable comment on the company. Nira Maharaj said, "RF Communications remains a strong growth driver, fueling the company's profitability. Harris has had to increase production capacity at the New York facility to keep up with demand. Too, management has indicated it intends to augment its work force by hiring about fifty more engineers by this summer, and add more employees in other areas."

The *Value Line* analyst also said, "Falcon III radios continue to play a starring role. HRS has begun introduction of the next generation of this product, JTRS Falcon III radios. The newer version of the radio is enhanced with video capacity on the battlefield and higher data capacity."

■ For the full fiscal year 2007, revenue was $4.2 billion, a 22 percent increase compared to fiscal year 2006. GAAP (according to generally accepted accounting principals) income was $480 million or $3.43 per diluted share, compared to $238 million or $1.71 per diluted share in the prior year. Non-GAAP net income for fiscal year 2007, excluding charges associated with cost-reduction actions, asset impairments, acquisition costs and the gain associated with the creation of Harris Stratex Networks, was $391 million or $2.80 per diluted share, a 26 percent increase compared to the prior year.

"Our fourth quarter results indicate solid momentum across each of our business segments, with double-digit organic growth and record-setting levels of new orders," said CEO Howard L. Lance, on August 7,

2007. "Our government businesses delivered excellent revenue growth on both a year-over-year and a sequential basis, while our commercial segments had significant sequential revenue and orders growth and improved operating performance."

▪ For the full fiscal year 2007, revenue was $4.2 billion, a 22 percent increase compared to fiscal year 2006. GAAP net income was $480 million or $3.43 per diluted share, compared to $238 million or $1.71 per diluted share in the prior year. Non-GAAP net income for fiscal year 2007, excluding charges associated with cost-reduction actions, asset impairments, acquisition costs and the gain associated with the creation of Harris Stratex Networks, was $391 million or $2.80 per diluted share, a 26 percent increase compared to the prior year.

▪ In June, 2007, Harris was awarded an IDIQ contract by the Joint Program Executive Office of the Joint Tactical Radio System (JPEO JTRS) to supply the U.S. Department of Defense with next-generation Falcon III multiband handheld radios and vehicular systems. The contract has a one-year maximum value of $2.7 billion and a five-year maximum value of $7 billion. Under the contract, orders will be awarded based on competitive bidding between Harris and the incumbent supplier.

▪ In July of 2007, Harris was awarded another IDIQ contract for its Falcon III radios by the U.S. Marine Corps. Harris is the sole supplier on the contract, which has a potential value of $212 million. The company has already received two orders totaling $158 million against the contract for radios to be installed on the new Mine Resistant Ambush Protected (MRAP) vehicles and other applications. In addition, Harris was awarded a $26 million contract in early August for Falcon II and Falcon III radios on the Navy version of the MRAP.

SECTOR: **Information Technology**
BETA COEFFICIENT: **1.30**
10-YEAR COMPOUND EARNINGS PER SHARE GROWTH: **7.8%**
10-YEAR COMPOUND DIVIDENDS PER SHARE GROWTH: **1.5%**

	2007	2006	2005	2004	2003	2002	2001	2000
Revenues (Mil)	4,243	3,475	3,001	2,519	2,093	1,876	1,955	1,807
Net Income (Mil)	391	310	202	126	90	83	101	70
Earnings per share	2.80	2.22	1.46	0.94	0.68	0.63	0.75	0.48
Dividends per share	0.44	0.32	0.24	0.20	0.16	0.10	0.10	0.20
Price high	66.9	49.8	45.8	34.6	19.7	19.3	18.5	19.7
low	45.9	37.7	26.9	18.9	12.7	12.0	10.4	10.4

AGGRESSIVE GROWTH

Hewlett-Packard Company

3000 Hanover Street ▫ Palo Alto, CA 94304 ▫ (866) 438-4771 ▫ Web site: *www.hp.com* ▫ Dividend reinvestment plan available ▫ Fiscal years end October 31 ▫ Listed: NYSE ▫ Ticker symbol: HPQ ▫ S&P rating: B+ ▫ Value Line financial strength rating: A++

On January 22, 2008, Hewlett-Packard announced that it had signed a definitive agreement to acquire Exstream Software, LLC, a privately held leading provider of enterprise software that streamlines the creation and delivery of personalized documents and other communications materials.

Exstream's technology, when combined with HP's presence in document output management and printing market leadership, helps businesses design, manage and publish structured and unstructured content in a fully personalized manner via print and online.

"Businesses—whether a bank, healthcare provider, or utility company—need to communicate relevant, personalized information to their customers through a broad range of channels," said David Murphy, senior vice president, Web Services and Software Business, IPG, HP. "We expect that the acquisition of Exstream will allow HP to address a broader set of customers and be a strong leader in the fast-growing document automation market."

"We are very happy to join with HP to accelerate our ability to help businesses around the world to efficiently develop and deploy personalized communications," said Richard Troksa, chief executive officer and president, Exstream Software. "The combination of Exstream's solutions and HP's print software expertise will provide customers with a more comprehensive approach to delivering reliable and targeted business communications."

About Exstream Software

Ranked among the world's fastest growing technology companies, Exstream provides enterprise software solutions for businesses around the world to streamline document creation processes and produce higher quality, relevant communications of all types for delivery through print/mail and online channels. Customers in many industries benefit by getting communications to market as much as 85 percent faster, reducing document production costs up to 80 percent and as much as tripling customer response.

Company Profile

Hewlett-Packard is a technology solutions provider to consumers, businesses and institutions globally. The company's offerings span IT infrastructure, global services, business and home computing, and imaging and printing. As of October 31, 2006, the company's annual revenue totaled $91.7 billion.

- HPQ serves more than 1 billion customers in more than 170 countries on six continents.
- HPQ has about 150,000 employees worldwide.
- HPQ's 2006 *Fortune* 500 ranking: Number eleven.
- HPQ's mission is to invent technologies and services that drive business value, create social benefit and improve the lives of customers—with a focus on affecting the greatest number of people possible.
- HPQ dedicates $3.5 billion annually to its research and development of products, solutions and new technologies.

Hewlett-Packard is:

- Number one globally in the inkjet, all-in-one and single-function printers, mono and color laser printers, large-format printing, scanners, print servers and ink and laser supplies.
- Number one globally in x86, Windows®, Linux and UNIX servers.
- Number one in total disk and storage systems.
- Number two globally in notebook PCs, Pocket PCs, workstations, and blade servers.
- Awarded Outstanding Customer Service for Consumers.
- Number one position in server brand loyalty for ProLiant servers.
- Hewlett-Packard ranks A+ for management of investment risks arising from material, environmental, social, employment and ethical impacts by Core Ratings.
- Number eight in the first global index that evaluates how well the world's 100 largest companies account for their impact on society and the environment. Hewlett-Packard is

the only domestic company to appear in the top ten of the Accountability Rating developed by AccountAbility and csrnetwork.

■ Number one in computer and peripherals industry for intangible value analysis reporting—including governance, human capital and emerging market issues—by Innovest Strategic Value Advisors, Inc., a leading independent research firm for the SRI community. HP ranked fifth for environmental reporting.

■ Number ten globally and number one in the United States in Environment, Social Impact Ratings by the *Economist*.

Shortcomings to Bear in Mind

■ Hewlett-Packard will never make it as an income stock. The company pays only $.32 dividends per year, and that amount has not changed in several years.

Reasons to buy

■ On March 15, 2008, Standard & Poor's *Stock Reports* gave HPQ a BUY rating. Thomas W. Smith, CFA, said, We believe that global demand for PCs will grow at a strong pace in calendar 2008, albeit slower than in the boom year of 2007. We foresee more moderate growth for printers and other segments. We expect HPQ's broad product and customer base to aid its efforts to add market share."

■ On April 11, 2008, *Value Line* gave the company a 2 rating, which is similar to a BUY, rather than a STRONG BUY. George A. Niemond said, "Hewlett-Packard is expanding rapidly in emerging markets, which should cushion the blow from a slowdown in the domestic economy. Hewlett also has a diverse customer base, with roughly one-third of sales each to enterprises, small and mid-sized businesses, and consumers. What's more, it does less business than its peers in the financial segment, where IT spending could be hit especially hard. The company is also expanding its sales force, which ought to help it capture additional business and improve account penetration."

■ On November 15, 2007, Hewlett-Packard announced that 3M Company, a $22.9 billion diversified technology company, had purchased the HP Neoview data warehousing platform to enhance its global business intelligence capabilities.

After evaluating several offerings, 3M chose HP Neoview to provide the company with a comprehensive view of historical and real-time information to help make business decisions faster.

Neoview will enable integration and analysis of 3M's financial data, including the company's general ledger, so that 3M can react in near real time to everyday opportunities and threats.

"We are looking for a new level of price/performance to help grow our business through enhanced business intelligence solutions," said Peter Godfrey, director, global information technology infrastructure, 3M. "As a long-time data warehouse user, we are excited to get the new Neoview platform in house and to prove its capabilities."

The HP Neoview data warehouse platform integrates hardware, software and services to offer customers a comprehensive view of essential business information, such as metrics on product sales, customer trends, production and operational effectiveness. This allows for real-time decision making and historical analysis.

"Our customers are some of the world's largest businesses and Neoview is precisely tuned to enable the volumes of information they generate every second to be better leveraged for business advantage," said Ben Barnes, vice president and general manager, Business Intelligence Software, HP. "HP Neoview offers 24x7 availability built on cost-effective, industry-standard hardware. Having gone in search of replacements for our competitors' data warehousing solutions, customers agree that the return on investment with Neoview is unmatched in the industry."

3M's HP Neoview solution is paired with software from leading business intelligence software vendor Business Objects and leading data integration software provider Informatica.

- "Chief Executive Mark Hurd, fifty-one, who took the reins in 2005 from the ousted Carly Fiorina, gets much of the credit for Hewlett's impressive showing," said a *Barron's* article on February 25, 2008. Author Mark Veverka went on to say, "He 'has executed as well as or better than anyone else in computer hardware,' says David Bailey, hardware analyst at Goldman Sachs, who calls H-P his No. 1 stock pick."

Mr. Veverka also said, "Under Hurd, H-P has proven it can do more than cut costs, although that remains important. 'We expect to remove significantly more costs this year than last year,' he says. 'We will take these savings . . . to fund investments that improve the efficiency of H-P and create growth opportunities for us.'"

- On July 23, 2007, Hewlett-Packard announced that it had signed a definitive agreement to purchase Opsware Inc., a market-leading data center automation software company, through a cash tender offer for $14.25 per share, or an enterprise value (net of existing cash and debt) of $1.6 billion on a fully diluted basis.

The acquisition will enhance HP's portfolio of Business Technology Optimization (BTO) software. Combining Opsware's solutions with HP's enterprise IT management software will deliver a comprehensive and fully integrated solution for IT automation. Opsware is the latest in a series of strategic software acquisitions, including Mercury Interactive and Peregrine Systems, which expands HP's leadership in BTO.

- On December 10, 2007, Hewlett-Packard announced that it had signed a definitive agreement to acquire NUR Macroprinters Ltd., a manufacturer of industrial wide-format digital inkjet printers.

Based in Lod, Israel, NUR is a leading supplier of UV-curable and solvent inkjet printers for display graphics, serving commercial printing companies, sign printers, screen printers, billboard and media companies, photo labs and digital print service providers.

The acquisition expands HP's Graphic Arts portfolio of digital presses and wide-format printers and furthers HP's Print 2.0 strategy to digitize analog prints by extending the company's overall digital content creation and publishing platform. With the acquisition, HP will be able to offer additional midrange UV platforms and technologies.

SECTOR: **Information Technology**
BETA COEFFICIENT: **1.10**
10-YEAR COMPOUND EARNINGS PER SHARE GROWTH: **6.1%**
10-YEAR COMPOUND DIVIDENDS PER SHARE GROWTH: **0%**

		2007	2006	2005	2004	2003	2002	2001	2000
Revenues (Mil)		104,286	91,658	86,696	79,905	73,061	72,346	45,226	48,782
Net Income (Mil)		7,264	6,198	4,708	4,067	3,557	2,409	1,739	3,561
Earnings per share		2.68	2.18	1.62	1.33	1.16	0.79	0.89	1.73
Dividends per share		0.32	0.32	0.32	0.32	0.32	0.32	0.32	0.32
Price	high	53.5	41.7	30.3	26.3	23.9	24.1	37.9	77.8
	low	38.2	28.4	18.9	16.1	14.2	10.8	12.5	29.1

Honeywell International, Inc.

101 Columbia Road □ P. O. Box 2245 □ Morristown, NJ 07962-2245 □ (973) 455-2222 □ Dividend reinvestment plan available
Web site: *www.honeywell.com* □ Ticker symbol: HON □ Listed: NYSE □ S&P rating: B □ Value Line financial strength rating: A+

On April 8, 2008, Honeywell announced that it had been chosen to supply the latest generation of its HTF7000 turbofan propulsion system family for Embraer's new MSJ and MLJ business aircraft. The contract is valued at more than $23 billion, including aftermarket over the life of the agreement.

"The HTF7500-E engine will feature new technology to achieve reduced emissions, improved fuel efficiency and will maintain our design emphasis on reliability and dispatchability. It will be backed by our industry-leading maintenance service plan," said Rob Wilson, president, Business and General Aviation. "Honeywell designed the E-Engine with an acoustic signature well under stage four noise requirements and with improved combustor technology that will reduce NOx emissions substantially below current ICAO levels while still delivering best-in-class fuel economy."

"We are delighted that Honeywell engines will power the new Embraer MSJ and Embraer MLJ business jets," said LuÁs Carlos Affonso, Embraer executive vice president, Executive Jets. "The HTF7000 series already enjoys high levels of customer satisfaction, and the new technologies incorporated in the HTF7500E engine will further increase its efficiency."

Honeywell's $23 billion win follows a March win at Gulfstream valued at $3 billion, an Air Tran win earlier this year valued at $1 billion and an Airbus A350 win announced in the fourth quarter valued at $16 billion.

"We are delivering a propulsion system that will incorporate the newest technologies while building on a proven design that is delivering a benchmark level of reliability in this thrust class," Wilson said. "With more than 360 HTF7000 engines in worldwide service

that have accrued more than 365,000 hours of operation since entering service four years ago, the HTF7000 is delivering better than 99.95 percent dispatch reliability for our customers."

"Honeywell's 24/7/365 support approach and focus on worldwide asset availability was seen as a differentiator in the selection. Our new state of the art technical operations center is now providing real time technical solutions to support the growing global fleet," said Gregg Cohen vice president, Customer and Product Support. "The support approach coupled with the engine's design for maintainability has proven benefits to the operators. One of our authorized service centers has successfully demonstrated the capability to complete hot section inspections on-wing."

"The HTF7000 is proving it is truly an on-condition engine," Wilson said. "The unique combination of new technology and a demonstrated heritage of rugged reliability, make this engine uniquely suited for high utilization operations such as fractional ownership programs and other high time operators."

Company Profile

Honeywell can trace its roots back to 1885, when an inventor named Albert Butz patented the furnace regulator and alarm. He formed the Butz Thermo-Electric Regulator Company in Minneapolis on April 23, 1886, and a few weeks later invented a simple, yet ingenious device that he called the "damper flapper."

Here's how it worked. When a room cooled below a predetermined temperature, a thermostat closed the circuit and energized an armature. This pulled the stop from the motor gears, allowing a crank attached to the main motor shaft to turn one-half revolution. A chain connected to the crank opened the furnace's air damper to let in air. This made the fire burn hotter. When the temperature rose to the preset level, the thermostat signaled the motor to turn another half revolution, closing the damper and damping the fire. The temperature correction was automatic. Over the years, many Honeywell products have been based upon similar, but more complicated closed-loop systems.

Honeywell Now

Honeywell is a diversified technology and manufacturing leader, serving customers worldwide with aerospace products and services (40 percent of sales); control technologies for buildings, homes and industry (31 percent of sales); automotive products (15 percent of sales); specialty materials (14 percent of sales). It is one of the thirty stocks that make up the Dow Jones Industrial Average and is also a component of the Standard & Poor's 500 Index.

Honeywell globally manages its business operations through four segments:

Aerospace

The Aerospace segment primarily makes cockpit controls, power generation equipment, and wheels and brakes for commercial and military aircraft. It is also a leading maker of jet engines for regional and business jet manufacturers. Demand for the company's aircraft equipment is driven primarily by expansion in the global jetliner fleet, particularly those jets with 100 or more seats. Since 1993, the global airliner fleet has grown at a 3 percent annual pace. The Aerospace segment is also a major player in the $35-billion global aircraft maintenance, repair and overhaul industry, which is growing at a 2.2 percent annual rate.

Automation and Control Solutions

Honeywell's Automation and Control Solutions segment is best known as a global maker of home and office climate controls equipment. It also makes home automation systems, energy-efficient lighting controls, as well as security and fire alarms.

Specialty Materials

The Specialty Materials operation makes specialty chemicals and fibers, which are sold primarily to the food, pharmaceutical, and electronic packaging industries.

Transportation Systems

The Transportation System segment consists of a portfolio of brand name car-care products, such as Fram filters, Prestone antifreeze, Autolite spark plugs, and Simonize car waxes. The unit is also a major large truck brake manufacturer.

Shortcomings to Bear in Mind

- The company's record of growth has been disappointing, at least through 2006. In the prior ten years, earnings per share inched ahead from $1.81 to $2.52, a compound annual growth rate of only 3.4 percent. During that same period, dividends grew from $0.45 to $0.91, a growth rate of 7.3 percent. When dividends grow faster than earnings, that sounds a negative note. On the plus side, with CEO Dave Cote at the helm, better tidings are in prospect.

Reasons to Buy

- "2007 was another terrific year for Honeywell," said Mr. Cote. "Our great positions in good industries, together with favorable macro trends, drove growth across each of our four business segments in 2007. The year's highlights included major contract wins, more than $1 billion in acquisitions, and approximately $4 billion in share repurchases, all driving shareowner value.

"While we anticipate softer global economic conditions in 2008, we remain confident in Honeywell's ability to outperform," added Cote. "We will continue to invest in innovation, expand globally, and execute on productivity initiatives to drive double digit earnings per share growth and higher free cash flow in 2008."

- On April 22, 2008, Argus Research Company had this favorable comment, according its analyst, Rashid Dahod: "The company continues to benefit from strong global demand, particularly in the Aerospace segment and Specialty Materials, with improvements in Automation & Control, as well. Despite some pressure in the Transportation segment in the first quarter, the overall outlook for 2008 remains solid, and global growth, coupled with productivity gains, offset domestic weakness." The stock was rated a BUY.

■ Writing for the Standard & Poor's *Stock Reports* on April 21, 2008, Richard Tortoriello rated the stock a BUY, with this reasoning, "Given our expectation that growth in the emerging markets will benefit HON's ACS segment and that the Aerospace segment, where business and commercial jet demand remains high, will continue to improve, we believe HON can continue to increase revenues and improve profitability."

■ Business aviation is in the midst of one of its strongest up cycles in decades and Honeywell remains well positioned in the market, according to its fifteenth annual Business Aviation Outlook.

In the report, Honeywell predicted shipments of about 12,000 new aircraft valued at $195 billion by original equipment manufacturers through 2016. The most optimistic business-jet outlook yet, it forecasts that business jet makers will top 1,000 deliveries in a single year for the first time ever in 2007.

"Industry growth is moving into unprecedented territory," said Mr. Wilson. "2006 shaped up as a record year for the industry. If current growth projections for the global economy hold, 2007 should be even better and will set a new all-time high delivery record."

The forecast is substantially more bullish than Honeywell's optimistic assessment from the previous year, which predicted deliveries of 9,900 business jets valued at $156 billion between 2005 and 2015. The outlook also predicted the industry would not hit the 1,000-unit delivery mark until 2013.

SECTOR: **Industrials**
BETA COEFFICIENT: **1.15**
10-YEAR COMPOUND EARNINGS PER SHARE GROWTH: **4.6%**
10-YEAR COMPOUND DIVIDENDS PER SHARE GROWTH: **6.8%**

		2007	2006	2005	2004	2003	2002	2001	2000
Revenues (Mil)		34,589	31,367	27,653	25,601	23,103	22,274	23,652	25,023
Net Income (Mil)		2,444	2,083	1,736	1,281	1,344	1,644	1,672	2,293
Earnings per share		3.16	2.52	1.92	1.49	1.56	2.00	2.05	2.83
Dividends per share		1.00	0.91	0.83	0.75	0.75	0.75	0.75	0.75
Price	high	62.3	45.8	39.5	38.5	33.5	40.9	53.9	60.5
	low	43.1	35.2	32.7	31.2	20.2	18.8	22.2	32.1

CONSERVATIVE GROWTH

Hormel Foods Corporation

1 Hormel Place ❑ Austin, MN 55912-3680 ❑ (507) 437-5007 ❑ Dividend reinvestment plan available ❑ Fiscal years end on the last Saturday of October ❑ Listed: NYSE ❑ Web site: *www.hormel.com* ❑ Ticker symbol: HRL ❑ S&P rating: A+ ❑ Value Line financial strength rating: A

On August 23, 2007, Hormel Foods Corporation announced it had purchased privately held Burke Corporation, a manufacturer and marketer of pizza-toppings and other fully cooked meat products, for $110 million. The company anticipates annual net sales of $125 million, and expects the deal to be accretive to its fiscal 2008 earnings.

"Hormel Foods is a leader in pepperoni, and the addition of Burke Corp. strengthens our position in the pizza-topping industry by expanding our offerings to foodservice customers," said CEO Jeffrey M. Ettinger of Hormel Foods. "This acquisition increases our production efficiencies and adds manufacturing capabilities, enabling Hormel Foods to grow in this important category."

Burke Corp. manufactures and markets pizza-toppings and other fully cooked meat products primarily for restaurants, foodservice establishments, and manufacturers of frozen entrées and appetizers. Product lines include traditional pizza meat toppings, meatballs, Mexican meat fillings, and breakfast meats.

"The cultural similarities between Hormel Foods and Burke Corp. made the decision to move forward with this transaction an easy one," said CEO Bill Burke Jr. "Our new relationship with Hormel Foods will allow us to continue, and even strengthen, our focus on customers and fellow Team Members, who consistently produce high quality products."

Burke Corp. operates its main facility in Nevada, Iowa, and another in Ames, Iowa. These facilities increase Hormel Foods' production capabilities of fully cooked meat products and pizza-toppings.

Burke Corp. was established in 1974 by William J. Burke Sr. and has 239,000 square feet of production capacity. As part of Hormel Foods' Refrigerated Foods business segment, Burke Corp. will continue to be run by Bill Burke Jr.

Company Profile

Founded by George A. Hormel in 1891 in Austin, Minnesota, Hormel Corporation is a multinational manufacturer of consumer-branded meat and food products, many of which are among the best-known and trusted in the food industry. The company, according to management, "enjoys a strong reputation among consumers, retail grocers, and foodservice, and industrial customer for products highly regarded for quality, taste, nutrition, convenience and value."

The company's larger subsidiaries include Jennie-O Turkey Store, the nation's largest turkey processor; Vista International Packaging, Inc., a manufacturer of casings; and Hormel Foods International Corporation, which markets Hormel products throughout the world.

The company's business is reported in five segments: Refrigerated Foods, Grocery Products, Jennie-O Turkey Store, Specialty Foods, and All Other.

The company's products include hams, bacon, sausages, franks, canned luncheon meats, stews, chilies, hash, meat spreads, shelf-stable microwaveable entrees, salsas, and frozen processed meats.

These selections are sold to retail, foodservice, and wholesale operations under many well-established trademarks that include: Black Label, by George, Cure 81, Always Tender, Curemaster, Di Lusso, Dinty Moore, Dubuque, Fast'n Easy, Homeland, Hormel, House of Tsang, Jennie-O-Kid's Kitchen, Layout Pack, Light & Lean 100, Little Sizzlers, May Kitchen, Old Smokehouse, Peloponnese, Range Brand, Rosa Grande, Sandwich Maker, Spam, and Wranglers.

These products are sold in all fifty states by a Hormel Foods sales force assigned to offices in major cities throughout the United States. Their efforts are supplemented by sales brokers and distributors.

The headquarters for Hormel Foods is in Austin, Minnesota, along with it Research and Development division and flagship plant. Company facilities that manufacture meat and food products are situated in such states as Iowa, Georgia, Illinois, Wisconsin, Nebraska, Oklahoma, California and Kansas. In addition, custom manufacturing of selected Hormel Foods products is performed by various companies that adhere to stringent corporate guidelines and quality standards.

Hormel Foods International Corporation (HFIC), a wholly owned subsidiary in Austin, has established a number of joint venture and licencing agreements in such countries as Australia, China, Colombia, Costa Rica, Denmark, England, Japan, Korea, Mexico, Panama, the Philippines, Poland, Spain, among others. HFIC exports products to more than forty countries.

Shortcomings to Bear in Mind

▪ Food companies are hurting because of higher costs of raw materials, such as wheat, largely a byproduct of brisk demand for ethanol.

Reasons to Buy

▪ "We were pleased to end the year with a strong finish that allowed us to deliver respectable full year results in a challenging environment. The strength of the fourth quarter's results provides good momentum heading into fiscal 2008," said Mr. Ettinger on November 20, 2007. "I was encouraged to see that despite significantly higher grain markets, Jennie-O Turkey Store increased year-over-year segment profit this quarter. Improved product mix, operations efficiencies and better recovery of higher costs through pricing were the key drivers."

Mr. Ettinger also said, "As indicated during our Investor Day in October, we expected that our Grocery Products segment would be down. While the Grocery Products results were disappointing, primarily caused by a soft quarter from the SPAM family of products and VALLEY FRESH chunk meats, we continued to have success building our HORMEL COMPLEATS microwave tray business. We also had strong results from our chili business, up double-digit for the quarter. We expect the Grocery Products segment will have a slow start in fiscal 2008 and the results will improve as the year progresses.

"The lower Specialty Foods segment results were primarily due to a very difficult year-ago comparison. This segment has delivered exceptional top and bottom line growth over the last two years. As we have indicated in the past, we expect the long-term growth rate of this segment to be similar to our total company growth rate goals of 5 percent top-line and 10 percent bottom-line.

"The Refrigerated Foods segment has been a strong performer all year and the fourth quarter was no exception. Our strategy to be the industry leader in value-added protein has proven successful and we continue to strengthen our portfolio with innovation. The acquisition of Burke Corporation in August has been a great addition to our portfolio and was accretive to this quarter's results.

"Considering the higher input cost challenges we faced, I am pleased with the results. I believe our balanced model of packaged foods and protein products in addition to our blend of foodservice and retail sales, provides the right combination of stability in difficult environments, yet offers upside opportunity when conditions turn favorable."

▪ "We think the company is well-positioned for longer-term growth, with profitability expected to benefit as higher margin, value-added products become a larger part of the company's business," said Joseph Agnese, writing in the Standard & Poor's *Stock Reports* on January 22, 2008.

▪ Value-added products are helping the Jennie-O Turkey Store. This segment now offers a broad selection of value-added branded products such as Thanksgiving Tonight oven-roasted turkey breast, which "delivers holiday flavor and everyday convenience."

Demand for value-added turkey items, moreover, are growing faster than that for traditional products.

▪ Developing new products takes some effort. For Hormel, it means asking customers "about features that make their lives better." A case in point is the award-winning kid-friendly plastic packaging "of our popular Kid's Kitchen brand of microwave-ready foods."

■ "Time-starved consumers now spend about half their food dollars on meals prepared away from home," said a company officer. "We're capturing an increasing portion of those food-service sales by aiming for center-of-the-plate entrees that simplify food prep for foodservice operators, while tempting today's sophisticated palates. Our cafÃ© product line features exotic entrees such as barbacoa meat, pork ossobuco, carnita meat, and stuffed pork loins with Greek or Italian seasoning."

■ On March 7, 2008, Argus Research Company rated Kellogg a BUY, with this analysis by Erin Ashley Smith, "Kellogg has been a consistent performer over the past few years, reflecting its overall strong fundamentals and investments in building its brands. We expect the company to continue to deliver solid results in 2008."

■ On February 1, 2008, Justin Hellman, an analyst with *Value Line*, had this com-

ment, "Fiscal 2008 should be a solid year, with share net likely climbing at a double-digit pace. Though cost pressures are not expected to ease, Hormel, which continues to move away from its historic meat-packing roots, will probably be able to offset the headwinds with strategic price hikes. Indeed, the company's commitment to growing its value-added portfolio will probably give it a leg up on its competitors and support a margin recovery in the coming periods."

■ The company's recent acquisition of Diamond Crystal Brands Nutritional Products and Cliffdale Farms further strengthened Hormel Foods's brand presence in the fast-growing managed health care foods business. Hormel Foods is among the top providers in this field, which has strong growth prospects. The sixty-plus population worldwide is expected to double between 2000 and 2025.

SECTOR: Consumer Staples
BETA COEFFICIENT: .75
10-YEAR COMPOUND EARNINGS PER SHARE GROWTH: 12%
10-YEAR COMPOUND DIVIDENDS PER SHARE GROWTH: 9.1%

	2007	2006	2005	2004	2003	2002	2001	2000
Revenues (Mil)	6,193	5,745	5,414	4,780	4,200	3,910	4,124	3,675
Net Income (Mil)	302	286	254	232	186	189	182	170
Earnings per share	2.17	2.05	1.82	1.65	1.33	1.35	1.30	1.20
Dividends per share	0.74	0.56	0.52	0.45	0.42	0.39	0.37	0.35
Price high	41.8	39.1	35.4	32.1	27.5	28.2	27.3	21.0
low	30.0	31.9	29.2	24.9	19.9	20.0	17.0	13.6

CONSERVATIVE GROWTH

Idex Corporation

630 Dundee Road □ Northbrook, IL 60062 □ (847) 498-7070 □ Dividend reinvestment plan not available □ Web site: *www.idexcorp.com* □ Ticker symbol: IEX □ Listed: NYSE □ S&P rating: A− □ Value Line financial strength rating: B+

On June 12, 2007, IDEX Corporation announced the acquisition of Quadro Engineering, a leading provider of particle con-

trol solutions for the pharmaceutical and bio-pharmaceutical markets. Quadro's core capabilities include fine milling, emulsification and special handling of liquid and solid particulates for laboratory, pilot phase and production scale processing within the pharmaceutical and bio-pharmaceutical markets. Headquartered in Waterloo, Ontario, Canada, Quadro will be operated as a standalone unit within the company's Fluid & Metering Technologies segment.

For the year ended December 31, 2006, Quadro had revenues of $22 million (USD). The cash consideration was $31 million and is expected to be accretive to IDEX's earnings beginning in 2008.

Commenting on the acquisition, IDEX CEO Larry Kingsley said, "We are extremely pleased by Quadro Engineering's decision to become part of IDEX. Quadro is a technology leader in customized, critical particle control applications, providing a basis for us to serve selective, high growth sanitary applications in developing markets worldwide. Quadro's capabilities expand IDEX's ability to provide customized solutions for the movement, transformation, measurement and dispense of high value fluids and, now, solids."

Quadro Engineering president Keith McIntosh stated, "We are excited to become a part of IDEX and its Fluid & Metering Technologies business. IDEX is a recognized leader in applied engineered solutions. We have an expanded global footprint and the technology to provide our customers with a complete solution for the safe, sanitary and efficient transformation and delivery of high value fluids and solids."

Company Profile

According to a company spokesman, "We serve a highly diverse set of customers, who look to our company to provide applied engineered fluidic and mechanical solutions to their exacting specifications, anywhere in the world. Ours are the recognized brand names of the industrial world. We produce hundreds of products that touch people's lives every day. Whether you're drinking clean water, printing a photograph, buying paint for the kitchen, putting fuel in your car, or just bushing your teeth, chances are an Idex product was involved in the value chain."

Idex's business units are organized into four groups:

- Fluid & Metering Technologies
- Health & Science Technologies
- Dispensing Equipment
- Fire & Safety/Diversified Products

"Our businesses design, manufacture and market an extensive array of highly engineered, fluid-handling devices and other engineered equipment to customers in a variety of industries around the world.

"End markets include paints and coatings, fire and rescue, industrial machinery, chemical processing, life sciences/medical, petroleum/LPG, water and wastewater treatment, transportation equipment, food and beverage, pharmaceuticals and many others."

Fluid & Metering Technologies
- Liquid Controls
- Pulsafeeder
- Versa-Matic
- Viking Pump
- Warren Rupp

"These businesses design, produce and distribute some of the most recognized names in positive displacement pumps and flow meters, compressors, injectors, and other fluid-handling pump modules and systems.

"Our application-specific pump and metering solutions serve a diverse range of growing end markets including:

- Industrial infrastructure (fossil fuels, alternative fuels, oil & gas, water and wastewater)

- Chemical processing
- Food & beverage
- Pulp & paper
- Transportation
- Plastics & resins
- Electronics & electrical
- Construction & mining
- Machinery
- Numerous other specialty niche markets

Health & Science Technologies
- Gast Manufacturing
- Micropump
- Rheodyne
- Sapphire Engineering
- Upchurch Medical
- Upchurch Scientific

"These business units design, produce and distribute a wide range of precision fluidics solutions from very high precision, low flow rate pumping solutions required in analytical instrumentation, clinical diagnostics and drug discovery to high performance molded and extruded, biocompatible medical devices and implantables. Through this platform, Idex is also expanding its capability in air compressors used in medical, dental and industrial applications, as well as its expertise in precision gear and peristaltic pump technologies that meet OEMs' (original equipment makers) exacting specifications.

Dispensing Equipment
- FAST & Fluid Management
- Fluid Management

"These business units produce highly engineered equipment for dispensing, metering and mixing colorants, paints, inks and dyes, hair colorants and other personal care products; and paint refinishing components. This proprietary equipment is used in a variety of retail and commercial industries around the world.

Fire & Safety/Diversified Products
- BAND-IT
- Hale Products—Fire Suppression
- Hale Products—Hydraulic Equipment

"The businesses in this group manufacture engineered stainless steel band clamping systems and pumps, rescue tools, and other components and systems for the fire and rescue industry. Our high-quality stainless steel bands, buckles, preformed clamps, band clamping systems and related installation tools are used worldwide in industrial and commercial markets. They are used to secure exhaust system heat and sound shields, industrial hose fittings, traffic signals and signs, electrical cable shielding, identification and bundling, marine pilings, and many other 'hold-together' applications.

"The group also includes the world's leading manufacturer of truck-mounted fire pumps, 'Jaws of Life' rescue and recovery tools, and vehicle control devices and systems. Hale is further designated in two categories—fire suppression and hydraulic equipment."

Shortcomings to Bear in Mind
■ Idex has a solid record of earnings growth. However, this has not been translated into a consistent record of dividend growth. From 1999 through 2003, the dividend was unchanged, at 37 cents per share. I prefer companies that raise their dividends nearly every year.

Reasons to Buy
■ "We are pleased with our overall performance in 2007," said CEO Kingsley on February 5, 2008. "Growth in the Fluid and Metering Technologies segment was driven by strong global demand in the process control and infrastructure-related end markets. In the Health and Science Technologies segment, strong growth in the core health and science end markets was adversely impacted by declines in specific pneumatic and industrial OEM customers. Performance in the

Dispensing Equipment segment was driven by strong demand for replenishment orders in the U.S. large retail channel market and solid performance in Europe. Despite softness in our fire suppression business, our overall Fire & Safety/Diversified Products segment performed well as a result of product innovation and international growth.

"For the full year 2008, we expect performance in the Fluid and Metering Technologies segment to be driven by continued strong global investment in the infrastructure-related markets and process control industries. Within the Health and Science Technologies segment, the strength of the core analytical instrumentation, IVD and biotechnology markets as well as new OEM platforms will continue to be offset by the residual effect of two OEM contracts, unfavorably impacting full year segment growth by approximately 400 basis points. Despite softness in the North American housing market, growth in the Dispensing Equipment segment will be fueled by anticipated replenishment programs for large U.S. retailers and continued paint channel expansion in global markets. We expect our Fire and Safety/Diversified Products segment to continue to perform well, driven by growth in demand for band clamping applications and global expansion of our rescue tools business, offset in part by continued weak-

ness in the North American fire suppression market.

"Given these trends and current market conditions, we expect full year 2008 total revenue growth in the range of 13 to 15 percent (with organic revenue growth of 4 to 6 percent, acquisitions of 6 percent and foreign currency translation of 3 percent) and EPS in the range of $2.10 to $2.18 compared to $1.90 in the prior year. In addition, 2008 free cash flow is projected to exceed net income by 10 to 20 percent."

■ On November 14, 2007, IDEX announced it had entered into a definitive agreement to acquire Nova Technologies Corporation (NTC), a leading provider of metering technology and flow monitoring services for the water and wastewater markets. NTC develops products and provides comprehensive integrated solutions that enable industry, municipalities and government agencies to analyze and measure the capacity, quality and integrity of wastewater collection systems. This essential process of flow monitoring and measurement plays a determining role in the upgrade of municipalities' wastewater infrastructure. Headquartered in Huntsville, Alabama, with regional sales and service offices throughout the United States and Australia, NTC has annual revenues of about $70 million.

SECTOR: **Industrials**
BETA COEFFICIENT: **1.05**
10-YEAR COMPOUND EARNINGS PER SHARE GROWTH: **9.2%**
10-YEAR COMPOUND DIVIDENDS PER SHARE GROWTH: **8.1%**

		2007	2006	2005	2004	2003	2002	2001	2000
Revenues (Mil)		1,358	1,155	1,011	928	798	742	727	704
Net Income (Mil)		155	147	110	86	62	54	33	63
Earnings per share		1.90	1.81	1.39	1.11	0.83	0.74	0.47	0.92
Dividends per share		0.48	0.38	0.32	0.29	0.25	0.25	0.25	0.25
Price	high	45.0	35.7	30.3	27.3	18.8	17.6	16.5	16.0
	low	30.4	26.0	24.3	17.7	11.5	11.4	11.1	10.1

Illinois Tool Works, Inc.

3600 West Lake Ave. □ Glenview, IL 60025-5811 □ (847) 657-4104 □ Dividend reinvestment plan available □ Web site: *www.itw.com* □ Listed: NYSE □ Ticker symbol: ITW □ S&P rating: A+ □ Value Line financial strength rating: A+

With several hundred diverse operations, Illinois Tool Works is not an easy company to describe. To cut through this plethora of confusion, here are some comments made by company spokesmen that tend to shed some light on the extremely successful company.

- "How do our Miller welding machines end up in such faraway places? It's called performance. When our customers are building pipelines in the middle of nowhere, they need portable, reliable equipment that will get the job done. As a leading manufacturer of arc welding and cutting equipment, Miller is one of the most trusted brand names in the world. Whether our customers are working on a construction site in Hong Kong, a manufacturing plant in Mexico or a pipeline in Alaska, we equip them with the welding machines they need to keep their projects flowing smoothly."

- "Peek into most commercial kitchens around the world, and you're bound to find at least one of our Hobart products in the mix. As a leading provider of commercial food equipment for the food-service and food-retail industries, Hobart produces the high-performance appliances our customers need to keep their kitchens and stores running smoothly. Whether they require warewashing (industry lingo for dishwasher) and refrigeration, baking and cooking appliances, or scales and wrapping systems, we're got a full range of products to help satisfy any appetite."

- "Stand in line at any supermarket in the world, and you're likely to find our Zip-Pak technology in quite a few shopping carts. That's because it's used in many major branded and private-label product categories in the market today. We pioneered the zipper feature decades ago and now hold more than 200 patented zipper solutions. These innovations not only help our customers keep their products fresh, but also make it easier for consumers to open and close the packages."

Company Profile

Illinois Tools's record of sustained quality earnings is the result of a very practical view of the world. The company relies on market penetration—rather than price increases—to fuel operating income growth. What's more, the company's conservative accounting practices serve as a reliable yardstick of financial performance. These results then generate the cash needed to fund ITW's growth through both investing in core businesses and acquisitions.

Illinois Tool Works designs and produces an array of highly engineered fasteners and components, equipment and consumable systems and specialty products and equipment for customers around the world. A leading diversified manufacturing company with nearly 100 years of history, ITW's some 650 decentralized business units in forty-five countries employ about 49,000 men and women who are focused on creating value-added products and innovative customer solutions.

Engineered Products in North America

Product Categories: Short lead-time plastic and metal components and fasteners, and specialty products such as adhesives, fluid products and re-sealable packaging.

Major Businesses: Buildex, CIP, Deltar, Devcon, Drawform, Fastex, Fibre Glass Evercoat, ITW Brands, Minigrip/Zip-Pak, Paslode, Ramset/Red Head, Shakeproof, TACC, Texwipe, Truswal, and Wilsonart.

Primary End Markets: Construction, automotive, and general industrial.

Engineered Products International

Products Categories: Short lead-time plastic and metal components and fasteners, and specialty products such as electronic component packaging.

Major Businesses: Bailly Comte, Buildex, Deltar, Fastex, Ispra, James Briggs, Krafft, Meritex, Novadan, Paslode, Pryda, Ramset, Resopal, Rocol, Shakeproof, SPIT, and Wilsonart.

Primary End Markets: Construction, automotive, and general industrial.

Specialty Systems North America

Products Categories: Longer lead-time machinery and related consumables, and specialty equipment for applications such as foodservice, and industrial finishing.

Major Businesses: Acme Packaging, Angleboard, DeVilbiss, Gerrard, Hi-Cone, Hobart, ITW Foils, Miller, Ransburg, Signode, Valeron, Unipac, and Vulcan.

Primary End Markets: Food institutional, and retail, general industrial, construction, and food, and beverage.

Specialty Systems International

Product Categories: Longer lead-time machinery, and related consumables, and specialty equipment for applications such as foodservice, and industrial finishing.

Major Businesses: Auto-Sleeve, Decorative Sleeves, DeVilbiss, Elga, Foster, Gema, Gerrard, Hi-Cone, Hobart, ITW Foils, Mima, Orgapack, Ransburg, Signode, Simco, Strapex, and Tien Tai Electrode.

Primary End Markets: General industrial, food institutional, and retail, and food, and beverage.

Leasing and Investments

This segment makes opportunistic investments in the following categories: mortgage entities; leases of telecommunications, aircraft, air traffic control, and other equipment; properties; affordable housing; and a venture capital fund.

Shortcomings to Bear in Mind

■ On April 17, 2008, Standard & Poor's *Stock Reports* gave the stock a lackluster two stars, tantamount to a HOLD, with this reason by Mathew Christy, CFA: "While we expect contributions from acquisitions, share repurchases, and favorable international conditions in many of ITW's end markets to continue over the next twelve months, we believe that our outlook is largely reflected in the price of the stock."

Reasons to Buy

■ The stock has historically traded at a premium to the market, but based on its exceptional performance over the years, it would appear to be warranted. With some 650 businesses, Illinois Tool offers investors wide diversification by product line, geographic region and industry. This helps insulate the company from weakness in any one sector. Over the years, this has resulted in consistent performance despite the cyclicality of the automotive and construction sectors.

■ In 2007, revenues increased 17 percent, operating income grew 10 percent, income from continuing operations rose 9 percent and diluted income per share from continuing operations was 11 percent higher than the year-ago period. Revenues were $16.171 billion compared to $13.799 billion for full-year 2006. Operating income was $2.624 billion versus $2.385 billion. Income from continuing operations was $1.826 billion compared to $1.681 billion and diluted income per share from continuing operations was $3.28 versus $2.95. Total company operating margins of 16.2 percent for full-year 2007 were 110 basis points lower than 2006, even though base revenue margins improved 40 basis points on a year-over-year basis.

The company's free operating cash flow was a robust $694 million in the fourth quarter and $2.1 billion for the full year. Free cash was used, in part, to acquire fifteen companies during the fourth quarter representing $165 million of acquired revenues. For full-year 2007, the company completed fifty-two acquisitions totaling $995 million of annualized revenues and paid less than one time revenues for these transactions. During the fourth quarter, the company also paid $799 million to repurchase 14.4 million shares as part of its ongoing, open-ended buyback program. For the full year, ITW paid $1.8 billion to repurchase 32.4 million shares.

"Despite slowing in a number of North American end markets, we were helped by the strength of our international end markets and improved contributions from our acquisitions to produce a fourth quarter highlighted by both double digit revenue and earnings growth," said CEO David B. Speer. "While we expect 2008 to be a challenging year, we believe the company will benefit in the upcoming year from our increasingly diversified end markets and geographies as well as our acquisition activity."

■ "Acquisitions remain a key component of the company's growth strategy," said Mario Ferro, writing for *Value Line Investment Survey* on March 21, 2008. "Illinois picked up fifty-two businesses last year, representing just under $1 billion in annualized revenues. About three-quarters of this

was from international markets, and we estimate a similar amount and geographic breakdown for 2008."

■ On April 17, 2008, Argus Research Company called Illinois Tool a BUY, with this comment by Rashid Dahod, "Despite ongoing weakness in the North American homebuilding sector, ITW has continued to post solid revenue and profit growth, and management expects this to continue into 2008, with sustained strength in international operations."

■ "Innovation is a core strength of our global culture and is valued and reinforced throughout our worldwide business," said Mr. Speer in 2008. "The number of patents we hold, and the number of patent application filings, are clear signs of our creative attitude. Today, we have 21,636 patents and pending applications around the world, and we consistently rank in the top 100 of patent recipients in the United States. Our patent activities showcase the global nature of our business as well—in 2007 we were issued 287 U.S. patents and 1,212 foreign ones. Via the prestigious ITW Patent Society, our most creative thinkers gather during the year to share the latest insight and product breakthroughs with patent leaders from other parts of the company. This knowledge sharing helps spur idea generation throughout our businesses and results in direct customer benefits."

SECTOR: Industrials
BETA COEFFICIENT: 1.00
10-YEAR COMPOUND EARNINGS PER SHARE GROWTH: 11.1%
10-YEAR COMPOUND DIVIDENDS PER SHARE GROWTH: 17.2%

		2007	2006	2005	2004	2003	2002	2001	2000
Revenues (Mil)		16,171	14,055	12,922	11,731	10,036	9,468	9,293	9,984
Net Income (Mil)		1,870	1,718	1,495	1,340	1,040	932	806	958
Earnings per share		3.36	3.01	2.60	2.20	1.69	1.51	1.32	1.58
Dividends per share		1.12	0.71	0.59	0.52	0.47	0.45	0.41	0.38
Price	high	60.0	53.4	47.3	48.4	42.4	38.9	36.0	34.5
	low	45.6	41.5	39.3	36.5	27.3	27.5	24.6	24.8

Ingersoll-Rand Company Ltd.

Clarendon House ❑ 2 Church Street ❑ Hamilton HM 11 Bermuda ❑ (201) 573-3113 ❑ Dividend reinvestment plan available
❑ Web site: *www.irco.com* ❑ Ticker symbol: IR ❑ Listed: NYSE ❑ S&P rating: Not rated ❑ Value Line financial strength ating: A++

On December 17, 2007, Ingersoll-Rand announced that it had executed a definitive agreement to acquire Trane Inc., formerly American Standard Companies Inc., in a transaction valued at $10.1 billion. Trane is a global leader in indoor climate control systems, services and solutions with expected 2007 revenues of $7.4 billion.

CEO Herbert L. Henkel said, "The combination of Ingersoll-Rand and Trane will create a global, diversified industrial company with projected pro forma 2008 revenues of $17 billion. The new Ingersoll-Rand portfolio will include an $11 billion Climate Control business which will offer high value equipment, systems and services necessary for delivering solutions across the temperature spectrum for indoor, stationary, and transport applications worldwide.

"As a result of expected revenue and cost synergies, we are confident that this acquisition will improve Ingersoll-Rand's future earnings growth potential. We believe the new Ingersoll-Rand will be capable of sustaining annual organic revenue growth averaging 5–7 percent and EPS growth exceeding 15 percent per year, both in excess of our former growth guidance. In particular, assuming timely consummation of the proposed acquisition, we anticipate earnings of $4.00 per share in 2008.

"This acquisition represents a significant next step in Ingersoll-Rand's decade-long transformation to become a leading global diversified industrial company, with strong market positions across the climate control, industrial and security markets," said Mr. Henkel. "The acquisition of Trane meets our long-term objectives of significantly increasing consistency of revenue and income streams, adding strong brands and market positions, and further strengthening the organic growth potential of our portfolio. Trane's leadership position in the global commercial and residential climate control industry enhances our own highly regarded Hussmann and Thermo King brands."

Company Profile

Ingersoll-Rand is a global provider of products, services, and integrated solutions to industries as diverse as transportation, manufacturing, construction, and agriculture. The company brings to bear a 100-year-old heritage of technological innovation to help companies be more productive, efficient, and innovative. Examples include cryogenic refrigeration that preserves agricultural produce worldwide, biometric security systems for airports, corporations, and government facilities, the efficient harnessing of air to drive tools and factories, and versatile, compact vehicles for construction and efficient movement of people and goods. In every line of business, Ingersoll-Rand enables companies and their customers to turn work into progress. The company operates five business segments:

Climate Control Technologies provides solutions to transport, preserve, store and display temperature-sensitive products, and includes the market-leading brands of Hussmann® and Thermo King®.

The Compact Vehicle Technologies segment includes Bobcat® compact equipment and Club Car® golf cars and utility vehicles.

Construction Technologies includes Ingersoll-Rand® road pavers, compactors, portable power products, general-purpose construction equipment and attachments.

Industrial Technologies provides solutions to enhance customers' industrial and energy efficiency and provides equipment and services for compressed air systems, tools, fluid and material handling, and energy generation and conservation.

Security Technologies includes mechanical and electronic security products; biometric and access-control technologies; security and scheduling software; integration and services.

Shortcomings to Bear in Mind

■ On January 11, 2008, Ingersoll-Rand announced that it had taken a noncash charge to earnings of discontinued operations of $449 million ($277 million after tax) relating to the company's liability for all pending and estimated future asbestos claims through 2053. This charge results from an increase in the company's recorded liability for asbestos claims by $538 million, from $217 million to $755 million, offset by a corresponding $89 million increase in its assets for probable asbestos-related insurance recoveries, which now total $250 million.

■ Ingersoll-Rand has a Beta of 1.30, which means that it is somewhat more likely to rise and fall than the general market. A Beta of 1.0 would indicate volatility in line with the market, and a Beta of less than one would be a company that is even less volatile. For ultraconservative investors, Ingersoll-Rand might not be your cup of tea. That's why I have tabbed the stock for Aggressive Growth.

Reasons to Buy

■ Full-year 2007 net revenues were $8,763 million, a 9 percent increase compared with net revenues of $8,034 million in 2006. Excluding acquisitions and currency, revenues increased by 6 percent. Operating income for 2007 totaled $1,057.8 million compared with $998.5 million in 2006. Operating margin for 2007 was 12.1 percent, compared with 12.4 percent in the prior year. Higher revenues and productivity improvements were partially offset by cost inflation, unfavorable product mix

and restructuring costs. Excluding restructuring costs, the 2007 operating margin was 12.4 percent, equal to 2006.

The company reported full-year 2007 EPS of $13.43 ($3,966.7 million). Earnings per share from discontinued operations were $10.95 ($3,233.6 million). Discontinued operations includes gains on the sale of discontinued construction machinery businesses equal to EPS of $11.04; a charge of -$0.94 per share related to increasing asbestos reserves for the fourth quarter; and earnings equal to approximately $0.85 per share from the earnings and retained costs from discontinued businesses. EPS from continuing operations were $2.48 ($733.1 million). Full-year results also include restructuring costs equal to EPS of -$0.06.

The company reported 2006 EPS of $3.20 ($1,032.5 million), including EPS of $0.83 ($267.5 million) from discontinued operations and EPS of $2.37 ($765.0 million) from continuing operations.

The company continued to be a strong cash generator with full-year available cash flow in 2007 of $714 million. Full year available cash flow also includes a $217 million tax payment.

■ On September 4, 2007, Ingersoll-Rand announced that it had signed an agreement to purchase privately owned Officine Meccaniche Industriali srl (OMI), a leading European provider of compressed-air treatment equipment.

OMI manufactures a line of compressed-air treatment products, including air dryers, filters, chillers, and system controllers, that maximize the productivity and reliability of compressed air systems for a variety of industrial and manufacturing applications. Founded in 1989, OMI is based in northeast Italy in Fogliano Redipuglia, Gorizia Province, and has an additional facility in Logatec, Slovenia.

"The acquisition of OMI reflects our intention to build upon one of our core business platforms relating to industrial productivity," said Mr. Henkel. "With its strong distribution channels throughout Europe,

Asia and Latin America, OMI advances our leadership as a global provider of innovative and comprehensive compressed-air systems and extends our line of Ingersoll-Rand compressed air products and services."

- Writing for the Standard & Poor's *Stock Reports* on March 8, 2008, analyst Christopher Lippincott said, "We believe IR's organic growth (that is, without including acquisitions) prospects remain healthy due to overseas strength, although some of its U.S. business units may display slower growth. In our view, IR's portfolio re-balancing, including the sale of the Road Development and Bobcat businesses, has reduced its capital intensity and cyclicality."

- On February 20, 2008, Argus Research Company called Ingersoll-Rand a BUY. Rashid Dahod said, "We continue to believe that Trane will make a good addition to IR's existing Climate Control Technologies portfolio." He went on to say, "The commercial component of Trane's air conditioning business should generate solid returns, based on its strong commercial backlog. In addition, we note that the residential component has performed relatively well despite the weakness in the U.S. housing market. We expect IR to realize both cost and revenue synergies from the acquisition."

- On November 30, 2007, Ingersoll-Rand announced that it had completed the sale of its Bobcat, Utility Equipment and Attachments business units to Doosan Infracore for gross proceeds of approximately $4.9 billion, and net cash proceeds of about $3.75 billion.

The combined businesses manufacture and sell compact equipment, including skid-steer loaders, compact track loaders, mini-excavators and telescopic tool handlers; portable air compressors, generators, and light towers; general-purpose light construction equipment; and attachments. For full-year 2006 these businesses collectively generated $2.6 billion in revenues. The sale includes manufacturing facilities in Gwinner and Bismarck, North Dakota; Carrollton, Georgia; Litchfield, Minnesota; Petersburg, Virginia; Wujiang, China; Dobris, Czech Republic; Lyon and Pontchateau, France; Slane, Ireland; and Tredegar, Wales.

"With the sale of Bobcat, Utility Equipment and Attachments, Ingersoll-Rand has become a true diversified industrial company, positioned to deliver consistent financial performance over the long term and across all phases of the economic cycle," said CEO Henkel.

"Collectively, this transaction and the sale of our Road Development business in April 2007 generated net cash proceeds of approximately $4.8 billion. We will continue to use a balanced approach in our investment priorities of organic growth, acquisitions and share repurchases. We prefer to use the proceeds of the sale to augment profitable growth by funding innovation and new-product development efforts and to make acquisitions that enhance our strategic business platforms."

SECTOR: **Industrials**
BETA COEFFICIENT: **1.30**
10-YEAR COMPOUND EARNINGS PER SHARE GROWTH: **7.9%**
10-YEAR COMPOUND DIVIDENDS PER SHARE GROWTH: **9.5%**

		2007	2006	2005	2004	2003	2002	2001	2000
Revenues (Mil)		8,763	11,409	10,547	9,394	9,876	8,951	9,682	8,798
Net Income (Mil)		733	1,033	1,054	830	594	367	246	546
Earnings per share		2.48	3.20	3.09	2.37	1.72	1.08	0.74	1.68
Dividends per share		0.72	0.68	0.57	0.44	0.36	0.34	0.34	0.34
Price	high	56.7	49.0	44.0	41.5	34.1	27.2	25.2	28.9
	low	38.2	35.0	35.1	29.5	17.3	14.9	15.2	14.8

Intel Corporation

2200 Mission College Boulevard □ Santa Clara, CA 95054-8119 □ (408) 765-9785 □ Dividend reinvestment plan available □ Web site: *www.intc.com* □ Listed: Nasdaq □ Ticker symbol: INTC □ S&P rating: B+ □ Value Line financial strength rating: A++

On March 18, 2008, Intel and Microsoft joined force with academia to create two Universal Parallel Computing Research Centers (UPCRC), aimed at accelerating developments in mainstream parallel computing, for consumers and businesses in desktop and mobile computing.

The new research centers will be located at the University of California, Berkeley (UC Berkeley), and the University of Illinois at Urbana-Champaign (UIUC). Microsoft and Intel have committed a combined $20 million to the Berkeley and UIUC research centers over the next five years. An additional $8 million will come from UIUC, and UC Berkeley has applied for $7 million in funds from a state-supported program to match industry grants. Research will focus on advancing parallel programming applications, architecture and operating systems software. This is the first joint industry and university research alliance of this magnitude in the United States focused on mainstream parallel computing.

Parallel computing brings together advanced software and processors that have multiple cores or engines, which when combined can handle multiple instructions and tasks simultaneously. Although Microsoft, Intel and many others deliver hardware and software that is capable of handling dual- and quad-core-based PCs today, in the coming years computers are likely to have even more processors inside them.

"Intel has already shown an 80-core research processor, and we're quickly moving the computing industry to a many-core world," said Andrew Chien, vice president, Corporate Technology Group and director, Intel Research. "Working with Microsoft and these two prestigious universities will

help catalyze the long-term breakthroughs that are needed to enable dramatic new applications for the mainstream user. We think these new applications will have the ability to efficiently and robustly sense and act in our everyday world with new capabilities: rich digital media and visual interfaces, powerful statistical analyses and search, and mobile applications. Ultimately, these sensing and human interface capabilities will bridge the physical world with the virtual."

"Driven by the unprecedented capability of multicore processors, we're in the midst of a revolution in the computing industry, which profoundly affects the way we develop software," said Tony Hey, corporate vice president of External Research at Microsoft Research. "Working jointly with industry and academia, we plan to explore the next generation of hardware and software to unlock the promise and the power of parallel computing and enable a change in the way people use technology."

Company Profile

It has been more than three decades since Intel introduced the world's first microprocessor, making technology history. The computer revolution that this technology spawned has changed the world. Today, Intel supplies the computing industry with the chips, boards, systems, and software that are the "ingredients" of computer architecture. These products are used by industry members to create advanced computing systems.

Intel architecture platform products

Microprocessors, also called central processing units (CPUs) or chips, are frequently described as the "brains" of a computer, because they control the central processing of data in personal computers (PCs), servers, workstations and other computers. Intel offers microprocessors optimized for each segment of the computing market. Chipsets perform essential logic functions surrounding the CPU in computers, and support and extend the graphics, video, and other capabilities of many Intel processor-based systems. Motherboards combine Intel microprocessors and chipsets to form the basic subsystem of a PC or server.

Wireless communications and computing products

These products are component-level hardware and software focusing on digital cellular communications and other applications needing both low-power processing and re-programmable, retained memory capability (flash memory). These products are used in mobile phones, handheld devices, two-way pagers, and many other products.

Networking and communications products

System-level products consist of hardware, software and support services for e-Business data center and building blocks for communications access solutions. These products include e-Commerce infrastructure appliances; hubs, switches and routers for Ethernet networks; and computer telephony components. Component-level products include communications silicon components and embedded control chips designed to perform specific functions in networking and communications applications, such as telecommunications, hubs, routers and wide area networking. Embedded control chips are also used in laser printers, imaging, storage media, automotive systems, and other applications.

Solutions and services

These products and services include e-Commerce data center services as well as connected peripherals and security access software.

Major Customers

- Original equipment manufacturers of computer systems and peripherals.
- PC users, who buy Intel's PC enhancements, business communications products and networking products through reseller, retail and OEM channels.
- Other manufacturers, including makers of a wide range of industrial and telecommunications equipment.

Shortcomings to Bear in Mind

- Intel does not have a very impressive record of growth, at least not in the past ten years. Earnings per share are only modestly higher than they were in 1997. What's more, EPS has declined from the prior year four times in that span: 1998, 2001, 2002, and 2006.

Reasons to Buy

- On January 15, 2008, CEO Paul Otellini said, "2007 was a breakthrough year for innovation at Intel. We realized the benefits of our investments in new products and our efforts to drive efficiencies. Our customers embraced the Intel Core micro-architecture, extending our competitive leadership and driving a significant gain in operating results. We enter 2008 with the best combination of products, silicon technology and manufacturing leadership in our history."
- On March 25, 2008, Argus Research Company rated Intel a BUY, with this comment by Wendy Abramowitz: "In a surprise move, Intel raised its dividend for the second time in a row. INTC now carries a yield of 2.6 percent, which is above average for a semiconductor stock. In our view, boosting the yield was the right move for Intel; investors should feel more comfortable owning a stock with both growth and income potential."
- On November 28, 2007, Intel announced an upgrade of its popular software tools suite for Mac OS X Leopard, the sixth major version of Apple's advanced operating system. The latest 10.1 version of the Intel® C++ Compiler and Intel® Fortran

Compiler, as well as the Intel® Threading Building Blocks, Intel® Math Kernel Libraries and Intel® Performance Primitives, have been optimized for Apple's Leopard and Xcode 3.0 development environment launched last month.

The combination of Intel's compilers, Leopard and Xcode 3.0 provides unprecedented support for Mac developers to take full advantage of Intel multicore processors. Intel's compilers contain auto-parallelizing capabilities, libraries and Threading Building Blocks for Mac OS X, and Leopard is fully optimized for multicore environments with new developer APIs and tools for developing multithreaded applications.

Several Mac developers, including Apple's own Leopard development team, Adobe and Autodesk, have used Intel's compilers since the Mac OS X tools suite was introduced in January 2006.

"Leopard, Xcode and Intel's compilers give developers powerful new tools to squeeze even more performance out of the latest Intel processors," said Bertrand Serlet, Apple's senior vice president of software engineering. "Intel's software works well in our Xcode environment, and the Intel engineering team does a great job supporting our Apple engineers and Mac OS X developers."

"The Intel C++ Compiler has been a critical tool in the delivery of the industry's most complete cross-platform suite of professional video tools Adobe Production Premium," said Bill Hensler, vice president of Dynamic Media for Adobe. "Intel has done a great job delivering a set of software tools that allows Adobe engineers to create outstanding products that revolutionize how the world engages with ideas and information."

"One of the unique advantages of Autodesk Maya is that it runs on multiple platforms. Creative professionals have long had an affinity for Apple products, and the Maya software's availability on Apple's Mac OS X allows them to use their platform of choice," said Kevin Tureski, director of product development, Autodesk Media and Entertainment. "With Apple's switch to Intel processors and with multicore Mac Pro machines becoming commonplace, we need compilers that allow us to multithread Maya. We rely on the Intel C++ compiler for our threading work because of its support for OpenMP and performance-critical sections of code."

■ On September 10, 2007, an article written by the Associated Press said, "Intel Corp. held a groundbreaking ceremony Saturday for its first chip factory in China, expanding its presence in the booming Chinese computer industry and boosting Beijing's campaign to lure foreign high-tech investment.

"The US $2.5 billion facility, one of the biggest single foreign investments in China, will be Intel's first silicon-wafer fabrication plant in Asia and its eighth worldwide. It is due to open in 2010 with a workforce of 1,200.

"The new factory, dubbed 'Fab 68,' will produce chipsets, which connect microprocessors to other computer components. Intel says it chose not to equip the plant with its most advanced processes because of U.S. restrictions on high-tech exports.

"'China is obviously such a booming economy. We very much felt like it was important to be near our customers,'" said Kirby Jefferson, the Dalian plant's general manager, in an interview ahead of the ceremony.

"Santa Clara, California-based Intel says China already is its second-largest market after the United States and is expected to be the world's biggest information technology market by 2010."

SECTOR: **Information Technology**
BETA COEFFICIENT: **1.35**
10-YEAR COMPOUND EARNINGS PER SHARE GROWTH: **2%**
10-YEAR COMPOUND DIVIDENDS PER SHARE GROWTH: **31.1%**

	2007	2006	2005	2004	2003	2002	2001	2000
Revenues (Mil)	38,334	35,382	38,826	34,709	30,141	26,764	26,539	33,726
Net Income (Mil)	6,976	5,044	8,700	7,516	5,641	3,117	1,291	10,535
Earnings per share	1.18	.086	1.40	1.16	0.85	0.46	0.19	1.51
Dividends per share	0.45	0.40	0.32	0.16	0.08	0.08	0.08	0.07
Price high	28.0	26.6	28.8	34.6	34.5	36.8	38.6	75.8
low	18.8	16.8	21.9	19.6	14.9	12.9	19.0	29.8

CONSERVATIVE GROWTH

International Business Machines Corporation

New Orchard Road □ Armonk, New York 10504 □ (800) 426-4968 □ Direct dividend reinvestment plan available □ Web site: *www.ibm.com* □ Listed: NYSE □ Ticker symbol: IBM □ S&P rating: A □ Value Line financial strength rating: A++

"IBM Corp. is unveiling its next-generation mainframe computer Tuesday, touting the z10 as a more powerful and energy-efficient alternative for data centers that use many small servers and face rising power and cooling costs," said David Ho, writing for the Cox News Service on February 26, 2008.

"The more than 6-foot-tall mainframe was designed to handle growing demands on computer facilities driven by Internet traffic and transactions, IBM said. The z10 can handle about 2 billion transactions each day.

"The mainframe is the product of a five-year, $1.5 billion project involving a global Big Blue team of more than 5,000 people, including software developers in Austin, Texas.

"'It's the beginning of a new version of the mainframe that's going to become more relevant to today's business problems, particularly for larger corporations,' said Carl Greiner, an analyst with the Ovum Inc. consulting firm who was briefed on the announcement.

"About 20 percent of data centers use mainframes, while more than 60 percent use servers based on chips from Intel Corp. or Advanced Micro Devices Inc., Greiner said.

"While it is unlikely IBM can hinder that dominance, 'the mainframe is getting a rebirth on some of the economic benefits it can provide and some of the environmental benefits,' he said.

"A single z10 has the computing capacity of nearly 1,500 desktop computers but uses 85 percent less energy, said David Gelardi, IBM's vice president of mainframe systems and performance. He said the z10 also occupies far less space."

Company Profile

Big Blue is the world's leading provider of computer hardware. IBM makes a broad range of computers, notebooks, mainframes, and network servers. The company also develops software (it's number two, behind Microsoft) and peripherals. IBM derives about one-third of its revenues from an ever-expanding service arm that is the largest in the world. IBM owns Lotus Development, the software pioneer that makes the Lotus Notes messaging system.

The company's subsidiary, Tivoli Systems, develops tools that manage corporate computer networks. Finally, in an effort to keep up with the times, IBM has been making a concerted effort to obtain a slice of the Internet business.

Shortcomings to Bear in Mind

- There must be something wrong with IBM. If you find out, let me know.

Reasons to Buy

- On January 14, 2008, IBM announced fourth-quarter 2007 diluted earnings of $2.80 per share from continuing operations, an increase of 24 percent, compared with diluted earnings of $2.26 per share in the fourth quarter of 2006. The company also reported fourth-quarter revenue of $28.9 billion, an increase of 10 percent as reported, including 6 points of currency benefit, compared with the fourth quarter of 2006.

IBM reported full-year 2007 diluted earnings of $7.18 per share, including 5 cents per share relating to the sale of the Printing Systems Division in the second quarter, an increase of 18 percent, compared with diluted earnings of $6.06 per share in 2006. The company also reported full-year revenue of $98.8 billion, an increase of 8 percent, including 4 points of currency benefit. IBM's cash balance at the end of 2007 was more than $16 billion, with strong free cash flow performance.

"The broad scope of IBM's global business—led by strong operational performance in Asia, Europe and emerging countries—drove these outstanding results," said CEO Samuel J. Palmisano. "IBM is well-positioned as we begin 2008 as a result of our global business reach, solid recurring revenue stream and strong financial position. We are on track to achieve our long-term earnings-per-share roadmap objective in 2010."

- On November 12, 2007, IBM and Cognos® announced that the two companies had entered into an agreement for IBM to acquire Cognos, a publicly held company based in Ottawa, Ontario, Canada, in an all-cash transaction at a price of $5 billion USD or $58 USD per share, with a net transaction value of $4.9 billion USD.

The acquisition of Cognos supports IBM's Information on Demand strategy, a cross-company initiative announced on February 16, 2006 that combines IBM's strength in information integration, content and data management and business consulting services to unlock the business value of information. Integrating Cognos, the twenty-third IBM acquisition in support of its Information on Demand strategy, will enable new business insights to be delivered to a broader set of people across an organization, beyond the traditional users of business intelligence.

IBM said the acquisition fits squarely within both its acquisition strategy and capital allocation model, and that it will contribute to the achievement of the company's objective for earnings-per-share growth through 2010.

"Customers are demanding complete solutions, not piece parts, to enable real-time decision making," said Steve Mills, senior vice president and group executive, IBM Software Group. "IBM has been providing Business Intelligence solutions for decades. Our broad set of capabilities—from data warehousing to information integration and analytics—together with Cognos, position us well for the changing Business Intelligence and Performance Management industry. We chose Cognos because of its industry-leading technology that is based on open standards, which complements IBM's Service Oriented Architecture strategy."

- On November 13, 2007, a *Wall Street Journal* column written by Robert Cyran and John Foley, had this comment: "It is easy to see why IBM boss Sam Palmisano likes the business. Software is both solidly profitable—although it only accounts for about a fifth of IBM's sales, it accounts for 40 percent of profit—and growing. Moreover, the industry is undergoing seismic change. Rather than purchasing so-called best-of-breed software from several vendors, customers are moving toward big providers such as IBM, SAP and Oracle that offer one-stop shopping. So IBM's purchase of Cognos—which sells programs that help clients interpret information from databases—isn't surprising.

"Software acquisitions also tend to make financial sense, which explains why there have been so many of them. When one software group acquires another, the purchaser often can cut a quarter of the target's operating costs. And IBM should be able to sell Cognos software to a lot more clients."

■ On February 26, 2008, Wendy Abramowitz, an analyst with Argus Research Company, said, "BUY-rated International Business Machines has modestly increased EPS guidance for the year. The improved outlook is partially supported by additional stock repurchasing, but we also believe that new product offerings, acquisitions, and the company's global footprint will aid growth this year."

■ Standard & Poor's *Stock Reports* was equally enthusiastic on April 5, 2008, giving the stock its highest rating, a STRONG BUY, with this comment by Thomas W. Smith, CFA, "IBM's results should benefit, in our view, from a widening of margins, reflecting cost cutting and improved profitability of its portfolio lines."

■ "Just after Palmisano took charge of Big Blue six years ago, the prognosis was poor," said a *Barron's* writer, Andrew Bary, on March 24, 2008. The article was titled, "World's Best CEOs". "The services division was being savaged by lower-cost IT outfits in Bangalore, and the personal-computer division was running into cut-throat competition.

"That all began to change when Palmisano sold the PC business to Lenovo, on the theory that the PC's dominance had been replaced by mobile phones. He also invested heavily in overseas operations and began spending to buy software companies and then push their products through IBM's giant sales force, thus carrying out his strategy of boosting margins by moving into faster-growth businesses."

■ "International Business Machines Corp. said it achieved a breakthrough in developing a three-dimensional semiconductor chip that can be stacked on top of another electronic device in a vertical configuration long sought by engineers to reduce size and power use," said William M. Bulkeley, writing for the *Wall Street Journal* on April 12, 2007.

"IBM said the new chips, which feature tiny wires leading down through the semiconductor, may appear in cell-phones and other communication products made by customers of the East Fishkill, NY, semiconductor foundry as soon as next year.

"Semiconductors are normally connected to each other through wires around their periphery. Chip manufacturers have worked for years to develop ways to connect one type of chip to another vertically, but they haven't been able to achieve such links without using up huge amount of space on the chip, reducing the room for circuitry and processing power."

■ Technology is giving the health care industry a potent weapon against counterfeit drugs. With the latest offering from IBM, pharmaceutical companies can create an electronic certificate of authenticity (known as an electronic pedigree or ePedigree) for every drug that passes through the supply chain. And, all participants in the supply chain—manufacturers, distributors, pharmacies and hospitals—can access historical data on individual bottles or packages of medicine.

"This system has the potential to improve the integrity of the entire drug supply chain by allowing users to quickly authenticate pharmaceutical products through direct data exchange with trading partners," said Christian C. Clauss, director, Sensor Information Management, IBM Software Group.

The ePedigree feature is a key capability of the new version of IBM's WebSphere RFID Information Center. Amerisource-Bergen, a "big three" pharmaceutical distributor, is already using IBM's RFID

Information Center, as is a large global pharmaceutical manufacturer.

The ePedigree feature will also help comply with new and emerging regulations such as those that will take effect in California in 2009.

"IBM's approach to ePedigree is unique in that it enables ePedigree compliance without significant impact to the existing business processes and legacy IT systems," said Shay Reid, AmerisourceBergen, vice president, Integrated Solutions. "This system will be a helpful tool in our industry to comply with mandates, various trading partner requirements, and enable new business use cases."

■ On August 1, 2007, an IBM official said the company would consolidate some 3,900 computer servers onto about 30 System z mainframes running the Linux operating system. The company expects the new setup to use about 80 percent less energy than the current arrangement. The switch is part of Project Big Green, a commitment by IBM to sharply reduce data center energy consumption for the company and its clients.

"The mainframe is the single most powerful instrument to drive better economics and energy conservation at the data center today," said James Stallings, general manager, IBM System z mainframe. "By moving globally onto the mainframe platform, IBM is creating a technology platform that saves energy while positioning our IT assets for flexibility and growth."

SECTOR: **Information Technology**
BETA COEFFICIENT: **0.95**
10-YEAR COMPOUND EARNINGS PER SHARE GROWTH: **9.1%**
10-YEAR COMPOUND DIVIDENDS PER SHARE GROWTH: **13.2%**

	2007	2006	2005	2004	2003	2002	2001	2000
Revenues (Mil)	98,786	91,424	91,134	96,503	89,131	81,186	83,067	88,396
Net Income (Mil)	10,418	9,492	7,934	8,448	7,583	3,579	7,495	8,093
Earnings per share	7.18	6.06	4.91	4.39	4.34	3.07	4.69	4.44
Dividends per share	1.35	1.10	.078	0.70	0.66	0.60	0.55	0.51
Price high	121.5	97.4	99.1	100.4	94.5	124.0	124.7	134.9
low	88.8	72.7	71.8	81.9	73.2	54.0	83.8	80.1

AGGRESSIVE GROWTH

International Paper Company

400 Atlantic Street ❑ Stamford, CT 06921 ❑ (901) 419-4957 ❑ Dividend reinvestment plan available ❑ Web site: *www .internationalpaper.com* ❑ Ticker symbol: IP ❑ Listed: NYSE ❑ S&P rating: B+ ❑ Value Line financial strength rating: B+

On March 17, 2008, International Paper signed an agreement with Weyerhaeuser to purchase its Containerboard, Packaging and Recycling (CBPR) business for $6 billion in cash, subject to postclosing adjustments. International Paper expects to close the deal in the third quarter of 2008. Because the transaction is a purchase of assets rather than of stock, International Paper will realize a tax benefit that has an estimated net present value of approximately $1.4 billion. Taking this benefit into account, the net purchase price is about $4.6 billion.

"This deal represents a compelling opportunity for International Paper and our shareowners at a very attractive valuation," said CEO John Faraci. "Integrating Weyerhaeuser's CBPR business into our North American packaging platform fits very well with our strategy to improve our earnings, cash flow and returns by strengthening existing businesses. We expect the combined packaging business will generate stronger cash flow and higher EBITDA margins than either standalone business."

Carol Roberts, senior vice president of International Paper's packaging business, said she sees low integration risk and considerable upside potential in the deal. "Weyerhaeuser has low-cost, well-run assets that complement our existing mill and converting system and offer significant synergies," she said. "The acquisition expands our geographic presence in the U.S. and Mexico and diversifies our customer base in key product lines. All of this will make our packaging business more competitive, more profitable and better able to serve customers."

Company Profile

International Paper is a global uncoated paper and packaging company with primary markets and manufacturing operations in the United States, Europe, Latin America, and Asia, complemented by xpedx, an extensive North American merchant distribution system. With annual sales of about $22 billion, the company has operations in more than twenty countries and employs some 60,000 people worldwide.

International Paper has a long-standing policy of using no wood from endangered forests. The company supports mutual recognition of forest certification standards. Management has encouraged the adoption of CERFLOR, the SFI Standard and other systems recognized by the global Programme for the Endorsement of Forest Certification (PEFC) council. The PEFC-endorsed systems around the globe, including the SFI program, now account for an area larger than the combined forest area of all twenty-five member countries of the European Union.

Facilities

In the United States, International Paper operates eighteen pulp, paper, and packaging mills, ninety-four converting and packaging plants, and five wood products facilities. Operations in Europe, Asia, and Latin America include eight pulp, paper and packaging mills and forty-four converting and packaging plants. The company distributes printing, packaging, graphic arts, maintenance and industrial products principally through more than 250 distribution branches located primarily in the United States.

Shortcomings to Bear in Mind

- In the past, earnings per share have been most unimpressive, with no consistent pattern. Dividends, as well, have been stuck in a rut for many years at $1.00 per share—with no sign of a positive change.

Reasons to Buy

- "We increased profits before special items by 52 percent in 2007, which is strong evidence that the transformation we began in 2005 is continuing to pay off," said Mr. Faraci on February 7, 2008. "We've steadily expanded our margins through internal cost controls and by focusing on the right customers and product segments within our key businesses. Our global investments are adding to revenue and profit growth and helping to offset some demand decline in North America."

- On April 4, 2008, *Value Line Investment Survey* gave International Paper its highest rating for Timeliness, with this comment by Orly Seidman, "We expect double-digit share-net gains this year and next. Last year, management dedicated itself to improving productivity. Though input prices rose, and will likely continue their upward trend over the next few years, cost-saving initiatives helped lift IP's bottom line, as should synergies from these new packaging resources."

- On September 24, 2007, International Paper announced it had begun production of high-performance lightweight linerboard at its Pensacola, Florida, mill. Startup of the project allows International Paper to economically produce linerboard grades with greater strength characteristics while using less wood fiber. The company expects to ramp up machine production during the fourth quarter and estimates average production of 50 to 60 percent of the machine's capacity for that period.

The product line provides the dual benefits of premium performance and sustainability. Sourced with 100 percent virgin wood fiber, the lightweight linerboard has excellent performance properties. It is fully recyclable and recoverable and allows customers to reduce their overall volume of packaging.

"Our Pensacola machine is the first of its kind in North America, designed to deliver lighter-weight grades with unmatched performance to provide our customers with the competitive advantage they need to win in today's packaging marketplace," said Glenn Landau, vice president and general manager of International Paper's containerboard business. "Across the globe, our customers demand packaging that meets their changing needs. This machine will provide the high-quality linerboard they have come to expect from IP."

In early 2006, International Paper announced plans to convert its Pensacola mill from a 350,000 ton-per-year uncoated paper machine to a 500,000 ton-per-year lightweight linerboard machine. The conversion was part of International Paper's strategy to strengthen its existing uncoated paper and packaging businesses. Related changes within the company's containerboard business include the previously announced closure of the 200,000-ton Terre Haute, Indiana, mill slated for Oct. 1.

"With the global demand for containerboard growing at 4 percent, we believe our customers' demand matches our capacity," Mr. Landau said.

The mill conversion and paper machine rebuild began in the first quarter of 2007 and involved hundreds of mill employees and significant contracted engineering and construction support. "This was one of the largest capital projects we've undertaken in North America in the past several years. Our employees and the firms that worked to complete this project deserve the credit for a job well done," said Michael Exner, International Paper vice president of containerboard manufacturing. "Now our goal is to operate the mill safely and productively to manufacture high-quality board on a consistent basis," he added.

■ On September 19, 2007, Tully's Coffee Corporation, a fully handcrafted coffee roaster, became the first major coffee retailer to adopt a fully renewable and compostable paper cup for its hot beverages. Tully's has simultaneously established an in-store collection program to divert the used cups and other compostable food waste from local landfills to organic composting facilities. These materials will eventually be composted and "recycled" to enrich soil rather than be lost to the landfill.

Tully's program features the innovative ecotainer™ hot cup from International Paper. Unlike conventional paper hot cups that are lined with a petrochemical plastic to prevent leaking, the ecotainer hot cup is lined with a bio-plastic made from a renewable resource—corn. This coating material requires less energy to manufacture and is greenhouse gas neutral. In addition, the cup is the only commercially available 100 percent compostable hot cup certified by the Biodegradable Products Institute (BPI).

"Our ecotainer hot cup is designed to maximize use of renewable materials, to reduce energy and greenhouse gas emissions required to make the product, and to offer an alternative to land-filling packaging waste," said Austin Lance, vice president and general manager of International Paper's Foodservice Business. "Tully's is among the leaders in achieving the full environmental benefit that this product was designed to deliver."

■ On November 6, 2007, International Paper announced it would invest $10 million to convert its Louisiana Mill in Bastrop, Louisiana, to 100 percent market and fluff pulp production. Conversion of the mill will begin later this year with equipment upgrades to be completed by the fall of 2008.

"Moving the mill from paper to pulp production, combined with key cost reduction measures, makes strategic sense for us," said Wayne Brafford, senior vice president of International Paper's printing and communications papers sector. "It allows us to operate the Louisiana mill competitively and meet global demand for our softwood and fluff pulp while reducing our uncoated freesheet capacity by about 250,000 tons."

The mill will cease production of uncoated freesheet, such as office paper and envelopes, as well as other specialty papers. Instead it will have the capacity to make up to 450,000 tons per year of primarily softwood pulp, used in tissue, towels, paper and packaging, as well as fluff pulp, used in diapers and personal hygiene products. The mill's bristols production, used for products such as index cards and file folders, will be shifted to other mills in the International Paper system.

SECTOR: Materials
BETA COEFFICIENT: 1.10
10-YEAR COMPOUND EARNINGS PER SHARE GROWTH: 10.1%
10-YEAR COMPOUND DIVIDENDS PER SHARE GROWTH: 0%

		2007	2006	2005	2004	2003	2002	2001	2000
Revenues (Mil)		21,890	21,995	24,097	25,548	25,179	24,976	26,363	28,180
Net Income (Mil)		1,168	635	513	634	382	540	214	969
Earnings per share		2.70	2.18	1.06	1.30	0.80	1.12	0.44	2.16
Dividends per share		1.00	1.00	1.00	1.00	1.00	1.00	1.00	1.00
Price	high	41.6	38.0	42.6	45.0	43.3	46.2	43.3	46.2
	low	31.0	30.7	27.0	37.1	33.1	31.3	30.7	26.3

CONSERVATIVE GROWTH

Johnson Controls, Inc.

P. O. Box 591 ▫ Milwaukee, WI 53201-0591 ▫ (414) 524-2375 ▫ Direct dividend reinvestment plan available ▫ Fiscal years end September 30 ▫ Web site: *www.johnsoncontrols.com* ▫ Listed: NYSE ▫ Ticker symbol: JCI ▫ S&P rating: A+ ▫ Value Line financial strength rating: A

On August 21, 2007, a fleet of advanced, Dodge Sprinter plug-in hybrid delivery vans began operating within the United States, powered by Lithium-ion (Li-ion) batteries developed by Johnson Controls-Saft Advanced Power Solutions (JCS). The test fleet is helping to usher in a new age of extremely fuel-efficient and environmentally friendly, urban transportation.

"Advances in Lithium-ion battery technology are bringing the reality of plug-in hybrids closer to commercialization," said Mary Ann Wright, who leads the JCS joint venture and is

vice president and general manager of Johnson Controls' hybrid battery business.

According to Ms. Wright, the Dodge Sprinter is an ideal vehicle to carry a large battery pack and still have ample room readily accessible for use as a delivery vehicle. Fleets of Sprinter plug-in hybrids were put into service in Los Angeles, New York, and Kansas City in 2006 during the first phase of Chrysler and Daimler's plug-in hybrid development program. Powered by Johnson Controls-Saft nickel-metal hydride (NiMH) and Li-ion battery packs, the Sprinter vans have provided valuable data to accelerate the development of future battery technology.

The Li-ion battery packs in Sprinter plug-in hybrids will be 47 percent lighter compared to previous NiMH systems and deliver more power than today's conventional hybrid batteries.

"Advanced battery technology is the single most important enabler in making all types of electric vehicles practical," says Ms. Wright. "Plug-in hybrids, conventional hybrids, electric vehicles (EVs) and hydrogen fuel cell vehicles will benefit from Lithium-ion technology. Johnson Controls-Saft is determined to deliver state-of-the-art batteries to power advanced, environmentally friendly vehicles."

Plug-in hybrids can travel much farther on emission-free electric power than conventional hybrids, and are particularly well suited for urban delivery vehicles operating in heavy traffic and making frequent stops. Plug-ins can be charged overnight using less-expensive off-peak electricity. Very large battery packs, however, are needed to store the electric energy for daily use.

"The Dodge Sprinter plug-in hybrids will be placed in multiple locations within the United States," Wright added. "The technology will be exposed to different drive cycles yielding information to develop the next generation of Lithium-ion batteries."

Johnson Controls-Saft is a joint venture that has brought together Johnson Controls—the world's leading supplier of automotive batteries and a company deeply experienced in integrated automotive systems solutions—with Saft, a French advanced energy storage solutions provider with extensive Li-ion battery expertise.

Company Profile

"Our mission to exceed customer expectations gives us the latitude to bring a powerful set of capabilities to our markets and tap into emerging needs and trends," said CEO John M. Barth. "Throughout our 120-year history, Johnson Controls has continued to transform itself for continued success, and 2005 is no exception. The impending acquisition of York International doubles our market opportunity, and by combining our controls expertise with HVAC equipment, we will be advantaged in the marketplace and have strengthened capabilities to penetrate the huge building services market. In the automotive battery market, where we are the undisputed leader, we extended our leadership from the Americas and Europe to Asia, and are prepared to be a strong player in the hybrid vehicle market.

"In automotive interiors, we established a blueprint for continued profitable growth by accelerating cost reductions, leveraging our global footprint and investing in innovative products. We are responsive to the various strategies of our customers, and Johnson Controls has the financial strength to deliver on their expectations."

Johnson Controls is strengthening its market leadership through the company's businesses:

Interior Experience focuses on the world's largest automakers and responds to their individual requirements, providing innovative interior components and systems that offer best-in-class functions and features. Johnson Controls offering includes seats, instrument panels, cockpits, electronics, door and overhead systems, as well as navigation and entertainment systems, designed to make the driving experience more comfortable, safe and enjoyable.

Building Efficiency enables facility managers to optimize comfort and energy efficiency in their buildings. As rising fuel prices make energy management even more essential, Johnson Controls helps its customers improve their building systems and reduce their energy-related costs by providing a single source of integrated heating/cooling, lighting, fire, and security products and services, supported by the largest building services force in the world.

Power Solutions services both automotive original equipment manufacturers and the battery aftermarket by providing advanced battery technology, coupled with systems engineering, marketing and service expertise. Johnson Controls produces more than 80 million lead-acid batteries annually, and offers nickel-metal-hydride and lithium-ion battery technology to power hybrid vehicles.

Shortcomings to Bear in Mind

■ Johnson Controls does considerable business with the automotive industry, which has a history of doing poorly during bad times.

■ *Value Line Investment Survey* had this negative comment on March 28, 2008, according to analyst Iason Dalavagas, "Over the 3-to-5-year period, these shares have below-average appreciation potential."

Reasons to Buy

■ On January 7, 2008, Johnson Controls announced the acquisition of Metro Mechanical, Inc, a mechanical services company located in Phoenix. Specific terms of the agreement were not disclosed.

Metro Mechanical, Inc. provides retrofit, maintenance and repair services for commercial, industrial and institutional customers throughout the Phoenix region. The company has some 200 employees.

"Acquiring Metro Mechanical, Inc. allows us to expand our offerings and deliver enhanced service to customers in Phoenix," said Steven Kallan, general manager, Phoenix service branch of Johnson Controls. "We are committed to continuing Metro Mechanical's dedication to customer service that has contributed to its position of leadership for over thirty-three years."

"Johnson Controls brings worldwide credibility, expanded capacity and a great vision for the growing Phoenix market," said Nick Ganem, president of operations, Metro Mechanical, Inc. "The employees of both organizations are committed to providing the best service in the market place and will now be able to offer a broader range of services to our customers."

About Metro Mechanical, Inc.

For three generations Metro Mechanical has supplied the finest commercial and industrial HVAC, sheet metal, plumbing, process piping and fire protection for a prestigious list of customers throughout the Valley of the Sun. The company excels in all phases of retrofit, optimization, modification, service, maintenance, and custom fabrication.

■ The company's automotive business is expected to expand in the years ahead as automakers continue outsourcing seating and interior systems in North America and Europe, as well as in emerging global markets.

What's more, the company's development of innovative features and application of new technologies for the automotive interior will strengthen the company's leadership position, as Johnson Controls makes its customers's vehicles more comfortable, convenient and safe.

■ The company engineers, manufactures and installs control systems that automate a building's heating, ventilating and air conditioning, as well as its lighting and fire-safety equipment. Its Metasys Facility Management System automates a building's mechanical systems for optimal comfort levels while using the least amount of energy. In addition, it monitors fire sensors and building access, controls lights, tracks equipment maintenance and helps building managers make better decisions.

■ The company's Controls Group does business with more than 7,000 school districts, colleges, and universities as well as over 2,000 health care organizations. These customers benefit from performance contracting, a solution that lets them implement needed facility repairs and updates without up-front capital costs. Performance contracting uses a project's energy and operational cost savings to pay its costs over time. For instance, using a performance contract, Grady Health System in Atlanta was able to complete energy efficiency upgrades that will generate $20 million in savings over the next ten years.

- On July 25, 2007, Johnson Controls announced a three-for-one split of its stock. The split became effective October 2, 2007, to shareholders of record September 14, 2007. The company also declared a regular quarterly cash dividend of $.33 per share, which was paid as $.11 on a postsplit basis.

Mr. Barth said, "Johnson Controls is focused on improving its returns to shareholders through the combination of sustained profitable growth, improving our return on invested capital, business diversification and improved cash flows to maintain a strong

capital structure while investing in value accretive acquisitions." He added that the company anticipates continuing to increase its cash dividend in line with earnings growth.

Fiscal 2007 marked Johnson Controls' thirty-second consecutive year that it has increased its dividend. The company's last stock split, on a two-for-one basis, was in January 2004. Since then the company's share price has approximately doubled.

- On March 15, 2008, Standard & Poor's *Stock Reports* rated Johnson Controls a BUY. Efraim Levy, CFA, said, "We expect growth to exceed that of peers, and with greater earnings stability. We project that diversification in geography, products and customers will help JCI withstand weakness at the domestic auto manufacturers."

SECTOR: **Consumer Discretionary**
BETA COEFFICIENT: **1.15**
10-YEAR COMPOUND EARNINGS PER SHARE GROWTH: **15.8%**
10-YEAR COMPOUND DIVIDENDS PER SHARE GROWTH: **12.1%**

		2007	2006	2005	2004	2003	2002	2001	2000
Revenues (Mil)		34,624	32,235	27,883	25,363	22,646	20,103	18,427	17,155
Net Income (Mil)		1,252	1,028	909	818	683	601	542	472
Earnings per share		2.09	1.75	1.50	1.41	1.20	1.09	0.85	0.85
Dividends per share		0.44	0.37	0.33	0.28	0.24	0.22	0.21	0.19
Price	high	44.5	30.0	25.1	21.1	19.4	15.5	13.8	10.9
	low	28.1	22.1	17.5	16.5	12.0	11.5	8.0	7.6

CONSERVATIVE GROWTH

Johnson & Johnson

One Johnson & Johnson Plaza ◻ New Brunswick, NJ 08933 ◻ (800) 950-5089 ◻ Dividend reinvestment plan available ◻ Web site: *www.jnj.com* ◻ Listed: NYSE ◻ Ticker symbol: JNJ ◻ S&P rating: A+ ◻ Value Line financial strength rating: A++

On November 15, 2007, Johnson & Johnson announced a series of organizational changes, including the creation of a new strategy and growth organization to sharpen its focus on opportunities outside its traditional areas of interest and in the growing intersections of health care and the creation of two new business operating groups. The changes are

designed to accelerate growth for Johnson & Johnson by building on the unique strengths afforded by the company's broad base of businesses and decentralized structure.

A new Office of Strategy and Growth will identify opportunities for future growth that are distinct from those being pursued by the company's existing businesses; a

Surgical Care Group will focus on advancing technologies, solutions and services to enhance patient care in the surgical setting; and a Comprehensive Care Group will create portfolios to address some of the world's most chronic and pervasive conditions, such as metabolic disorders, through the convergence of technologies, products and services.

"These decisions recognize that a new environment is emerging in human health and well-being," said CEO William C. Weldon. "They reflect our assessment of the best way for us to capture and develop the opportunities associated with those changes and they capitalize on the unique, broadly based, decentralized approach of Johnson & Johnson."

Company Profile

Johnson & Johnson is the largest and most comprehensive health care company in the world, with 2006 sales of more than $53 billion. JNJ offers a broad line of consumer products, ethical and over-the-counter drugs, as well as various other medical devices and diagnostic equipment.

The company has a stake in a wide variety of endeavors: anti-infectives, biotechnology, cardiology and circulatory diseases, the central nervous system, diagnostics, gastrointestinals, minimally invasive therapies, nutraceuticals, orthopaedics, pain management, skin care, vision care, women's health, and wound care.

Johnson & Johnson has more than 200 operating companies in fifty-four countries, selling some 50,000 products in more than 175 countries.

One of Johnson & Johnson's premier assets is its well-entrenched brand names, which are widely known in the United States as well as abroad. As a marketer, moreover, JNJ's reputation for quality has enabled it to build strong ties to health care providers.

Its international presence includes not only marketing, but also production and distribution capability in a vast array of regions outside the United States. One advantage of JNJ's worldwide organization: Markets such as China, Latin America and Africa offer growth potential for mature product lines.

The company's well-known trade names include Band-Aid adhesive bandages, Tylenol, Stayfree, Carefree and Sure & Natural feminine hygiene products, Mylanta, Pepcid AC, Neutrogena, Johnson's baby powder, shampoo and oil, and Reach toothbrushes.

The company's professional items include ligatures and sutures, mechanical wound closure products, diagnostic products, medical equipment and devices, surgical dressings, surgical apparel and accessories, and disposable contact lenses.

Shortcomings to Bear in Mind

▪ Don't invest in Johnson & Johnson if you are looking for instant riches. This is an ultra-conservative stock, not an aggressive one. This is made clear if you examine the Beta coefficient, which is a mere .55. That is fine if you are afraid of your shadow and can't stand the thought of risking your hard-earned cash in the stock market. But if you are more aggressive, you will suffer in a rising market, since a Beta of .55 means JNJ will rise only 5.5 percent when the market climbs 10 percent.

Reasons to Buy

▪ Net earnings and diluted earnings per share for the 2007, as reported, were $10.6 billion and $3.63, decreases of 4.3 percent and 2.7 percent, respectively, as compared with 2006. Full-year 2007 net earnings included after-tax charges of $807 million for in-process research and development; $528 million for restructuring; an after-tax, noncash charge of $441 million for the write-down of the intangible asset related to NATRECOR (nesiritide); and a gain of $267 million for international tax restructuring. Full-year 2006 net earnings included after-tax charges for in-process research and development of $448 million and an after-tax gain of $368 million associated with the termination of the Guidant acquisition agreement. Excluding these special items, net earnings for 2007 were $12.1 billion and earnings per share were $4.15, representing increases of 8.6 percent and 10.4 percent, respectively, as compared with the same period in 2006.

"Despite challenges in certain markets, our broad base of businesses allowed us to achieve solid results in 2007, building on our foundation of long-term profitable growth," said CEO Weldon. "It was a year of significant progress in our pipeline; the successful integration of Pfizer Consumer Healthcare; and the creation of new organizational structures focused on future growth."

■ On April 15, 2008, Standard & Poor's *Stock Reports* rated the company a BUY. Robert M. Gold said, "JNJ's deal with Pfizer added brands such as Listerine, Nicorette, Visine and Neosporin. We believe revenue and cost synergies will drive cash EPS (earnings per share) accretion by 2008, and we think the deal will boost revenue and cash flow visibility amid challenging medical device and pharmaceutical conditions."

■ Argus Research Company also regarded Johnson & Johnson a BUY. On January 28, 2008, Martha Freitag, CFA said, "The company's product pipeline remains on track with seven to ten applications planned for approval of new medications that could reach the market in 2008 through 2010."

■ "This stock may prove to be an excellent long-term option if recent stock market turbulence continues," said Tom Nikic, writing for *Value Line Investment Survey* on February 29, 2008.

"JNJ's three-to-five-year capital appreciation potential is just about in line with the *Value Line* median. Too, the allure of this high-quality issue is magnified when the current economic environment is taken into account. Indeed the struggling economy bodes ill for many businesses, but

not for JNJ. The healthcare industry is not strongly influenced by the economy."

■ Johnson & Johnson has thirty-four drugs with annual sales exceeding $50 million; twenty-four drugs with annual sales of more than $100 million; and more than 100 drugs that are sold in more than 200 countries.

■ Johnson & Johnson Consumer Products Company introduced a revolutionary liquid bandage that is changing the way consumers treat minor cuts and scrapes. Band-Aid Brand Liquid Bandage provides superior protection and optimal healing and stays on hard-to-cover areas like fingers and knuckles.

The bandage creates a clear seal that keeps out water and germs to help prevent infection and promote quick healing. It stays on until it naturally sloughs off as the wound heals. Band-Aid Brand Liquid Bandage contains 2-octyl cyanoacrylate, the same base material found in Dermabond Topical Skin Adhesive, a prescription device marketed by Ethicon Products. Both are manufactured by Closure Medical Corporation. Used by physicians to close wounds and incisions in place of stitches or staples, Dermabond adhesive acts as a barrier that seals out bacteria that can lead to infection.

■ "Our medical device and diagnostics (MD&D) franchises continue to comprise the world's largest medical technology business," said Mr. Weldon on March 12, 2008. "We treat some of the world's most pervasive medical conditions with a more comprehensive approach than any other company in this field. In 2007, these businesses achieved sales of $21.7 billion, with total growth of 7.2 percent. This was solid growth in light of a significant decline in the market for drug-eluting stents (DES), which took a toll on sales of the CYPHER Sirolimus-eluting Coronary Stent. Excluding the impact of the DES market decline, we saw strong total growth of nearly 13 percent in our MD&D franchises."

■ Mr. Weldon goes on to say, "We enjoy strong competitive positions across our diverse franchises, with more than 80 percent of MD&D sales coming from businesses in the number one or number two market positions. Our vision care business surpassed the $2 billion mark for the first time in its history.

"These businesses achieved a number of important product launches and regulatory approvals, including U.S. approval of the REALIZE Adjustable Gastric Band, a device for treatment of morbid obesity; the ANIMAS 2020 Insulin Pump, the smallest full-featured insulin pump on the market; and GENESEARCH Breast Lymph Node (BLN) Assay, a novel molecular diagnostic tool for detecting the spread of breast cancer to the lymph nodes while the patient is undergoing surgery. This assay helps breast cancer patients and their doctors avoid the challenges of a second surgery to remove cancerous lymph node tissue following results of a biopsy. It was cited by *Time* magazine as the second-leading medical breakthrough of 2007.

"We are well positioned in 2008 with a robust pipeline and strategic development programs in Orthopaedics, biosurgicals, bariatric surgery, vision care, and other major categories."

■ Mr. Weldon also said, "Thanks to the power of our operating model and the character of the people we attract, we have been able to deliver exceptionally consistent performance decade after decade. In 2007, we achieved:

- Our seventy-fifth consecutive year of sales increases.
- Our twenty-fourth consecutive year of earnings increases, adjusted for special items.
- Our forty-fifth consecutive year of dividend increases.

"This is a track record matched by few, if any, companies in history."

SECTOR: **Health Care**
BETA COEFFICIENT: **.55**
10-YEAR COMPOUND EARNINGS PER SHARE GROWTH: **11.6%**
10-YEAR COMPOUND DIVIDENDS PER SHARE GROWTH: **14.5%**

		2007	2006	2005	2004	2003	2002	2001	2000
Revenues (Mil)		61,095	53,324	50,514	47,348	41,862	36,298	32,317	29,139
Net Income (Mil)		10,576	11,053	10,411	8,509	7,197	6,651	5,668	4,800
Earnings per share		3.63	3.73	3.35	2.84	2.40	2.18	1.84	1.63
Dividends per share		1.66	1.46	1.28	1.10	0.93	0.82	0.70	0.62
Price	high	68.8	69.4	70.0	64.2	59.1	65.9	61.0	53.0
	low	59.7	56.6	59.8	49.2	48.0	41.4	40.3	33.1

CONSERVATIVE GROWTH

Kellogg Company

One Kellogg Square ❑ P. O. Box 3599 ❑ Battle Creek, MI 49016-3599 ❑ (269) 961-6636 ❑ Dividend reinvestment plan available ❑ Web site: *www.kelloggcompany.com* ❑ Ticker symbol: K ❑ Listed: NYSE ❑ S&P rating: A— ❑ Value Line financial strength rating: B++

On December 12, 2007, Kellogg announced that it is expanding its W.K. Kellogg Institute for Food and Nutrition Research (WKKI) located in Battle Creek,

Michigan, to continue to meet business needs and to achieve continued growth. The 157,000-square- foot pilot plant and office space addition will expand Kellogg Company's existing global center for research and innovation activities. The $40 million expansion and $14 million investment in pilot plant equipment (over the next ten years) falls within Kellogg Company's previously reported capital expenditure guidance.

Since the WKKI facility opened in 1997, Kellogg Company's net sales have doubled from $6 billion to almost $12 billion, and net sales from innovation have also almost doubled. In addition, numerous process capabilities have been added to WKKI as the company extended its business into new categories, and the number of employees in the facility almost doubled to support these new technologies and the company's growth.

The WKKI expansion will enable Kellogg to continue to fuel top-line growth through additional pilot plant space, enhanced process scalability and additional space for a flexible team environment and total technical community. The addition will also ensure WKKI continues to be a "best in class" facility, allowing the company to continue to successfully retain and recruit world-class research and development talent.

"Innovation is a core component of Kellogg's business strategy and we have a proven track record of delivering results from our innovations," said CEO David Mackay. "In 2006, 17 percent of net sales or almost $1.9 billion dollars were delivered through innovations launched in the last three years. The expansion of the WKKI facility ensures we can continue to drive strong innovation and supports our goal of delivering sustainable growth for our shareholders."

Company Profile

Dating back to 1906, Kellogg is the world's leading producer of cereal and a leading producer of convenience foods, including cookies, crackers, toaster pastries, cereal bars, frozen waffles, meat alternatives, pie crusts, and cones.

The company's brands include Kellogg's®, Keebler®, Pop-Tarts®, Eggo®, Cheez-It®, Nutri-Grain®, Rice Krispies®, Special K®, Murray®, Austin®, Morningstar Farms®, Famous Amos®, Carr's®, Plantation®, and Kashi®.

Kellogg icons such as Tony the Tiger™, Snap! Crackle! Pop!™, and Ernie Keebler™ are among the most recognized characters in advertising. The company's products are manufactured in nineteen countries and marketed in more than 160 countries around the world.

Shortcomings to Bear in Mind

■ Over the past ten years, earnings per share and dividends per share have inched ahead at a snail's page.

Reasons to Buy

■ On January 30, 2008, Kellogg Company reported strong 2007 earnings. Fourth quarter earnings were $0.44 per share. Annual earnings were $2.76 per share, representing the sixth consecutive year that the company has met or exceeded its long-term EPS targets.

Reported net earnings for full-year 2007 were $1,103 million, a 10 percent increase over last year's $1,004 million. Earnings were $2.76 per diluted share, an increase of 10 percent from $2.51 per share in 2006. Reported net earnings in the fourth quarter of 2007 were $176 million, or $0.44 per diluted share, compared to $182 million, or $0.45 per share, in fourth quarter of 2006. This result included a double-digit increase in advertising investment, significantly higher commodity, fuel, energy, and benefit cost inflation and upfront investment charges of $0.03 per share versus $0.08 per share in 2006. For the full year, upfront investment charges were $0.18 per share versus $0.14 per share in 2006. In addition, Kellogg recently announced acquisitions relating to Bear Naked, Inc.; and the Gardenburger brand in the U.S.; as well as the January 2008 acquisition of The United Bakers Group in Russia.

"Despite significant additional cost pressures in 2007, our company posted another year of strong growth," said Mr. Mackay. "And for the first time, we generated more than $1 billion of cash flow. We also continued to invest cash back into the company's growth through higher up-front costs, a double-digit increase in advertising and several recent acquisitions."

Reported net sales in 2007 increased by 8 percent to $11.8 billion; fourth quarter sales were $2,794 million, representing 8 percent growth from the fourth quarter of 2006. Internal net sales growth, which excludes the effect of foreign-currency translation and acquisitions, was 5 percent for the full year as well as 5 percent for the fourth quarter.

- "The No. 1 cereal maker may be the best-managed U.S. food company," said Andrew Bary, writing for *Barron's* on February 11, 2008. He also said, "Kellogg has taken share from archrival General Mills in cereal and has built a strong snack-food business with products such as NutriGrain bars and Rice Krispies Treats."

- Heart disease is the leading cause of death in the United States. Most people who suffer from heart disease are victims of its two principal risk factors: high blood pressure and high cholesterol. In response to this serious health crisis, Kellogg introduced Smart Start Healthy Heart in 2005, the only nationally distributed cereal with oat bran, potassium and low sodium, ingredients that can help lower both blood pressure and cholesterol. The cereal has been certified by the American Heart Association.

Kellogg Company's legacy is based on the philosophy that people can improve their health by eating a balanced diet and exercising. Medical experts agree that there are steps that people can take to reduce the risks of heart disease, including making changes to their diets.

"When it comes to heart health, we can literally take our lives into our own hands by making lifestyle changes that can help lower risks of heart disease," said Andrea Pennington, M.D., author of "The Pennington Plan," noted lifestyle expert and past medical director of the Discovery Health Channel. "Smart Start Healthy Heart is an excellent choice for people trying to take simple and immediate steps to improve their heart health."

Smart Start Healthy Heart joins the Smart Start lineup, including Smart Start Antioxidants and Smart Start Soy Protein, products that offer health benefits for people who are actively seeking ways to improve their health. The new cereal is a combination of lightly sweetened toasted oat bran flakes and crunchy whole grain wheat and oat clusters.

To commemorate the introduction of this new product, Kellogg launched "Simple Start to a Healthy Heart," an initiative aimed at increasing Americans' awareness of the risks of heart disease and actions they can take to address those risks.

- On February 8, 2008, Kellogg announced plans for a host of new products hitting store shelves, as the Kellogg Company continues its focus on innovation.

Since WKKI opened in 1997, the company's net sales from innovation have almost doubled. In addition, the company's investment in research and development has increased significantly from $106.4 million in 2002 to $179.3 million in 2007.

"We're proud of our proven track record of delivering results from our innovations," said Dr. Donna Banks, senior vice president, global innovation. "In 2007, approximately 17 percent of net sales or almost $2 billion dollars were delivered through innovations launched in the last three years. We're very excited about the expansion of our WKKI facility and about our new product offerings launching this year."

Kellogg Company's recently launched new products include:

Health and Wellness: Wholesome Cereals and Snacks. New adult cereals provide tasty ways to stay on track with diet and weight-management goals, while kids can enjoy whole-grain goodness in two new great-tasting cereals. New, flavorful snacks also offer more options for snacking healthier without sacrificing great taste.

■ Animal Planet™ Wild Animal Crunch™ lets kids go wild with a vanilla-chocolate flavored, whole-grain cereal that's a good source of fiber. Available in January in four collectors' packages featuring real photographs of meerkats, polar bears, pandas and seals.

■ Mini-Wheats® Unfrosted cereal allows consumers to enjoy the lightly toasted, whole-grain flavor of Mini-Wheats cereal with no added sugar. Product was available nationwide last October.

■ Special K Bliss™ bars feature tantalizing, sweet fruit-flavored pieces, crispy cereal and a chocolatey bottom layer. The bars are available in two exciting flavor combinations—Chocolatey Dipped Raspberry and Chocolatey Dipped Orange—and are 90 calories. Special K Bliss bars hit store shelves in January.

■ Pop-Tarts® Toaster Pastries with One Serving of Whole Grain contain one serving (16 grams) of whole grain in each pastry, almost doubling the amount of whole grains the average American gets in their diet. Get the whole grains you need in two favorite Pop-Tarts flavors—Strawberry and Brown Sugar Cinnamon. Product was available beginning in January.

■ "Annual double-digit earnings growth to 2010-2012 is very achievable," said William G. Ferguson, an analyst for *Value Line Investment Survey*, on February 1, 2008. "The main reason for our confidence in Kellogg's ability to sustain growth is that the company has never wavered on spending for product innovations, brand building, and advertising, even during this difficult cost environment. Going forward, we expect Kellogg to invest more in advertising (as a percentage of sales) and marketing than most of its industry peers."

■ On March 7, 2008, Argus Research Company called Kellogg a BUY. Erin Ashley Smith said, "Kellogg has been a consistent performer over the past few years, reflecting its overall strong fundamentals and investments in building its brands. We expect the company to continue to deliver solid results in 2008."

SECTOR: Consumer Staples
BETA COEFFICIENT: .70
10-YEAR COMPOUND EARNINGS PER SHARE GROWTH: 5%
10-YEAR COMPOUND DIVIDENDS PER SHARE GROWTH: 3.6%

	2007	2006	2005	2004	2003	2002	2001	2000
Revenues (Mil)	11,776	10,907	10,177	9,614	8,812	8,304	8,853	6,955
Net Income (Mil)	1,103	1,004	980	891	787	711	533	652
Earnings per share	2.76	2.51	2.26	2.14	1.92	1.73	1.31	1.61
Dividends per share	1.24	1.14	1.06	1.01	1.01	1.01	1.01	1.00
Price high	56.9	51.0	47.0	45.3	38.6	37.0	34.0	32.0
low	48.7	42.4	42.4	37.0	27.8	29.0	24.3	20.8

Kimco Realty Corporation

3333 New Hyde Park Road □ Suite 100 □ New Hyde Park, NY 11042-0020 □ Listed: NYSE □ (866) 831-4297 □ Direct dividend reinvestment plan available □ Web site: *www.kimcorealty.com* □ Ticker symbol: KIM □ S&P rating: A+ □ Value Line financial strength rating: B++

On January 7, 2008, Kimco Realty announced the following major acquisition, disposition, and financing activity for the fourth quarter 2007. During the quarter, the company acquired four shopping center properties totaling 830,000 square feet for approximately $116.6 million in California, Arizona, and Mexico. The company disposed of nine shopping center properties totaling 1.3 million square feet for approximately $226.3 million. Year-to-date, the company has acquired eighty-one shopping center properties totaling 8.8 million square feet for $2.2 billion and disposed of 55 shopping center properties totaling 6.1 million square feet for $891.0 million. Transactions between Kimco affiliated entities are excluded from these totals.

Company Profile

Kimco Realty Corporation is the largest publicly traded real estate investment trust (REIT) that owns and operates a portfolio of neighborhood and community shopping centers (measured by gross leasable area). The company has specialized in the acquisition, development and management of well-located shopping centers with strong growth potential. Kimco has interests in 720 properties, comprised of 645 shopping centers, thirty-two retail store leases, and other projects totaling about 104 million square feet of leasable area in forty-two states, Canada and Mexico.

Since incorporating in 1966, Kimco has specialized in the acquisition, development, and management of well-located centers with strong growth potential. Self-administered and self-managed, the company's focus is to increase the cash flow and enhance the value of its shopping center properties through strategic re-tenanting, redevelopment, renovation and expansion, and to make selective acquisitions of neighborhood and community shopping centers that have below market-rate leases or other cash flow growth potential.

A substantial portion of KIM's income consists of rent received under long-term leases, most of which provide for the payment of fixed-base rents and a pro rata share of various expenses. Many of the leases also provide for the payment of additional rent as a percentage of gross sales.

KIM's neighborhood and community shopping center properties are designed to attract local area customers and typically are anchored by a supermarket, discount department store, or drugstore, offering day-to-day necessities rather than high-priced luxury items. Among the company's major tenants are Kmart, Wal-Mart, Kohl's, and TJX Companies.

Kimco's core strategy is to acquire older shopping centers carrying below-market rents. This space is then released at much higher rates.

Funds from Operations

REITs are not valued by earnings per share (EPS), but rather by funds from operations (FFO) per share. FFO is calculated by adding net income and depreciation expense and then subtracting profits from the sale of assets. If a REIT pays out 90 percent or more of its taxable income in dividends, it is exempt from paying federal income taxes. FFO per share is in excess of net income because depreciation is added in. This means that a REIT such as Kimco pays out only about 66 percent of its FFO in dividends, with the balance of 34 percent available for acquisitions and improving existing properties.

Shortcomings to Bear in Mind

- As most investors are aware, dividends under a new federal tax law are now taxed at a maximum rate of 15 percent. Unfortunately, this does not apply to dividends paid out by REITS. That's because real estate investment trusts generally don't pay corporate income tax.
- On March 15, 2008, Standard & Poor's *Stock Reports* gave Kimco a HOLD rating. On the other hand, the analyst, Robert McMillan, had these kind words for the company, "We believe that KIM, as one of the largest owners and operators of neighborhood and community shopping centers in the United States with a broad array of established relationships, will generate above-average rent growth, and that it deserves to trade at a premium to peers. We also view its success in establishing portfolios in Canada and Mexico as a positive."

Reasons to Buy

- Bridget Adams, writing for Argus Research Company, also had encouraging comments on January 29, 2008. "We believe that the company will be able to weather the impact of the disappointing same-store data reported in December, thanks to the diversity and strategic positioning of its portfolio. In particular, we note that no single tenant accounts for more than 3.3 percent of the company's base rent." She goes on to say, "We believe that Kimco's Mexican development pipeline (with yields of 12 percent to 16 percent) and, to a lesser extent, the U.S. pipeline (with yields of 9 percent to 11 percent) will continue to drive growth."
- In the same vein, *Value Line Investment Survey* also chipped in with these thoughts on January 18, 2008. Sigourney B. Romaine said,

"We think Kimco will fare relatively well if the economy slows in 2008. That's because most of its shopping centers offer consumer staples that people will continue to buy if times get harder than we believe will happen."

Highlights for 2007

- Increased 2007 FFO per diluted share by 17.2 percent over 2006 FFO per diluted share
- Averaged growth in same-store net operating income of 4.5 percent over the past eight quarters
- Increased the FFO contribution from investment management programs by over $57 million or 44 percent from 2006
- Recognized $39.3 million of promoted income upon the sale of twenty-one assets from KROP
- Significantly increased market position in Mexico with the acquisition of fifty new properties or development projects totaling 5.4 million square feet for $332 million
- Entered market in Chile with a new joint venture and acquisition of four shopping centers
- Acquired eighty-one shopping centers totaling 8.8 million square feet for $2.3 billion
- Disposed of fifty-five shopping centers totaling 6.1 million square feet for $891 million
- Recognized $57.2 million of income from preferred equity investments, including approximately $24 million in residual participation from the sale or re-financing of eighteen investments
- Recognized $75.5 million, net of tax, from investment in Albertson's
- Completed an offering of $300 million, 5.70 percent senior unsecured notes
- Completed a $460 million preferred stock offering
- Increased the amount of the company's various credit facilities by $650 million
- Kimco's customers include some of the strongest and most rapidly growing chains in the United States, such as Costco, Home

Depot, Best Buy, Wal-Mart, Value City, Target, and Kohl's.

■ Nearly all of the company's revenue is contractual. This means that even when a retailer's sales slump, it does not change the rent they must pay to Kimco under the lease agreement or the value of the company's real estate.

■ Knowledge of local markets and trends is crucial to success in the real estate sector. Kimco's decentralized asset management staff—situated in such cities as New York, Los Angeles, Chicago, Philadelphia, Dallas, Phoenix, Tampa, Charlotte, and Dayton, provides knowledge of real estate developments that are analyzed by professionals on the scene.

■ Kimco's success comes not by accident but as the careful product of business principles that have remained firmly in place since the company was founded in the 1950s. The company invests in properties that are undervalued assets, where management knows it will be able to capitalize on the margin between the price at which it can buy the property and the price at which it can lease it. The average rent on properties in Kimco's portfolio remains below the market, providing the company with significant upside potential.

■ On July 10, 2006, Kimco Realty and Pan Pacific Retail Properties, Inc. announced that the two companies had entered into a definitive merger agreement.

Under the terms of the agreement, Kimco acquired all of the outstanding shares of Pan Pacific for a total merger consideration of $70 per share in cash. Kimco may elect to issue up to $10 per share of the total merger consideration in the form of Kimco common stock to be based upon the ten-day average closing price of Kimco shares two trading days prior to the Pan Pacific stockholders' meeting to approve the transaction. The election to issue Kimco common stock may be made up to fifteen days prior to the Pan Pacific stockholders' meeting and may be revoked by Kimco at any time if the revocation would not delay the stockholders' meeting for more than ten business days.

The transaction has a total value of about $4 billion, including Pan Pacific's outstanding debt totaling approximately $1.1 billion and approximately $2.9 billion in equity value. Kimco has received financing commitments totaling up to $3.0 billion, which it may use to fund all or a portion of the total merger consideration.

Pan Pacific's portfolio totals 138 properties, encompassing approximately 22.6 million square feet. Kimco expects to target a substantial number of the properties for its strategic co-investment programs. These programs have produced solid investment returns and growth while further expanding Kimco's investment and property management business.

SECTOR: Financials
BETA COEFFICIENT: 1.00
10-YEAR COMPOUND EARNINGS PER SHARE GROWTH: 10.6%
10-YEAR COMPOUND DIVIDENDS PER SHARE GROWTH: 9.9%

	2007	2006	2005	2004	2003	2002	2001	2000
Rental Income (Mil)	682	594	506	517	480	433	450	459
Net Income (Mil)	423	428	364	282	244	226	236	205
Earnings per share	1.65	1.70	1.52	1.19	1.11	1.08	1.03	0.96
Funds from Operations	2.59	2.21	2.00	1.78	1.62	1.52	1.50	1.35
Dividends per share	1.52	1.44	1.27	1.16	1.10	1.05	0.98	0.91
Price high	53.6	84.0	33.4	29.6	22.9	16.9	17.0	14.9
low	33.7	61.3	25.9	19.8	15.1	13.0	13.6	10.9

Lowe's Companies, Inc.

1000 Lowe's Boulevard ☐ Mooresville, NC 28117 ☐ (704) 758-3579 ☐ Direct dividend reinvestment plan available ☐ Web site: *www.lowes.com* ☐ Fiscal years end Friday closest to January 31 of following year ☐ Listed: NYSE ☐ Ticker symbol: LOW ☐ S&P rating: A+ ☐ Value Line financial strength rating: A+

"Customers have always looked for ways to make their homes unique, and Lowe's always strives to offer the most innovative products," said a company official in 2007. "We stock more than 40,000 products at everyday low prices in twenty distinct product categories, including everything needed to decorate and enhance the home.

"We continue to improve our offering and innovative products and brands customers know and trust. Our inspiring product lines offer value at all points along the price continuum and feature premium brands such as John Deere mowers, power tools by DeWalt, fashion plumbing by Kohler, and millwork from Therma-Tru, to name just a few.

"We added new products and merchandise sets during 2006, offering customers many new choices. In appliances, we strengthened our already strong lineup with the new Frigidaire Elements kitchen line, an exclusive at Lowe's. This, along with high-efficiency laundry products from Bosch, Samsung, Maytag, and Whirlpool, demonstrate our commitment to offer brands that are compelling and innovative.

"In composite decking, we are adding Trex, the leading brand in the industry, and we are strengthening our grill lineup with Char-Broil TEC gas grills that feature patented infrared technology. In 2007, we will enhance our paint offering with high-quality Valspar Signature Colors, Valspar Duramax, and Valspar Ultra Premium brands. The Martha Stewart Colors palette will also be available exclusively at Lowe's.

"While national brands are important, in some product categories brand is less impor-

tant, and style, quality and other features, including price, drive the purchase decision.

"We use our Lowe's-owned brands, such as Real Organized storage organization, GardenPlus lawn and landscaping products and Portfolio lighting for product line extensions to offer customers more choices with great value."

Company Profile

Lowe's Companies, Inc. is the second-largest domestic retailer of home-improvement products serving the do-it-yourself and commercial business customers. (Home Depot is number one.) Capitalizing on a growing number of U.S. households (about 100 million) the company has expanded from fifteen stores in 1962. The company sells more than 40,000 home-improvement products, including plumbing and electrical products, tools, building materials, hardware, outdoor hard lines, appliances, lumber, nursery and gardening products, millwork, paint, sundries, cabinets and furniture. Lowe's has often been listed as one of the "100 Best Companies to Work for in America."

The company obtains its products from about 6,500 merchandise vendors from around the globe. In most instances, Lowe's deals directly with foreign manufacturers, rather than third-party importers.

In order to maintain appropriate inventory levels in stores and to enhance efficiency and distribution, Lowe's operates seven highly automated, efficient, state-of-the-art regional distribution centers (RDCs). RDCs are strategically situated in North Carolina, Georgia, Ohio, Indiana, Pennsylvania, Washington, and Texas.

In 2000, the company broke ground in Findlay, Ohio, on an $80 million regional distribution center. Completed in October 2001, the 1.25-million-square-foot facility employs 500 people and supplies products to some 100 stores throughout the lower Great Lakes region.

Lowe's serves both retail and commercial business customers. Retail customers are primarily do-it-yourself homeowners and others buying for personal and family use. Commercial business customers include building contractors, repair and remodeling contractors, electricians, landscapers, painters, plumbers, and commercial building maintenance professionals.

During 1999, Lowe's acquired Eagle Hardware & Garden, a thirty-six-store chain of home-improvement and garden centers in the West. The acquisition accelerated Lowe's' West Coast expansion and provided a stepping-stone for the company into ten new states and a number of key metropolitan markets.

In recent years, the company has been transforming its store base from a chain of small stores into a chain of home-improvement warehouses. The current prototype store (the largest in the industry) has 150,000 square feet of sales floor and another 35,000 dedicated to lawn and garden products. The company is in the midst of its most aggressive expansion in company history. Lowe's is investing $2 billion a year and opening more than one store each week.

Shortcomings to Bear in Mind

■ On February 25, 2008, Lowe's reported net earnings of $408 million for the quarter ended February 1, 2008, a 33.4 percent decline over the same period a year ago. Diluted earnings per share declined 30.0 percent to $0.28 from $0.40 in the fourth quarter of 2006. For the fiscal year ended February 1, 2008, net earnings declined 9.5 percent to $2.81 billion while diluted earnings per share declined 6.5 percent to $1.86.

Reasons to Buy

■ "Fourth quarter and fiscal year 2007 sales fell short of our plan as we faced an unprecedented decline in housing turnover, falling home prices in many areas and turbulent mortgage markets that impacted both sentiment related to home improvement purchases as well as consumers' access to capital," said CEO Robert A. Niblock. "While our results fell short of our expectations, I want to thank our more than 215,000 employees whose customer focus allowed us to capture market share in both the quarter and the year. Those market share gains combined with appropriate expense management in a very challenging environment for the home improvement industry allowed us to deliver respectable annual earnings per share.

"As we look to fiscal 2008, we know the next several quarters will be challenging on many fronts as industry sales are likely to remain soft," Niblock continued. "We remain focused on what we can control: providing great customer service while managing expenses and offering customers the best shopping experience in home improvement. As the year progresses, the recent Federal Reserve interest rate cuts and the approved fiscal stimulus package are expected to lend support to the broader economy and the consumer. As a result, many of the headwinds facing the housing market and the home improvement industry should lessen, and consumers' confidence in investing in and improving their homes should improve."

■ On February 26, 2008, Standard & Poor's *Stock Reports* gave Lowe's a BUY rating. Michael Souers said, "We think the aging of homes, home ownership rates near historical highs, and the increased net worth of baby boomers are powerful long-term demographic drivers that should help mitigate the continued slowdown in housing turnover we see for 2007 and 2008. In addition, despite concerns about interest rates and overall consumer spending, we believe consumers will continue to allocate a fair portion of their discretionary income to home improvement projects, as they view their homes as investments."

■ On February 25, 2008, Argus Company Research also viewed Lowe's as a BUY. Christopher Graja, CFA, said "While the shares remain under the cloud of a difficult housing market, we think the ratio of reward-to-risk remains favorable for patient investors. On a fundamental basis, the company's financial strength is solid. Lowe's has operating margins that are well above the retail average, investment-grade debt ratings, and ownership of about 86 percent of its stores (big buildings on busy roads). Moreover, the company appears to be gaining market share in many categories.

"In our view, the company has all four of the attributes we look for in a retail stock: the ability to boost sales by opening stores, adding new products and taking market share; the ability to increase margins through improving logistics and foreign imports; the ability to generate and deploy cash flow to new stores, dividends and share buybacks; and the potential for some multiple expansion."

■ "Lowe's stores feature wide, bright aisles, easy-to-read store signs and well-stock shelves, ensuring customers will find shopping our store an unparalleled experience in the home-improvement industry," said a company spokesman in 2007. "It is part of our culture to ensure customers have a great shopping experience in our stores.

"Therefore, each of our stores receives routine maintenance, enhancing the customer experience. Our departments are updated with new merchandise sets, creating more powerful product presentations, while providing customers clear, concise information to make the shopping experience easier. We combine attractive product displays with convenience and functionality, giving customers an inviting shopping environment. In 2006, we invested more than $650 million in our existing store base."

■ To enhance its extensive line of national brands, such as DeWalt, Armstrong, American Standard, Olympic, Owens Corning, Sylvania, Harbor Breeze, and Delta, the company is teaming up with vendors to offer preferred brands exclusive to Lowe's. These include Laura Ashley, Sta-Green, Troy-Bilt, Alexander Julian, among others.

In categories where preferred brands are not available, Lowe's has created its own brands, including Kobalt tools, Reliabilt doors and windows, and Top Choice lumber.

SECTOR: Consumer Discretionary
BETA COEFFICIENT: 1.00
10-YEAR COMPOUND EARNINGS PER SHARE GROWTH: 21.7%
10-YEAR COMPOUND DIVIDENDS PER SHARE GROWTH: 26.7%

		2007	2006	2005	2004	2003	2002	2001	2000
Revenues (Mil)		48,283	46,926	43,243	36,464	30,838	26,491	22,111	18,779
Net Income (Mil)		2,809	3,105	2,770	2,176	1,844	1,471	1,023	810
Earnings per share		1.86	1.99	1.73	1.36	1.18	0.95	0.65	0.53
Dividends per share		0.32	0.18	0.11	0.08	0.06	0.04	0.04	0.04
Price	high	35.7	34.8	34.9	60.5	30.3	25.0	24.5	16.8
	low	21.8	26.2	25.4	23.0	16.7	16.3	11.0	8.6

Lubrizol Corporation

29400 Lakeland Boulevard □ Wickliffe, OH 44092-2298 □ (440) 347-1206 □ Dividend reinvestment plan available
□ Web site: *www.lubrizol.com* □ Listed: NYSE □ Ticker symbol: LZ S&P rating: B+ □ Value Line financial strength rating: B+

On September 3, 2007, Lubrizol and Croda International plc reached an agreement for Lubrizol to purchase Croda's refrigeration lubricant business, with its annual revenues of $84 million.

The acquisition includes Croda's polyol ester and alkyl benzene refrigeration lubricant technology, Emkarate and Icematic brand names, customer lists, manufacturing know-how, and complementary intellectual property, but no manufacturing facilities.

"This business complements our existing refrigeration lubricants business, which is served by our subsidiary, CPI Engineering Services, Inc., headquartered in Midland, Michigan," said Val Pakis, Lubrizol Additives' vice president of industrial products. "This is an example of Lubrizol's strategy to grow through bolt-on acquisitions that enhance existing product lines."

Phase out of ozone-depleting refrigerant gases and conversion to environmentally friendly chemistries required by the Montreal protocol and the Kyoto Accord are expected to drive market growth for new refrigeration lubricants. In addition, demand for refrigerators and air conditioners in developing countries is increasing, providing strong growth for the related lubricants.

Company Profile

Lubrizol in an innovative specialty chemical company that produces and supplies technologies that improve the quality and performance of its customers' products in the global transportation, industrial, and consumer markets. Lubrizol's business is founded on technical leadership. "Innovation provides opportunities for us in growth markets as well as advantages over our competitors," according the Lubrizol

10-K publication (which is published annually by all public companies and is far more extensive and detailed than an annual report). From a base of some 2,800 patents, "we use our product development and formulation expertise to sustain our leading market positions and fuel our future growth. We create additives, ingredients, resins, and compounds that enhance the performance, quality and value of our customers' products, while minimizing their environmental impact. Our products are used in a broad range of applications, and are sold into stable markets such as those for engine oils, specialty driveline lubricants, and metalworking fluids, as well as higher growth markets such as personal care and pharmaceutical products and performance coatings and inks. Our specialty materials products are also used in a variety of industries, including construction, sporting goods, medical products, and automotive industries."

The 10-K goes on to say, "We are an industry leader in many of the markets in which our product lines compete. We also produce products with well-recognized brands names, such as "Anglamol (gear oil additives), Carbopol (acrylic thickeners for personal care products), Estane (thermoplastic polyurethane), and TempRite (chlorinated polyvinyl chloride resins and compounds used in plumbing, industrial, and fire-sprinkler systems).

"We are geographically diverse, with an extensive global manufacturing, supply chain, technical, and commercial infrastructure. We operate facilities in twenty-seven countries, including production facilities in twenty-one countries and laboratories in nine countries, in key regions around the world through the efforts of about 7,800 employees. Including the 2004 acquisition of Noveon International for the period ended December 31, 2004, we derived about 48 percent of our consolidated total revenues from North America, 28 percent from Europe, 18 percent from the Asia/Pacific and the Middle East regions, and 6 percent from Latin America. We sell our products in more than 100 countries."

Shortcomings to Bear in Mind

■ "We are disappointed with the overall results from the Lubrizol Advanced Materials segment," said CEO James Hambrick on February 8, 2008. "The very strong performance of our Consumers Specialties product line was overshadowed by margin and mix challenges in Engineered Polymers and demand weakness in Performance Coatings. The success of our third and fourth quarter pricing action gives us some confidence that consumers are recognizing the need for suppliers to recover the unprecedented increases in raw material costs. While encouraging, we will still need to take further actions during 2008 to restore margins to an acceptable level. Additionally, we must also position for increased volume growth. We are encouraged by the state of new products that all Advanced Materials product lines have underway as well as the increased geographic presence of these businesses."

Reasons to Buy

■ On a more positive note, Mr. Hambrick also said, "I am very pleased with our performance in the fourth quarter, which contributed to our record operating performance in 2007, our fourth consecutive year of earnings growth. We finished the year with strong demand and established a new mark for volume in a fourth quarter. We experienced sales growth in all geographic regions with international market growth outpacing North American demand. We also advanced our strategic agenda by closing our refrigeration lubricants acquisition in the quarter. In short, our performance reflects the ongoing successful transformation of Lubrizol and the underlying strength, diversity and resiliency of our businesses."

■ The company's 10-K had this comment on its acquisition of Noveon: "With the acquisition of Noveon International, we have accelerated our program to attain a substantial presence in the personal care and coatings markets by adding a number of higher-growth, industry-leading products under highly recognizable brand names, including Carbopol, to our already strong portfolio of lubricant and fuel additive products and consumer product ingredients.

"Additionally, Noveon International has a number of industry-leading specialty materials businesses, including TempRite chlorinated polyvinyl chloride and Estane thermoplastic polyurethane, that generate strong cash flow. We believe that the Noveon International acquisition meets the core tenets of our stated strategy to:

• Maintain technology leadership.
• Apply our formulation expertise to extend applications into new markets.
• Expand the global breadth of our businesses.

"The lubricant additives segment is the leading global supplier of additives for transportation and industrial lubricant," said the company's recent 10-K publication. "We pioneered the development of lubricant additives over seventy-five years ago and continue to maintain leadership in the $5 billion industry today. Our customers rely on our products to improve the performance and lifespan of critical components, such as engines, transmissions and gear drives for cars, trucks, buses, off-highway equipment, marine engines, and industrial applications."

The 10-K also said, "Our products serve to increase cost-effectiveness by reducing friction and heat, resisting oxidation, minimizing deposit formation, and preventing corrosion and wear. Through our in-house research, development and testing programs, we have the capability to invent and develop a broad range of proprietary chemical components, including antioxidants, anti-wear agents, corrosion inhibitors, detergents, dispersants, friction modifiers and viscosity modifiers."

- The 10-K goes on to say, "Our engine additives products hold a leading global position for a wide range of additives for passenger car, heavy-duty diesel, marine diesel, stationary gas and small engines. We also produce fuel additives and refinery and oilfield products.

"Our customers, who include major global and regional oil companies, refineries and specialized lubricant producers and marketers, blend our additive products with their base oil and distribute the finished lubricant to end users via retail, commercial or vehicle original equipment manufacturer channels. Passenger car motor oils and diesel engine oils are more than 80 percent of our engine additive sales."

- In 2006, Lubrizol announced plans to make a multimillion dollar investment to increase production capacity at its Avon Lake, Ohio facility. The facility, part of its Specialty Chemicals segment (Noveon), increased production of its Estane thermoplastic polyurethane (TPU) by about one third.

The additional capacity, which came on line in late summer of 2007, facilitated meeting increased customer demands for Estane TPU in the Americas. In addition, the increased capacity positions Noveon to meet growing customer needs worldwide.

"With production facilities in the United States, Europe and Asia, Noveon continues to deliver on its commitment to serve the growing needs of the industry by providing local sourcing in addition to manufacturing facility around the world," said Don Bogus, president of Noveon, Lubrizol's Specialty Chemicals segment. "The Avon Lake expansion will allow us to continue to maintain the high level of service Estane TPU customers have to come to expect from Noveon."

Expansion plans included adding Estane TPU resin manufacturing equipment and associated auxiliary equipment. The new polymerization line was designed to use the best available technology and manufacturing practices from within Noveon's global Estane TPU operations.

Noveon offers one of the largest portfolios of TPU technology in the world. Noveon's broad product portfolio includes TPU resins for a wide variety of recreational, industrial, automotive, textile and medical applications. With an extensive range of hardness levels, from 70A to 80D, Noveon TPU resins bridge the gap between flexible rubbers and rigid thermoplastics.

- "Our BUY recommendation is based on total return potential, said Richard O'Reilly, CFA, writing for the Standard & Poor's *Stock Reports* on March 3, 2008. The mid-2004 acquisition of Noveon greatly changed LZ's business mix, in our view, reducing its low-growth lubricant additives business to about two-thirds of total sales and expanding its industrial and consumer-related product lines."

SECTOR: **Materials**
BETA COEFFICIENT: **.95**
10-YEAR COMPOUND EARNINGS PER SHARE GROWTH: **4.2%**
10-YEAR COMPOUND DIVIDENDS PER SHARE GROWTH: **1.4%**

		2007	2006	2005	2004	2003	2002	2001	2000
Revenues (Mil)		4,499	4,041	3,622	3,156	2,049	1,980	1,839	1,771
Net Income (Mil)		283	106	189	139	91	126	94	103
Earnings per share		4.05	2.62	2.36	2.48	2.04	2.45	1.84	1.94
Dividends per share		1.16	1.04	1.04	1.04	1.04	1.04	1.04	1.04
Price	high	70.0	50.8	44.5	37.4	34.4	36.4	37.7	33.9
	low	48.8	38.0	35.2	29.4	26.5	26.2	24.1	18.3

McCormick & Company, Inc.

18 Loveton Circle □ P. O. Box 6000 □ Sparks, MD 21152-6000 □ (410) 771-7244 □ Web site: *www.mccormick.com*
□ Direct dividend reinvestment plan available □ Fiscal years end November 30 □ Listed: NYSE □ Ticker symbol:
MKC □ S&P rating: A+ □ Value Line financial strength rating: B++

On November 14, 2007, McCormick announced that it had signed a definitive agreement with Unilever to purchase the assets of Lawry's for $605 million in cash.

- Lawry's manufactures and sells a variety of marinades and seasoning blends under the well-known Lawry's and Adolph's® brands.
- Annual sales of this business are approximately $150 million, primarily in the U.S. and Canada.
- The acquisition supports the company's long-term outlook to grow sales 4–6 percent.

The Lawry's business includes a full line of seasoning blend products under the Lawry's and Adolph's brands that are marketed in grocery stores and other consumer outlets, and account for 65 percent of sales. Another 23 percent of sales are Lawry's wet marinades, which lead the category in the U.S. market. Sales to food service customers represent the remaining 12 percent. The acquisition includes the rights to the brands as well as related inventory and a small number of dedicated production lines. It does not include any manufacturing facilities or employees.

The acquisition is expected to be immediately accretive to earnings. The purchase price is approximately nine times EBITDA (earnings before interest, tax, depreciation, and amortization). CEO Robert J. Lawless had this comment: "The acquisition of attractive consumer brands to complement our existing portfolio of flavors for food is one of our key objectives. Lawry's is a well-known brand that has achieved a high level of consumer acceptance over the years.

"We are excited about the opportunity to enter the growing marinades category and to achieve synergies through the utilization of our manufacturing assets to produce the seasoning blends. We intend to invest a portion of the synergies we achieve to reinvigorate sales growth through innovation and focused marketing.

"With its strong heritage in delivering distinctive full flavors to main meals, Lawry's will be an excellent addition to our portfolio of products."

Company Profile

McCormick, the world's foremost maker of spices and seasonings, is committed to the development of tasty, easy-to-use new products to satisfy consumer demand.

When investors hear the name McCormick, they think of the spices they use every day. Indeed, McCormick is the world's largest spice company. Yet, the company is also the leader in the manufacture, marketing, and distribution of such products as seasonings and flavors to the entire food industry. These customers include foodservice and food-processing businesses, as well as retail outlets. This industrial segment was responsible for 49 percent of sales and 33 percent of operating profits. A majority of the top 100 food companies are MKC's customers.

Founded in 1889, McCormick distributes its products in about 100 countries.

McCormick's U.S. consumer business (47 percent of sales and 67 percent of operating profits), its oldest and largest, is dedicated to the manufacture and sale of consumer spices, herbs, extracts, proprietary seasoning blends, sauces, and marinades. They are sold under such brand names as McCormick, Schilling, Produce Partners, Golden Dipt, Old Bay and Mojave.

Many of the spices and herbs purchased by the company are imported into the United States from the country of origin. However, significant quantities of some materials, such as paprika, dehydrated vegetables, onion and garlic, and food ingredients other than spices and herbs originate in the U.S.

McCormick is a direct importer of certain raw materials, mainly black pepper, vanilla beans, cinnamon, herbs and seeds from the countries of origin.

The raw materials most important to the company are onion, garlic and capsicums (paprika and chili peppers), which are produced in the United States; black pepper, most of which originates in India, Indonesia, Malaysia, and Brazil; and vanilla beans, a large portion of which the company obtains from the Malagasy Republic and Indonesia.

Shortcomings to Bear in Mind

- This is not a stock that will make you rich. Its Beta is a very low .70, which means it fluctuates far less than the market. If the market rises 10 percent, for instance, McCormick would rise only 7 percent. However, in a declining market, its low Beta could protect you from disaster.

- On March 7, 2008, Standard & Poor's *Stock Reports* gave the company a mediocre HOLD rating. Even so, Tom Graves, CFA, had this favorable comment, "Regarding the pending Lawry's acquisition, we like the idea of MKC expanding into related businesses. We believe that long-term prospects for the company to generate free cash flow are favorable."

- Similarly, Value Line gave the stock a 3 rating, which is essentially a neutral stance. However, Iason Dalavagas said, "The stock has an Above-Average (2) Safety rank, along with a high score for Price Stability, so conservative investors may find these shares appealing."

Reasons to Buy

- On January 23, 2008, McCormick reported results for the fourth quarter and fiscal year ended November 30, 2007. For fiscal year 2007, earnings per share were $1.73 compared to $1.50 in 2006. On a comparable basis, excluding restructuring activities, the company increased earnings per share 12 percent, to $1.92 in 2007, compared to earnings per share of $1.72 in 2006.

CEO Alan D. Wilson commented, "We exceeded our goals for sales and profit growth in 2007 with strong contributions from both the consumer and industrial businesses. Sales growth of 7 percent exceeded our 4 to 6 percent objective for 2007 with the benefit of favorable foreign exchange rates and higher pricing. Success with new products, revitalization efforts, marketing programs and our acquisition strategy drove an additional portion of the increase.

"During 2007 we made great progress with our restructuring program. Since the program began we have realized $45 million in annual savings and are on track to reach up to $55 million by the end of the program in 2008. This is an outstanding achievement which is ahead of our original $50 million goal, and a reflection of the planning, focus and effort of employees throughout McCormick. In 2007, these significant cost reductions as well as pricing actions partially offset steep increases in the cost of several raw materials including pepper, wheat, soy oil and cheese.

"We increased earnings per share 12 percent from 2006 on a comparable basis, well ahead of our initial 8 to 10 percent goal for 2007. Sales growth, cost reductions, improved performance by our joint ventures and lower shares outstanding each contributed to an outstanding increase in our profits. In November we announced a 10 percent increase in the quarterly dividend per share."

- The market environment for McCormick's consumer products—such as spices, herbs, extracts, proprietary seasoning blends, sauces, and marinades—varies worldwide. In the United States, for instance, usage is up, and consumers are seeking new and bolder tastes.

Although many people use prepared foods and eat out, a *Parade Magazine* survey reports that 75 percent of families polled eat dinner together at least four nights a week. A study conducted by National Panel Diary indicates that 70 percent of all meals are prepared at home, and a Canned Food Association Survey reports that 51 percent of women eighteen to sixty-four actually "scratch-cook" meals six times a week.

■ In the company's industrial business, said Mr. Lawless, "Our customers are constantly seeking new flavors for their products. In this environment, the ability to identify, develop and market winning flavors is essential. We flavor all kinds of products—spaghetti sauce, snack chips, frozen entrees, yogurt, a pack of chewing gum. In restaurants, we provide seasonings for a gourmet meal, salad dressings at a casual dining chain, and coating and sauce for a quick-service chicken sandwich.

"To anticipate and respond to changing tastes in markets worldwide, we are investing in research and development staff, equipment, instrumentation, and facilities.

These investments enable us not only to create innovative products but also to use sensory skills to make sure that the flavors we deliver are winners in the marketplace."

■ Worldwide, the retail grocery industry continues to consolidate, creating larger customers. What's more, in many of McCormick's markets, the company has multiyear contracts with customers to secure the shelf space for its products. McCormick's capabilities in category management and electronic data interchange, along with its high-quality products and service, also forge a link to its increasingly larger customers.

■ The company's past successes and future potential are rooted in the strength of the McCormick name. As a consequence, the company is now experiencing a 95 percent brand-awareness rating in the United States. This leadership role in the food industry ensures that consumers will enjoy a McCormick product at nearly every eating occasion. Grocery store aisles present more than 700 well-known products from major processors that rely on McCormick for seasoning or flavor.

SECTOR: **Consumer Staples**
BETA COEFFICIENT: **.70**
10-YEAR COMPOUND EARNINGS PER SHARE GROWTH: **10.3%**
10-YEAR COMPOUND DIVIDENDS PER SHARE GROWTH: **10.3%**

		2007	2006	2005	2004	2003	2002	2001	2000
Revenues (Mil)		2,916	2,716	2,592	2,526	2,270	2,045	2,372	2,124
Net Income (Mil)		230	202	215	214	199	180	147	138
Earnings per share		1.73	1.50	1.56	1.52	1.40	1.29	1.05	1.00
Dividends per share		0.80	0.72	0.64	0.56	0.46	0.42	0.40	0.38
Price	high	39.7	39.8	39.1	38.9	30.2	27.3	23.3	18.9
	low	33.9	30.1	29.0	28.6	21.7	20.7	17.0	11.9

The McGraw-Hill Companies, Inc.

1221 Avenue of the Americas □ New York, NY 10020-1095 □ (212) 512-4321 □ Direct dividend reinvestment program available □ Web site: *www.mcgraw-hill.com* □ Listed: NYSE □ Ticker symbol: MHP □ S&P rating: not rated □ Value Line financial strength rating: A+

On September 4, 2007, Standard & Poor's, the leading provider of financial market intelligence, owned by McGraw-Hill, announced it had acquired IMAKE Consulting, a leading provider of software and services to the structured finance market, and ABSXchange, an end-to-end solution provider for structured finance data, analytics and modeling.

IMAKE Consulting has been providing data, analytics and modeling software and services to the structured finance community since 1991. IMAKE's clients include issuers, investment banks, ratings agencies, trustees and accounting firms. Its premier product, Analytics-on-Demand, is both an Internet-based and client-network-enabled analytical tool providing structured finance market participants with an end-to-end enterprise solution for analyzing and valuing structured finance transactions. IMAKE's software is used by Standard & Poor's in Europe.

ABSXchange provides an end-to-end solution for structured finance data, analytics and modeling. ABSXchange's clients include issuers, trading desks, investors, research houses, rating agencies, risk managers, credit departments, structurers, servicers, and trustees. Its premier product, @ Investors Connection, is an Internet-based Web portal providing data, reporting and cash flow analysis to the structured finance market.

"The acquisition of IMAKE and ABSXchange will further enhance our existing in-depth surveillance process and enable Standard & Poor's to expand its

suite of end-to-end solutions for the structured finance market," said Vickie Tillman, executive vice president of Ratings Services at Standard & Poor's.

Company Profile

The McGraw-Hill Companies is a leading global information services provider aligned around three powerful and enduring forces essential to economic growth worldwide: the need for knowledge, the need for capital, and the need for transparency. MHP has built strong businesses with leading market positions in financial services, education, and business information to meet those needs.

McGraw-Hill Financial Services

- Standard & Poor's sets the standard for the global investment community by providing highly valued investment data, analysis, and opinions to financial decision-makers through its three businesses.

- Credit Market Services, which includes the world's largest network of credit ratings professionals, provides ratings for a wide array of credit obligations, as well as risk management and credit performance evaluation services.

- Investment Services provides institutional and retail investors with a wide range of investment information, analysis and opinions in equities, fixed-income, foreign exchange and mutual fund markets. The S&P indexes are used more than any other index group around the world.

- Corporate Value Consulting is the U.S. market leader in providing valuation and value analysis for financial reporting, tax, business combinations, corporate restructuring, capital allocation, and capital structure purposes.

McGraw-Hill Education

- McGraw-Hill Education is a global leader in education and professional information. With a broad range of products—from traditional textbooks to the latest in online and multimedia offerings—the company helps teachers teach and learners learn.
- The School Education Group is the domestic leader in the pre-K to 12 school market, providing educational, supplemental and testing materials across all subject areas.
- Through its Higher Education, Professional and International businesses, the company is a leader in the globally expanding market for college and post-college and post-graduate education, and the company's professional publishing businesses serve the rapidly expanding needs of the global scientific, health care, business, and computer technology fields.

McGraw-Hill Information and Media Services

Information and Media Services provides information, business intelligence and solutions that business executives, professionals and governments worldwide use to remain competitive in their fields and in the global economy.

- Well-known brands in this unit include *BusinessWeek*, the number one global business magazine. The franchise also includes BusinessWeek

Online, conferences and events, and BusinessWeek TV. This business also includes Platts (the key provider of price assessments with the petroleum, petrochemical and power markets).

- McGraw-Hill Construction and Aviation Week, which serve the needs of construction, and aviation professionals worldwide, and ABC-affiliated television stations in Bakersfield, California; Denver, CO; Indianapolis, Indiana; and San Diego, California.

Shortcomings to Bear in Mind

- "McGraw-Hill finished off the year on a weak note," said Simon R. Shoucair, writing for *Value Line Investment Survey* on February 15, 2008. "Although strong showings in the first nine months of 2007 produced a solid full-year earnings comparison, the ongoing subprime mortgage debacle caught up with the company's financial services unit, Standard & Poor's, in the fourth quarter. The deteriorating structured finance market hurt issuances during the span. S&P's Credit Market Services's fourth quarter revenues declined by 14.1 percent, year over year, to $524.9 million."

Reasons to Buy

- On January 24, 2008, McGraw-Hill reported 2007 diluted earnings per share of $2.94, an increase of 22.5 percent versus $2.40 in 2006. The 2007 results include a $0.03 diluted per share gain on the divestiture of a mutual fund data business and an $0.08 restructuring charge mainly for employee severance costs for a reduction of 611 positions. The 2006 results included a one-time charge of $0.04 for the elimination of the company's stock option restoration program, a $0.06 charge for restructuring, and $0.04 for a deferral of revenue for the transformation of Sweets from primarily a print catalog to a bundled print and online service.

Net income for 2007 increased 14.9 percent to $1.0 billion compared to 2006. Revenue in 2007 grew by 8.3 percent to $6.8 billion versus 2006. Including the $0.08 restructuring charge in the fourth quarter of 2007, diluted earnings per share for the period were $0.43 compared to $0.56 in 2006, which included a $0.03 restructuring charge.

Net income for the fourth quarter of 2007 was $140.6 million versus $204.8 million in 2006. Revenue declined 1.5 percent to $1.6 billion in the fourth quarter of 2007.

"We promised and produced a double-digit gain in earnings per share and margin improvement in Financial Services and McGraw-Hill Education in 2007 despite challenging conditions," said CEO Harold McGraw III. "In the fourth quarter, our diversification strategy at Financial Services helped buffer us against the steep downturn in capital markets. A solid fourth quarter finish in the U.S. college and university market enabled McGraw-Hill Education to turn in a better than expected performance. To fortify our growth prospects, we restructured business operations in the fourth quarter."

■ S&P Indexes are the foundation for a growing array of investment funds and exchange-traded products that continue to generate new revenue. The company receives fees based on assets and trading activity. In addition, the recent volatility of the stock market has increased the revenue stream. Currently, more than $700 billion is invested in mutual funds tied to the S&P indexes.

■ Europe contributes almost half of McGraw-Hill's international revenue, growing at a double-digit rate. With a push from the new Monetary Union, the European market will be a springboard for growth in many of the company's key businesses. Here are some expectations:

- European companies that once financed their growth mainly by borrowing from banks are shifting to the issuance of corporate bonds instead, while nontraditional financial instruments also boom. Those are both large opportunities for Standard & Poor's Rating Services, which has built the world's largest network of ratings professionals.

- Increases in investments by Europeans building retirement funds—the result of a transition to privately funded pension plans—will accelerate demand for global financial information. These are pluses for Standard & Poor's Financial Information Services.

- The continued growth of English in business communications and as a second language in everyday use widens. These will benefit the company's educational products and the European edition of *BusinessWeek*.

- The promise of the global economy depends on educational training. This is a plus for McGraw-Hill's global publishing activities—most notably the company's business, finance, engineering, information technology and English instruction products.

■ In the construction industry, The McGraw-Hill Construction Information Group (MH-CIG) is the foremost source of information crucial to new construction projects and planning. MH-CIG has increasingly turned to the Internet and other electronic tools to gather and distribute information.

Dodge Plans is the latest of several MH-CIG electronic products stemming from print media. It provides access—online or by CD-ROM twice weekly—to the plans, specifications and bidding requirements for more than 60,000 new construction and renovation projects.

■ The McGraw-Hill Professional Book Group publishes nearly 800 titles per year in computing, business, science, technical, medical and reference markets. The group continues to expand by creating publishing

alliances with partners such as Oracle and Global Knowledge, transforming key reference titles into Internet-based services. In addition, the Professional Book Group offers electronic products, ranging from Internet subscription services to CD-ROMs, and is building its capabilities in on-demand publishing.

SECTOR: **Consumer Discretionary**
BETA COEFFICIENT: **.95**
10-YEAR COMPOUND EARNINGS PER SHARE GROWTH: **14.9%**
10-YEAR COMPOUND DIVIDENDS PER SHARE GROWTH: **8.6%**

	2007	2006	2005	2004	2003	2002	2001	2000
Revenues (Mil)	6,772	6,255	6,004	5,250	4,828	4,640	4,646	4,308
Net Income (Mil)	1,014	882	844	736	629	572	380	481
Earnings per share	2.94	2.40	2.21	1.91	1.64	1.48	1.23	1.21
Dividends per share	0.82	0.73	0.66	0.60	0.54	0.51	0.49	0.47
Price high	72.5	69.2	54.0	45.8	35.0	34.9	35.5	33.9
low	43.7	46.4	40.5	34.3	25.9	25.4	24.4	21.0

GROWTH AND INCOME

MDU Resources Group, Inc.

1200 W. Century Avenue ▢ P. O. Box 5650 ▢ Bismarck, ND 58506-5650 ▢ (701) 530-1057 ▢ Direct dividend reinvestment plan available ▢ Web site: *www.mdu.com* ▢ Listed: NYSE ▢ Ticker symbol: MDU ▢ S&P rating: A ▢ Value Line financial strength rating: A+

On January 8, 2008, MDU Resources Group announced that its indirect wholly owned subsidiary, Fidelity Exploration & Production Company (Fidelity), had signed a purchase and sale agreement to acquire natural gas properties located in Rusk County, Texas.

The agreement includes the purchase of 97 billion cubic feet equivalent (Bcfe) of proven reserves and 36 Bcfe of estimated probable reserves. Current net production from these assets is 17.5 million cubic feet equivalent per day. The purchase price for these properties was $235 million, or $2.42 per thousand cubic feet equivalent of proven reserves, subject to accounting and purchase price adjustments customary with acquisitions of this type.

These assets were purchased from EnerVest, Ltd. and certain of its affiliated parties and co-venturers. Fidelity will be the operator of the newly acquired assets and expects to drill approximately twenty-five wells in 2008 to further develop the properties. The acquisition is expected to be accretive to 2008 earnings per share and financed through a combination of internal funds and other borrowings.

"This acquisition is in an area where we have experience and fits well with our existing operations. These lower-risk development properties strengthen our strategy of having a balanced portfolio of assets and add production in an actively developing area," said CEO Terry D. Hildestad. "There is long-term development potential within these high-quality proven reserves and upside potential from the unproven reserves. Combined with our active exploratory programs in the Bakken Play in North Dakota and the Paradox Basin in Utah, we expect to be well-positioned for the future."

Company Profile

MDU Resources Group, Inc. is a natural resource company. The company's diversified operations, such as oil and gas and construction materials should help MDU Resources grow at a better rate than electric utilities that depend entirely on their electric business.

MDU Resources Group has a number of operations:

Electric Distribution

Montana-Dakota Utilities Company generates, transmits and distributes electricity, and provided related value-added products and services in the Northern Great Plains.

Natural Gas Distribution

Montana-Dakota Utilities Company and Great Plains Natural Gas Company distribute natural gas and provide related value-added products and services in the Northern Great Plains.

Utility Services

Operating throughout most of the United States, Utility Services, Inc. is a diversified infrastructure construction company specializing in electric, natural gas and telecommunication utility construction, as well as interior industrial electrical, exterior lighting and traffic stabilization.

Independent Power Production

Centennial Energy Resources owns electric generating facilities in the United States and Brazil. Electric capacity and energy produced at these facilities is sold under long-term contracts to nonaffiliated entities.

Pipeline and Energy Services

WBI Holdings, Inc. provides natural gas transportation, underground storage and gathering services through regulated and nonregulated pipeline systems and provides energy marketing and management throughout the United States. Operations are situated primarily in the Rocky Mountain, Midwest, Southern and Central regions of the United States.

Natural Gas and Production

Fidelity Exploration & Production Company is engaged in oil and natural gas acquisition, exploration and production throughout the United States and in the Gulf of Mexico.

Construction Materials and Mining

Knife River Corporation mines and markets aggregates and related value-added construction materials products and services in the western United States, including Alaska and Hawaii. It also operates lignite and coal mines in Montana and North Dakota.

Shortcomings to Bear in Mind

- Public utilities are often hurt by rising interest rates, since they have to borrow money to build new facilities. As the economy strengthens, it seems logical to assume that interest rates will climb from the depressed levels of recent years.
- "The Construction Materials division is feeling the effects of weakness in residential construction," said Paul E. Debbas, CFA, an analyst with *Value Line Investment Survey*, on February 8, 2008. "This segment's net income fell 10 percent last year, to $77 million, and we think there will be little (if any) recovery in 2008. In addition, the Construction Services operation, which provides such services to utilities, will have a tough act to follow after a year in which net income soared 58 percent, to $43.8 million."

Reasons to Buy

- "We believe that MDU's diverse business model will continue to drive earnings growth and that the stock will appreciate further, aided by the company's higher-return, nonregulated operations, improving balance sheet strength, and the fair and balanced regulation in its service territories (South Dakota, Minnesota and Montana)," said Gary F. Hovis, writing for Argus Research Company on January 25, 2008. The service gave MDU a BUY rating. "In addition, we anticipate moderate growth in the company's utility customer base, as well as higher sales of electricity and natural gas."

■ MDU Resources has an established position in the coal bed natural gas fields in the Powder River Basin of Wyoming and Montana. This provides the company's natural gas and oil production segment with additional reserve potential of low-cost coal bed natural gas.

In addition, MDU continues enhancing production from its existing gas fields in Colorado and Montana. The company's strong reserve position, both onshore and offshore in the Gulf of Mexico, provides this group a large geographic base upon which to expand.

■ On August 2, 2007, MDU Resources announced the acquisition of Lone Mountain Excavation and Utilities, LLC, based in Las Vegas, Nevada Lone Mountain is a specialty excavation and utilities contractor. Lone Mountain will become an indirect affiliate of MDU Construction Services Group, Inc., a wholly owned subsidiary of MDU Resources. Earnings from the acquisition are expected to be accretive to MDU Resources earnings per share.

"Lone Mountain will strengthen our service offering and increase the opportunity for CSG companies to offer a more complete construction package to general contractors and owners in the Las Vegas market," said John Harp, CEO of MDU Construction Services Group.

"CSG has thrived in the Las Vegas market. Our CSG companies are among the best in the business, and Lone Mountain will only add to that outstanding package of companies," said Mr. Hildestad.

■ On July 5, 2007, MDU Resources Group announced that it had acquired Ames Sand & Gravel, Inc., a ready-mix concrete company headquartered in Fargo, North Dakota.

Ames will become part of Knife River Corporation, the construction materials and mining subsidiary of MDU Resources. Financial details of the acquisition were not disclosed. MDU Resources anticipates the acquisition will be accretive to 2007 earnings per share.

"We are pleased to announce the acquisition of Ames," said Mr. Hildestad. "Ames has a proud history as a successful, well-managed company. Additionally, as a materials-based company, it is a good strategic fit for our corporation as we continue to focus on growing our core businesses—construction materials, energy and utility resources."

"We are excited to bring Ames into Knife River," said William Schneider, CEO of Knife River. "This acquisition allows us to begin operating in one of the strongest and fastest-growing markets in eastern North Dakota and western Minnesota. It bridges the gap between our existing operations in Bismarck, ND, and St. Cloud, MN."

■ On September 5, 2007, MDU Resources Group, Inc. announced that it had acquired Quality Concrete & Materials Co., Ltd., a ready-mix concrete and materials supplier headquartered in Beaumont, Texas.

Quality will become part of Knife River Corporation, the construction materials and mining subsidiary of MDU Resources. MDU Resources anticipates the acquisition will be accretive to 2007 earnings per share.

"We are pleased to announce our expansion into the Southeast Texas market through the acquisition of Quality Concrete & Materials," said Mr. Hildestad.

"Quality's strong market presence in an area that is experiencing robust industrial and commercial growth will be of great benefit to our construction materials business."

Quality operates ten ready-mix concrete plants, two material distribution yards and three pug mills throughout Southeast and Central Texas. In total, it produces in excess of 400,000 cubic yards of ready-mix per year, and it distributes between 1 million to 2 million tons of aggregates per year for internal and third-party use through its material yards. Revenues from its operations total nearly $50 million annually.

"Quality is an excellent addition to Knife River," said Mr. Schneider,. "It is a profitable and well-managed company and it reinforces our strategic commitment to grow our materials business."

SECTOR: Utilities
BETA COEFFICIENT: .85
10-YEAR COMPOUND EARNINGS PER SHARE GROWTH: 15.7%
10-YEAR COMPOUND DIVIDENDS PER SHARE GROWTH: 5.8%

		2007	2006	2005	2004	2003	2002	2001	2000
Revenues (Mil)		4,248	4,071	3,455	2,719	2,352	2,032	2,224	1,874
Net Income (Mil)		432	315	275	206	175	148	156	110
Earnings per share		2.36	1.74	1.53	1.17	1.03	0.92	1.02	0.80
Dividends per share		0.58	0.52	0.49	0.47	0.44	0.42	0.40	0.38
Price	high	31.8	27.0	24.7	18.5	16.3	14.9	17.9	14.7
	low	24.4	21.8	17.0	14.5	10.9	8.09	.97.9	

AGGRESSIVE GROWTH

Medtronic, Inc

710 Medtronic Parkway N. E. ▫ Minneapolis, MN 55432-5604 ▫ (763) 505-2692 ▫ Listed: NYSE ▫ Dividend reinvestment plan available ▫ Web site: *www.medtronic.com* ▫ Ticker symbol: MDT ▫ Fiscal years end April 30 ▫ S&P rating: A ▫ Value Line financial strength rating: A++

On October 10, 2007, Medtronic announced a U.S. Food and Drug Administration (FDA) advisory committee had unanimously recommended the company's Endeavor® drug-eluting stent for conditional approval as a treatment for coronary artery disease. This action positions the Endeavor stent to become the first new drug-eluting stent to be introduced in the United States since 2004.

Meeting on October 10 in Gaithersburg, Maryland, FDA's Circulatory System Devices Panel voted unanimously to recommend the Endeavor stent for approval with conditions related to product labeling and postmarket study requirements. The advisory committee recommended that the product's labeling reflect the clinical trial protocol use of dual anti-platelet therapy and the available professional society guidelines on their use. The panel also recommended a postmarket single-arm registry of at least 5,000 patients followed to a minimum of five years with a primary endpoint of very late stent thrombosis (ARC defined) and a secondary endpoint evaluating death and myocardial infarction. This recommendation is consistent with Medtronic's proposal for a postmarket study.

The FDA usually follows the recommendations of its advisory committees.

"We are very pleased with the outcome of today's panel meeting and appreciate the advisory committee's careful consideration of the extensive data on the Endeavor stent," said Scott Ward, president of Medtronic's cardiovascular business. "We will continue to work with the FDA to bring the Endeavor stent to the U.S. market as soon as possible so that patients and physicians in the U.S. can benefit from this next-generation technology. We believe that Endeavor provides the optimal combination of safety, efficacy and deliverability."

The Endeavor drug-eluting stent is commercially available in more than 100 countries outside the United States. In the United States, it remains an investigational device and is not yet approved for commercial use.

Medtronic presented the advisory committee with clinical data on more than 2,100 patients who have been treated with the Endeavor stent as participants in the ENDEAVOR Clinical Program, including 1,287 patients studied for two years and 675 patients studied for three years. The volume of data from the ENDEAVOR Clinical Program represents the largest body of scientific evidence ever submitted to the FDA to support the approval of a new drug-eluting stent.

Highlights from the clinical studies of the Endeavor stent include the following findings:

- Endeavor reduced restenosis in patients by more than 60 percent over its bare metal stent comparator, Medtronic's Driver® bare metal stent, at nine months.
- The reduction in restenosis is sustained over time as Endeavor showed a 92.8 percent freedom from target lesion revascularization (TLR) at three years, meaning less than 8 percent of patients had to return for a repeat procedure in the three years after receiving the stent.
- Endeavor patients had low rates of cardiac death, myocardial infarction (MI) and stent thrombosis with long-term follow-up to three years.
- 99 percent of Endeavor clinical patients have survived without a cardiac death beyond three years after implant; 97.3 percent of the Endeavor clinical patients have been free from heart attack at three years.

- There is no evidence of increased stent thrombosis risk within one year (0.7 percent Endeavor vs. 1.3 percent Driver per ARC definite/probable) or in years one to three (0.1 percent Endeavor vs. 0.2 percent Driver) in patients treated with the Endeavor stent compared with those treated with the Driver bare metal stent.
- In the ENDEAVOR IV clinical trial at nine months, the overall stent thrombosis rate was 0.8 percent (protocol defined), and there were no stent thrombosis observed after six months.

"The Endeavor drug-eluting stent significantly reduces restenosis and the need for repeat procedures while maintaining an excellent long-term safety profile," according to Martin B. Leon, Columbia University Medical Center, New York, and principal investigator of the ENDEAVOR III and ENDEAVOR IV Clinical Trials. "Importantly, rates of cardiac death, myocardial infarction and stent thrombosis are exceptionally low with the Endeavor stent out to three years of patient follow-up. The device's consistently strong clinical performance will make the Endeavor stent a welcome addition to the practice of interventional cardiology in the United States."

Company Profile

Medtronic is the world's leading medical technology company, providing lifelong solutions for people with chronic disease. Here are its key businesses:

Medtronic Cardiac Rhythm Management develops products that restore and regulate a patient's hearth rhythm, as well as improve the heart's pumping function. The business markets implantable pacemakers, defibrillators, cardiac ablation catheters, monitoring and diagnostic devices, and cardiac re-synchronization devices, including the first implantable device for the treatment of heart failure.

Medtronic Cardiac Surgery develops products that are used in both arrested and beating heart bypass surgery. The business also markets the industry's broadest line of heart valve products for both replacement and repair, plus autotransfusion equipment and disposable devices for handling and monitoring blood during major surgery, as well as cardiac ablation devices to treat a variety of heart conditions.

Medtronic Vascular develops products and therapies that treat a wide range of vascular diseases and conditions. These products include coronary, peripheral and neuro-vascular stents, stent graph systems for diseases and conditions throughout the aorta, and distal protection systems.

Medtronic Neurological and Diabetes offers therapies for movement disorders, chronic pain, and diabetes. It also offers diagnostics and therapeutics for urological and gastrointestinal conditions, including incontinence, benign prostatic hyperplasia (BPH), enlarged prostate and gastroesophageal reflux disease (GERD).

Medtronic Spinal, ENT and SNT develops and manufactures products that treat a variety of disorders of the cranium and spine, including traumatically induced conditions, deformities, and tumors.

Shortcomings to Bear in Mind

- On October 15, 2007, Medtronic said that it had voluntarily suspended worldwide distribution of the Sprint Fidelis* family of defibrillation leads because of the potential for lead fractures. In addition, the company recommends against new implants of the leads (Sprint Fidelis Models: 6930, 6931, 6948, 6949).

The Sprint Fidelis leads are used to deliver therapy in defibrillators only, including Implantable Cardioverter Defibrillators (ICDs) and Cardiac Resynchronization Therapy—Defibrillators (CRT-Ds). About 268,000 Sprint Fidelis leads have been implanted worldwide. This action does not affect Medtronic pacemaker patients.

"There is nothing more important to us than the safety and well-being of patients,"

said CEO Bill Hawkins. "We take all matters of product quality very seriously and believe this action is the right thing to do given currently available information."

Reasons to Buy

- Medtronic is a pioneer in the emerging field of medicine that promises to restore normal brain function and chemistry to millions of patients with central nervous system disorders. The company's implantable neuro-stimulation and infusion systems treat disorders by modulating the nervous system with electrical stimulation, chemicals, and biological agents delivered in precise amounts to specific sites in the brain and spinal cord.

- Since its origin, Medtronic has held a clear market leadership in cardiac pacing, chiefly with pacemakers designed to treat bradycardia (hearts that beat irregularly or too slow) and more recently, tachyarrhythmia (hearts that beat too fast or quiver uncontrollably, called tachycardia and fibrillation). Today, more than half the cardiac rhythm devices and leads implanted throughout the world come from Medtronic.

- The worldwide coronary vascular market is estimated at $4 billion and is expected to grow because it serves significant, unmet medical needs. Medtronic's coronary vascular products include several types of catheters used to unblock coronary arteries, stents that support the walls of an artery and prevent more blockage, and products used in minimally invasive vascular procedures for coronary heart disease, the chief cause of heart attack and angina.

- Medtronic's cardiac surgery group offers superior products to support cardiac surgeons, including tissue heart valves that are best represented by the Freestyle stentless valve, the Mosaic stented tissue valve, and the Hall mechanical valve. In addition, the company is expanding its leadership in cardiaccannulae used to connect a patient's circulatory system to external perfusion systems used in conventional and minimally invasive surgeries.

- "We continue to like this top-quality equity for the long haul," said George Rho, analyst with *Value Line Investment Survey*, on February 29, 2008. "Valuations have contracted steadily since peaking in 2000. Considering this premier medical devices maker's fundamental vitality, along with its secular growth prospects, it's difficult to envision further material compression. Indeed, our view is that the current valuation sets the stage for superior price gains out to 2011–2013, even assuming only a modest expansion of the P/E ratio."

- Diabetes afflicts more than 170 million people worldwide and about 20 million in the United States. It's the most costly chronic condition, with annual expenditures exceeding $130 billion in the U.S. alone. People with diabetes are also much more likely to suffer from numerous other medical complications, including cardiovascular disease, kidney disease, blindness, and amputation. As the world leader in external insulin pumps, Medtronic is expanding its product offering to help insulin-dependent diabetes patients better manage their glucose levels and their disease.

SECTOR: **Health Care**
BETA COEFFICIENT: **.60**
10-YEAR COMPOUND EARNINGS PER SHARE GROWTH: **15.7%**
10-YEAR COMPOUND DIVIDENDS PER SHARE GROWTH: **15.2%**

		2007	2006	2005	2004	2003	2002	2001	2000
Revenues (Mil)		12,299	11,292	10,055	9,087	7,665	6,411	5,552	5,015
Net Income (Mil)		2,798	2,687	2,270	1,959	1,600	984	1,282	1,111
Earnings per share		2.41	2.21	1.86	1.63	1.30	0.80	0.85	0.90
Dividends per share		0.41	0.36	0.31	0.28	0.25	0.20	0.12	0.15
Price	high	58.0	59.9	58.9	53.7	52.9	49.7	62.0	62.0
	low	44.9	42.4	48.7	45.5	42.2	32.5	36.6	32.8

CONSERVATIVE GROWTH

Meredith Corporation

1716 Locust Street ❑ Des Moines, IA 50309-3023 ❑ (515) 284-2633 ❑ Dividend reinvestment plan not available ❑ Fiscal years end June 30 ❑ Listed: NYSE ❑ Web site: *www.meredith.com* ❑ Ticker symbol: MDP ❑ S&P rating: A− ❑ Value Line financial strength rating: A

Meredith Corporation, one of America's leading media and marketing companies, announced on February 19, 2008, multiyear licensing agreements to publish *Child* magazine in India and *Parents* in Greece. With these new agreements, Meredith's international reach will extend to twenty properties in nine countries.

Child India will be published monthly by Media Transasia India Ltd., which launched *Better Homes and Gardens* in India under license from Meredith in 2007. *Parents Greece* will be published monthly by Daily Press Magazines S.A., an affiliate of the Daily Press Group.

Under terms of the licensing agreement with Media Transasia, an English-language version of *Child* magazine is expected to launch in India by summer 2008. The magazine's full name will be *Child India*, a *Parents* publication. It will leverage the editorial platforms of Meredith's extensive parents brands, including *Child, Family Circle, American Baby* and *Parents*.

"We're very pleased to broaden our relationship with Media Transasia India, further extending the reach of our *Parents* brands and content in Asia," said John Zieser,

Meredith's chief development officer, noting that Meredith currently has licensing agreements for *Parents* in China and Indonesia. "This agreement cements *Parents'* presence in Asia's three most populous countries, offering advertisers the opportunity to reach these growing consumer markets."

"*Child* has great potential in India," said Rasina Uberoi, vice president of Media Transasia. "Regardless of where you live, the joys and anxieties of raising a child are universal. *Child* will be the magazine that Indian parents turn to when looking to find expert advice or share their experiences."

Parents Greece is expected to launch by summer 2008, and represents Meredith's first extension of a parenthood brand in Europe. Athens-based Daily Press, founded in 2000, currently publishes two daily newspapers, one weekly newspaper and several magazine titles under license, including *Jolie, L'Officiel,* and *BBC Olive.*

Company Profile

Meredith Corporation is one of America's leading media and marketing companies. Its business centers on magazine and book publishing, television broadcasting, interactive media, and integrated marketing. The company's roots go back to 1902, when it was an agricultural publisher.

The Meredith Publishing Group is the country's foremost home and family publisher. The group creates and markets magazines, including *Better Homes and Gardens, Ladies' Home Journal, Country Home, Creative Home, Midwest Living, Traditional Home, WOOD, Hometown Cooking, Successful Farming, MORE, Renovation Style, Country Gardens, American Patchwork & Quilting, Garden Shed, Do It Yourself, Garden, Deck and Landscape, Decorating,* and about 150 special-interest publications.

In 2002, the company acquired American Baby Group, a publisher with titles geared toward mothers-to-be and young mothers. American Baby's magazines include: *American Baby, First Year of Life, Childbirth, Healthy Kids en Espanol, Pimeros 12 Meses,* and *Espera.* American Baby produces television shows; owns six consumer-sampling programs; provides custom publishing; and owns the American Baby Family Research Center and two Web sites. The company expected the acquisition to attract younger readers and to tap the fast growing domestic Hispanic market.

The Publishing Group also creates custom marketing programs through Meredith Integrated Marketing, licenses the *Better Homes and Gardens* brand and publishes books created and sold under Meredith and Ortho trademarks. Meredith has some 350 books in print and has established marketing relationships with some of America's leading companies, including Home Depot, Daimler-Chrysler and Carnival Cruise Lines. Meredith's most popular book is the red-plaid *Better Homes and Gardens New Cook Book.*

The Meredith Broadcasting Group includes fourteen television stations in locations across the continental United States, in such cities as Atlanta; Phoenix; Portland, Oregon; Hartford-New Haven, Connecticut; Kansas City, Missouri; Nashville; Greenville-Spartanburg-Anderson, South Carolina; Asheville, North Carolina; Las Vegas; Flint-Saginaw, Michigan; and Bend, Oregon. The network affiliations include CBS (five affiliates), NBC (one), UPN (one), and FOX (four).

Meredith's consumer database contains more than 80 million names, making it one of the largest domestic databases among media companies. These databases enable magazine and TV advertisers to precisely target marketing campaigns. In addition, the company has an extensive Internet presence, including branded anchor tenant positions on America Online.

Shortcomings to Bear in Mind

- The company's profits depend heavily on advertising revenues. The recession in the early part of the decade was particularly hard on advertising, which can be a volatile factor. When companies are hurting, they often lay off employees and pare back advertising.

Reasons to Buy

■ On July 25, 2007, Meredith Corporation reported fiscal 2007 net earnings per share of $3.31, a 16 percent increase over the prior year. Total revenues increased 3 percent to $1.6 billion, including 6 percent growth in advertising revenues. For the fourth quarter, net earnings per share increased 8 percent to $1.05 and total revenues grew 2 percent to $428 million.

"In fiscal 2007, we delivered another year of solid performance and strong returns to Meredith shareholders," said CEO Stephen M. Lacy. "Our Publishing Group posted strong advertising growth in the second half of the fiscal year, led by key brands such as *Better Homes and Gardens, Family Circle* and *More*. Our Broadcasting Group produced record political advertising and grew nonpolitical revenues as well. Online revenues and audience metrics grew at a rapid rate across all lines of business. And we positioned ourselves for future growth through key strategic investments, particularly in the online and broadband areas."

Highlights during Fiscal 2007:

■ Meredith Publishing Group advertising revenues increased 6 percent in the second half of fiscal 2007 over the prior year period, a trend that is continuing into fiscal 2008. Titles such as *More* and *Family Circle*, along with Meredith's Special Interest Publications, had a very strong year. Advertising revenues at *Better Homes and Gardens* surged more than 10 percent in the second half of fiscal 2007, buoyed by a magazine redesign and new creative and sales leadership.

■ Meredith Broadcasting Group delivered a record $33 million in net political advertising revenues. Also, local nonpolitical advertising revenues increased 4 percent. Meredith Video Solutions launched the company's first broadband video network and increased production of broadcast-quality video for use by Meredith's television stations and Web sites, as well as custom video for clients.

■ Internet page views climbed nearly 15 percent, driving revenue growth of approximately 50 percent. Meredith relaunched its flagship Web site *www.bhg.com* and introduced a parenting superportal *www.parents.com*. Additionally, the company redesigned all television station Web sites.

■ Meredith strengthened its consumer and custom marketing interactive capabilities through the acquisition of three online businesses: Genex, an interactive marketing services firm that specializes in online customer relationship marketing; New Media Strategies, an interactive word-of-mouth marketing company; and Healia, a consumer health search engine specializing in finding high quality and personalized health information online.

■ Meredith generated approximately $170 million of earnings from continuing operations and nearly $175 million in free cash flow, increased its dividend rate by 16 percent, repurchased more than 1 million shares of its common stock and reduced debt by $90 million in fiscal 2007.

■ "Americans are coming home," said a company spokesman. "Research shows they are devoting more time to their homes and their families, and the Meredith Publishing Group is ideally positioned to serve them. Through our century-long commitment to quality service journalism, we have built a reputation as a trusted source of information. Our subscription magazines, special interest publications, book, Web sites and other materials are respected resources for Americans seeking to enrich their homes through remodeling, decorating, gardening and cooking."

■ On October 23, 2007, Meredith announced a multiyear licensing agreement with Wal-Mart Stores for the design, marketing and retailing of a wide range of home products based on the *Better Homes and Gardens* brand. This new line of home products is expected to be available exclusively in Wal-Mart stores by the fall of 2008.

Merchandise to be developed includes items in popular home categories such as bedding and throws; bath accessories; dinnerware and kitchen textiles; and decorative pillows. *Better Homes and Gardens'* creative staff will take an active role in product design. These products will reflect *Better Homes and Gardens'* high standards and timeless style. They will delight the Wal-Mart shopper with stylish colors, patterns and designs that have broad appeal.

"This represents the largest extension of products bearing the *Better Homes and Gardens* brand in its eighty-five-year history," said Mr. Lacy. "We're excited to be partnering with Wal-Mart in bringing the *Better Homes and Gardens* style into the homes of millions of American shoppers."

■ Meredith serves more than 80 million American consumers each month through its magazines, books, custom publications, Internet presence and television stations. What's more, the company's database contains 80 million names, with 300 data points on seven of the ten domestic home-owning households.

■ "We are optimistic about the company's long-term growth prospects," said Simon R. Shoucair, an analyst with *Value Line Investment Survey*, on February 15, 2008. "Strong performance from the company's diversified media portfolio, coupled with the growing and profitable array of online digital and video initiatives, all augur well for revenue and profit growth over the long haul."

■ The company's products dominate the industry sweet spot of Americans in the thirty-five to fifty-four age group, the nation's largest purchasers. This age group does a disproportionate amount of spending in Meredith specialties—remodeling, decorating, cooking, and gardening.

SECTOR: **Consumer Discretionary**
BETA COEFFICIENT: **.75**
10-YEAR COMPOUND EARNINGS PER SHARE GROWTH: **10.5%**
10-YEAR COMPOUND DIVIDENDS PER SHARE GROWTH: **11.9%**

		2007	2006	2005	2004	2003	2002	2001	2000
Revenues (Mil)		1,616	1,598	1,221	1,162	1,080	988	1,053	1,097
Net Income (Mil)		162	145	128	111	91	70	71	71
Earnings per share		3.31	2.86	2.50	2.14	1.80	1.38	1.55	1.71
Dividends per share		0.69	0.60	0.52	0.43	0.37	0.35	0.33	0.31
Price	high	63.4	57.3	54.6	55.9	50.3	47.8	39.0	41.0
	low	48.1	45.0	44.5	48.2	36.9	33.4	26.5	22.4

AGGRESSIVE GROWTH

Nabors Industries Ltd.

515 West Greens Road □ Suite 1200 Houston, TX 77067 □ (281) 874-0035 □ Dividend reinvestment plan is not available □ Web site: *www.nabors.com* □ Listed: NYSE □ Ticker symbol: NBR □ S&P rating: not rated □ Value Line financial strength rating: B++

"While North American onshore drilling faces challenges due to capacity additions and spending cutbacks, we view NBR as somewhat protected through long-term contracts, its emphasis on larger operators, and segment diversification (particularly the International segment)," said Michael Kay, writing for Standard & Poor's *Stock*

Reports on January 24, 2008. "In addition, we remain bullish on NBR's drilling prospects related to unconventional natural gas, given the higher technology content needed for drilling such wells."

Company Profile

Nabors is the largest land-drilling contractor, with about 600 land drilling rigs. The company conducts oil, gas and geothermal land drilling operations in the lower forty-eight states, Alaska, Canada, South and Central America, the Middle East, the Far East, and Africa. What's more, NBR is one of the largest land well-servicing and workover contractors in the United States and Canada.

Nabors owns about 700 land workover and well-servicing rigs in the United States, primarily in the southwestern and western United States and about 215 land workover and well-servicing rigs in Canada. Nabors is also a leading provider of offshore platform workover and drilling rigs and owns forty-three platform, nineteen jack-up units and three barge rigs in the United States and multiple international markets.

Land Rigs

A land-based drilling rig generally consists of engines, a drawworks, a mast (or derrick), pumps to circulate the drilling fluid (mud) under various pressures, blowout preventers, drilling string, and related equipment.

The engines power the different pieces of equipment, including a rotary table or top drive that turns the drill string, causing the drill bit to bore through the subsurface rock layers. Rock cuttings are carried to the surface by the circulating drilling fluid. The intended well depth, bore hole diameter, and drilling site conditions are the principal factors that determine the size and type of rig most suitable for a particular drilling job.

Platform Rigs

Platform rigs provide offshore workover, drilling and re-entry services. The company's platform rigs have drilling and/or well-servicing or workover equipment and machinery arranged in modular packages that are transported to, and assembled and installed on, fixed offshore platforms owned by the customer.

Fixed offshore platforms are steel tower-like structures that either stand on the ocean floor or are moored floating structures. The top portion, or platform, sits above the water level and provides the foundation upon which the platform rig is placed.

Jack-up Rigs

Jack-up rigs are mobile, self-elevating drilling and workover platforms equipped with legs that can be lowered to the ocean floor until a foundation is established to support the hull, which contains the drilling and/or workover equipment, jacking system, crew quarters, loading and unloading facilities, storage areas for bulk and liquid materials, helicopter landing decks, and other related equipment. The rig legs may operate independently or have a mat attached to the lower portion of the legs in order to provide a more stable foundation in soft bottom areas.

Shortcomings to Bear in Mind

▪ If the high price of oil and natural gas bring on a worldwide recession, the demand for these energy products could recede substantially and lead to a reduction in drilling.

Reasons to Buy

▪ On February 5, 2008, CEO Gene Isenberg said, "Our 2007 results represent the second-best year in our company's history, with earnings per share from continuing operations just 5 percent below 2006's record level, despite a decline of $381 million or 30 percent in the operating income contribution of our North American rig operations, excluding Alaska. This minimal impact is attributable primarily to offsetting growth of nearly $200 million in several units, including International, Alaska, Oil and Gas, and Other Operating Segments. It is bolstered further by a lower share count and effective tax rate. The year's $3.13 diluted result, while down slightly, still represents an increase of $1.16 per diluted share from continuing operations over the $1.97 per diluted share achieved in 2005, which was previously the second best year. The results of the fourth quarter again reflect a mix of positive developments and some delays and disappointments, but I expect that future quarters will see diminishing potential for the adverse. Since we last reported new builds we have received nineteen additional commitments for new rigs, bringing the total number of new rig commitments since early 2005 to 140 drilling rigs and thirteen coiled tubing/stem drilling rigs. The 19 new rigs are all for our International operations, bringing to forty the number of new rigs in that unit.

"Our international operating income for the quarter increased from $63 million in the prior year to $92 million setting its eighth consecutive quarterly record. Operating income for the full year increased from $209 million in 2006 to $332 million in 2007, also setting a new record for the seventh year in a row. We expect 2008 will also show substantial increases since the majority of the prospective improvement is defined by the deployment of additional rigs already under term contracts and the renewal of existing contracts at current market prices."

■ On February 6, 2008, Argus Research Company gave Nabors a BUY rating, with this comment, in the words of analyst Philip Weiss, CFA, CPA. "As one of the largest onshore drilling and well-servicing contractors in North America, Nabors has captured a good portion of the drilling activity in the United States and Canada. The company's sizable fleet of workover rigs helps production firms maximize production from existing wells."

■ On September 21, 2006, Nabors Industries announced it had entered into a Letter of Intent to acquire the Moncla Companies for an undisclosed price. The principal assets consist of fifty-six workover and well-servicing rigs, thirteen truck-mounted swabbing and testing units, rental equipment, various auxiliary equipment and real estate. The land rig fleet is composed of twenty-eight 350-to-450 horsepower and twenty-one 500-to-900 horsepower heavy workover rigs while the offshore fleet consists of seven 500-to-1,000 horsepower barge workover rigs. Moncla's headquarters, central training and maintenance facility and principal operations are located in Lafayette, Louisiana, with extended operating yards located in Mississippi and Southeast Texas.

Mr. Isenberg commented on the acquisition, "We view this as an excellent opportunity to expand into one of the few markets we do not serve through the acquisition of the most highly regarded well-servicing operation in the region. It also serves as a good platform for deployment of our new 400- and 500-horsepower state-of-the-art Millennium rigs. We do expect the transaction to be accretive to both our near and longer-term results. We expect the existing Moncla management team will remain with Nabors and continue to run the various operations. We are delighted to welcome all of the Moncla customers and employees to the Nabors family of companies."

Charlie Moncla, president of Moncla Companies, commented, "Over the last twenty-two years, we have expanded the scope of our services and the geographies we cover. Today, we are the largest, privately held well-servicing company in the United States. I want to thank all of our loyal customers and dedicated employees for the success we have achieved. We believe the market outlook for our services is very favorable and that the resources of Nabors will better position Moncla Companies to pursue these favorable market opportunities. I have a deep respect for Nabors and believe our employees and customers will benefit from this transaction."

■ On September 22, 2006, Nabors Industries Ltd. and First Reserve Corporation announced their agreement to form NFR Energy LLC, a new joint venture to invest in oil and gas exploitation opportunities worldwide. Each party will hold an equal interest in the new entity and has committed to fund its proportionate share of $1 billion in equity. With third-party debt, reinvestment of cash flows, and the partners' ability to expand their equity commitments, NFR can invest more than twice its initial equity. The new company will pursue development and exploitation projects with both existing customers of Nabors and other operators in a variety of forms including operated and nonoperated working interests, joint ventures, farm-outs, and acquisitions.

Mr. Isenberg commented on the new partnership, "We are delighted to co-invest with the leading energy directed private equity firm. This combination will allow each party to benefit from the extensive expertise, experience, relationships and asset base of the other thus providing an enhanced platform for undertaking larger and more lucrative opportunities. This new venture will enable both partners' E&P clients and constituents to exploit opportunities more rapidly and efficiently utilizing the capital, expertise, and other assets, such as Nabors newest state-of-the-art rigs, through this venture."

William E. Macaulay, First Reserve's CEO, commented, "We see great potential in combining First Reserve's and Nabors' respective strengths in the largest and best-funded venture ever of its kind. We expect NFR's unprecedented combination of capital, experience, expertise and assets to provide for the rapid and profitable growth of a worldwide onshore E&P company. Our relationship with Nabors spans several decades and multiple industry cycles. While Nabors' rigs will be enabling assets in an era of active E&P spending, we will staff and capitalize the company to grow and succeed in any environment."

First Reserve is the oldest and largest private equity firm specializing in the energy industry. Founded in 1983, First Reserve was the first private equity investment firm to actively pursue building a broadly diversified global investment portfolio of companies involved in the various sectors of the energy industry. Since 1992, First Reserve has raised over $12.7 billion for its buyout-focused funds. Throughout its twenty-three-year history, the strong franchise that the firm has developed by investing exclusively in companies involved in the energy industry has served as a competitive advantage for First Reserve.

SECTOR: **Energy**
BETA COEFFICIENT: **.95**
10-YEAR COMPOUND EARNINGS PER SHARE GROWTH: **19.9%**
10-YEAR COMPOUND DIVIDENDS PER SHARE GROWTH: **no dividend**

		2007	2006	2005	2004	2003	2002	2001	2000
Rev (Mil)		4,939	4,820	3,551	2,394	1,880	1,466	2,121	1,327
Net Income (Mil)		931	1,081	660	302	192	108	348	136
Earnings per share		3.25	3.60	2.01	0.96	0.63	0.36	1.09	0.45
Dividends per share		—	—	—	—	—	—	—	—
Price	high	36.4	41.4	40.0	27.2	22.9	25.0	31.6	30.3
	low	26.0	27.3	23.1	20.0	16.1	13.1	9.0	14.1

Nordson Corporation

28601 Clemens Road ❑ Westlake, OH 44145 ❑ (440) 414-5344 ❑ Dividend reinvestment plan available
❑ Web site: *www.nordson.com* ❑ Fiscal years end October 31 ❑ Ticker symbol: NDSN ❑ Listed: Nasdaq
❑ S&P rating: B+ ❑ Value Line financial strength rating: B++

"Every time you open a cereal box, guzzle a soft drink, talk on your cell phone, drive a car, pick up a hammer, feed your dog, bleach your clothes or frost a cake, changes are good that you'll come into contact with Nordson," said Sandra Ward, writing for *Barron's* on October 1, 2007.

The *Barron's* article goes on to say, "Now is probably a good time to get better acquainted with Nordson, whose headquarters are in Westlake, Ohio, but whose reach extends to more than fifty countries. It holds leading market shares in its main businesses, and with 70 percent of its revenues coming from overseas, it is well cushioned from economic deceleration in the United States. The weak dollar is an added boon."

In addition, Ms. Ward said, "Nordson's well-regarded chief executive, Ed Campbell, is confident that strength in his global business 'will more than offset' any weakness in the United States, which he thinks could be under pressure for the next six to nine months, as demand softens. What's more, the bulk of Nordson's U.S. exposure lies in less-cyclical consumer-nondurables industries—food and beverages and staples. So Campbell expects the impact from the housing crisis, high energy prices and auto-industry difficulties to be muted."

Finally, the *Barron's* writer said, "Nordson certainly isn't reluctant to share its successes with investors: It has increased its dividend every year for the past forty-three years and, even after paying the dividend, its cash flow per share usually exceeds its net income."

Company Profile

Nordson Corporation is one of the world's leading producers of precision dispensing equipment that applies adhesives, sealants and coatings to a broad range of consumer and industrial products during manufacturing operations. The company also manufactures equipment used in the testing and inspection of electronic components as well as technology-based systems used for curing and surface treatment processes. Headquartered in Westlake, Ohio, Nordson has more than 3,800 employees worldwide, and direct operations and sales support offices in thirty countries.

Nordson products are used around the world in the appliance, automotive, bookbinding, construction, container, converting, electronics, food and beverage, furniture, medical, metal finishing, nonwovens, packaging, semiconductor, life sciences, and other diverse industries.

The company's strategy for long-term growth is based on a customer-driven focus that is global in scope. Consistent with this strategy, more than two-thirds of the company's revenues are generated outside the United States.

Major manufacturing, research and development facilities

Alabama, California, Florida, Georgia, Ohio, Pennsylvania, and Rhode Island in the United States, as well as in China, Germany, India, The Netherlands and the United Kingdom.

Worldwide operations

Nordson's more than 3,800 employees are located in direct operations and sales support offices in thirty countries. The company has working relationships with more than 165 distributor organizations, expanding its worldwide presence to fifty-seven countries.

Markets served:

Appliance, automotive, bookbinding, circuit board assembly, electronics, food and beverage, furniture, medical, metal finishing, nonwovens products, packaging, semiconductor, telecommunications, and other diverse industries.

Shortcomings to Bear in Mind

▪ Over the past ten years, the compound annual growth of earnings per share and dividends has been uninspiring, just over 6 percent.

Reasons to Buy

▪ On December 18, 2007, Nordson Corporation reported record sales and earnings for the fourth quarter, which ended October 31, 2007. Sales for the fourth quarter reached $290.8 million, a 20.4 percent increase over sales for the same period of 2006. Acquisitions accounted for 11.6 percent of the increase and core volume added 4.4 percent, with the remainder coming from the effects of currency translation.

On a diluted basis, fourth-quarter earnings per share were $.87, as compared to the prior year's $.87 from continuing operations and $.82 including discontinued operations. The current quarter's results include a charge of $.01 for short-term purchase accounting for acquired inventory.

"We had a very strong finish to the year, with record fourth quarter sales and operating profit," said CEO Edward P. Campbell. "We generated significant volume growth during the quarter in all segments and each geographic region, grew operating profit by 17 percent and, after normalizing the effect on last year's earnings of nonrecurring tax benefits, grew earnings per share from continuing operations by 14 percent."

Annual sales for the year, which ended October 31, 2007, reached a record $993.6 million, an 11.4 percent increase over sales of $892.2 million a year ago. Acquisitions accounted for 7.9 percent of the growth, currency accounted for 3.4 percent, and core growth accounted for 0.1 percent. Full year diluted earnings per share were $2.65 as compared to the prior year's $2.86 from continuing operations and $2.65 including discontinued operations. The current year's results include a charge of $.16 for short-term purchase accounting for acquired inventory. The effective tax rate in the current quarter is 33.2 percent as compared to the prior year's rate of 28.4 percent on continuing operations. The prior year rate benefited from certain nonrecurring tax benefits. Excluding the $0.16 short-term purchase accounting charge in the current year and applying the current year effective tax rate to prior year results, earnings per share from continuing operations increased 5.2 percent over 2006.

▪ On August 23, 2007, Nordson announced that it had acquired TAH Industries, a manufacturer of motionless mixer dispensing systems for two component adhesives and sealants. The company is headquartered in Robbinsville, New Jersey, and employs 180 people. TAH Industries specializes in the design and production of disposable plastic mixers and cartridge dispense systems, meter mix dispense valves and accessories. The company's products are used in the dental, construction, automotive, life science, food, DIY, marine and aerospace industries.

Nordson acquired TAH Industries for $45 million and expects the acquisitions to be neutral to slightly dilutive to 2007 fiscal year earnings. For the twelve months ending July 2007, TAH had revenues of $24.5

million, operating margins of 17 percent and EBITDA of $5.5 million, in each case on an unaudited basis and after adjusting for nonrecurring private company expenses. From 2004 to 2006, revenues grew at an average rate of 16 percent per year.

"TAH Industries complements Nordson's core manufacturing capabilities in the area of precision injection molding as well as our experience of working with material formulators around the world," said Mr. Campbell. "In addition, TAH's presence in life science markets enhances Nordson's ability to provide customers with a full range of solutions, including surface treatment and dispensing."

■ "Nordson ought to post impressive earnings gains out to 2011-2013," said Christopher Robertson, an analyst with *Value Line*, on April 25, 2008. "The company is growing rapidly in the Asia-Pacific area, and we believe that the growth rates are sustainable. After all, that region currently accounts for only about 15 percent of total sales, and there is ample room to expand. Meanwhile, demand for industrial products in Eastern Europe ought to bolster sales in that region. These gains should compensate for the weakness that we anticipate in the United States."

■ On March 15, 2008, Thomas White rated Nordson a BUY, with this comment by its analyst, "The capital goods team at Thomas White projects that over the next twelve months an investment in Nordson will return over 15 percent. These results should outperform the market and outperform 90 percent of the stocks in its industry. We recommend taxable investors buy Nordson and hold it for long-term capital gain."

■ Ford Equity Research called Nordson a BUY on February 9, 2008, with this comment by its analyst, "The Ford research team projects that Nordson will outperform the market over the next six to twelve months. Our decision is based on systematic analysis, which balances Nordson's quality and trend of its earnings growth, relative to fundamental valuation and its timeliness."

■ On July 25, 2007, Nordson announced that it had received a 2007 Governor's Excellence in Exporting Award from the Ohio Department of Development. The "E" Awards program recognizes companies and organizations that have demonstrated outstanding performance in exporting or heightened awareness of exporting as a vital component of Ohio's economy. Nordson's products are exported to fifty-seven countries and the company has direct operations in thirty countries. Governor Ted Strickland presented Nordson with the award during a ceremony held at the Statehouse Atrium in Columbus on July 18.

SECTOR: **Industrials**
BETA COEFFICIENT: **1.20**
10-YEAR COMPOUND EARNINGS PER SHARE GROWTH: **6.4%**
10-YEAR COMPOUND DIVIDENDS PER SHARE GROWTH: **6.2%**

	2007	2006	2005	2004	2003	2002	2001	2000
Revenues (Mil)	994	892	839	794	667	648	731	741
Net Income (Mil)	90.7	97.7	78.3	63.3	35.2	22.1	24.6	47.5
Earnings per share	2.65	2.86	2.14	1.73	1.04	0.66	0.74	1.67
Dividends per share	0.73	0.67	0.64	0.62	0.61	0.57	0.56	0.52
Price high	61.6	57.8	45.8	43.8	36.0	33.4	32.3	33.0
low	44.3	38.7	29.5	32.2	20.5	21.3	20.7	18.1

Norfolk Southern Corporation

Three Commercial Place ▫ Norfolk, VA 23510-2191 ▫ (757) 533-4810 ▫ Dividend reinvestment plan available ▫ Web site: *www.nscorp.com* ▫ Ticker symbol: NSC ▫ Listed: NYSE ▫ S&P rating: B+ ▫ Value Line financial strength rating: B+

Freight transportation is undergoing immense change, and it favors railroads. Demand for rail transportation is expanding in all major business sectors: coal, intermodal and general merchandise.

A dynamic convergence of circumstances is driving this demand, while shaping a structural change in the basic nature of the transportation business:

■ Rising freight volumes have strained the capacity of highways, increasing congestion.

■ Driver and equipment shortages are increasing costs for trucking companies.

■ Fuel prices favor the inherent efficiency advantages of railroads. One intermodal train pulled by two locomotives can haul the equivalent of up to 300 trucks. Trucking companies are converting business to rail, accelerating growth in intermodal traffic. Norfolk Southern meanwhile has built the most extensive intermodal network in the East.

■ Intermodal traffic has been very successful for railroads in general. This involves moving truck trailers and containers that normally would be hauled over the highway. In the past, intermodal business did not apply to shorter hauls, those of 500 miles or less. More recently, railroads have even been competing successfully in this sector, as well. One reason for growth in intermodal business is the problem that truckers have had in hiring drivers. Turnover among drivers has been high because drivers are averse to being away from home several weeks at a stretch.

■ Changing ocean shipping patterns have led to a surge of intermodal traffic at East Coast ports. Traditionally, Asian imports have moved by ship to the U.S. West Coast, and then by rail inland. Now, more and more traffic from Asia is routed through the Panama Canal to East Coast ports. Both coasts have seen triple-digit growth of imports from Asia.

■ Norfolk Southern has positioned itself to take on additional business and handle it effectively and efficiently. New systems have enhanced operating efficiency, service and capacity.

■ The Thoroughbred Operating Plan and the Coal Transportation Management System are driving improved service and capacity for Norfolk Southern's general merchandise and coal networks.

Company Profile

Norfolk Southern Corporation is one of the nation's premier transportation companies. Its Norfolk Southern Railway subsidiary operates 21,500 route miles in twenty-two states, the District of Columbia, and Ontario, Canada, serving every major container port in the eastern United States and providing superior connections to western rail carriers. NS operates the most extensive intermodal network in the East and is North America's largest rail carrier of automotive parts and finished vehicles.

Shortcomings to Bear in Mind

■ Norfolk Southern is a cyclical company, not a growth company. Look at its records of earnings per share for evidence. In the past ten years, earnings per share have fluctuated up and down from a high of $3.68 in 2007 to a low of $0.55 in 2000. Only rarely have EPS risen to $2. The dividend record is equally spotty. For several years, the company paid $.80, from 1997 through 2000. The following year, the dividend payout was slashed to $0.24 and is only $1.16 at present.

Reasons to Buy

- On January 23, 2008, Argus Research Company called Norfolk Southern a BUY, with this comment by Kevin Tynan, "As the economic and equity markets enter a troublesome phase, rail stocks should provide both defense and growth for value-oriented investors. While rail volumes were disappointing in 2007, pricing strength combined with system efficiency has enabled the early reporting rails to post better-than-expected results."

- "The company's operating metrics are top-notch," said analyst Garrett Sussman, writing for *Value Line Investment Survey* on March 7, 2008. "Effective hedging has helped Norfolk Southern to offset much of the increases in diesel prices over the past few months. Fuel costs rose only a few percentage points last year, while energy prices climbed to dramatically high levels. Reduced compensation and material costs also helped to widen the operating margin."

- On November 14, 2007, a company spokesman said, heavy machinery grinds away brick, concrete and solid rock as a railroad tunnel near Cowan, VA, gets its roof raised to accommodate taller trains. This is the beginning of a three-year engineering project to increase intermodal freight capacity by raising vertical clearances in twenty-eight tunnels on a Norfolk Southern rail line between the port of Hampton Roads, Virginia, and Chicago known as the Heartland Corridor. The first phase of the tunnel work began in October.

When the project is completed in early 2010, containerized freight moving in double-stack trains will be able to shave off about 200 miles and up to a day's transit time between the East Coast and the Midwest. Currently, double-stack trains must take longer routes by way of Harrisburg, Pennsylvania, or Knoxville, Tennessee. The Heartland Corridor goes across Virginia, through southern West Virginia and north through Columbus, Ohio.

"The Heartland Corridor is one of the most significant railroad engineering projects of modern times," said Tim Drake, NS vice president, engineering. "We're excited to get started. We're at the beginning of something big—a true partnership that will benefit the nation's economy and create a competitive advantage for railroad shippers and receivers, our public partners and our communities."

Stack trains require a minimum vertical clearance of twenty feet, nine inches. The methods of increasing clearances vary from lowering track to notching corners into an arched roof to digging out and installing a new roof. In one case, the top of the tunnel may be removed altogether, turning the tunnel into a "cut," a process known as "daylighting." Tunnel lengths range from 174 feet (the one to be daylighted at Big Four, West Virginia) to the Cowan Tunnel's 3,302 feet.

In early 2008, work will have begun on three other tunnels in Virginia, near Eggleston and Pembroke, and eight tunnels along eleven miles of track in southern West Virginia between Antler and Gordon. The remaining tunnels, all in West Virginia (except for one in Kentucky), will be modified in two more phases, first proceeding eastward to Coopers, West Virginia, then westward. In addition, overhead clearances will be increased on seven railroad bridges, three overhead bridges, three railway signals and three sets of overhead wires.

Meanwhile, Norfolk Southern trains continue to run through the corridor, serving coal and other customers in the region. Where practical, trains have been rerouted, permitting sections of track to be closed for ten hours at a time, five days a week, for the next three years. Norfolk Southern has formulated plans to minimize the impact of the construction on coal customers. Accurate and timely information about service changes and delays will be communicated throughout the construction period. Close communication and joint planning with customers on expected volumes and changes in coal sourcing also will enhance efforts as the project progresses.

■ On July 12, 2007, the company announced that the Michigan Central Railway would initiate freight rail service over 384 route miles of rail line in Michigan and Indiana in first-quarter 2008 under a joint venture to be formed by Norfolk Southern Railway Company and Watco Companies, the parent company of the newly formed Michigan Central.

"The new Michigan Central will preserve and enhance freight rail service in southern Michigan," said David C. Eyermann, Michigan Central's interim president. "The company will be headquartered in Kalamazoo and will employ 118 people. In the first year alone we plan to invest more than $6 million to improve track and equipment to capitalize on the rail-served economic development opportunities we envision for the region. A critical component of industrial growth and job creation is a vibrant freight rail network, and we are excited about the partnerships we will establish with shippers doing business in southern Michigan, as well as with state and local governments on the Michigan Central network."

The new Michigan Central will operate over freight rail line segments between Ypsilanti and Kalamazoo; between Jackson and Lansing; and between Grand Rapids and Elkhart, Indiana. The Michigan Central also will acquire Norfolk Southern's trackage rights on the Amtrak-owned line between Kalamazoo and the Michigan/Indiana state line. The transaction is subject to regulatory approval by the Surface Transportation Board (STB) in Washington, D.C. Norfolk

Southern and Watco will make the required filings with the STB later this month.

"Our focus will be to grow the business and add value for our customers and the Michigan economy," Eyermann said. "We will have a marketing team based in Kalamazoo that will be tasked to move additional freight traffic by rail. These officers will be meeting with customers and communities on a daily basis to find ways to move more freight via the railroad."

■ According to an October 15, 2007, article in *Barron's* by Teresa Rivas, "Burlington isn't the only railroad that has caught [Warren] Buffett's eye. Although more recent figures aren't available, filings with the Securities and Exchange Commission in May (2007) showed that his holdings include 6.4 million shares off Norfolk Southern (NSC), or a 1.62 percent stake, and 10.5 million Union Pacific (UNP) shares, a 3.9 percent stake."

■ On December 28, 2007, Norfolk Southern completed the installation of a 50-kilowatt wind turbine at its Bellevue Yard in Ohio to power the yard's wastewater treatment plant. The wind turbine consists of three twenty-four-foot rotor blades mounted on an eighty-foot tower and is estimated to generate more than 100,000 kilowatt hours annually.

"The Bellevue wind turbine is the first of its kind on Norfolk Southern, and we believe that its success will act as a catalyst for other sustainable energy initiatives on the railroad," said Chuck Wehrmeister, vice president, Safety and Environmental. "We truly appreciate the interest officials from both Erie County and the City of Bellevue expressed in the use of alternative renewable energy."

SECTOR: Industrials
BETA COEFFICIENT: 1.15
10-YEAR COMPOUND EARNINGS PER SHARE GROWTH: 6.4%
10-YEAR COMPOUND DIVIDENDS PER SHARE GROWTH: 3.8%

		2007	2006	2005	2004	2003	2002	2001	2000
Revenues (Mil)		9,432	9,407	8,527	7,312	6,468	6,270	6,170	6,159
Net Income (Mil)		1,464	1,481	1,281	870	529	460	362	210
Earnings per share		3.68	3.57	3.11	2.18	1.35	1.18	0.94	0.55
Dividends per share		1.16	0.72	0.48	0.36	0.30	0.26	0.24	0.80
Price	high	59.8	57.7	45.8	36.7	24.6	27.0	24.1	22.8
	low	45.4	39.1	29.6	20.4	17.3	17.2	13.4	11.9

CONSERVATIVE GROWTH

Northern Trust Corporation

50 South La Salle Street ❑ Chicago, IL 60675 ❑ (312) 444-4281 ❑ Dividend reinvestment plan not available ❑ Web site: *www.northerntrust.com* ❑ Ticker symbol: NTRS ❑ Listed: Nasdaq ❑ S&P rating: A− ❑ Value Line financial strength rating: A

On November 5, 2007, Suzanne McGee, writing for *Barron's*, had this comment, "'We don't need a transformational acquisition, nor do we need to sell to a larger firm in order to compete,'" says President Rick Waddell, who becomes CEO in January (2008); he replaces William Osborn, who will continue as chairman. "'We are independent and we want to maintain that independence, and execute on our core strategies.'

"At some point, the bank could become attractive to an acquirer like UBS, which is rumored to be interested in expanding its business with America's ultrarich. But in the rarefied world of private banking, observers say, an unsolicited offer is unlikely; Northern would probably have to change its mind and initiate the deal.

"Meanwhile, its tradition and 'high-touch' culture remains very much intact. For instance, even Waddell is required to meet with some 300 clients a year—one-on-one in his office or their homes, or at conferences or other events. 'It helps build trust and confidence,' he explains.

"Alois Pirker, senior analyst with research firm Aite Group in Boston, says, 'Northern is reaching more and more wealthy individuals, and it's well positioned to be the quarterback, the organization that is the glue in the relationship that those individuals have with all kinds of different service providers.'

"To the extent that Northern Trust forges those relationships, they are likely to be long lasting."

Company Profile

Northern Trust Corporation, founded in 1889, is a multibank holding company headquartered in Chicago that provides personal financial services and corporate and institutional services through the corporation's principal subsidiary, The Northern Trust Company, and other bank subsidiaries located in the following eighteen states: Illinois, Arizona, California, Colorado, Connecticut, Delaware, Florida, Georgia, Massachusetts, Michigan, Minnesota, Missouri, Nevada, New York, Ohio, Texas, Washington, and Wisconsin.

Global offices are situated in Amsterdam, Bangalore, Beijing, Dublin, Hong Kong, Limerick, London, Singapore, Tokyo, and Toronto. The corporation also owns two investment management subsidiaries, Northern Trust Investments, N.A. and Northern Trust Global Advisors, Inc. As of March 31, 2007, Northern Trust Corporation had approximately $60 billion in banking assets, more than $756 billion in assets under management and $3.8 trillion in assets under custody.

Northern Trust Corporation's Major Business Segments:

Northern Trust Corporation organizes client services around two principal business units: Personal Financial Services (PFS) and Corporate and Institutional Services (C&IS). Northern Trust Global Investments (NTGI) provides investment products and services to clients of both PFS and C&IS.

Personal Financial Services (PFS) offers personal trust, estate administration, private banking, residential real estate mortgage lending, securities brokerage, and investment management services to individuals, families and small businesses. PFS operates through a network of eighty-four offices in eighteen states: Illinois, Arizona, California, Colorado, Connecticut, Delaware, Florida, Georgia, Massachusetts, Michigan, Minnesota, Missouri, Nevada, New York, Ohio, Texas, Washington, and Wisconsin. In distinctive, full-service facilities, experienced Northern Trust people work in a client service culture that is unparalleled in the industry.

Corporate and Institutional Services is a leading provider of trust, global custody, investment, retirement, commercial banking, and treasury management services worldwide.

Northern Trust's institutional clients reside in over forty countries and include corporations, public retirement funds, foundations, endowments, governmental entities, and financial institutions.

Shortcomings to Bear in Mind

■ Northern Trust is not without major competitors. Competition in Personal Financial Services varies by geographic market but may include domestic and foreign financial institutions, trust companies,

asset management firms, and brokerage firms.

Northern Trust's main domestic competitors in master trust/custody are State Street Corporation, The Bank of New York Company, Inc., Mellon Financial Corporation, and J.P. Morgan Chase & Co. For Treasury Management Services, Northern Trust's main U.S. competitors include Wachovia, Bank of America, Mellon Financial Corporation, and J.P. Morgan Chase & Co.

Reasons to Buy

■ On February 2, 2008, Channel Trend regarded Northern Trust as a BUY. Its analyst said, "The research team at Channel Trend projects that NTRS will outperform the market over the next six to twelve months. Our decision reflects a disciplined analysis of the stock's relationship to its projected future price and its estimated fair value."

■ On March 22, 2008, Standard & Poor's *Stock Reports* said Northern Trust was a BUY, with this comment by its analyst, Frank Braden, CFA: "Despite the recent runup in noninterest expenses, we view NTRS as a well-run custody bank with solid credit quality. We have a positive view of the company's product and geographic diversity, coupled with a healthy operating outlook. We believe the company's leading position in the affluent market, and its focus on ultrawealthy clients, should result in above-peer average revenue and earning growth in a stable or modestly rising equity market."

■ "Credit quality is very good, as evidenced by a the very low 0.04 percent ratio of loan losses to average loans for 2007," said Douglas G. Maurer, CFA, an analyst with *Value Line*, on March 21, 2008. "Northern Trust has a conservative orientation and has avoided the very large writeoffs reported by other financial firms."

■ "Clients are at the center of everything we do," said then CEO William A. Osborn in 2007. "Since 1889, Northern Trust has distinguished itself by our commitment to exceptional client service and the importance of building and maintaining strong, long-lasting relationships. Our clients's needs drive every product and service decision we make and the location of every office we open.

"This client-centered focus has been integral to Northern Trust's growth over the years. By remaining true to our focused business strategy and to the principles upon which we were founded—a commitment to unquestioned integrity and honesty, a dedication to excellence in client service, a continuous search for innovative solutions and a passion to improve the communities in which we do business—Northern Trust has evolved into a dynamic global financial services enterprise."

- On January 16, 2008, CEO Waddell said, "Our focused business model continued to generate excellent results in the fourth quarter of 2007, amidst a challenging capital and credit market environment. Record operating earnings for the quarter and full year were driven by strong growth in trust, investment and other servicing fees, foreign exchange trading income, and net interest income, while the quality of our loan portfolio continued to be exceptionally strong.

"Northern Trust's success in the marketplace was evidenced by double-digit growth in client assets, with assets under custody increasing 17 percent, to $4.1 trillion, global custody assets growing 23 percent, to $2.1 trillion, and assets under management increasing 9 percent, to $757.2 billion, versus last year. We enter 2008 in excellent financial condition with a continued focus on serving the needs of personal and institutional clients."

- In 2007, a company spokesman said, "The physical presence of our Personal Financial Services (PFS) business is unrivaled; no other bank in the United States has as many offices focused exclusively on the affluent market. Our locations are within a forty-five-minute drive of about half of the nation's millionaire households. Each office

has an experienced team of asset management, fiduciary, and private banking professionals on staff who reside in the communities where our clients live and work. This close proximity to clients is just one characteristic that makes Northern Trust unique.

"The number of households within the $1 million to $10 million range is expected to grow eight percent annually through this decade, and the number of households with $10 million or more is expected to grow 10 percent annually—compared with the overall projected U.S. household growth of less than two percent annually. These projections, fueled by the tremendous wealth creation in the United States economy and other factors, reinforce our consistent and well-defined growth strategy. Northern Trust is positioned well for future growth through expanding and existing relationships and by capturing new business within our target markets."

- "In Corporate and Institutional Services, we completed the integration of Baring Asset Management's Financial Services Group hedge fund, property, and other fund administration in the United Kingdom and Ireland," said Mr. Osborn in 2007. We are the largest administrator of offshore private equity funds in Europe and have the largest number of funds administered in Dublin. We also completed at year-end the migration of Insight Investment Management (Global) Limited's back- and middle-office investment operation to our strategic platform—nearly $200 million in assets. This outstanding success positions Northern Trust well for future outsourcing opportunities."

- Mr. Osborn also said, "We experienced dramatic growth in the Asia-Pacific region, as we celebrated our ten-year anniversary in Singapore. We were selected to provide global custody, investment mandate compliance monitoring, and performance measurement services to China's multibillion dollar National Social Security Fund—the first institutional retirement fund in China to invest overseas. On January 23, 2007, Northern

Trust announced that it was chosen to act as custodian for the New Zealand Superannuation Fund, which is expected to grow from US $8 billion to US $76 billion by 2025."

■ Mr. Osborn went on to say, "Through our five offices in Asia-Singapore, Hong Kong, Japan, China, and Bangalore, India—we continue to expand Northern Trust's reach into new markets such as New Zealand, which provides a strong foundation for our future growth in the Asia-Pacific region.

SECTOR: **Financials**
BETA COEFFICIENT: **1.15**
10-YEAR COMPOUND EARNINGS PER SHARE GROWTH: **9.3%**
10-YEAR COMPOUND DIVIDENDS PER SHARE GROWTH: **10.5%**

	2007	2006	2005	2004	2003	2002	2001	2000
Total Assets (Mil)	67,611	60,712	53,414	45,277	41,450	39,478	39,665	36,022
Net Income (Mil)	727	665	584	506	418	447	488	485
Earnings per share	3.24	3.00	2.64	2.33	1.95	1.97	2.11	2.08
Dividends per share	1.03	0.94	0.84	0.76	0.68	0.68	0.68	0.62
Price high	83.2	61.4	55.0	51.3	48.8	62.7	82.3	92.1
low	56.5	49.1	41.6	38.4	27.6	30.4	41.4	46.8

CONSERVATIVE GROWTH

Omnicom Group, Inc.

437 Madison Avenue □ New York, NY 10022 □ (212) 415-3393 □ Direct dividend reinvestment plan available □ Web site: *www.omnicomgroup.com* □ Ticker symbol: OMC □ Listed: NYSE □ S&P rating: A+□ Value Line financial strength rating: B++

On September 3, 2007, Omnicom Group, the leading global advertising and marketing services group, acquired, through its Diversified Agency Services division (DAS), a majority ownership interest in Consultech, a leading health care market consulting and marketing communications company based in China.

With offices in Beijing and Shanghai, Consultech offers a wide range of marketing services to multinational and local health care companies covering strategic consulting, marketing research, marketing communications, and advertising. Consultech's clients include Novartis, Novo Nordisk, Xian-Janssen, Ipsen, and China Resources Corp.

"Through Consultech joining Omnicom, we have strengthened our ability to deliver a full scope of services to our healthcare clients in China," said David Stark, CEO of DAS Asia-Pacific Healthcare. "During 2007 we have already seen strong growth in our healthcare footprint in China through our association with Consultech. Moreover, Consultech's solid healthcare credentials and know-how are helping other Omnicom networks in China deliver their own specialized marketing services to healthcare clients. The formalization of our relationship can only help speed our total growth."

Jiang Song, managing director of Consultech, said, "Our decision to join Omnicom opens a new era of development for us. Our deep understanding of the Chinese healthcare market and extensive experience in consulting and marketing communications combined with Omnicom's global resources and networks further enhances Consultech's ability to provide the best services to healthcare companies in China."

"Over the last three years, there has been a growing consensus between the global and regional management of pharmaceutical companies on the importance of bringing best practices in healthcare marketing communications to the local marketing and product management teams," said Mr. Stark. "Many healthcare marketers in China tell me that they are looking to implement best practices and need the know-how and leadership that Omnicom companies can provide. For many years, we have successfully demonstrated our ability to deliver such leading services in many Asia Pacific markets (notably Japan), and we are particularly excited about the huge China opportunity."

Company Profile

Founded in 1986, Omnicom Group is a strategic holding company that manages a portfolio of global market leaders. Its companies operate in the disciplines of advertising, marketing services, specialty communications, interactive/digital media and media buying services. Omnicom Group includes:

- Three global advertising brands: BBDO Worldwide, DDB Worldwide, and TBWA Worldwide
- Leading U.S.-based national advertising agencies: Arnell Group, Goodby, Silverstein & Partners, GSD&M, Martin|Williams, Merkley Newman Harty|Partners, and Zimmerman Partners
- Diversified Agency Services (DAS) DAS consists of a global enterprise of more than 100 companies that provide services in direct marketing/consultancy, public relations, promotional marketing, and specialty communications.
- Omnicom Media Group (OMG)

Omnicom's leading media agencies are part of OMG. The group consists of two full service media companies, OMD Worldwide and PHD Network, as well as several media specialist companies.

Recognition and Rankings
- Omnicom Group's agency brands are consistently recognized as being among

the world's creative best. Omnicom global advertising agency networks, BBDO Worldwide, DDB Worldwide, and TBWA Worldwide once again dominated the International Advertising Festival at Cannes, winning fifty-seven awards, or more than twice as many of any rivals, including the Grand Prix, the industry's most prestigious.
- *Forbes* magazine elected Omnicom to the *Forbes* Platinum 400 list of the Best Big Companies in America.
- *The Wall Street Journal* ranked Omnicom Group Number One in its peer group for our ten-year average annual total return to shareholders.

Shortcomings to Bear in Mind

According to a company spokesman, "The businesses in which we participate are highly competitive. Key competitive considerations for keeping existing business and winning new business include our ability to develop creative solutions that meet client needs, the quality and effectiveness of the services we offer, and our ability to efficiently serve clients, particularly large international clients, on a broad geographic basis.

"While many of our client relationships are long-standing, companies put their advertising, marketing and corporate communications services business up for competitive review from time to time. We have won and lost accounts in the past as a result of these reviews. To the extent that we are not able to remain competitive, our revenue may be adversely affected, which could than affect our results of operations and financial condition."

Reasons to Buy
- On February 15, 2008, Argus Research Company rated Omnicom a BUY. Analyst Wendy Walker said, "Omnicom is a fundamentally strong company with well-diversified global operations in a competitive industry." She went on to say, "The company has not seen any cutbacks in

client spending, and its net new business wins hold promise for continued top-line strength. International gains continue to outpace Omnicom's domestic growth rate, and we see opportunity for meaningful profit increases in emerging markets, where the company has been building ground-up operations for lack of acquisition targets."

■ On February 12, 2008, Standard & Poor's *Stock Reports* also had a BUY rating on Omnicom. James Peters, CFA, said, "We see OMC's operating margin remaining at about 13 percent in 2008. While we expect OMC to realize operating leverage from higher revenues on its fixed costs, we also see the company continuing to invest heavily in its infrastructure to maintain above peer revenue growth and profitability."

■ On February 15, 2008, *Value Line Investment Survey* looked fondly on Omnicom, giving it a 2 rating, which is tantamount to a BUY. Alan G. House said, "Omnicom's immense size puts it in a lucrative competitive position for the three- to five-year pull. We look for earnings to reach $4 a share during this time frame. Our optimism assumes a decent global economic backdrop. We believe that if a recession does occur in the near term on the domestic front, conditions will have recovered by 2010-2012."

■ On September 20, 2007, Omnicom Group expanded its Omnicom University Advanced Management Program (AMP) to Asia by holding its first executive leadership development program in Shanghai, China. The four-day program, which gathered more than fifty future leaders of Omnicom companies working in the Asia Pacific, the United States, and Europe, was held at the China Europe International Business School.

Omnicom University is Omnicom's in-house global leadership development faculty. It forms the core of Omnicom's commitment to attract, retain and motivate talent. Created in 1995 by Tom Watson, vice chairman emeritus of Omnicom Group, in conjunction with then Harvard Business School Professor Len Schlesinger, Omnicom University is regarded as one of the world's foremost executive education experiences. Traditionally taught at the Babson Executive Conference Center in Wellesley, Massachusetts, the program was extended to Vevey, Switzerland in 2005.

"The ability to attract the best people and to nurture and retain them is a key priority for us as we continue to grow our business in Asia Pacific," commented Michael Birkin, Omnicom's vice chairman and chairman and CEO, Asia Pacific. "Our decision to bring Omnicom University to China reflects our strong belief that providing very talented people with advanced opportunities to learn and develop is critical to our success in this region."

"The Omnicom University Advanced Management Program, a unique initiative in our industry, clearly demonstrates Omnicom's global commitment to the professional development of our executives. This focus on attracting, retaining and developing the best talent is particularly important in a region where localization is essential to sustain the significant growth our agencies are experiencing" added Serge Dumont, Omnicom senior vice president and president, Asia Pacific. "Given the strategic importance of Asia and China to our clients and to our agencies, we are truly excited to host this prestigious program for the first time in Asia Pacific."

"After thirteen years and the completion of the program by more than 1,000 executives, Omnicom University has promoted positive change throughout the Omnicom network," said Tom Watson, founder and dean of Omnicom University. "Our core teaching concept, the Service Profit Chain, has created a common culture and values throughout the organization. Many of our senior managers consider Omnicom University 'the best educational experience of their career.'"

■ Omnicom Group is a leading global marketing and corporate communications company. Omnicom's branded networks and numerous specialty firms provide advertising, strategic media planning and buying, direct and promotional marketing, public relations and other specialty communications services to over 5,000 clients in more than 100 countries.

- On November 30, 2006, Omnicom Group announced that it had acquired a majority stake in 180 Amsterdam.

Founded in 1998 by managing partners Alex Melvin, Guy Hayward, and Chris Mendola, 180 Amsterdam is one of the most awarded independent agencies in the world. Its work is regularly featured in the Clio, One Show, D&AD, and Cannes Advertising Festivals. In 2004, 180 Amsterdam was recognized as the world's third most awarded agency at the Cannes Lions International Advertising Festival. Its

founding client, adidas, was awarded the Advertiser of the Year accolade at the 2006 Cannes Festival.

180's management lineup is completed by managing partner Peter Cline and executive creative directors Andy Fackrell and Richard Bullock.

"Led by an outstanding management team, 180 is at the leading edge of international creativity. We are delighted to welcome 180 to our portfolio of award winning, world-class creative agencies," said CEO John Wren.

180 Amsterdam is an international agency that employs 100-plus people from over twenty-five countries. 180's client roster includes Motorola, Omega Watches, Amstel, Sony Electronics USA, Amnesty International, and adidas International.

SECTOR: **Consumer Discretionary**
BETA COEFFICIENT: **1.00**
10-YEAR COMPOUND EARNINGS PER SHARE GROWTH: **15.6%**
10-YEAR COMPOUND DIVIDENDS PER SHARE GROWTH: **10.1%**

	2007	2006	2005	2004	2003	2002	2001	2000
Revenues (Mil)	12,694	11,377	10,481	9,747	8,621	7,536	6,889	6,154
Net Income (Mil)	976	864	791	724	676	644	503	435
Earnings per share	2.95	2.50	2.18	1.95	1.80	1.72	1.35	1.20
Dividends per share	0.60	0.50	0.46	0.44	0.40	0.40	0.39	0.35
Price high	55.4	53.0	45.7	44.4	43.8	48.7	49.1	50.5
low	45.8	39.4	37.9	33.2	23.3	18,3	29.5	34.1

AGGRESSIVE GROWTH

Oshkosh Corporation

2307 Oregon Street ▫ Post Office Box 2566 ▫ Oshkosh, WI 54903-2566 ▫ (920) 233-9332 ▫ Web site: *www.oshkoshtruckcorporation.com* ▫ Dividend reinvestment plan available ▫ Fiscal years end September 30 ▫ Listed: NYSE ▫ Ticker symbol: OSK ▫ S&P rating: A ▫ Value Line financial strength rating: B+

On December 20, 2007, Oshkosh Corporation (formerly Oshkosh Truck) announced that, with Ideal Innovations, Inc. (I-3), and Ceradyne, Inc., it had been awarded a firm-fixed-priced delivery order for six Mine Resistant Ambush Protected (MRAP) II test vehicles by the U.S. Marine Corps Joint MRAP program office. The vehicles are to be

delivered in the first quarter of calendar year 2008 and will be used for further government testing of their Explosively Formed Penetrator (EFP) resistant capabilities. The Bull™ is produced on an Oshkosh® MTVR (medium tactical vehicle replacement) chassis.

"Oshkosh Truck understands the complex mobility and protection requirements of armored vehicles, and with many companies competing for these contracts, it says volumes that Oshkosh was only one of two companies selected," said CEO Robert G. Bohn.

"The Oshkosh Truck armored vehicles are engineered to help protect U.S. troops against asymmetric warfare threats such as mines and IEDs, and we are proud to supply troops with armored vehicles to help keep them safer in the theater."

The contract awarded to I-3, Oshkosh Truck and Ceradyne is worth $18,100,000, and is a developmental effort to purchase test vehicles and armor coupons for enhanced MRAP survivability and mobility tests. The MRAP II contracts will also contain ordering options for production quantities.

The MRAP II test vehicles and armor coupons will be delivered to Aberdeen Test Center. Manufacturing of these vehicles will be performed in Wixom, Michigan, Costa Mesa, California, and Oshkosh, Wisconsin, and work is expected to be completed July 2008. This contract was competitively procured. The Marine Corps Systems Command, Quantico, Virginia, is the contracting activity.

Company Profile

Oshkosh Corporation is a manufacturer of a broad range of specialty commercial, fire and emergency and military trucks and truck bodies. It sells mostly to customers in domestic and European markets. The company sells trucks under the Oshkosh and Pierce trademarks; truck bodies under the McNeilus, MTM, Medtec, Geesink and Norba trademarks; and mobile and stationary compactors under the Geesink Kiggen trademark.

Oshkosh began business in 1917 and was among the early pioneers of four-wheel drive technology.

The company's commercial truck lines include refuse truck bodies, rear and front-discharge concrete mixers, and all-wheel drive truck chassis. Its custom and commercial fire apparatus and emergency vehicles include pumpers; aerial and ladder trucks;

tankers; light-, medium- and heavy-duty rescue vehicles; wildland and rough-terrain response vehicles; and aircraft rescue and firefighting vehicles and ambulances, and snow-removal vehicles.

As a manufacturer of severe-duty, heavy-tactical trucks for the United States Department of Defense, Oshkosh Truck manufactures vehicles that perform a variety of demanding tasks, such as hauling tanks, missile systems, ammunition, fuel, and cargo for combat units. More than 6,500 Oshkosh trucks have been in service in Iraq.

Shortcomings to Bear in Mind

- The company is benefiting from the Iraq war and would lose government business if the war ended or if a substantial number of troops were brought home.

Reasons to Buy

- On March 6, 2008, Oshkosh Corporation received a contract modification from the U.S. Army to the current family of heavy tactical vehicles (FHTV) contract, ordering the manufacture of 1,084 heavy expanded mobility tactical trucks (HEMTT) in the A4 configuration. This contract modification raises the total of Oshkosh® HEMTT A4s currently under contract to 1,745, for a total contract modification of more than $321 million. The Oshkosh HEMTT A4 production will begin in July 2008.

An original contract modification was awarded on February 1, 2008, while the second modification designated the vehicle models to be manufactured as HEMTT A4s. The Oshkosh Defense Group will continue to manufacture product-improved HEMTT A2s until the A4 upgrades take effect in July. The most recent improvements to the HEMTT A2 are a fully air conditioned cab and cab structural changes that makes installation of add-on-armor in the field quicker and easier.

The HEMTT's thirteen-ton payload and off-road capabilities make it the backbone for the U.S. Army's logistics fleet. Since its introduction in 1985, the HEMTT has helped keep the Army on the move during major conflicts such as Operations Desert Storm and Iraqi Freedom. The vehicle also fulfills critical resupply missions in its different configurations, including fuel servicing, load handling system (LHS), and cargo variants.

■ "We believe OSK's growth prospects are strong, and we have confidence in management's ability to execute its strategic initiatives over the long term," said Pearl Wang, an analyst writing for Standard & Poor's *Stock Reports* on February 20, 2008. "Moreover, we expect favorable conditions to continue in many of the end markets that OSK serves." S&P gave Oshkosh a BUY rating on March 15, 2008.

■ On February 29, 2008, *Value Line Investment Survey* had this comment by analyst Jason A. Smith, "The appeal of this stock lies in it long-term prospects. The addition of JLG at the end of 2007 has so far proved to be a worthwhile investment, given its contributions and the level of diversity the new segment brings."

■ Daren Fonda, writing for *SmartMoney* in May 2008, had this comment, "Oshkosh is the Army's sole supplier of heavy tactical vehicles, and spending is already set to increase 110 percent through September. Even if troops start heading home, those vehicles will need replacing after years of abuse. Military revenue accounts for 22 percent of Oshkosh's total $6.3 billion and is growing 20 percent annually. The firm also makes construction equipment and should profit from an increase in infrastructure spending—which Obama supports, for instance."

■ On July 27, 2007, Oshkosh Corporation, Ceradyne, Inc., and Ideal Innovations, Inc. (I-3) announced an agreement to further develop, produce and market the Bull™ armored vehicle. The Bull is intended to address the increasing need for protection from improvised explosive devices (IED),

mine blasts and high-threat, explosively formed projectiles (EFP) and will be built on a combat-proven Oshkosh Truck chassis.

The Bull advanced technology armored solution, conceived by I-3 in 2005 and developed with Ceradyne in 2006, has been tested by the Army Test Center, Aberdeen, Maryland, and demonstrated to be capable of protecting vehicle occupants against IED, EFP, and mine blast threats. It is designed to meet current IED threats, and is intended to withstand the increasingly prevalent and higher EFP threats now faced by the U.S. military.

"It is our mission to help protect the brave men and women of the U.S. military against the most dangerous threats, and together with Ceradyne and I-3, we intend to build the best vehicles to protect our soldiers against the higher threat weapons used by our enemies," said Mr. Bohn. "We believe the Bull will be a great addition to Oshkosh Truck's long history of setting the standard for serving our troops in the field."

Joel P. Moskowitz, CEO of Ceradyne, said, "This team will bring the United States military an advanced, integrated armor solution and survivability system to our soldiers and Marines. The Oshkosh Truck chassis, which will serve as the primary mobility platform for the Bull, has already been used successfully in combat. When combined with the Bull's special armor, it provides a highly survivable mobile armored vehicle that will serve our military well."

Bob Kocher, CEO of I-3 added, "We believe that the Bull's integrated cab and advanced armor produced by Ceradyne combined with Oshkosh Truck's highly capable and reliable chassis, and both companies' extensive production capabilities, will provide our deployed soldiers effective protection from IEDs and EFPs."

■ "Sitting high in the cab of the hulking lime-green TerraMax truck, a driver can be excused for instinctively grabbing the steering wheel. There's no need. TerraMax is a self-driving vehicle, a prototype designed to navigate and obey traffic rules—all while the people inside, if there are any, do anything but drive," said an article written for the Associated Press by Dinesh Ramde on October 3, 2007.

"During a recent test on property owned by manufacturer Oshkosh Truck Co., Terra-Max barreled down a dusty road with its driver seat empty. It stopped at a four-way intersection and waited as staged traffic resolved.

"If the Defense Department gets its way—about as long as a typical sport utility vehicle and almost twice as high—could represent the future of transportation for the military's ground forces."

■ On June 4, 2007, Oshkosh introduced the new HT-Series™ snow tractor at the Airfield Operations Area (AOA) annual conference in Milwaukee, Wisconsin. The HT-Series snow tractor is engineered and designed as a Multi-Tasking Equipment (MTE) vehicle and is built specifically for airport snow removal operations.

A multitasking, all-purpose vehicle in the truest sense of the word, the HT-Series snow tractor can perform a myriad of functions, including plowing, brooming, scraping and deicing.

"We've spent a great deal of time and resources meeting with our customers to discuss their needs and priorities for multitasking equipment," said Tim Kiefer, vice president of Airport/Municipal Products at Oshkosh Truck. "The result is the HT-Series snow tractor. It's the most versatile and best performing multitasking unit available today and will lead the segment in North America from day one."

SECTOR: **Industrials**
BETA COEFFICIENT: **1.15**
10-YEAR COMPOUND EARNINGS PER SHARE GROWTH: **33.4%**
10-YEAR COMPOUND DIVIDENDS PER SHARE GROWTH: **17.5%**

	2007	2006	2005	2004	2003	2002	2001	2000
Revenues (Mil)	6,307	3,427	2,960	2,262	1,926	1,744	1,445	1,324
Net Income (Mil)	268	206	160	113	75.6	59.6	50.9	48.5
Earnings per share	3.58	2.76	2.18	1.57	1.08	0.86	0.74	0.74
Dividends per share	0.40	0.37	0.22	0.13	0.08	0.09	0.09	0.09
Price high	65.8	65.7	46.2	34.5	26.4	16.3	12.4	11.0
low	44.8	42.6	30.3	23.9	13.1	11.5	8.0	5.4

AGGRESSIVE GROWTH

Parker Hannifin Corporation

6035 Parkland Boulevard ▢ Cleveland, OH 44124-4141 ▢ (216) 896-3000 ▢ Web site: *www.parker.com*
▢ Dividend reinvestment plan available ▢ Fiscal years end June 30 ▢ Listed: NYSE ▢ Ticker symbol: PH
▢ S&P rating: A— ▢ Value Line financial strength rating: B++

On August 6, 2007, Parker Hannifin Corporation, the global leader in motion and control technologies, announced the acquisition of the assets of Silver Cloud Manufacturing, a maker of electromagnetic and radio frequency interference shielding products and display filters for a variety of electronics applications.

Silver Cloud will operate as part of Parker's sealing and shielding business within the company's Industrial North America segment. "Silver Cloud's unique lamination technology and anti-reflective chemistry knowledge are used to create products that are used in control panels, monitors, handhelds, voting booths, in-flight entertainment screens, and medical devices," said Heinz Droxner, president of Parker's global Seal Group. "This acquisition puts Parker among the leaders in this market niche and also offers potential synergies with the Tecknit acquisition we completed last year."

"Silver Cloud combines proprietary materials with custom display filters to produce unique configurations that add value to a wide range of OEM products," said Silver Cloud president and general manager Bill Riland. "Parker is an excellent fit for us and should help us to continue growing our business profitably."

Company Profile

The company's key sectors are:

Aerospace

Parker's cooling technology is used to boost the computing power of mobile military computers by up to five times to facilitate remote intelligence capabilities.

Automation

Parker invented the world's smallest motorized syringe assembly for high throughput autosamplers used in the life sciences market. By synchronizing adaptive fluidic and motion control systems and by developing strategic partnerships, Parker is delivering pre-engineered solutions that improve precision, and dramatically increase productivity by four times for OEM (original equipment manufacturers) leaders in the drug discovery process.

Climate & Industrial Controls

The company's electronic superheat control system provides temperature control, a wireless interface, a "smart defrost" function for added energy efficiency, and intelligent diagnostic capabilities to keep supermarket refrigeration systems running at optimal performance.

Filtration

Parker's innovative low-pressure fuel systems are getting smarter and lasting longer with new brushless pumps that optimize fuel flow during all engine cycles for agriculture equipment.

Fluid Connectors

Parker assists the oil and gas market with high-pressure capability hoses that provide greater flexibility and safe, economical handling of methanol used to force oil to the surface from sub-sea wells.

Hydraulics

Parker's next generation hydraulic pumps and motors are quieter, more compact, and more efficient. With the company's new H1A axial piston pump, it can now offer OEMs in the turf care and similar markets, a complete hydrostatic transmission.

Instrumentation

Process industries extract and analyze pipeline samples to determine their composition and maximize production yields. The sample must then be disposed of properly to ensure environmental compliance. Parker's new vent master system promises to replace complex pumping systems while maintaining stable pressure and flow as the sample is analyzed and discharged through disposal points such as flares and incinerators.

Seal

With Parker's ever-advancing materials and sealing processes, the company provides tangible performance benefits in the most critical aerospace, fluid power, energy, oil and gas, and transportation applications. Aggressive fluids, harsh chemicals, high-temperature, and high-pressure are no match for Parker's wide range of sealing systems.

Shortcomings to Bear in Mind

- This stock is not for the faint of heart, with a Beta of 1.25. In addition, earnings per share, although robust of late, can suffer sinking spells, as they did in 2001 and 2002, when EPS fell from $1.99 to $.75 and $1.15.

Reasons to Buy

- On December 7, 2007, Parker Hannifin and FedEx Ground, a unit of FedEx Corp., announced they had agreed to test a Class 6 vehicle employing hybrid hydraulic technology that seeks to improve fuel mileage by greater than 50 percent and significantly reduce engine emissions.

The new vehicles will rely on a Parker series hybrid hydraulic drive that eliminates the conventional transmission, along with its weight and maintenance, while improving drive train power density. Primary pump/motor components developed by Parker leverage additional technologies developed by the EPA to create a true series hybrid drive as opposed to a parallel system that would increase vehicle weight. The system captures, stores and deploys energy by recovering inertial energy and optimizing engine efficiency, using Parker hydraulic technology.

"This relationship with FedEx Ground marks the latest chapter in Parker's ten-year history of energy saving hydraulic drive systems for commercial vehicles," said Dr. Joseph A. Kovach, vice president of Technology and Innovation for Hydraulics at Parker. "We are extremely pleased FedEx Ground is working with us as a collaborator for this program."

- On March 18, 2008, Argus Research Company called Parker-Hannifin a BUY, and its analyst, Rashid Dahod, said, "The company has maintained its earnings momentum, propelled in part by continued sales growth in the Aerospace segment and the Industrial International segment. Its success reflects its recent contract award from Cessna Aircraft Company and its

Chomerics division's Performance Excellence Award from Boeing."

- On March 19, 2008, Parker Aerospace was selected by Gulfstream Aerospace, a wholly owned subsidiary of General Dynamics, to supply the flight control actuation system for its brand new G650 business jet aircraft.

The Parker Control Systems Division will design and manufacture the G650's fly-by-wire flight control actuation system, including the primary aileron, rudder, elevator, and spoiler flight control actuation and control electronics.

The G650 fly-by-wire flight control actuation system uses state-of-the-art actuation technology. This system incorporates electrohydrostatic and electrohydraulic technologies to allow enhanced aircraft performance, redundancy, and safety. These technologies were proven during Gulfstream's recently completed Advanced Flight Control System demonstration program, also supported by Parker's Control System Division.

In addition to the flight control system, Parker's Hydraulic Systems Division will provide engine-driven hydraulic pumps, auxiliary electric motor pumps, and electro-hydrostatic motor pump units for flight controls, as well as landing gear retraction and door actuators on the new G650. These products will satisfy the hydraulic power generation needs of the aircraft and support a significant portion of the utility actuation requirements.

The Parker Electronic Systems Division will supply the fluid quantity indicator (FQI) on the aircraft. This indicator measures and controls maintenance of the engine oil and hydraulic fluids.

The G650's ecology bottle and hydraulic selector valve are new wins for the Parker Air and Fuel Division on Gulfstream aircraft. The division will also provide oil and hydraulic replenishment reservoirs and oil selector valves on the aircraft.

Parker Aerospace vice president and Control Systems Division general manager Carl Moffitt said, "Parker has supported Gulfstream's primary flight control needs for more than forty years. We are extremely proud to continue this relationship and to be a part of this new and exciting aircraft."

■ For the 2007 fiscal year, the company surpassed $10 billion in sales for the first time in its eighty-nine-year history. Sales reached a record $10.7 billion, an increase of 14.2 percent from $9.4 billion in the previous year. Income from continuing operations increased 30 percent to $830.0 million compared to $638.3 million a year ago, and earnings per diluted share from continuing operations increased 32.8 percent to $7.01 compared to $5.28 a year ago. Cash flow from operating activities reached a record $955.0 million, or 8.9 percent of sales.

"In surpassing the $10 billion sales milestone, we continue to demonstrate our propensity to grow," said CEO Don Washkewicz. "Our compound annual growth rate over the last thirty-five years is in excess of 11 percent. This year, we grew by more than 14 percent, or more than three times GDP. This exceeded our Win Strategy goal to grow both organically and through disciplined acquisitions at a 10 percent compound annual rate. Of the 14 percent growth, 5 percent was organic, 6 percent was from strategic acquisitions, and the remainder was from the effects of foreign currency exchange

rates. We're especially pleased with gains we've made in our Industrial International segment, where revenues grew by 34 percent and operating income grew by 51 percent. Margins in this segment also reached an all time high and continue to approach those in our North American segment. Overall, our revenues and profits are more balanced regionally than ever before, which speaks to the growing demand around the world for our motion and control technologies. By executing our Win Strategy, we delivered record earnings per share in the quarter and for the year. Total shareholder return for the year was 28 percent, or 35 percent higher than the S&P 500, and our return on invested capital remains at the top quartile among our peers.

"We also generated close to $1 billion in annual cash flow from operating activities, which allowed us to both maintain our strong balance sheet and use cash wisely to invest in our company. We continued to invest in strategic acquisitions this year, purchasing eleven companies that added nearly $260 million in annualized revenues. We spent $433 million to repurchase 5.4 million shares, and we made discretionary contributions of $161 million to our pension funds. In fiscal 2007, we increased dividends 13 percent, paying out approximately $121 million to shareholders, maintaining our dividend increase record that spans fifty-one years."

SECTOR: Industrials
BETA COEFFICIENT: 1.25
10-YEAR COMPOUND EARNINGS PER SHARE GROWTH: 11%
10-YEAR COMPOUND DIVIDENDS PER SHARE GROWTH: 7.4%

	2007	2006	2005	2004	2003	2002	2001	2000
Revenues (Mil)	10,718	9,386	8,215	7,107	6,411	6,149	5,980	5,355
Net Income (Mil)	830	638	548	346	196	130	341	368
Earnings per share	4.67	3.57	3.03	1.85	1.15	0.75	1.99	2.21
Dividends per share	0.69	0.61	0.52	0.51	0.49	0.48	0.47	0.45
Price high	86.6	58.7	50.8	52.3	39.9	36.6	33.4	36.0
low	50.4	43.4	37.9	34.5	23.9	23.0	20.7	19.7

Patterson Companies, Inc.

1031 Mendota Heights Road □ St. Paul, MN 55120-1419 □ (651) 686-1775 □ Web site: *www.pattersondental.com*
□ Dividend reinvestment plan not available □ Fiscal years end last Saturday in April □ Listed: Nasdaq □ Ticker symbol:
PDCO □ S&P rating: B+ □ Value Line financial strength rating: A

Patterson Dental is the exclusive North American distributor of the CEREC 3D dental restorative system. Reflecting strong ongoing demand for the CEREC system, which is fundamentally changing the way dentists perform crown, inlay and onlay procedures, the company believes this new technology equipment has gained full clinical acceptance.

Unlike traditional crown procedures that require two office visits for the patient, a CEREC procedure is completed in just one appointment. By strengthening office productivity and enabling the dentist to perform more restorative procedures, CEREC technology is generating new revenue opportunities for dental practices. CEREC procedures also result in improved clinical outcomes with numerous advantages for the patient. It is a conservative treatment that requires no impressions or temporary caps, and the ceramic, metal-free crown is tooth-colored, highly durable, and biocompatible.

Patterson Dental also is the leading provider of digital radiography systems, which rank high on the wish list of most dentists. Unlike traditional film-based X-rays, digital systems create instant images. The resulting increase in office productivity enables dentists to treat more patients. The benefits of digital radiography are increased when it is integrated with the appropriate software, including Patterson's proprietary EagleSoft line. This integration creates an electronic database that combines the patient's dental record with digital information from the X-ray, intr-oral camera, CEREC and other digital equipment. With a current market penetration of only about 20 percent, it is believed that digital radiography eventually will be installed in most dental offices.

Company Profile

Patterson Companies, Inc. is a value-added distributor serving the dental, companion-pet veterinarian and rehabilitation supply markets. The company recently changed its name from Patterson Dental Company to reflect its expanding base of business, which now encompasses the veterinary and rehabilitation supply markets, as well as its traditional base of operations in the dental supply market.

Dental Market

As Patterson's largest business, Patterson Dental Supply provides a virtually complete range of consumable dental products, equipment, and software, turnkey digital solutions, and value-added services to dentists and dental laboratories throughout North America.

Veterinary Market

Webster Veterinary Supply is the nation's second-largest distributor of consumable veterinary supplies, equipment, diagnostic products, vaccines and pharmaceuticals to companion-pet veterinary clinics.

Rehabilitation Market

AbilityOne Products Corp. is the world's leading distributor of rehabilitation supplies and non-wheelchair assistive patient products to the physical and occupational therapy markets. The unit's global customer base includes hospitals, long-term-care facilities, clinics, and dealers.

Shortcomings to Bear in Mind

- "HOLD-rated Patterson Companies, Inc. posted mixed results in its fiscal third quarter," said David H. Toung, writing for Argus Research Company on March 5, 2008. "While sales growth picked up from the prior quarter, this was a mixed blessing, as the business segment with the smallest profit margin showed the strongest growth. Another factor that pressured margins was an unfavorable shift in product mix in the Dental segment."
- On February 29, 2008, *Value Line Investment Survey* had this comment by Erik A. Antonson: "This equity is no longer timely. Indeed, we now expect it to run in tandem with the broader market in the coming six months. Moreover, we advise most investors to start heading for the hills."

Reasons to Buy

- On February 21, 2008, CEO James W. Wiltz said, "We are encouraged by Patterson's third quarter operating results, which were driven in large part by the performance of our Patterson Dental unit. In addition to solid sales of consumable dental supplies, our dental business benefited from a strong rebound in equipment sales. We are also encouraged by the 10 percent year-over-year sales growth of our CEREC line. Now that the market transition to CEREC's new software and crown milling chamber is largely behind us, we are starting to see a growing level of momentum in CEREC system sales."
- On November 5, 2007, Patterson announced the acquisition of Advanced Practice Systems (known in the marketplace as PTOS Software), the developer and marketer of the industry-leading practice management software for physical therapists.

  PTOS practice management software provides physical therapists with billing, scheduling, documentation and business management capabilities. PTOS has established a leading share in the highly fragmented physical therapy software market

and is endorsed by the leading provider networks in the rehabilitation market.

David P. Sproat, president of Patterson Medical, said, "The acquisition of PTOS software makes another step forward in our drive to expand and strengthen Patterson Medical's full-service, value-added business platform. While PTOS will not have a material impact on current operations, we believe this product line is strategically important, since it should enable Patterson Medical to attract new customers as well as deepen relationships with our existing customer base."

- Dental market growth drivers:

- Graying of America generating demand for dental services, since older individuals require more dental care than any other age group.
- Consumers are spending more on oral health.
- People are keeping natural teeth longer.
- Technological advances are improving clinical outcomes.
- There is an increased demand for specialty procedures.
- There is a strong demand for new-generation equipment needed to strengthen office productivity.
- Dentists per capita are declining, resulting in more business per dentist.
- There is a growing number of dentists who are updating basic equipment.
- There is an expansion of dental insurance coverage.

- Webster Veterinary Supply serves the $2.2 billion domestic companion-pet veterinary supply market, which the company believes to be growing at a 6 percent to 7 percent rate. Small-animal or companion-pet veterinarians are the largest and fastest-growing segment of the overall veterinary market.

  A variety of factors are driving the growth of this segment, including rising pet ownership. It is currently estimated that about

31 million U.S. households own dogs, while 27 million own cats. Consistent with the growth of pet ownership, annual consumer spending on veterinary care is far higher today than it was a decade ago. The willingness of owners to spend more on their pets is related in part to the advent of new procedures and drugs that significantly improve clinical outcomes.

■ Patterson Companies entered the estimated $5 billion worldwide rehabilitation-supply market in fiscal 2004 by acquiring AbilityOne Products Corp., the world's leading distributor of rehabilitation supplies, equipment, and non-wheelchair assistive living products. As the only one-stop shop in the rehabilitation marketplace, AbilityOne provides its customers with the convenience of a single source of supply for all of their product needs.

AbilityOne owns many of the leading brands on the global rehabilitation market, including Sammons, Preston, and Rolyan in the United States and Homecraft in Europe. As a result, no competitor comes close to matching the breadth, and leadership positions of AbilityOne's offerings, which include:

• Braces, splints, and continuous passive motion machines for the orthopedic market.
• Dressings, dining, and bathing devices for the assistive-living segment.

• A full range of rehabilitation equipment, including treatment tables, mat platforms, and stationary bicycles.
• Clinical products, such as exercise bands, weights, balls, and mats.
• Walkers, canes, and wheelchair accessories in the mobility category.

■ Sales of Patterson Medical (formerly AbilityOne Corporation) increased 33 percent in fiscal 2005, to $295.3 million. Excluding the May 2004 acquisition of Medco Supply Company—a leading national distributor of sports medicine, first aid and medical supplies—and the impact of currency adjustments related to its foreign operations, Patterson Medical's internally generated sales increased about 11 percent during 2005. Given favorable demographics and Patterson Medical's industry-leading position, the company view's the rehabilitation market as an excellent long-term growth opportunity for PDCO. According a company spokesman, "By extending our proven value-added business model to this unit and by making selective acquisitions, we intend to further build Patterson Medical's position of market dominance."

SECTOR: **Health Care**
BETA COEFFICIENT: **.70**
10-YEAR COMPOUND EARNINGS PER SHARE GROWTH: **19.7%**
10-YEAR COMPOUND DIVIDENDS PER SHARE GROWTH: **No dividend**

	2007	2006	2005	2004	2003	2002	2001	2000
Revenues (Mil)	2,798	2,615	2,421	1,969	1,657	1,416	1,156	1,040
Net Income (Mil)	208	198	184	150	116	95	76	64
Earnings per share	1.51	1.43	1.32	1.09	0.85	0.70	0.57	0.48
Dividends per share	—	—	—	—	—	—	—	—
Price high	40.1	38.3	53.8	43.7	35.8	27.6	21.1	17.3
low	28.3	29.6	33.4	29.7	17.7	19.1	13.8	8.2

Paychex, Inc.

911 Panorama Trail South □ Rochester, NY 14625-0397 □ (585) 383-3406 □ Web site: *www.paychex.com*
□ Dividend reinvestment plan available □ Fiscal years end May 31 □ Listed: Nasdaq □ Ticker symbol: PAYX
□ S&P rating: A+ □ Value Line financial strength rating: A

On October 8, 2007, Jay Palmer, writing for *Barron's,* had this comment on Paychex, "Beyond the current fiscal year, which ends next May, there is no reason to believe that growth will slow. Its main drivers are a steady rise in the number of clients and the increased popularity of the human-resources operations. The new customers, produced both by referrals from current clients and through the efforts of Paychex's sales team, are coming from cities in which Paychex already operates.

"'We could expand into new cities and will do so slowly,' says CEO Jon Judge. 'But as long as our client numbers are rising satisfactorily, we don't need to do so,' he adds, explaining that margins are lower in new territory for three to five years as operations are established. 'At the moment, our footprint is optimal.'

"For now, Paychex is a rare combination of growth machine and cash cow. 'We have been growing since Moses was four,' quips Judge, noting that this year some 75 percent of new income will be distributed to shareholders, even as the $1 billion stock buyback goes forward. 'We have no cap on our payout, as we are always looking at ways to return money to shareholders, since holding money in the balance sheet is not a good use of cash.'"

Company Profile

Paychex, Inc. is a leading provider of payroll, human resource, and benefits outsourcing solutions for small- to medium-sized businesses. The company offers comprehensive payroll services, including payroll processing, payroll tax administration, and employee pay services, including direct deposit, Readychex, and check signing. Human resource services include 401(k) plan record keeping, workers' compensation administration, section 125 plans, a professional employer organization, time and attendance solutions, and other administrative services for businesses. Paychex was founded in 1971. The company has more than 100 offices and serves more than 543,000 payroll clients nationwide.

Primary Paychex Payroll Services

If there is such a thing as an "average" Paychex client, it is probably represented by the Aquatic Center of Rochester, New York, where they can report their time sheet information by phone, fax, or the Internet, and payroll checks and reports arrive by their chosen delivery method. Other payroll-related services used by the company's core customers include:

- Payroll tax computation, filing, and deposits.
- State unemployment insurance support.
- Electronic filing services for businesses required to deposit payroll or business taxes electronically.
- New-hire reporting.
- Employee pay options, including paper checks, direct deposit, and Visa payroll debit card.
- Laser check signing and insertion of checks in security envelopes.
- Time and attendance solutions that improve productivity and accuracy.
- Online services that extend the convenience of the Internet to the handling of payroll, payroll reports, time sheets, and linking of payroll data to a general ledger.

Shortcomings to Bear in Mind

■ As you might expect, Paychex has a high PE ratio, based on a strong record of earnings. I would not pay more than twenty-five times earnings.

Reasons to Buy

■ On February 6, 2008, *The Outlook*, a publication of Standard & Poor's, gave Paychex a BUY rating, with this comment. "This provider of human resources and benefits services trails rival Automatic Data Processing, but has a strong presence in the small- and medium-sized business market, which we believe is an attractive and growing segment. Despite a slowdown in job growth in recent months, we still look for the overall market for processing services to increase by about 5 percent over the next five years."

■ "The average Paychex client has seventeen employees, although our offerings are the answer for the smallest business to larger ones with more complex needs," said Mr. Judge in 2007. "Among our core clients, we continue to see more usage of our suite of online products. More than 180,000 clients are enrolled in at least one of our online services. This year, we saw a 50 percent jump in the number of customers using our Paychex Online Reports alone. Paychex Major Market Services (MMS) marked its tenth anniversary in 2006. Over 33,000 businesses with fifty or more employees, or with more complex payroll and HR needs, rely on MMS for an integrated solution that includes payroll, time and attendance products, and Paychex HR Online, our Internet-based human resources management system. MMS revenue climbed 27 percent this year, to $225 million."

■ Mr. Judge went on to say, "We are also the market leader in offering a total HR outsourcing solution, serving over 295,000 worksite employees through our Paychex Premier Human Resources product and our professional employer organization, Paychex Business Solutions. Revenue from our Paychex Premier product grew by 57 per-

cent during fiscal 2006, to $52.6 million. PEO revenue was up 25 percent, to $67.1 million.

■ "We opened a whole new distribution system for our Paychex 401(k) Record keeping service in fiscal 2006, allowing our clients and financial advisor partners access to more investment choices," said Mr. Judge. "This lets us go to current payroll clients who have 401(k) plans, but who don't use Paychex for their record-keeping, and offer them a chance to use our 401(k) service while keeping their current investment choices. This new approach also means we can partner with stockbrokers and insurance agents as the record-keeper for their 401(k) customers. This is the kind of leadership that helped us once again rank as the top 401(k) record-keeper in an industry survey, as measured by the number of plans sold. More than 38,000 businesses are now Paychex 401(k) clients. Our Retirement Services revenue was up 16 percent, to $106.1 million last year."

■ Mr. Judge goes on to say, "Through our licensed insurance agency, we provide an ever-growing number of Paychex clients with workers's compensation insurance services. Fifty-two thousand clients use this great service that includes a budgeting tool to help manage their costs. The Paychex Insurance Agency ranks sixteenth in the nation among the biggest public and bank-owned insurance agencies, according to a leading industry publication."

Strategy for the Future

■ "We absolutely value our accomplishments, but we also know that being the best means expanding our opportunities—by looking ahead, planning for the strategic horizon, and ensuring that the appropriate investments are being made to seed a successful future for Paycheck," said Mr. Judge in fiscal 2007. "Our international expansion is part of that future. As the fiscal year ended, we had just opened our third and fourth offices in Germany, which gives us virtually a national footprint. In addition, to offices in Berlin and Hamburg, we are now operating in Dusseldorf and Munich. We have over 500 payroll clients in Germany."

- He went on to say, "Time and attendance solutions are also part of our strategy for the future. The evolution of this exciting suite of products for us includes an online time and labor management system targeting our MMS clients. Another big growth area for Paychex is health and benefits. We now offer health insurance to businesses nationwide, simplifying the process for our clients and researching their options through relationships we have with national and regional insurers."

- The CEO concluded with these comments, "Paychex has been on an extraordinary journey to become the foremost provider in our industry. We started down the path to outsourcing leadership as a payroll company for small businesses. As their needs grew, so did our offerings—evolving to add products like Taxpay, direct deposit, and other pay options for employees. The addition of

employee handbooks ultimately launched a whole new division—Paychex Human Resource Services. The pace of growth in our HR services keeps accelerating, moving from 401(k) record-keeping and flexible spending accounts to our total outsourcing HR solutions and health benefits."

- "These shares are ranked 2 for Timeliness," said Adam Rosner, writing for *Value Line* on February 22, 2008. "Further, our projections indicate Paychex stock offers above-average appreciation potential for the next 3 to 5 years. Although the issue still offers investors a moderate yield, we think the impressive increase in the dividend is a good indicator that business remains healthy."

- On March 28, 2008, writing for Standard & Poor's *Stock Reports*, Dylan Cathers said, "Our BUY recommendation is based on valuation as well as our positive long-term view of the company. We see PAYX's earnings benefiting from solid execution, higher retention rates, falling attrition, and strong profitability."

SECTOR: **Information Technology**
BETA COEFFICIENT: **.95**
10-YEAR COMPOUND EARNINGS PER SHARE GROWTH: **20.4%**
10-YEAR COMPOUND DIVIDENDS PER SHARE GROWTH: **27.4%**

		2007	2006	2005	2004	2003	2002	2001	2000
Revenues (Mil)		1,887	1,675	1,445	1,294	1,099	955	870	728
Net Income (Mil)		515	465	369	303	294	274	255	190
Earnings per share		1.35	1.22	0.97	0.80	0.78	0.73	0.68	0.51
Dividends per share		0.79	0.61	0.51	0.47	0.44	0.42	0.33	0.22
Price	high	47.1	42.4	43.4	39.1	40.5	42.2	51.0	61.3
	low	36.1	33.0	28.8	28.8	23.8	20.4	28.3	24.2

CONSERVATIVE GROWTH

PepsiCo, Inc.

700 Anderson Hill Road □ Purchase, NY 10577-1444 □ (914) 253-3055 □ Dividend reinvestment plan available □ Web site: *www.pepsico.com* □ Listed: NYSE □ Ticker symbol: PEP □ S&P rating: A+ □ Value Line financial strength rating: A++

On March 20, 2008, PepsiCo and The Pepsi Bottling Group announced that they have agreed to jointly acquire a 75.53 percent stake in Russia's leading branded juice company, JSC Lebedyansky, excluding the company's baby food and mineral water business, for US$ 1.4 billion.

Lebedyansky is the world's sixth-largest juice manufacturer and the largest in Russia, with an estimated market share in Russia of around 30 percent and annual revenues in 2007 of $800 million from its juice business.

"This agreement provides us with a strong platform for continued expansion in one of the world's fastest growing juice markets and advances the global transformation of Pepsi-Co's product portfolio," said Michael White, PepsiCo international CEO and vice chairman of PepsiCo. "Combining Lebedyansky's strengths with those of PepsiCo, one of the world's largest makers and sellers of branded juice, and The Pepsi Bottling Group, our largest bottler, will create vast opportunities. We are committed to investing in Lebedyansky's brands and building an even brighter future for this great Russian company."

"Russia represents our biggest growth market, and we are making smart investments that further enhance our business there," said Eric Foss, president and CEO of The Pepsi Bottling Group. "Adding Lebedyansky's strong brands and capable people to the powerful PBG-PepsiCo partnership will enable us to be at the forefront of the continued expansion of the Russian juice category."

Company Profile

The company consists of the snack businesses of Frito-Lay North America and Frito-Lay International; the beverage businesses of Pepsi-Cola North America, Gatorade/Tropicana North America and PepsiCo Beverages International; and Quaker Foods North America, manufacturer and marketer of ready-to-eat cereals and other food products. PepsiCo brands are available in nearly 200 countries and territories.

Many of PepsiCo's brand names are over 100 years old, but the corporation is relatively young. PepsiCo was founded in 1965 through the merger of Pepsi-Cola and Frito-Lay. Tropicana was acquired in 1998, and PepsiCo merged with The Quaker Oats Company, including Gatorade, in 2001.

Frito-Lay North America and Frito-Lay International

PepsiCo's snack food operations had their start in 1932 when two separate events took place. In San Antonio, Texas, Elmer Doolin bought the recipe for an unknown food product—a corn chip—and started an entirely new industry. The product was Fritos brand corn chips, and his firm became the Frito Company.

That same year in Nashville, Tennessee, Herman W. Lay started his own business distributing potato chips. Mr. Lay later bought the company that supplied him with product and changed its name to H.W. Lay Company. The Frito Company and H.W. Lay Company merged in 1961 to become Frito-Lay, Inc.

Today, Frito-Lay brands account for more than half of the U.S. snack chip industry.

PepsiCo began its international snack food operations in 1966. Today, with operations in more than forty countries, it is the leading multinational snack chip company, accounting for more than one quarter of international retail snack chip sales. Products are available in some 120 countries. Frito-Lay North America includes Canada, and the United States. Major Frito-Lay International markets include Australia, Brazil, Mexico, the Netherlands, South Africa, the United Kingdom, and Spain.

Often Frito-Lay products are known by local names. These names include Matutano in Spain, Sabritas and Gamesa in Mexico, Elma Chips in Brazil, Walkers in the United Kingdom, and others. The company markets Frito-Lay brands on a global level, and introduces unique products for local tastes.

Major Frito-Lay products include Ruffles, Lay's, and Doritos brands snack chips. Other major brands include Cheetos cheese flavored snacks, Tostitos tortilla chips, Santitas tortilla chips, Rold Gold pretzels, and SunChips multigrain snacks. Frito-Lay also sells a variety of snack dips and cookies, nuts, and crackers.

Pepsi-Cola North America and PepsiCo Beverages International

PepsiCo's beverage business was founded at the turn of the century by Caleb Bradham, a New Bern, North Carolina druggist, who first formulated Pepsi-Cola. Today consumers spend about $33 billion on Pepsi-Cola beverages. Brand Pepsi and other Pepsi-Cola products—including Diet Pepsi, Pepsi-One, Mountain Dew, Slice, Sierra Mist, and Mug brands—account for nearly one-third of total soft drink sales in the United States, a consumer market totaling about $60 billion.

Pepsi-Cola also offers a variety of noncarbonated beverages, including Aquafina bottled water, Fruitworks, and All Sport.

In 1992, Pepsi-Cola formed a partnership with Thomas J. Lipton Co. Today Lipton is the biggest selling ready-to-drink tea brand in the United States. Pepsi-Cola also markets Frappuccino ready-to-drink coffee through a partnership with Starbucks.

In 2001, SoBe became a part of Pepsi-Cola. SoBe manufactures and markets an innovative line of beverages including fruit blends, energy drinks, dairy-based drinks, exotic teas, and other beverages with herbal ingredients.

Outside the United States, Pepsi-Cola soft drink operations include the business of Seven-Up International. Pepsi-Cola beverages are available in about 160 countries and territories.

Gatorade/Tropicana North America

Tropicana was founded in 1947 by Anthony Rossi as a Florida fruit packaging business. The company entered the concentrate orange juice business in 1949, registering Tropicana as a trademark.

In 1954, Rossi pioneered a pasteurization process for orange juice. For the first time, consumers could enjoy the fresh taste of pure not-from-concentrate 100 percent Florida orange juice in a ready-to-serve package. The juice, Tropicana Pure Premium, became the company's flagship product.

In 1957 the name of the company was changed to Tropicana Products, headquartered in Bradenton, Florida. The company went public in 1957, was purchased by Beatrice Foods Co. in 1978, acquired by Kohlberg, Kravis & Roberts in 1986 and sold to The Seagram Company Ltd. in 1988. Seagram purchased the Dole global juice business in 1995. PepsiCo acquired Tropicana, including the Dole juice business, in August 1998.

Today the Tropicana brand is available in sixty-three countries. Principal brands in North America are Tropicana Pure Premium, Tropicana Season's Best, Dole Juices, and Tropicana Twister. Internationally, principal brands include Tropicana Pure Premium and Dole juices along with Frui'Vita, LoÃza and Copella. Tropicana Pure Premium is the third largest brand of all food products sold in grocery stores in the United States.

Gatorade sports drinks was acquired by the Quaker Oats Company in 1983 and became a part of PepsiCo with the merger in 2001. Gatorade is the first isotonic sports drink. Created in 1965 by researchers at the University of Florida for the school's football team, The Gators, Gatorade is now the world's leading sport's drink.

Quaker Foods North America

The Quaker Oats Company was formed in 1901 when several American pioneers in oat milling came together to incorporate. In Ravenna, Ohio, Henry D. Seymour and William Heston had established the Quaker Mill Company and registered the now-famous trademark.

The first major acquisition of the company was Aunt Jemina Mills Company in 1926, which is today the leading manufacturer of pancake mixes and syrup.

In 1986, the Quaker Oats Company acquired the Golden Grain Company, producers of Rice-A-Roni.

PepsiCo merged with the Quaker Oats Company in 2001. Its products still have the eminence of wholesome, good-for-you food, as envisioned by the company over a century ago.

Shortcomings to Bear in Mind

■ According to one analyst, there is some risk from unfavorable weather conditions in the company's markets, inability to meet volume and revenue growth targets, increased popularity of low-carbohydrate diets, and consumer acceptance of new product introductions.

Reasons to Buy

■ On January 8, 2008, PepsiCo announced that it had reached a definitive agreement to purchase Penelopa, Bulgaria's leading producer and seller of branded nuts and seeds. Penelopa, founded ten years ago by current owner Yanko Lolov, sells peanuts, sunflower seeds, and other savory snacks throughout Bulgaria, principally through its dedicated national direct distribution system. The company operates one plant, located in Sliven, and employs nearly 200 people.

"Penelopa is an outstanding company that will dramatically increase our presence in Bulgaria, a consumer market enjoying robust economic growth, as well as in the broader Balkans region," said Mr. White. "Furthermore, Penelopa's line of high quality nuts and seeds is very consistent with our global focus on addressing consumers' growing interest in health and wellness."

■ On September 14, 2007, PepsiCo and Unilever announced they had agreed to expand their international partnership for the marketing and distribution of ready-to-drink tea products under the Lipton brand, the world's best-selling tea brand.

The new agreement adds eleven countries to the partnership's existing Lipton ready-to-drink tea business. The business in these countries—eight in Europe (Germany, Italy, France, Netherlands, Switzerland, Austria, Belgium, and Portugal) as well as Korea, Taiwan and South Africa—had combined systems sales to the trade of around Euro 300m in 2006. The new agreement effectively completes the partnership and creates the leading global ready-to-drink tea business.

■ On March 22, 2008, Standard & Poor's *Stock Reports* rated PepsiCo a BUY with this comment by Esther Y. Kwon, CFA, "Our recommendation reflects our view of PEP's domestic and international growth opportunities, strong pricing power and healthy cash flow."

■ Argus Research Company also gave Pepsi a BUY rating on March 11, 2008. Erin Ashley Smith said, "PepsiCo plans to drive growth in 2008 through expansion in international markets, stronger marketing and product development efforts, and improved relationships with retailers."

■ For its part, *Value Line* gave Pepsi a favorable 2 rating with this comment by Tom Nikic: "We think earnings growth will be healthy in 2008. The PepsiCo International division should be a strong driver of growth."

SECTOR: **Consumer Staples**
BETA COEFFICIENT: **.75**
10-YEAR COMPOUND EARNINGS PER SHARE GROWTH: **12%**
10-YEAR COMPOUND DIVIDENDS PER SHARE GROWTH: **11.3%**

	2007	2006	2005	2004	2003	2002	2001	2000
Revenues (Mil)	39,474	35,137	32,562	29,261	26,971	25,112	23,512	25,480
Net Income (Mil)	5,658	5,642	4,078	4,174	3,494	3,313	2,660	2,540
Earnings per share	3.41	3.34	2.39	2.44	2.01	1.85	1.47	1.42
Dividends per share	1.43	1.13	1.01	0.85	0.63	0.60	0.58	0.56
Price high	79.0	66.0	60.3	55.7	48.9	53.5	50.5	49.9
low	61.9	56.0	51.3	45.3	36.2	34.0	40.3	29.7

> INCOME

Piedmont Natural Gas Company, Inc.

P. O. Box 33068 ❏ Charlotte, NC 28233 ❏ (704) 731-4226 ❏ Dividend reinvestment program is available
❏ Fiscal years end October 31 ❏ Listed NYSE ❏ Web site: *www.piedmontng.com* ❏ Ticker symbol: PNY
❏ S&P rating: A− ❏ Value Line financial strength rating: B++

For the 2007 fiscal year, the company reported net income of $104.4 million, or $1.40 per diluted share. These results compare with net income of $97.2 million, or $1.28 per diluted share, for the 2006 fiscal year. CEO Thomas E. Skains commented, "We are pleased with the progress of the Company during fiscal year 2007, a year in which we continued to invest in natural gas infrastructure to serve our growing markets, streamline and consolidate our business processes and operations, and enhance our customer service and satisfaction levels. Our nonutility joint venture investments, with a strong performance from South-Star Energy and Hardy Storage going into service in 2007, made positive contributions to our earnings growth." Mr. Skains went on to say, "We have made significant progress in all aspects of our business and our customers and shareholders are seeing the benefits."

System throughput for fiscal year 2007 totaled 206 million dekatherms, compared with 198.7 million dekatherms for the previous year. The increase was primarily due to greater transportation deliveries to power generation customers and overall customer growth. Weather for the year was 12 percent warmer than normal and 7 percent warmer than 2006.

Margin for the year was essentially flat compared to the prior year. While margin was positively influenced by customer growth in the company's service areas, it was partially offset by warmer than normal weather and customer conservation. Additionally, a regulatory order required the discontinuance of an accounting practice that also adversely impacted margin for the year by ($5.4

million), or ($.04) per share. Operations and maintenance expenses for the year decreased $4.9 million from the previous fiscal year primarily due to cost reductions from the company's 2006 management restructuring program and from the implementation of the automated meter reading project completed earlier in the year. These decreases were partially offset by increased expenses associated with outside services and employee benefits.

Company Profile

Incorporated in 1950, Piedmont Natural Gas is an energy services company, primarily engaged in the transportation, distribution and sale of natural gas and propane to residential, commercial and industrial customers in North Carolina, South Carolina, and Tennessee.

The company is the second-largest natural gas utility in the Southeast, serving 960,000 customers. Piedmont Natural Gas and its nonutility subsidiaries and divisions are also engaged in acquiring, marketing, transporting, and storing natural gas for large-volume customers, in retailing residential and commercial gas appliances.

Other business interests in which the company is engaged that are not subject to state utility regulation include the sale of propane and investments in a natural gas pipeline and an interstate LNG (liquefied natural gas) storage facility and marketing natural gas and other energy products and services to deregulated markets.

PNY's Joint Ventures

- SouthStar Energy Services LLC—an equity participant (or part owner) in Georgia's largest retail natural gas marketer.

- Pine Needle LNG Company, LLC—an equity participant in a liquefied natural gas facility that's among the nation's largest.
- Cardinal Pipeline Company, LLC—an equity participant in a 102-mile intrastate pipeline serving portions of North Carolina.
- EasternNC Natural Gas—an equity participant in a venture that is expanding natural gas distribution into fourteen counties in eastern North Carolina.

Shortcomings to Bear in Mind

■ The company has benefited from extraordinary growth in its service territory. However, customer growth can be a double-edged sword, as it is expensive to continuously expand an underground pipe system to keep up with new construction. On the other hand, Piedmont has effectively lowered its cost to connect a customer to about $1,800, a significant decline over prior years. Analysts, moreover, expect this cost to continue to decline, which would contribute to future earnings growth.

Reasons to Buy

■ On March 20, 2008, Net Davis Research, Inc. had this comment: "Both the Fundamental Risk Model and the Technical Model for PNY remain in the favorable zone. Consequently, the stock remains on its BUY rating."

■ Columbine Capital gave the stock a BUY rating on March 20, 2008, with this comment: "Columbine evaluated Piedmont by comparing the company to its peers on a series of individual analytical tools that represent proven measure's of a firm's business value, its long-term growth characteristics, and the behavior of its investors."

■ On March 20, 2008, Ford Equity Research had this to say: "The Ford research team projects that Piedmont will outperform the market over the next six to twelve months. Our decision is based on systematic analysis, which balances Piedmont's quality and trend of its earnings growth, relative to fundamental valuation and its timeliness."

■ Piedmont Natural Gas has an impressive record of acquisitions:

- Effective January 1, 2001, the company purchased for cash the natural gas distribution assets of Atmos Energy Corporation, situated in the city of Gaffney and portions of Cherokee Country, South Carolina. It added 5,400 customers to PNY's operations.
- Effective September 30, 2002, the company purchased for $26 million in cash substantially all of the natural gas distribution assets of North Carolina Gas Service, a division of NUI Utilities, Inc. This added 14,000 customers to PNY's distribution system in the counties of Rockingham and Stokes, North Carolina.
- Effective September 30, 2003, the company purchased for $417.5 million in cash 100 percent of the common stock of NCNG from Progress Energy, Inc., a natural gas distributor serving some 176,000 customers in eastern North Carolina.
- In 2004, the company completed the permanent debt and equity financing of its acquisition of NCNG. Mr. Skains said, "We established our historically strong capital structure with an equity capitalization of 56 percent, as of October 31, 2004. In April, the rating agencies recognized these accomplishments by raising their outlook for Piedmont to 'stable' along with credit ratings of 'A' and 'A3'. Your company is financially strong

and well-positioned to take advantage of future strategic opportunities in a disciplined fashion."

According to another officer of the company, "The primary reasons for these acquisitions are consistent with our strategy of pursuing profitable growth in our core natural gas distribution business in the Southeast. The reasons for the acquisitions and the factors that contributed to the goodwill include:

- A reasonable purchase price, slightly above book value.
- The prospect of entering a market contiguous to our existing North Carolina service areas where, as a combined company, we could realize on-going system benefits.
- The prospect of acquiring an operation that could be integrated into our existing business systems and processes.
- The opportunity to grow within a regulatory environment with which we are familiar."

■ Piedmont Natural Gas enjoys an economically robust and diverse service area that is among the fastest growing in the nation. The company's three-state service area consists of the Piedmont region of the Carolinas—Charlotte, Salisbury, Greensboro, Winston-Salem, High Point, Burlington, and Hickory in North Carolina and Anderson, Greenville, and Spartanburg in South Carolina—and the metropolitan area of Nashville, Tennessee. Both *Plant Sites and Parks* and *Site Selection* magazines continue to rank the Carolinas and Tennessee among the best in the nation for business relocation and expansion and business climate.

The center of the Piedmont Carolinas area is the Greater Charlotte urban region—sixth largest in the nation—with over 6 million people within a 100-mile radius. Charlotte is the nation's second-largest financial center. It is headquarters city for Bank of America, the nation's second-largest bank, and for First Union National bank, the sixth largest. Wachovia Corporation, the nation's fifth-largest bank, is headquartered in Winston-Salem.

Charlotte/Douglas International Airport, with over 500 flights per day and 23 million passengers annually, is US Airways' largest hub and the twentieth busiest airport in the world.

The Nashville region is a diverse center of a retail trading area of over 2 million people, where health care is the largest industry. It is also home to major transportation, publishing, printing, financial, insurance and communications companies as well as twenty colleges and universities.

■ An important factor in analyzing any public utility is the region's regulatory environment. In Piedmont's states, regulators have generally been supportive of the company's regulatory needs over the past few years. In the opinion of Daniel M. Fidell and Tracey W. McMillin, analysts with A. G. Edwards, "Our conclusion is based on several factors, such as purchased gas and weather normalization mechanisms in rates that serve to smooth the impact of changes in gas prices and abnormal weather conditions. In addition, PNY has benefited from fair and timely rate relief in the past to recover costs associated with extensive system growth."

SECTOR: **Utilities**
BETA COEFFICIENT: **.85**
10-YEAR COMPOUND EARNINGS PER SHARE GROWTH: **4.2%**
10-YEAR COMPOUND DIVIDENDS PER SHARE GROWTH: **5.1%**

	2007	2006	2005	2004	2003	2002	2001	2000
Revenues (Mil)	1,711	1,925	1,761	1,530	1,221	832	1,108	830
Net Income (Mil)	104	97	101	95	74	62	65	64
Earnings per share	1.40	1.28	1.32	1.27	1.11	0.04	1.01	1.00
Dividends per share	1.00	0.96	0.92	0.86	0.82	0.79	0.76	0.72
Price high	28.9	28.4	25.8	24.4	22.0	19.0	19.0	19.7
low	22.0	23.2	21.3	19.2	16.6	13.7	14.6	14.3

CONSERVATIVE GROWTH

Praxair, Inc.

39 Old Ridgebury Road □ Danbury, CT 06810-5113 □ (203) 837-2354 □ Dividend reinvestment plan available □ Web site:
www.praxair.com □ Listed: NYSE □ Ticker symbol: PX □ S&P rating: A □ Value Line financial strength rating: A

On September 17, 2007, Praxair and Foster Wheeler North America Corp. (a U.S. subsidiary of Foster Wheeler Ltd.) signed a multiyear agreement that calls for the joint pursuit of certain demonstration projects that will incorporate clean coal technologies and integrated oxy-coal combustion systems into coal-fired electric generating plants to facilitate capture and sequestration of carbon dioxide (CO_2).

The combination of the two companies' technologies and systems expertise would enable a coal-fired generating plant to reduce carbon dioxide stack emissions by more than 90 percent as compared to a conventional coal-fired plant of similar size. Generating plants that burn opportunity fuels such as biomass and petroleum coke in combination with coal would also be able to effect similar reductions in CO_2 emissions. The two companies agreed to share technical information to ensure successful integration of the combined systems.

Under the agreement, Foster Wheeler will develop and supply steam generators using oxy-coal combustion technology that can be installed in new or existing coal-fired power plants. Oxy-coal combustion creates a highly concentrated stream of CO_2

from a steam generator to facilitate carbon capture and sequestration. Foster Wheeler expects that its first applications of oxy-coal combustion technology would involve the company's circulating fluidized-bed (CFB) steam generators, which have already gained global market acceptance for their efficiency, fuel flexibility, and relatively low emissions. Foster Wheeler expects that oxy-coal combustion technology will be applicable to pulverized-coal (PC) steam generators as well.

Praxair has a long history of advancing oxygen-based combustion and gas-processing technologies that bring substantial productivity and environmental benefits to customers in many industries. For this project, Praxair will provide the upstream oxygen-supply facilities, applying its design, engineering and construction expertise in building large cryogenic air-separation plants that produce the large volumes of oxygen necessary for clean-coal projects. Praxair also will provide the downstream CO_2 capture and gas-processing technologies and equipment, based on its experience as one of the world's leading CO_2 suppliers. Praxair's control systems and integration capabilities also will be a key component of the project.

Company Profile

Praxair, Inc. is a global *Fortune* 500 company that supplies atmospheric, process and specialty gases, high-performance coatings, and related services and technologies. Praxair, which was spun off to Union Carbide shareholders in June 1992, is the largest producer of industrial gases in North and South America; it is the third-largest company of its kind in the world.

Praxair's primary products are: atmospheric gases—oxygen, nitrogen, argon, and rare gases (produced when air is purified, compressed, cooled, distilled and condensed), and process and specialty gases—carbon dioxide, helium, hydrogen, semiconductor process gases, and acetylene (produced as by-products of chemical production or recovered from natural gas).

The company also designs, engineers and constructs cryogenic and noncryogenic supply systems. Praxair Surface Technologies is a subsidiary that applies metallic and ceramic coatings and powders to metal surfaces in order to resist wear, high temperatures and corrosion. Aircraft engines are its primary market, but it serves others, including the printing, textile, chemical and primary metals markets, and provides aircraft engine and airframe component overhaul services. Praxair adopted its name in 1992, from the Greek word "praxis," or practical application, and "air," the company's primary raw material. PX was originally founded in 1907 when it was the first company to commercialize cryogenically separated oxygen. Over the century of its existence, Praxair has remained a leader in the development of processes and technologies that have revolutionized the industrial gases industry. The company introduced the first distribution system for liquid gas in 1917, and developed on-site gas supply by the end of WWII. In the 1960s, Praxair introduced noncryogenic means of air separation, and since then has continued to introduce innovative applications technologies for various industries. PX holds almost 3,000 patents. Praxair serves a wide range of industries: food and beverages, health care, semiconductors, chemicals, refining, primary metals and metal fabrication, as well as other areas of general industry.

Shortcomings to Bear in Mind

- On April 5, 2008, Standard & Poor's *Stock Reports* rated Praxair a HOLD. That's the only negative comment I can find.

Reasons to Buy

- On April 7, 2008, Argus Research Company preferred a BUY rating, "with a price target of $97," said analyst Bill Selesky.
- On March 14, 2008, *Value Line Investment Survey* gave Praxair its highest rating, a 1 for Timeliness. Simon R. Shoucair said, "Surface technologies is rallying nicely. This segment has improved significantly, as strong coatings sales to aerospace customers and rising demand for industrial gas turbine coatings have primarily driven sales growth."
- On December 3, 2007, Praxair and Yara International ASA of Norway formally launched a joint venture, Yara Praxair AS, effective November 30, to develop growth opportunities in the industrial gases sector in Scandinavia.

The intention to form the venture was announced in May and the European Commission cleared Praxair's acquisition of a 50 percent stake in Yara International's industrial gases business on November 28.

Yara International ASA, with 2006 revenue of more than USD $8 billion, is a leading chemical company that converts energy and nitrogen from the air into essential products for farmers and industrial customers. As the number one global supplier of mineral fertilizers and agronomic solutions, it helps provide food for a growing world population. Its industrial product portfolio includes environmental protection agents that safeguard air and water purity and preserve food quality. Yara's global workforce of 7,000 employees represents great diversity and talent enabling Yara to remain a leading performer in its industry.

■ "Globally, Praxair's business is strong," said CEO Steve Angel on February 26, 2008. "In Mexico, our sales have grown at about 15 percent per year, reflecting increasing demand from the domestic manufacturing sector. Last year, we acquired a local industrial gases business, which added about $75 million in sales and strengthened our production and distribution network in that country.

"In South America, the startup of new plants to supply metals and petrochemical customers generated a 19 percent increase in sales, while cost controls and productivity improvements resulted in an operating profit increase of 23 percent. Our joint venture in the distribution of liquefied natural gas in Brazil with the state-owned oil company, Petrobras, has been very successful and has led to new contracts with more than a dozen other industrial customers."

■ Mr. Angel also said, "Our European business continued strong growth, particularly in Germany and Spain. We formed a joint venture with Yara International ASA of Norway to develop new opportunities in the on-site gas businesses as well as promising enhanced-oil-recovery projects in the North Sea. The venture combines Yara's strong market position and name recognition in the Scandinavian region with Praxair's operational expertise and technologies. The global reach of both companies also offers the potential for additional collaboration in other parts of the world."

■ The CEO goes on to say, "Across Asia, demand for electronic gases from semiconductor and flat-panel liquid-crystal-display producers in Korea and Taiwan remained strong. We expect significant sales growth in China over the next two years as a number of new projects startup for customers in the petrochemicals, metals and electronics markets. In India, we are actively participating in the modernization of India's infrastructure, working with customers in the metals, petrochemicals, transportation, and pharmaceutical sectors."

■ The largest construction project in Praxair's history—two new hydrogen plants in Texas—now supply refinery customers along Praxair's 340-mile pipeline. These plants doubled Praxair's hydrogen capacity on the U.S. Gulf Coast.

Demand for the company's hydrogen on the Gulf Coast is expected to grow 20 percent annually through 2010 for the following reasons:

• More stringent limits on sulfur content in motor fuels.
• The need to process crude oil containing higher levels of sulfur.
• The role hydrogen can play in expanding existing refining capacity.
• Increased processing of tar sands in Canada.
• New regulatory requirements for locomotives, off-road vehicles, and marine engines scheduled to be implemented later in the decade.

■ Praxair's applications technologies have improved air and water quality and increased energy efficiency for customers in dozens of industries. Most recently, Praxair and BP opened a hydrogen fueling station at Los Angeles International Airport to support Governor Schwarzenegger's hydrogen highway initiative. In its own operations, the company is on track to meet its goals of reducing energy intensity by 18 percent and greenhouse gases emissions intensity by 8 percent over the next ten years.

■ Hydrogen is part of a comprehensive portfolio of bulk and specialty gases, technologies and services Praxair provides refining and chemical customers worldwide. For example, Praxair supplies more than fifty refineries and petrochemical plants from its 280 miles of pipeline along the Texas and Louisiana Gulf Coast. Other Praxair pipeline enclaves serving these industries are situated in Ecorse, Michigan; Edmonton, Alberta, Canada; Salvador, Brazil; Antwerp, Belgium; and Beijing, China.

SECTOR: **Materials**
BETA COEFFICIENT: **1.10**
10-YEAR COMPOUND EARNINGS PER SHARE GROWTH: **11%**
10-YEAR COMPOUND DIVIDENDS PER SHARE GROWTH: **18.5%**

		2007	2006	2005	2004	2003	2002	2001	2000
Revenues (Mil)		9,402	8,324	7,656	6,594	5,613	5,128	5,158	5,043
Net Income (Mil)		1,177	988	726	697	585	548	432	432
Earnings per share		3.62	3.00	2.20	2.10	1.77	1.66	1.50	1.49
Dividends per share		1.20	1.00	0.72	0.60	0.46	0.38	0.34	0.31
Price	high	92.1	63.7	54.3	46.2	38.3	30.6	28.0	27.5
	low	58.0	50.4	41.1	34.5	25.0	22.4	18.3	15.2

CONSERVATIVE GROWTH

The Procter & Gamble Company

P.O. Box 599 □ Cincinnati, Ohio 45201-0599 □ (800) 742-6253 □ Direct Dividend reinvestment plan available □ Web site: *www.pg.com* □ Listed: NYSE □ Fiscal years end June 30 □ Ticker symbol: PG □ S&P rating: A+ □ Value Line financial strength rating: A++

Net sales in fiscal 2007 increased 12 percent to $76.5 billion. Sales were up behind 9 percent volume growth, including the impact of an additional three months of Gillette in fiscal 2007. Growth was driven by initiative activity such as Gillette Fusion, Pantene brand restage, Olay Definity and Regenerist, Dolce & Gabbana "The One," Always Clean, Tide Simple Pleasures, Gain Joyful Expressions, Swiffer upgrade, and Pampers Caterpillar Flex.

Price increases added 1 percent to net sales and favorable foreign exchange contributed 2 percent. Organic sales were up 5 percent with each reportable segment delivering year-on-year growth.

Net earnings grew 19 percent during the fiscal year to $10.3 billion. Net earnings increased behind sales growth and an 80-basis point improvement in operating margin. Diluted net earnings per share increased 15 percent to $3.04, including an estimated $0.10-$0.12 dilution impact from Gillette. Gillette dilution was better than the company's expectations primarily due to faster-than-expected cost synergies.

Gross margin improved 60-basis points to 52.0 percent during the fiscal year. (There are 100 basis points in a percentage.) Higher commodity costs hurt gross margin by over 60-basis points but were more than offset by scale leverage from strong organic volume growth, cost savings projects and Gillette cost synergies. The favorable mix impact of the additional three months of Gillette results in fiscal 2007 contributed approximately 30-basis points to gross margin.

SG&A as a percent of sales improved 20-basis points in fiscal 2007 to 31.8 percent driven by lower overhead spending as a percentage of net sales. Overhead spending improved as volume scale leverage, Gillette-related cost synergies and overhead cost controls more than offset the impact of higher Gillette acquisition-related expenses.

The company's operating cash flow for the fiscal year was $13.4 billion, an increase of 18 percent versus the prior year. Operating cash increased primarily behind higher earnings. Working capital increased during the year primarily to support business growth. Capital expenditures were 3.9 percent of net sales, in line with the prior year and slightly better than the company's 4 percent target. Free cash flow was $10.5 billion for the year and free cash flow productivity was 101 percent during the year, well above the company's 90 percent target.

Company Profile

Procter & Gamble dates back to 1837, when William Procter and James Gamble began making soap and candles in Cincinnati. The company's first major product introduction took place in 1879, when it launched Ivory soap. Since then, P&G has traditionally created a host of blockbuster products that have made the company a cash-generating machine.

Procter & Gamble is a uniquely diversified consumer-products company with a strong global presence. P&G today markets its broad line of products to nearly 5 billion consumers in more than 160 countries.

Procter & Gamble is a recognized leader in the development, manufacturing and marketing of superior quality laundry, cleaning, paper, personal care, food, beverage, and health care products, including prescription pharmaceuticals.

Among the company's nearly 300 brands are Tide, Always, Whisper, Didronel, Pro-V, Oil of Olay, Pringles, Ariel, Crest, Pampers, Pantene, Vicks, Bold, Dawn, Head & Shoulders, Cascade, Iams, Zest, Bounty, Comet, Scope, Old Spice, Folgers, Charmin, Tampax, Downy, Cheer and Prell.

Procter & Gamble is a huge company, with 2005 sales of more than $56 billion. In the same fiscal year (which ended June 30, 2005), earnings per share advanced from $2.32 to $2.53. Dividends also climbed—as they have for many years—from $0.93 to $1.03. The company has nearly 110,000 employees working in more than eighty countries.

The Acquisition of Gillette

In 2005, Procter & Gamble acquired Gillette Company for about $57 billion. "This merger is going to create the greatest consumer products company in the world," said Warren E. Buffett, CEO of Berkshire Hathaway, Inc., Gillette's largest shareholder. "It's a dream deal."

Here is what Gillette looks like:

Founded in 1901, The Gillette Company is the world leader in male grooming, a category that includes blades, razors, and shaving preparations. Gillette also holds the number-one position worldwide in selected female grooming products, such as wet shaving products and hair epilation devices.

The company holds the number one position worldwide in manual and power toothbrushes and is the world leader in alkaline batteries.

According to the company, "Our focus is on placing resources behind Gillette's three core businesses: grooming, batteries and oral care. Our core businesses account for nearly 80 percent of our sales and 90 percent of our profits. We are—in all three—the undisputed global leader.

"Some of our core brands include:

- Gillette Mach3
- Gillette for Women Venus
- Gillette Series
- Right Guard
- Duracell Copper Top
- Oral-B
- Braun Oral-B
- Braun

Gillette manufacturing operations are conducted at thirty-four facilities in fifteen countries. Products are distributed through wholesalers, retailers and agents in over 200 countries and territories.

Shortcomings to Bear in Mind

- "Retailers are sometimes competitors as well as partners," said CEO A. G. Lafley. "Their own brands are growing as the retailers, themselves, grow. Private labels, or store brands, strive to match innovation quickly and try to present a compelling value alternative in many categories. This is healthy, in my opinion. It requires that we continue to lead innovation and price P&G products competitively. Further, the growing strength of store brands underscores the importance of always being the number-one or number-two brand in any category. Brands that can't maintain this leadership stature will find it difficult to compete effectively with the best store brands. Based on our internal global share measures, we have the number one or number two brand in seventeen of our nineteen key global categories—categories that account for about 70 percent of sales and earnings. P&G is in a strong position, and ready to become an even better retail partner."

Reasons to Buy

■ P&G is the global leader in Baby Care, Feminine Care, and Fabric Care, with 32 percent to 36 percent global shares in these major categories. In the company's strongest large markets, however, Procter & Gamble has shares that exceed 50 percent. What's more, the Gillette Blades and Razors business is still growing, with global shares in excess of 70 percent.

■ Procter & Gamble has more than doubled sales in faster-growing, higher-margin categories, such as beauty, health care, and home care. According to a company spokesman, "More than 70 percent of the company's growth, or roughly $20 billion in net sales, has come from organic growth and strategic acquisitions in these businesses. Well over half of P&G sales now comes from these faster-growing higher-margin businesses."

■ P&G interacts with more than 4 million consumers a year in nearly sixty countries. "We conduct more than 10,000 research studies each year and invest more than $200 million per year in consumer and market understanding. Our research spans more than twenty-five product categories, providing a more complete understand-

ing of consumers than companies focused more narrowly on a few categories. We see innovation opportunities that others do not see," said a company official in fiscal 2007.

■ In a recent U.S. survey by Cannondale Associates, retailers were asked to rank manufacturers on a number of competencies. P&G was ranked number one in virtually every category:

• Clearest company strategy
• Brands most important to retailers
• Best brand marketers overall
• Most innovative marketing programs

■ Procter & Gamble in known for product innovation. More than 8,000 scientists and researchers are accelerating the pace of new products. The company has a global network of eighteen technical centers in nine countries on four continents. What's more, P&G holds more than 27,000 patents and applies for 3,000 more each year. Not surprisingly, the company is among the ten top patent-producing companies in the world—well ahead of any other consumer-products manufacturer.

■ "Long-term prospects look good," said Orly Seidman, writing for *Value Line Investment Survey* on April 4, 2008. "The breadth of Procter's portfolio, coupled with its branding initiatives, should help brighten the 2010-2012 horizon. Innovation and improving its offerings of household staples should help P&G maintain its position in a highly competitive environment as domestic discretionary spending continues to decline."

■ On February 9, 2008, Thomas White, a research organization, gave Procter & Gamble a BUY rating, with this comment: "The consumer staples team at Thomas White projects that over the next twelve months an investment in P&G will return over 15 percent. These results should outperform the market and outperform 90 percent of the stocks in its industry."

■ Procter & Gamble was given a BUY rating by Channel Trend on March 22, 2008. The report said, "The research team at Channel Trend projects that P&G will outperform the market over the next six to twelve months. Our decision reflects a disciplined analysis of the stock's relationship to its projected future price and its estimated fair value."

■ "Our STRONG BUY opinion reflects our confidence that PG will deliver consistent sales and earnings growth near the high end of its peer group over the next several years, benefits from the Gillette acquisition, and growth prospects in new markets and categories," said Loran Braverman, CFA,

writing for Standard & Poor's *Stock Reports* on February 25, 2008.

■ Procter & Gamble believes in product quality. One of the reasons given for the company's problems in 2000 was its refusal to get into the lower-quality, lower-cost private-label business. That just goes against the grain.

P&G believes that the consumer will reward even minor product advantages, and it will not launch a brand if it does not have a competitive advantage. Then, it will continually improve its products and make every effort to maintain that advantage. Tide, for example, has been improved more than seventy times over the years.

SECTOR: **Consumer Staples**
BETA COEFFICIENT: **.65**
10-YEAR COMPOUND EARNINGS PER SHARE GROWTH: **10.3%**
10-YEAR COMPOUND DIVIDENDS PER SHARE GROWTH: **11%**

	2007	2006	2005	2004	2003	2002	2001	2000
Revenues (Mil)	76,476	68,222	56,741	51,407	43,377	40,238	39,244	39,951
Net Income (Mil)	10,340	8,684	7,257	6,481	5,186	4,352	2,922	4,230
Earnings per share	3.04	2.64	2.53	2.32	1.85	1.54	1.04	1.24
Dividends per share	1.28	1.15	1.03	0.93	0.82	0.76	0.70	0.64
Price high	75.2	64.2	59.7	57.4	50.0	47.4	40.9	59.2
low	60.4	52.8	51.2	48.9	39.8	37.1	28.0	26.4

CONSERVATIVE GROWTH

Raytheon Company

870 Winter Street ❑ Waltham , MA 02451 ❑ (781) 522-3000 ❑ Dividend reinvestment plan available ❑ Web site: *www.raytheon.com* ❑ Ticker symbol: RTN ❑ Listed: NYSE ❑ S&P rating: B ❑ Value Line financial strength rating: A+

On September 20, 2007, Raytheon Company announced that it had entered into an agreement to acquire Oakley Networks, a leading developer of cyber-security technology.

Oakley Networks was founded in 2001 to deliver security solutions to the U.S. government and *Fortune* 500 companies to protect their most critical information technology assets from abuse or misuse. The Oakley platform uniquely combines a broad enterprise monitoring solution with highly visual investigation and forensics tools that

protect against a full range of cyber threats. The company, which is based in Salt Lake City, Utah, has 200 employees.

"We're very excited to add Oakley's capabilities to our own portfolio," said Michael D. Keebaugh, president, Raytheon Intelligence and Information Systems. "We believe that Oakley's portfolio of products and technology, combined with Raytheon's software systems integration expertise, will allow us to provide the robust information security solutions our customers need."

Derek Smith, CEO of Oakley Networks, said, "Combining Raytheon's global expertise and capability with our unique cybersecurity solutions will provide customers with the very best protection available to sustain the confidentiality, integrity and availability of their critical networks, while preserving vital information sharing capability."

Company Profile

Raytheon is a global leader in technology-driven solutions that provide integrated mission systems for the critical defense and nondefense needs of its customers. Raytheon's integrated businesses assure mission success with a broad range of products and services in government electronics, space, information technology, technical services, business, aviation and special mission aircraft.

Raytheon's businesses:

Integrated Defense Systems

Integrated Defense Systems is Raytheon's leader in Joint Battlespace Integration providing affordable, integrated solutions to a strong international and domestic customer base, including the U.S. Missile Defense Agency, the U.S. Armed Forces, and the Department of Homeland Security.

Network Centric Systems

Raytheon Network Centric Systems (NCS), headquartered in McKinney, Texas, develops and produces mission solutions for networking, command and control, battlespace awareness, and air traffic management. Programs include civilian applications, command and control systems, integrated communications systems, and netted sensor systems. NCS serves all branches of the United States military, the National Guard, the Department of Homeland Security, the Federal Aviation Administration, and other U.S. national security agencies, as well as international customers.

Intelligence and Information Systems

At Raytheon Intelligence and Information Systems (IIS), the company transforms data into knowledge. IIS is a leading provider of intelligence and information solutions that provide the right knowledge at the right time, enabling our customers to make timely and accurate decisions to achieve mission goals of national significance.

Raytheon Technical Services Company LLC

RTSC provides technical, scientific, and professional services for defense, federal, and commercial customers worldwide.

It specializes in mission support, counter-proliferation and counter-terrorism, base and range operations, and customized engineering services.

Missile Systems

Missile Systems designs, develops, and produces missile systems for critical requirements, including air-to-air, strike, surface Navy air defense, land combat missiles, guided projectiles, exoatmospheric kill vehicles, and directed energy weapons.

Space and Airborne Systems

Raytheon Space and Airborne Systems (SAS) is a leader in designing and developing integrated systems for crucial missions. For decades, Raytheon has supported military and civil customers with focused, forward-looking technology.

Shortcomings to Bear in Mind

- Raytheon does not have a consistent record of earnings increases. In the 1997-2007 span, for instance, earnings per share made no real progress. In 1997, EPS were $3.01 and did not again reach that level until 2007. In the same span, dividends have been lackluster, at 80 cents a share until 2005.

Reasons to Buy

■ On February 14, 2008, Raytheon said it would have a major presence at DEFEXPO India 2008 in Delhi, India, on February 16-19. As a global technology leader, Raytheon displayed a number of products and services that are applicable to India's stated goals of modern-ization of military and civilian systems.

"Our portfolio is broad, and it fits nicely with India's long-term plans for updating its defense capabilities in areas including the fighter competition, air and missile defense, space and beyond," said Walter Doran, president of Raytheon Asia for Raytheon International, Inc. "India is a key emerging market for us in Asia, and we believe our advanced technology capa-bilities can be tailored to support India's unique needs in coming years."

■ On December 13, 2007, Raytheon MK 57 Vertical Launching System (VLS) program for the Zumwalt-class destroyer (DDG 1000) was recognized by the Department of Defense and the National Defense Industrial Association (NDIA) as a 2006 Top 5 DoD program award winner for excellence in systems engineering.

Co-developed by Raytheon Integrated Defense Systems (IDS) and BAE Systems, the MK 57 VLS provides critical ship self defense capabilities and is designed to fire all missile types in the U.S. Navy inven-tory and projected to be in inventory for the foreseeable future. The first shipboard deployment of the system is planned for the Zumwalt-class destroyer, the U.S. Navy's next-generation, multimission destroyer.

"This award is a projection of the cus-tomer's confidence in the MK 57 VLS and our team's ability to deliver world-class sys-tems," said IDS' Bill Marcley, director of Zumwalt Mission Systems Equipment. "Ray-theon applies its engineering innovation and expertise to the development of systems and capabilities that are reliable, affordable and tailored to meet the needs of the warfighter."

Members from Raytheon's joint govern-ment-industry team were presented with the award during NDIA's 10th Annual Systems Engineering Conference, in San Diego, Cal-ifornia. AFADTS (Advanced Field Artillery Data System), another Raytheon program, also received one of the Top 5 awards.

Integrated Defense Systems is Raythe-on's leader in Joint Battlespace Integration providing affordable, integrated solutions to a broad international and domestic cus-tomer base, including the U.S. Missile Defense Agency, the U.S. Armed Forces, and the Department of Homeland Security.

■ On September 28, 2007, a Raytheon Company partnership with the U.S. Army was named the winner of the Defense Department's 2007 Secretary of Defense Performance Based Logistics (Sub-System Level) Award.

The partnership on Improved Target Acquisition System (ITAS) Contractor Logistics Support was cited by DoD for dra-matically improving the mission success of the ITAS through innovative performance based logistics.

Against a requirement of 90 percent, the Raytheon ITAS CLS team achieved an aver-age operational readiness rate of 99.7 percent for the Army's 782 ITAS. That performance—along with significant improvement in repair times—has resulted in an estimated cost sav-ings of nearly $300 million for the Army.

The award acknowledges the outstand-ing government-industry partnership of Ray-theon's Network Centric Systems Contractor Logistics Support team and the Army in estab-lishing a benchmark program for maintenance and mission support for the ITAS program.

"We're very proud of the work done by the ITAS CLS team with the Army," said Glynn Raymer, vice president of Combat Sys-tems at Network Centric Systems. "This award recognizes our unwavering commitment to supporting our men and women in uniform, the outstanding combat readiness and perfor-mance of the ITAS, as well as our customer's satisfaction with the overall system."

Network Centric Systems is in the first year of a ten-year, firm-fixed-price contract to provide performance-based logistics and mission support for this Army and Marine Corps tactical system. The contract requires Raytheon to provide worldwide logistics support to Army and Marine Corps operations at garrison locations, training centers, and in combat operations around the world. The ITAS CLS program is managed out of Raytheon's McKinney, Texas, facility with field service representatives located around the world, including Iraq and Afghanistan.

■ In a report dated February 16, 2008, Standard & Poor's *Stock Reports* gave Raytheon a BUY rating. Richard Tortoriello said, "Despite changes in Congressional leadership, we think defense budgets will continue to increase at least moderately, given our view of significant current and potential future military threats. We also believe that RTN's leading positions in missiles and defense electronics situate it well to provide products for defense against these threats. We see RTN as well positioned to capture foreign business, for missile defenses and other defense products, with allies including Australia, the United Kingdom, Japan, and other countries in the Middle East and Asia."

■ On February 1, 2008, Argus Research Company rated Raytheon a BUY, with this comment by analyst Suzanne Betts, "The outlook for 2008 remains bright, as Raytheon has a solid backlog and diverse revenue base."

■ *Value Line* gave Raytheon its best rating for Timelines, 1, on March 21, 2008, with this analysis by Morton L. Siegel, "Orders were quite strong last year, which generated a backlog of $36.6 billion, at year-end, over 170 percent of 2007's sales. The company's increasing acceptance as a supplier of military hardware around the globe to America's friends and allies is illustrated by foreign sales amounting to 20 percent of the total last year. Meanwhile, the foreign backlog amounted to 26 percent of the total at year-end, which augurs well for increasing penetration of the overseas markets."

SECTOR: **Industrials**
BETA COEFFICIENT: **.95**
10-YEAR COMPOUND EARNINGS PER SHARE GROWTH: **2.4%**
10-YEAR COMPOUND DIVIDENDS PER SHARE GROWTH: **2.5%**

	2007	2006	2005	2004	2003	2002	2001	2000
Revenues (Mil)	21,301	20,291	21,894	20,245	18,109	16,760	16,867	16,895
Net Income (Mil)	2,578	1,155	942	661	535	861	489	498
Earnings per share	3.80	2.56	2.08	1.49	1.29	2.15	1.35	1.46
Dividends per share	1.02	0.96	0.88	0.80	0.80	0.80	0.80	0.80
Price high	65.9	54.2	40.6	41.9	34.0	45.7	37.4	33.3
low	1.03	9.43	6.02	9.32	4.32	6.32	4.01	7.9

GROWTH AND INCOME

Rohm and Haas Company

100 Independence Mall West ❑ Philadelphia, PA 19106 ❑ (215) 592-3000 ❑ Dividend reinvestment plan not available ❑ Web site: *www.rohmhaas.com* ❑ Ticker symbol: ROH ❑ Listed: NYSE ❑ S&P rating: A– ❑ Value Line financial strength rating: B++

On September 24, 2007, Rohm and Haas announced the launch of TianBa™ 2000, a new coatings product that has been developed to meet Chinese customers' needs. This product introduction clearly demonstrates Rohm and Haas' commitment to provide swift response and innovative products to meet local customers' needs. TianBa™ 2000 was exhibited to Chinese customers for the first time at the China Roofing and Waterproofing Exhibition on September 24.

TianBa 2000 is the new generation flexible acrylic copolymer with broad applicability for use in cement-based and non-cement-based waterproof coatings, flexible plastering mortar for thermal insulation systems, external flexible putties, ceramic tile adhesives, and mortar repair. Extensive studies demonstrate that TianBa 2000 has better waterproofing, flexibility, and alkali resistance than similar existing products. TianBa 2000 is environmentally advanced technology, which is low-odor and low in volatile organic compounds.

"The launch of TianBa 2000 is a significant break through for both the Chinese and global coatings markets," said Bruce Hoechner, general manager for Paint and Coatings Materials in Asia-Pacific. "TianBa 2000 significantly expands our technology offerings for waterproof coatings applications and demonstrates our continued commitment to local markets."

Company Profile

Founded in 1909, Rohm and Haas is a global pioneer in the creation and development of innovative technologies and solutions for the specialty materials industry. The company's technologies are found in a wide range of industries including: Building and Construction, Electronics and Electronic Devices, Household Goods and Personal Care, Packaging and Paper, Transportation, Pharmaceutical and Medical, Water, Food and Food Related, and Industrial Process.

Innovative Rohm and Haas technologies and solutions help to improve life every day, around the world. ROH is the source of a remarkable array of sophisticated materials that help its customers create better products, so their customers can lead more comfortable lives. The company's products, and the ultimate commercial products of its customers, serve many and diverse markets, from building and construction to electronics, to personal care and household products.

Markets the company serves:

Automotive

From the cars, trains, ships and planes we ride in to the highways and roads the world drives on, the company's innovative products help make traveling more comfortable, safer, reliable, and enjoyable.

Building and Construction

From rooftops to foundations, from walls to floors, and the insulation and plumbing in-between, Rohm and Haas creates the innovative materials used throughout our surroundings to bring peace of mind and improve quality of life. Ever since ROH pioneered acrylic waterborne chemistry for high-quality interior and exterior paints and coatings, it has been leading the way with environmentally sustainable technology for the building and construction markets.

Electronics and Electronic Devices

With a focus on inventing new materials that make electronic devices faster, smaller, more powerful and less expensive, Rohm and Haas offers leading-edge chemistry used to make semiconductor chips and printed wiring boards found in today's most sophisticated electronic devices.

Food and Retail

The company's ion exchange resins purify apple and citrus juices, soft drinks and dairy products, and they have helped sugar producers make white granulated sugar and other sweeteners for more than forty years. Rohm and Haas also helps ensure that food processing operations run trouble-free and at peak efficiency with cleaners to remove soil and with polymers to control scale in evaporators and other equipment. In addition, the company offers the most complete line of salt-related products under our Morton Salt brand.

Household and Personal Care

The company's chemistry is in products you use everyday—softening your water, boosting the cleaning power of laundry detergents and other household products, keeping finished products like lotions, shampoos, and conditioners from spoiling after purchase, and increasing the protective power of sunscreens. ROH also provides a wide array of preservatives for both industrial and personal care applications. Its strength in microbial protection is demonstrated through a wide variety of personal care products.

Industrial

Rohm and Haas works closely with customers to understand their unique operating challenges and design custom solutions to help them succeed. The company's petrochemical and chemical industry experts, for example, support its customers in developing novel polymer-based catalysts, improving catalytic and purification processes, and running refining processes. In mineral processing, our ion exchange technology recovers precious metals from ores, and the company's composites support, stabilize, and seal walls in mines. In other industries, its resins purify medicines, recover uranium for reactor fuel, and capture heavy metals to optimize manufacturing costs and minimize waste handling problems.

Packaging

The global packaging industry looks to Rohm and Haas to help it efficiently and cost-effectively produce these products and create more attractive and protective packages than ever before. From packaging for just about any food, one can think of flexible overnight mail envelopes and boxes, to plastic and glass bottles, to hardware containers, the company's chemistry produces packaging that encloses, covers, sticks and protects the material that is inside.

Paper

As a coating specialist, Rohm and Haas backs its broad product line in hollow sphere plastic pigments, binders, rheology modifiers, and dispersants with world-class technical service and support for our customers.

The company is also a leading supplier of bleaching chemicals for paper and textiles.

Water

As one of the most powerful names in water treatment, Rohm and Haas offers a wide range of high quality solutions for virtually every application, from the biggest industrial plants to municipalities to the home.

Shortcomings to Bear in Mind

■ On February 25, 2008, Standard & Poor's *Stock Reports*' analyst, Richard O'Reilly, CFA said, "We have a HOLD on the shares, based on total return potential. We view the company's fundamentals as favorable, although we expect volume growth to remain modest in 2008."

Reasons to Buy

■ On January 28, 2008, CEO Raj L. Gupta said, "We completed the year on a strong note with record sales contributed by robust organic growth, particularly in our Electronic Materials business. Growth in the company's chemical businesses in Rapidly Developing Economies along with favorable performance for our Salt business also helped to deliver a strong quarter."

■ On November 14, 2007, Rohm and Haas and Basin Water, Inc. announced the formation of an exclusive alliance that brings together the technologies, the R&D strength and the global infrastructure of Rohm and Haas Ion Exchange Resins with the systems design, deployment and operating strengths of Basin Water. The alliance will address the need for quality water across a broad range of market segments in the United States and Canada. Initially serving the potable water market, the alliance will also focus on developing new technology to address other groundwater treatment issues, produced water from oil and gas operations, and emerging water recovery applications. New offerings for the potable water market will be jointly developed to include media for the selective removal of inorganic contaminants, synthetic organics, such as MTBE and 1,2,3-TCP, and nitrate destruction/brine recycle technology.

The alliance will be marketed via the Basin Water business model that provides guaranteed performance and guaranteed costs over the lifetime of a project. As part of the alliance, Basin Water will have exclusive access to Rohm and Haas ion exchange resin technology for selected markets. Rohm and Haas will continue to offer its Advanced Amberpack™ system and Amberlite™ PW line of resins for drinking water markets outside of the alliance territory and for traditional industrial water treatment markets globally.

According to Michael M. Stark, president and COO of Basin Water, the alliance with Rohm and Haas will enhance Basin Water's ability to provide reliable, quality supplies of water to its traditional markets and will energize the company's move toward offering new technologies that will provide water solutions in a growing base of applications. "Rohm and Haas is one of the world's leading-edge companies in water treatment technology. We are excited at the opportunity to work with

them in putting that technology to work for our customers," he said. "By engaging in this Alliance, Basin Water gains immediate access to technology and an R&D infrastructure that would have taken us years to develop by ourselves. Together, the Alliance will represent a new concept in delivering solutions to the growing need for quality water in both the public and private sector with an evolving array of state-of-the-art technologies. We believe the market will find this offering very appealing," he added.

Kim Ann Mink, vice president and global general manager for Rohm and Haas Ion Exchange Resins, adds, "Through this Alliance with Basin Water, we now have a strong, reliable channel through which we can expand our depth and breadth of technologies to improve drinking water and to manage the residuals associated with the treatment process. Together, I am confident we can deliver to the market new solutions for many pressing water treatment challenges."

SECTOR: **Materials**
BETA COEFFICIENT: **1.20**
10-YEAR COMPOUND EARNINGS PER SHARE GROWTH: **5.3%**
10-YEAR COMPOUND DIVIDENDS PER SHARE GROWTH: **8.9%**

	2007	2006	2005	2004	2003	2002	2001	2000
Revenues (Mil)	8,897	8,230	7,994	7,300	6,421	5,727	5,666	5,879
Net Income (Mil)	721	755	676	486	374	339	189	381
Earnings per share	3.41	3.49	3.02	2.17	1.68	1.53	0.86	1.73
Dividends per share	1.48	1.28	1.12	0.97	0.86	0.82	0.80	0.78
Price high	62.7	54.0	50.0	45.44	3.14	2.63	8.74	9.4
low	47.0	41.9	39.5	35.9	26.3	30.2	24.9	24.4

AGGRESSIVE GROWTH

Schlumberger Limited

5599 San Felipe, 17th Floor ❑ Houston, TX 77056 ❑ (713) 375-3535 ❑ Dividend reinvestment plan is not available
❑ Web site: *www.slb.com* ❑ Ticker symbol: SLB ❑ Listed: NYSE ❑ S&P rating: B+ ❑ Value Line financial strength rating: A+

"You could call Schlumberger the stealth oil major," said Stanley Reed, writing for *BusinessWeek* on January 14, 2008. "Sure, giants such as ExxonMobil, Chevron, and

BP dominate headlines in the global quest for crude. But they couldn't do it without Schlumberger. The company helps them scope out pockets of oil thousands of feet below the earth's surface, conjuring up their layer-cake images on the computer screen, and then threading drill bits through the richest bands.

"Schlumberger has figured out better than anyone else how the global oil game has changed, and it's helping to drive that change. The company is increasing its cooperation with Big Oil's most prominent rivals, state-owned oil companies, and it's helping a group of smaller upstarts that are seeking to get into the business, such as hedge funds and private equity outfits."

Company Profile

Schlumberger Limited is the world's leading oilfield services company supplying technology, information solutions and integrated project management that optimize reservoir performance for customers working in the oil and gas industry. Founded in 1926, today the company employs more than 76,000 people of over 140 nationalities working in some eighty countries.

The company comprises two business segments:

Schlumberger Oilfield Services supplies a wide range of products and services from formation evaluation through directional drilling, well cementing and stimulation, well completions and productivity to consulting, software, information management and IT infrastructure services that support core industry operational processes.

WesternGeco is the world's largest seismic company and provides advanced acquisition and data processing services.

Schlumberger has principal offices in Houston, Paris and The Hague.

Organization

Schlumberger manages its business through twenty-eight GeoMarket regions, which are grouped into four geographic areas: North America, Latin America, Europe, Commonwealth of Independent States and Africa, and Middle East and Asia. The GeoMarket structure offers customers a single point of contact at the local level for field operations and brings together geographically focused teams to meet local needs and deliver customized solutions. Working together with the company's technology segments, the GeoMarkets provide a powerful conduit through which information and know-how flow to the customers, and through which Schlumberger engineers and geoscientists maximize technological synergies over the entire life of the field.

The company was founded by the two Schlumberger brothers who invented wireline logging as a technique for obtaining downhole data in oil and gas wells. Today, it continues to build on the industry's longest track record of providing leading-edge exploration and production technology to develop new advancements—from reservoir to surface. Schlumberger has always invested significant time and money on research and engineering as a long-term strategy to support and grow its technology leadership. Short-term business cycles do not affect this. In 2006, the company invested $619 million in R&D for its oilfield activities. Schlumberger invests more each year in R&D than all other oilfield services companies combined.

Shortcomings to Bear in Mind

■   Although earnings have made impressive strides in recent years, dividends have lagged far behind. In the period of 1996 through 2004, for instance, dividends per share stayed stagnated at the $0.38 level. More recently, however, the company has made excellent strides in changing this pattern, with the current dividend at $0.70.

Reasons to Buy

■   On January 18, 2008, CEO Andrew Gould made these comments on the company's 2007 results: "Schlumberger revenues in 2007 grew by 21 percent, driven by strong demand for oilfield services particularly in the Eastern Hemisphere and Latin America. All Technologies showed double-digit improvement, with Drilling and Measurements, Well Testing, and Integrated Project Management recording the highest overall growth rates.

"In the fourth quarter strong sequential revenue growth contributed significantly to overall performance, but a less favorable Oilfield Services revenue mix, lower pricing in U.S. land operations, and a number of exceptional and seasonal weather effects led to less than satisfactory margins.

"In addition, strong WesternGeco Multiclient sales failed to offset lower Marine utilization for the quarter due to several vessels dry docking or seasonally transiting to new contracts with consequent margin decline.

"During the second half of 2007, IPM mobilized and started seventeen drilling rigs for the Mezosoico and Alianza projects in Mexico. The fourth-quarter results included the expensing of significant startup costs associated with both projects.

"However, with the exception of pricing for certain Oilfield Services activities on land in North America, the events in the quarter were largely seasonal or reflected the startup cost of new IPM activities and do not represent a change in the underlying trends.

"Shorter-term growth presents a more complex picture than the immediate past. Natural gas drilling in North America is not expected to vary greatly in the absence of any severe weather in the remaining winter months. High utilization of the existing offshore rig fleet and limited new builds entering the market during the year will not only limit growth, but also make activity vulnerable to operating efficiency. However, growth in land activity outside North America will remain strong, while seismic exploration services worldwide will remain in high demand both on land and offshore as the industry gears up for the expanding exploration cycle.

"Within this context, technology that assists our customers in mitigating risk in exploration and development projects, increasing recovery factors and improving operational efficiency will remain at a premium.

"In the longer term however, current levels of drilling are insufficient to meaningfully slow decline rates, improve reservoir recovery or add sufficient new production capacity. The explosion in exploration licenses awarded in the last three years, the continual expansion of the number of new offshore rigs being ordered for delivery through and beyond the end of the decade, and the industry-wide, as well as our own plans to increase both capex and research and development spend are clear indicators of future growth. It is our view that only a global economic recession that lowers demand can flatten this trend.

"In line with this overall positive outlook, I am pleased to announce that the Board of Directors has increased the quarterly dividend for the fourth consecutive year."

■ Schlumberger services and solutions combine domain expertise, best practices, safe and environmentally sound well site operations, innovative technologies, and high-quality support aimed at helping its customers increase oilfield efficiency, lower finding and producing costs, improve productivity, maximize reserve recovery, and increase asset value in a safe, environmentally sound manner.

Today, Schlumberger Oilfield Services solutions include open-hole and cased-hole wireline logging; drilling services; well services, such as cementing, coiled tubing, stimulations and sand control; well completion services including well testing and artificial lift; interpretation and consulting services; and integrated project management. Strong technical and operational support to the field is vital to the success of any complex global operation that includes remote locations. The key is to provide real-time linkage with world-class experts and knowledge, delivering the latest and best problem-solving capabilities—anywhere, anytime. The company's InTouchsupport.com knowledge management tool improves field access to Schlumberger technology centers through the most advanced IT tools, twenty-four hours a day, seven days a week.

Enhancing core E&P operations to improve production, increase reserves and drill better wells requires the integration of innovative information technology. Schlumberger Information Solutions (SIS) offers a unique combination of people and processes, technology and infrastructure, and real-time IT enablers-delivering key value-adding solutions to overcome a myriad of challenges confronting industry operational processes. SIS offers information management, software technology and infrastructure services. Combined with the domain experience available through the Business Consulting group, these enable oil and gas companies to enhance their workflows and achieve their goals.

As the industry's focus is moving toward maximizing post-plateau production and ultimate recovery, oil companies have to face more and more resource intensive projects. Integrated Project Management (IPM) is the Schlumberger response to this challenge and a significant growth area for Schlumberger. IPM activity is characterized by long-term relationships between the customer and Schlumberger. It offers a combination of engineering, process management and understanding of Schlumberger segment technologies. As well as providing technology and expertise, Schlumberger often works with local subcontractors to harness local knowledge and experience. Schlumberger has achieved a number of successes in IPM in particular in Mexico. The Burgos project for example, now in its seventh year, has delivered 237 completed wells, which include the drilling of 2.3 million feet of hole. The benefits to the customer have included accelerated production, reduced capital expenditure and increased efficiency.

- Schlumberger offers its clients four key advantages:

- Deep domain knowledge of exploration and production operations gained through seventy-five years of experience
- The service industry's longest commitment to technology and innovation through a network of twenty-three research, development, and technology centers
- A global reach in more than eighty countries coupled with strong local experience and the diversity in thought, background and knowledge that more than 140 nationalities bring
- A commitment to excellence in service delivery anytime, anywhere

- "We are maintaining our BUY rating on Schlumberger and raising our target price to $120 from $106," said David B. Rewcastle on April 9, 2008, writing for the Argus Research Company. He went on to say, "Given the company's earnings performance, its expected ramp-up activity and its technological lead over competitors, we see a strong probability for further upside for SLB shares. We also note that Schlumberger's strategy of becoming a 'local operator' in every geographical market is helping it win some of the industry's largest and most lucrative comprehensive contracts from national oil companies, via its Integrated Project Management efforts."

- On April 12, 2008, Standard & Poor's *Stock Reports* gave the company a BUY rating, with this comment by Stewart Glickman, CFA: "We believe SLB is well positioned to benefit from growing demand for oilfield services technology, particularly in frontier regions, such as the Middle East, Africa, and Eastern Europe."

SECTOR: **Energy**
BETA COEFFICIENT: **1.00**
10-YEAR COMPOUND EARNINGS PER SHARE GROWTH: **12.7%**
10-YEAR COMPOUND DIVIDENDS PER SHARE GROWTH: **6.3%**

		2007	2006	2005	2004	2003	2002	2001	2000
Revenues (Mil)		23,277	19,230	14,309	11,480	13,893	13,474	13,746	9,611
Net Income (Mil)		5,177	3,747	2,022	1,236	911	694	809	735
Earnings per share		4.18	3.04	1.67	1.03	0.78	0.60	0.71	0.64
Dividends per share		0.70	0.48	0.41	0.38	0.38	0.38	0.38	0.38
Price	high	114.8	74.8	51.5	34.9	28.1	31.2	41.4	44.4
	low	56.3	47.9	31.6	26.3	17.8	16.7	20.4	26.8

CONSERVATIVE GROWTH

Sigma-Aldrich Corporation

3050 Spruce Street □ St. Louis, MO 63103 □ (314) 771-5765 □ Dividend reinvestment plan not available □ Web site: *www .Sigma-Aldrich.com* □ Ticker symbol: SIAL □ Listed: Nasdaq □ S&P rating: A+ □ Value Line financial strength rating: A

On October 4, 2007, Sigma-Aldrich announced that it had entered into a collaboration with the Institute of Research in Immunology and Cancer (IRIC) of the Université de Montréal. This collaboration, made possible through grants from Genome Quebec and contributions by Sigma-Aldrich, will leverage Sigma's RNA Interference (RNAi) technologies for the purpose of identifying potential new drug targets.

Sigma-Aldrich and the Université de Montréal have signed an agreement whereby the Institute's High Throughput Screening facility gains access to Sigma-Aldrich's RNAi intellectual property portfolio and its MISSION® shRNA library collection for both human and mouse genomes. This agreement marks the latest in a number of licensing and research collaborations the company has made as an ongoing commitment to bring cutting-edge technologies to researchers worldwide. By adopting the MISSION shRNA library as their platform for RNAi screening, Université of Montréal will be utilizing the collective expertise of The RNAi Consortium (TRC), which consists of a partnership among the Broad Institute, MIT, Harvard, Dana Farber, Sigma-Aldrich as well as other research organizations and major pharmaceutical companies. In exchange, Sigma-Aldrich plans to utilize feedback from the collaboration to further its understanding of specific target function and to continue the development of tools for high throughput drug discovery.

"We are eager to work with the Universite de Montreal to provide researchers access to the Sigma-Aldrich MISSION RNAi portfolio of products and intellectual property," said David Smoller, PhD, president of Sigma-Aldrich's Research Biotechnology business unit. "RNAi is becoming the leading technology used by researchers for the advancement of drug discovery, commitment to this technology by the University and the investment of Canadian government positions the facility to be a leader in this effort."

Company Profile

Sigma-Aldrich is a leading life science and high technology company. The company's biochemical and organic chemical products and kits are used in scientific and genomic research, biotechnology, pharmaceutical development, the diagnosis of disease, and as key components in pharmaceutical and other high technology manufacturing. Sigma-Aldrich has customers in life science companies, university and government institutions, hospitals, and industry. The company operates in thirty-six countries and has over 7,600 employees providing excellent service worldwide.

Shortcomings to Bear in Mind

■ On April 2, 2008, Standard & Poor's *Outlook* gave Sigma-Aldrich a lackluster HOLD rating, with this comment: "The stock trades at a premium P/E to the S&P 500, and we believe it is worth holding in light of the company's long-term earnings and dividend growth record."

Reasons to Buy

■ On February 12, 2008, CEO Jai Nagarkatti said: "We are very pleased to have posted record results again in 2007. Annual sales exceeded $2 billion for the first time in our company's history. And our efforts to expand margins through Process Improvement activities combined with lower interest costs enabled us to grow our EPS more rapidly than sales, despite a higher effective tax rate. Key initiatives supporting our customer centric focus enabled us to deliver sales exceeding $500 million for the third successive quarter."

■ On September 26, 2007, SAFC®, a member of the Sigma-Aldrich Group, announced a $29 million investment to significantly expand its drug substance capabilities in high-potency biologics at the Sigma-Aldrich facility in Jerusalem, Israel. The site enhancement will enable SAFC Pharma™ to provide process development and cGMP manufacturing to customers requiring large-scale, high-potency, toxic or hazardous drug substances (large molecule HPAPIs).

The biologics area exploits over thirty years of Sigma-Aldrich's expertise in research, development and scale-up of fermentation-derived products in Israel and close technology links to Israel's academic

and R&D communities. Scheduled for completion in the first quarter of 2009, the 50,000 square-foot high-potency fermentation expansion will focus production on secondary metabolites (antibiotic-like molecules), cytotoxins and large-molecule proteins. A 30,000-square-foot area of the new facility has been designed to be Biosafety Level 2 compliant and enabling manipulation of human pathogens. Site capabilities include 1,000- and 4,000-liter tank capacities for bacterial and fungal fermentation.

The new capabilities are expected to expand SAFC Pharma's High Potent Active Pharmaceutical Ingredient (HPAPI) offering to include fermentation-derived HPAPI manufacturing, complementing the multi-step organic synthesis flagship facility at its Madison, Wisconsin location.

Commenting on the investment, Frank Wicks, SAFC president, said, "This expansion builds on the fermentation track record of our Jerusalem facility while adding significantly to our HPAPI capacity. It is consistent with SAFC's strategy to extend the range and scope of coverage in niche technologies and APIs for biologics sectors."

■ On March 8, 2008, Thomas White upgraded Sigma-Aldrich to a BUY, with this comment by its analyst: "The healthcare team at Thomas White projects that over the next twelve months an investment in SIAL will return from 8 percent to 15 percent. These results should outperform the market and outperform 70 percent of the stocks in its industry. We recommend taxable investors buy SIAL and hold it for the long-term capital gain."

■ Ford Equity Research upgraded Sigma-Aldrich to BUY on February 16, 2008, with this comment: "The Ford research team projects that SIAl will outperform the market over the next six to twelve months. Our decision is based on systematic analysis, which balances SIAL's quality and trend of its earnings growth, fundamental valuation and its timeliness."

■ On September 13, 2007, Sigma-Aldrich and Ingenuity Systems announced a partnership to develop a revolutionary new search capability to enhance the Sigma-Aldrich Web-based customer experience. Under the terms of the agreement, Sigma-Aldrich will leverage Ingenuity's knowledge base and integrate its search technology into Sigma-Aldrich's life science product portfolio. Ingenuity's knowledge base is the world's largest and highest quality repository of biological and chemical networks created from millions of expert curated relationships among proteins, genes, complexes, cells, tissues, drugs, and diseases.

The new search capability will be freely available to researchers to enable them to rapidly locate and purchase the Sigma-Aldrich products most relevant to their research. The search capability will enable researchers to understand those products in a content-rich environment of highly relevant biological and chemical relationships.

Dr. Smoller said, "Customers will not only be able to now utilize our search tools such as Your Favorite Gene™ (*http://www.sigma.com/yfg*), a Web-based tool that enables life science researchers to match gene information to thousands of Sigma-Aldrich products against their gene of interest, but this partnership will also extend customers' searches to much broader biological queries around disease, function, and pathways."

Jake Leschly, CEO of Ingenuity, added, "Today's increasing emphasis on a systems view of biology is requiring scientists to design their experiments based on a more complete and dynamic understanding of biology. Through this innovative partnership with Sigma-Aldrich, we will enable researchers to leverage the breath of Ingenuity's knowledge and technology to gain scientific insight and to immediately translate this into more effective experimental designs and better selection of Sigma-Aldrich products."

■ On February 14, 2008, Sigma-Aldrich announced an exclusive partnership with Atlas Antibodies to distribute Prestige Antibodies™, developed by the Human Proteome Resource, to the proteomics and cell biology research communities. Initially consisting of 1,800 antibodies, the library is expected to grow by several thousand per year with the goal of producing at least one antibody to all 22,000 nonredundant human proteins by 2015. Through this partnership, Sigma-Aldrich is granted exclusive distribution rights in the U.S. and all regions outside of Europe, with co-exclusive distribution rights in Europe.

Prestige Antibodies are highly characterized and offer significant value to the research community. Each antibody is highly validated for specificity and accompanied by over 500 immunohistochemical images, which are displayed in the publicly accessible Human Protein Atlas. In addition, Prestige Antibodies are optimized on a single protocol and tailored for high throughput operations, providing significant time and cost savings for researchers. The antibodies are designed to have low cross-reactivity to other human proteins and to work in a variety of applications and tissue preparations. All Prestige Antibodies are tested in multiple assurance steps to ensure that they are the most specific products on the market.

"We are delighted to have been chosen as the exclusive distributor of Prestige Antibodies, and we expect to release substantial additions to the catalog annually," said Dr. Smoller. "By making these high quality and highly validated antibodies accessible to proteomics and cell biology researchers worldwide, Sigma-Aldrich is helping to further promote the study of disease."

Atlas Antibodies is a biotech company established in 2006 to produce the antibodies identified by the Human Proteome Resource (HPR), a major component of the Human Proteome Organization (HUPO) that is systematically exploring the human proteome using antibody-based proteomics. As the library developed by Atlas Antibodies grows each year, Sigma-Aldrich will expand its catalog of Prestige Antibodies.

"Sigma-Aldrich offers a recognized brand name and an established distribution network that will help us bring our antibodies to market," said Marianne Hansson, co-founder and CEO of Atlas Anti-

bodies. "This partnership will enable Atlas Antibodies to reach all of the proteomics and cell biology researchers who will benefit from the unprecedented specification of the Prestige Antibodies."

SECTOR: Information Technology
BETA COEFFICIENT: .90
10-YEAR COMPOUND EARNINGS PER SHARE GROWTH: 10.9%
10-YEAR COMPOUND DIVIDENDS PER SHARE GROWTH: 13.5%

		2007	2006	2005	2004	2003	2002	2001	2000
Revenues (Mil)		2,039	1,798	1,667	1,409	1,298	1,207	1,179	1,096
Net Income (Mil)		311	276	258	233	193	131	141	139
Earnings per share		2.34	2.05	1.88	1.67	1.34	0.89	0.94	0.83
Dividends per share		0.46	0.42	0.38	0.26	0.21	0.17	0.17	0.16
Price	high	56.6	39.7	33.6	30.8	29.0	26.4	25.7	20.4
	low	37.4	31.3	27.7	26.6	20.5	19.1	18.1	10.1

AGGRESSIVE GROWTH

St. Jude Medical, Inc.

One Lillehei Plaza □ St. Paul, MN 55117 □ (651) 766-3029 □ Dividend reinvestment program is not available □ Web site: www.sjm.com □ Listed: NYSE □ Ticker symbol: STJ □ S&P rating: B+ □ Value Line financial strength rating: A

On September 18, 2007, St. Jude Medical announced that the U.S. Food and Drug Administration (FDA) had approval of its first radiofrequency (RF) wireless devices to treat patients with heart failure and with potentially lethal heart arrhythmias. The Promote™ RF CRT-D (cardiac resynchronization therapy defibrillator) and Current™ RF ICD (implantable cardioverter defibrillator) feature radiofrequency telemetry for wandless communication with programmers used by physicians to interrogate and program devices.

RF telemetry enables secure, remote communication between the implanted device and the programmers in a clinician's office or hospital. Wireless communication occurs while the device is being implanted and when patients see physicians for follow-up visits, allowing for efficient, more convenient care and device management. Previously

available in Europe, FDA approval brings this advanced technology to U.S. patients as well.

The devices use a dedicated range of frequencies designated for medical devices called the MICS (Medical Implant Communications Service) frequency band, which helps to prevent interference from other electronic signals. The MICS technology also includes the capability to choose between ten channels in order to optimize the telemetry link and avoid interference.

The Promote RF CRT-D and Current RF ICD are built on St. Jude Medical's next generation "Unity" device platform. This consolidated electronics platform will enable St. Jude Medical to more quickly introduce devices with new features and diagnostics, as they become available, because the basic platform for all of the devices is the same. In addition, the consolidated platform's expanded capabilities can support more advanced algorithms and features for better patient management. Furthermore, programming during device follow-up will be streamlined, as all software interfaces for new St. Jude Medical pacemakers, ICDs and CRT devices will be the same.

The Promote RF CRT-D allows physicians to electronically reconfigure left ventricular (LV) leads to help optimize the pacing performance of the device without the need to physically reposition the lead. (A lead is a thin, insulated wire, connected to the heart tissue on one end and to the device on the other end. It transmits electrical impulses to the heart, and information from the heart back to the implanted device, so physicians can use it for diagnoses. LV leads are placed in the lower left chamber of the heart.)

Company Profile

St. Jude Medical, Inc. is dedicated to the design, manufacture, and distribution of cardiovascular medical devices of the highest quality, offering physicians, patients, and payers unmatched clinical performance and demonstrated economic value. The company's product portfolio includes pacemakers, implantable cardioverter defibrillators (ICDs), vascular closure devices, catheters, and heart valves.

In the Cardiac Rhythm Management therapy area, St. Jude Medical has assembled a broad array of products for treating heart rhythm disorders—including atrial fibrillation—as well as heart failure. Its innovative product lines include sophisticated ICDs, state-of-the-art pacemaker systems, and a variety of diagnostic and therapeutic electrophysiology catheters.

Atrial fibrillation, a quivering chaotic rhythm in the upper chamber of the heart (atria) is the world's most common cardiac arrhythmia, affecting more than 5 million people worldwide. It reduces the normal output of the heart, is a known risk factor for stroke, is often associated with heart failure, and can greatly impair a person's quality of life. AF is encountered by all of the company's physician customers—and today it remains one of the most difficult conditions for the medical profession to treat.

In addition to its electrophysiology catheters, the company develops catheter technologies for the Cardiology/Vascular Access therapy area. Those products include industry-leading hemostasis introducers, catheters, and the market's leading vascular closure device. From access to closure, those products represent a complete set of tools for vascular access site management.

In the Cardiac Surgery therapy area, the company has been the undisputed global leader in the mechanical heart valve technology for more than twenty-five years. St. Jude Medical also develops a line of tissue valves and valve-repair products. In 2003, the company expanded its presence in cardiac surgery with a minority investment in Epicor Medical, Inc., which is developing a unique surgical approach for atrial fibrillation.

St. Jude Medical products are sold in more than 120 countries. The company has twenty principal operations and manufacturing facilities around the world.

Shortcomings to Bear in Mind

▪ To be sure, St. Jude is an exceptional company with an impressive record. However, the market knows this and gives it a lofty P/E ratio, sometimes more than thirty times earnings.

Reasons to Buy

▪ On January 25, 2008, an independent investigator clinical trial showed that atrial fibrillation (AF) is effectively treated using the Epicor(™) Cardiac Ablation System, when treated concomitantly to corrective heart surgery. The trial results were published in the December edition of *The Annals of Thoracic Surgery*. St. Jude Medical manufactures and distributes the Epicor system.

The investigators reported that more than 83 percent of all patients, followed for at least six months after surgery, were free from AF. In addition, 86 percent of the patients followed for at least eighteen months remained free from AF. The investigators reported that there were no device or ablative procedure-related adverse events and specifically noted an absence of esophageal, coronary, or phrenic nerve damage.

The clinical trial is the first in the United States to examine the safety and efficacy of high-intensity focused ultrasound (HIFU) therapy for the treatment of AF. The prospective trial was conducted from February 2005 to February 2007 at Mission Hospitals in Asheville, North Carolina. A cohort of 129 patients (who had an ablation performed concomitant to another, already-scheduled cardiac procedure and who were followed at least six months) were assessed in the study. Freedom-from-AF rates were determined through rigorous postoperative physical examinations, electrocardiogram testing, and twenty-four-hour Holter monitoring at six, twelve, and eighteen months postablation.

The results confirmed the findings of a European multicenter trial published in the September 2005 *Journal of Thoracic and Cardiovascular Surgery*. The investigators in the European clinical trial reported an 85 percent freedom-from-AF rate at six months postprocedure—the study's primary efficacy end point—in patients concomitantly treated for AF with the Epicor Cardiac Ablation System.

"Recent published reports point to a strong justification to treat AF at the time of other cardiac surgeries in an attempt to improve the long-term patient outcomes of those procedures," said Mark A. Groh, M.D., the lead investigator of the study. "Our study indicates that ablation using high intensity focused ultrasound can provide a safe and effective option for AF treatment during other heart surgeries."

- On November 26, 2007, St. Jude Medical announced U.S. Food and Drug Administration (FDA) approval of its Epic™ Stented Tissue Valve with Linx™ AC Technology. Identical in design to the company's Biocor™ Valve, which currently leads the tissue valve industry in U.S. market share growth, the Epic Valve also incorporates patented anti-calcification technology designed to protect against tissue mineralization, or hardening.

An estimated 100,000 Americans undergo heart valve replacement annually and the majority of them receive tissue valves.

"The Epic Valve sets a new standard for addressing tissue mineralization and potentially extending long-term valve durability," said Vibhu Kshettry, M.D., director of Cardiac Surgery at the Minneapolis Heart Institute at Abbott Northwestern Hospital, Minneapolis, and a principal investigator in the Epic clinical study. "Enhanced durability, combined with a design that facilitates the implant procedure, makes the Epic Valve an ideal prosthesis."

When physicians choose tissue valves for patients, durability is a key consideration. Valve durability is affected by both mechanical stress and tissue calcification. The Epic Valve is designed to address both issues to deliver long-term performance. A recently published paper concluded that over seventeen years, the Biocor design reduced tissue fatigue from mechanical stresses. In addition, the Biocor Valve has more than twenty years of clinical experience.

- *Value Line Investment Survey* gave St. Jude Medical its highest rating for Timeliness on February 29, 2008. Erik A. Antonson said, "St. Jude Medical stock may be a safe selection during these times of uncertainty."

- "We are maintaining our BUY rating on St. Jude Medical Inc.," said David H. Toung on January 23, 2008. "Even discounting the one-time benefit from

Medtronic's recall of ICD leads, St. Jude delivered a strong performance in cardiac rhythm management (CRM) devices in the fourth quarter. It is clearly benefiting from the expansion of its sales force."

■ On April 9, 2008, Standard & Poor's *Stock Reports* awarded St. Jude a BUY rating. Robert M. Gold said, "We are concerned about the sluggishness that we see throughout ICD markets. However, we think the global ICD market can grow by about 7 percent in 2008, and we expect faster growth from St. Jude as it continues to gain market share."

■ On August 21, 2007, St. Jude Medical announced regulatory approval from the Ministry of Health, Labor and Welfare (MHLW), in addition to reimbursement approval, for the Angio-Seal™ STS Plus Vascular Closure device.

Angio-Seal STS Plus is designed to provide physicians with an improved method of sealing catheterization sites, allowing patients increased comfort and offering hospitals improved efficiencies. Approved for both percutaneous peripheral and cardiac interventional catheterization procedures, the device enables physicians to quickly seal femoral artery punctures made during those procedures.

The device offers a significant advantage over the Angio-Seal Millennium vascular closure platform, which has been used in Japanese catheterization labs since 2004. With the addition of a self-tightening suture, the Angio-Seal STS Plus allows vascular closure to be completed entirely in the catheterization lab, saving labor and reducing the length of time required to complete the procedure.

Nearly 10 million catheterizations are performed worldwide each year. In these procedures, a catheter, or thin tube, is inserted into the femoral artery in the leg. Physicians then deliver diagnostic tools or interventional therapies, such as balloons, stents, and medications, through the catheter to the point of treatment.

SECTOR: **Health Care**
BETA COEFFICIENT: **.80**
10-YEAR COMPOUND EARNINGS PER SHARE GROWTH: **21.2%**
10-YEAR COMPOUND DIVIDENDS PER SHARE GROWTH: **no dividend**

	2007	2006	2005	2004	2003	2002	2001	2000
Revenues (Mil)	3,779	3,302	2,915	2,294	1,932	1,590	1,347	1,179
Net Income(Mil)	652	548	394	410	339	276	203	156
Earnings per share	1.85	1.47	1.04	1.10	0.92	0.76	0.57	0.46
Dividends per share	—	—	—	—	—	—	—	—
Price high	48.1	54.8	52.8	42.9	32.0	21.6	19.5	15.6
low	34.9	31.2	34.5	29.9	19.4	15.3	11.1	5.9

AGGRESSIVE GROWTH

Staples, Inc.

500 Staples Drive ▫ Framingham, MA 01702 ▫ (800) 468-7751 ▫ Web site: *www.staples.com*
▫ Direct dividend reinvestment plan is available ▫ Fiscal years end Saturday closest to January 31
▫ Listed: Nasdaq ▫Ticker symbol: SPLS ▫ S&P rating: B+ ▫ Value Line financial strength rating: A+

On August 16, 2007, Staples said that it is revolutionizing the creation and printing of business cards by being the first national retailer to offer a way to get business cards within minutes of being designed. The world's largest office products company announced Business Cards in Minutes, a new service that makes it easy for customers to design, proof and print professional-quality business cards in as fast as thirty minutes, versus the standard industry delivery time of three to seven days.

The Business Cards in Minutes technology, powered by Logoworks by HP, is available only at Staples Copy & Print Centers nationwide. Customers can now design customized cards right at the counter and have them printed quickly on the spot. The service also lets customers print as few as 100 cards at a time, compared to the industry-standard minimum of 250, allowing greater flexibility to update cards on-demand. Once created, business cards are stored for future customization and printing at any Staples nationwide.

"By offering this new convenience, Staples is doing for business cards what 'instant photo' did for photo processing," said Rob Schlacter, vice president of Business Services, Staples, Inc. "We just made it much easier for our customers and we see a great opportunity to grow this service with both small businesses and individuals who want 'social cards' for sharing personal and online information with family and friends."

Staples has found that business cards aren't just for businesses anymore. Test market results revealed that everyone from teens to soccer moms are using Business Cards in Minutes to create highly personalized social cards that make staying connected easy.

Business Cards in Minutes allows customers to quickly produce full-color business cards while they wait. At the Staples Copy & Print Center counter, Logoworks software provides an easy step-by-step process for selecting a card template, colors and fonts and personalizing contact details and inserting a logo. Customers can choose from a large database of categorized logos, upload a custom logo or scan an existing business card to be reprinted.

Business Cards in Minutes expands Staples' offerings of affordable, on-demand copy and print services for small businesses and

consumers, alike. Prices vary based on quantity and type of paper, but a standard order costs $19.99 for 100 black and white cards ($3 for each additional 100) or $29.99 for 100 colored cards ($6 for each additional 100).

Company Profile

Staples, Inc. launched the office supplies superstore industry with the opening of its first store in Brighton (near Boston), Massachusetts, in May 1986. Its goal was to provide small business owners the same low prices on office supplies previously enjoyed only by large corporations. Staples is now a $16 billion retailer of office supplies, business services, furniture and technology to consumers and businesses from home-based businesses to *Fortune* 500 companies in the United States, Canada, the United Kingdom, France, Italy, Spain, Belgium, Germany, the Netherlands, and Portugal. Customers can shop with Staples in any way they choose, by either walking in, calling in or logging on.

Staples is the largest operator of office superstores in the world, serving customers in 1,600 office superstores, mail order catalogs, e-commerce and a contract business.

The company operates three business segments: North American Retail, North American Delivery, and European operations.

The company's North American Retail segment consists of the company's U.S. and Canadian business units that sell office products, supplies, and services.

Staples North American Delivery segment consists of the company's U.S. and Canadian contract, catalog and Internet business units that sell and deliver office products, supplies, and services directly to customers.

Staples European Operations segment consists of the company's business units, which operate 201 retail stores in the United Kingdom (93), Germany (53), the Netherlands (40), and Portugal (14) and Belgium (1). The company also sells and delivers office products and supplies directly to businesses throughout the United Kingdom and

Germany. The company's delivery operations comprise the catalog business (Staples Direct and Quill Corporation), the contract stationer business (Staples National Advantage and Staples Business Advantage) and the Internet e-commerce business (Staples.com). Quill, acquired in 1998, is a direct mail catalog business, serving more than 1 million medium-sized businesses in the United States.

In 2002, SPLS acquired, for $383 million, Medical Arts Press, a leading provider of specialized printed products and supplies for medical offices. In 2002, the company acquired Guilbert's European mail order business for about $788 million.

At the retail level, stores operate under the names Staples-The Office Superstore and Staples Express. The prototype store had, up until recently, about 24,000 square feet of sales space, which the company reduced to 20,000 in fiscal 2003. Stores carry about 8,500 stock items.

Express stores are much smaller, with between 6,000 square feet and 10,000 square feet of sales space. They also handle fewer items, generally about 6,000, and are situated in downtown business sectors. By contrast, the larger units tend to be situated in the suburbs.

Sales by product are: North American Retail, 59 percent; North American Delivery, 28 percent; and Europe, 13 percent. Sales by product line are: office supplies and services, 42 percent; business machines and telecommunications services, 30 percent; computers and related products, 21 percent; and office furniture, 7 percent.

Shortcomings to Bear in Mind

■ Staples management is convinced that buying back its own stock is a sound strategy. As of January 2008, the company had returned 23 million shares to its buyback program and plans to continue buying even more. To be sure, this increases earnings per share, even when profits are flat. On the other hand, many analysts—myself included—are convinced that it would be better to invest those funds in other ways, such as buying another company or improving facilities.

Reasons to Buy

■ "New store openings will continue as planned even with economic headwinds," said Mary Beth Wiedenkeller, an analyst with *Value Line Investment Survey*, on April 11, 2008. "The company plans to open over 100 stores in 2008, after launching 159 locations in 2007. And Staples has identified ten major markets in which it is likely to set up a presence in the next several years."

■ "While our BUY rating reflects our expectation for the shares to outperform the S&P 500 on a risk-adjusted basis, we particularly like the company's prospects relative to other specialty retailers," said Christopher Graja, CFA, writing for Argus Research Company on March 4, 2008. "We think that within the specialty retail sector, Staples's financial strength, international exposure, and emphasis on businesses, rather than consumers, may be favorable attributes."

■ On April 5, 2008, Standard & Poor's *Stock Reports* said Staples was a BUY. Michael Souers said, "We believe business spending trends and a solid job market bode well for SPLS. The North American Delivery division's recent performance has been stellar, in our opinion, and we anticipate continued strong results. In addition, we think strong results from new Chicago, Miami, and Denver stores indicate further growth in untapped domestic metropolitan areas."

■ "America's retailers are taking it on the chin as consumers get walloped by the housing slump, rising gasoline prices, and the credit crunch," said Gene Marcial, writing for *BusinessWeek* on November 26, 2007. "But some money pros are snapping up shares of Staples, the world's largest office-products company." The article goes on to quote Alan Lancz, president of investment adviser Alan B. Lancz & Associates: "Despite the very difficult retail environment, Staples continues to demonstrate its superiority vs. its peers, aided by strong foreign sales and increasing profit margins."

■ "Another way we are differentiating ourselves is with Staples brand products," said CEO Ron Sargent in 2007. "Staples brand products offer high quality and great value to our customers, drive brand loyalty and are more profitable. They're also a great way to provide innovative solutions to our customers. We launched more than 600 new Staples brand products in 2006, including hundreds of back-to-school products, an LCD computer monitor, and innovative shredders. Most notably, Staples launched the MailMate shredder, a breakthrough product designed to shred junk mail in the kitchen. We're already sold hundreds of thousands of MailMates, and today Staples is the largest reseller of shredders in the world. And the great news is we still have plenty of room to grow. In 2006, 20 percent of our sales came from Staples brand products, and we expect to increase brand penetration to 30 percent over the next several year. Sourcing more of the products we sell directly from factories will further increase the profitability of Staples brand products. We significantly increased our direct sourcing in 2006 and benefited from the growing capabilities of our buying office in Shenzhen, China."

■ Mr. Sargent, now in this eighth year in the corner office, has no plans to let up. He says there's room for 25 percent growth in the industry-wide count of 3,200-plus office superstores in North America. Staples plans to grow its own base 5 percent for the next few years, as well as opening smaller stores in downtown markets. In total, Sargent figures Staples can add about 100 stores a year for the next few years.

■ Staples has a solid balance sheet, with 88 percent of its capitalization in shareholders' equity. Total interest coverage, moreover, is impressive, at twenty-nine times.

SECTOR: **Consumer Discretionary**
BETA COEFFICIENT: **1.10**
10-YEAR COMPOUND EARNINGS PER SHARE GROWTH: **18.2%**
10-YEAR COMPOUND DIVIDENDS PER SHARE GROWTH:*

	2007	2006	2005	2004	2003	2002	2001	2000
Revenues (Mil)	19,373	18,161	16,079	14,448	13,181	11,596	10,744	10,674
Net Income (Mil)	996	974	834	708	552	417	307	264
Earnings per share	1.38	1.32	1.04	0.93	0.75	0.63	0.44	0.39
Dividends per share	0.29	0.17	0.13	—	—	—	—	—
Price high	27.7	28.0	24.1	22.5	18.6	15.0	13.0	19.2
low	19.7	21.1	18.6	15.8	10.5	7.8	7.3	6.9

*Dividends paid only since 2004t.

AGGRESSIVE GROWTH

Stryker Corporation

P. O. Box 4085 ◻ Kalamazoo, MI 49003-4085 ◻ (616) 385-2600 ◻ Web site: *www.strykercorp.com*
◻ Listed: NYSE ◻ Dividend reinvestment plan not available ◻ Ticker symbol: SYK ◻ S&P rating: A+
◻ Value Line financial strength rating: A

Highlights for the Year Ended December 31, 2007

■ Net sales increased 16.6 percent (14.0 percent constant currency) to $6,001 million.

■ Orthopaedic implant sales increased 14.8 percent (11.8 percent constant currency).

■ MedSurg Equipment sales increased 19.3 percent (17.4 percent constant currency).

- Diluted net earnings per share from continuing operations increased 26.7 percent from $1.87 to $2.37 and adjusted diluted net earnings per share from continuing operations increased 20.0 percent from $2.00 to $2.40.
- Net earnings increased 30.8 percent to $1,017 million and diluted net earnings per share increased 29.1 percent from $1.89 to $2.44.

"Our strong fourth quarter financial results capped another excellent year, our seventh consecutive year of double-digit sales growth," said CEO Stephen P. MacMillan. "Domestic sales were particularly strong, as every key franchise achieved double digit growth in the fourth quarter and international sales were also solid, especially behind the continued expansion of our MedSurg franchises."

Net earnings from continuing operations for the year ended December 31, 2007, were reduced by a $12.7 million intangible asset impairment charge (net of $7.1 million income tax benefit) recorded in the second quarter to write off patents associated with intervertebral body fusion cage products. Net earnings from continuing operations for the year ended December 31, 2006, were reduced by a $52.7 million charge to write off purchased in-process research and development associated with the first quarter 2006 acquisition of Sightline Technologies, Ltd.

Net earnings from continuing operations for the year ended December 31, 2007, were $986.7 million, representing a 27.9 percent increase over net earnings from continuing operations of $771.4 million for the year ended December 31, 2006. Diluted net earnings per share from continuing operations for the year ended December 31, 2007, increased 26.7 percent to $2.37 compared to $1.87 for the year ended December 31, 2006.

Company Profile

Stryker Corporation was founded in 1941 by Dr. Homer H. Stryker, a leading orthopedic surgeon and the inventor of several ortho-

pedic products. The company now ranks as a dominant player in a $12 billion global orthopedics industry. SYK has a significant market share in such sectors as artificial hips, prosthetic knees and trauma products.

Stryker develops, manufactures and markets specialty surgical and medical products worldwide. These products include orthopedic implants, trauma systems, powered surgical instruments, endoscopic systems, and patient care and handling equipment.

Through a network of 374 centers in twenty-six states, Stryker's Physiotherapy Associates division provides physical, occupational and speech therapy to orthopedic and neurology patients. The physical therapy business represents a solid complementary business for Stryker, in view of the high number of its surgeon customers who prescribe physical therapy following orthopedic surgery.

A major component of Stryker's success is the optimal use of resources in manufacturing and distribution. Taking advantage of both information technology and leading-edge workflow management practices, the company monitors quality and service levels at its sixteen plants throughout North America and Europe for continuous improvement. This attention to operations has resulted in the inclusion of Stryker facilities in the elite *IndustryWeek* Best Plants list twice in the last three years. The Stryker Instruments plant in Kalamazoo, Michigan, was named one of the Best Plants in 2000, and the Howmedica Osteonics facility in Allendale, New Jersey, was honored in 1998.

Shortcomings to Bear in Mind

- David H. Toung, writing for Argus Research Company on January 14, 2008, had this negative comment: "Despite the company's strong earnings and sales performance over the last five years, Stryker faces challenges in 2008. Smith & Nephew introduced a hip restructuring product that is cutting into the sales of Stryker's total hip replacement device."

- Because of its great record, Stryker usually sells at a fat multiple of thirty times earnings or more.

Reasons to Buy

- On December 6, 2007, Stryker announced that the board of directors had declared a year-end cash dividend of thirty-three cents per share, an increase of 50 percent over the twenty-two cent dividend declared in December 2006.

"Our accelerating revenue growth in 2007 combined with our strong overall financial position have put us in the position of being able to significantly increase our dividend for the second year in a row," commented Mr. Stephen P. MacMillan.

- Analysts believe that industry trends are setting the stage for continued growth for Stryker in the years ahead. Virtually all market dynamics point in that direction. These are the key factors:

- The population as a whole is aging. In fact, the target population for orthopedic implants for knees and hips is expected to increase 68 percent in the next nine years, according to a report issued by Gerard Klauer Mattison & Company, Inc., a brokerage firm headquartered in New York City.
- Mild inflation in average selling prices for orthopedic implants in the United States compares favorably to the declining price environment of the past decade.
- Consolidation among orthopedic implant and device manufacturers over the past few years has greatly decreased the number of competitors in sectors such as orthopedic implants, spinal devices, arthroscopy products and other orthopedic products. This serves to consolidate market share and mitigates price competition.
- Advances in orthopedic technology—much of which has taken place in the past decade—have markedly decreased

operating and recovery times. These advances have decreased the amount of time a surgeon must spend with each patient, thus giving the surgeon more time to perform more operations in a period. Consequently, according to the Gerard Klauer Mattison report, "we believe that procedural volume will increase."

For its part, Stryker has set itself up to benefit from these microeconomic dynamics, according to the report issued by this same brokerage house. "For example, Stryker has strategically used acquisitions over the past few years to broaden and deepen its product portfolio. Furthermore, innovation in orthopedic implants and instrumentation has provided the company with certain competitive advantages that should be important ingredients for gaining market share in the coming years."

- The company has achieved these distinctions:

- Ranked 1 in *Fortune* magazine's America's Most Admired Companies in Medical Products and Equipment
- Ranked 11 in *Barron's* 500 Best Companies for Investors
- Ranked 30 overall and 4 in Healthcare Equipment & Services in *BusinessWeek's* Top Fifty Companies of the S&P 500

- In 2007, CEO MacMillan said, "We promised a turnaround in our orthopedic implant business, and is it well underway, with five consecutive quarters of improved performance, while the orthopedic industry as a whole was slowing down. We have far outstripped our competitors in knees, posting double-digit growth for a remarkable 23 quarters in a row, due in part to the introduction of Triathlon into the global marketplace. With the recent launch of our new LFIT Anatomic Femoral Heads, featuring new, more anatomically sized heads and our high-performing X3 polyethylene liners, we expect to further strengthen our hip replacement business."

- Mr. MacMillan goes on to say, "We developed a game plan to expand our Med-Surg business internationally, and this effort produced very positive results in these highly competitive markets. By building out the international sales force, we have taken advantage of underdeveloped markets outside the United States. Additionally, releases of next-generation Instruments and Endoscopy products during the second half of the year have reinvigorated domestic growth. These favorable trends in the United States point out fundamental strengths, especially because they occurred at the same time that we were creating several new, highly focused sales forces to better serve our customers. We work tirelessly to be in tune with the needs of our customers. As one example, our investment in surgical navigation—one of the most sought-after medical technologies—have made our Navigation business unit the fastest-growing in the company."
- The CEO also said, "Our Spine business, which became a separate division with a dedicated U.S. sales organization in 2004, has delivered exceptional growth and has almost

quadrupled in sales since 2001. Spine turned in another excellent performance in 2006, and we opened a new spine manufacturing facility in Neuchatel, Switzerland. We also successfully completed our first interim analysis of the data from FlexiCore lumbar disc clinical trial, which will allow an earlier filing of our premarket approval (PMA) application to the U.S. Food and Drug Administration (FDA)."

- "This issue is favorably ranked for the year ahead," said George Rho, writing for *Value Line* on February 29, 2008. "Earnings are expanding rapidly, and the slowing economy isn't likely to be a significant impediment. These characteristics have helped SYK stock perform superbly over the years. And we think it will continue to fare well over the next three to five years."
- On April 12, 2008, Standard & Poor's *Stock Reports* said Stryker was a BUY. Robert M. Gold said, "We think Stryker will sustain high double-digit earnings growth through 2008, driven by new product launches, rising gross margins and well-managed operating costs."

SECTOR: **Health Care**
BETA COEFFICIENT: **.90**
10-YEAR COMPOUND EARNINGS PER SHARE GROWTH: **22.5%**
10-YEAR COMPOUND DIVIDENDS PER SHARE GROWTH: **22.0%**

	2007	2006	2005	2004	2003	2002	2001	2000
Revenues (Mil)	6,001	5,406	4,872	4,262	3,625	3,012	2,602	2,289
Net Income (Mil)	1,017	778	644	586	454	346	272	221
Earnings per share	2.44	1.89	1.57	1.43	1.12	0.88	0.67	0.55
Dividends per share	0.22	0.11	0.11	0.09	0.07	0.05	0.04	0.035
Price high	76.9	55.9	56.3	57.7	42.7	33.8	31.3	28.9
low	54.9	39.8	39.7	40.3	29.9	21.9	21.7	12.2

CONSERVATIVE GROWTH

Sysco Corporation

1390 Enclave Parkway ▫ Houston, TX 77077-2099 ▫ (281) 584-1458 ▫ Web site: *www.sysco.com*
▫ Dividend reinvestment plan available ▫ Fiscal years end the Saturday closest to June 30 ▫ Listed: NYSE
▫ Ticker symbol: SYY ▫ S & P rating: A+ ▫ Value Line financial strength rating: A++

With the advent of two household incomes, with both husband and wife working outside

the home, it is not surprising that no one wants to come home after eight hours at the office and still have to face cooking supper. Not to mention cleaning up after the repast.

Today, about half of Americans' food dollars are spent on meals prepared away from home. That figure far surpasses the 37 percent that was spent on away-from-home meals in 1972. It reveals how heavily our society now depends on foodservice operations to satisfy consumers' nutritional needs by providing a variety of quality meals at affordable prices.

According to a company officer, "We are in a wonderful industry with great upside potential. Two-income families have more disposable income to spend. As the population ages, the fifty- and sixty-five-year-olds also have more time and money to eat meals cooked in someone else's kitchen.

"In addition, retirees are healthier and living longer, and many are in retirement communities that serve meals on site. Of course, the twenty-to-forty-year-old segment has grown up with parents who worked outside the home, so eating out comes naturally to them, and many just don't have the time, skills or desire to cook."

Company Profile

As they go about their lives, many people encounter the familiar Sysco trucks, bearing giant blue lettering, delivering products to customers. Few are aware, however, of Sysco's far-reaching influence on meals served daily throughout North America. As the continent's largest marketer and distributor of foodservice products, Sysco operates 150 distribution facilities across the United States and Canada (including eighty-four broadline facilities, seventeen hotel supply locations, sixteen specialty produce facilities, fifteen SYGMA distribution centers, twelve custom-cutting meat locations, and two distributors specializing in the niche Asian foodservice market). These distribution facilities serve about 415,000 restaurants, hotels, schools, hospitals, retirement homes and other locations where food is prepared to be eaten on the premises or taken away

and enjoyed in the comfort of the diner's chosen environment.

Sysco is by far the largest company in the foodservice distribution industry. In sales, Sysco dwarfs its two chief competitors, U.S. Foodservice and Performance Food Group.

Shortcomings to Bear in Mind

- On January 28, 2008, Standard & Poor's *Stock Reports* gave Sysco only three stars (five stars is the top rating), with this comment: "Risks to our recommendation and target price include a slowing of growth rates, given SYY's significant size and reach, sharp increases in gas prices, and a potential slowdown in restaurant sales."

Reasons to Buy

Fiscal 2007 Highlights
- Sales increased 7.4 percent to $35.04 billion from $32.63 billion in fiscal 2006.
- Net earnings were $1.00 billion compared to $855.3 million in the prior fiscal year, an increase of 17.0 percent.
- Diluted EPS increased 17.6 percent to $1.60 compared to $1.36 in fiscal 2006.

"We delivered solid sales and excellent earnings growth in the fourth quarter as our operating companies successfully supported their customers in a market that experienced significant food cost inflation," said CEO Richard J. Schnieders. "Looking at fiscal 2007 overall, sales growth met our expectations and we are especially pleased with the nearly 18 percent EPS growth that accompanied it. It is particularly gratifying to achieve a major milestone of one billion dollars in net earnings for the first time."

- Mr. Schnieders also said, "Throughout Sysco's history, our growth has consistently outpaced that of the foodservice industry. We are encouraged with the progress of our national supply chain, sourcing, and integrated delivery initiatives to date and remain confident that the successful execution of these initiatives going forward will position us well to participate in the growth and success of our customers for years to come. Therefore, although industry growth has moderated somewhat in recent years, over the long term we are targeting 7 percent to 9 percent annual nominal sales growth, excluding the impact of major acquisitions. With our continuing improvement in operating leverage capabilities, we expect to convert this sales growth into low- to mid-double digit annualized EPS growth."

■ On March 20, 2008, Ned Davis of Research, Inc. had this comment: "Both the Fundamental Risk Model and the Technical Model for SYY remain in the favorable zone. Consequently, the stock remains on its BUY rating."

■ "BUY-rated Sysco reported strong third-quarter sales, earnings, and operating margin growth despite the challenging U.S. economy and its impact on the foodservice and restaurant industry," said Erin Ashley Smith, writing for Argus Research Company on April 28, 2008. "The growth was driven by productivity initiatives and an increase in the number of broadline customers, as Sysco focused on building strong relationships with clients."

■ *Value Line* rated the company a 2 (similar to a BUY) on February 1, 2008. George A. Niemond said, "We like Sysco shares. The top-quality issue is Timely and has good three-to-five-year price appreciation potential."

■ "When you eat in a hospital, school, hotel or chain restaurant, there's a good chance the food—or at least the napkin—comes from Sysco," said Klaus Kneale, writing for *Forbes* magazine on April 21, 2008. "The nation's biggest food-service distributor (15 percent market share) is sometimes confused with Cisco Systems. But unlike the tech sector, food service has never had a meltdown."

■ On October 4, 2007, Sysco announced a move that will improve service to its customers in the Houston market area and create the opportunity to help provide the Houston Food Bank a new home.

Sysco Food Services of Houston, Inc., the company's Houston subsidiary, plans to construct a high-efficiency, environmentally friendly warehouse/office complex on a site in a proposed industrial park at the southwest corner of Interstate 45 and Beltway 8 in Harris County, Texas. Groundbreaking is anticipated as soon as the required permits are issued. One element key to the process was Sysco's assistance in working with the Houston Food Bank to occupy Sysco's current facility off Interstate Highway 10 just east of downtown. Sysco has long been a significant supporter of the Food Bank, providing both monetary and in-kind food donations, as well as employee volunteer time.

Keith Miller, CEO of the Houston operation, said, "Houston is truly a vibrant city with a sophisticated foodservice clientele. Our new facility is designed to better accommodate our customers and the restaurants, hotels, hospitals and others who expect the best the foodservice world can offer. Houston has been very good to us and I can't imagine anything better than helping the Food Bank grow to support our community as we continue to grow with our customers and help our employees achieve their career goals."

Brian Greene, CEO of the Houston Food Bank said, "Our move into the Sysco facility will allow us to feed many thousands more than the 80,000 people currently fed each week through the food bank's network of nearly 400 hunger relief agencies. The Sysco facility matches all of our needs. It has the warehousing capacity that will allow us to reach our goal of distributing 120 million pounds of food by 2016."

Mr. Miller said Sysco believes the high-speed product retrieval system that will be installed in the new warehouse is state-of-the-art in the foodservice distribution industry and that the new facility will be one of the most efficient of its kind ever built. The company also has dedicated nearly 4,000-square-feet of space for its business review process that helps customers improve their businesses. "Our customers' success has helped make us one of Sysco's flagship companies," Mr. Miller explained. "In addition, Sysco has been voted one of the best places to work in the Houston market over the past five years."

■ According to industry sources, there are nearly 900,000 foodservice locations in the United States—such as restaurants, hospitals, nursing homes, cruise ships, summer camps, sports stadiums, theme parks, schools, colleges, hotels, motels, corporate dining rooms and cafeterias, and retirement homes—and more than 63,000 in Canada.

■ Whether dining in an upscale restaurant or picking up pasta as the entrée for a meal at home, people spend less time on food preparation than ever before. They want variety and flavor in the foods they choose to eat, yet their time to prepare meals is constantly in competition with work and leisure activities. More than ever, people are turning to meals prepared away from home for greater convenience, quality and, most of all, choice.

It is a trend that started in World War II, as women began to work outside the home. Business cafeterias, coffee shops, school lunchrooms and restaurants broadened the range of dining choices for people who were used to much simpler fare. Twenty-five years ago, not many consumers could identify kiwi fruit. During the past three decades, foodservice offerings have moved from fruit cocktail with a cherry on top to kiwi and other exotic fare; from steak and potatoes to fajitas with all the trimmings.

■ As the largest distributor of foodservice products in North America, Sysco assists customers in creating a vast array of dining choices. Menus have greatly improved since a French chef named Boulanger offered a choice of soups, or "restorative" to patrons who paused at his inn to refresh themselves as they traveled during the 1700s. The sign in French read "restaurant," and his establishment may have been the first to offer a menu.

Today's diverse menu choices could not have been imagined then—raspberries from Australia served fresh in Wisconsin in January; gourmet pesto sauce rich with garlic, fresh basil and pine nuts delivered to a Vancouver chef's doorstep; or artfully prepared hearts of lettuce served in Arizona college cafeterias each day. Providing choices from soup to nuts, and everything in between, Sysco leads the way in helping chefs in restaurants, schools, business cafeterias, health care locations, lodging, and other facilities increase the variety and quality of food choices in North America.

■ Sysco keeps margins high by selling products under its own label, a strategy it began a year after its founding. It saves on national advertising and passes some of the savings along to its customers. Its private-label business carries an estimated 24 percent gross margin, or 10 percent more than it earns on national brands.

SECTOR: **Consumer Staples**
BETA COEFFICIENT: **.80**
10-YEAR COMPOUND EARNINGS PER SHARE GROWTH: **14%**
10-YEAR COMPOUND DIVIDENDS PER SHARE GROWTH: **17.3%**

		2007	2006	2005	2004	2003	2002	2001	2000
Revenues (Mil)		35,042	32,628	30,282	29,335	26,140	23,351	21,784	19,303
Net Income (Mil)		1,001	855	961	907	778	680	597	454
Earnings per share		1.60	1.35	1.47	1.37	1.18	1.01	0.88	0.68
Dividends per share		0.72	0.66	0.58	0.48	0.40	0.36	0.28	0.22
Price	high	36.7	37.0	38.4	41.3	37.6	32.6	30.1	30.4
	low	29.9	26.5	30.0	29.5	22.9	21.2	21.8	13.1

Target Corporation

1000 Nicollet Mall ❑ Minneapolis, MN 55403 ❑ (612) 370-6735 ❑ Direct dividend reinvestment plan available ❑ Web site: *www.target.com* ❑ Fiscal years end Saturday closest to January 31 of following year ❑ Listed: NYSE ❑ Ticker symbol: TGT ❑ S&P rating: A+ ❑ Value Line financial strength rating: A

"Delivering a merchandise assortment that is distinctive, exclusive and unexpected in design and value is a key focus in our effort to connect with our guests and differentiate Target from our competitors," said CEO Bob Ulrich in 2007. "We continue to introduce unique specialty brands, expand our premium owned and licensed brands and offer a carefully edited assortment of trusted national brands.

"For example, in 2007 we are launching Proenza Schouler as the next GO International collection in women's apparel, and based on our success with Rafe for Target handbags, we are extending this concept to women's accessories. In Bath and Beauty and Toys, we continue to develop and refine our assortments of exclusive European brands that were introduced at Target in 2006, and in consumer electronics, we are dramatically improving our presentation and selection of nationally branded flat-panel televisions."

Mr. Ulrich goes on to say, "To ensure that we have the right combination of merchandise to delight our guests (translated: customers), we balance the excitement of our signature brands with the convenience of our everyday essentials. In particular, we continue to enhance our offerings of food and basic household commodities and improve our ease of shopping for pharmacy and over-the-counter medications through new store growth, greatly expanded assortments and innovative product introductions. By strengthening our commitment to our selection, competitive pricing and in-stock reliability in key replenishable categories, we position Target as the preferred shopping destination for all our guests's needs and wants."

Company Profile

Target Corporation (formerly Dayton Hudson Corporation) was formed in 1969 through the merger of two old-line department store companies, Dayton Corporation and J. L. Hudson Company. In 1990, TGT acquired another venerable retailer, Marshall Field & Company. The department stores (once run separately, but now under the Marshall Field umbrella) have since been eclipsed by TGT's fast-growing Target division, which accounts for the bulk of revenues and profits.

Target is the nation's fourth-largest general merchandise retailer, specializing in large-store formats, including discount stores, moderate-priced promotional stores, and traditional department stores. The company operates Target stores, Marshall Field's, and Mervyn's stores.

At the end of October 2005, Target operated 1,400 stores in forty-seven states. The Target operation is the company's strongest retail franchise and is its growth vehicle for the future. Most of the remaining units operate under Mervyn's banner. These 266 outlets handle soft goods. Finally, the department store segment consists mostly of sixty-two Marshall Field's department stores.

Target stores are situated largely in such states as California, Texas, Florida, and the upper Middle West. Mervyn's are clustered largely in California and Texas.

In 2000, the company formed target.direct, the direct merchandising and electronic retailing organization. The business combines the e-commerce team of Target with its direct merchandising unit into one integrated organization. The target.direct organization operates seven Web sites, which support the store and catalog brands in an online environment and produces six retail catalogs.

Shortcomings to Bear in Mind

■ Because Target has a greater proportion of trendy, discretionary merchandise and has been rapidly increasing its credit-card business, analysts consider it more sensitive to economic swings than its chief rival Wal-Mart.

■ The retail business is always subject to competitive pressures from such outstanding companies as Bed Bath & Beyond, Wal-Mart, Costco, Lowe's, and Home Depot. Here's what the company has to say, according to its latest 10-K: "Target's retail merchandising business is conducted under highly competitive conditions in the discount segment. Its stores compete with national and local department, specialty, off-price, discount, grocery and drug store chains, independent retail stores and Internet businesses which handle similar lines of merchandise. Target also competes with other companies for new store sites."

On a more positive note, the 10-K goes on to say, "Target believes the principal methods of competing in its industry include brand recognition, customer service, store location, differentiated offerings, value, quality, fashion, price, advertising, depth of selection and credit availability."

Reasons to Buy

■ On February 26, 2008, Target Corporation reported net earnings of $1,028 million for the fourth quarter ended February 2, 2008, a thirteen-week period, compared with $1,119 million in the fourth quarter ended February 3, 2007, a fourteen-week period. Earnings per share in the fourth quarter decreased 4.7 percent to $1.23 from $1.29 in the same period a year ago. All earnings per share figures refer to diluted earnings per share.

For the full fiscal year 2007, a fifty-two-week period, net earnings were $2.849 billion, compared with $2.787 billion in fiscal 2006, a fifty-three-week period. Earnings per share increased 3.9 percent to $3.33 from $3.21 a year ago.

"Our financial performance in 2007 fell short of our expectations as the pace of sales and earnings slowed considerably in the second half of the year," said Mr. Ulrich. "As we enter 2008, we remain keenly focused on the disciplined execution of our core strategy, positioning Target to deliver improved financial results, even in the face of continued challenges in the current economic environment."

Full-Year Results

For fiscal 2007, total revenues increased 6.5 percent to $63.367 billion from $59.490 billion in 2006, fueled by the contribution from new store expansion, a 3.0 percent increase in comparable store sales, and contribution from credit card operations, offset by the impact of an extra fiscal week in 2006. On a fifty-two-week over fifty-two-week basis, total revenues in 2007 increased 8.4 percent. Total revenues include retail sales and net credit card revenues. Comparable-store sales are sales from stores open longer than one year.

■ "The credit card operation has accounted for an increasing percentage of operating profits in recent years," said David R. Cohen, an analyst with *Value Line Investment Survey*, on February 8, 2008. "Expansion of the company's customer base, along with ongoing leveraging of administrative and marketing expenses related to the Target Visa card, resulted in a 24 percent gain, year to year, in the first nine months of fiscal 2007. Barring a sale of a sizable amount of credit card receivables, this trend should continue for a while."

■ On January 17, 2008, the company said that DwellStudio, one of the country's leading modern home furnishings companies, introduced a new home and baby collection, DwellStudio for Target. Launching exclusively in Target stores and at Target.com, the DwellStudio for Target line consists of a graphic and colorful array of bed linens for adults and nurseries, nursery furniture, baby layette and a variety of accessories for the kitchen and table.

Founded by designer Christiane Lemieux, DwellStudio has won accolades for pioneering modern textiles through consistent use of uncommon color combinations and vivid patterns. "Modern today means a mix of colors, prints and textures. These unexpected pairings help achieve a contemporary look," says Ms. Lemieux. "This concept translates well into our new line. The result is a signature look that is fresh and distinctly DwellStudio for Target."

■ On January 14, 2008, Target announced that every product in its premium owned food brand, Archer Farms, contains zero grams of added trans fat. Available exclusively at Target and SuperTarget® stores across the country, Archer Farms is the first national proprietary food brand to eliminate added trans fats from its entire product portfolio, based on the Food and Drug Administration's (FDA) definition of zero grams added trans fat. The Archer Farms collection features more than 2,000 products made from the finest ingredients, which have all been formulated without adding unhealthy trans fats.

In an ongoing effort to empower its guests to make smart, nutritious food decisions, Target has dedicated the past several months to reformulating selected products so the entire Archer Farms collection meets the FDA standard for labeling items as zero grams of added trans fat. For example, while bakery treats typically contain trans fats, guests will find Archer Farms products such as triple berry pies, lemon cookies, blueberry muffins and tiramisu desserts with zero grams of added trans fats. This initiative expands upon a concerted effort from Target to offer its guests the tools they need to live healthier lives and raise healthy families.

In 2006, Target expanded its Archer Farms brand to include affordable organic food products. The same year, all SuperTarget produce departments became certified organic by the U.S. Department of Agriculture's (USDA) National Organic Program—the strictest, third-party certification available.

"Removing added trans fat has quickly become a priority among the health community and for good reason. Regardless of age or gender, consuming food products with added trans fats presents a host of long-term health concerns," says Dr. Susan Mitchell, Target health and nutrition expert. "The Archer Farms line offers premium, affordable snacking and meal options made from the finest ingredients for those looking to steer clear of added trans fat."

Created with the finest ingredients, the Archer Farms food collection provides guests with everything from elegant hors d'oeurvres and gourmet spreads, to European-style baked goods and meals on the go. Delivering on its "Everyday Incredible" promise, Archer Farms combines the highest quality foods with affordable prices.

SECTOR: **Consumer Discretionary**
BETA COEFFICIENT: **1.10**
10-YEAR COMPOUND EARNINGS PER SHARE GROWTH: **15%**
10-YEAR COMPOUND DIVIDENDS PER SHARE GROWTH: **12.7%**

	2007	2006	2005	2004	2003	2002	2001	2000
Revenues (Mil)	63,367	59,490	52,620	46,839	48,163	43,917	39,888	36,903
Net Income (Mil)	2,849	2,787	2,408	1,885	1,841	1,654	1,419	1,264
Earnings per share	3.33	3.21	2.71	2.07	2.01	1.81	1.56	1.38
Dividends per share	0.56	0.42	0.38	0.30	0.26	0.24	0.22	0.21
Price high	70.8	60.3	60.0	54.1	41.8	46.2	41.7	39.2
low	48.8	44.7	45.6	36.6	25.6	24.9	26.0	21.6

AGGRESSIVE GROWTH

Teva Pharmaceutical Industries, Ltd.

5 Basel Street ❑ P.O. Box 3190 ❑ Petach Tikva Israel 49131 ❑ (215) 591-8912 ❑ Dividend reinvestment plan not available ❑ Web site: *www.tevapharm.com* ❑ Listed: Nasdaq ❑ Ticker symbol: TEVA ❑ S&P rating: not rated ❑ Value Line Financial Rating: A

Teva Specialty Pharmaceuticals, the U.S. respiratory therapy unit of Teva Pharmaceutical Industries Ltd., and UCB announced on January 16, 2008, an agreement to co-commercialize Teva's U.S. respiratory medicines. The initial product to be jointly promoted in the United States is Teva's ProAir® HFA (albuterol sulfate) inhalation aerosol. ProAir HFA is the number-one branded hydrofluroalkane (HFA) albuterol sulfate inhaler in the United States. Additionally, the agreement provides UCB future joint promotion opportunities with other products in development by Teva Specialty Pharmaceuticals.

"Over the last months we have undertaken a rich, strategic review globally across regions, therapy areas and business units," said William S. Marth, CEO of Teva North America. "The respiratory therapy area has been identified as a key growth area given the incidence of asthma, allergic rhinitis, and COPD (chronic obstructive pulmonary disease). Our collaboration with UCB, a company known for excellence in the respiratory market, will help us achieve a stronger presence in this growing therapeutic area."

"UCB is focused on discovering and commercializing medicines to treat serious conditions, including asthma, and we are committed to expanding our portfolio because we believe ProAir HFA has the potential to improve patient treatment options," said Fabrice Egros, CEO, UCB North America. "We look forward to working with Teva Specialty Pharmaceuticals for the benefit of the many Americans who suffer from this condition."

UCB is a global leader in the biopharmaceutical industry dedicated to the research, development and commercialization of innovative pharmaceutical and biotechnology products in the fields of central nervous system disorders, allergy/respiratory diseases, immune and inflammatory disorders, and oncology. Employing 12,000 people in more than forty countries, UCB achieved revenue of $4.6 billion (3.5 billion euro) in 2006 on a pro forma basis. UCB is listed on the Euronext Brussels Exchange. Worldwide headquarters are located in Brussels, Belgium, and U.S. headquarters are located in Atlanta, Georgia.

What Are Generic Drugs?

"All drugs—whether prescription or over the counter—have a nonproprietary name (also called a generic name, it's the name of a drug that's not subject to being trademarked), but only some are sold as generic drugs," said Robert S. Dinsmoor, a contributing editor of *Diabetes Self-Management*, a leading publication devoted to the treatment of diabetes. "If and when a drug can be sold as a generic depends on when the patent (or patents) held by the developer of the drug expire. A patent gives the drug developer the exclusive right to market the drug under its brand name for a certain amount of time."

Mr. Dinsmoor went on to explain, "Generic drugs usually sell for a fraction of the cost of the brand-name drugs. Generic metformin, for example, costs about two-thirds as much as the brand-name product. The price drop that occurs when generics enter the market is attributable to several factors, including competition and the lower overhead of generic-drug manufacturers. When companies compete with each other to sell the same product, market theory argues that prices will tend to go down. Manufacturers of generics are also able to offer lower price because, unlike the developer of the original brand-name drug, they do not have to recoup large investments in research and development or engage in expensive marketing and advertising campaigns."

Company Profile

Teva was founded in Jerusalem in 1901 as a small wholesale drug business that distributed imported medicines loaded onto the backs of camels and donkeys to customers throughout the land. The company was called Salomon, Levin and Elstein, Ltd., after its founders.

Teva Pharmaceutical Industries Ltd. is a global pharmaceutical company specializing in generic drugs. The company has major manufacturing and marketing facilities in Israel, North America and Europe.

Teva's scope of activity extends to many facets of the industry, with primary focus on the manufacturing and marketing of products in the following categories:

■   Human pharmaceuticals. Teva produces generic drugs in all major therapeutic realms in a variety of dosage forms, from tablets and capsules to ointments, creams and liquids. Teva manufactures innovative drugs in niche markets where it has a relative advantage in research and development.

■   Active Pharmaceutical Ingredients (API) competitively distributes its API to manufacturers worldwide as well as supports its own pharmaceutical production. Through its API division, the company offers raw materials used by drug manufacturers. API produces more than 190 different bulk chemicals or active ingredients for use in human pharmaceuticals. Teva's acquisition of Sicor added complementary API operations to its existing capabilities.

These activities, which comprise the core businesses of the company, account for 90 percent of Teva's total sales.

Shortcomings to Bear in Mind

■   In 2006, Medicare began providing a drug benefit to senior citizens, which will boost the industry sales. Unfortunately, analysts say the generic drug industry is becoming more competitive. Low cost, India-based companies are gaining a bigger foothold in the United States while technological advances lower the barriers to entry in the field. And there's debate over just how lucrative the Medicare drug benefit will be since those implementing it will try to extract the lowest possible prices.

Meanwhile, deals known as "authorized generics" may ultimately hurt the industry. Under the current law, the first generic company to file for approval to make a medicine receives 180 days to sell the product exclusively. This enables the company to make a significant portion of money before competitors enter, driving down costs.

On the other hand, pharmaceutical companies have recently been giving permission to a generic company to make its drug right before the patent expired, effectively ending 180 days of exclusivity for the other company. While two providers means lower prices for consumers, it also means lower profits for generic makers that can ultimately harm their business.

Reasons to Buy

■ On February 12, 2008, CEO Shlomo Yanai said, "2007 was an outstanding year for Teva—a year in which we achieved record-breaking results across the board, fortified our leadership in key markets, and significantly grew our business."

Mr. Yanai continued, "Surpassing Teva's unprecedented growth in 2006 posed a major challenge for us going into 2007. We not only met this challenge but in fact exceeded our own ambitious targets—a clear demonstration of the unique strengths and capabilities that we believe will enable Teva to continue its tradition of continuous, profitable growth and value creation for our shareholders. We expect the significant momentum that we generated in 2007 to continue throughout 2008, resulting in another excellent year for Teva."

■ Teva Pharmaceutical Industries Ltd. and Bentley Pharmaceuticals, Inc. announced on March 31, 2008, that they have entered into a definitive agreement under which Teva will acquire Bentley.

Teva will acquire Bentley, which at closing will consist solely of the generic pharmaceutical operations, for an aggregate cash purchase price of approximately $360 million.

Bentley manufactures and markets a portfolio of about 130 pharmaceutical products in various dosages and strengths, as both branded generic and generic products, to physicians, pharmacists and hospitals. Bentley markets its products primarily in Spain, but also sells generic pharmaceuticals in other parts of the European Union. These efforts are supported by finished dosage and active pharmaceutical ingredient manufacturing facilities. Bentley's generic pharmaceutical operations generated revenues of approximately $114 million for the year ended December 31, 2007.

Commenting on the transaction, Mr. Yanai said: "This is an important acquisition for Teva, as the combination of Teva Spain and Bentley will provide us with a platform to capture a leading position in the fast-growing Spanish generic pharmaceutical market. Spain was identified as one of our target markets in the strategic review we conducted last year. We are extremely pleased that we will have Bentley's strong management and work force, complementing our existing management team, to support our growth strategy."

"We are excited about today's announcement. By separately selling Bentley's generic operations while spinning off its drug delivery business, we believe that we are maximizing shareholder value," added James R. Murphy, Bentley's CEO. "Our generic pharmaceutical operations will serve as the platform on which Teva can build a leading position in Spain. Becoming part of the world's leading generic pharmaceutical company and gaining access to its extensive resources and expertise in generic R&D, manufacturing and marketing will enable us to better serve our customers in bringing to market high quality and affordable generic pharmaceuticals."

■ On April 18, 2008, *Value Line Investment Survey* called Teva a 2, the same as a BUY. J. Susan Ferrara said, "Management is laying the groundwork for long-term growth. In fact, it plans to double the size of the business by 2012, with sales reaching $20 billion and profit margins surpassing 20 percent. Widening the global footprint, especially within such emerging markets as Latin America and parts of Europe, and expanding the pipeline of generics and branded drugs will figure importantly here."

■ Market Edge Research rated the stock a BUY on March 24, 2008, with this comment, "The current financial condition of TEVA is very strong as evidenced by the large number of positive fundamental factors. The stock represents a good value when compared to other stocks in its industry group and appears likely to experience further price appreciation."

■ On March 22, 2008, Standard & Poor's *Stock Reports* gave the stock its highest rating, five stars, or STRONG BUY. Phillip M. Seligman said, "We see demand for generic drugs continuing to rise strongly, as the U.S. and other countries seek to limit increases in drug spending. With the largest generic drug portfolio among peers, and 160 ANDAs (generic drug filings) awaiting FDA clearance as of February 7, 2008, we think Teva will continue to gain market share via the offer of one-stop shopping."

SECTOR: HEALTH CARE
BETA COEFFICIENT: .75
7-YEAR COMPOUND EARNINGS PER SHARE GROWTH: **35.1%**
7-YEAR COMPOUND DIVIDENDS PER SHARE GROWTH: **30.7%**

	2007	2006	2005	2004	2003	2002	2001	2000
Revenues (Mil)	9,408	8,400	5,250	4,799	3,276	2,519	2,077	1,750
Net Income (Mil)	1,952	1,867	1,072	965	691	410	278	148
Earnings per share	2.38	2.30	1.59	1.42	1.04	0.76	0.53	0.29
Dividends per share	0.39	0.30	0.27	0.16	0.14	0.09	0.06	0.07
Price high	47.1	44.7	45.9	34.7	31.2	20.1	18.6	19.7
low	30.8	29.2	26.8	22.8	17.3	12.9	12.1	8.0

CONSERVATIVE GROWTH

3M Company

3M Center, Building 225-01-S-15 □ St. Paul, MN 55144-1000 □ (651) 733-8206 □ Web site: *www.MMM.com* □ Listed: NYSE □ Dividend reinvestment plan available □ Ticker symbol: MMM □ S&P rating: A+ □ Value Line financial strength rating: A++

On January 4, 2008, 3M announced that it is now providing consumer electronics manufacturers with a revolutionary advancement in the emerging field of miniature projection technology. 3M scientists developed a breakthrough ultracompact, LED-illuminated projection engine designed for integration into virtually any personal electronic device. Roughly the size of a wireless earpiece and less than half an inch thick, the 3M mobile projection engine delivers brilliant VGA resolution images and is available today.

With the expansion of digital media now accessible by mobile devices, consumers need the convenience of larger displays. "3M mobile projection engines achieve the size, efficiency, image quality and affordability needed for consumer adoption of this promising new product category," said Mike Kelly, executive vice president, 3M Display and Graphics Business. "This development continues 3M's long history as a global leader in advanced projection display technology. What is really exciting is that this technology is available now."

When deployed in a host platform, such as a mobile phone, 3M's technology can project a forty-inch or larger image with no-speckle and a high-fill factor that ensures superior image quality. Each engine uses an advanced liquid crystal on silicon (LCOS) electronic imager in conjunction with proprietary 3M optics technology.

Company Profile

Minnesota Mining and Manufacturing—now known as 3M Company—is a $24 billion diversified technology company with leading positions in industrial, consumer and office, health care, safety, electronics, telecommunications, and other markets. The company has operations in more than sixty countries and serves customers in nearly 200 countries.

3M has a vast array of products (more than 50,000), including such items as tapes, adhesives, electronic components, sealants, coatings, fasteners, floor coverings, cleaning agents, roofing granules, fire-fighting agents, graphic arts, dental products, medical products, specialty chemicals, and reflective sheeting.

The company's Industrial and Consumer Sector is the world's largest supplier of tapes, producing more than 900 varieties. It is also a leader in coated abrasives, specialty chemicals, repositionable notes, home cleaning sponges and pads, electronic circuits, and other important products.

The Life Sciences Sector is a global leader in reflective materials for transportation safety, respirators for worker safety, closures for disposable diapers and high-quality graphics used indoors and out. This sector also holds leading positions in medical and surgical supplies, drug-delivery systems, and dental products.

3M has a decentralized organization with a large number of relatively small profit centers, aimed at creating an entrepreneurial atmosphere.

Shortcomings to Bear in Mind

▪ On March 24, 2008, Market Edge Research said to SELL MMM, with this comment: "The stock's recent price momentum has been negative, but it has been outperforming the market when compared to the S&P 500. The recent negative price performance indicates that further price appreciation at this time is unlikely."

Reasons to Buy

▪ On January 29, 2008, CEO George W. Buckley said, "We made good progress on our growth plan in 2007, and we will continue this effort in 2008. By investing in our many enduring franchises, strategic acquisitions and new plants to streamline our supply chain, we are securing 3M's future as a faster-growing and more efficient enterprise."

3M reiterated its 2008 earnings expectations. The company expects 2008 earnings to be a minimum 10 percent increase over its 2007 earnings-per-share of $4.98, which excludes special items.

"We will continue to balance growth and operational excellence in order to meet our commitments to our shareholders and customers around the world," said Mr. Buckley.

MMM has many strengths:

• Leading market positions. Minnesota Mining is a leader in most of its businesses, often number one or number two in market share. In fact, 3M has created many markets, frequently by developing products that people didn't even realize they needed.

• Strong technology base. The company draws on more than thirty core technologies—from adhesives and nonwovens to specialty chemicals and microreplication.

• Healthy mix of businesses. 3M serves an extremely broad array of markets—from automotive and health care to office supply and telecommunications. This diversity gives the company many avenues for growth, while also cushioning the company from disruption in any single market.

- Flexible, self-reliant business units. 3M's success in developing a steady stream of new products and entering new markets stems from its deep-rooted corporate structure. It's an environment in which 3M people listen to customers, act on their own initiative, and share technologies and other expertise widely and freely.
- Worldwide presence. Minnesota Mining has companies in more than sixty countries around the world. It sells its products in some 200 countries.
- Efficient manufacturing and distribution. 3M is a low-cost supplier in many of its product lines. This is increasingly important in today's value-conscious and competitive world.
- Strong financial position. 3M is one of a small number of domestic companies whose debt carries the highest rating for credit quality.

■ On January 30, 2008, Argus Research Company regarded 3M at a BUY, with this comment by Rashid Dahod: "The company is reaping the benefits of its diverse portfolio, with positive sales growth in all of its business lines."

■ On November 15, 2007, 3M and Aearo Technologies Inc. announced that they had entered into a definitive agreement for 3M's acquisition of Aearo for a total purchase price of $1.2 billion, to be financed through a combination of cash and other borrowings. Aearo is a global leader in the personal protection industry and manufactures and markets personal protection and energy absorbing products.

Aearo will significantly expand 3M's occupational health and environmental safety platform by adding hearing protection as well as eyewear and fall protection product lines to 3M's existing full-line of respiratory products. It provides a broad platform for accelerated growth. This acquisition enables 3M to provide industrial, military and construction customers as well as consumers with a more complete personal protection solution.

"Aearo complements and significantly broadens our core safety and personal protection business, a space which is growing fast and of strategic importance to the company," said Mr. Buckley. "The combination of 3M's technology, our global reach and well-known safety brand with Aearo's strong product portfolio and brands positions 3M as the global leader in personal protective equipment products. Our powerful international distribution network will enable us to enhance and leverage this asset going forward."

Aearo has achieved the leading global market positions in hearing and eye protection through the strength of its brand names such as E-A-R, Peltor, AOSafety, and SafeWaze, and its reputation for developing high-quality, innovative products and strong market competitiveness. The company has demonstrated a strong track record of consistent market beating growth and profitability, with sales increasing at a compound annual growth rate of more than 12 percent over the past five years to $508 million.

The complete Aearo product line includes passive hearing, communication headsets, eye protection, head and face protection and fall protection. The company also markets systems solutions and proprietary energy absorbing materials, which are incorporated into other manufacturers' products to control noise, vibration, shock and temperature.

■ 3M supplies a wide variety of products to the automotive market, including high-performance tape attachment systems; structural adhesives; catalytic converter mounts; decorative, functional and protective films; and trim and identification products.

■ On September 13, 2007, 3M announced that it had entered into a definitive agreement to acquire Abzil Industria e Comercio Ltda., a manufacturer of orthodontic products based in Sao Jose do Rio Preto, Sao Paulo, Brazil.

Abzil is a successful player in the fast-growing Brazilian orthodontic market. The company's brackets, bands, tubes, and wires are widely recognized as some of the highest quality orthodontic products available in the country. "Abzil's strong brand and product portfolio complement our full line of orthodontic solutions and will allow us to better serve customers in Brazil and beyond," said Paul Keel, president, 3M

Unitek. "We see strong technical and sales synergies as well as manufacturing opportunities with Abzil," added Luigi Faltoni, managing director, 3M Brazil.

"Abzil and 3M together are a natural fit," said Tufy Lemos Filho, owner and president, Abzil. "We will draw on the strength of 3M's global resources and expertise to provide a broader product offering for orthodontic professionals."

SECTOR: **Industrials**
BETA COEFFICIENT: **.90**
10-YEAR COMPOUND EARNINGS PER SHARE GROWTH: **11.2%**
10-YEAR COMPOUND DIVIDENDS PER SHARE GROWTH: **6.1%**

		2007	2006	2005	2004	2003	2002	2001	2000
Revenues (Mil)		24,462	22,923	21,167	20,011	18,232	16,332	16,079	16,724
Net Income (Mil)		4,096	3,851	3,111	2,990	2,403	1,974	1,430	1,782
Earnings per share		5.60	5.06	3.98	3.75	3.09	2.50	1.79	2.32
Dividends per share		1.92	1.84	1.68	1.44	1.32	1.24	1.20	1.16
Price	high	97.0	88.4	87.4	90.3	85.4	65.8	63.5	61.5
	low	72.9	67.0	69.7	73.3	59.7	50.0	42.9	39.1

AGGRESSIVE GROWTH

The TJX Companies, Inc.

770 Cochituate Road □ Framingham, MA 01701 □ (508) 390-2323 □ Dividend reinvestment plan not available □ Fiscal years end the last Saturday in January □ Listed: NYSE □ Web site: *www.tjx.com* □ Ticker symbol: TJX □ S&P rating: A+ □ Value Line financial strength rating: A+

"Struggling retailers and cost-conscious consumers are likely to present opportunities for TJX," said Joel Schwed, writing for *Value Line Investment Survey* on February 8, 2008. "The unusually large amount of excess merchandise at retailers and department stores, from which the company gets its products, should provide for an excellent selection, and puts TJX in a strong buying position. Furthermore, the economic strain on consumers, while weighing on overall spending, should drive new customers to its stores, as they search for bargains."

Mr. Schwed also said, "TJX shares should match the stock market over the coming year. And we project solid earnings gains for the next three to five years."

Company Profile

The TJX Companies, Inc. is the leading off-price apparel and home fashions retailer in the U.S. and worldwide, with $16 billion in revenues in 2005, eight businesses, and more than 2,300 stores, and ranked 138th in the most recent *Fortune* 500 rankings. TJX's off-price concepts include T.J.Maxx, Marshalls, HomeGoods, and A.J. Wright, in the U.S., Winners and HomeSense in Canada, and T.K. Maxx in Europe. Bob's Stores is a value-oriented, casual clothing and footwear superstore in the northeastern United States. The company's off-price mission is to deliver a rapidly changing assortment of quality, brand name merchandise at prices that are 20-60 percent less than department and specialty store regular prices, every day. Its target customer is a middle to upper-middle income shopper, who is fashion and value conscious and fits the same profile as a department store shopper, with the exception of A.J. Wright, which reaches a more moderate-income market, and Bob's Stores, which targets customers in the moderate to upper-middle income range.

T.J. Maxx

T.J. Maxx was founded in 1976 and is the largest off-price retailer of apparel and home fashions in the United States. T.J. Maxx offers brand name family apparel, giftware, home fashions, women's shoes, and lingerie, and emphasizes accessories and fine jewelry, at prices 20-60 percent below department and specialty store regular prices. T.J. Maxx customers fit the same profile as a department and specialty store shopper, a savvy consumer who is fashion and value conscious. T.J. Maxx, which operated 799 stores at the end of 2005, has further growth opportunities in the United States. The average store size of a T.J. Maxx store is 30,000 square feet.

Marshalls

Marshalls is the second largest off-price retailer in the United States and was acquired by TJX in 1995. With a product assortment very similar to T.J. Maxx, Marshalls offers brand name family apparel, giftware, home fashions, and accessories. Marshalls also offers expanded footwear assortments for the entire family and a broader men's department. Marshalls customers have a very similar profile to those who shop at department and specialty stores. The Marshalls chain, operating 715 stores at the end of 2005, continues to grow

in many markets across the U.S. Marshalls stores are an average of 32,000 square feet.

Winners

Winners, operating 174 stores in Canada by the end of 2005, has grown into the leading off-price family apparel retailer in that country since it was acquired by TJX in 1990. Patterned after T.J. Maxx, Winners offers brand name family apparel, giftware, fine jewelry, home fashions, accessories, lingerie, and family footwear. Winners stores average 30,000 square feet. Winners' customer profile is very similar to that of T.J. Maxx and Marshalls. As at the other divisions, the Winners customer typically shops for her entire family, seeking excellent value on brand name fashions. Management expects to net eleven additional Winners stores in 2006 and believes that Canada can support 200 Winners stores.

HomeSense

With its launch in 2001, HomeSense introduced the home fashions off-price concept to Canada. Similar to HomeGoods in the United States, HomeSense offers customers a wide, rapidly changing selection of giftware, home basics, accent furniture, rugs, lamps, accessories, and seasonal items. At year-end 2005, HomeSense operated fifty-eight stores with a typical store size of 24,000 square feet. The company added ten HomeSense stores in 2006. Ultimately, it believes the Canadian market can support eighty HomeSense stores.

T.K. Maxx

T.K. Maxx, a T.J. Maxx-like off-price apparel and home fashions concept, operated 197 stores in the United Kingdom and Ireland at the end of 2005. T.K. Maxx has been very well received since its launch in 1994 introduced the off-price concept to the U.K., offering a unique shopping experience to that market. Today, T.K. Maxx is the only major off-price retailer in any

European country. With stores averaging 30,000 square feet in size, T.K. Maxx offers great values on family apparel, women's footwear, jewelry, lingerie, accessories, and home fashions. T.K. Maxx added a total of 15 stores in 2006. Management sees the United Kingdom and Ireland supporting 300 stores in the long term.

HomeGoods

HomeGoods, a chain of off-price home fashions stores, operated 251 stores at the end of 2005. HomeGoods offers an exciting and rapidly changing selection of home décor merchandise, including giftware, home basics, accent furniture, lamps, rugs, accessories, and seasonal merchandise at great values. This chain operates in a standalone and superstore format, which couple HomeGoods with a T.J. Maxx or Marshalls. Standalone HomeGoods stores average 27,000 square feet. In the year 2006, Home-Goods netted ten new stores. Ultimately, the company believes that the U.S. market could support 650 HomeGoods stores.

A.J. Wright

A.J. Wright, launched in 1998, operates similarly to the company's other off-price concepts, but targets the moderate-income customer. A.J. Wright offers outstanding values on family apparel and footwear, accessories, home fashions, giftware, including toys and games, and special, opportunistic purchases. Prices at A.J. Wright are 20 to 70 percent below regular prices at national discount chains and budget department stores. At year-end 2005, A.J. Wright operated 152 stores. A.J. Wright stores average 26,000 square feet. A.J. Wright netted 8 new stores in 2006. Longer-term, TJX believes that the United States could potentially support 1,000 stores.

Bob's Stores

Bob's Stores, which was acquired by TJX in 2003, is a value-oriented, casual, clothing and footwear superstore. Bob's Stores offers customers casual, family apparel and footwear, workwear, activewear, and licensed team apparel. This concept targets a moderate- to upper-middle income customer and its stores average 46,000 square feet. Bob's Stores operated thirty-five stores in the northeastern United States at the end of 2005, and TJX opened one Bob's Store in 2006.

Shortcomings to Bear in Mind

▪ Retail stocks can have their ups and downs, principally because of the shifts in the economy. Then, too, they can lose market share when new competitors appear on the scene.

Reasons to Buy

▪ On February 20, 2008, CEO Carol Meyrowitz said, "We are very pleased with our performance in 2007. Our strategies yielded strong operating results and margin growth, even in the challenging retail environment. Driving profitable sales remains our top priority, and we have delivered another great year on top of a great year by solidly executing the fundamentals of our flexible, global, off-price model. We were extremely disciplined in managing inventories, which gave us the ability to buy into current trends and offer great brands and fashions at compelling values. New merchandising initiatives and improved marketing highlighted our values and helped drive customer traffic. Further, expense management continued to be a key focus across the Company. In 2008, we will remain focused on many of these same strategies to drive profitable sales growth, and will continue pursuing growth vehicles to expand our brand presence both domestically and internationally."

▪ On February 20, 2008, a company spokesman said, "For the fiscal year ending January 31, 2009, the company expects earnings per share from continuing operations in the range of $2.20 to $2.25, which represents a 15 percent to 18 percent increase over the $1.91 adjusted earnings per share from continuing operations in Fiscal 2008 (detailed above). This guidance includes an expected $.09 per share benefit from the 53rd week in the company's Fiscal 2009 calendar. Excluding this benefit, this guidance represents a 10 percent to 13 percent increase over last year. This range is based upon estimated consolidated comparable store sales growth of 2 percent to 3 percent, of which approximately 0.5 percentage points is due to the impact of foreign currency exchange rates."

■ "As household budgets get squeezed, consumers are likely to spend more at discount retailers—and TJX, owner of T. J. Maxx, is one of the best. The company has reported favorable comparable-store sales

for all but two of its thirty years in business." said Mara Der Hovanesian, writing for *BusinessWeek* on September 3, 2007.

■ "On February 13, 2008, Argus Research Company's analyst, Christopher Graja, had this comment: "Our research suggests that TJX is doing a better job of delivering a 'treasure hunt' atmosphere, in which shoppers find name-brand merchandise at discount prices. We believe that more appealing designer clothing as well as a consistent flow of shoes and accessories is helping to attract customers. Under CEO Carol Meyrowitz, management has placed a strong emphasis on merchandising and has encouraged the company's approximately 400 buyers to take more risks and to negotiate great deals from more than 10,000 venders."

SECTOR: **Consumer Discretionary**
BETA COEFFICIENT: **.95**
10-YEAR COMPOUND EARNINGS PER SHARE GROWTH: **13.7%**
10-YEAR COMPOUND DIVIDENDS PER SHARE GROWTH: **21.8%**

	2007	2006	2005	2004	2003	2002	2001	2000
Revenues (Mil)	18,647	17,405	16,058	14,913	13,328	11,981	10,709	9,579
Net Income (Mil)	777.8	738	690.4	683.4	658.4	578.4	540.4	538.1
Earnings per share	1.66	1.63	1.29	1.34	1.28	1.08	0.97	0.93
Dividends per share	0.36	0.28	0.24	0.18	0.14	0.12	0.09	0.08
Price high	32.5	29.8	26.0	26.8	23.7	22.5	20.3	15.8
low	25.7	22.2	20.0	20.6	15.5	15.3	13.6	7.0

AGGRESSIVE GROWTH

T. Rowe Price Group, Inc.

100 East Pratt Street ❑ Baltimore, MD 21202 ❑ (410) 345-2124 ❑ Dividend reinvestment plan not available ❑ Web site: *www.troweprice.com* ❑ Ticker symbol: TROW ❑ Listed: Nasdaq ❑ S&P rating: A ❑ Value Line financial strength rating: A+

On January 16, 2008, global investment management firm T. Rowe Price officially opened its second building at its Colorado Springs campus, doubling its capacity and positioning the firm to support anticipated growth needs. Located at 2220 Briargate Parkway, T. Rowe Price's expanded facilities include a 145,000 square foot, three-story

building and an additional parking structure and will accommodate 650 associates, bringing capacity at the Colorado Springs campus to nearly 1,400 associates.

T. Rowe Price currently employs more than 670 people in Colorado Springs, a 28 percent increase since June 2006 when the expansion plans were announced. Since it first opened a Colorado Springs office in November 1998, the firm has grown from less than $150 billion in assets under management to $396.8 billion as of September 30, 2007.

The Colorado Springs campus complements similar operations centers in Owings Mills, Maryland, and Tampa, Florida, and provides flexibility in servicing investors throughout the United States, as well as enhanced capability to serve the investment and administrative needs of the firm's shareholders and clients located in the western states. At complete build-out the thirty-one-acre site has the potential to accommodate four buildings and approximately 2,000 associates. T. Rowe Price also recently announced plans to expand its facilities in Owings Mills.

Employees in Colorado Springs provide investment guidance and various client services to individual investors, retirement plan participants, and 401(k) plan administrators.

"Our expansion in Colorado Springs reflects the continued growth of our business as well as our goals to provide world-class service to our clients and a world-class work environment for our associates," said CEO Edward C. Bernard. "While T. Rowe Price continues to expand its operations around the world, Colorado Springs remains a strong fit with our culture and a critical part of our success. We expect that to continue for many years to come."

"We continue to be very pleased with the talent pool, business environment and community relationships in Colorado Springs, as well as our partnership with the Colorado Springs Economic Development Corporation," said Chris Hufman, vice president of T. Rowe Price Services, Inc. and general manager of the Colorado Springs Investment Services Center. "These were driving factors in our decision to expand, and should continue to support our firm's future growth and longstanding commitment to the area."

Company Profile

Founded in 1937, Baltimore-based T. Rowe Price is a global investment management firm with $308.1 billion in assets under management as of September 30, 2006. The firm provides a broad array of separate account management, sub-advisory services, and mutual funds for institutional and individual investors, retirement plans, and financial intermediaries.

T. Rowe Price's disciplined, risk-aware investment approach focuses on diversification, style consistency, and fundamental research.

The company's investment approach strives to achieve superior performance but "is always mindful of the risks incurred relative to the potential rewards. Our consistent investment philosophy helps mitigate unfavorable changes and takes advantage of favorable ones. We provide our clients with world-class investment guidance as well as attentive service."

Founded in 1937 by Thomas Rowe Price Jr., the company offers separately managed investment portfolios for institutions and a broad range of mutual funds for individual investors and corporate retirement accounts. Mutual funds are pooled investments representing the savings of many thousands of individuals that are invested in stocks, bonds, and other assets managed by a portfolio manager or managers in the hope of either outperforming a market average—such as the S&P 500 or the Dow Jones Industrial Average—or meeting a similar goal. No-load funds are sold without a sales commission. However, this does not infer there is no cost. All mutual funds have expenses, such as salaries, office rent, advertising, travel and the like. This averages about 1.6 percent per year, but does not include the cost of buying and selling stocks. T. Rowe Price is a low-cost manager.

In founding his firm, Mr. Price followed a very simple principle: What is good for the client is also good for the firm. Rather than charge a commission, as was then the practice in the securities business, Mr. Price charged a fee based on the assets under management.If the client prospered, so did T. Rowe Price.

Mr. Price is best known for developing the growth stock style of investing. Although he was trained as a chemist, he had a passion for investing. Mr. Price believed that investors could earn superior returns by investing in well-managed companies in fertile fields whose earnings and dividends could be expected to grow faster than inflation and the overall economy. The core of Mr. Price's approach, proprietary research to guide investment selection and diversification reduce risk, has remained part of the firm's bedrock principles.

Today, growth stock investing is one of the many investment styles the firm currently follows. T. Rowe Price also employs value-oriented, sector-focused, tax-efficient, and quantitative index-oriented approaches in managing mutual funds and institutional portfolios.

Shortcomings to Bear in Mind

- Because of its impressive record of growth, this stock is rarely on the bargain counter. It has a P/E that is well above the market.
- If you are a conservative investor, this may not be the stock for you. T. Rowe Price has a Beta coefficient of 1.40, which means it fluctuates 40 percent more than the market, both up and down. A Beta of 1.00, by contrast, would indicate a stock that is much less volatile, or about the same as the overall market.

Reasons to Buy

- On September 10, 2007, T. Rowe Price Associates announced that it is expanding its international fund lineup with a new fund focusing on the emerging markets of Africa and the Middle East.

The T. Rowe Price Africa & Middle East Fund is a no-load fund that seeks long-term capital growth by investing primarily in stocks of companies located or with primary operations in these regions. The primary markets the fund invests in include Bahrain, Egypt, Jordan, Kenya, Lebanon, Morocco, Nigeria, Oman, Qatar, South Africa, and United Arab Emirates.

Other potential markets as they develop include: Algeria, Botswana, Ghana, Kuwait, Mauritius, Namibia, Tunisia, and Zimbabwe.

The political and economic risks in the region make these markets susceptible to extreme volatility and sudden and possibly severe price declines. In addition, the fund has a high risk/reward profile since it can invest in small- and mid-cap stocks in emerging markets and has a relatively concentrated portfolio, which will typically consist of twenty-five to fifty companies.

Financial companies represent the largest sector exposure, as commercial banks are benefiting from rapidly growing economies. "Many of these companies are experiencing significant revenue growth as demand for both retail and business credit increases," a company portfolio manager said. "Significant reform of banking and pension markets in many states should further encourage loan growth in both the Middle East and Africa."

- "We are upbeat about the company's operating performance over the three-to-five-year time frame," said Frederick L. Harris, III, writing for *Value Line Investment Survey* on February 22, 2008. "One major positive is that a number of its mutual funds have an excellent total-return record, compared to their respective peer groups. Product introductions and further restructuring efforts should help T. Rowe Price, too."

- On October 4, 2006, T. Rowe Price launched an enhanced suite of Advisory Planning Services to assist those saving for retirement, approaching retirement, or already retired, as well as those just seeking a thorough evaluation of their overall investment portfolio.

As part of the services, the firm provides a complete portfolio evaluation and a detailed personalized recommendation for a suitable investment strategy and how much the individual should be saving to meet retirement goals, or spending in retirement. The recommendation is based on discussions that the investor has with a T. Rowe Price advisory counselor and a detailed questionnaire that helps provide insight on the client's personal financial preferences—

such as desired retirement date, achieving a high monthly income, or leaving a legacy to heirs—and investment experience, risk tolerance, and current financial situation.

The services also utilize state-of-the-art financial modeling technology that incorporates proprietary software to assess how the recommended strategy might perform based on 1,000 hypothetical market scenarios.

SECTOR: **Financials**
BETA COEFFICIENT: **1.40**
10-YEAR COMPOUND EARNINGS PER SHARE GROWTH: **15.7%**
10-YEAR COMPOUND DIVIDENDS PER SHARE GROWTH: **17.1%**

	2007	2006	2005	2004	2003	2002	2001	2000
Revenues (Mil)	2,228	1,815	1,516	1,280	996	924	1,028	1,212
Net Income (Mil)	671	530	431	337	227	194	195	269
Earnings per share	2.40	1.90	1.58	1.26	0.89	0.76	0.76	1.04
Dividends per share	0.68	0.68	0.48	0.40	0.35	0.33	0.31	0.27
Price high	65.5	48.5	37.7	31.7	23.8	21.4	22.0	25.0
low	44.6	34.9	27.1	21.9	11.9	10.7	11.7	15.1

CONSERVATIVE GROWTH

United Parcel Service, Inc.

55 Glenlake Parkway N. E. ❑ Atlanta, GA 30328 ❑ (800) 877-1503 ❑ Direct dividend reinvestment plan is available ❑ Web site: *www.ups.com* ❑ Listed: NYSE ❑ Ticker symbol: UPS ❑ S&P rating: B+ ❑ Value Line financial strength rating: A

On September 13, 2007, the U.S. Departments of State and Transportation reached an agreement that now allows UPS and other air carriers to expand air operations to and from Japan.

The agreement provides UPS the authority to operate six daily flights between the U.S. and Nagoya, Japan, in addition to its daily service to Tokyo and Osaka. Nagoya, the fourth largest city in Japan, offers UPS significant opportunities to continue expanding its business in Asia. In addition, UPS will be able to connect these flights to its new air hub in Shanghai, China.

"With the world's second largest gross domestic product, Japan is a tremendous opportunity for UPS's customers world-

wide," said Alan Gershenhorn, president of UPS International. "The new access that comes with this landmark agreement will allow UPS to better serve customers in Japan and around the world and gain an even stronger foothold in the region."

"With the establishment of our hub in Shanghai and its formal opening next year, the opening of air lanes between Nagoya and Shanghai will improve our services to customers throughout Asia, especially China and Japan," added Ken Torok, president, UPS Asia Pacific.

UPS has operated in Japan since 1987 and transitioned to a wholly owned international express delivery operation in 2004. The company's operations cover fifteen metropolitan areas, offering express delivery, customs brokerage and supply chain management services. UPS currently offers seventy-eight weekly flights to and from Tokyo and Osaka.

Japan is one of the more than forty countries and territories UPS serves in Asia. The company operates air hubs in Taipei, Hong Kong, Singapore and the Philippines and will formally open its hub in Shanghai in 2008.

Company Profile

United Parcel—also known as Big Brown— is one of the largest employee-owned companies in the nation. With a fleet of 88,000 vehicles and 600 aircraft, UPS delivers 13.5 million packages and documents each day, or well over 3 billion a year.

The company's primary business is the delivery of packages and documents throughout the United States and in over 200 other countries and territories. In addition, UPS provides logistic services, including comprehensive management of supply chains, for major companies worldwide.

United Parcel has built strong brand equity by being a leader in quality service and product innovation in its industry. UPS has been rated the second-strongest business-to-business brand in the United States in a recent Image Power® survey and has been *Fortune* magazine's Most Admired Transportation Company in the mail, package and freight category for sixteen consecutive years.

UPS entered the international arena in 1975. It now handles over 1.2 million international shipments each day. What's more, its international package-delivery service (17 percent of revenues) is growing faster than its domestic business, and this trend is likely to continue. The company is also moving to expand its presence in Asia. In 2001, the Department of Transportation awarded UPS the right to fly directly from the U.S. to China.

Nonpackage businesses, although only 8 percent of revenues, comprise the company's fastest-growing segment. These operations include UPS Logistics Group and UPS Capital Corporation. A truck leasing business was sold in 2000. The logistics business provides global supply chain management, service parts logistics, and transportation and technology services. UPS Capital, launched in 1998, provides services to expedite the flow of funds through the supply chain.

The UPS shares sold in late 1999 represent about 10 percent of the company's total ownership. The rest is still owned by about 125,000 of its managers, supervisors, hourly workers, retirees, foundations and descendants of the company's early leaders. The company sold only Class B shares to the public. Each share has one vote, compared with the Class A stock, which has ten votes per share.

Shortcomings to Bear in Mind

■ UPS is not immune to business cycles. If there is a recession in 2008, the company is likely to experience a negative impact on its sales and earnings.

Reasons to Buy

■ On January 30, 2008, UPS reported adjusted diluted earnings per share of $1.13 for its fourth quarter, an 8.7 percent increase over last year. Revenue improved 6.1 percent driven by a double-digit increase in international export volume, growth and firm pricing in the U.S. package business and market-leading shipment gains at UPS Freight.

During the quarter, the company announced the ratification of a new five-year agreement with the International Brotherhood of Teamsters, eight months before expiration of the existing contract. As a result, $6.1 billion was paid to withdraw approximately 45,000 UPS employees from the Central States multi-employer pension plan and expensed to the U.S. Package segment in the quarter. Including the impact of that charge, diluted earnings per share fell to a loss of $2.46 for the three-month period.

"In 2007, UPS delivered on its forecast in an economic environment that became increasingly challenging over the year," said CFO Scott Davis. "We achieved this through sound execution in all parts of our business. In addition, we reached an historic labor contract with the Teamsters. I would like to thank UPSers around the world for their efforts."

The fourth quarter produced solid growth in spite of a sluggish U.S. economy. Consolidated average daily package volume reached a record level of 17.7 million pieces, an increase of 359,000 per day. Adjusted net income for the quarter benefited from a lower effective tax rate.

For the full year, the company delivered a record 3.97 billion packages, an average of 15.8 million per day. Consolidated revenue climbed 4.5 percent to $49.7 billion. Adjusted diluted earnings per share were $4.17, an increase of 8 percent compared to 2006 and at the midpoint of UPS's earnings guidance for 2007. Before adjustments, operating profit equaled $578 million and diluted earnings per share totaled $0.42.

▪ "These shares are timely," said Christopher T. Wells, an analyst with *Value Line Investment Survey*, on March 7, 2008. The service gave FedEx a 2 rating, its second best. "Looking out three to five years, we anticipate that the steps taken, both with infrastructure abroad as well as the removing of future pension responsibilities, should give the company flexibility to pursue expansion opportunities where they arise. Although there will be challenges for the company for a time from the slowing economy, UPS is poised to expand its strong position in the coming years."

▪ UPS obtains the vast majority of its revenue from small-package deliveries here at home. On the other hand, overseas shipments, finance and supply-chain management are growing at a fast clip—and that's where the company believes its future is headed.

▪ UPS stands out from the crowd in scores of ways:

- The company's mobile radio network transmits more than 3 million packets of tracking data each day.
- The company's maintenance capacity allows the transmission of more than 22 million instructions per second.
- UPS shipping tools are embedded in more than 65,000 customer Web sites.
- Using global positioning satellite technology, has the capacity to pinpoint a package within thirty feet of its location.
- UPS Supply Chain Solutions has operations in more than 120 countries. The Supply Chain Solutions Group provides logistics and distribution services, international trade management, and transportation and freight using multimodal transportation.
- UPS Supply Chain Solutions files more than 4 million customer entries in the United States, making it the nation's largest broker.
- UPS Supply Chain Solutions has hundreds of engineers to help remap supply chains for greater efficiency and market responsiveness.
- UPS Supply Chain Solutions was rated as the number one logistics provider in *Inbound Logistics* annual Top 10 3PL Excellence Award survey.
- UPS is ranked as the largest third-party logistics provider in North America by *Traffic World* magazine.
- UPS has 4,500 retail locations worldwide—more than all other franchised shipping chains put together.
- In the United States and Canada, UPS has more than 41,000 drop boxes.
- There are 7,500 third-party retail pack-and-ship locations.
- The company operates 1,400 customer centers with its operating facilities worldwide.
- UPS has more than 12,900 in-store shipping locations and commercial counters.

- The company serves more than 850 airports around the world, flying more than 1,800 flight segments each day.
- UPS operates the eleventh-largest airline in the world.
- Local country management people average fourteen years of UPS experience.
- With expanded air rights to Hong Kong, UPS now offers direct service to its two largest hubs in Europe and Asia and enhanced service to China's fastest-growing express and cargo region.
- The company has under construction a $135 million, 30,000-square-meter facility at Cologne/Bonn Airport in Germany. It will be the largest UPS facility outside the United States.
- UPS has a ninety-seven-year history of revenue growth.
- UPS is one of seven companies in the United States that has a triple-A credit rating from both Standard & Poor's and Moody's.
- Active and former employees and their families own more than 50 percent of UPS stock. That may be why you rarely see a UPS driver walking—they insist on running at top speed.

■ "From delivery of an envelope to the movement of heavy freight—locally or internationally, via air or ground, whether commercial or residential—UPS offers comprehensive shipping, tracking, visibility, customs, financial and supply chain management services," said the company's chief financial officer, D. Scott Davis.

"Our integrated global network gives us unsurpassed operational flexibility that ensures the highest levels of customer satisfaction in the industry. This single network supports multiple products with varying time-of-day delivery guarantees. The result: a business model that allows for economies of scope and scale, optimum use of assets and industry-leading margins.

"UPS's worldwide network is supported by the most sophisticated information technology (IT) in the transportation industry. We have invested $20 billion in IT over the past two decades, creating a centralized global infrastructure that sustains business continuity and quality of service at all times. Our customers can take advantage of our IT platform by linking their systems directly into the UPS global network. This seamless integration allows us to provide unique solutions that help customers improve their profitability and access new markets."

SECTOR: Industrials
BETA COEFFICIENT: .80
10-YEAR COMPOUND EARNINGS PER SHARE GROWTH: 17.7%
10-YEAR COMPOUND DIVIDENDS PER SHARE GROWTH: 17%

		2007	2006	2005	2004	2003	2002	2001	2000
Revenues (Mil)		49,692	47,547	42,581	36,582	33,485	31,272	30,321	29,771
Net Income (Mil)		447	4,202	3,870	3,333	2,898	3,182	2,425	2,795
Earnings per share		4.17	3.86	3.47	2.90	2.55	2.84	2.10	2.38
Dividends per share		1.68	1.52	1.32	1.12	0.92	0.76	0.76	0.68
Price	high	79.0	84.0	85.8	89.1	74.9	67.1	62.5	69.8
	low	68.7	65.5	66.1	67.2	53.0	54.3	46.2	49.5

United Technologies Corporation

One Financial Plaza □ Hartford, CT 06103 □ (860) 728-7912 □ Listed: NYSE □ Dividend reinvestment plan available
□ Web site: *www.utc.com* □ Listed: NYSE □ Ticker symbol: UTX □ S&P rating: A+ □ Value Line financial strength A++

Earnings per share in 2007 climbed to $4.27, and net income of $4.2 billion increased 15 and 13 percent, respectively, from 2006 results. Revenues increased 14 percent, to $54.8 billion, including 9 points of organic growth, 3 points from foreign exchange, and 2 points from acquisitions. Full year cash flow from operations was $5.3 billion and capital expenditures were $1.2 billion.

"UTC had a powerful close to 2007 and expects continuing good performance in 2008. Although the U.S. economic outlook is mixed, UTC's balance across geographic and product markets should sustain yet another year of double digit earnings per share growth," said CEO George David.

"Organic growth was 9 percent for 2007, a fourth year in a row at comparable levels. Markets across the board were good for us with the single exception of North American Residential for Carrier. Commercial aerospace volumes for UTC in total grew organically at 11 percent, as did our commercial construction businesses combined in Otis and Carrier at 10 percent.

"In 2007, all six UTC businesses grew operating profits at double digit rates, and we expect the same in 2008. Even with the significant deterioration in its North American Residential market, Carrier grew its operating profit overall at 12 percent on strong performances in its three other global businesses. Accordingly, UTC confirms its prior guidance range for 2008 earnings per share of $4.65 to $4.85, up 9 percent to 14 percent, respectively."

Company Profile

United Technologies provides high-technology products to the aerospace and building systems industries throughout the world. Its companies are industry leaders and include:

Pratt & Whitney

Large and small commercial and military jet engines, spare parts and product support, specialized engine maintenance and overhaul and repair services for airlines, air forces, and corporate fleets; rocket engines and space propulsion systems; and industrial gas turbines.

Chubb

Security and fire protection systems, integration, installation and servicing of intruder alarms, access control and video surveillance, and monitoring, response and security personnel services; installation, and servicing of fire detection and suppression systems.

Hamilton Sundstrand

Aircraft electrical power generation and distribution systems; engine and flight controls; propulsion systems; environmental controls for aircraft, spacecraft and submarines; auxiliary power units; product support, maintenance and repair services; space life support systems; industrial products including mechanical power transmissions, compressors, metering devices, and fluid handling equipment.

Sikorsky

Military and commercial helicopters; fixed-wing reconnaissance aircraft; spare parts and maintenance services for helicopters and fixed-wing aircraft; and civil helicopter operations.

UTC Power

Combined heat, cooling and power systems for commercial and industrial applications and fuel cell systems made by UTC Fuel Cells for commercial, transportation and space applications, including the U.S. space shuttle program.

Carrier

Heating, ventilating and air conditioning (HVAC) equipment for commercial, industrial and residential buildings; HVAC replacement parts and services; building controls; commercial, industrial, and transport refrigeration equipment.

Carrier emphasizes energy-efficient, quiet operation and environmental stewardship in its new residential and commercial products. The new WeatherMaker residential air conditioner using Puron, a non-ozone-depleting refrigerant, provides the domestic market with low operating costs and sound levels—about the same as a refrigerator's. The Puron unit gives Carrier a healthy lead over competitors, as chlorine-free refrigerants become the standard.

Otis

Elevators, escalators, moving walks and shuttle systems, and related installation, maintenance and repair services; modernization products and service for elevators and escalators.

Shortcomings to Bear in Mind

▪ A new CEO will take the reins in the spring of 2008. Will he be as successful as Mr. David? Only time will tell.

Reasons to Buy

▪ Pratt & Whitney scored a major coup by being chosen by the Pentagon as the lead engine supplier on both versions of the Joint Strike Fighter, as well as the F-22 fighter, two of the miliary's highest-profile new programs. Pratt is also tapping into markets it once chose to leave to others, aggressively seeking commercial-engine overhaul and maintenance business that could be valued at more than $1 billion a year. What's more, the company also has seized on an opportunity provided by the nation's power woes: It expects to sell fifty-four modified JT8D engines for industrial electric generation for major power companies in need of cheap and quickly obtainable electric power.

▪ Otis Elevator Company won the contract to supply elevators and escalators for Beijing's biggest public transit project, a new facility under construction in preparation for the Olympic Summer Games in Beijing in 2008. Otis will supply and install eleven elevators and thirty-eight escalators for the Transit Center.

▪ The Comanche is a new helicopter under development for the U.S. Army by the Boeing-Sikorsky team. This sophisticated piece of hardware will more accurately and effectively relay critical information from the battlefield to the command center than any other system in place today. Sikorsky is part of United Technologies' Flight Systems, one of the company's four segments.

While it has the ability to carry out light attack missions, the Comanche will mainly serve as a reconnaissance aircraft that will coordinate the many aircraft and ground forces involved in a combat mission. For this reason the U.S. Army has called the Comanche critical to the twenty-first century Objective Force.

The Comanche is designed, manufactured, and tested by the Boeing-Sikorsky team, with help from over fifteen leading aerospace manufacturers. In addition to Sikorsky, another one of UTX's subsidiaries, Hamilton Sundstrand, will provide the electrical power generating system and the environmental control system for the Comanche.

The battlefield of the twenty-first century will be almost entirely digitalized. As such, the Comanche, which carries highly advanced electronic equipment, will be essential for receiving and processing intelligence and sending it on to other assets. This aircraft can visually detect and classify targets seven times quicker than any other U.S. Army surveillance device today, and it can hand off precise coordinates to shooters within seconds. What's more, it can operate any time of the day and in all weather conditions. The Comanche has been undergoing rigorous testing for almost ten years. Initial deployment is scheduled for the end of the decade.

- On April 17, 2008, Standard & Poor's *Stock Reports* gave United Technologies four stars, or BUY. Richard Tortoriello said, "We believe a combination of strong management and favorable global trends, including global aerospace and commercial construction and infrastructure demand, will lead to above-average growth for UTX going forward. Although we see U.S. economic growth slowing, we expect international results as well as a weak dollar to bolster results at UTX. In addition, we think management's focus on production issues and bolstering profits at Sikorsky will continue to result in improved growth and profit margins in this segment."

- On April 21, 2008, Argus Research Company rated United Technologies a BUY. Its analyst, Suzanne Betts, said, "The company continues to benefit from a strong global footprint and particular strength in the aerospace markets. All six of its business units delivered double-digit profit growth, contributing to the 24 percent increase in earnings."

- On March 30, 2007, United Technologies announced an offer to purchase Rentokil Initial's Initial Electronic Security Group (IESG) for a purchase price of £595 million ($1.16 billion). Rentokil Initial's board of directors indicated its intention to accept UTC's offer subject to satisfaction of customary conditions. UTC also announced its intention to divest its manned guarding businesses in the United Kingdom and Australia.

IESG is the electronic security division of Rentokil Initial. It is headquartered in Blackburn, U.K., with reported sales of approximately £300 million, or $580 million, in 2006, and operating margins of about 14 percent. IESG has operations in the U.K., Netherlands, France, and the United States and employs 3,400 people in more than 100 branch locations. IESG sells integrated security systems, intrusion detection, CCTV, access control, and security software.

"This acquisition builds UTC's scale and capability in the electronic security business which we regard as attractive in national markets where we have significant presence," said Mr. David. "This acquisition strengthens particularly our position in Europe and expands our product and service offerings to a broader range of customers there. We expect our usual strong synergies and good financial returns from the combination.

"We have at the same time decided to divest low-technology manned guarding businesses in Australia and the U.K. These transactions together meaningfully transition UTC's fire and security portfolio toward higher margin and growth opportunities."

SECTOR: **Industrials**
BETA COEFFICIENT: **1.05**
10-YEAR COMPOUND EARNINGS PER SHARE GROWTH: **15.1%**
10-YEAR COMPOUND DIVIDENDS PER SHARE GROWTH: **15.2%**

		2007	2006	2005	2004	2003	2002	2001	2000
Revenues (Mil)		54,759	47,740	42,725	37,445	31,034	28,212	27,897	26,583
Net Income (Mil)		4,224	3,732	3,069	2,788	2,361	2,236	1,938	1,808
Earnings per share		4.27	3.71	3.03	2.76	2.35	2.21	1.92	1.78
Dividends per share		1.28	1.02	0.88	0.70	0.57	0.49	0.45	0.42
Price	high	82.5	67.5	58.9	53.0	48.4	38.9	43.8	39.9
	low	61.8	54.2	48.4	40.4	26.8	24.4	20.1	23.33.3

AGGRESSIVE GROWTH

Varian Medical Systems, Inc.

3100 Hansen Way ❑ Palo Alto, CA 94304-1030 ❑ (650) 424-5782 ❑ Dividend reinvestment plan not available
❑ Web site: *www.varian.com* ❑ Fiscal years end on Friday nearest September 30 ❑ Ticker symbol: VAR
❑ Listed NYSE ❑ S&P rating: B+ ❑ Value Line financial strength rating: A

On February 20, 2008, Varian Medical Systems announced a series of educational symposia about its revolutionary Rapid Arc™ radiotherapy technology for faster and more precise cancer treatments. These symposia offer clinicians the opportunity to learn more about a technology that makes it possible to deliver image-guided, intensity-modulated radiation therapy (IMRT) two to eight times faster than is possible with conventional IMRT or helical tomotherapy.

"RapidArc represents a major medical advance that will revolutionize the way image-guided IMRT is planned and delivered for thousands and thousands of patients," said Dow Wilson, president of Varian's Oncology Systems business. "Interest in RapidArc is tremendous and we're finding that our radiation oncology clinicians are eager to learn how to implement it in their centers, so we're holding several events including symposia and webinars to address this interest."

RapidArc, which recently received two FDA clearances for the treatment hardware and the treatment planning software module in Varian's Eclipse™ treatment planning system, quickly delivers a complete volumetric IMRT treatment in a single arc of the treatment machine around the patient. Varian has started taking orders for RapidArc, and began delivering it to customers in the spring of 2008.

"RapidArc should make more precise and faster radiotherapy a more affordable and more accessible treatment option for more cancer patients," said Mr. Wilson. "Varian is again providing technology advances that extend the versatility of a treatment system, adding volumetric arc therapy to other advanced capabilities including fixed-beam IMRT, image-guidance and stereotactic, electron and respiratory-gated treatments.

"No other company offers this level of options for customizing treatments according to each patient's specific needs on one treatment machine. Doctors can use the advances of RapidArc for prostate and head and neck treatments, and still offer world-class fixed beam IMRT treatments with motion management for lung and breast tumors and electron treatments for patients with superficial lesions."

Company Profile

Varian Medical Systems is the world's leading manufacturer of integrated radiotherapy systems for treating cancer and other diseases; it is also a leading supplier of X-ray tubes for imaging in medical, scientific and industrial applications. Established in 1948, the company has manufacturing sites in North America and Europe and in forty sales and support offices worldwide.

In 1999, the company (formerly Varian Associates, Inc.) reorganized itself into three separate publicly traded companies by spinning off two of its businesses to stockholders via a tax-free distribution.

Since then, the company has significantly broadened its product and business offerings, acquired new businesses, and set records for sales and net orders. More importantly, Varian put itself at the forefront of a radiotherapy revolution that is making a dramatic difference in the struggle against cancer.

About three out of every ten people will be afflicted with some form of cancer. The good news is that their chances of surviving, of beating cancer, have greatly improved, thanks to recent advances in radiation therapy—many of which have been led by Varian Medical Systems.

The company has three segments:

Varian Oncology Systems

Varian Oncology Systems is the world's leading supplier of radiotherapy systems for treating cancer. Its integrated medical systems include linear accelerators and accessories, and a broad range of interconnected software tools for planning and delivering the sophisticated radiation treatments available to cancer patients. Thousands of patients all over the world are treated daily on Varian systems. Oncology Systems works closely with health care professionals in community clinics, hospitals, and universities to improve cancer outcomes. The business unit also supplies linear accelerators for industrial inspection applications.

Varian X-Ray Products

Varian X-Ray Products is the world's premier independent supplier of X-ray tubes, serving manufacturers of radiology equipment and industrial inspection equipment, as well as distributors of replacement tubes. This business provides the industry's broadest selection of X-ray tubes expressly designed for the most advanced diagnostic applications, including CT scanning, radiography, and mammography. These products meet evolving requirements for improved resolution, faster patient throughput, longer tube life, smaller dimensions and greater cost efficiency. X-Ray Products also supplies a new line of amorphous silicon flat-panel X-ray detectors for medical and industrial applications.

Ginzton Technology Center

The Ginzton Technology Center acts as Varian Medical Systems' research and development facility for breakthrough technologies and operates a growing brachytherapy business for the delivery of internal radiation to treat cancer and cardiovascular disease. In addition to brachytherapy, current efforts are focused on next-generation imaging systems and advanced targeting technologies for radiotherapy. The center is also investigating the combination of radiotherapy with other treatment modalities, such as bioengineered gene delivery systems.

Shortcomings to Bear in Mind
■ Varian typically sells for a high price/earnings ratio, which makes is more vulnerable to any changes in outlook.

Reasons to Buy
■ Jay Palmer, writing for *Barron's* on October 22, 2007, had this to say concerning Varian: "Two of the competitors getting

the most attention—TomoTherapy (TTPY) and Accuray (ARAY)—came public just this past spring and together handle annual sales amounting to less than 20 percent of Varian's $1.6 billion.

"Yes, those outfits could get bigger— and they have both blathered about that. But Varian isn't a pushover. All indications are that it has held on to just about all of its 50 percent-plus share of sales in its market segment. CEO Tim Guertin figures that while the company may have lost a few points of market share in the quarter ending in March, the slide did not continue into the April-to-June period."

Mr. Palmer also said, "Varian, it appears, is still in an excellent position to capitalize on the long-term trends in cancer. The company remains the leading provider of integrated systems for treating cancers with radiation therapy, and it's a top supplier of the x-ray tubes used for diagnostic detection and imaging. That last business also promises to give the company a top role in the growing business of airport and transportation security, since its machines can also be used to scan bags and containers."

■ According to recent studies, more than 6 million people worldwide succumb to cancer each year. Nearly twice as many others are diagnosed with the disease. In some countries, cancer is a leading cause of death among children. Mostly though, it is a disease primarily of aging, with people fifty or older—the "baby boomers"—now accounting for nearly 80 percent of diagnosed cases. In the United States, the chances that you'll eventually develop cancer are one in three if you are female, one in two if you are male. In a very real sense, cancer victimizes not only patients, but also their families and friends, colleagues and neighbors. Ultimately, the disease affects us all. The social and economic costs are staggering.

The fact is that half of U.S. patients receive radiotherapy as part of their treatment. Now, thanks to the new technology that Varian Medical Systems has helped to develop, radiotherapy is poised to play an even stronger role in cancer treatment, and many more patients could be cured by it. It's technology that is being implemented in all corners of the world.

■ With certain cancers, the odds of surviving are improving markedly, thanks to the growing use of a radiotherapy advance called intensity modulated radiation therapy, or IMRT. IMRT is being used to treat head and neck, breast, prostate, pancreatic, lung, liver, and central nervous system cancers. IMRT makes it possible for a larger and more effective dose of radiation to be delivered directly to the tumor, greatly sparing surrounding, healthy tissues. This is expected to result in a higher likelihood of cure with lower complication rates.

The clinical outcomes using IMRT are extremely promising. A study of early stage prostate cancer has shown that the higher radiation doses possible with IMRT have the potential to double the rate of tumor control to more than 95 percent. Using IMRT, clinicians were able to deliver high doses while reducing the rate of normal tissue complications from 10 percent to 2 percent. Similar results have been reported by doctors using IMRT to treat cancers of the head and neck.

Varian Medical Systems has joined forces with GE Medical Systems to combine the latest in diagnostic imaging results with advanced radiotherapy technologies in what are called See & Treat Cancer Care imaging and treatment tools. This approach enables physicians to see the distribution of malignant cells more clearly and treat them more effectively with precisely targeted radiation doses using IMRT.

■ Varian Medical Systems has long been the world's leading supplier of radiotherapy equipment. Now, the company's Smart-Beam IMRT system, the culmination of twelve years and $300 million of development effort, is already making a difference for thousands of patients.

Today, a little more than 500 of the world's 5,700 radiotherapy centers for cancer treatment have acquired a set of integrated tools for SmartBeam IMRT from Varian Medical Systems.

Almost one-fifth of them are now offering it to their patients, and many others are close behind.

In addition to promising outcomes and public demand for better care, new Medicare and Medicaid reimbursement rates are expected to help accelerate the rapid adoption of IMRT by both hospitals and free-standing cancer centers in the United States. In international markets, public health systems are under pressure to reduce patients' waiting periods by updating systems with more effective treatment technology that can treat more patients.

SECTOR: **Health Care**
BETA COEFFICIENT: **.95**
10-YEAR COMPOUND EARNINGS PER SHARE GROWTH: **10.2%**
10-YEAR COMPOUND DIVIDENDS PER SHARE GROWTH: **None**

		2007	2006	2005	2004	2003	2002	2001	2000
Revenues (Mil)		1,777	1,598	1,383	1,236	1,042	873	774	690
Net Income (Mil)		240	223	207	167	131	946	853	
Earnings per share		1.83	1.65	1.50	1.18	0.92	0.67	0.50	0.41
Dividends per share		—	—	—	—	—	—	—	—
Price	high	53.2	61.7	52.9	46.5	35.7	25.7	19.3	17.8
	low	37.3	41.1	31.6	30.8	23.7	15.8	13.5	7.1

AGGRESSIVE GROWTH

Vulcan Materials Company

1200 Urban Center Drive □ Birmingham, AL 35242-2545 □ (205) 298-3191 □ Direct dividend reinvestment plan available □ Web site: *www.vulcanmaterials.com* □ Listed: NYSE □ Ticker symbol: VMC □ S&P rating: A— □ Value Line financial strength rating: B++

On November 16, 2007, Vulcan Materials announced the completion of its acquisition of Florida Rock Industries, a leading producer of construction aggregates, cement, concrete and concrete products in the Southeast and Mid-Atlantic states. The purchase price was $4.2 billion.

The acquisition further diversifies the geographic scope of Vulcan's operations, providing the company with an enhanced presence in attractive Florida markets and other high-growth Southeast and Mid-Atlantic states, while also providing Vulcan more than 2 billion tons of aggregates

reserves in markets where reserves are increasingly scarce.

Company Profile

Vulcan Materials is the nation's largest producer of construction aggregates and a major producer of asphalt and ready-mix concrete. Construction materials consist of the production, distribution, and sale of construction aggregates and other construction materials and related services. Construction aggregates include crushed stone, sand and gravel, rock asphalt, and re-crushed concrete. Aggregates are employed in virtually all types of construction, including highway construction and maintenance, and in the production of asphaltic and Portland cement concrete mixes. Aggregates also are widely used as railroad ballast.

In June 2005, VMC sold its chemicals business to a subsidiary of Occidental Chemical Corporation. The decision to sell the chemicals business reflected the company's desire to focus on its construction materials business

Vulcan operates primarily in the United States, and its principal product—aggregates—is consumed in virtually all types of publicly funded construction. In the most recent year, aggregates accounted for 72 percent of net sales. From 283 aggregates production facilities and sales yards, the company shipped a record 260 million tons to customers in twenty-two states, the District of Columbia and Mexico. Vulcan's top ten states accounted for 85 percent of total aggregates shipments.

According to a company spokesman, "Our current of 11.1 billion tons of zoned and permitted aggregates reserves represents a net increase of 3.6 billion tons since the end of 1995. We believe that these reserves are sufficient to last, on average, 44.9 years at the current annual production rates."

Besides its aggregates business, the company produces and sells asphalt and concrete in California, Texas, Arizona, and New Mexico. "While aggregates are our primary business, vertical integration between aggregates and downstream products can be managed effectively in certain markets to generate acceptable financial returns," said the official.

"Demand for our products is dependent on construction activity. The primary end uses include public infrastructure (e. g., manufacturing, industrial, retail and office) and private residential construction. Historically, construction spending in the public sector has generally been more stable than private construction spending. Government appropriations and expenditures are typically less interest-rate sensitive than private-sector spending."

Customers for Vulcan's products include heavy construction and paving contractors; residential and commercial building contractors; concrete products manufacturers; state, county and municipal governments; railroads; and electric utilities.

Customers are served by truck, rail, and water networks from the company's production facilities and sales yards. Due to the high weight-to-value ratio of aggregates, markets generally are local in nature, often consisting of a single metropolitan area or one more counties or portions thereof when transportation is by truck alone. Truck deliveries account for about 85 percent of total shipments. What's more, sales yards and other distribution facilities located on waterways and rail lines substantially increase the company's geographic market reach through the availability of rail and water transportation.

Shortcomings to Bear in Mind

■   Environmental and zoning regulations have made it increasingly difficult for the construction aggregates industry to expand existing quarries or to develop new quarries in some markets. On the other hand, says a company officer, "Although we cannot predict what government policies will be adopted in the future regarding environmental controls that affect the construction materials industry, we believe that future environmental control costs will not have a material adverse affect on our business. Furthermore, future land use restrictions in some markets could make zoning and permitting more difficult. Any such restrictions while potentially curtailing expansion in certain areas, could also enhance the value of our reserves at existing locations."

■   "Although the persistent woes of the housing segment are weighting heavily on the broader market in general, they are taking a heftier toll on the building materials industry," said Jason A. Smith, writing for *Value Line* on April 4, 2008. "And Vulcan, despite its significant exposure to the non-residential markets and the recent acquisition of Florida Rock Industries, has not been able to avoid the wrath of investors."

Reasons to Buy

■ On February 13, 2008, CEO Don James said, "Our business generated improved results in 2007 despite weaker demand for our products. The sharp downturn in residential construction activity was only partially offset by increased levels of highway construction and nonresidential construction. The pricing environment for aggregates remained favorable during 2007. The average selling price for aggregates increased 13 percent in 2007, despite a 9 percent decline in aggregates shipments.

"The past year also was highlighted by Vulcan's purchase of Florida Rock Industries on November 16, 2007. This acquisition, which includes significant aggregates reserves in attractive markets, continues our long-term strategy to position our company in markets where reserves are limited and where demand for aggregates is expected to grow at above-average rates. The short time that Vulcan owned Florida Rock during this seasonally weak period, coupled with the one-time earnings effects from the transaction, resulted in the acquisition providing limited contribution to 2007 EBITDA. Integration of this acquisition is proceeding smoothly and according to our plans."

■ On February 19, 2007, Vulcan Materials announced that it had signed a definitive agreement for Vulcan Materials to acquire Florida Rock in a cash and stock transaction valued at approximately $4.6 billion. The acquisition, which has been unanimously approved by both companies' boards of directors, will significantly enhance Vulcan Materials' strategic position and long-term growth opportunities by greatly expanding its presence in attractive Florida markets

and in other high-growth Southeast and Mid-Atlantic states. The combined company will have aggregates reserves totaling approximately 13.9 billion tons, an increase of more than 20 percent over Vulcan Materials' stand-alone aggregates reserves, and 2006 pro forma aggregates shipments of 300 million tons, an increase of approximately 18 percent compared to Vulcan Materials' stand-alone shipments.

■ "Despite decades of consolidation, the aggregates industry remains highly fragmented," said Mr. James. "Public companies account for about 40 percent of U.S. production. Vulcan, the largest U.S. producer of aggregates, supplies only about 8 percent of the total U.S. demand. With over 5,000 companies in the industry, and over 60 percent of those privately held, there are numerous candidates for acquisition. These include both medium and large multi-quarry companies, and smaller operations that can serve as bolt-on enhancements to existing facilities and markets."

In 2005, for instance, Mr. James, said, Vulcan acquired a quarry in Tennessee near Chattanooga: a quarry in the north Atlanta market; and a quarry and three sand and gravel plants in northwestern Indiana to expand "our presence in that state. We also acquired five aggregates production facilities and five associated asphalt plants in Arizona. Three of these operations are in Phoenix and enhance our existing facilities there. The other two operations are in Tucson, a new market for Vulcan."

■ On February 15, 2008, Argus Research Company gave Vulcan Materials a BUY rating. Its analyst, Bill Selesky, said, "Vulcan's concrete and cement shipments are particularly exposed to the housing market. We do, however, believe that Vulcan's earnings are far more insulated than those of most peers, as it also has substantial end markets in highway and infrastructure construction, which are not as economically sensitive as the residential construction market."

SECTOR: **Materials**
BETA COEFFICIENT: **1.30**
10-YEAR COMPOUND EARNINGS PER SHARE GROWTH: **8.4%**
10-YEAR COMPOUND DIVIDENDS PER SHARE GROWTH: **12%**

		2007	2006	2005	2004	2003	2002	2001	2000
Revenues (Mil)		3,328	3,342	2,895	2,454	2,892	2,797	3,020	2,492
Net Income (Mil)		451	468	388	261	223	190	223	220
Earnings per share		4.54	4.69	3.73	2.52	2.18	1.86	2.17	2.29
Dividends per share		1.96	1.48	1.16	1.04	0.97	0.94	0.90	0.84
Price	high	128.6	93.8	76.3	55.5	48.6	50.0	55.3	48.9
	low	77.0	65.8	52.4	41.9	28.8	32.4	37.5	36.5

CONSERVATIVE GROWTH

Walgreen Company

200 Wilmot Road □ Mail Stop *2261 □ Deerfield, IL 60015 □ (847) 914-2972 □ Direct dividend reinvestment program is available □ Fiscal years end August 31 □ Web site: *www.walgreens.com* □ Ticker symbol: WAG □ S&P rating: A+ □ Value Line financial strength rating: A+

"Walgreen Company thrived for decades by opening stores faster than its competitors—a new location pops up every sixteen hours—and by pushing out more prescriptions per year than any other chain," said Amy Merrick, writing for the *Wall Street Journal* on March 19, 2008.

"But facing pressure from rivals, a weak economy and cracks in the health system, Walgreen is changing its time-tested formula. Instead of simply bottling pills, it is refashioning itself into a broad health-care provider.

"On Monday, the Deerfield, IL-based company announced plans to buy I-trax Inc. and Whole Health Management, two companies that run a total of 350 health centers at corporate offices. The centers offer services from treating simple illnesses to counseling patients on managing diabetes.

"Walgreen expects to open more pharmacies at work sites and to attract employees, their family members and retirees to its stores. The acquired companies will form part of Walgreen's new health and wellness division and will include Take Care Health Clinics, which operate 136 clinics inside Walgreen stores.

The article goes on to say, "'This is only the beginning of our presence in the sector,' Walgreen chief executive Jeffrey Rein said in a conference call with analysts. In the U.S., there are more than 7,600 office sites with 1,000 or more employees that could support a health-care center, he said."

Company Profile

Walgreens, one of the fastest-growing retailers in the United States, leads the chain drugstore industry in sales and profits. Sales for fiscal 2005 reached $42.2 billion, produced by 4,953 stores in forty-five states and Puerto Rico (up from 4,582 stores a year earlier).

Founded in 1901, Walgreens today has 179,000 employees. The company's drugstores serve more than 4.4 million customers daily and average $8.3 million in annual sales per unit. That's $747 per square foot, among the highest in the industry. Walgreens has paid dividends in every quarter since 1933 and has raised the dividend in each of the past twenty-five years.

Stand-Alone Stores

Competition from the supermarkets has convinced Walgreens that the best strategy is to build stand-alone stores. Since the rise of managed care, many pharmacy customers now make only minimal co-payments for prescriptions. That leaves convenience as the major factor in choosing a pharmacy. The free-standing format makes room for drive-thru windows, which provide a speedy way for drugstore customers to pick up or drop off prescriptions.

On the other hand, the company's stand-alone strategy is more expensive. Walgreen insists on building its units on corner lots near an intersection with a traffic light. Such leases normally cost more than a site in a strip mall.

More than a Pharmacy

Home meal replacement has become a $100-billion business industry-wide. In the company's food section, Walgreens carries staples as well as frozen dinners, desserts, and pizzas. In some stores, expanded food sections carry such items as fruit, and ready-to-eat salads.

In the photo department, the company builds loyalty through a wide selection of products and the service of trained technicians. Walgreens experimented with one-hour photo service as early as 1982, but it was in the mid-1990s before, according to CEO Dan Jorndt, "We really figured it out." Since 1998, one-hour processing has been available chain-wide, made profitable by "our high volume of business. We've introduced several digital photo products that are selling well and are evaluating the long-term impact of digital on the mass market."

Shortcomings to Bear in Mind

- The company reported a decline in fourth quarter earnings in 2007, due in part to lower reimbursements on some popular generic drugs and higher expenses.

Net earnings for the fourth quarter declined 3.8 percent to $397 million or 40 cents per share (diluted) versus last year's $412 million or 41 cents per share (diluted).

"This quarter was negatively impacted by lower generic drug reimbursements, combined with higher salary and store expenses, and higher advertising costs," said CEO Jeffrey A. Rein. "Our expenses weren't in line with the level of reimbursements we were receiving. Managing both expenses and lower reimbursements on some generic drugs is my top priority. We're going to fix this, and at the same time continue our aggressive growth plan."

Reasons to Buy

- On October 1, 2007, Walgreens announced its thirty-third consecutive year of record earnings and sales. Fiscal year net earnings increased 16.6 percent to $2.04 billion versus last year's $1.75 billion. Net earnings per share for fiscal 2007 increased 18.0 percent to $2.03 per share (diluted) versus $1.72 per share (diluted) the previous year.

For the fifty-two-week period ending Aug. 11, Walgreens increased its market share in fifty-nine of its top sixty product categories compared to food, drug, and mass merchandise competitors, as measured by A.C. Nielsen.

Prescription sales, which accounted for 65.0 percent of total sales in fiscal 2007, climbed 10.5 percent in the fourth quarter and 14.7 percent for the year. Prescription sales in comparable drugstores rose 6.5 percent in the quarter and 9.5 percent for the year, while the number of prescriptions filled in comparable drugstores rose 4.0 percent in the quarter and 5.7 percent for the year.

Overall, Walgreens filled 583 million prescriptions in fiscal 2007, an increase of 10.0 percent from the previous year. Walgreens now fills nearly 17 percent of all retail prescriptions in the country.

■ Including acquisitions, Walgreens expansion program resulted in a record net gain of 536 new stores in fiscal 2007. As of August 31, the company operated 5,997 stores in forty-eight states and Puerto Rico versus 5,461 a year ago, and anticipates opening 550 new stores in fiscal 2008, with a net increase of more than 475 stores after relocations and closings. Walgreens is on track to exceed its goal of operating 7,000 stores in 2010.

"We have a three-part strategy for growth, and the first part is to continue what we do best—grow stores," said president Greg Wasson. "We're committed to organic store growth, yet at the same time we're more open to acquisitions when the right opportunity arises.

"The second part of our growth strategy is expanding into adjacent sectors of pharmacy and healthcare service. For example, in August we acquired Option Care, Inc., a national specialty pharmacy and home infusion services provider. This move makes us the fourth-largest specialty pharmacy provider in the country and the largest home infusion provider.

"The final part of our growth strategy is using our existing store space to drive customer traffic through new services like printer cartridge refills and convenient care clinics. We have more than sixty-five clinics open today, and by the end of calendar 2008 our goal is to have more than 400."

Take Care Health Systems, the wholly owned subsidiary of Walgreens that manages the clinics, is opening clinics in nine new markets this fall, including Cincinnati, Cleveland, Houston, Las Vegas, Miami, Nashville, Tennessee, Orlando, Florida, Tampa, Florida, and Tucson, Arizona. Combined with expansion in existing markets, up to 100 new Take Care Health Clinics will open this fall.

Walgreens estimates more than $2 billion in capital investments for fiscal 2008.

This reflects expenditures for new stores, technology and a new distribution center in Connecticut scheduled to open in fiscal 2009.

■ Favorable demographics include 77 million aging baby boomers (forty-five to sixty-four years old) and their estimated increased usage. For instance, the typical forty-year-old takes six-plus prescriptions annually; at fifty it reaches eight; at sixty the annual rate is eleven; and at seventy the number of prescriptions reaches fifteen.

■ On September 12, 2007, Walgreen completed its acquisition of Option Care, Inc., which provides a full spectrum of specialty pharmacy and home infusion services from a national network of more than 100 pharmacies in thirty-four states. Its services are used by patients with acute or chronic conditions that can be treated at home, in a physician's office or at any one of OptionCare's ambulatory infusion sites. OptionCare's services also include respiratory therapy and home medical equipment at some locations.

The acquisition positions Walgreens as the largest home infusion therapy provider in the country and expands its respiratory therapy and durable medical equipment services at some locations. It also makes Walgreens the nation's fourth-largest specialty pharmacy provider.

"Our increased resources instantly expand our ability to provide patients and payors with national access to these services," said Stanley B. Blaylock, Walgreens Health Services vice president of specialty pharmacy and home care. "Providing service in this expanding space will help members, payor clients and referral sources to better manage patients' conditions, their care and the associated costs. This also expands our opportunities to gain greater access to limited-distribution biotech medications for our clients and patients."

Mr. Blaylock added, "The acquisition is another step toward positioning ourselves as a provider of a variety of patient-focused healthcare services. We're moving beyond traditional pharmacy in ways that are beneficial to patients and help payors better manage their overall medical and pharmacy spending."

OptionCare president Paul Mastrapa said, "Both companies are very clinically focused and make a strong cultural fit. With OptionCare's more than twenty-five years of experience in providing home care services, both organizations are leaders in the healthcare industry and have established providers with dedicated management and staff who believe we can help our patients live better lives."

SECTOR: Consumer Staples
BETA COEFFICIENT: .75
10-YEAR COMPOUND EARNINGS PER SHARE GROWTH: 16.5%
10-YEAR COMPOUND DIVIDENDS PER SHARE GROWTH: 12.2%

		2007	2006	2005	2004	2003	2002	2001	2000
Revenues (Mil)		53,762	47,409	42,202	37,502	32,505	28,681	24,623	21,207
Net Income (Mil)		2,041	1,751	1,478	1,360	1,176	1,019	886	756
Earnings per share		2.03	1.72	1.52	1.32	1.14	0.99	0.86	0.74
Dividends per share		0.38	0.27	0.22	0.18	0.15	0.15	0.14	0.14
Price	high	49.1	51.6	49.0	39.5	37.4	40.7	45.3	45.8
	low	35.8	39.6	38.4	32.0	26.9	27.7	28.7	22.1

GROWTH AND INCOME

Wells Fargo & Company

420 Montgomery Street ❑ San Francisco, CA 94163 ❑ (415) 396-0523 ❑ Direct dividend reinvestment plan available
❑ Web site: *www.wellsfargo.com* ❑ Listed: NYSE ❑ Ticker symbol: WFC ❑ S&P rating: A ❑ Value Line financial strength rating: A+

"What big bank is most likely to find the safest, fastest route through the United States's dangerous credit mess? Wells Fargo is an excellent bet," said Mark Veverka, writing for *Barron's* on February 18, 2008.

"Partially, it's about what Wells isn't. Unlike most of its peers that have been badly dinged, the San Francisco-based bank doesn't have a big capital-markets operation exposed to credit derivatives, structured-investment vehicles, or mortgage-backed securities. It isn't slowed by a huge book of subprime residential-mortgage loans, and its balance sheet can withstand more bullets than most.

"The nation's only triple-A-rated bank in the eyes of both major credit agencies hasn't had to seek outside capital from a giant sovereign wealth fund in Singapore or Abu Dhabi; its biggest shareholder is Warren Buffett's Berkshire Hathaway, in Omaha. Buffett has been a long-time supporter of the bank's respected management team, and Berkshire just raised its Wells position to 9.4 percent."

Company Profile

Wells Fargo & Company is a diversified financial services company, providing banking, insurance, investments, mortgages, and consumer finance from more than 6,250 stores, the Internet (*wellsfargo.com*) and other distribution channels across North America. Wells Fargo Bank, N.A. Is the only "AAA"-rated bank in the United States.

As of March 31, 2007, Wells Fargo had $486 billion in assets, was the fifth-largest among its domestic peers, and the market value of the stock ranked third among its peers.

In community banking, Wells Fargo has 3,120 stores in twenty-three states, 23 million customers and is the nation's most extensive banking franchise.

Wells Fargo Card Services

In the realm of card services, WFC has:

- 6.0 million credit card accounts
- $6.2 billion in average consumer credit cards outstanding
- The nation's number two issuer of credit cards
- 15.48 million debit card accounts

Wells Fargo is the number one originator of home mortgages and the number two servicer of residential mortgages. Combined, the company's retail and wholesale lending operations fund about one of every eight homes financed annually in the United States.

Here is a summary of the company's home mortgage operations:

- Serving all fifty states through more than 2,000 mortgage and Wells Fargo banking stores, and the Internet
- The nation's number one retail home mortgage lender
- 4.9 million customers
- Originations: $470 billion
- Servicing: $753 billion

Credit Card Group

A leading provider of home equity and personal credit accounts with a combined portfolio of $64 billion. Sales channels include Retail Banking, Wells Fargo Home Mortgage, CCG Direct-to-Consumer (wellsfargo.com, telesales, and direct mail), wholesale and third-party mortgage

brokers, finance companies, indirect dealer programs, and other third-party partners. In summary, this is how WFC stacks up:

- One of America's largest and fastest-growing providers of home equity and personal credit
- Serving more than 2.1 million customer households
- Largest lender of prime home equity (loans and lines of credit)
- First to introduce Home Asset Management Account, which combines a mortgage and home equity line of credit, enabling customers to finance a home in an all-in-one process
- Number one in personal credit market share in Wells Fargo banking states
- Largest provider of auto loans, excluding captive finance companies

Shortcomings to Bear in Mind

■ Wells Fargo reported diluted earnings per common share of $2.38 for 2007 compared with $2.47 in 2006. As most investors are aware, 2007 was not a good year for banks, and Wells Fargo performed better than most.

"Despite the industry headwinds and challenging economic environment, our outstanding team members produced record revenue for both the fourth quarter and full year," said CEO John Stumpf. "We expect the environment to remain challenging in 2008, particularly in the consumer sector, but we're as committed as ever to satisfying all our customers' financial needs and believe we have the right strategy and team in place to do just that. Our talented team did exceptionally well in fundamental areas such as account, revenue and deposit growth and we expanded distribution and cross-sell to both consumer and commercial customers."

Reasons to Buy

■ On September 18, 2007, Wells Fargo & Company announced the latest addition to its mobile banking services, Wells Fargo Mobile℠ for small businesses, a browser-based solution that gives small business owners nationwide access to their business and personal financial information at anytime, from anywhere.

Once enrolled in the Wells Fargo Mobile service, small business customers can check balances of their small business and personal deposit and credit accounts, view transaction history, and transfer money between eligible Wells Fargo accounts on any Web-enabled mobile device by accessing the mobile banking through www.wf.com.

"Mobile banking is ideal for our small business customers, who benefit from the convenience of checking their account balances or making money transfers easily and quickly while on the go," says Jim Smith, executive vice president and managing head of Wells Fargo's Internet Services Group. "The Wells Fargo Mobile service gives small businesses an 'extended office' with access to account information through their mobile devices."

"Most of our small business customers also hold personal accounts at Wells Fargo, and the ability for them to view their financial information in one place is important," said Eskander Matta, senior vice president, Wells Fargo Internet Services Group. "Wells Fargo Mobile offers small business customers the choice of which accounts—business, personal or both—they want to view on their mobile device."

Wells Fargo was the first financial institution to introduce access to banking accounts on the Internet in 1995. Additional new mobile solutions for both consumer and business customers that were announced this year include:

■ In May, Wells Fargo became the first major U.S. financial services company to offer a mobile service for businesses with the introduction of the CEO Mobile℠ service.

■ In June, Wells Fargo and Visa USA announced an extensive mobile pilot to test consumer mobile payments and services

■ In July, Wells Fargo Mobile℠, a browser-based mobile banking solution available to all of its customers nationwide, was introduced.

■ On November 15, 2007, a company official said, "The small business lending market totaled $126 billion in 2006, with Wells Fargo holding steady as America's number-one small business lender for the fifth consecutive year. With an 18 percent year-over-year increase in its 2006 lending, Wells Fargo extended $21 billion to small business owners nationwide (in loans under $100,000), according to the 2006 Community Reinvestment Act (CRA) data. CRA data measures small business lending based on loan originations, providing the industry's most comprehensive set of small business lending figures."

"CRA data is an important barometer for small business lending because it tracks loan originations, which represent the total amount extended to a business," said Marc Bernstein, EVP and head of Small Business Lending for Wells Fargo. "Wells Fargo's 18 percent increase in year-over-year lending affirms our ongoing commitment to small businesses. With an average loan size of just under $26,000, Wells Fargo is the leading small business lender for loans under $100,000, extending more than 820,000 loans nationwide. With 95 percent of all small businesses generating less than $2 million in annual revenues, tracking loans under $100,000 is a key measure of how financial institutions are meeting the capital needs of small business owners."

"As a small business owner, the continued support of financial institutions is critical to my success," said Lisa Johnson, founder and CEO of Chicago-based Gourmet Kitchens. "Since we started over eighteen years ago, obtaining credit has helped us grow from a company of seven employees into a multimillion dollar business with over 300 employees. Growing a business requires all types of assistance; you need a lot of support and a bank that can be there as your capital needs change."

Wells Fargo was also the number-one lender to small businesses in low- and moderate-income neighborhoods (for loans under $100,000), with over 160,000 loans totaling more than $4.3 billion dollars.

Wells Fargo ranked number one for loans under $100,000 in eighteen states: Alaska, Arizona, California, Colorado, Idaho, Iowa, Minnesota, Montana, Nebraska, Nevada, New Mexico, North Dakota, Oregon, South Dakota, Texas, Utah, Washington, and Wyoming.

"As America's leading small business lender, we continually look for ways to understand and meet all the financial needs of small business owners," said Rebecca Macieira-Kaufmann, EVP and head of Wells Fargo's Small Business segment. "By offering a wide range of products and resources, such as our Small Business Webcast Series, Wells Fargo helps small business owners to succeed financially—in business and personally."

■ On December 5, 2007, Wells Fargo Private Bank released the findings of its Wealth Lifecycle study, which measures the attitudes and views of U.S. high net worth (HNW) individuals toward a wide range of life's most important issues, including money, family, work, and values.

A notable finding in regard to money revealed that even though HNW individuals are focused on planning for retirement, planning for their health care and minimizing taxes, they also place great importance on giving, volunteerism, and caring for loved ones. About three-quarters (74 percent) of respondents indicated that they are generous with their money, and the majority said that making a difference in the world (65 percent) and volunteering in their community (57 percent) are important to their overall happiness.

"It's clear from these results that high net worth individuals are focused on making a difference in the world, in their communities, and in their families. Not all high net worth individuals manage their lifestyles and money the same way, but most are focused on balancing their personal, professional and financial goals with their desire to make a difference through philanthropy or helping loved ones," said Christine Deakin, executive vice president and head of Client Solutions, Strategy and Marketing for Wells Fargo Private Bank.

SECTOR: Financials
BETA COEFFICIENT: .85
10-YEAR COMPOUND EARNINGS PER SHARE GROWTH: 10.5%
10-YEAR COMPOUND DIVIDENDS PER SHARE GROWTH: 14.3%

	2007	2006	2005	2004	2003	2002	2001	2000
Loans (Millions)	344,800	306,900	296,100	269,600	249,182	192,772	168,738	157,405
Net Income (Mil)	8,060	8,480	7,670	7,014	6,202	5,710	3,423	4,026
Earnings per share	2.38	2.49	2.25	2.05	1.83	1.66	0.99	1.17
Dividends per share	1.18	1.12	1.00	0.93	0.75	0.55	0.50	0.45
Price high	38.0	37.0	32.4	32.0	29.6	27.4	27.4	28.2
low	29.3	30.3	28.8	27.2	21.7	19.1	19.2	15.7

INDEX OF STOCKS
BY CATEGORY

Aggressive Growth

- Alcoa
- Apache Corporation
- Boeing Company
- Carnival Corporation
- Cash America Int'l
- Caterpillar, Inc.
- Cintas
- Coach
- CONSOL Energy
- Costco Wholesale
- Deere & Company
- Devon Energy
- Dover
- EnCana Corporation
- Fastenal Company
- FedEx Corporation
- FMC Corporation
- Goodrich
- Harris Corporation
- Hewlett Packard
- Ingersoll-Rand
- Intel
- International Paper
- Medtronic
- Nabors Industries
- Nordson
- Oshkosh Corporation
- Parker Hannifin
- Patterson Companies
- Paychex
- Schlumberger
- St. Jude Medical
- Staples
- Stryker
- Target Corporation
- Teva Pharmaceutical
- TJX
- T. Rowe Price
- Vulcan Materials Co.

Conservative Growth

- Air Products
- Bard, C.R.
- Becton, Dickinson
- Campbell Soup
- Canadian National
- Clorox
- Colgate-Palmolive
- CVS/Caremark Corporation
- Dentsply Int'l
- Donaldson
- Ecolab
- Energen
- General Dynamics
- Grainger, W.W.
- Hormel Foods
- Idex
- Illinois Tool Works

International Business Machines

Johnson Controls

Johnson & Johnson

Kellogg

Lowe's Companies

McCormick & Co.

McGraw-Hill

Meredith

Norfolk Southern

Northern Trust

Omnicom Group

PepsiCo

Praxair

Procter & Gamble

Raytheon

Sigma-Aldrich

Sysco Corporation

3M Company

United Parcel

United Technologies

Varian Medical

Walgreen

Growth & Income

Abbott Laboratories

AT&T

ChevronTexaco

Coca-Cola

ConocoPhillips

Dominion Resources

DuPont

Eaton Corporation

Emerson Electric

Entergy

ExxonMobil

FPL Group

General Electric

General Mills

Gentex

Honeywell

Kimco Realty

Lubrizol

MDU Resources

Rohm & Haas

Wells Fargo

Income

Piedmont Nat'l Gas

About the Author

John Slatter has a varied investment background and has served as a stockbroker, securities analyst, and portfolio strategist. He is now a consultant with Klopp Investment Management, a firm in Cleveland, Ohio, that manages investment portfolios on a fee basis.

Slatter has written hundreds of articles for such publications as *Barron's*, *Physician's Management*, *Ophthalmology Times*, *The Writer*, and *Better Investing*, as well as for brokerage firms he has worked for, including Hugh Johnson & Company and Wachovia Securities. His books include *Safe Investing*, *Straight Talk about Stock Investing*, and twelve prior editions of *The 100 Best Stocks You Can Buy*.

He has been quoted in such periodicals as the *Cleveland Plain Dealer*, the *New York Times*, *Gannett News Service*, *Burlington Free Press*, *Wall Street Journal*, *Cincinnati Enquirer*, *Toledo Blade*, *Dayton Daily News*, *Buffalo News*, *Christian Science Monitor*, and *Money* magazine. He has also been quoted in a number of books, including *The Dividend Investor* and *Stocks for the Long Run*, and he has been interviewed on a number of radio stations and by the CNBC daily television program *Today's Business*.

In August 1988, Slatter was featured in a *Wall Street Journal* article concerning his innovative investment strategy that calls for investing in the ten highest-yielding stocks in the Dow Jones Industrial Average. This approach to stock selection is sometimes referred as "The Dogs of the Dow," a pejorative reference that Mr. Slatter does not believe is justified, since the stocks with high yields have, in the past, included such blue chips as Merck, IBM, 3M, General Electric, AT&T, Caterpillar, DuPont, ExxonMobil, J.P. Morgan Chase, and Altria.

He lives in Essex Junction, Vermont, and can be reached at (802)879-4154.